D0773128

BUILDING STATES AND NATIONS

BUILDING STATES AND NATIONS

Analyses by Region

Volume II

Edited by

S. N. EISENSTADT

and

STEIN ROKKAN

⑤ SAGE PUBLICATIONS / **Beverly Hills** / **London**

For information address:

SAGE PUBLICATIONS, INC.
275 South Beverly Drive
Beverly Hills, California 90212

SAGE PUBLICATIONS LTD
St George's House / 44 Hatton Garden
London EC1N 8ER

Printed in the United States of America

International Standard Book Number 0-8039-0257-3

Library of Congress Catalog Card No. 73-77873

FIRST PRINTING

PREFACE

A PROGRAMME FOR COMPARATIVE CROSS-NATIONAL RESEARCH: THE ACTION OF THE INTERNATIONAL SOCIAL SCIENCE COUNCIL

The International Social Science Council was established by UNESCO in 1951 as a central organization for the advancement of projects of cooperation across disciplines and across countries. The Council's mission is to internationalize the social sciences: to help social scientists across all regions link up with each other in their concrete work; exchange information; test out techniques in new settings; compare models, procedures, and findings across cultures and across political systems.

The Council has tried a variety of strategies in its efforts to internationalize the social sciences. In 1962, just over ten years ago, the Council launched a programme to advance joint work on the infrastructure, the methodology and the theory of comparative cross-cultural and cross-national research.

The programme was initially centered on the coordination of efforts to build up data resources for comparative analysis. Publications such as *Comparing Nations,*[1] *Data Archives for the Social Sciences,*[2] and *Quantitative Ecological Analysis,*[3] all helped to generate interest in the development of better infrastructures for cross-national research.

To establish a firmer framework for these efforts of cooperation and coordination, the ISSC in 1966 established a Standing Committee on Social Science Data. This body concerns itself not only with the maintenance of an active network of communication among data archives, but also with technical matters such as the diffusion of management and retrieval systems and of social science computer programs.

The Council took stock of its initial endeavours at an important meeting in Paris in 1965.[4] The scholars assembled strongly recommended that the Council take steps to broaden its programme: it should pay more attention to the methodology of comparisons, and it should help forward efforts of systematic confrontation of theories. To move forward on the methodology front, the Council was able to persuade UNESCO to organize a number of "data confrontation seminars" and training courses designed to acquaint younger research workers with the techniques of cross-national comparison. This programme was later supported under a grant by the Volkswagen Foundation, which allowed the Council to launch a series of summer schools for training in comparative research and also to organize several seminars on problems in the methodology of comparisons and in the development of theories of the sources of variability across cultures and territorial units.

The stock-taking conference in 1965 also strongly recommended that the Council establish close links with historians in exploring the possibilities of systematic comparisons of cultures and systems in greater time depth. During 1966-1967, the Council prepared a plan for a series of encounters between historians and generalizing social scientists over issues in the theory of development. This plan was submitted to UNESCO, and it proved possible to finance a series of seminars and larger conferences on issues of national political development. The first such encounter took place in 1968.[5] This was followed in 1970 by a major cross-regional conference on "State Formation and Nation-Building" in Cérisy-la-Salle in Normandy,[6] by regional conferences in Asia and in Latin America, and by a technical workshop on data resources for historical comparisons of national development.[7]

This series of meetings generated a number of important reports and papers. To ensure wide circulation of these texts, UNESCO published a selection of papers from the Cérisy Conference[8] and asked the International Social Science Council to assemble the broader body of contributions in a separate publication. The task of editing this collection was entrusted to two of the Directors of the UNESCO project, Professors S. N. Eisenstadt and Stein Rokkan. They commissioned a number of additional chapters to fill lacunae and to round off the presentations region by region. They also took steps to prepare an extensive bibliography of the literature on state formation and nation-building.

The results of these various efforts can be studied in the two volumes of this Council publication, *Building States and Nations.* In the first volume the editors have assembled a series of general discussions of *models and concepts* in the study of macro-political change and added a number of papers on the *data resources* for comparative research on such processes. The second volume presents a series of papers on major variations in political development across the world; it is organized by *region* and offers analyses of the sources of diversity within each of the distinctive areas of common cultural and/or political inheritance.

We believe that this collection offers a useful source of information on current thinking and research on national political development, and we hope that the recommendations and the suggestions recorded in this volume will help to give direction and structure to future comparative studies in this field. The International Social Science Council is ready to continue its efforts to advance systematic exchanges and encounters at the borderline between history and social science and will be much encouraged if the work reported on in these pages will inspire new initiatives by younger scholars interested in cross-cultural and cross-national comparisons.

This volume would never have seen the light of day without the help so freely given by so many friends and colleagues. We are particularly indebted to Marie-Anne de Franz of the Department of Social Sciences in UNESCO: as an historian working with social scientists, she believed firmly in our project and helped it forward at every step. We are also most grateful to S. N. Eisenstadt, Rajni Kothari, and Candido Mendes for all they did to advance our project. Among the many who helped us produce this volume in Paris, in Bergen, and at Yale, we would single out for special thanks Elina Almasy, Astrid Blom, Kirsti Saelen, Marianne Serck-Hanssen, Joan Warmbrunn, and Lydia Stevens. We finally wish to thank all the authors for both the quality of their contributions and for their patience in answering our queries and in awaiting publication of these volumes.

Bergen and Paris,   *Samy Friedman*
1 February 1973.   *Stein Rokkan*

NOTES

1. R. L. Merritt and S. Rokkan, eds., Comparing Nations, New Haven, Yale University Press, 1966.

2. S. Rokkan, ed., Data Archives for the Social Sciences, Paris, Mouton, 1966.

3. M. Dogan and S. Rokkan, eds., Quantitative Ecological Analysis in the Social Sciences, Cambridge, Mass., M.I.T. Press, 1969.

4. See Stein Rokkan, ed., Comparative Research Across Cultures and Nations, Paris, Mouton, 1968.

5. See the report by Stein Rokkan in the following chapter.

6. See the report by Stein Rokkan below, and the one by Rajni Kothari in Chapter 3 of this volume.

7. See Chapter 5 of this volume: "Data Resources for Comparative Research on Development: A Review of Recent Efforts," by Stein Rokkan.

8. International Social Science Journal, Vol. 23, No. 3, 1971.

CONTENTS

BUILDING STATES AND NATIONS

I.

EUROPE—WEST AND EAST

CHAPTER 1

BUILDING CONSOCIATIONAL NATIONS

Hans Daalder

HANS DAALDER is Professor of Political Science at the University of Leiden. He has done extensive research on politics in The Netherlands and in Britain, on legislative behavior, on Marxism, and on comparative development in Europe and in new states. He has contributed to various symposia (for example, R. A. Dahl, editor, *Political Opposition in Western Democracies;* and J. LaPalombara and M. Weiner, editors, *Political Parties and Political Development.* His major book is *Cabinet Reform in Britain.*

Of late, the term "consociational" has been increasingly used to characterize a certain pattern of political life in which the political elites of distinct social groups succeed in establishing a viable, pluralistic state by a process of mutual forbearance and accommodation. In modern social science, the word was first used by David Apter.[1] The term was further elaborated into a general classificatory concept by Arend Lijphart.[2] Independently of him and sometimes under different terms like *Proporzdemokratie* or *Konkordanzdemokratie,* Gerhard Lehmbruch,[3] Jürg Steiner,[4] and Rodney Stiefbold[5] have sought to analyse comparable types of political experience.

The word consociatio originated with Johannes Althusius.[6] It is significant that a term first adopted to analyse the development of a new polity in the Low Countries in the early seventeenth century, is now being revived in the study of comparative political development in the twentieth century. A process of building-up a new political society from below, to some degree by the consent of participating communities, in which deliberate compromises by elites carefully circumscribe and limit the extent to which political power can be wielded by one political centre, may be a relatively rare political phenomenon. Yet it provides at least a significant footnote to the prevailing mood in the study of nation-building which so often proceeds from the assumption that nationhood should be forged from above, by the deliberate imposition of a "modern" state on traditional society.

The term "consociational democracy" has been used by Lijphart to characterize the political life of European countries (the Low Countries, Austria, Switzerland) as well as countries on other continents (e.g. Israel, Lebanon, Uruguay, Colombia). This chapter will deal only in its conclusion with the general model of consociational democracy. Its major emphasis will be on a two-country comparison prompted by the suggestion of Stein Rokkan that a treatment of the Dutch and Swiss cases of nation-building might open "fascinating possibilities of comparative historical analysis."[7] Inevitably, in the context of a short chapter, the argument will proceed mainly in the form of propositions that stand in need of more detailed historical substantiation.

Comparison presupposes common as well as contrasting characteristics. In the first section of this chapter, common elements in the political development of the Netherlands and Switzerland will be traced. In the second section, the focus will shift to differences between the two countries. The chapter will conclude with some remarks on more theoretical questions that are prompted by a comparison of Dutch and Swiss experiences in nation-building with those of other countries.

COMMON CHARACTERISTICS OF SWISS AND DUTCH NATION-BUILDING PROCESSES

Both the Netherlands and Switzerland provide examples of states that attained international sovereignty with only minimal internal consolidation. Some violence did occur both in the processes of external demarcation and internal integration; but nationhood typically grew through extensive processes of accommodation and compromise. In the typology of European states[8] the two countries resemble the United Kingdom and Sweden in their centuries-old status as independent polities that show strong traditions of continuous representative organs and that grew slowly—but without reversals—into modern democratic societies. But unlike these two countries, nationhood was achieved without dynastic guidance or early central government. Like Italy and Germany, the modern state developed through unification of once highly dispersed political communities. But whereas conquest and foreceful unification stood at the cradle of Italian and German statehood, Swiss and Dutch statehood as well as nationhood were formed on the whole by compact and accommodation.

If one seeks to account for the Dutch and Swiss developments, the following factors would seem to stand out.

Geopolitical Factors

Otto Hintze long ago drew attention to the importance for later developments of the specific location of certain countries at the periphery of the Holy Roman Empire.[9] Due to the weakness of central authority in the Empire, independent dukedoms, bishoprics, counties, cities, cantons, and provinces maintained themselves with a high degree of political self-sufficiency and independence when in other countries like France, Spain, the United Kingdom, and the Scandinavian countries, dynastic rule resulted in centralized statehood. The development notably of the United Kingdom and France as strong power centres on the international scene, assisted the further development of political independence of Switzerland and the Netherlands: Swiss independence after the fifteenth century was strengthened by a special relationship with France, and Dutch nationhood was achieved not the least because Habsburgs, Bourbons, and Stuarts were unwilling to see political control over the European Delta go to any one of them.

A second common geopolitical factor between the Netherlands and Switzerland is their location at some of the most important trade routes of Europe. This location led to the early development of mercantile cities. Both in the Netherlands and in some of the more important Swiss cantons, cities thus gained a dominant position that they also extended over the surrounding countryside. But these cities remained at the same time highly particularist political communities. Both in the Netherlands and in some of the more important Swiss cantons, cities thus gained a dominant position that they also extended over the surrounding countryside. But these cities remained at the same time highly particularist political communities. Both in the Netherlands and in Switzerland a polycephalous city network developed in which no single city could become the "capital city" for the whole country. Switzerland as well as the Netherlands remained for a long time, much to the dislike of nineteenth-century unifiers like Friedrich List, a *Konglomerat von Munizipalitäten*.[10] Moreover, in both countries strong rural cantons and provinces retained an indepedent political title beside the more prosperous city-dominated polities.

Third, for geographic reasons, neither country saw the development of large land ownership. Communal grazing practices in Switzerland, common needs for the protection of land against the ever-present threat of the sea and rivers in the Lowlands, made for an early development of self-reliant peasant communities. If not always in practice, this arrangement provided at least in political theory for the idea of self-governing communes administered by commoners. Later political developments could, therefore, be inspired by ancient traditions.

The Peculiar Development of Sovereignty

Both in the Netherlands and in Switzerland, independent national existence was originally decided by the force of arms. Territorial consolidation was achieved only by extensive military battles against foreign claimants and, to some extent, at least in Switzerland, by a show of strength against internal dissidents. Local military conflicts decided the course of later frontiers, and military alliances began the process of later development of national identity. To state that nationhood emerged from the completely voluntary association of free communities, would therefore be an unwarranted simplification. In the Netherlands, the seven United Provinces conquered Brabant and Limburg in the 1620s and 1630s and ruled them as dependent territories for 150 years. Switzerland for long was a patchwork of *Urkantone,* associated cantons and a host of dependencies of which Tessin and Vaud were the most important. The essence of Dutch and Swiss political life remained for very long a motley arrangement of particularist communities, not national cooperation among equals.

Yet this very particularism had important consequences for later developments. Interestingly, even the more important, potentially more powerful provinces and cantons did not aspire to become central administrative capitals. And even in dependent territories, local traditions and local governments were permitted to persist. A measure of traditionalist self-sufficiency could eventually substantiate later claims for a separate identity on a par with former overlords. The very dispersed power structure gave ample scope, moreover, for local elites to maintain themselves, and for the confederation as a whole to continue irrespective of political changes within any of the constituent political communities. If there was hardly any national political life, there were also no strong national cleavages or conflicts.

Both the Netherlands and Switzerland emerged therefore as independent political societies without either a strong central government apparatus or an articulate national identity. Common affairs were decided ad hoc by political procedures that resembled international conferences rather than legitimate national government. Neither the United Provinces nor the Swiss Confederation knew a central army or a central bureaucracy. There were no organs of state that could act directly on the individual and there was no concept of common citizenship.

Does this mean that one cannot speak of a Dutch or a Swiss nationality in this period? The answer is somewhat in the nature of a *petitio principii.* If one defines "the central factor of nation-building" as "the orderly exercise of a nation-wide public authority,"[11] the answer must be negative, as no such nationwide public authority existed. If one speaks of nations only when there has been a "process whereby people *transfer* [my italics] their commitment and loyalty from smaller tribes, villages, or petty principalities to the larger central political system,"[12] the conclusion must be equally negative. But one could also argue that at least one condition of nationality—sovereign political existence—had been fulfilled. And if one defines nationality more in terms of at least some consciousness of tegetherness rather than as an exclusivist transfer of loyalties to a new state, signs of an incipient nationhood could be found at least among the leading political strata of Swiss and Dutch society.

The Persistence of Pluralism in Modernization

The French Revolution, undoubtedly, had a major effect on the development of Dutch and to a lesser extent on that of Swiss nationhood. In the Netherlands, French occupation brought a lasting unitary state, common citizenship, common laws, and equal rights for the various religions. In Switzerland, the institutions of the Helvetic Republic proved abortive, but old inequalities between the cantons disappeared and virtually equal rights were secured for the main languages. Eventually, Switzerland too moved to more definite forms of (federal) statehood in 1848.

But the drive of radical forces for unification (as represented by the Dutch *Patriotten beweging* or the Swiss Helvetic Society towards the end of the eighteenth century, or again by innovative radicals around 1848) never succeeded in achieving a sharp break with older pluralist traditions. If thinkers of the French Enlightenment put the twin concepts of absolutism and individualism against what they conceived as the dead weight of privileged corporate interests, Dutch and Swiss traditions consistently regarded an entrenched pluralism as the safeguard of liberties. Admittedly, these old liberties (in the plural) might frustrate individual equality and individual liberty (in the singular). Yet, corporate rights were regarded as important in themselves, as well as a protection against threatening claims by an omnipotent new state.

The formation of the Dutch and Swiss nations could therefore become the result of a slow process of genuine national integration, rather than that of deliberate nation-building. It would be difficult to point to one social group, or one political centre, or one legal institution that might be regarded as the chief nation-building force.

Data on elite recruitment (whether on Dutch Cabinet personnel[13] or on Swiss members of Parliament[14] show that elite positions in the nineteenth century were shared widely by all the major regions of the country. National integration first evolved slowly on the level of accommodating elites, to filter down later to the more parochial orders of society. The slow development of a stronger national sentiment in the population at large was therefore in the main complementary to, rather than destructive of, older local allegiances.

In Dutch and Swiss nineteenth-century history one also looks in vain for a salient role of the usual agencies of nation-building: the army, the bureaucracy, national schools.

National armies appeared relatively late on the Dutch and Swiss scenes. Although they may have played some role in the political socialization of recruits into a developing national political culture—a role so often attributed to armies[15]—a definite sense of national identity preceded the introduction of compulsory military service.

Especially in Switzerland, the national bureaucracy has remained of relatively modest dimensions, not the least because the cantonal governments retained very major political and administrative functions in the federal structure. In the Netherlands also, which was a unitary state from 1795 onwards, the central bureaucracy remained of modest size until the early twentieth century. Recruitment to higher civil service roles has retained many of the features of earlier particularist elite practices. To this day, the Swiss and the Dutch bureaucracy remain in many respects not only nationalizing agencies, but also points of brokerage between highly differentiated subgroups of society.

Schools have undoubtedly played an important role in fostering the development of national sentiment. But in Switzerland control over education has, in practice, remained a highly regionalized and localized affair. In the Netherlands, an attempt by secular, liberal elite groups in the second part of the nineteenth century to build up a centralized school system soon ran into strong opposition from Calvinists and Catholics who successfully fought for autonomy of religious schools under their own control.[16] An inspection of the course content of Dutch and Swiss schools would probably reveal an insistence on both national and subnational allegiances, typically regarded as fully compatible.

Thus, older traditions of elite accommodation, which had grown from the necessities of the highly dispersed power structure of the pre-1789 confederations, could be carried over into the modernization process. Older pluralist elite attitudes facilitated the gradual settlement of participation demands from new social groupings in society. Both in Switzerland and in the Netherlands verbal adherence to ancient ideals of accountable government had gone together in practice with effective rule by relatively narrow—albeit also pluralist—elite groups. But typically, these groups had enjoyed a high degree of legitimacy. The franchise was extended only slowly, and older practices by which policies were preferably determined in negotiations and compromises outside the public market place, have retained a strong hold in the political culture. Both the Netherlands and Switzerland substantiate two of Stein Rokkan's hypotheses: (a) "The stronger the inherited traditions of representative rule, whether within estates, territorial assemblies or city councils, the greater the chances of early legitimation of opposition"; and (b) "the stronger the inherited traditions of representative rule, the slower, and the less likely to be reversed, the processes of enfranchisement and equalization."[17]

Finally, in the two countries, a strong emphasis on the need to insure that political power could not become concentrated in one political centre, has continued to form part of the political culture. More so in Switzerland than in the Netherlands, local governments have been kept strong and relatively independent political sites.[18] In both countries, central government institutions have been so arranged as to insure a definite duality between the executive and the legislature. Within each, older pluralist traditions and modern electoral devices have seen to it that political power has been divided over a variety of political parties: the distance that separates even the largest party from the majority point has been greater in Switzerland and in the Netherlands than in practically any other European countries[19] Coalition government is ingrained both within the official government structures and in the decision-making processes of the large number of interest groups.

In sum, ancient pluralism has facilitated the development of a stable, legitimate, and consistently pluralist modern society.[20] Both the Netherlands and Switzerland are countries with strong subcultural divisions. yet, of the six possible ways to deal with subcultural conflicts according to Robert A. Dahl,[21] violence and repression as well as secession or separation have been remarkably absent. Instead, a respect for autonomy, a habitual reference to proportional representation, and sometimes a willingness to abide by mutual veto rather than undiluted majority decisions[22] have been characteristic features of Dutch and Swiss political culture. And this instinctive respect for diversity has, paradoxically, eased modern processes of assimilation.

CONTRASTS BETWEEN DUTCH AND SWISS NATION-BUILDING PROCESSES

If "the inevitablity of gradualness" in a consistently pluralist evolution is the most obvious common characteristic of the two countries, certain differences between them should also be noted.

Geopolitical Factors

Geographic factors have differentiated Dutch and Swiss political development on the following points.

First, Dutch geography provided less durable barriers to processes of social mobility than did the Swiss terrain. Particularism was therefore more easily broken up once the homogenizing processes of political modernization set in. The most conspicuous illustration of this process is the relatively unhindered development of one national language. To this day Frisian remains a separate language spoken by a few hundred thousand persons; in addition there are numerous slowly disappearing Dutch dialects, but there was never any real issue about the acceptance of the original tongue of the burghers of the cities of the Netherlands as the national language. This fact, in turn, facilitated easy communication throughout the country, and paved the way for stronger assimilatory processes than could be found in Switzerland.

Second, Switzerland is a land-locked country, the Netherlands very much a sea-faring nation. The latter country acquired a colonial empire, and also developed other strong overseas links. At the same time, the Netherlands psychologically stood for a long time—to use a habitual Dutch metaphor—with its back against the European continent (strong trading links with the hinterland notwithstanding). The Dutch self-image was therefore relatively little influenced by the country's precarious position as a small European state at the borders of larger European powers. Switzerland, on the other hand, was acutely conscious of its larger neighbours. The very fact that Swiss citizens spoke the languages of three larger neighbouring states—and that each of these tended to define nationality in linguistic terms—made it imperative to separate the concept of nationhood from any possible link with seemingly objective "national" criteria of language, culture, or ethnic descent.[23] Of the two countries, the

Netherlands became the more homogeneous, unconsciously nationalized society; Switzerland the more heterogeneous, diversified State which embraced a self-conscious 'political' definition of nationhood.[24]

Differences in Political Centralization

Since 1795, the Netherlands has been the more centralized political community, but even before, some vestiges of centralization could be found in the Low Countries. The Dutch Republic, after all, developed when mediaeval traditions inspired particularist societies in the sixteenth century to revolt against the Burgundians who seemed destined to become the most successful centralizing dynasty of Europe.[25] If the Dutch Revolt arrested this drive towards centralization, some remnants of it could yet be found in some of the curious political organs of the Dutch Republic. Notably, the office of the *stadtholder* (literally, the Sovereign's *remplaçant*) retained vestiges of earlier centralizing practices, and provided a political base for the Orange dynasty that had no counterpart in Swiss history. Technically, the *stadtholders* were servants of each of the provinces, and for long periods the city aristocracies successfully kept the Orange princes from power. But the office carried the command of fleet and army, and eventually developed even before the arrival of the unitary state into a unifying force, complete with court and court circle.

Much more than the Swiss Confederation, the Dutch Republic was for a time an active participant on the international scene. Some of the Orange princes—as well as the Grand-Pensionary of Holland—were actively involved in high diplomatic manoeuvres. The Dutch fleet, and the Dutch colonies, also made for a stronger international presence. This more active international stance hardly contributed towards internal consolidation. In the seventeenth and eighteenth centuries, activist foreign policies were settled in the most narrow circles, in which the otherwise highly particularist representatives of the Province of Holland had a decisive voice. Typically, activism in foreign policy was more characteristic of the loosely structured Dutch Republic than of the nineteenth-century centralized kingdom. But the role played by the Republic in international affairs created at least a self-conscious image of the international importance of the Netherlands, which later nationalist historians could exploit on behalf of nationalist mythology.

Both during the days of French supremacy, and after the defeat of Napoleon, there was a definite revulsion against centralized structures in both countries. But whereas Switzerland reverted almost completely to the old order in 1813, the Netherlands knew its period of strongest autocratic rule after 1815. Fears of the older diversity caused the new kings to obtain strong powers. Control over local governments remained strongly centralized, and to this day the appointment of provincial governors and local mayors rests with the central government.[26] Decisive powers were explicitly vested in the national government. Ever since 1813, Dutch political life has tended to be national in scope: constitutional conflicts centred on the national institutions, and political oppositions tended to develop as contestants in one national political arena.

In contrast, nineteenth- and twentieth-century developments in Switzerland have been far less centralistic in nature. Not only after 1813, but also after the formation of a genuine political federation in 1848, Swiss politics has remained a very specific compromise between local, regional, and national forms of government. The Swiss *Gemeinde* has retained many characteristics of autonomous polities, including lifelong administrative and sentimental ties with persons born within its boundaries. The Swiss cantons have remained powerful bodies, with great diversities in structure and policies. And even in the national institutions, regional interests hold an important place. The Swiss Upper House (like the American Senate) continues to give absolute parity to cantons, large or small; the Dutch *Eerste Kamer* is also elected by the provincial councils but only after a complex weighting arrangement makes the vote of each councillor proportional to population. The Swiss Executive *(Bundesrat),* composed of only seven members, preserves a careful balance between linguistic and regional interests, unlike the much larger Dutch Cabinets that are formed almost exclusively with an eye to the relative strength of political parties. Also in the election of the Lower House—as well as the day-to-day functioning of political parties—regional forces play a much greater role in Switzerland than in the Netherlands. Being more important than Dutch local government posts, cantonal government positions provide much greater sources of leverage for local politicians within their national parties than can be found in the Netherlands.

Differences in the Cleavage Structure

The much greater, continuing influence of regional factors in Swiss political life strongly affects the degree of politicization of various cleavages. This factor may perhaps be best illustrated in the very different manner in which religious factors have affected the growth of national integration.

Both the Netherlands and Switzerland belong to the mixed religious belt in Europe in which Protestants and Catholics live side by side. In the

United Provinces, Calvinism became the established church, even though Catholics never numbered less than a third of the Dutch population. Catholics not only lived in the conquered provinces of Brabant and Limburg, but also formed large minorities—and locally even majorities—in the western parts of the country. Switzerland did not know a national established church; the effective independence of each of the cantons made for the development of specific Catholic and specific Protestant cantons (true to the old Augsburg formula of *cuius regio eius religio*). Much more so than in the Netherlands, religion was therefore tied to specific regional positions.

This factor had great effect on later developments. The localization of religion in Switzerland in particular cantons exacerbated regional strife. It polarized conflict to such an extent that religious conflict led to the regional *Sonderbund* war in 1847.[27]

In the Netherlands, on the other hand, national unification after 1795 had insured equal rights for all religious groups throughout the state. But both the secular claims of the new state and the widespread processes of secularization in society at large provoked Calvinists and Catholics to demand autonomy for their churches and denominational control over education. This issue made religion the dominant dividing line in the formation of modern political parties in the latter part of the nineteenth century. Paradoxically, religion therefore became both an integrative and a divisive force. It split mixed religious local communities, and built strong organizational links among like-minded believers across the nation. The strong institutional build-up of Calvinist and Catholic organizations led to a strong segmentation of the Dutch nation in separate subcultural communities of Calvinists, Catholics, and more secular groups. But this new division, while splitting the country along a new dimension, integrated and nationalized political life.

The subordination of regional to religious cleavages can be best illustrated by the example of the Dutch Catholics. About half the number of Dutch Catholics live in the two southern provinces of Brabant and Limburg. These provinces shared a common history, similar patterns of speech, and religious outlook with neighbouring Belgium. Belgian Catholicism exercised a strong influence on these southern provinces, not the least because a Catholic hierarchy had disappeared in the north when Calvinists captured the leadership of the Dutch Revolt at the end of the sixteenth century. Until very late, only weak administrative links and at most tenuous integrationist contacts on the level of a narrow political elite linked Brabant and Limburg between 1650 and 1850 with the remainder of the Netherlands. These circumstances would seem to make Brabant and

Limburg natural candidates for secessionist stirrings. Why then did these not materialize?

The explanation probably lies in differences in the timing of political mobilization. Brabant and Limburg remained for a long time the least developed, most traditional part of the Netherlands. Northern Catholics, on the other hand—living as distinct minority groups in a part of the country that modernized earliest—developed a more definite political consciousness than their southern brethren. Sensitive to the massive Protestantism that surrounded them, these Catholic minorities demanded a return of the Roman Catholic hierarchy in order to secure their identity with a definite organizational base. The resurrection of the Catholic heirarchy in 1853—and later joint political action for other Catholic interests—strengthened organizational links between Catholics of all parts of the country. The fight on behalf of separate Catholic interests simultaneously promoted the integration of Brabant and Limburg in the Dutch nation.

In both the Netherlands and Switzerland, then, religion was an important cleavage line. But the much greater political centralization of the Dutch state made religion less a regional than a national source of political conflict. Much more so than in Switzerland, regional factors were subordinated to national partisan alignments. If in Switzerland religion was one factor in a highly diversified society, in the Netherlands the contest between Calvinists, Catholics, and more secular elements of the society became of overriding importance; in this process a strongly integrated, but religiously segmented political community developed.

We can make this statement more general. Partly due to the much greater role of regional factors, Swiss political culture is more highly fragmented than Dutch political culture.[28] Factors of class, religion, language, and regionalism intersect one another at numerous points. None of these factors have assumed dominant importance, and in many cases the potential for politicization of any one cleavage line has been minimized by rival claims of other possible divisions. Swiss politics, too, might be dubbed "the politics of accommodation."[29] But accommodationist practices are diffused among many more sites and arenas than in the Netherlands, where religion (and to a lesser extent class) came to subordinate other potential cleavages as the basis on which political organizations were formed and political decisions made.

CONSOCIATIONAL DEMOCRACY AND DUTCH
AND SWISS EXPERIENCE

In this final section, we shall raise, on the basis of Swiss and Dutch experience, some more general theoretical questions. These are important if one seeks to generalize from the experiences of these two countries to wider issues of possible models of nation-building. Two issues deserve special attention: (a) to what extent is consociationalism a matter of free choice for political elite groups? and (b) is the model of consociationalism restricted to nations of smaller size?

Consociationalism as Free Choice?

In the argument of Arend Lijphart,[30] consociational democracy should be seen above all as a result of "deliberate efforts to counteract the immobilizing and unstabilizing effects of cultural fragmentation," under-taken by leaders of rival subcultures; Lijphart defines consociational democracy as "government by elite cartel designed to turn a democracy with a fragmented political culture into a stable democracy." Implicit in this reasoning is the statement that certain political societies develop such sharp cleavages, that only the "deliberate joint effort by the elites [can] stabilize the system."

Lijphart's argument is directed against the writings of a generation of scholars who have ascribed the stability of political systems to a combination of a homogeneous political culture and a group structure in which "crosscutting cleavages" make for overlapping memberships and hence for political moderation. He attributes a vital importance to the stance of political elites who may turn the expected dangers of a fragmented political culture into a "self-denying prophecy," by counter-acting the divisive effects through conscious policies of accommodation. He mentions certain conditions that should be fulfilled for a successful consociational democracy: (1) ... that the elites have the ability to accommodate the divergent interests and demands of the subcultures; (2) ... that they have the ability to transcend cleavages and to join in a common effort with the elites of rival subcultures; (3) [that they have] a commitment to the maintenance of the system and to the improvement of its cohesion and stability; (4) finally ... that the elites understand the perils of political fragmentation.

These are demanding conditions, but they remain largely on the level of free choice by strategic elite groups. The major theme of the earlier part of this chapter has been that, in the Netherlands and Switzerland, traditions of pluralism and political accommodation long preceded the processes of political modernization. Against Lijphart's views of consociational democracy as the outcome of a desire on the part of elites to counteract the potential threat of political divisions, one might put forth the reverse thesis: earlier consociational practices facilitated the peaceful transition towards newer forms of pluralist political organization in these two countries. Consociationalism, in this view, is not a response to the perils of subcultural splits, but the prior reason why subcultural divisions never did become perilous.

Whereas our analysis starts from a developmental perspective of centuries, Lijphart gives a critical analysis of certain general sociological models that have a somewhat static character. In doing so, Lijphart remains, to some extent, hostage to some of the mechanistic fallacies that underlie the literature on political cleavages. This body of literature often assumes, without adequate political analysis, that social divisions automatically translate themselves into political conflicts, hence the search for cross-cutting cleavages to dampen the explosive potential of polarized cleavage lines. Hence also Lijphart's quest for counteracting forces on elite level when he finds societies in which cross-cutting cleavages seem replaced by mutually reinforcing dividing lines. Both views tend to neglect the important question of what forces make for the politicization, or nonpoliticization of dividing lines. Under general terms like "subcultural splits," "segmentation," "fragmentation," "cleavages," all manner of social divisions are regarded as loaded with potential political content. Rarely are different cleavage lines distinguished according to their potential for politicization. Too little attention is paid to the issue of whether earlier politicization of one cleavage line may prevent the exploitation of other possible cleavages. Elite cultures are regarded too much as a dependent variable only: Lijphart's elites act to counteract the perils of "objective" cleavages. In our view, on the other hand, the elite culture is in itself a most important independent variable that may go far to determine how cleavages are handled in a political society, to what extent they become loaded with political tension, and to what degree subcultural divisions are solved in a spirit of tolerance and accommodation, or by violence and repression.

The importance of these theoretical matters for the comparative study of nation-building processes should be obvious. The view of elite culture as an important independent variable forces one to take a long developmental perspective. Differences between existing nation-states are seen to be to a considerable extent the product of earlier forms of state formation.[31] Similarly, the future of nation-building efforts in the new states becomes highly dependent on prior elite experiences. Prevailing ideological outlooks in the new states are not favourable for consociationalist choices. Older pluralist traditions in the new states are strong, but they are regarded generally by present-day political elites as obstacles that should be cleared away, rather than as building-stones from which a new, pluralist nation might be constructed. Later developments will depend to a very large extent on choices now taken. The importance of stressing the various alternative roads to modern statehood, including the consociational one, lies in the need to destroy the widespread assumption that *Blut und Eisen* is the "normal" path to nation-building.[32]

Consociationalism—A Luxury of Small Nations?

Both the Netherlands and Switzerland are smaller nations. It has often been argued that their specific political experiences are related to that fact. A standard argument holds that smaller nations can practice a certain pattern of political life that larger states could not endure, exactly because these latter states cannot escape the international responsibilities their size forces on them.[33] According to this theory, larger states carry a greater political load. They must have certain institutions that allow them to act with sufficient decisiveness. Considerations of defence necessitate a larger army that in turn requires a strong bureaucracy. The need to act rules out the cumbersome accommodationist styles of Swiss or Dutch politics; for that reason electoral systems like proportional representation or accommodationist coalition systems on the level of the cabinet or chief executive are impracticable. In the particular case of Switzerland (or the Netherlands before 1940), the stance was moreover facilitated by the fact that the surrounding powers liked to see neutral states in charge of strategic locations. Even this factor implied neutrality by imposition; it gave these countries a licence for internal tolerance and cumbersome pluralism that larger nations could not afford.[34]

It is not easy to assess the justification of this body of reasoning. Undoubtedly, countries like Switzerland and the Netherlands fared better in international politics than did many of the larger states, and to the extent to which small size assisted this development, it helped them to maintain the accommodationist practices of older times. But should one grant the argument that larger states must carry the burden of international politics as distinct from actually carrying, let alone preferring to carry it? Did not the once-subject inhabitants of Tessin consciously prefer in 1798 to join the archaic Swiss Republic rather than join an incipient national state in Italy because they preferred internal freedoms to foreign grandeur? Did not in the early nineteenth century many *Kleinstaatler* in Germany foresee the dangers that the development of a large, new German state might spell both for internal freedoms and external aggressiveness?

The statement that smaller states carry in fact a smaller load in international politics remains debatable. Handling a foreign environment and the impact of foreign influences within their boundaries pose large problems for small states. Not the least of these is survival itself. The Netherlands' and Switzerland's survival among the states of Europe may possibly be due in some measure to their ability to handle not only internal diversity, but also foreign-imposed loads.

NOTES

1. David Apter, The Political Kingdom in Uganda: a Study in Bureaucratic Nationalism. Princeton University Press, 1961, pp. 24-25.

2. See his "Typologies of Democratic Systems," Comparative Political Studies, No. 1, 1968, pp. 3-44; and "Consociational Democracy," World Politics, Vol. 21, 1968-69, pp. 207-25.

3. See his Proporzdemokratie, Tübingen, 1967; and "A Non-Competitive Pattern of Conflict Management in Liberal Democracies: the Cases of Switzerland, Austria and Lebanon," paper presented to the Brussels Congress of the International Political Science Association, 1967.

4. Jürg Steiner, Gewaltlose Politik und Kulturelle Vielfalt: Hypothesen Entwickelt am Beispiel der Schweiz, Bern and Stuttgart, 1970.

5. Rodney Sticfbold, Elite-Mass Opinion Structure and Communication Flow in a Consociational Democracy (Austria), paper presented to the annual meeting of the American Political Science Association, Washington, 1968.

6. For a useful short summary see Otto Gierke, Natural Law and the Theory of Society 1500 to 1800, ed. and trans. by Ernest Barker, Boston, 1957, pp. 70-79.

7. Stein Rokkan, Citizens, Elections, Parties—Approaches to the Comparative Study of the Processes of Development, Oslo, Norway University Press, 1970, p. 118.

8. Ibid., Part I, especially Chapter 3; see also Hans Daalder, "Parties, Elites and Political Developments in Western Europe," in Joseph LaPalombara and Myron Weiner (eds.), Political Parties and Political Development, Princeton, Princeton University Press, 1966, pp. 44-52.

9. Otto Hintze, "Typologie der Ständischen Verfassung des Abendlandes," Historisches Zeitschrift, Vol. 141, 1930, pp. 224-48.

10. Quoted by Hans Kohn, Nationalism and Liberty—the Swiss Example, London, 1956, p. 57.

11. Reinhard Bendix, Nation-building and Citizenship—Studies of our Changing Social Order, New York, 1964, p. 18.

12. Gabriel A. Almond and G. Bingham Powell, Jr., Comparative Politics—a Developmental Approach, Boston, Little, Brown, 1966. p. 36.

13. A machine-readable bibliographical file on all Dutch cabinet ministers since 1848 is available in the Leiden Department of Political Science, based on material

originally collected by Mattei Dogan and Maria Scheffervan der Veen. In the context of a larger study of the Dutch Parliament, a similar file is being prepared on all members of the Dutch Parliament from 1848 to the present.

14. E. Gruner and K. Frei, Schweizerische Bundesversammlung 1848-1920, Bern, 1966, 2 vols.

15. See in particular Lucian W. Pye, Aspects of Political Development, Boston, Little, Brown, 1965, Chapter XI.

16. See Hans Daalder, "The Netherlands: Opposition in a Segmented Society," in Robert A. Dahl (ed.), Political Oppositions in Western Democracies, New Haven, Conn., 1966 p. 199ff.

17. Rokkan, op. cit., pp. 82-83.

18. On the concept of political "site," see Dahl, op. cit., p. 338ff.

19. See the classificatory table, "Smaller European Democracies by the Likelihood of Single-party Majorities and the Distribution of Minority Party Strength," in Rokkan, op. cit., p. 94.

20. This article concentrates above all on the distinct properties in the national development of Switzerland and the Netherlands. These countries have, of course, many other features in common with European states. Most of the general indicators specified by Rokkan, in his "Methods and Models in the Comparative Study of Nation-building," p. 65ff. would be highly relevant for a study of Dutch and Swiss experience. Swiss and Dutch national development might also be contrasted with that of the United States. In fact, both countries often resemble Huntington's "American" pattern of development more than his "European" type (whether "British" or "Continental"). See Samuel P. Huntington, "Political Modernization: America vs. Europe," World Politics, Vol. 18, 1965-66, pp. 378-414.

21. These six possible ways of solving subcultural conflicts are (a) violence and repression, (b) secession or separation, (c) mutual veto, (d) autonomy, (e) proportional representation, and (f) assimilation—see Dahl, op. cit., pp. 358-59.

22. Typically, the Swiss referendum has in practice become much more a weapon wielded by minorities who seek to resist majority decisions taken by the federal Parliament than an expression of will by "the" soveriegn Swiss people as a whole.

23. It has been argued that Switzerland owes its continued political independence to the very circumstance that it was not a German-speaking state only, but a multilingual political community. According to the historian William Martin, the conquest of French-speaking parts by the original Swiss Confederation in 1536 determined the very existence of a Swiss state:

> On ne saurait exagérer l'importance de cette conquête. Elle est comparable á celle du Tessin et la dépasse de beaucoup. Ce fut pour la Confédération une nouvelle naissance. Sans qu'il soit permis de refaire L'histoire, on peut affirmer que si la Suisse était restée purement allemande, elle n'aurait pas pu défendre son indépendence contre le mouvement des nationalités modernes qui a tendu à la création de grands Etats sur une base linguistique. Au moment où les Bernois ont conquis le Pays de Vaud, ils n'ont peut-être pas saisi toute la portée nationale de leur acte, car la diversité des langues n'étonnait alors aucun esprit. Mais la conquête n'en a pas moins régénéré, et peut-être sauvé, la Confédération.

William Martin, Histoire de la Suisse—Essai sur la Formation d'une Confédération d'Etats, Lausanne, 1943, p. 112 as quoted by Kohn, op. cit., pp. 19-20, footnote 1.

24. For a discussion on the definition of "nation"—and the political overtones in the debate about defining "nationhood"—older studies like those of C. A. Macartney,

characterized by "an administrative and legal order subject to change by legislation, to which the organized activities of the administrative staff, which are also controlled by regulations, are oriented." This system of order claims binding authority, not only over the members of the state—the citizens, most of whom have obtained membership by birth—but also to a very large extent over all action taking place in the area of its jurisdiction. It is thus a compulsory organization with a territorial basis. Hence, the claim: "to monopolize the use of force is as essential to it as its character of compulsory juridisdiction and continuous operation."

Nation, as Weber writes, "means above all that *it is proper* to expect from certain groups a specific sentiment of solidarity in the face of other groups. Thus, the concept belongs in the sphere of values." But as Weber also notes,

> there is no agreement on how these groups should be delimited or about what concerted action should result from such solidarity. In ordinary language, "nation" is, first of all not identical with the "people of a state," that is, with the membership of a given polity. Numerous polities comprise groups who emphatically assert the independence of their "nation" in the face of other groups; or they comprise merely *parts* of a group whose members declare themselves to be one homogeneous "nation" (Austria is an example for both [before World War I]). Furthermore, a "nation" is not identical with a community speaking the same language; . . . this by no means always suffices. . . . As a rule, however, the pretension to be considered a special "nation" is associated with a common language as a culture value of the masses. . . . Solidarity, instead, may be linked with . . . religious creed . . . [or] connected with differing social structure and mores and hence with "ethnic" elements. . . . Yet above all, national solidarity may be linked to memories of a common political destiny with other nations. . . . It goes without saying that "national" affiliation need not to be based upon common blood. Indeed especially radical "nationalists" are often of foreign descent . . . it seems that a group of people under certain conditions may attain the quality of a nation through specific behavior, or they may claim this quality as an "attainment"—and within short spans of time at that.[6]

As the degree of compliance with the demands of obedience by state authority can vary widely, and states differ in their natures, so an unbroken scale of quite varied and high changeable attitudes toward the idea of the "nation" is found among social strata within single groups to which language usage ascribes the quality of "nation." The scale extends from emphatic affirmation to emphatic negation and finally complete indifference, as may be characteristic of the citizens of Luxembourg and of nationally "unawakened" peoples. "Different strata do not have homogeneous or historically constant attitudes toward the idea."[7]

These texts of Weber are particularly applicable to Spain, where the degree of national consciousness, both of the Spanish and of the peripheral linguistic-cultural-historic groups, varies widely from regions with "un-

National States and National Minorities, London, 1934; Royal Institute of International Affairs, Nationalism. London, 1939; E. H. Carr, Nationalism and After, London, 1945; and Alfred Cobban, National Self-determination, Oxford, 1945, remain highly relevant.

25. For a very good analysis, see B.H.M. Vlekke, The Evolution of the Dutch Nation, New York, 1945.

26. It is again illustrative, however, of the forces of pluralism in the Netherlands that these central appointees nevertheless developed into highly independent magistrates rather than into "prefects" on behalf of the centre.

27. It testifies to the lasting strength of accommodationist practices in Switzerland that immediately after the civil war victors and vanquished sat together in elaborating the Swiss Constitution of 1848 that retained much of the older regional particularism and to a large degree depoliticized religious cleavages.

28. See especially the theoretical study on Switzerland by Steiner, op. cit.

29. This phrase is the well-chosen title of Arend Lijphart's important study, The Politics of Accommodation—Pluralism and Democracy in the Netherlands, Berkeley, Calif., 1968.

30. The following quotes are all from Arend Lijphart, "Consociational Democracy," World Politics, January 1969, p. 212ff.

31. See the article mentioned in note 2 above.

32. See Hans Daalder, "Government and Opposition in the New States," Government and Opposition, No. 1, 1966, pp. 205-26.

33. These views are particularly evident in the writings of Ferdinand Hermens, Carl J. Friedrich, and Barrington Moore. See on this same point Lijphart, "Consociational Democracy," op. cit., p. 217; Lehmbruch, Proporzdemokratie, and Rokkan, op. cit., p. 88ff.

34. In a similar vein, the greater freedom characteristic of the United Kingdom and the United States is often explained by their ability to avoid entanglements in large-scale land wars.

CHAPTER 2

EARLY STATE-BUILDING AND LATE PERIPHERAL NATIONALISMS AGAINST THE STATE: THE CASE OF SPAIN

Juan Linz

JUAN LINZ is Professor of Sociology and Political Science at Yale University. He has carried out research on parties, elections, elites, entrepreneurs, local leadership, intellectuals, and authoritarian regimes. His work has focused on Spain, Germany, Italy, and Brazil; and he has been active in international cooperative networks in sociology and political science. He is Chairman of the Research Committee on Political Sociology of the International Political Science Association and the International Sociological Association.

Spain represents some interesting problems for those concerned with the building of political systems encompassing large geographical areas but diverse social structures, historical traditions and languages. In 1966, with 31,871,000 inhabitants, it was by population the seventeenth largest country in the world and the fifth in Europe. However, it was only about the thirty-sixth in GNP per capita, with $645.[1] It is therefore a middle-sized country whose economic development, by European standards, has been retarded, even though rapid in recent years. In addition, that development is very unevenly distributed between regions.[2] One of these, Catalonia, with a distinctive personality, a glorious medieval history, a different language spoken by a large part of the population and a high level of industrialization in 1960 had almost four million inhabitants, not much less than that of Finland and larger than Norway and Ireland at that

Author's Note: This essay should be read in conjunction with another more specifically focused on the linguistic question and regional nationalism: Juan J. Linz, "Politics in a multilingual society with a dominant world language," in Jean Guy Savard and Richard Vegneault, eds., *Les états multilingues. Problems et Solutions. Multilingual States: Problems and Solutions,* Quebec, Presses de l'Université Laval, 1974.

time. If the Catalan-speaking areas outside of Catalonia proper are added, the figure might be between 5.9 and 6.8 million.[3]

The unity of the peoples and the lands of Spain has not remained unquestioned in the last hundred years despite the fact that the Spanish state—or was it only the crown?—had incorporated all of the present territory by 1512. Since the turn of the century regional nationalisms have questioned the existence of a Spanish nation and even a Spanish state. Spain therefore is a case of early state-building where the political, social and cultural integration of its territorial components—nation-building—was not fully accomplished. The state has been and is exposed to serious crises even when it has been far from ever breaking down, even in periods of Civil War such as that between 1936 and 1939, since that conflict was mainly about control of the state rather than about its existence. The ambivalent relation between the Spanish state (with few interruptions a unitary state since the eighteenth century and particularly since 1839) and modern nationalism on its peripheries might be of interest to students of political entities that have attained statehood in recent decades but whose nationhood is not unquestioned.

The problem has been excellently formulated by the great French historian Pierre Vilar when he writes:

L'Espagne, état unifié, d'une structure ancienne et de solide apparence, a tendu, sous l'influence des "renaissances" nationales du siècle dernier, a se désagréger comme les empires incohérents d'Europe centrale et orientale, et a laisser revivre des souvenirs politiques mediévaux, au moment meme ou les vieux royaumes allemands, ou les glorieuses cités italiennes, achevaient de se fondre en Etats modernes. Curieuse *contre-expérience.*[4]

STATE, NATION AND NONNATION-STATE, NATION-STATE

Before going further, we should clarify our use of the terms "state" and "nation," and therefore state- and nation-building—the processes leading to a more or less perfect realization of those social forms. Since entire bookshelves have been filled with volumes on those concepts it would be futile to discuss the literature in detail and to expect precise definitions. Let us quote Max Weber to define what we mean by "state":

A compulsory political organization with continuous operations will be called a "state" insofar as its administrative staff successfully upholds the claim to the *monopoly* of the *legitimate* use of force in the enforcement of its order.[5]

A state is a modern, essentially postfeudal form of political organization

TABLE 1

Population of Regions with Distinctive Languages and/or a Historical or Geographical Distinctiveness and Their Attitudes Toward Nationalism or Administrative Autonomy and Percentage of Their Population in Relation to the National Total[a] (1970 census)

I Regions with a tradition of local nationalism

Catalonia	14.9—from which one should substract those born outside of the province of residence
Basque country	(three provinces) 5.7—from which one should subtract those born outside of the province and the electorate not identified with the nationalists

II Region with a tradition of administrative and fiscal autonomy but not necessarily favorable to linguistic autonomy or local nationalism

Navarre   1.3

III Regions susceptible to linguistic and administrative autonomy appeals but not actively committed to such demands

Galicia   7.8

Levante   8.6 more specifically Valencia and Castellón

Balearic Islands 1.5

(Levante and the Balearic Islands might come under the influence of a greater Catalonia appeal)

IV Region with some tradition of local administrative autonomy; but Castilian-speaking and economically dependent on the central government

Canary Islands   3.5

a. These figures allow different combinations in favor of quite different political solutions to the problem of national diversity. The hard core "non-Castilian nationalism"—Catalonia and the Basque country (ignoring for the moment the Castilian oriented immigrants and sectors of the population)—would draw 20.6 percent. Galicia, where the linguistic nationalism has not been so strong, and Levante and Baleares, where the local language does not have the significance nor, in Levante, the diffusion of Catalan, would add another 17.9%, making the absolute, and obviously exaggerated maximum of population in favor of linguistic pluralism 38.5 percent with the rest showing little or no sympathy to their claims. The addition of regions with traditions of local administrative autonomy would bring this figure up to 43.5 percent with the remainder of the country almost firmly committed to a centralistic unitary state.

awakened" people to those with extremist "nationalistic" minorities, and varies in time, from periods of only "provincialist" feelings to those of a true "nationalism." However, we want to retain the fundamental distinction between the *state*—an organization based on certain chances of compliance with authority and the capacity for enforcement—and the solidarities based on certain attitudes and sentiments reflected in certain behaviors, that transform a social group into a *nation*. When both processes coincide—creation of an organization for the exercise of authority, and development of a specific sense of solidarity in the face of other groups—we will speak of a *nation-state*. Since that sentiment of solidarity is based on intensive social communication between members of a group, it is an inevitable concomitant of a modern economy and of the social mobilization that goes with political democracy. This accounts for the tendency, since the nineteenth century, to fuse both processes, state-building and nation-building. The question might even be asked: in an era of democratic values, is it possible to create a state—or even hold it together—without a parallel process of nation-building?

Analytically, the processes have to be kept distinct. Only such conceptual clarity will allow us to understand how Spain is for most Spaniards a nation-state, invoking in them a sense of solidarity that no other group affiliation produces; for important minorities, it has been and is likely to remain only a state with whose authority they comply in their behavior, attributing to it more or less legitimacy, depending on their attitudes toward the regimes exercising power within Spain's borders and the coercive capacities of those regimes. For those minorities Spain is a state, but not their nation, and therefore not a nation-state. Those minorities identifying with a Catalan or particularly a Basque nation might be small, but they demonstrate failure by Spain and its elites to nation-build, whatever their success in state-building. Sometimes Spaniards, whatever views they held about the social and economic system their state should create and about which social classes should control its apparatus, had to ask those who claimed other national identities if they were willing to recognize that state or aspired to create new nation-states. Very often those who had strongly identified with the state built through centuries by the Castilian core and the elites from the whole peninsula that had collaborated in the process, as if it were the expression of a Spanish nation, felt that their fellow citizens should identify equally strongly with a Spanish nation rather than consider Spain just as a state, a nonnation-state. Many of the great polemics in the pamphlet literature and the bitter debates in the halls of the legislatures of the last hundred years turn around these questions. These differences have resulted in conflicts about symbols—like flags and anthems—riots, legal prosecutions, army interventions, and heightened consciousness of conflicting solidarities. Obviously such symbolic conflicts mask and are a reflection of other strains, often economic, but it would be a great mistake to ignore their independent significance. Leaving aside the affect in their statements, the distortions of the number of people involved with those issues, and the intensity of their feelings, Spanish political leaders have often perceived the problem in much the same terms as an analytical social scientist—arguing bitterly about a Spanish "state," a Spanish "nation" and "peripheral nations."

Prat de la Riba, the great leader of the Lliga, formulated the problem in these texts:

> But we did not doubt, no, we did not. We saw the national spirit, the national character, the national thought; we saw the law, we saw the language; and from the law the language and the organism; the national thought, the character and the spirit, bring the Nation; that is, a society of people who speak a language of their own and have the same spirit that manifests itself or is characteristic for the whole variety of the whole collective life.

> And we saw more: we saw that Catalonia had a language, a law, an art of its own, that it had a national spirit, a national character, a national thought: Catalonia was, therefore, a nation.

> So all the confusions were destroyed, all the doubts: The Nation (Catalonia) was a life, organic, natural, entity. It existed in face of the laws that did not recognize it. And by the fact of being natural it distinguished itself clearly from the artificial creations of man, among them fundamentally, the State.

> The State remained fundamentally differentiated from the Nation, because the State was a political organization, a power independent externally, supreme in the interior with material force of men and monies to maintain its independence and authority.[8]

At the other end of the Pyrennees, in 1906, a Capucine monk, Evangelista de Ibero, wrote in a Basque nationalist catechism, *Ami Vasco,* a series of ideological definitions which contrast nation and state:

I. Nation.
1 - What is a nation? The ensemble of men or peoples who have a same origin, a same language, a same character, the same customs, the same fundamental laws, the same glories, the same tendencies and aspirations, and the same destinies.
2 - Of all those properties, which constitutes essentially a nationality? In the first place, the blood, race or origin; in the second place, the language. The other qualities are nothing but the consequence of the other two, most specifically of the first.

II. State
7 - What is the State? Considered not in its formal and directing element but in its material or directed element, (*sic*), we could define it: The ensemble of peoples or individuals who live subject to the same sovereign authority.
8 - Is the nation the same as the state? Absolutely not. The nation is something natural, that is, something created by nature itself; the state is something artificial, dependent on human will. The nation is indestructible, as long as the race subsists; the states are formed and broken by the whims of kings and

conquerors. The nation binds its elements with bonds of blood and language: the state, only with the tie of the authority that governs them.[9]

Significantly, the PNV (Partido Nacionalista Vasco) representatives in the Republican government during the Civil War, insisted on the use of the term "state" in their pronouncements.

SUBORDINATION OF MEDIEVAL POLITICAL UNITS UNDER A SINGLE MONARCH—FIRST STEPS IN STATE-BUILDING

In the course of the Middle Ages, feudal lords and kings of different territories of the Iberic peninsula, by conquest and marriages, created a number of political units, the larger ones being, in the middle of the fourteenth century, the crown of Aragón; Castile; Portugal; Navarre; and the last Moorish enclave, the kingdom of Granada. Starting from the Asturian reduit, and the Pyrennaic focae of resistance, the Christians had slowly reconquered the Peninsula from the Moors. Navarre had remained isolated by the advance of Castile-León and Aragón, maintaining its separate identity until 1512. The other two Pyrennaic states, Aragón and Catalonia, were united under the Count of Barcelona, Ramón Berenguer IV, in 1137, curtailing the imperial ambitions of the Castilian king Alphons VII. The new kingdom was to expand southward to Valencia, across the sea to Mallorca, and over the Pyrenees into Languedoc and the Provence, but would be checked by the French nucleus. The Castilian move toward the Mediterranean, through Murcia, would stop its southward expansion and redirect its efforts toward the Mediterranean, particularly southern Italy.[10] Castile-León also failed in subordinating or incorporating the Kingdom of Portugal, founded 1134, that advanced southward along the Atlantic parallel to the dominant power in the interior of the peninsula. As in France the royal marriage policies attempted to incorporate the neighboring kingdoms. That policy was crowned by the marriage of Ferdinand of Aragón and Isabella of Castile in 1469, and their joint rule over both kingdoms with each maintaining its own institutions. The conquest of Granada in 1492 and the incorporation of Navarre into Castile in 1515 completed the territorial unification of most of the peninsula under one crowned head, but as a union it was no more than dynastic. In 1580, Philip II became king of Portugal by inheritance, but that union would be broken in 1640.[11]

The union of Castile and Aragón—including the three crowns of the Aragonese confederation: the kingdom of Aragón, the principality of Catalonia and the kingdom of Valencia, with their distinct institutions—

was not a union of equal partners. The two territories were at very different stages of development, and the world setting offered different opportunities to each component, particularly with the shift of the focus of history from the Mediterranean to the Atlantic, so well analyzed by Fernand Braudel.[12] The end of the Reconquista, the discovery of the New World, and the wool trade with northern Europe offered Castile the opportunity and the resources to turn outward toward Europe and the wider world. The Catalan-Aragonese empire of the thirteenth and fourteenth centuries, in the fifteenth had entered, particularly in Catalonia, into a commercial, social, and political crisis, resulting from the general economic depression of the Mediterranean world. A conflict siding the king, peasants, and artisans against the nobility and merchant oligarchy which controlled the traditional institutions, had plunged the principality into a civil war. The pacification by Ferdinand after he assumed power in 1479, instead of laying the foundations of absolute royal power such as the monarchs of Castile were beginning to enjoy, resurrected and reinvigorated the old contractual state and its institutions which protected subjects against the abuse of royal power.[13] After 1479, therefore, the monarchy combined territories with very different political institutions and social structures, some closer to the model of the emerging patrimonial monarchies, others closer to the estate societies[14] that emerged in Europe on the borders of the more centralized monarchies, with some elements, in the case of Catalonia and particularly Barcelona, of the city states[15] of Italy, the Hanse, the Low countries, and Switzerland. In the crown of Aragón lands the representative institutions would retain for some time a strength they had already started to loose in Castile and which would atrophy under the new Habsburg dynasty. Castile would be a kingdom with a strong center, the court of a powerful monarch surrounded by a bureaucracy and a court nobility; initially, there would be strong cities but their power would decay (after an unsuccessful uprising); the seaward oriented Kingdom would be forced by its European involvements—Flanders and Italy—to an early Primat der Aussenpolitik. The parts of the monarchy were also unequal in territorial and population resources (see Table 2).

As J. H. Elliot writes:

The Catalan-Aragonese federation, oriented towards the Mediterranean, commercial in spirit, cosmopolitan in outlook, had little in common with a Castile whose social organization was geared to the needs of crusading warfare and whose mental horizons had been limited by centuries of political and cultural isolation. The gulf between the two was made still wider by their differing political traditions and institutions. Each, it was true, possessed parliamentary institutions, or Cortes, but the Cortes of Castile, which had never attained legislating power,

TABLE 2

Area and Population of the Spanish Monarchy at the End of the Sixteenth Century

	Area Sq. Km.	Population	Density Inhabitants Sq. Km.	Area in %	Popula- tion in %
Kingdom of Castile	378,000	6,910,000	18.2	65.2	72.8
Crown of Aragon	100,000	1,180,000	11.8	17.2	12.4
Kingdom of Navarre	12,000	145,000	12.1	2.1	1.5
Kingdom of Portugal	90,000	1,250,000	14.0	15.5	13.3
	580,000	9,485,000	14.0	100	100

SOURCE: Juan Reglá and Guillermo Céspedes del Castillo, **Imperio, Aristocracia, Absolutismo**, Vol. III of the **Historia social y económica de España y América**, ed. by Jaime Vicens Vives, Barcelona, Teide, 1957, p. 13.

emerged from the Middle Ages isolated and weak, and with little prospect of curbing an energetic monarch. Those of Valencia, Catalonia and Aragón, on the other hand, shared the legislative power with the Crown and were well buttressed by laws and institutions which derived from a long tradition of political liberty. The king's powers in the States of the Crown of Aragón for the administering of justice, the exacting of tributes or the raising of armies were hedged about with legal restrictions. At every turn, a ruler would find himself limited by the fueros, the laws and liberties he had sworn to observe, and each of the territories possessed a standing body, like the Catalan Diputacio whose function was to defend the national liberties against the arbitrary power of the Crown . . . Apart from sharing common sovereigns, neither Castile nor the Crown of Aragón underwent any radical institutional alteration which might begin the slow process of merging them into a single State . . . The nature of this union, as much as the unequal strength of the two partners, played its part in determining the course taken by the Spanish history during the XVI century. It set the pattern for the acquisition of further territories by the Kings of Spain. Each new territory acquired through marriage or inheritance, like the great Habsburg inheritance of 1504, was added as the Crown of Aragón had been added, with the retention of its own laws and privileges; and fresh conquests remained the possession of the conqueror, and not the common property of all. America fell, not to Spain, but to Castile alone.[16]

THE SEVENTEENTH CENTURY CRISIS IN THE STATE-BUILDING PROCESS

The Catalan rebellion of 1640 and the secession of Portugal in 1665, recognized in 1668, exemplify the difficulties of monarchic-bureaucratic state-building, as the rebellion of the Netherlands in 1560 had shown the difficulties of holding together widely separate domains under an imperial rule in Europe.[17] Studying the nature of the relation between the monarch, his ministers, and the institutions of the different kingdoms and their societies will help us understand the obstacles to large state-building endeavors before nationalism, which, however, leave a critical heritage to the nation-building phase. The Catalan uprising is one of the "six contemporaneous revolutions" of the seventeenth century studied comparatively in a book of that title by the British historian Roger Bigelow Merriman, that attempts to break with tradition to see the Puritan revolution, the Commonwealth, and the Protectorate as isolated phenomena.[18] Five antimonarchical rebellions shook the continent in the middle decades of the seventeenth century when the authority of the king of Spain, even when he did not then have that title, was successively challenged in Catalonia and permanently in Portugal; the French monarchy was shaken to its foundations by that strange revolt of the lawyers and the princess known as the Fronde; finally, the stadtholderate, with its centralized monarchical tendencies was forced to give way to the pensionary government in the Netherlands and did not regain control for twenty-two years. The three revolutions against the Spanish monarch were all of an essentially peripheral character, but as Merriman points out, all "were serious matters, and had caused the authorities in Madrid much trouble and anxiety, but the fact remains that the Spanish government was never confronted with revolution in the heart of its own dominions at all [in] the same fashion as were England, France, and Holland." The Naples revolt led by a fisherman generally named Masaniello, taken over after his death by an aristocrat named Massa, and again by a blacksmith named Annese, could not sustain the proclaimed republic and had to turn, like the Catalan revolutionaries, to the protection of another foreign power: France. Only the Portuguese rebels, thanks largely to international support and the existence of a Portuguese empire, were able to create a new state sufficiently homogeneous in its European home-base to become one of its oldest pure nation-states.[19]

Merriman points out some of the parallels in all six revolutions. In the first place, the immediate though not always the most fundamental cause of every one of them was financial. The emerging modern state with its international commitments—particularly overtaxing the resources of Castile, head of a loose confederation of kingdoms—engaged in almost constant wars and demanded changes in the fiscal relation of the component parts of the Crown that started the revolts. Second, in five of the six, the outbursts originally were directed against dominant and unpopular ministers rather than against the monarchs. Third, while all broke out at the end of the period known as the century of the Wars of

Religion, religious questions affected them little, except in England. After the expulsion of the Jews in 1492, the quick end of the few Protestant foci and the expulsion of the Moriscos, religious problems would not affect the efforts of state- or nation-building in Spain until the nineteenth century. Before the last century, the influence of the Crown over the national church would make the Catholic religion important in the tradition of all components of the monarchy and a collaborator in the process of state-building due to centuries of struggle against Islam and later against the Reformation or Protestant countries. In fact, the identification of the state and even the nation with Catholicism became and has remained, among many Spaniards, so strong that they are willing almost until the present to identify anti-Catholic with anti-Spanish. This would be an obstacle to secular state- and nation-building in the nineteenth and twentieth centuries when important leaders, particularly of the Republics, sought to create a secular state and nation. For reasons that deserve more investigation, some territories of the periphery, particularly the Basque country, developed a more intense religiosity, even when at odds with the official hierarchy in the last decades, so that the defense of traditional rights of the periphery, and later of its cultural identity, became strongly tied to the clergy, particularly the lower clergy and some of the orders, often adding a religious dimension to the center-periphery conflicts. Fourth, the rulers and their officials, and to lesser extent some of the supporters of Cromwell, perceived the basic revolutionary character and the possibility of contagion from the English revolution.

In the seventeenth century, the King of Spain faced the problem of annuling such "rights, privileges, franchises, and exemptions enjoyed by subjects as prejudice the authority of the prince."[20] This, in the opinion of hostile historians was out of a lust for the power of the king, his prime minister, or the Castilian bureaucrats and nobles. Other historians recognized an inevitable requirement for the maintenance of Spanish power in the world, the needs of common defense in men and moneys that the King could not meet within the framework of traditional institutions. Once a Castilian state had been created by Charles V and Philip II, that fact created unbearable inequality between the kingdoms. The power of the monarch in Castile meant that it had to carry the load of the empire and its foreign policy commitments even when its elite inevitably enjoyed the power and prestige of the state, provoking the jealousy of the periphery.

A secret memorandum prepared for Philip IV by the Conde Duque de Olivares, dated 25 December 1624, provided a detailed description of the nature of government in the Spanish monarchy and its problems. Its main theme was expressed in these often quoted terms:

> The most important thing in Your Majesty's Monarchy is for you to become king of Spain: by this I mean, Sir, that Your Majesty should not be content with being king of Portugal, of Aragón, of Valencia and count of Barcelona, but should secretly plan and work to reduce these kingdoms of which Spain is composed to the style and laws of Castile, with no difference whatsoever. And if Your Majesty achieves this, you will be the most powerful prince in the world.[21]

The Conde Duque suggested three possible ways to achieve this aim. The first "and the most difficult to achieve, but the best, if it can be managed" was to favor the people of other kingdoms, "introducing them into Castile, marrying them to Castilians," and, "by admitting them into the offices and dignities of Castile, to prepare the way for a natural union. The second was to start negotiations when he had an army and a fleet unoccupied, so that he could negotiate from strength"

> The third way, although not so justified, but the most effective, would be for Your Majesty—assuming you have these forces—to go in person as if to visit the kingdom where the business is to be done; and there to bring about some great popular tumult. Under this pretext, the troops could intervene. And in order to restore calm and prevent any further recurrence of the troubles, the laws could be reorganized (as if the country had been newly conquered) and brought into conformity with those of Castile.

In the same memorandum he wrote:

> There is the greatest justification for discontent in those other kingdoms and provinces, which have not only put up with government for so many years without the presence of the king, but are also regarded as unfitted for honors and unequal to the other vassals. . . .

The first alternative is peaceful integration by increased communication in this case between elites and between them and the king; the second, imposition from a position of strength, accepted by the local power structures; the last, a coup d'etat. Historical circumstances made any of the three unviable, and probably unintentionally the rebellion of 1640 appeared to be the third, but due to the international commitments of the monarchy, the forces were not available to carry it out.

The problem faced by the Crown in trying to build a modern patrimonial monarchical state in Catalonia, and previously, to a lesser extent, in Aragón and Valencia, resulted from the development in the late Middle Ages of an "estate state," Ständestaat, of the type studied in comparative perspective by Otto Hintze.[22] As a seventeenth century commentator described it:

In Catalonia, the supreme power and jurisdiction over the province belongs not to His Majesty alone, but to his Majesty and the three estates of the province, which together possess supreme and absolute power to make and unmake laws, and to alter the machinery of the government of the province . . . The laws we have in Catalonia are laws compacted between the king and the land, and the prince can no more exempt himself from them than he can exempt himself from a contract.[23]

Each king on his accession would swear that they should be inviolably observed by himself and his officials. The community expressed its will through the sessions of the Cortes, and when they were not sitting, by means of the *Diputació,* a standing committee of six men, two from each estate. They were elected through the *insaculació,* whereby the names of eligible persons were drawn at random. The representation of the king in his absence, which since the Habsburgs was almost permanent, was attributed to a viceroy who could be a non-Catalan and who was the head of civil and military administration. His orders came from Madrid and his dispatches addressed to the king would be considered by a collegiate body, the council of Aragón, that would make recommendations to the king.

The fiscal foundations of royal authority were exceptionally precarious. All secular taxation was in the hands of the Diputació, from whose resources the Crown benefited only very marginally. Its own major source of revenue was ecclesiastical, but that source had been farmed out to the bankers of the Crown. The royal patrimony in Catalonia was only the ghost of a patrimony compared to the Duke of Cardona and the Church and the barons. The income of the Crown from all secular sources was less than half of the income of the city of Barcelona alone and only a quarter of the income enjoyed by the Diputació. As Elliot writes, there could be no better commentary on the king of Spain's weakness in the principality. Even with a contribution by the Diputació the salaries of the officials had to come from Crown estates in Valencia. There were no funds to perform many functions of government, for example, prosecution of bandits who had increased with population pressure and economic crisis. Troops often could not be paid.

Royal, baronial, ecclesiastical, and mixed jurisdictions all existed side by side, with their immunities and privileges. In the countryside the inhabitants would fight desperate rearguard actions to save themselves from falling by default completely under the control of the local aristocracy. The 2,385 administrative units (*llocs*) were apportioned as follows: baronial jurisdiction 1,114, royal jurisdiction 681, ecclesiastical jurisdiction 589. Royal authority in the countryside, for example, in prosecuting banditry, depended on close cooperation between baronial and royal officials. Another series of immunities were those of the agents of the Inquisition, numerous due to the border character of the area, and the ecclesiastical ones.

However, the most important part of the Constitution specified the privileges and immunities of the aristocracy. The Diputació, controlled by a few influential nobles and by the Barcelona city oligarchy, could be counted on to protest any infringment of aristocratic interests. After each Cortes, where the Crown appeared to obtain subsidies, the aristocracy was a little stronger. As long as the king imposed respect to the nobility, as did Philip II, government could function, even though badly. With hands tied by the Constitutions and by lack of financial means, without strong support from Madrid, the viceroys could not maintain order. In 1615 an economic and social crisis, reflected in banditry, created a condition in which the choice became security or Constitutions, creating a unique opportunity to castilianize Catalonia under the pretext of restoring order. A conflict between the two duties of the king—to uphold the Constitutions and to see that his subjects were properly governed, between "legality" and "necessity"—became inescapable. Elliot summarizes the problem in these terms:

> In this lies the interest, and the tragedy, of the seventeenth century conflict between Castilian and Catalan. This conflict arose out of the divergence between the ideal Catalonia and Catalan reality, between the imaginary and the actual relationship of the Catalans and their king, between the medieval laws of Catalonia and the stark modern needs of Castile. The king would allege necessity; the Catalans would cling to legality.[24]

Let us note a certain parallel with Third World countries that have adopted liberal-democratic institutions, but whose real situations are far from congruent with them, where necessity leads to violations, while important sectors cling to the ideal, questioning the legitimacy of those acting in terms of reality.

One policy undertaking was the taming of the nobles with the support of the towns, the alliance of the people with the Crown, but it was unsuccessful when a new viceroy engaged in a conflict with the Diputació, which represented all three traditional classes of Catalan society.

To understand the transition from estate society and representation to patrimonial or semibureaucratic monarchical government, the need for that transition, and the difficulties in accomplishing it in this case, what the Catalans called Castilianization, it is important to realize the true state of the key institutions and their mutual relationship. We cannot go into such detail, but let us note that the Crown had not managed to keep the Diputació and the city disunited, inevitably it had antagonized the nobility while its financial demands prevented a coalition with the cities, and its military presence aroused the populace and made it willing to follow dissident elites. The presence in Barcelona of masses of harvesters led to a riot and the assassination of the viceroy (1640), precipitating the rebellion of the Principado. However, the Catalans failed in their effort to create a Catalan republic linked with France. The presence of French troops created discontent, as had those of the King of Spain previously. In 1651 the Spanish monarch could reconquer his domain, without changing the Constitution, even when in 1659 he was to lose part of his Catalan domain to France. Between the two great powers Catalonia had proven unable to regain its historical sovereignty, despite the fact that in some respects its historical and social personality was more distinct than Portugal's.

The situation of the principality is well summarized by Elliot:

> Catalonia's traditional form of government may have been admirably suited to the days before the union of Crowns, but times had changed. In the words of one commentator who, although Catalan, was unsympathetic to Catalonia's claims: "the form of the empire and of the Monarchy has altered, and our province no longer possesses a king who rules in it alone, but one who rules over all four quarters of the earth."

> The Castilians, could not appreciate the intensity of feeling with which the Catalans looked on their laws and institutions, and there was some justification for *their* belief that those laws were simply a cloak to shield certain interested groups from the punishment they deserved.[25]

These quotations reflect well the problems of a transition from a decadent and ossified estate society to a more centralized modern administration, from a small political unit where the ruler could be personally present to a large one in which he could not be personally in contact with the affairs of each of his domains, but where he had only the necessary traditional authority to arbitrate among the complex social and institutional forces in conflict, or to impose his will.

However, the union of monarchies could have continued inefficiently and ineffectively for many years without economic or military integration had it not been for the international commitments of Spain in Europe and overseas, often with different consequences for different units of the monarchy. (At this time the defense of Portuguese possessions in Brazil prevented an armistice with the Netherlands that would have allowed a more successful struggle with France, but the possessions could not be given up at the risk of alienating that Crown country.) The sudden catastrophic decline in American silver remittances, the indebtedness of the Crown, the cost of the maintenance of troops in a moment of international tension made it inevitable that Castilian government councils and the *arbitristas* (men commenting on the problems of the state who might be considered the first economists) should suggest that the burdens be distributed in proper proportion. They could not continue to fall only on the head of the monarchy—Castile, where the king had the power to impose his will—when it was blocked by the political and social structure of the other kingdoms.

The policy advocated by the Conde Duque de Olivares, whatever his errors in execution, tactics, and timing, was not the result of an arbitrary will, but of constraint by the change in scale of political units. To some degree we can say that modern state-building was in part the result of the Primat der Aussenpolitik. The different processes of state-building in the larger European monarchies that had such important consequences when the more or less absolute monarchies had to incorporate new social strata and create or expand representative institutions in response to democratic ideologies in the nineteenth century (as Hintze, Palmer, Rokkan, Daalder, among others, have stressed), were largely determined by the difference between large and small politics, empires and second-rate powers. In the Spanish case the delay in building the Spanish state in the period of maximum glory, the prestige of its kings and influx of wealth from America, made the task more difficult in a period of decadence. The delay, in turn, was the result of the early success in Castile, of the need to go slowly, considering the problems of the extra-Spanish territories of the Crown in Italy and Central Europe that would have been threatened by such institutional changes. The advantage offered in the administration of overseas Spain of incorporation into Castile rather than the transfer of the complex institutions of the Crown of Aragón was another factor.

One of the leading Spanish historians, Claudio Sánchez-Albornoz, has formulated the problem in these terms:

> Neither in their own mind nor in that of their collaborators emerged the idea to articulate all Spaniards into a state unity, of whatever form. Charles and Philip organized, it is true, the modern Castilian state, but in doing so they accentuated the obstacles that arose in the task of Spain. Because they placed Castile, converted central political axis of the monarchy and fiscal basis of it, and the other peninsular kingdoms on different levels, transformed into mere satellites of similar significance to the other European states inserted into the general framework of their large empire . . . It is the enormous responsibility of Charles V and Philip II to have neglected to unite Spain. Spain can claim against them a great debt. Even those most hostile to the very idea of Spain in the peripheric regions admit that in the eighteenth century there emerged everywhere, even in Catalonia a Spanish patriotism.[26]

The reading of the historians of the Spanish monarchy in the sixteenth and seventeenth centuries suggest a slight modification to our initial theme: *Spain: a case of partial early state-building in Castile and delayed state-building of Spain.* The memories of that early phase of frustrated state-building haunted Spanish politicians in the late nineteenth and early twentieth centuries. Not by accident the anthem of the Catalan nationalists is *Els Segadors,* reminding them of the "Corpus of Blood" in which the Spanish viceroy was killed in 1640. Medieval and early modern history is one of the main battlegrounds of the nationalist historians against any nation-building efforts: efforts of fiscal and military penetration in the nineteenth century, particularly in the Basque case. Frustrated state-building in the most glorious period of cultural splendor and world prestige allows a separate sense of history among an important minority among the elites of the periphery. The ideal image of their institutions, rather than the reality, allows them to link them with the democratic-liberal period on an ideological level, without, however, the positive real links we find in the Netherlands or in some Nordic states. A glorious estate-representative tradition, rather than contributing to the consolidation of a modern democratic Spanish state, as it did in other countries, has become a component of the antistate sentiments and interests in the periphery. As an ideology it was used to mobilize some of its populations against that liberal-democratic state emerging in the center of the monarchy and Andalusia, supported by the army, in the nineteenth century.

After the instauration of the Bourbon dynasty and the defeat of the supporters of Archduke Charles in the War of Succession (1700-1715), Philip V introduced deep changes in the Constitution of the monarchy doing away with much of the traditional limits to royal authority in the lands of the Crown of Aragón.[27] The monarch and his ministers reformed the structure of government, the local administration, the tax system and administration, even the university. New offices modeled after the French administration were created. The nobility which had sided with the pretender were deprived of their lands, even when they were returned to noble status after they recognized the new authority. The Enlightenment penetrated into Spain and influenced many reforms, considerable economic progress took place, and all promised that the state-building process would go on successfully, even when internationally Spain had lost its preeminence as a power, and its cultural creativity was reduced.[28] Regional tensions never were more lulled; Catalonia with its new access to the overseas market experienced an economic revival, and at the time of the war with the French revolutionaries and Napoleon, a new Spanish patriotism, if not nationalism, was dramatically demonstrated. The French looked for collaborationists, but had little success except for a small attempt at secession under their protection in Guipúzcoa (1794). The Jacobinism of the French, who desired to incorporate the province rather than support independence, dwarfed the attempt.

In a paradoxical way the bitter conflict in Catalonia, which contributed to its siding with the Archduke Charles against the Bourbon heir of Charles II in 1700, led to the most successful period of Spanish state-building, to unification of the country through the abrogation of the Catalan Constitution in the Decreto de Nueva Planta (1716), and with it, the disappearance of a legal and ideologico-historical basis for resistance to the state in Catalonia. In contrast in the Basque country, outside of the mainstream of Spanish life until the end of the eighteenth century, and after rapid industrialization at the turn of this century, the persistence of medieval institutions until 1839, decapitated even at a later date (1876), served as a basis for the emergence of a nationalist movement that questioned not only a Spanish nation-state but a nonnational-state in a much more radical way than the majority of Catalan nationalists. The self-confidence of the eighteenth century Bourbon state after subjecting the lands of the Crown of Aragón to the centralizing tendencies following the French model, delayed even more the process of state-penetration in the Basque periphery. Delayed state-building made nation-building in the nineteenth century—under unfavorable circumstances—even more difficult in that region.

THE PERIPHERY AGAINST THE CENTER: PRE-NATIONALIST TENSIONS IN THE NINETEENTH CENTURY

Around 1800 the conflicts within the royal family, as well as the reaction against the reformers resulting from the French Revolution, started a crisis of legitimacy of the monarchy, but only the Napoleonic invasion in 1808 and the popular revolutionary response against it, was to plunge the country into a century of conflict.[29] Those tensions or civil wars between liberals and partisans of the ancient regime, between secularizers and clericals, and later between social classes, initially had no relation to regional and linguistic differences, but, through a complex set of circumstances would be fought out largely in the lands on the periphery of the old Castilian Spain and thereby activate their sentiments of historical distinctiveness and of grievance against the central authorities. The Carlist rebellion in Navarre did not emphasize originally the defense of the *Fueros*—the distinctive political, administrative, and financial institutions of the kingdom—and the supporters of the Liberal branch of the dynasty were equally interested in those privileges, but in the course of the war and in the peace of 1839 that ended the seven year long war, the

Fueros had come to join the Carlist trilogy of God, Country, and King.[30] The lack of sociologically oriented research on the bases of support of Carlism, like the work of Tilly on the Vendée[31] makes it difficult to estimate the weight of peripheral anticentralist sentiments compared to religious, economic, social, and other factors, in the fight between Carlist peripheral Spain and the Liberal supporters of Isabel II in the Castilian center and Andalusia. When one analyses the internal conflicts of Spain in the nineteenth century until the Restoration, one should not forget that the main divisions cut through the society and politics of the peripheral regions, countryside versus cities, mountain areas versus plains and valleys. It should be stressed that the three largest cities of the Basque country resisted, except for very short periods, the encirclement and siege by the Carlists, that the mountain interior of Catalonia reacted politically differently from the city of Barcelona.[32] However, those conflicts left a legacy of questioning the authority of the state, of hostility to the parties of the Liberal monarchy, and of Catholic questioning of the new political order that would not allow the integration of certain sectors of opinion into a system not characterized by efficiency when confronted with difficult problems like the loss of the last colonies in 1898, social unrest and anarchist terrorism, or a costly and unpopular war in Morocco. Unfortunately, we have no scholarly studies of the political behavior of elites, clergymen, and others in the Basque country and Catalonia by which to follow in detail the process of desintegration of the former support of Carlism and its two splinters, the Jaimistas and Integristas, and of Catholic and Fuerist candidates (around the turn of the century), to locate some of the strata and elites that would end support of the Lliga—the right-wing of Catalan autonomism—and the Partido Nacionalista Vasco PNV). The history of part of the peripheral opposition might well have started as a religious cleavage, reinforced perhaps by socio-economic crisis situations, slowly turning into a regionalistic, autonomist sentiment, and finally toward nationalist parties.

But let us turn back to the early decades of the nineteenth century. Spanish political liberalism was an Andalusian development, and not a Catalan one, nor one of the Basque-Navarrese periphery, even when in both there were, particularly in the cities, groups sympathizing with the Constitutionalists of Cádiz. Let us not forget that despite its economic development Barcelona was not the only modern economic center of Spain, that in the Sevilla-Cádiz area and later in Málaga, we would find germs of economic growth, a commercial bourgeoisie, which in the course of the century would lose it impetus, perhaps absorbed by a surrounding latifundist aristocratic-bourgeois rural society.

In Catalonia, when the Constitution was reinstated in 1820 after the absolutist period (1814-1820), the consequences of the yellow fever, bad crops, and consequent crisis in the countryside, allowed the royalists and the clergy to arouse the peasantry, that was used to support a counter-government of a royalist Regency, in favor of a return to a purified traditional monarchical rule.[33] Their manifestos referred to the Fueros and privileges abrogated or ignored by the Constitutionalists, and a promise to extend them in Catalonia. The Liberals defeated the uprising militarily, but the intervention of the Holy Alliance reestablished the absolute rule of the king (1823). However, the new regime, partly due to the French presence, did not purge all Liberals from the army and the bureaucracy, nor reestablish the Inquisition, nor fuse the professional army with the royalist militias, so that the ultras felt disappointed. Those dissatisfied—in Catalan the *malcontents*—rose in 1827, but only in the Catalan countryside. A politico-ideological conflict was superimposed or converged with a socio-economic crisis. The movement was repressed and the new governor, a hateful figure, established a regime of terror against the subversives but also against the Liberals. In this whole period the Church, to defend its conservative positions and to reach the masses, had turned to pamphlets and sermons in Catalan against the dangers of Liberalism. The Liberals in turn favored the policies directed toward a greater uniformity in the kingdom, accepting the new division in provinces, and so forth. Only in the late twenties, partly in response to the propaganda of the "royalists," did a certain "provincialist" sentiment appear on issues like the administrative unity of Catalonia.

The years 1833 to 1844 brought the bourgeois revolution and the dynastic war between those defending the rights of the minor Isabel II against her uncle Carlos. In 1834 a new moderate Constitution—The *Estatuto Real*—was proclaimed and favorably received in Barcelona, but even before, some guerrilla bands outside of the city had appeared against the Liberals. The textile manufacturers organized in the *Comisión de Fábricas* supported the Liberal monarchy, manufacturers were elected to the Parliament in 1834, and the sale of church properties benefited the bourgeoisie. However, soon the more radical popular elements and the mob—the murris or miserables—turned to burning churches and convents, and the tax collecting offices at the gates and, after an attempt to reestablish order, the largest textile mill. The situation, to be repeated in future decades, was one where a growing industrial bourgeoisie faced a two-fronted threat: the Carlist reactionaries rising up in the countryside and provincial towns, the radicalized petty bourgeoisie dissatisfied with "moderate freedom" agitating on the basis of the citizens guard, the mob (created by the economic crisis and the disorganization in the country-side), and the central government, weakened by the Carlist wars, unable to respond effectively. In this context a *Junta Auxiliar Consultiva* was constituted by the authorities in an effort to control those who had made the revolution on the street, in which the more radical elements, future members of the progressive party, gained the upper hand. It proposed extraordinary Cortes, appealing to Catalan sentiment: "Catalans the political division of the provinces of Catalonia will never destroy our affections and interests. Catalans, union and freedom." It invited similar juntas in Valencia and Zaragoza jointly to organize an armed force, but their passive response, like that of the other Catalan juntas, defeated its ambitions. It obtained the appointment of a liberal general as captain general and dissolved, but another junta, with representatives of each of the four provinces of Catalonia, continued.

A threefold split divided Catalan society between Carlist religious reactionaries, the moderates (supporters of the 1834 Constitution: civil servants, businessmen, professors, often with a long liberal tradition) and the progressives with Jacobin ideas, involved in secret societies, recently returned from exile, ideological and strongly anticlerical. Each of them, in turn, was faction-ridden.

The moderates regained control of the city government and reorganized the militia, with the support of the Spanish army. It goes beyond our purposes to summarize the different phases of that struggle between 1836 and 1839, the ups and downs of the different sides, and the violent fights in the city. One aspect stands out: the Liberal leaders of the Commission of Factories stated: "there was no other solution than the presence of the Captain General to save this city; and his entry among the blessings and tears of a grateful people, represents an outstanding and timely service to the national welfare."[34] The military authority in 1837 constituted a *Consejo Superior Central de Cataluña* ignoring to some extent the new provincial, departmental, politico-administrative division of Spain. It reflected the importance of the unifying elements of the region, its common problems, but also the ineffectiveness of the central government in a period of civil war and turmoil in large parts of the country. Increasingly in coming decades the army intervened in national politics, and in Catalonia imposed its will on the conflicting forces.

After the defeat of the Carlists in Catalonia in 1840, the progressives became dissatisfied with the moderate liberals in power. In Catalonia the progressives had considerable strength in the provinces, and even in the city of Barcelona they obtained 3,000 votes, compared to 5,800 for the moderates, despite a censitary suffrage. The working class, discontented by a depression, received General Espartero, identified with the Progressives, with great enthusiasm. The actions of the militia, tolerated by the army, allowed the general to press the Queen Regent for a change of government. The popular pressure and the lack of support of the army soon led to the abdication of the Queen Mother and the appointment of General Espartero as a regent. The new government did not stop the centralizing tendencies of Spanish liberalism, and followed a free trade policy that ran counter to the Catalan interests, so that the Progresistas who had welcomed him soon felt betrayed. A democratic wing of liberalism, supported by the workers of Barcelona, and the moderates, for different reasons, developed a new hostility against the administration, the world of affairs and the economic policies of Madrid. The period 1842-1843 is one of urban riots, of juntas, and of disrespect for decisions coming from the capital. A revolt in Barcelona against Espartero and his repression was successful, but leaderless. The junta that emerged with a confused program is summarized by Vicens Vives:

> Union and pure *españolismo* (Spanish patriotism) among all free Catalans, without allowing any kind of division among all those who belong to the great liberal community; independence of Catalonia from the Court until the restoration of a just, free and independent government, with nationality [sic], honor and intelligence; protection to agriculture, commerce and industry; administrative clean-up; justice for all; integrity and order.[35]

The slogan would be "Down with Espartero! Justice and protection of the national industry!"

Here we find a pattern to be repeated until the 1934 events: Barcelona resisting the central government, often on the basis of its particular interests and issues, but claiming to act in the name of Spain and its broader national interests against the Madrid government. As on some other occasions, many of the leading Catalan men of the time did not want to commit themselves to the movement which had to turn toward the left in search of support. Faced with the reaction of the central government and its army, and feeling threatened by the popular revolution, desirious to disarm the mob—the *patuleia*—the bourgeoisie had to capitulate or withdraw from exercising control. The defeat of the rebellion by Espartero led to a repression and new centralizing measures in taxation and the draft. However, not long afterwards a movement was started in Andalusia by a coalition of moderates and *progresistas,* finding support among army officers in Catalonia. It overthrew Espartero, creating a new *Junta Suprema* located in Barcelona and connected with those of other parts of Spain that transferred power to another general. Soon the moderates forgot their former progressive allies. The conflicts turned about taxation, smuggling, the draft, appointment of municipalities, the dissolution of the juntas, and who should have the armed power, the government through the army, or the citizens through the militia. Again the city divided between the more popular element pejoratively called *Jamancios* (a gypsy term) and the bourgeoisie. The broad movement, labeled centralist, was soon militarily defeated; an honorable capitulation forced the dissolution of the more popular units of the militia. The provincialist liberalism was defeated in 1844. Except for two years, the moderates were to rule Spain until 1868, under the sign of a desire for peace, coinciding with an expansive swing of the business cycle. The moderate period was one of consolidation of the Spanish, moderately liberal, and not too democratic state. Basic legislation shaping Spanish society well into the present was passed: the 1857 education bill of Claudio Moyano, the 1845 fiscal reforms of Mon, the Civil Procedure Code of 1855, the Mortgage and Property Registration Law of 1863, and the like. All these laws disregarded regional differences and did away with the last remainders of legal particularism and privileges of Catalonia. They introduced an educational system in Castilian, but Catalonia, except for a recession in 1853-1854, prospered and accepted the process.

Peace and prosperity, however, allowed the emergence of a new generation of men who, without questioning the Spanish state, developed a reformist consciousness, often linking with historical tradition on a Catholic basis, often trying to integrate the former Carlists into the Liberal monarchy. This position led them to a preregionalist position, to use the expression of Vicens Vives, critical of the rationalist centralism. Demographic pressures changed relations between the owners, particularly the new bourgeois owners of church lands, and the rural population provoked a rural jacquerie (the war of the matiners) in 1846-1848, exploited by the Carlists, but that was unsuccessful. The Spanish 1854 revolution found considerable echo among the Barcelona working class protesting the introduction of labor-saving machinery and the economic crisis, but no tie was established between their protest and the progressive middle classes, and the democrats could only hold out for a short time in the northeastern corner of Catalonia that later would be a stronghold of federal republicanism. A successful campaign in Morocco by a Catalan general produced a brief wave of Spanish nationalism in Catalonia.

However, underneath, a critical attitude toward the Spanish state, its politicians, and bureaucracy was increasing mainly against their corruption, their distortion of democracy, their desire to regulate centralistically, their neglect of economic interests of the manufacturers. The interest group of the latter successfully brought together men of different ideological tendencies for the election campaign of 1850. The idea that the provinces could do something against or independently of the "cesaristic centralism" of Madrid appeared significantly in an article entitled "Catalanism is not provincialism" (1855) by a law professor who later would be minister of the Crown for a short period in one of the regenerationist cabinets and as a follower of Savigny, a defender of local legal traditions against unifying codification.

This consciousness coincides with the beginning of a cultural revival under the sign of romanticism, poetry competitions, a revitalized press, the organization by Clavé of singing societies to lure the workers away from drinking. Let us note the similarity with some of the folk-oriented movements in Scandinavian countries, linked with temperance societies, concerned with the moral degradation of the working class. A complex process of social and cultural mobilization was initiated in this period with the creation of interest groups like the protectionist lobby of the Fomento del Trabajo Nacional (1867); the Liceo Opera Association (1844); cultural associations and clubs like the Ateneo (1860), the Casino Mercantil Barcelonés (1864), the Juegos Florales (1859), imitating the provençal medieval poetry competitions, new newspapers, and the like which would become even more active in the eighties and nineties.

It seems doubtful that these tendencies could not have been absorbed by a successful Spanish state, party system, and general renewal movement, but in the coming decades the Spanish state would be far from successful, and the economic, educational, political underdevelopment of a large part of Spain would alienate many Catalans from it. Ultimately, legitimacy is dependent on efficacy, and the standards to judge it are relative. Except for the period between the 1869 revolution and the Restoration in 1876, the Spanish state was performing relatively well in the latter half of the 19th century, considering the standards of its underdeveloped and provincial areas, but not those sectors of the population more open to the world, particularly Catalonia, that became increasingly interested in the changes taking place in politics, the economy, intellectual life, music, and the arts across the Pyrennaic border.

The September revolution of 1868 which for many historians is the delayed 1848 European revolution in Spain, offered the Catalan opponents of the system an opportunity to intervene in a general Spanish political and social change, although with a somewhat different emphasis.[36] Initiated in Andalusia with the support of part of the army and navy, hailed by the professors and students of the university of Madrid, it was received enthusiastically in a Barcelona that had been suffering the consequences of the cotton crisis provoked by the American Civil War, the depression of 1866, and a crash of the stock exchange in 1866. The leading figure of the army, General Prim, was closely connected with Barcelona business circles and popular among the lower bourgeoisie. His assassination and the failure of the monarchy under a Saboyan king after the ouster of Isabel II, led to a Republic in which two main currents would emerge: a unitary one and a federalist one. Men from Barcelona played a leading role in the new regime, arousing the jealousy of Madrid. The federalist revolt in parts of Catalonia was one manifestation of the discontent with centralist formulas, as the revival of Carlism was a reflection of the hostility of many Catalans to the secularizing tendencies of the revolution, leading to a three-year war in some of the rural areas.[37] The Carlist pretender attempted to mobilize regional sentiments by declaring the decrees of Philip V abrogated, but outside of the peasant areas under the influence of the clergy and local elites, his move did not find response. The Republic had come "where we least expected it, overnight," with the abdication of the Saboyan king, Amadeo. The more radical elements proclaimed a federal Catalan state and the internationalistas (the working class) appeared on the horizon, with uprisings in some parts of Spain, bringing to the bourgeoisie the image of the French Commune. The elections to the constituent assembly took place within a climate of indifference and moderate republicans won over the federalists, who afterwards attempted a coup. Again a *Junta de Salvación y Defensa de Cataluña* appeared on the scene. The tensions unleashed in an industrial society and in a class-divided countryside with a large agricultural proletariat, the revival of populist reaction under the banner of Carlism, and the differences between centralists and federalists, created a crisis of the new regime that soon led the Catalan bourgeoisie to support the men preparing the Restoration. The now powerful industrial and financial bourgeoisie was to play an important role in bringing the king back, but felt ambivalent about their choice after having for so long advocated greater freedom, jury trial, universal suffrage, and federalism.

A recurrent pattern in modern Spanish history had appeared: short periods of high revolutionary enthusiasm carried by the hopes of broad segments of the citizenry, activation of radical masses pushed by poverty, withdrawal of the moderate reformist element, defeat of the forces of change by the intervention of the army, establishment of a conservative government, and a relatively prolonged period of peace and prosperity— without, however, arriving at a solution of basic underlying problems or creating fully legitimate institutions. Peace and prosperity, with few moving ideals, seems to be characteristic of such periods: the moderate decade (1856-1866), the Restoration (1876-until the crisis at the end of

World War I), and later the Franco Regime (1939 to the present), contrasting with periods of political mobilization like the eighteen thirties, the revolution of 1854, and the "bienio" until 1856, the revolution of 1868 and the Republic from 1873-1874, the unrest and attempts of reformist-bourgeoisie-trade unionism and regionalism coalition in 1917, the Second Republic and Civil War (1931-1939). Catalonia, an advanced industrial region with a powerful bourgeoisie, a large lower middle class, and a growing working class, received the periods of change with enthusiasm and often initiated them. But soon its different classes divided on how far change should go, with the more radical element taking power and the moderates looking for the reestablishment of order, often turning to the authoritarian-conservative elements of the rest of Spain, particularly the army, for help. Not long after, however, that same bourgeoisie started feeling frustrated in its desire to push forward toward a more liberal, democratic, "European" type of politics, contributing to initiating the cycle again.

Let us stress that by the last quarter of the century Catalonia had experienced for almost three-quarters of a century, though perhaps in a more acute and conscious manner, crises parallel to those of other parts of Spain. Its more complex economy in an underdeveloped country probably made the Spanish crisis more acute, and exposed the region to the international business cycles, creating social and consequently political problems. The failure of government often led to local or particularistic solutions, but regionalistic and particularly nationalistic parties had not appeared. Let us not forget that federalism, led by Pi y Margall, a Catalan living in Madrid, inspired by Proudhon, and strongly supported in Catalonia, was a nationwide movement with a program for the country—so was the broad though less enthusiastic support among the Catalan upper bourgeoisie for the Restoration.

However, between the middle and the turn of the century, one variable changed: different segments of Catalan society, first the upper bourgeoisie and later the middle classes, thought that a more effective solution could be found within the regional framework by administrative and political self-government and even within a Catalan state built on the basis of nationalism. Frustrated in an effort to gain power in Madrid, the Catalan bourgeoisie dreamed of power in Catalonia; however, as Solé-Tura stresses, in his book, *Catalanism i revolució burgesa,* from a somewhat Marxist perspective, the social structure gave the Catalan bourgeoisie a marked institutional and ideological instability:

It converted it into an intimately reactionary class that in the Spanish context played a revolutionary role, a corporativist, traditionalist, conservative class that proposed itself to modernize, liberalize the country, an essentially urban and industrial class, profoundly tied to a countryside that was extremely conservative and immobilist.[38]

He writes mainly on the movement of the Lliga in the first decades of this century and its ideological leader Prat de la Riba, but even for an earlier phase it is true that the Catalan bourgeoisie was consolidating itself as a class in a relatively advanced stage of capitalist development, when the proletariat began to acquire sufficient strength to act as an independent force. Perhaps we would shift the emphasis somewhat: It is not only the late capitalist development that makes an alliance between proletariat and bourgeoisie on a liberal-democratic program against oligarchic preindustrial interests difficult (even when such an alliance exists in the fight for protective tariffs). We would stress other factors as well, some of a more political and institutional nature. Foremost was the crisis of legitimacy of the state and its institutions provoked by the Carlist wars, the emergence of a tradition of localized revolutionary or semirevolutionary power: the *juntas* tradition initiated with the fight against Napoleon. The weakness of central government encourages an early democratization; for example, the expansion of suffrage in 1837 goes beyond that in most European countries; universal male suffrage is introduced by the 1868 revolution.[39] The crisis in the Establishment caused by the French invasion (incipient even before) the weakness of the aristocracy compared to Prussia, for example, due to the policies of the absolute monarchy,[40] the division between collaborationists and patriots, liberals, and absolutists, did not allow a clear-cut conflict between bourgeoisie and aristocracy and indirectly weakened the unity of the antiaristocratic forces. The ties established between the new social classes (business and professional and the country side) through the acquisition of land from the Church and the municipalities made an alliance with the lower classes on a platform of land-reform difficult except on an anticlerical basis. A relatively permanent alliance between the lower classes and the bourgeoisie on the basis of a regionalistic-nationalistic community of sentiment, like that developed by many nationalistic-irredentist movements, was not feasible, even though often expressed by regional-nationalist leaders and ideologists, because that identity was not strong enough, particularly in the urban proletariat. In the twentieth century with the massive migration of Castilian-speaking workers to the highly industrial areas, such a possibility became even more remote. Class interests linked the peripheral bourgeoisies to the owning and conservative strata of the rest of Spain and to the state-maintaining middle classes; when threatened by the lower classes, the workers, or the lumpenproletariat, that coincidence would become effective. It would be only a coincidence of interests, however, rather than a broad collaboration in the tasks of governing through a conservative party. The style of life of a manufacturing and commercial bourgeoisie and a land-owning nobility or middle class were too different for a real understanding. So was the style of the Castilian bureaucratic, military, and professional middle classes, dependent on the state rather than on bourgeois industriousness. Occasional attempts to regenerate the body politic, like some of the attempts of reform within the Conservative party at the end of the century, or even the Primo de Rivera pronunciamiento, initially would bring the peripheral bourgeoisies to support a nationwide move, but the differences in style and values, and the desire to concentrate on regional problems was ultimately to lead to their withdrawal or alienation.

THE CRISIS OF THE SPANISH STATE AND THE PERIPHERAL NATIONALISMS AT THE TURN OF THE CENTURY

In the latter part of the 19th century the tensions moved from religious-ideological conflicts to those of regional-culture and class. Despite labor unrest in the cities and countryside (often coinciding with more strictly political crises), it took considerable time before these conflicting forces became institutionalized in large trade union federations and a socialist workers party (PSOE) of considerable strength, particularly if we compare the Spanish data with those for Italy.[41] The peasant jacqueries, the incidents of violence, the anarchist terrorism, late in the 19th century should not lead us to overestimate the extensions and penetration of the class cleavage compared to its latent intensity.[42] On the contrary, the center-periphery tensions during this period did not weaken. In the first decade of the century, they already found a large organized expression in the electoral success of Catalan parties, far larger than the labor protest.[43] Simplifying things enormously, one could say that the phasing of conflicts, challenges, and problems was religious-ideological, periphery-center, urban and rural proletariat-owning classes. However, elements of the religious-secular conflict fused, particularly in the Basque country, into the periphery-center problem; the conflicts between industrial-bourgeois structures and a preindustrial agrarian-bureaucratic society got channeled into one of the center-periphery conflicts (the Catalan), and the labor-owning classes in industrial Spain where superimposed in a skewed way on the cultural-linguistic-periphery versus center conflict. The standard sequence of penetration, integration, participation and identity, crises or challenges, does not coincide fully with this historical sequence.[44]

Each of the problems found only a partial solution or none, so that with the Republic in 1931, all accumulated, and some of those having at one point, like the religious, been partly compromised, were reopened. The weakness of the Spanish state in the whole period limited its degree of penetration; the conflicts of the 19th century placed serious barriers before an integration process that seemed inevitable. Participation was formally extended very early, but the great differences in economic and cultural development in a largely agrarian society, and for that matter inequalitarian in a large part of the country, led to distortion in the form of the *caciquismo.* The identity creation process was delayed or broken by the lack of satisfactory solution to the other challenges. The sum of halfway solutions, or temporary solutions to these four problems ultimately produced a serious legitimacy crisis, first of the Restoration in 1923 and then of the Monarchy and unitary state in 1931. The legitimacy of the Restoration was largely by default: it was the best system possible under the circumstances, but not the ideal system for anybody. As it consolidated, the contradiction between reality and ideal, between "official country" and some parts of the "real country," plus lack of efficacy and effectiveness in solving many problems, created that crisis of legitimacy. With so many unsolved or partially solved problems and with a dubious legitimacy the regime could not undertake serious efforts to solve problems of distribution. With the Republic, the level of economic development and social mobilization and the "historical time" in Europe should have placed distribution problems in the first place on the agenda of the regime, but its leaders felt that they had to attempt a final solution to the other crises: the army reform, the secularizing legislation, and the Catalan Estatuto were voted before the Agrarian reform, and little fiscal or social security legislation was enacted.[45] Consequently, the disappointed hopes of the masses led to the crisis in Spring, 1936.

FROM REGIONALISM TO CATALAN NATIONALISM. FROM CONSERVATIVE NATIONALISM TO LEFT NATIONALISM: LLIGA TO ESQUERRA. BETWEEN THE SPANISH STATE AND THE WORKING CLASS.

The Restoration monarchy created in Catalonia a period of peace and coincided initially with a period of prosperity. Cultural life bloomed. With the literary revival of the *Renaixena,* Barcelona became a modern metropolis; the city opened its doors to foreign intellectual and artistic influences. The two dynastic parties controlled the elective offices, and many leading manufacturers or men closely connected with them occupied seats in parliament. Only in a few districts were non-Catalans elected by the two-party system. The machines of Conservatives and Liberals were parallel to the competing banking houses of Girona and Arnus. However, this system entered in crisis in the last decade of the century under the converging pressure of working class protest and Catalan nationalism, precipitated by a financial and economic crisis and the 1898 defeat by the United States, with the loss of the last remnants of the empire, which reinforced the world depression of the first years of the century.

A number of factors converged, some coming from the period of prenationalist center-periphery tensions we discussed before, to create a broad, diffuse, and internally differentiated Catalan movement in search of political expression. Historians diverge somewhat in assigning weights to those various factors, and it is not always easy to distinguish underlying conditions from precipitant events and how much weight to assign to the latter. Jesús Pabón in his biography of Cambó, leader of the Lliga, notes four sources: the cultural and literary revival based on renewed interest in the language and history; the fight for tariff protection that mobilizes the bourgeoisie and leads it to accept the autonomist formulae proposed by the romantic intellectuals; the Carlist dissidence we already discussed, as reinterpreted by some Catholic writers.[46] The Catalan historian Vicens Vives wants to trace it farther back to a broad sentiment expressed in the provincialism of the 1820s and 1830s, and the writings of moderate Catholics like Balmes, regionalist journalists like Mañé y Flaquer, bishops like Morgades and Torras y Bages, and professors like Milá Fontanals and Duran y Bas, that is, in center positions.[47] But he, like other writers, ends by stressing the question asked on repeated occasions: Can we, Catalans, continue participating in a system that is decaying, that is out of tune with the times, and whose inefficacy is patent? The loss of Cuba, and the economic consequences particularly in Catalonia, awakened this crisis consciousness. The critique of parliamentarism, as it developed out of a corrupted suffrage, was another element. From conservatives like Mañé y Flaquer to ex-Federalists like Almirall, the hostility against the professional politicians grew. Almirall, for example, wrote: "War against politics, war against the parties that ruin and dishonor the country! " Let us not forget that a similar sentiment was to find expression in Aragón and Castile under the leadership of Joaquín Costa, between 1898 and 1902 in the Liga Agraria, the taxpayers league, the assembly of chambers of commerce in Zaragoza and the Unión Nacional. These movements outside of Catalonia did not reach organizational maturity and some of their best elements, for example, a man like Santiago Alba, were absorbed by the old parties.

It would be a mistake, made sometimes by the Marxist interpretations of Catalanism, to underestimate the importance of the cultural and historicist revival which through the study of Catalan history contributed to discovering and praising the resistance to assimilation by the Spanish state. The codification of civil law in 1889 provoked a bitter struggle for the survival of a distinctive legal tradition led by Duran y Bas, a professor and parliamentarian inspired by the ideas of the German historical school of law, particularly Savigny, that fought a similar battle in Germany against the enactment of the BGB.

The Marxists are, however, right in stressing the importance of the fight for tariff protection against the liberal 1869 tariff policy and a planned commercial treaty with England (1885). It was the defense of the interests of the national bourgeoisie that activated the manufacturers to create interest groups, organize meetings, write petitions, and contribute decisively to the founding of the *Lliga de Catalunya* in 1887. The defense against that treaty, and concern for the legal tradition brought together real economic interests among the men of the cultural revival of the Renaixenca and the Centre Català, to present in 1885 the petition called the *Memorial de greuges* (of complaints) significantly entitled: "Memorial in the defense of the moral and material interests of Catalonia," submitted to the king in 1885.

The movement was to have a strong appeal to the students through the Centro Escolar Catalanista, founded in 1887, which produced the leadership cadres for the next decades. The encounter with Europe, through the study of history, philology, law; the openness to new musical currents, particularly Wagner; the discovery of impressionism; the modernist architecture which flourished in the buildings of Gaudi for the bourgeoisie, created a feeling of superiority over provincial Spain and the official cultural life of Madrid, which reinforced the self-confidence based on the economic achievements of a manufacturing bourgeoisie in an underdeveloped country, so well described by Albert Hirschman.[48]

Ideologically the Catholic conservative, antirationalist tradition of Balmes, expressed by Bishop Torras y Bages and the radical tradition of Proudhonian Federalism, transformed into Catalanism by Almirall, contributed from opposite extremes to the new state of mind. Ultimately they would diverge again, dividing the Catalanist movement because their roots and assumptions about society and politics were radically different, but in the meantime they had achieved the "secession" of Catalan life and politics from the system of Restoration Spain.

The crisis provoked by some incidents between the army and Catalanists and the attempts of the Liberals under army pressure to introduce repressive legislation were to precipitate in 1906 the massive vote for a strange coalition from Carlists to Republicans, called the Solidaridad Catalana.[49] Out of that campaign, surrounded by the halo of heroism as a consequence of an attempt against his life, emerged a young lawyer and businessman Francisco Cambó, as leader of the Lliga. One of the most intelligent, European, moderate, bourgeois politicians of Spain, he was torn between his calling to statewide Spanish leadership and his role as a leader of a minoritarian peripheral nationalism. These notes found among his papers reflect this dramatically:

> In 1919 in the debates on integral autonomy Alcalá Zamora (then a Liberal deputy) attacked me saying: Your honor attempts to be, at the same time, Bolivar of Catalonia and Bismarck of Spain. They are contradictory aspirations, and it is necessary that you choose between them. In this accusation Alcalá Zamora expressed in a successful formula the whole drama of my life. Because it is true that since very young, I had that double ideal: to give freedom to Catalonia and greatness to Spain.[50]

It is not easy to account for the secession of Catalan political life from that of the remainder of Spain, first in the form of regionalist-autonomist political movements with their own party since 1900, the Lliga, and increasingly channeled into a nationalistic movement that would culminate in the Catalan left led by Maciá and Companys under the Republic (1931-1939). By secession from the national political life we mean the giving up by the leaders of Catalonia, except those of the anarcho-syndicalist labor movement, of the idea of solving the problems of a rapidly changing society in Catalonia by contributing within Spain-wide parties or movements to their solution for the whole country. Most of the men making that crucial choice were not secessionists from the Spanish state, separatists, nor were their demands always incompatible with a statewide process of regeneration, from the right or the left. However, their "particularism" (in the sense used by Ortega y Gasset in his *Invertebrate Spain*,[51] not too different from the one introduced into sociology by Talcott Parsons) created tensions and ultimately conflicts which contributed to defeating any transformation of the Spanish polity. Sympathizers with the Catalan efforts of renewal might argue against this broad and somewhat simplified formulation that the most responsible leaders of Catalonia in the twentieth century, with considerable political sense, were often willing to search for allies in Spanish politics, to support some of their efforts, to coordinate some of their policies, to contribute to important political, social, and economic changes in the whole country. This was certainly the relationship developing between Cambó and Maura, the leading Conservative politician, in the first decade of the century, and his avowed position in his later political testament, the insightful political essay, *Por la Concordia* (1927).[52] It was also the basis for the understanding between Companys, the leader of the Catalan left (the Esquerra), and Azaña, the leader of the left-bourgeoisie and intelligentsia who aimed, with more or less support of the Socialists, to build the Spanish Republic in 1931-1933. Certainly the role of Cambó as a regional leader of a renewed Spanish Conservative party, or of Companys as a lieutenant rather than as an ally of Azaña, could have changed the destiny of Spain.

Another possibility, implicit in the old Federalist program of Pi y Margall, abandoned for nationalism by his former sumpathizer Almirall, was the creation of a federal Spain with power widely decentralized. This ideal was defeated with the first Republic and perhaps was impracticable in Spain, with the great and persistent differences in economic, social, cultural, and religious development and consequently of social and political mobilization, and with centuries of centralistic government in large part of the country. With the Catalan shift to nationalism, federalism found expression in attempts to form a coalition of cultural-linguistic minorities and the encouragement of Basque nationalism; but the slow mobilization of Galicia, due to its rural isolation and backwardness, the lack of success of such efforts in other linguistically heterogeneous areas of the so-called greater Catalonia, and above all the numerical minority of all those regions in the Spanish population, condemned any such efforts to failure. They only served to arouse a Castilian-Spanish nationalism that, as Cambó describes it in *Por la Concordia,* contained in itself secessionist elements, and that played an important part in the reaction of the Liberal Party to Catalanist demands and later in that of the Radical Party (born, let us not forget, in the conflict between the Castilian speaking lower classes of Barcelona against the Catalanist bourgeoise for the control of city hall in Barcelona, under the leadership of Lerroux). Rightly the Catalan leaders, when they think of a federal Spain, monarchical or republican, in contrast to one in which regions with a distinctive history, language and culture, would have a special status (as it was argued basically by Prat de la Riba and Almirall, on opposite sides of the ideological spectrum, and on the basis of different traditions), see such a possibility only in an Iberian federation including Portugal. Only its incorporation would create the balance in population, resources, and cultural weight of the components of a multi-national state, based on the model of the segmented pluralism, Proporzdemokratie, consociational democracy, developed by Val Lorwin, Lehmbruch and Lijphart, so important to the work of Stein Rokkan on alternative paths to nation-building. Only Spaniards concerned with the regional integration problem, like Madariaga from a Spanish perspective, hope for an integration of Portugal into a larger political unit. However, the strength of Portuguese nationality has made such ideas idle dreams.

WHY NO "CONSOCIATIONAL" SOLUTION?

Why should it have been impossible to work out Spanish problems by alliances between politically skilled leaders in the periphery—specifically Catalonia—and national political leaders in Madrid? Let us try to sketch a tentative answer that would require considerable research and analysis of specific crises to put forward with more assurance. The comparison with the difficulties created for the consolidation of the Weimar Republic by the ambivalent relations between the Zentrum leadership and that of the Bavarian People's Party, or between Czech leaders and the nonnationalist Slovaks, or the Serb politicians with the Croation Agrarians, in contrast to situations where statewide parties with strong regional loyalties and leaders undertook the task, like the Belgian, would be helpful in finding an answer.

A basic problem is created by the different style of politics in the center and the periphery without integration, however loose, into statewide parties. Inevitably, separate organizations, symbols, and constituencies ultimately put serious limits and strains on any coalition between state or regime-builders at the center and spokesmen of the periphery. The main one, underlined by all biographers of Cambó (unfortunately there is no scholarly study of the role of Companys), is that inevitably they are forced to formulate problems in different terms when speaking locally and with their potential allies at the center. Without being able to impose on their constituency a middle course for the sake of a larger organization and its purposes, such an alliance, even when sincerely entered into by the leaders, is difficult to defend.

Inevitably the appeals used by the Lliga in mobilizing Catalonia to exert its pressure on Madrid contained elements felt as a threat by Spanish politicians. The language used in the press, the speeches in Barcelona, could not be acceptable to them, whatever assurance might be given in private. Specific issues, like economic policies and taxation, became charged with emotional elements in the course of the debate. The emergence of autonomous institutions like the *Mancomunidad* (a coordination of activities of the administration of the four Catalan provinces dominated by Barcelona and the Lliga), inevitably led to a dual leadership: one in parliament and even in government in the capital, and another in the region, which spoke different political languages. The division of labor between Cambó and Prat de la Riba, apparently without provoking difficulties among them, certainly involved ambivalences that would contribute ultimately to crisis in that party. However, the most serious consequence of the inevitable ambivalences of such a two-arena politics is that they allowed opponents to question the good faith of the cooperating leaders, accusing them of betraying their main constituencies for the sake of power, or broad goals to specific interests.

The understanding between national leaders and those of the periphery was always precarious because the overloading of the Spanish political system with difficult problems, ultimately caused by delayed economic development, late secularization, and foreign commitments of a second rate-power, prevented them from concentrating at an early stage on finding a solution. In addition, the fragmentation of forces at the regional level made it difficult for leaders to make unambiguous and public commitments, consolidating gains made rather than pressing more or less continuously for new ones, leaving their followers in doubt about the value of the compromise reached and in fear of being outflanked by competitors. Under such conditions it was impossible for the Lliga leadership to accept some of the reforms of Maura, or for Companys and his coalition partners in the Catalan regional government to accept a temporary setback when the tribunal of constitutional guarantees declared a Catalan rural tenancy law unconstitutional.[53]

In the fall of 1934 the Esquerra leader and head of the Catalan regional government found himself pressured by the more nationalist Estat Catalá Party in his government to take a rigid stand. On October 6, after his revolt against the central government he wryly commented: "Let's see if they also say that I am not Catalanist."[54] The centrifugal multiparty system in Catalonia obviously was the opposite of the "internal political cohesion of the subcultures" and the ability to carry them along posited by Lijphart and Daalder.

However, the obstacles to stable compromises in the Spanish case are not to be found only on one side. It is very difficult for leaders like Azaña because of the dominant position in terms of population, recent history, and language, of Castilian-speaking Spain. In the absence of an equilibrium of strength, concessions to the periphery could always appear as weakness if not treason by the leaders rather than solutions, an attitude particularly strong in the army that had developed a specific Spanish-Castilian nationalism. If we add that the lack of unity of leadership in the periphery did not fully sanction the compromise reached at great cost by Spanish leaders like Azaña, their situation ultimately was undermined. The suspicion and deep hatred of the right against Azaña for his relation with Companys is one example.

Opponents will press for unequivocal statements that threaten any compromises worked out, statements that would not be demanded of leaders with sectional constituencies within a statewide party. The ambivalences of a nationalist rhetoric used by an autonomist movement ultimately lead to the emergence of a more principled nationalist leadership, within the original party or outside and against it.

CLASS POLITICS AND NATIONALISM IN THE CENTER-PERIPHERY RELATIONS.

The problem would be compounded by the modern and complex class structure of Catalan society. In many other European societies the linguistic, cultural, peripheral oppositions challenging central power emerged in agricultural, economically underdeveloped regions, often from a society based on peasant communalism. Not so in Catalonia and the Basque country. Obviously some of the strongholds of regionalist nationalism in Catalonia, and especially in the Basque country, had those characteristics; the rural base and traditionalist values, linked with the Church, of a rural population speaking the vernacular are still an important component. However, both were fundamentally industrial areas, in fact the most industrialized in the country. Catalan agrarian society was not without class conflicts between owners and share-tenants, particularly in the vineyards. Conflicts along class lines within the Catalan community, between haute bourgeoisie, a petty bourgeoisie, and the lower classes, as well as between landowners and farmers, would divide Catalanism along left-right lines. In such a context it ultimately became impossible for any leader to speak as a "national" leader, and pragmatic agreements based on coincidence of interests or bargaining for specific advantages had to be suspected of betraying "national" interests for more narrow class interests. Without having to accept fully the Marxist interpretation of Ramos Oliveira[55] of the Catalanism of the Lliga as an instrument of the bourgeoisie to blackmail the Spanish government into making concessions favorable to the manufacturing interests, there is .no doubt that Madrid politicians were inclined to let the Catalans have a share in economic policy making (the protectionist tariff policy and turning over of economic ministries to Lliga leaders at some point) in the hope of quieting some of their other demands. The nationalist intelligentsia and the petty bourgeoisie that had become mobilized under the banners of regional nationalism would end by turning away from the Lliga leadership. Once the Esquerra gained power in Barcelona, the conservative interests could look for support in their class conflicts (concretely, in the regulation of tenancy relations in the thirties) to Madrid. The class cleavages *within* the periphery limited the flexibility that sectional movements have often shown in their relations with central governments. One condition for a consociational type of politics listed by Lijphard, internal cohesion within the subcultures, without which the leaders would not be able to carry their followers along and retain their loyalty, was missing in Spain.

The class division and ideological split in Catalan society and its expression in two major and antagonistic parties—Lliga and Esquerra—created a unique pattern of politics. The existence of two parliaments and governments, in Madrid and in Barcelona, combined with an electoral system favoring disproportionately winning coalitions and different election dates, made possible the dominance of opposite tendencies in both. This naturally made the already difficult cooperation between regional and central government even more difficult. So in the summer of 1934 a situation developed in which the Esquerra, in protest against the Radical-CEDA (Christian Democratic) supported government, withdrew from parliament; simultaneously, the Lliga, antagonized by the Esquerra-dominated government and legislature in Barcelona, withdrew its deputies there. The support of the central government interests negatively affected by Esquerra regional legislation—expressed by means of a constitutionality suit—exacerbated the nationalism of the Esquerra and its hostility to the Lliga, close to those agrarian interests. In turn the bourgeois-left Azaña, deeply hostile to the center-conservative, clerical-supported government, could say: "As Catalonia is the last rampart left to the Republic, the autonomous power of Catalonia is the last republican power standing up in Spain."[56] Such a position led Cambó to say:

> They speak always as if Catalonia were to be the bulwark of the Left in Spain and of the left orientation of the Republic. Within Catalonia parties have the right to express whatever sympathies they may wish; Catalonia collectively and in its name its government, has no right to make statements which might endanger the respect that the freedoms of Catalonia deserve of all those governing Spain. Catalonia, collectively, and specially the representative institutions of Catalonia, should not be the bulwark of anyone; they should only be the bulwark of Catalonia.[57]

Cambó rightly stresses how the cumulation of nationwide cleavages with the center-periphery nationalism cleavage is threatening to any consociational compromise when advocated by a regional government. The same could be said about a central government taking sides for the regional opposition. The dynamics of antagonistic two-party politics of left-right in two arenas almost inevitably poison the issues. If we add that the major participants find themselves pressured by extremists (whose support, given the electoral system, is decisive) like the Esquerra by the extreme nationalists of the Estat Catalá and the center by the centralist right in Madrid, the conflict is almost inevitable. The result was, October 6, 1934, the rebellion of the Catalan government of Companys against the Madrid government; a "Catalan republic within the federal republic of Spain" that lasted only a few hours.

NATIONALISM, CENTRAL GOVERNMENT AND IMMIGRANT WORKERS—A THREE-CORNERED CONFLICT

In addition, the two peripheral industrial societies divided along class lines. (This was less true of the Basque country, particularly since their leaders were not so prominently recruited from the big business bourgeoisie, which tended to identify with Spanish conservatism.) But much of the working class protest they faced was from an immigrant labor force affiliated with Spanish labor movements. Catalan politics makes no sense if this variable is not taken into account. The ethnic cultural conflict was overlaid on a bitter class struggle. Particularly in the case of Lerroux, lower class protest, through non-Catalan organizations was perceived as an instrument of centralism against the regional community. Obviously a *divide* et *impera* policy temptation might have led to some links between the central government, particularly Liberal governments, and the local petty bourgeois demagogue in the early years of the century. But there can be little doubt that even without any encouragement, important sections of the population of Barcelona would not have found a channel of expression through the Catalan parties. Similarly, the Basque nationalism initially saw in the Socialists a threat to the ethnic community and perceived the immigrant workers as a national and as a class threat. With the turn of the workers in Barcelona to anarcho-syndicalism, rapid industrialization and immigration, wartime inflation, and post-Russian revolution hopes, rigidity in the response of small family entrepreneurs and large corporations to labor, and sabotage of war production for the allies created in Barcelona some of the most bitter labor conflicts in

Spanish history. A three-cornered conflict emerged among employers, workers, and central authorities.[58] It ultimately led to the independent intervention of the army and police authorities and the subversion of government authority. That is one of the antecedents of the prounciamiento that in 1923 brought the Primo de Rivera distatorship. It would be impossible to summarize the complexities of that struggle, but it certainly heightened the process of political mobilization, of alienation from the ineffectiveness of the central government, caught between demands for repression and lack of authority to impose compromises on either side, rejected as a bourgeois government by a syndicalist working class and as an alien authority by the local bourgeoisie.

In Catalonia, an advanced industrial area open to cosmopolitan influences, and after a century of conflict between Liberalism and the Church, the secular-clerical cleavage, without being too deep in the Catalan community, once more made more difficult an undivided leadership capable of making compromises stick. The Lliga was not a pro-clerical party but was, like its voters, respectful toward the Church, and some high Church officials were not unsympathetic to moderate Catalanism. However, among the Catalan left the Jacobin anticlericalism had a certain appeal. In the Basque country the PNV identified deeply with the Church, hoping to build a separate social and perhaps political community that would help to defend religious values against the secularizing tendencies perceived as coming from the center and to isolate the Basques from the disbelief of many immigrant workers. This different position of left Catalanism and the PNV in relation to the role of the Church led to very different responses of the Azaña-led governments (1931-1933) to both regionalisms.

In a complex industrial society a nationalist movement could not for long hold the loyalties of different strata unless the feeling of oppression were unbearable, but this was not the case for many Castilianized segments of the population, nor for most of the working class for whom linguistic rights and administrative autonomy took second place compared to their conflicts with the employers. Since those employers were not Castilian but Catalan speaking, the conflict could not, as in some countries with peripheral nationalisms, be described primarily in ethnic terms. In fact to the extent that it was an ethno-linguistic conflict, it was between immigrant laborers and the local bourgeoisie. In the Basque country, where a big business elite had assumed a dominant role in the Spanish economy through its banks, its large corporations with plants in other parts of the country, its ties with the royal Court, and feeling Spanish, the PNV could take a more populistic stance, appealing to petty bourgeois

TABLE 3

Percentage of Persons Born in a Different Province than Where Registered in the Census

Province	1877	1887	1900	1910	1920	1930	1950
Madrid	45.4	43.4	41.7	38.7	39.9	46.9	44.3
Barcelona	19.5	20.5	22.2	26.2	29.3	36.0	37.8
Vizcaya	13.7	19.5	26.4	26.0	26.1	24.9	26.0
Spain	8.5	8.0	8.5	9.0	10.2	12.2	15.3

SOURCE: Jorge Nadal, La Población Española (Siglos XVI a XX), Barcelona, Ariel, 1966, p. 190.

anticapitalist sentiments and supporting its own trade union movement; the Solidaridad de Trabajadores Vascos. This nationalistic populism, closely linked with the lower and rural clergy, could bridge the class cleavages in a society with many small entrepreneurs, highly skilled and paid workers, well distributed rural property (often serving as complimentary income to the workers). However, leaving aside historically inherited cleavages, ultimately Basque nationalism could until recent years, maintain the unity of the nationalist movement (in contrast to the Lliga versus Esquerra split) at the cost of leaving outside of the movement most of the big business elite and the immigrant working class identifying with the Socialist Party. This minority status, even within the region, contributed to an even greater ideological purity along nationalist lines than in Catalonia.

To work out compromises (because they cannot be anything but that) between cultural minorities and the dominant nation, which many consider including those minorities, strong leadership is needed, or a participation of *all* leaders in the settlement. As we have noted, the internal division due to other issues, but often translated into nationalistic terms within the peripheric regions and the deep cleavages on other issues among Spanish politicians, made such a settlement by all parties concerned impossible. On the other hand, attempts by men of sufficient leadership to solve the problem in a divided country like Spain are highly controversial and their decisions are therefore questionable. If Azaña had contributed only to the 1931 settlement of the Catalan question it might have been more strongly supported, but his antimilitary and above all his anticlerical policies created a deep opposition which the right inevitably would extend to the Catalan settlement. The same was true for an earlier attempt at decentralization through the reform of local and provincial government undertaken by Maura, the bête noire of many liberals for his pro-Catholic attitude.

To complicate things further, early in 1931 the dominant Esquerra was acceptable to the bourgeois left, but the dominant party in the Basque country, the PNV, appeared strongly identified with the defense of the rights of the Church, the Jesuits, and had obtained much support on that basis, even in suggesting a separate Church and State settlement for the Basque country to escape the anticlerical legislation being enacted by Azaña. Under those circumstances the effort made to solve one regional problem could not be made for another. The leaders able to reach an accommodation with one movement might well not be the ones to reach it with another, which then would become even less hopeful about such solutions and want to assure a maximum of power for the future.

A problem that has been and probably will be a serious obstacle to efforts of accommodation with the peripheral nationalisms is that a large proportion of the population in the growing urban and industrial centers of Catalonia and the Basque country will be Castilian-speaking immigrants, mostly manual workers. Whatever assimilation could take place through intermarriage and the education of their children, would be obstructed by the continuing process of immigration of Castilian-speaking people required by industrial growth and in the case of Catalonia, reinforced by a birth rate differential. The dilemma is not too different from that of Switzerland or West Germany, where the alternatives have become slower growth or immigration without hope of assimilation. However, the situation of an Andalusian or Sicilian migrating to Switzerland is different from that of the same man moving to Barcelona or Milano. In Switzerland he does not plan to stay, or even if he does, he does not expect to be a citizen with a voice in the affairs of the country, and for the sake of economic improvement he may stand a certain amount of social discrimination. A second-class citizenship there might be tolerable, but anything similar within a more or less autonomous Catalonia or Basque country which he considers part of Spain, his country, would probably provoke serious conflicts. However, leaving aside prejudices and stereo-types—particularly strong in the Basque nationalist tradition—any official recognition of the local language as a privileged means of communication (in contact with the administration, the Courts, the army) inevitably would place him in a situation of inferiority unless he were willing and able to assimilate. This situation would be difficult for him to accept since he would be aware that the dominant social group could accept his Castilian language, all its members, except in rural isolated areas, being bilingual. Obviously, opportunities for rapid upward social mobility for himself and his children might facilitate an acceptance of denationalization from his Spanish-Castilian identity, but it does not seem probable that the nonvernacular immigrant community would split on the issue. Any effort at rapid and forceful assimilation likely to be advanced by nationalist extremists who want to even the scores with the Castilian assimilation policy of past decades would certainly lead to conflicts.

Lijphart has stressed the existence of external threats to the country among the three factors strongly conducive to the establishment or maintenance of cooperation among elites in a fragmented system.[59] This factor has not been significant in the case of Spain, whose renunciation since the Napoleonic invasion of a major power role, with sufficient size and military capability to prevent others from attacking her, has limited such threats. In addition, the linguistic-cultural minority areas are nobody's irredenta. It is significant that Cambó in *Por la Concordia* should argue for a solution of the Catalan problem:

> But the day that Spain would find itself involved in an external conflict, the power fighting against it would take good care to encourage rebellion in Catalonia; and as long as the poisoning of the Catalan problem continues it could achieve it with little effort.

And he continues to reinforce his argument:

> Those who have governed Spain in this quarter of a century know how the fear, spontaneous or induced, that some power could encourage revolutionary agitations in Catalonia, has led the governments to shameful diplomatic and commercial surrender.[60]

Despite Cambó's veiled threat, without real credibility, the turning of some extremist nationalists to foreign powers or leaders, like Wilson, for support or sympathy contributes to embittering relations with the majority rather than to a search for solution.

Furthermore, in contrast to other similar movements, neither Catalan nor Basque nationalism can link with an irredentism across the border. Their goal cannot be to secede and join another state, particularly since France is as centralistic as and probably more nationalist-assimilationist than Spain. Nor is there much reason for France to encourage any secession from Spain, since an independent Basque country could aspire to realize the ideal of $3+2 = 5 = 1$, incorporating two historical relatively underdeveloped Basque regions, now parts of France. And an independent Great Catalonia would perhaps consider Catalan-speaking Frenchmen its irredenta.

FROM FUEROS TO RAZA, FROM CARLISM TO THE
PARTIDO NACIONALISTA VASCO

The opposition to the Spanish state in the three Basque provinces—Vizcaya, Guipúzcoa, and Alava—and the former kingdom of Navarre, has a complex history, which shows some parallels to but also significant differences from that of Catalonia. Up to the nineteenth century, the relationship between the kingdom of Navarre and the different political institutions in the three Basque provinces with the Crown had been stable, without significant conflicts. The loyalty to Philip V in the succession war meant that there was no drastic change in the constitutional relationship with the Crown. There were the natural tensions between center and periphery, but only in the nineteenth century would the defense of a peculiar relationship to the central state become an issue. In the course of that conflict, Basque historians have built an ideological base on the defense of medieval and premodern institutions ranging from feudal to communal, both countryside and royal cities, with their privileges recognized by the Crown which they interpret as a democratic tradition, ignoring the oligarchic and feudal dimensions. In the eighteenth century, with American trade and the penetration of the Enlightenment, Guipúzcoa experienced a considerable development, reflected in the founding (1765) by a group of enlightened nobles of the Sociedad Bascongada de Amigos del País, a mixture of club, academy, and educational institution. This association, serving as a model for similar institutions in other parts of Spain, had among other avowed goals to "strengthen the union of the three Basque provinces." One of its goals was to encourage the economy (the entrepreneurial spirit) and the sciences. Each province continued to have its *juntas* or representative councils with their permanent committees: *Diputación General* in Guipúzcoa, *Regimiento* in Vizcaya and *Junta de interregno* in Alava, and a *corregidor* acting as royal representative.

In 1793, at the time of the war against the Revolution, the Diputación of Guipúzcoa proposed to the French the neutrality and independence of the province under the condition that the Catholic religion and the *Fueros* (traditional laws and customs) would be respected. The French political commissars rejected the proposal and demanded incorporation, rejecting the survival of feudal institutions, but other authorities accepted a collaborationist Diputación. In the meantime a number of municipal councils decided to fight the French and elected another Diputación. The sentiment of opposition to Godoy must have contributed to a broader conspiracy, but the peace with the Republic in 1795 ended the danger of secession. The events raised the issue of destroying the traditional

EARLY STATE-BUILDING AND LATE PERIPHERAL NATIONALISMS AGAINST THE STATE: THE CASE OF SPAIN

JUAN LINZ is Professor of Sociology and Political Science at Yale University. He has carried out research on parties, elections, elites, entrepreneurs, local leadership, intellectuals, and authoritarian regimes. His work has focused on Spain, Germany, Italy, and Brazil; and he has been active in international cooperative networks in sociology and political science. He is Chairman of the Research Committee on Political Sociology of the International Political Science Association and the International Sociological Association.

Spain represents some interesting problems for those concerned with the building of political systems encompassing large geographical areas but diverse social structures, historical traditions and languages. In 1966, with 31,871,000 inhabitants, it was by population the seventeenth largest country in the world and the fifth in Europe. However, it was only about the thirty-sixth in GNP per capita, with $645.[1] It is therefore a middle-sized country whose economic development, by European stand-ards, has been retarded, even though rapid in recent years. In addition, that development is very unevenly distributed between regions.[2] One of these, Catalonia, with a distinctive personality, a glorious medieval history, a different language spoken by a large part of the population and a high level of industrialization in 1960 had almost four million inhabitants, not much less than that of Finland and larger than Norway and Ireland at that

Author's Note: This essay should be read in conjunction with another more specifically focused on the linguistic question and regional nationalism: Juan J. Linz, "Politics in a multilingual society with a dominant world language," in Jean Guy Savard and Richard Vegneault, eds., *Les états multilingues. Problems et Solutions. Multilingual States: Problems and Solutions,* Quebec, Presses de l'Université Laval, 1974.

National States and National Minorities, London, 1934; Royal Institute of International Affairs, Nationalism. London, 1939; E. H. Carr, Nationalism and After, London, 1945; and Alfred Cobban, National Self-determination, Oxford, 1945, remain highly relevant.

25. For a very good analysis, see B.H.M. Vlekke, The Evolution of the Dutch Nation, New York, 1945.

26. It is again illustrative, however, of the forces of pluralism in the Netherlands that these central appointees nevertheless developed into highly independent magistrates rather than into "prefects" on behalf of the centre.

27. It testifies to the lasting strength of accommodationist practices in Switzerland that immediately after the civil war victors and vanquished sat together in elaborating the Swiss Constitution of 1848 that retained much of the older regional particularism and to a large degree depoliticized religious cleavages.

28. See especially the theoretical study on Switzerland by Steiner, op. cit.

29. This phrase is the well-chosen title of Arend Lijphart's important study, The Politics of Accommodation—Pluralism and Democracy in the Netherlands, Berkeley, Calif., 1968.

30. The following quotes are all from Arend Lijphart, "Consociational Democracy," World Politics, January 1969, p. 212ff.

31. See the article mentioned in note 2 above.

32. See Hans Daalder, "Government and Opposition in the New States," Government and Opposition, No. 1, 1966, pp. 205-26.

33. These views are particularly evident in the writings of Ferdinand Hermens, Carl J. Friedrich, and Barrington Moore. See on this same point Lijphart, "Consociational Democracy," op. cit., p. 217; Lehmbruch, Proporzdemokratie, and Rokkan, op. cit., p. 88ff.

34. In a similar vein, the greater freedom characteristic of the United Kingdom and the United States is often explained by their ability to avoid entanglements in large-scale land wars.

way, that government will cut in the least any of their rights."[62] The Basque senator who had used the word clarified his statement saying:

> Certainly speaking at the time and in the moment that I have of nationality, that senator [referring to some comment in the debate] will know very well that those provinces being part of Spain, I should not speak of a different nationality than the Spanish. But since in that great nationality there is an organization with a separate life, I use the term nationality in speaking of the Basque provinces. I know that perhaps the words "organizational autonomy" would have been more exact; in any case, if your Honor does not consider "nationality" convenient, I will substitute for it "special organization."[63]

After the 1868 revolution and the proclamation of Amadeo I, the Carlists attempted a rebellion in 1872, but success was limited and a compromise ended the uprising with the Diputación of Vizcaya proposing, in signing the armistice, to pay for the expenses caused, a solution accepted by the commander-in-chief of the troops fighting it. Guerrilla activity continued and intensified after the proclamation of the Republic, and the Carlist pretender returned to Spain to fight a war that lasted three years. The restored liberal King, Alphonse XII, in his victory proclamation to the troops, expressed his grief about the cost of the war, but saw their sacrifice limited to one generation. But "once founded by your heroism the constitutional unity of Spain, the fruit and the blessings of your victory will reach the most remote generations."

The Conservative Party leader, however, acted cautiously introducing ambiguous legislation unifying the draft and the tax system; the local councils would meet in the future under the provincial governors. Passive resistance was reflected in that none of the juntas proclaimed the king, and the government did not ask for such a proclamation. A new party emerged: the neo-fueristas led by Sagarminaga. The Diputaciones jointly presented their demands to the prime minister threatening resignation. The government decided to fix the tax contribution of each province leaving to them the method of collection and payment. The provincial councils resigned or were dissolved, with Vizcaya the economically most developed province, leading the resistance. Finally, the government opted for a compromise with the law of 1878, confirmed in the budget bill of 1887, agreeing to leave the tax legislation and administration to the Diputaciones, and demanded a fixed sum to be agreed upon. Basque Union and Basque Policy were the slogans of the 1879 elections, with those accepting this solution obtaining the majority under the censitary suffrage. The legislation meant the absence of direct taxes on property or business and that often the municipal indirect taxes, like that on wine, would be double.[64]

The next stage was the emergence of a nationalist movement that would compete bitterly not only with the two national dynastic parties, but also with the Carlists and the local oligarchic leaders running on tickets defending the reinstatement of the fueros. The nationalist movement was born in the growing industrial metropolis of Bilbao, its support coming mainly from the rural population, often led by the lower clergy, the native skilled working class organized in the Solidaridad de Trabajadores Vascos, partly as a reaction against immigrant workers from other parts of Spain and the secular socialist labor movement. It is difficult to describe sociologically the initial leadership, but it is certain that with a few outstanding exceptions like the shipowner, Sota, support did not come from the big bourgeoisie of Bilbao, tied to one or the other of the dynastic parties, or sometimes supporting the Fuerist candidates. Since the region had no university and its cultural life, except choral singing and folklore, was generally in Castilian and unsympathetic to the cultural revival of the vernacular, the intellectuals and writers were not an important stimulus, as in Catalonia. That role was played, like in some other European peripheral nationalisms, by the lower clergy, often in conflict with their superiors. Initially, a petit bourgeoisie, professionals and family entrepreneurs, must have been among the main supporters, allowing the movement to retain for a long time a populist dimension that allowed it to bridge the class cleavages within the ethnocultural community, an aspect that made it appealing to the clergy. The founder, Sabino Arana, came from a business family, and his father had sacrificed much of his time and money for the Carlist cause, for which he went abroad.

The movement, much more than Catalanism, owed its character to the personality of Arana. A somewhat sickly man, strongly religious since his youth, educated in a Carlist family milieu and by the Jesuits, he went to Barcelona for unknown reasons to study law, without, however, obtaining a degree. In that city his perhaps incipient nationalist ideas crystalized in a milieu where Catalan nationalism was gaining ascendancy in the university and business community and where the young man decided to devote his efforts to the language and history of his homeland. In 1888 he returned to Bilbao, to aspire to a chair of Basque language in the local lycee supported by the provincial administration. In the competition among six aspirants which he did not win, he aspired on the basis of writings on the local language. The same year the Carlist movement split between those holding on to the dynastic claims of the pretender and those opting to defend just the ideological goals of a Catholic traditional society, that would be called—with a term also used in France—Integrists.[65] Like Carlism before, it would be a clerical party. In 1885 the Socialist party, founded in Madrid in 1879, started proselytizing among the metal workers and miners of Vizcaya; 1890 saw the first large strike, and in 1891 the first socialist city councilor of Spain was elected there. The industrialists agitated in those years for tariff protection and created powerful pressure groups. In this context the young man formulated his protest against the denationalization of his homeland by the immigration, the growing identification with Spain, and the neglect of local language, history, and pride. At that time the minister of finance decided to balance the budget and to ask Navarre—whose agreement had not been revised since 1841—and the Basque provinces to raise their contributions. This provoked incidents: the burning of a Spanish flag, a riot in front of the prime minister's summer residence.

In this context Sabino Arana[66] published his book, *Biskaya por su independencia* ("Biskaya" is the Basque spelling for the Castilian "Vizcaya"), and argued against the division of parties in his fatherland—eight parties, three Catholic: Carlists, Integrists, Fueristas, and five liberal: Conservatives and Liberals and three republican parties. All parties claimed to defend the traditional interests of the region. The program formulated at the time spoke of "Biskaya organizing itself in the regime of Republican confederation" reestablishing the old law, "constituting itself, if not exclusively, mainly with families of Euskerian race," Euskerian language to be the official language. "With Biskaya, by race, language, faith, character and customs, a brother of Alava, Benabarra, Guipúzcoa, Laburdi, Navarra and Zuberoa, it will form a tie or confederation with those six people to form a whole called Euskalerria, without loss of its particular autonomy." The Confederation would be formed by the free will of each of the Basque states (which included the French Basque provinces). Otherwise the programatic statement only emphasized repeatedly the Catholic character of Vizcaya, the subordination of politics to religion. To defend those principles, an association—really a party—was founded, and a newspaper, already being published by Arana, became its organ, a flag became the symbol rallying the few followers. The persecution using the press laws was almost immediate and Sabino ended in jail. The appeal was soon directed to the farmers, and in addressing the workers the traditional communal society was opposed to bourgeois society. In 1898 the leader was elected to the provincial council of Vizcaya, a platform he used for symbolic protests and to take stands which reflected the puritanism of communal protest we find in some of the teetotaler movements of rural liberalism in northern Europe. Municipal elections in 1899 brought a regression of the Carlists and seats to the Nationalists as well as to the Socialists reflecting the rapid industrialization of the area. A number of voluntary associations served as communication channels and cover for this movement, which faced constant legal difficulties in operating openly. A telegram to Teddy Roosevelt congratulating him for granting independence to Cuba and attacking the oppression of his people, caused his prosecution, but after five months in jail, he was declared innocent. Shortly afterwards, in 1903, he died. The movement would grow slowly in the coming decades and acquire particular strength in the first period of the Second Republic with the opportunity to institutionalize the autonomy and with the anticlerical policy pushing many voters toward the autonomy as a hope for an island of greater freedom for the Church. But let us stop our historical analysis to note some of the distinctive features of Basque nationalism in contrast to Catalan nationalist movements.[67]

Basque nationalism has a stronger communal ethnocentric dimension directed against denationalization, in a broad sense, linguistic, but also caused by the changes in social structure concomitant with industrialization and consequent immigration. This introduced a strong populist element, with ethnic exclusiveness. Catalan nationalism, with more intellectual than folk roots, centered its nationalism more on language, which ultimately is something that can be acquired. The possibility of assimilation of the immigrant was never excluded, and the strength of the language, both in its daily use and in its literary revival, made Catalan nationalism less defensive and perhaps therefore less aggressive and offensive.[68]

The populist element was reinforced by the relative lack of success of the PNV among the big bourgeoisie of the Basque country, particularly the financial and manufacturing magnates of Bilbao, tied for a variety of reasons to the Spanish economy, the oligarchic parties, the Court. This allowed the party to be more successful among the native working class and to bridge, like similar movements in other parts of the world, the class cleavages of an industrial society. But it also isolated it from the pragmatism that good business sense introduced into the relations between the Lliga and the Spanish state. In contrast to the PNV some of minor left-Catalanist parties influenced by the Federalist heritage of the left, also emphasized less the purely romantic nationalist component.

The point is hard to document, but it seems clear that a large part of the Bilbao business elite, which created giant steel-mills, other industrial plants, and some of the most successful industrial investment banks, remained aloof from the incipient nationalist movement. In fact they became (perhaps, as the nationalist say, with bought votes of their workers or with those of the nonleftist immigrants) the backbone of the parties of the old regime under the monarchy, and later of the conservative monarchist nationalist right in the Republic. Bilbao financiers and great industrialists (with some outstanding exceptions) did not identify with Basque nationalism. One reassuring factor was the Crown's policy after the Restoration in 1874, as that of Amadeo de Saboya (1871-73), of granting titles to financiers and industrialists. Since the leading businessman and supporter of the Restoration in Catalonia refused a title, this policy did not have the same effect on Catalonia, as in Vizcaya. This created in the Northern industrial emporium another set of ties with Madrid. These ties between the Vizcayan big business and the center continued after the Civil War, and the managerial character of many large industries facilitated the interchange of personnel. Those not native to the Basque country moved into top positions in Bilbao as managers after a successful engineering career, and Basques occupied important positions outside of their region in industries promoted by the banks.[69]

There are indications that some men of this managerial team have moved into the government in recent years. In this sense the contrast between Vizcaya and Barcelona could not be greater: few non-Catalans hold positions in the Catalan industrial world and few Catalans move elsewhere. Their family capitalism remains essentially local, while the Bilbao financial capitalism is essentially national. In this sense developments initiated in the 19th century have been reinforced in recent decades by the separation of ownership and control and the growth of financial capitalism. Leading businessmen and a small group of anti-Basque intellectuals of the region, were among the main supporters of Franco, and a few of them were even in early, but not permanent, contact with the founders of Spanish Fascism, some of whom would occupy key positions under Franco. Therefore, it is not surprising that Basques from Vizcaya or connected with its milieu should play a role in the Franco Regime as data on the regional origin of cabinet members show, while the Catalans do not proportionately play such a role.[70]

These links between the Bilbao financiers and industrialists and the central power structure on the other side strengthened the socially progressive tendencies of a rural paternalist democracy in the PNV, which could evolve in the direction of Christian Democratic Parties. With the Basque national, and linguistic identity much weaker than the Catalan, its upsurge in the early years of the Republic and its appeal even in Navarra was strengthened by the hope that the (autonomy Estatuto) would allow them to regulate separately their relations with the Vatican, offering exemptions from the anticlerical and anti-Jesuit legislation. This was reflected in the vote for the party in the first elections and the intransigeant clerical position of the Basque-Navarrese representation in

Parliament during the constitutional debates. Once these hopes dwindled, class issues seem to have gained saliency and in the 1936 three-cornered election, votes shifted markedly toward the Right and the Left and away from the Nationalists, particularly in the district of Bilbao (the greatest industrial center). It is an irony of history that the centralistic political position of the Right during the so-called two black years and the conservative, clerical, centralist uprising of the army in 1936, convinced the Basque nationalists that they could not hope to achieve their goals on that side making them turn toward the Left—which initially had not been sympathetic to this clerical movement. This rapprochement and the support for the Estatuto—regional autonomy provided within the 1931 Constitution—sealed the strange alliance between the Catholic Basques and the militantly anticlerical Left.

This process creates some interesting problems for the sociologist: the cross cutting cleavages, which we so often see as a source of social integration, here contributed to added tensions because the nationalist overidentification with one issue and the subordination of others to it was strongly resented by those whose common cause was "betrayed" for its sake. The explanation lies in the strange nature of nationalist movements, the emotion creates a nonrational loyalty to a party which then is tactically much freer to choose sides as long as the primary objective can be pursued. Geographic isolation also limits personal ties with other groups, with whom one's interests and plight would otherwise be common: in this case, Catholic-clerical Spaniards elsewhere in the country where an anticlerical wave was making itself felt much more.

The Carlist background of the founder and probably many early followers of the PNV, combined with the religiosity of the region, led to a strange and initially obsessive identification between nationality and loyalty to Catholicism, which allowed the native clergy to support the party. This also gave the party a moralistic fervor, an opposition to cosmopolitan corrupting influences, not too different from some prohibitionist-ruralist movements against bourgeois-urban society. A big bourgeoisie like the Catalan, even when practicing Catholics, would never feel at home with that fusion of religious and national sentiment. In addition, the great secularization of large segments of Catalan urban society would never allow a clerical stand of the conservative Lliga. In fact, the petty bourgeois Catalanism would be anticlerical. The different position of both movements on the religious-secular cleavage would affect for some time the possible alliances of both nationalisms on the national scene.

The long survival of distinctive legal institutions of the premodern state period in the Basque provinces and Navarre, would lead to a differentiation in traditions and interests between them that would raise obstacles to the penetration of a party founded in Vizcaya. The ambivalences between defense of a prenationalist tradition and a new sentiment of community based on nationalism, would be a problem encountered by the PNV, not faced by the Catalan movements in their penetration in the four provinces of Catalonia. That continuity also led the Basque Party to be more concerned with the past, to build its legitimacy of arguments based on history, rather than on a concern with the future or specific demands.

The populist Basque nationalism maintained its political unity in the PNV in its complex maneuvers between the increasingly hostile Left and Right during the Republic, even when a small left bourgeois and less clerical party, Acción Vasca, made its appearance. The Castilian speaking base of the Right, the populism of the party, and the adroitness of the Basque Socialist leader Prieto, slowly brought the PNV closer to the Left. On July 19, 1936 after the military uprising, the party stated its position in these terms:

Faced with the events that take place in the Spanish State, that could have so direct and painful a repercussion on Euzkadi (the Basque country) and its destinies, the PNV declares—leaving unquestioned everything to which its ideology obliges it, an ideology that it reafirms today solemnly—that with struggle posed between citizenship and fascism, between republic and monarchy, its principles lead it inevitably to fall on the side of citzenship and the Republic, in harmony with the democratic and republican regime that was distinctive of our people in its centuries of freedom.[71]

Only after the approval of the Estatuto did a Basque enter the republican government in October 1936, in contrast to the Catalan Lliga and Esquerra that had participated repeatedly in Madrid governments. The Basques emphasized their identification with the democratic republic, their disagreement with the intemperate anticlericalism, their reservations about the future relations with the Spanish state and their separate surrender negotiated by their troops after the loss of Euzkadi with an Italian general that was rejected by Franco.

In recent years new nationalist organizations, farther to the Left like Euzkadi ta Azkatasuna (Basque nation and freedom), ETA, have appeared in the Basque underground challenging the dominance of the PNV, somewhat like the FNL Quebeçois has challenged the moderate French Canadian leadership.[72] The radical nationalist separatists bitterly attack the PNV leadership for its contacts with the republican opposition and the policy of participation in the Spanish state since 1936.

THE UNAWAKENED PERIPHERIES

A complete analysis of the tensions between periphery and center would require a study of those regions where some of the conditions for the emergence of nationalism existed—particularly a linguistic diversity and some potential grievances against the central government—but where the awakening of a national consciousness did not succeed. Such an analysis would have some of the advantages of a controlled experiment. Unfortunately, the lack of success of the limited attempts of arousing such a consciousness limits the available information. Table 4 gives a survey of the salient characteristics of these peripheries.

The lack of success of nationalism in the Balearic Islands and the three provinces of the kingdom of Valencia, particularly in the capital and the wealthy surrounding area, is surprising. The people in these areas speak variants of Catalan; they are physically close, particularly in the Balearic Islands, to Barcelona; they are exposed to many of the appeals of the Catalan nationalist ideology of Greater Catalonia; yet there is this striking absence of a nationalist or even autonomist movement in the Baleares, and it appeals to only small groups of intellectuals in Valencia.[73] The dominant parties in the kingdom of Valencia were Spanish parties or affiliated with them when they—as in the province of Valencia—assumed the labels "regional" or "autonomist." No movement in favor of granting an Estatuto under the Constitution of 1931 got underway. The Derecha Regional Valenciana was part of the CEDA that loyally followed the leadership of Gil Robles and the most progressive and republican wing of that party. The autonomists have grown out of the Radical Party and its leadership cooperated closely with that party on the national level, representing a secularized bourgeoisie in a region with a rich commercial agriculture and considerable industrialization. The wealthier peasantry finds the Catholic Derecha Regional a good channel for its interests, and a center bourgeois position linked with the Radicals, reflects the discomfort of the owning classes with a largely anarcho-syndicalist labor movement. The working class, when it votes, supports the parties of the bourgeois Left or the Socialists.

Why, at least in the past, has there been so little active regionalism, even less nationalism, and no solidarity with Catalanism in these largely Catalan speaking areas? The explanation is not easy and probably different in the various provinces.

In the Baleares despite the relative well being, a medium-high level of education, and some industrialization, "notable politics" continued well into the thirties. Before 1923 the rise to national leadership of a favorite

[text continues on page 90]

TABLE 4

Characteristics of Spanish Regions and Peripheral Nationalism

	Catalonia	Basque Country	Navarre	Galicia	Levante	Balearic Islands
Population 1970 (% of national total)	14.9	5.7	1.3	7.8	8.6	1.5
Linguistic Differentiation	Catalan	Basque	Partly Basque	Galician	Variants of Catalan	
% of housewives preferring regional language conversations	54	25	(not included in survey)	44	31	67
% in large urban centers	47	8		8	10	39
Index of familiarity with language	89	44		85	73	82
% preference for TV in vernacular	58	33		18	14	20
Historical Distinctiveness	1137 Union with Aragón 1469 Union with Castile 1716 Abolition of legal distinctiveness	Middle Ages part of Castile and Navarre 1839 Abolition of traditional institutions	1512 Incorporated into Castile-Aragón 1829 Separate legislature met last	Part of León united with Castile in Middle Ages	Medieval kingdoms of the Crown of Aragón 1469 Union, as part of it, with Castile 1707 Abolition of legal distinctiveness	
Peripheral Nationalism:						
Emergence	1882-1892	1894	Part of Basque	1907-1916	1932 ?	None
Initial success	1906	1930s		1936	None	None
Status Under the Republic 1931-1939:						
Estatuto	Approved 1932	Various projects 1930s Approved 1936	Refuses to join Basques	Initiated 1932 Supported in plebiscite 1936	No formal action Discussions 1932	No demand

TABLE 4 (Continued)

	Catalonia	Basque Country	Navarre	Galicia	Levante	Balearic Islands
Regional or Nationalist Parties						
% of regional vote 1936[a] In the case of Catalan parties a large proportion of those votes were gained in coalition with non-Catalan parties	Lliga Catalana (before 1933 Regionalista) Unió Democràtica de Catalunya Acció Catalana Esquerra Estat Catalá Bloc Obrero i Camperol Partido Socialista Unificado de Cataluña PSUC	PNV Acción Vasca Recently new splinters ETA PC de Euzkadi	PNV	ORGA PC de Galicia	Derecha Regional Valenciana (part of CEDA) Partido Autonomista	None
Economic Development and Public Finance						
Per capita income in ratio to national average in 1960	154 Barcelona 116 rest of Catalonia	165	117	75 Coastal Galicia 58 interior Galicia	116	108
Change 1960-1949	+21 Barcelona −4 rest of Catalonia	−15	+1	−15 Coastal Galicia −21 interior Galicia	+15	−3
Change 1967-1960	−8 Barcelona +4 rest of Catalonia	−17	+8	−2 Coastal Galicia +6 interior Galicia	−20	+20

TABLE 4 (Continued)

	Catalonia	Basque Country	Navarre	Galicia	Levante	Balearic Islands
Economic Development and Public Finance (continued)						
% of GNP	17.6	7.2	1.6	5.7	8.5	1.7
% of National direct and indirect taxes	31	13	1	5	9	2.3
% of expenditures	13	5	1	9	9	2.2
% of expenditures with respect to taxes	41	42	101	172	91	95
Municipal expenditures as % of national	21.0	6.7	2.3	4.4	7.2	1.3
Mobilization in voluntary Associations						
Number of associations per 1,000 inhabitants in region	43.8	38.4	42.1	13.9	32.3	42.6
Outside provincial capitals	30.5	28.0	36.5	9.0	25.0	33.0
Religiosity						
Inhabitants per priest 1967	1528 Barcelona 653 rest of Catalonia	535	273	978 Coastal Galicia 461 interior Galicia	1321	735
Seminarians per 10,000 inhabitants	2.3 Barcelona 9.5 rest of Catalonia	7.9	26.1	2.2 Coastal Galicia 17.0 interior Galicia	4.0	8.9

TABLE 4 (Continued)

	Catalonia	Basque Country	Navarre	Galicia	Levante	Balearic Islands
Migration						
Net migration rates 1901-1930	24.8	5.4	−19.0	−15.6	3.3	5.0
Net migration rates 1931-1960	25.0	17.7	−12.7	−12.8	9.4	6.8
Proportion of housewives not born in region	33	34	—	6	31	16
Identification of Social Groups with Nationalism						
% of housewives who consider themselves Catalana, Basque, etc.						
Total sample	42	36	—	72	31	74
Metropolitan sample	36	16	—	58	21	52
Intellectuals	Strong	Weak except for minority	No	Medium	Low, incipient	Low, very incipient
Clergy	Medium high	Strong	No	Weak	Weak	Weak, growing?
Big business	High with moderate nationalism	Only minority strongly	No	No	No	No
Middle class	Strong	Divided, strong	No	Weak	Medium low	Low
Peasantry	Strong	Strong	No	No	No?	No
Working class	No, except lower middle class	Native partly	No	No	No	No
Public Opinion Support for Decentralization						
% of total	48	40	50	20	22	26
% among with opinion	75	58	82	57	36	50

NOTE to Table 4

Population: Anuario Estadistico 1971

Linguistic differentiation: Data from a national sample survey of housewives, 1969, Fundacion FOESSA, Informe sociológico sobre la situación social de España 1970, Madrid, Euramerica, 1970, Chapter 18, pp. 1261-268 and Tables 18.40 to 18.85. The survey did not include the province of Gerona in Catalonia, Navarra, and the province of Lugo in Galicia. Therefore, the data are only indicative.

Regional or nationalist parties: The electoral law of the Republic that favored the majorities in large multimember constituencies encouraged the formation of electoral coalitions, and this makes it very difficult to determine the strength of individual parties. For example, in 1936 it is possible to determine the votes for the Lliga in Barcelona city, but not in the four other districts of Catalonia where it ran on coalition tickets. In 1936 Lliga candidates not in coalition obtained 16.4 percent of the Catalan vote, and another 20.3 percent on coalition tickets; Acció Catalana only ran separate candidates in Barcelona city which obtained 3.3 percent of the regional vote. The Esquerra candidates obtained 23.5 percent of the vote and alliances of the Esquerra with other left parties, 18.4 percent. Non-Catalan parties of the Right in opposition to the Lliga obtained 6.7 percent; the Radicales 2.8 percent; Acción Republicana 0.8 percent; the Communists 1.6 percent, that is, a total of approximately 12 percent. Data from Javier Tusell Gómez, Las elecciones del Frente Popular en España, Madrid, Edicusa, 1971. In the Basque country in 1936 according to the same source, the PNV obtained 43.7 percent of the vote, the Socialist and bourgeois left, 31.4 percent; the Communists 2.5 percent; the coalition of the right 18.5 percent to which we would have to add the Tradicionalistas (Carlistas) with 5.4 percent (dominant in Alava).

Economic development and public finance: The data for per capita income in relation to national average and changes over time, and for the GNP are from FOESSA, Informe sociológico, op. cit., Tables 4.56 and 4.59. The data on taxation and expenditures are from Ministerio de Hacienda, Secretaria General Técnica, Información estadística del Ministerio de Hacienda 1968, Madrid, 1970. Data for taxes from capitulo I and II of the budget and the contribution concertada for Alava and Navarra, pp. 35-39, minus the customs which are excluded since their collection is not fully related with the regional activity, and those collected in Madrid since there are no separate data for payments made in Madrid from expenditures of the central administration—the Dirección General del Tesoro—with the consequence that the calculations otherwise would include taxes collected in Madrid but not payments. For a more detailed analysis of the problems in using these data, see Miguel Beltrán Villalba, "Andalucia, el presupuesto y la redistribución de la renta," Anales de Sociología 1968-1969, 4-5, pp. 18-31, especially p. 20.

Mobilization in voluntary associations: Data for 1960 from the national registry of associations of the Ministry of Interior, collected and elaborated by the author. See Juan J. Linz, "Asociaciones voluntarias: la realidad asociativa de los españoles," Sociología española de los años 70, Madrid, Conferacion Española de Cajas de Ahorros, 1971, pp. 307-48.

Religiosity: Data from FOESSA, Informe sociológico, op. cit., Chap. 6, pp. 435-70, Tables 6.10 and 6.11.

Migration: Data from Alfonso G. Barbancho, Las migraciones interiores españolas. Estudio cuantitativo desde 1900, Madrid, Estudios del Instituto de Desarrollo Enconómico, 1967, Tables A7 and A19. The data refer to interregional migrations except for Navarra and Baleares where the province serves as a unit.

Identification of social groups with nationalism: Data from the FOESSA 1969 survey quoted above. Those who when asked: Are you ... (the word for those of a particular region), had answered "yes", "as if I were, or halfway" rather than "no", were asked: "¿Que se siente Vd. más ... o española?" ("What do you feel more ... [Catalan, f.ex.] or Spanish?" The "two step" formulation of the question introduces in Catalonia, the Basque country and Valencia, a certain bias since respectively 24, 32, and 29 percent (in the total sample) had answered "no" to the first question and, therefore, were not asked the second. Not so in Galicia and Baleares where the percentages were 5 and 11 percent. Certainly those saying "no" would probably have answered Spanish to the second—forced choice—question.

Public opinion support for decentralization: Data from a national sample survey of the Instituto de Opinión Pública.

son—Antonio Maura— might have been another factor. The relative isolation of the three main islands may also explain.[74]

In the case of Levante and its three provinces the Castelianization already centuries back, had gone very far not only among the elites but among the urban middle and working class and even in many rural areas.[75] The intellectual elite wrote mostly in Castilian, particularly the politically influential republican novelist Blasco Ibáñez. The secularized sector of Valencian society tended to be anticlerical, perhaps because its identification with nineteenth century bourgeois liberalism and the Republic, and the hostility to the Carlist revolt in the border area with Aragón. This sentiment might have been an obstacle to any influence of the Catalan Lliga, described by the Radical newspaper as the "separatist Barcelona bourgeoisie, monkish and old fashioned."[76] Another factor, perhaps a more important one, must have been the conflict of economic interests of the orange and orchard areas of Levante and the Catalans. As exporters of agricultural products, the merchants and peasants of Valencia were hurt by industrial protectionism that invited foreign retaliation and increased the cost of consumption articles. The success in the region in the critical years before World War I of the Democratic wing of the Liberal Party led by Canalejas must have been another factor. However, it would require more research to discover why neither the local Carlism, of some strength in the nineteenth century and the Federalism of the seventies, did not derive to regionalism and ultimately nationalism. In recent years, the relative absence of men of the region in the elite of the Franco regime—due to the moderate center, center left or right orientation of the political class under the Republic—plus the crisis of some agricultural exports facing the competition of other countries and as a result of the exclusion of Spain from the Common Market (which is affecting the relatively privileged economic position of the region), seems to have led some of the younger elites to have second thoughts about their linguistic Catalanism and regional identity.

Galicia poses an even more difficult question. As a relatively underdeveloped, largely agricultural region, with no immigration, the mass of the population particularly outside a few urban centers, has continued using the vernacular. At the turn of the century the region experienced a modest cultural revival in Galician. The economic condition of the peasantry, the problem of the complex divided property rights (*foros*), should have been a source of grievance, like the *rabassaire* question in Catalonia.

Among the factors that, without real research on the problems, suggest themselves, we might mention the following: the Castelianization of the urban elites and middle classes, whose opportunities were tied with the state—the bureaucracy, the professions, the army, and the navy—the oligarchic character of politics in rural areas where the worst forms of caciquismo predominated; the important role of some of those Galician politicians in Parliament and government; the powerful but not always respected role of a rural clergy of limited education in the many isolated hamlets; and the absence of other elites in the countryside. If the Galician clergy had choosen nationalism, things might have been different. The heavy transoceanic emigration, comparable in some respects to the Irish, probably drained the region of some of the most dynamic and intelligent lower- and lower-middle-class elements that might have interpreted the plight of their region in anticentralist terms. Galicia could have developed the nationalism or at least sectionalism of the underdeveloped areas feeling neglected by the central government, even when it probably has been and is a beneficiary of its activities. The relatively well distributed poverty in an area with minifundia limited the class conflict to the urban centers, where the anarcho-syndicalists had some strength. This naturally facilitated the exchanges between the central government and the local political class that had nothing to gain in any real mobilization, which anyhow would have been difficult given the poverty, low education, and ecological isolation due to the settlement pattern of the peasantry. Here again the incipient activity of a Solidaridad Gallega, created imitating the Solidaridad Catalana in 1907, attracted Republicans and Carlists and attempted an agrarian program. However the strength of Carlism had never been comparable to the Pyrennaic fringe, another obstacle to the emergence of Galician nationalism. Only short-lived movements like the Solidaridad Gallega, the Acción Gallega, and the Irmandades de Fala (1916)—with their newspapers—gave expression to Galician sentiments and interests. The movement always had a strongly intellectual character, without becoming a mass movement.[77] Significantly, Catalonia served as inspiration and the Lliga leadership offered sympathetic support. The Galician left bourgeois party under the Republic—the ORGA (Organización Republicana Gallega Autonomista)—was not a nationalist movement, but a close ally of Azaña's Izquierda Republicana. Recently, intellectuals and professionals have been expressing demands in favor of the Galician language and the agriculture of the region. The increased awareness of regional economic differences, and the still infrequent use of the vernacular by the Church will strengthen regional-national awareness in the future.[78]

In the Galician case, underdevelopment, the absence of an anticentralist elite—like the clergy in many parts of Europe—the low level of mobilization in any kind of voluntary association of the population, the massive outmigration, the integration of the local elite into the national elite—political and bureaucratic—were all obstacles to the emergence of another peripheral nationalism, despite the clear linguistic and socio-structural diversity.

A SYSTEMATIC BUT TENTATIVE CROSS-STATE COMPARISON

In the course of our analysis we have referred frequently to the obstacles to consociational solutions of the regional-linguistic conflicts. Using the factors listed by Lijphart, Daalder, Lorwin, Dahl, and some additional ones suggested by the Spanish experience, we have very tentatively characterized a number of European countries and Canada along those dimensions and scored them as favorable, perhaps favorable, perhaps unfavorable, and unfavorable to consociational solutions (see table 5). The comparison with Belgium and Switzerland, two democratic consociational democracies, seemed obvious, as did that with the U.K. in view of the similarities in the early state-building process, and that with Finland since it is a bilingual country in which the Swedish-speaking minority faced a large nationalist Finish population. Yugoslavia, a country in which an effort of nation-building had little success in the interwar years, but in which Tito has attempted to create a federal, multinational state, seemed worth taking into account. More questionable is the inclusion of Italy where the northern border minorities occupy a position difficult to compare with Spanish minorities, but where some other factors might be comparable.

It would take too much space to comment on each of the cross-state comparisons and even more to justify each of the ratings or descriptions for each country. The considerations entering in the choice of the thirteen dimensions—one or two irrelevant in some cases—can be founded in the literature already quoted and in our analysis in previous pages, particularly of the interaction between intraregional and intrastate cleavages, between the regional and the statewide or dominant nation party-systems.

Our very preliminary (let us stress it) analysis perhaps not unexpectedly leads to a highly favorable score in the case of Switzerland, Belgium, and Finland, a more dubious one for the U.K.—including Ulster—a slightly negative one for Canada, a negative one for Yugoslavia, and the most negative for Spain. Italy, if the size of the linguistic-cultural minorities were not so small, would find some of the same difficulties as Spain, but other factors would probably be more favorable. It is no accident that the

[text continues on page 97]

TABLE 5
Factors Favorable and Unfavorable to Consociational Solutions to State-Building and Stability in Multinational Societies

	Spain	Yugoslavia	Canada	Belgium
Size of national minorities or groups (% of population)				
Relative equality of groups		Serbia 41.2. Croatia 23.1 Slovenia 8.7 Macedonia 7.7 Others 19.3		Walonia 33.1 Flanders 51.3 Brussels 15.6
Large majority, but significant minority/ies	Non linguistic (Castilian) 60.2 Catalonia 14.9 Basque country 5.7 Valencia 8.6 Baleares 1.5 Galicia 7.8 Navarre 1.3		French 31.2	
Size of country	Medium	Medium	Medium	Small
Historical tradition of unity of state	Great pre-nationalist	Medium low	Medium	Medium nationalist
Foreign threats	Weak	Large	Low	Large
Total load of political system in modern times	High	High	Medium	Medium
Economic development				
General	Medium low	Low	High	High
Peripheral nationalism area	Catalonia high Basque country high Galicia low	Slovenia high Croatia high Macedonia low	Quebec medium	Flanders originally lower

TABLE 5 (Continued)

	Spain	Yugoslavia	Canada	Belgium
Class cleavages in linguistic minority	Catalonia: great Basque country: medium (perhaps increasing)	Not marked	Low increasing	Medium low
Religious or religious-lay cleavages	Catalonia: internal Basque country: cumulative	Croat-Slovene versus Serbs: cumulative	Cumulative	Moderately cumulative
Party system State wide parties	No	Now CP	Yes, Liberals	Statewide party system with regional dominance
Single or dominant subcultural or regional party/ies	Basque country until recently (PNV)	Partly until appearance of Croat Ustacha	Liberals also regionally dominant party	Recently
Multiple regional parties in conflict	Catalonia: deep left (Esquerra)-right (Lliga) conflict		Minor manifestations	Minor manifestations
Traditions of local self-government	Weak, but strong in the past	Weak	Medium	Strong
Nationalism of dominant group	Intense	Intense	Ambivalent	No clearly dominant group Brussels unifying center

TABLE 5 (Continued)

	Finland	Switzerland	United Kingdom	Italy
Size of national minorities or groups (% of population)				
Relative equality of groups				Core Italy 87.7 Trentino-Alto Adige 1.6 Aosta 0.2 Sicily 9.2
Very small minorities	Finnish 91.1 Swedish 7.0			
Large majority, but significant minority/ies		German 74 French 20 Italian 4 Romanch 1	England 82.5 Scotland 9.8 Wales 5.0 Northern Ireland 2.7	
Size of country	Small	Small	Large	Large
Historical tradition of unity of state	Medium high	Great pre-nationalist	Great but conflictive in Ireland	Medium high nationalist
Foreign threats	Very large	Medium	Weak	Medium weak
Total load of political system in modern times	Medium high	Low	Medium low	High
Economic development				
General	Medium low	High	High	Medium high
Peripheral nationalism area	Swedish minority high	Mixed	Scotland, Wales: low North Ireland: very low	All slightly lower Sicily: low

TABLE 5 (Continued)

	Finland	Switzerland	United Kingdom	Italy
Class cleavages in linguistic minority	Low	Low	Low	Low except for Sicily
Religious or religious-lay cleavages	None	Cross cutting	Cumulative and inter-nal in North. Ireland	Tyrol: slightly cumulative
Party system Statewide parties		Unique party system but statewide ideological currents and heterogeneity	Yes	Sicily: yes Trentino-Alto Adige-Friuli-Venecia Giulia yes except Germans
Single or dominant subcultural or regional party/ies	Single dominant minority party		Minority nationalist movements	Single minority representation parties
Multiple regional parties in conflict	No	No	No	No
Traditions of local self-government	Medium	Very strong	Medium strong	Weak
Nationalism of dominant group	Intense	No clearly dominant group. Prenational identity	Prenational state identity	Intense

NOTE: The information in this table has been taken from the national statistical yearbooks and a variety of monographic sources too long to quote in detail. The coding of the information has obviously many pitfalls and is often almost subjective.

We have made a judgement about the favorable or negative consequences of each variable for consociational solutions. In some cases, the variable was not clearly relevant and in others ambiguously favorable or unfavorable. Those clearly favorable were scored +2; those ambiguously favorable, +1; those clearly unfavorable, −2; and those ambiguously unfavorable, −1. The total score obtained that should range between maxima of +26 and −26 is only a very tentative measure, particularly since in a few of the countries some variables seem inapplicable, lowering the total score.

two with most unfavorable loadings would also be those that have experienced authoritarian rule: Spain and Yugoslavia.

SPANISH "STATE" AND "NATION-BUILDING" AND ITS OUTCOME IN HISTORICO-COMPARATIVE PERSPECTIVE

The union centuries ago of different crowns with different political institutions, reflecting different social structures, in turn related to different economic and military histories, therefore, did not immediately build a Spanish state. The king was not king of Spain, but king of Castile, of Aragón, count of Flanders, lord of Vizcaya, duke of Milan and so on. For each of these territories their sovereigns' possession of the others was incidental, a source of pride but otherwise of no immediate concern. As Oscar Jaszi has described it to us, the Habsburg monarchy—the Austrian-Hungarian empire—would retain much of a similar structure until 1918. Imperial Spain in the sixteenth and seventeenth centuries, particularly for its European domains, would allow us to ask the same question the historian of the dissolution of the Habsburg monarchy poses when he wrote:

> This experiment, which the greatest state of the European continent (leaving out Russia and the colonial empires) undertook with colossal military, economic, and moral forces through almost sixteen generations, was one of the greatest and most interesting attempts in world-history. Had this experiment been successful, it would have meant more from a certain point of view than all efforts of *state-building* (our emphasis) ever recorded. For, if the Habsburgs had been able really to unite those ten nations through a supranational consciousness into an entirely free and spontaneous cooperation, the empire of the Habsburgs would have surpassed the narrow limits of the nation and would have proved to the world that it is possible to replace the consciousness of national unity by a consciousness of a state community. It would have proved that the same problem which Switzerland and Belgium have solved on a smaller scale among highly civilized nations under particular historical conditions should not be regarded as a historical accident, but that the same problem is perfectly solvable even on a large scale and among very heterogeneous cultural and national standards.[79]

The Spanish Habsburgs faced the same problem when trying to build a state of Castile, Aragón—particularly Catalonia—Navarre, Portugal, forgetting now about Flanders, Naples and Sicily, and Milan. After limited success under Charles V—the Emperor—and I of Spain, Philip II, and more haltingly Philip III, the effort to maintain the traditional institutions under a monarchical confederation ultimately failed when Philip IV and his prime minister the Conde Duque de Olivares, attempted a higher level of integration—without initially and necessarily giving up the peculiar structure inherited from the past. That experience has been interpreted in different ways by historians, from those modern peripheral nationalists who saw in it a plot by an absolutist monarch and his malevolent prime minister to destroy the freedom of the people to those who stress the inevitability of greater unification, equality between the components of an empire and the vested interests of local oligarchies behind the resistance to the process. The question is, why was a solution like the Swiss or the Dutch ultimately not viable in the large European monarchies, and why were they pushed into the centralizing pattern? This pattern was perhaps first exemplified by the French monarchy, even before the emergence of modern nationalism with its unifying and equalizing tendencies, which after the defeat of the Gironde—as Hedwig Hintze has shown—completed the process with the uniforming departmental system, imitated in Spain, Portugal, and Italy.[80] Certainly there were exceptions, not without tensions, on the periphery—as Stein Rokkan rightly stresses.[81] Britain, leaving aside Ireland, succeeded in maintaining some of the premodern-state structures into our times, particularly in the union of England and Scotland, but even here the loss of empire, cultural nationalism, and inequalities in economic development are creating new strains, not totally different from those experienced by Spain in the nineteenth century. Another of the great centers of the monarchy-state-building stage, Sweden, had to give up its aspirations over Norway, Denmark, and Finland. The Austro-Hungarian Empire in some respects remained closer to the model that emerged out of the transition from the Middle Ages to modernity until into the age of nationalism. However, the pressures from two strong, peripheral centers—Prussia nad Piedmont—creating the German Empire and unified Italy, respectively, and the internal strains created by nationalism—German, Hungarian and that of the Slavic peoples—together with the inequalities in economic, social, and cultural development, under the precipitating event of defeat in World War I, led to its ultimate disintegration.[82]

Spain found it difficult to follow the model it initially was ready to follow—even under a strong monarch like Philip II: a federation of crown lands that might have succeeded (if we consider the doubtful analogy of the United Kingdom) or failed (if we consider the Swedish effort to hold together Nordic Europe on such a basis). Castile with its empire united with Portugal, having its own overseas territories, might have been a Western dual monarchy. For a number of reasons—whose inevitability is the object of dispute among historians and ideologists—the monarchs based on the Castilian center first attempted to create a Spanish monarchy under Philip IV—almost destroying the system—to complete the process-following the French model—under the Bourbons both in the absolutist and the liberal-centralizing phase. This attempt culminated in the provincial organization of 1833 and the defeat in 1839 of the Carlist rebellion and with it the defense of the *fueros*. However, the Spanish state never achieved what French kings and ultimately the Revolution did: to create the fully unified state and a nation-state with its linguistic-cultural and emotional integration. Despite all the political and administrative similarities, the Spanish fifty provinces are not the same as the 89 French departments, even under Franco after his stripping of Vizcaya and Guipúzcoa of the last fiscal privileges, and the destruction of the autonomy that Catalonia had slowly and effectively regained in the first three decades of this century. Navarre and Alava still maintain a distinct fiscal system, and the Navarrese provincial administration still has a distinctive character.[83] But, and this is much more important, as Pierre Vilar stated, while the autonomist, secessionist tendencies fostered by peripheral-centers are weak or dead in countries having achieved unification in the nineteenth century, the aspirations of Catalans, Basques, and even Galicians, are an important factor in Spanish contemporary politics. The ultimate outcome of the Spanish state-building process was not like the French, Portuguese, or even Italian or German, nor was it like the British. It did not fail—at least not yet—like the dual monarchy or the efforts of Scandinavian large monarchies, but did not fully—the more or less is a very debatable problem—succeed in building a nation-state even when there is a Spanish state—unlikely to disappear—and to a large degree and for most Spaniards a Spanish nation.

The ambivalent outcome of a long historical process is the peculiar Spanish problem, one likely to be repeated in many parts of the world. *Spain today is a state for all Spaniards, a nation-state for a large part of the population, and only a state but not a nation for important minorities.* Perhaps the explanation lies in the fact that Spanish state-building went on before the age of nationalism and that the era of nationalism coincided with a period of crisis of the Spanish state, bitter ideological conflicts, loss of its colonial empire, and economic backwardness and uneven development—a period in which the center, Madrid and its government, had little to offer to the periphery and limited resources for a successful policy of Castilianization.

The attempt went very far and achieved much that might be irreversible, but the limited integration of Castilian Spain with some of its peripheries had caused deep strains when the model of cultural-linguistic nationalism caught the imaginations of elites in the periphery: first professionals and intellectuals, then their business bourgeoisie, to penetrate finally into more popular strata, initially in the more industrially and commercially developed bourgeois Spain, but increasingly in other areas. The last century has been in part a period of peripheral nationalisms against the Castilian-created state, but that conflict has been superimposed, without fully cross-cutting upon the religious-secular conflict and that between the proletariat and the owning classes of city and country.

Uneven secularization of different regions of Spain and even more uneven economic development have not allowed Spain to follow the course of Belgium—where class and religious-secular alignments have cut across the Walloon-Flemish cleavage, allowing the emergence of a segmented-pluralist democracy. In view of the Belgium experience, it could be asked if the early introduction of proportional representation in Spain would have encouraged such a pattern somewhat more.[84] The split of Spanish labor between Socialists and Anarchists was another obstacle, particularly in view of the Anarchist strength in Catalonia with its electoral abstentionism and its occasional support to petty-bourgeois radical nationalism. The successive solution of nation-building crises of Belgium, that has made it possible to find consociational solutions to the linguistic question in recent years, was not possible in Spain, where conflicts accumulated unsolved or were reopened in the nineteen thirties.

The more advanced bureaucratic-monarchical development of Spain under the Bourbons and the centralistic-liberal state have prevented the emergence of a state consciousness distinct and compatible with multiple national identities like in Britain, rather than incomplete national consciousness. The terminological differences in describing the elements of the two political units illustrate the difference: British subjects are Englishmen, Scots, Welsh and—here the question becomes difficult—Irish or Ulstermen.[85] Spaniards are Catalans, Basques, Galicians, and increasingly Valencians or Malloreans—if the inhabitants of those two regions do not identify themselves as Catalans on account of their language; there is no single term for all other Spaniards: they are not Castilians, like the non-Scots and non-Welsh are Englishmen. Castilians, like the Andalusians, Aragonese, Extremeñans, have become Spaniards, but in a different form and degree than many Catalans and Basques. To them it makes no sense when the Catalans or Basques speak of them as Castilians, since they conceive of themselves primarily as Spaniards and only secondarily by their various regional identities, one of which is Castilian. In turn, for them, often, anti-Castilian sentiments are anti-Spanish sentiments since they tend to identify Spain with Castilian-speaking Spain. Faced with the ambivalence of the term Castilian, the peripheral nationalists often have to speak of Spain in the same terms that a Scot nationalist might speak of England without questioning the British allegiance. It is much more difficult to conceive Spain like the United Kingdom, rather than as a nation-state; its process of nation-building went farther but not far enough.

However, Spain in some respects is more like the multinational states of Europe—Belgium, Switzerland, Yugoslavia, Czechosolvakia, Finland—but there are decisive differences too: almost five centuries of some degree of political unification and common history, and much greater inequality in size of the component "nationalities," given the overwhelming proportion of Castilian-speaking Spaniards. It is like a Belgium where instead of the more or less half and half division between Walloons and Flemish, over two-thirds are Walloons. It is, therefore, very different from other multinational states in Europe with more equal proportions among nationalities.

A last analogy might deserve discussion, even when it would outrage most Spaniards: is Spain not like the Austro-Hungarian Empire before its dissolution and the ultimate failure of the efforts of germanization and magyarization? Partly yes, perhaps because both were initially created in the period of transition between the Middle Ages and the era of nationalism, without Vienna, Budapest, or Madrid being capable of assimilating their peripheries to a single standard language to the extent the French did, thanks to a strong state in a period of cultural dominance, active democratization, and national glory. Partly no, since the religious homogeneity, the linguistic similarity, and probably the economic integration, have made Spain a much more unified polity than the Austro-Hungarian dual monarchy, or even any of its two components, ever dreamt to be. In addition the Spanish peripheries would not experience the pull of adjacent autonomous political units, conceiving of their brethren on the other side of their borders as irredenta: like Serbia, Rumania, and, before, Italy, or even many pan-Germans perceiving Austria as an artificial unit in the era of nation-states. Certainly, Galicia could have experienced a Portuguese pull, given the linguistic affinity, but the relative weakness of Portuguese nationalism—another early state rather than nation born in the nineteenth century—and the crisis of the Portuguese state in the last century with the loss of Brazil and internal turmoil, prevented any such development. The element of unjustified Portuguese fear of annexation by Spain might also have prevented any claims to Galicia. The peripheral nationalism could count only with very limited encouragements by foreign powers, compared to those on the eastern periphery of the European monarchies, and the sympathies felt for Catalan· or Basque nationalists would never reach the emotional strength of those for the Poles or other Slavs. Nor did the independence fit into the plans of the great powers of the last century. France, while not fully unsympathetic, was ultimately aware that the potential nation-states seceding from Spain would have been a pole of attraction to the small Catalan and Basque minorities in France. Peripheral nationalism in the case of Spain was strictly internal and the advanced stage of state and even national integration before the era of nationalism and the continuing process of Castilianization, condemned them to generally limit their aspirations to autonomy rather than secession. Any step further was and still is condemned to defeat.[86] The "differential facts" were not great enough to make Catalonia or the Basque country a Spanish Ireland, to the despair of the nationalist extremists.

In the era of nationalism, Castilian-speaking Spain was not strong enough to assimilate the periphery to the degree France was capable of doing with Brittany and its small Catalan minorities. Spain, born in the era of state-building, could not undergo the deep emotional process of democratic nation-building that the Italians underwent—despite Massimo d'Azeglio's pessimistic dictum—and Germany experienced since political unification. The balance of forces between center and periphery, the historical, demographical, and cultural-linguistic weight of Castilian-speaking Spain, make it doubtful that it could become a truly multi-national state. Only the total disintegration of the Portuguese empire offers an extremely dim hope of an Iberian multinational state accepted sincerely by all component nations.[87] The tensions between peripheral nationalisms and a Castilian-speaking state are likely to continue in the future, with the periphery divided on the degree of autonomy it might find acceptable and the center torn about the degree of unification it will consider necessary. It will continue to be difficult for Castilian-speaking Spaniards not to identify "Spanish nationalism with a historico-political and cultural tradition shaped by Castile and loyalty to the Castilian language." No final optimal solution to the problem is in sight. It is therefore not surprising that some of the leaders of the periphery look forward to the total destruction of the European system of states (and nation-states) and its substitution by a European federation of "patries"— rather than nations—in which old and new nations, as well as nonnation and nonstate units, would become part of a larger polity. However the prospects of such a development still seem very far off. At present, at least, the problem of Spain's multilinguistic society has elements of insolvability, a fact that does not exclude partial solutions on an evolutive basis—somewhat like Belgium or Canada—far from satisfactory to all concerned. Spain might have succeeded in state-building, but has had somewhat less success in nation-building, even when it was close to it at the turn of the eighteenth and the first decades of the nineteenth century, as the reaction in all parts of the peninsula to the Napolenonic invasion shows.[88]

To avoid any wrong impression of a historic determinism, let us stress those unfavorable nineteenty-century circumstances that contrast with Italy in the Risorgimento and Germany under Bismarck. Spain in the nineteenth century lost an empire, rather than dreaming with one; religious-secular conflicts were especially acute since Spain had not experienced the Reformation; its economic and scientific revolution had been frustrated or failed; its cultural golden age was of the past; and its state was not a new creation arousing hopes but a discredited, inefficient machine. Under those circumstances, the legacy of incomplete, partly frustrated, state-building and dead or distorted representative institutions became a handicap in the new effort of nation-building. The addition to that historical legacy of the secular-clerical and the class conflict, plus the presence of the army filling the vacuum of a dynamic bourgeoisie at the center, ultimately account for the difficulties and breakdown of the great attempt of the 1876 Restoration regime. The inevitable appeal or necessity to participate in the colonial expansion process in Morocco—for which the country was not prepared—finally broke the camel's back in 1923. The Republic in 1931 in the most unfavorable moment in European history would resume it on new bases, taking into account the national sentiments of part of the periphery, but failed again—perhaps inevitably even with better leadership. The Franco experiment, based on absolutely opposite premises than the Republic, would seem to have succeeded, ruling the country over thirty years and allowing its economic development, but there are too many signs that too many of the problems of the past, particularly that of integrating the periphery, remain unsolved.[89]

A FUTURE SPANISH STATE AS A MULTINATIONAL SOCIETY?

Robert Dahl writes,

> Systems with marked subcultural pluralism may sometimes confront, . . . a set of unhappy and even tragic choices: a) a polyarchy that provides mutual guarantees to its minorities but cannot respond to demands for solutions to major problems sufficiently well to hold the allegiance of the people; b) a hegemony that tries to meet these problems by coercing, if need be, members of one or more subcultures; or if the subcultures are also regional, c) separation into different

countries. Only the last may enable polyarchy to survive among the dissenting minority. Thus the price of polyarchy may be the breakup of the country. And the price of territorial unity may be a hegemonic regime.[90]

Spain in the last century has faced this unhappy situation. In the nineteen thirties, rightly or wrongly and among other issues, separatism contributed much to the radicalization of parts of the Castilian middle class, the bohemian intelligentsia, and students; the idea of defending national unity and historical tradition appealed to them. Regionalism gave the Fascists an excuse to call for "national," rather than strictly partisan, demonstrations. The contribution of regional nationalism to precivil war tensions is illustrated in a speech by the monarchist-authoritarian leader Calvo Sotelo when he supposedly said "I prefer a red Spain rather than a broken Spain"—making a play on the words *roja* (red) and *rota* (broken). In another speech he said:

> We face two hordes: the anti-Catholic horde and the anti-patriotic. In dealing with them I recommend two different treatments. Against the godless horde, tolerance, attraction, persuasion, never force. But against the anti-national horde, against those who want to divide that unity elaborated by hundred thousand ancestors, there is only one solution: to inculcate in the young generations a sentiment of virility and intransigence, making them know that if they want to separate themselves from Spain, that political and economic independence will not be achieved but by the force of arms.[91]

The outcome of the conflict was violence and repression and an effort of assimilation often ineptly carried out, which in recent years has given way to a growing liberalization which, however, is far from satisfactory to the advocates of linguistic autonomy. Fontana Tarrats has described this process in these terms:

> In moments of unitary euphoria it chooses its own "quislings" rather than the "loyal" (Catalans) and when the results become visible one turns to the least enemy moors, or what is worse, one trusts the apparent successes of the "quislings" who hold on on the basis of treason and compromises. This is even true for eclesiastical politics[92]

Such a solution, however, seems possible only under an authoritarian, hegemonic regime—in Dahl's terminology.

Without falling into the assimilation by force, extreme centralism, the "Spanish" nationalist not unsympathetic to many of the grievances of the periphery (not only the nationalistic one but the "provinces") had another answer to the dilemma of twentieth century late nation-building (or rebuilding). Intellectuals like Ortega y Gasset, Menéndez Pidal, and Américo Castro,[93] and under the influence of Ortega, the founder of Spanish Fascism, José Antonio Primo de Rivera, found the answer in emphasizing a common historical destiny and a mission or task for the future. They all reject romantic cultural, linguistic, ethnic concepts of the nation in contrast to most nationalisms in Europe. For Catholic conservatives, that sense of purpose was lost with the Enlightenment and Liberalism and, therefore, a return to the past was to be an answer; for the Fascists more willing to accept the secularization of Spain, it was to be Hispanidad—the projection of Spain and its culture in America or a dynamic-imperialist policy in Africa; for others, mainly Liberals, a unification of the Iberic peninsula with Portugal. Unfortunately, none of those dreams has much chance to serve as an unifying myth and the more pragmatic goals of Spaniards—economic development, social justice, a better life for all, good government, even democracy or socialism—do not have that mythical task character. The activist missionary definition of a Spanish nation cannot compete with the realities of multinationalism whatever its weaknesses, nor can the excellence of Castilian as a language of a great culture ignore the competition of the vernaculars, real or contrived, in the cultural life of Spain.

In view of the difficulties of a negative as well as a positive integrative solution on the basis of the heritage of the last centuries, we must turn to the other alternatives offered by Dahl: mutual veto, autonomy, proportional representation or perhaps a combination of such solutions.[94] The ill-fated attempts of the Republic were in this direction, except for proportional representation, in both the Spanish state and in the regional governments.

A Spanish state uniting a multilingual and to some extent multinational society might still succeed, on a different basis than in the past, in a democracy born under favorable stars. The early fifties might have been such a moment—with the temporary weakening of the appeal of nationalism—and the strong appeal of constitutional-liberal-democracy, plus economic development and a modicum of social reform. I am not so certain that the present world and ideological conjuncture is equally favorable, but Spaniards—Basque, Catalan, Galician, Castilian-speaking—will have to try, within a spirit of compromise and without illusions about the difficulties. Castilian-speaking Spaniards will have to give up the idea of a Spanish nation created largely by them and accept a more decentralized, largely multilingual state.[95] The periphery, while enjoying a new sense of nationhood, will have to combine it with a loyalty to the multinational state, a loyalty expressed in an active participation in the central politics and government, a willingness to share in the burdens of common economic and social development (that will fall more on it given its greater economic development and the benefits it derived and derives from a common protected market), a respect for a common history of centuries and the symbols of the state. The periphery, mainly the economically developed, will also have to guarantee equal citizenship rights to those, mainly immigrant, but also Castilianized minorities who will not feel the new nationalism, nor the desire to use the regional languages, and who will reject assimilation forcefully, unwilling to accept second-class citizenship on account of their Castilian language in a Spanish state. Once everyone has accepted loyally a multinational state, rejecting any open or veiled threats of secession, working out reasonable compromises in economic matters—particularly taxation—guaranteeing the rights of Castilian-speaking minorities, the strength of each culture, the capacity of regional leaders, the demographic processes, and other factors will decide the relative strength of the nationalities, in some regions in favor of the peripheral nationalisms, in others in favor of the continuous strength of Castilian. Within the initial agreement no one can expect, however, final and stable solutions, but constant processes of accommodation that will tax the qualities of leadership of all participants.

The third main alternative of Dahl, secession, cannot be excluded and is certainly considered by the minority of extreme nationalists of the periphery. However, Salvador de Madariaga, a convinced federalist and opponent of Franco, warns (1967): "At the slightest sign of separatism in Spain the armed forces would launch on the scene to suppress it and the country would return without escape to dictatorship."[96] and Cambó in 1927 wrote:

> Faced with a Catalan rebellion all the class and party conflicts would stop, all the other problems would be solved or postponed, and Spain would rise against Catalonia with the same enthusiams and decision with which France rose against Germany in 1914.[97]

Independently of that, it seems doubtful that any politician of Catalonia and perhaps even less of the Basque country could, in a foreseeable future, create sufficient unanimity for a secessionist solution. Too many Catalans and Basques consider themselves Spaniards; the social, economic, historic, emotional, and other ties are too strong; the immigrants are too large a proportion of the population; the number of those not using the vernacular and uninterested in its preservation is too large. Under those circumstances the breakup of the country would not assure polyarchy in the new states either. In addition, the economic cost of losing a protected Spanish market would probably be too high. In case of secession, the nonperipheral nationalist parts of Spain would lose economically, but so would the peripheral areas since their industry would not be competitive with that of other European countries. Intellectuals might be willing to pay this cost, but businessmen and the working class, particularly the immigrants indispensable to economic progress, will not.

With secession realistically excluded, at least in the foreseeable future, only the other two alternatives of Dahl remain. A consociational solution seems more desirable.[98] Neither total pessimism about its viability that can only lead to secession or imposition nor total optimism, that would soon turn into disappointment and pessimism, can inspire such a solution. There is no one solution to the complex historically created impasses in the state and/or nation-building of Spain, but changing solutions based on the avoidance of crises and a spirit of compromise. The alternative unfortunately is authoritarian rule over all Spaniards, Castilian as well as Catalans, Basques, and others, and not necessarily by Castilians, but by men coming from all corners of Spain.

NOTES

1. Data may be found in International Bank for Reconstruction and Development, "Population and Per Capita Product," World Bank Atlas, Washington, September 1968.

2. On these regional differences in economic and social structure and their political implications, see Juan J. Linz and Amando de Miguel, "Within-National Differences and Comparisons: The Eight Spains," in Richard L. Merritt and Stein Rokkan, Comparing Nations, New Haven, Yale University Press, 1966, pp. 267-319. See also the basic and detailed study, Fundación FOESSA, Informe Sociológico Sobre la Situación Social de España, 1970; Madrid, Euramérica, 1970, a 1034-page report directed by Amando de Miguel, with economic and sociological data, including those from a national sample survey.

3. On the population of Catalonia and the Catalan "lands", see the chapters by Ernest Lluch and Eugeni Giralt, "La Població Catalana" in the Catalan ed. of Alfred Sauvy, La Població, Barcelona, Edicions 62, 1964, pp. 145-206.

4. Pierre Vilar, La Catalogne dans l'Espagne Moderne. Recherches sur les Fondements Economiques des Structures Nationales, Vol. I, Paris, SEVPEN, 1962, p. 131.

5. Max Weber, Economy and Society, ed. by Guenther Roth and Claus Wittich, New York, Bedminster Press, 1968, Vol. I, pp. 54, 56.

6. Ibid., pp. 922-23; selected paragraphs from a long text.

7. Ibid., p. 924.

8. Prat de la Riba, quoted by Jordi Solé-Tura, Catalanisme i Revolució Burgesa, La Sintesi de Prat de la Riba, Barcelona, Edicions 62, 1967, pp. 180-181.

9. Ami Vasco, by P. Evangelista de Ibero, published in 1906, quoted by Fernando Sarrailh de Ihartza, Vasconia, Buenos Aires, Ediciones Norbait, 1962?, p. 547.

10. For a graphic presentation of those historico-geographic developments in the Middle Ages, see Jaime Vicens Vives, España. Geopolítica del Estado y del Imperio, Barcelona, Editorial Yunque, 1940, pp. 74-79, 84-95, 98-101.

11. This process was not very different from the one that in the same period created the French monarchy under the French kings from their core lands of the Ile de France, southward, toward the Atlantic—in conflict with England—and toward the East. In that process the weakness of the estate element became manifest in the inability of the nobility to work with the cities in resisting the expansion of royal power—a process that was completed only by Francis I through marriage with the duchess of Britanny, and the acquisition of that territory by their son in 1532.

12. Fernand Braudel, La Méditeranée et le Monde Méditerranéen a l'époque de Philippe II, Paris, Armand Colin, 1966 (2nd ed.).

13. Jaime Vicens Vives, Política del Rey Católico en Cataluña, Barcelona, Destino, 1940, and Historia de los Remensas en el Siglo XV, Barcelona, CSIC, Instituto Jerónimo Zurita, 1945.

14. As defined by Max Weber, Economy and Society, op. cit., passim, and Otto Hintze, "Typologie der Ständischen Verfassungen des Abendlandes" and "Weltgeschichtliche Bedingungen der Repräsentativverfassung," in Staat und Verfassung, Göttingen, Vandenhoeck & Ruprecht, 1962, pp. 120-85).

15. See Max Weber, Economy and Society, "The Occidental City," op. cit., vol. 3 Ch. 16, pp. 1212-374.

16. J. H. Elliott, The Revolt of the Catalans. A Study in the Decline of Spain (1598-1640), Cambridge, Cambridge University Press, 1963, pp. 6-8.

17. For a general history of Spain under the Habsburgs, see J. H. Elliot, Imperial Spain 1469-1716, New York, St. Martin's, 1964 and John Lynch, Spain under the Habsburgs, 2 vols., Oxford, Basil Blackwell, 1965-1969.

18. Roger Bigelow Merriman, Six Contemporaneous Revolutions, Hamden, Conn, Archon, 1963, first published 1938. Merriman notes that the origins of the Puritan revolution were not so fully different even when the religious component and the leadership of Cromwell, together with the strength already acquired by the Commons, made it vastly more important in its actual achievements and implications for the future, than the other five. "The more extensive authority of the monarchs of Spain and France, kept constantly before the eyes of king James Stuart, by the Spanish ambassador Gondomar, was doubtless a fundamental cause of many of its worst mistakes" (p. 29). The French Fronde, for a number of reasons, left the monarchy more powerful than ever, in contrast to the English revolution. Hans Daalder in his paper "Building Consociational States" (in this volume) has already described the very different process undergone by the Netherlands since their almost accidental independence.

19. Then, as today, international intervention—sometimes hesitant and sometimes resolute, generally motivated by self-interest—interfered with some of the state-building by the great monarchies, but helped some of the smaller peripheral countries, particularly Portugal, whose rebellion was encouraged and supported by France, the Netherlands, and England (even when, in the case of Dutch-Portuguese relations, the high-handedness of the Dutch in pressing their commercial and colonial claims became an obstacle). The British support and recognition, symbolized in the marriage of Charles II with the Infanta Catherine of the new house of Braganza contributed to the consolidation of its independence. To ignore the impact of

international relations on state-building and revolutions, certainly would be a mistake for the past as for the present (see the chapters on "cross-currents" in Part III of Merriman, op. cit., and particularly those on Portugal and the other powers).

20. This is the notion of a "coup d'état" as formulated by the French political theorist, Gabriel Naude, in a book written in 1639, before the outbreaks, *Considerations Politiques sur les Coups d'Etat,* which lays down some insightful rules for those who attempt to subvert existing conditions, among them that they should assume an "attitude defensive" rather than "offensive." The coups d'état, for him still, are the acts of the existing authority of the state faced with subversion, called for among other things to "annul such rights, privileges, franchises, and exceptions enjoyed by subjects as prejudice the authority of the prince," or, when it is necessary, to ruin some power which has become too great and extensive to be put down by other means. For Naude, it seems, coups d'état were an instrument of state-building; ironically, they would become so again in the present stage of the process of state-building in some of the so-called Third World countries. On this and the writings of other political philosophers, foremost Hobbes in Leviathan (1651), as the reflection particularly in England and France of the state-building process and the revolutions against it, see Merriman, op. cit., Ch. II.

21. Quoted by Elliot, op. cit., p. 200.

22. Otto Hintze, op. cit., pp. 120-85.

23. Quoted by Elliot, op. cit., p. 45.

24. Ibid., p. 119.

25. Ibid., p. 180.

26. Claudio Sánchez-Albornoz, España: un Enigma Histórico, Buenos Aires, Editorial Sudamericana, 1956, pp. 479-80.

27. On this period see Henry Kamen, The War of Succession in Spain, 1700-1715, Bloomington, University of Indiana, 1969 and Joan Mercader i Riba, Felip V i Catalunya, Barcelona, Edicions 62, 1968.

28. On eighteenth century Spain, see Juan Mercader Riba and Antonio Domínguez Ortiz, "La Epoca del Despotismo Ilustrado," Vol. IV of the Historia Social y Económica de España y América, ed. by Jaime Vicens Vives, Barcelona, Teide, 1958; Richard Herr, The Eighteenth Century Revolution in Spain, Princeton, Princeton University Press, 1958; and the last two volumes of Pierre Vilar, op. cit.

29. Richard Herr, Good, Evil, and Spain's Rising against Napoleon, Ideas in History, 1965, pp. 157-81.

30. On Carlism, see Stanley Payne, "Spain," in Hans Rogger and Eugene Weber, The European Right, Berkeley, University of California Press, 1966, pp. 168-207; see pp. 168-81 and 205-06 for further references.

31. Charles Tilly, The Vendée, A Sociological Analysis of the Counterrevolution of 1793, New York, John Wiley, 1967. An example of the type of research possible and an interesting contribution for one province and the second Carlist war is Julio Aróstegui Sánchez, El Carlismo Alavés y la Guerra Civil de 1870-1876, Vitoria, Diputación Foral de Alava, Consejo de Cultura, 1970, with data on the social bases of Carlism.

32. Jaime Vicens Vives, Cataluña en el Siglo XIX, Madrid, Rialp, 1961, Ch. III, pp. 309-40, 368-70.

33. Ibid., Ch. III.

34. Ibid., p. 364.

35. Ibid., p. 379.

36. Clara E. Lida and Iris M. Zavala, ed., La Revolución de 1868, Historia, Pensamiento, Literatura, New York, Las Américas, 1970.

37. See C. A. M. Hennessy, The Federal Republic in Spain. Pi y Margall and the Federal Republican Movement 1868-74, Oxford, Clarendon Press, 1962. Also see Miguel Martínez Cuadrado, Elecciones y Partidos políticos de España (1868-1931), 2 vols., Madrid, Taurus, 1969, on the elections of 1869, 1871, 1872, 1873, for the areas of strength of Federal Republicans and Carlists.

38. Jordi Solé-Tura, Catalanisme i Revolució Burgesa, Barcelona, Ediciones 62, 1967, p. 24.

39. Joaquín Tomás Villarroya, El Sistema Político del Estatuto Real (1834-1836), Madrid, Instituto de Estudios Políticos, 1968, Ch. X, XI, pp. 427-533. See also Dieter Nohlen, "Spanien," in Dolf Sternberger and Bernhard Vogel (eds.), Die Wahl de Parlamente und anderer Staatsorgane, 2 vols, Berlin Walter de Gruyter, 1969, especially Vol. I, pp. 1229-284, and Table A−1 (p. 1269) for changes in the number of those eligible to vote and electoral participation (1834 to 1936).

40. Raymond Carr, "Spain," in A. Goodwin (ed.), The European Nobility in the Eighteenth Century, London, Adam and Charles Black, 1953, pp. 43-59.

41. Juan J. Linz, "The Party System of Spain, Past and Future," in Seymour M. Lipset and Stein Rokkan, Party Systems and Voter Allignments, New York, Free Press, 1967, pp. 197-282.

For the Catalanist parties, particularly the Lliga, and other parties in Catalonia, see the important work by Isidre Molas, *Lliga Catalana. Un estudi d'Estasiologia*. Vol. I: *Lliga Regionalista, Lliga Catalana. Un partit catalanista L'estructura del partit: La base humana*. Vol. 2: *L'estructura del partit: L'organització. El programa politic. Canas d'influència. El sistema de partits, La desaparició de Lliga Catalana*, Barcelona, Edicions 62, 1972.

42. An excellent review is Stanley G. Payne, The Spanish Revolution. A Study of the Social and Political Tensions that Culminated in the Civil War in Spain, New York, Morton, 1970, with detailed bibliographic references.

43. J. Linz, "The Party System," op. cit. p. 225.

44. For an attempt to use this sequence in Spanish history, and its limited applicability, see Stanley G. Payne, unpublished paper.

45. On this point see the outstanding work by Edward Malefakis, Agrarian Reform and Peasant Revolution in Spain. Origins of the Civil War, New Haven, Yale University Press, 1971, particularly Chs. 9, 15.

46. Jesús Pabón, Cambó, Vol. I (1918-1930); Vol. II, Part 1 (1918-1930), Part 2 (1930-1947); Barcelona, Alpha, Vol. I, 1952; Vol. II, 1969.

47. In addition to the already quoted works of J. Pabón and J. Vicens Vives, see Maximiano García Venero, Historia del Nacionalismo Catalán, Madrid, Editora Nacional, 1967, rev. ed. in 2 vols. See also Anton Sieberer, Katalonien gegen Kastilien, Zur Innenpolitischen Problematik Spaniens, Vienna, Saturn, 1936; E. Allison Peers, Catalonia Infelix, London, Methuen, 1937; Stanley Payne, "Catalan and Basque Nationalism," Journal of Contemporary History, Vol. I, No. 1, 1971, pp. 15-51; and Oriol Pi-Sunyer, "The Maintenance of Ethnic Identity in Catalonia," in O. Pi-Sunyer, (ed.), The Limits of Integration: Ethnicity and Nationalism in Modern Europe, Department of Anthropology Research Reports 9, University of Massachussetts, Amherst, 1971.

For the history of Catalonia, see also Ferran Soldevila, História de Catalunya, Barcelona, Alpha, 1934-35, and many papers, book reviews, collected in Jaime

Vicens Vives, Obra Dispersa, Catalunya Ahir i Avui, ed. by M. Batllori and E. Giralt, Barcelona, Editorial Vicens Vives, 1967.

For a general history that devotes considerable attention to the regional nationalisms, see Raymond Carr, Spain 1808-1939, Oxford, Clarendon, 1966, see especially pp. 538-58.

On Catalan thought in this period, see J. Ruiz i Calonja, Panorama del Pensament Català Contemporani, Barcelona, Editorial Vicens Vives, 1936 for a selection of texts with brief introductions.

48. Albert Hirschman, The Strategy of Economic Development, New Haven, Yale University Press, 1958, pp. 185-86. This feeling is reflected today in the different prestige of business activities and civil service and military careers in Catalonia (and also, but less so, in the Basque country) than in the rest of Spain; see Juan J. Linz and Amando de Miguel, "The Eight Spains," op. cit., and by the same authors, "El Prestigio de Profesiones en el Mundo Empresarial," Revista de Estudios Políticos, 128 and 129-30, 1963, and "La Percepción del Prestigio de las Ocupaciones Industriales y Burocráticas por los Jóvenes Españoles," Anales de Sociología, Vol. I, No. 1, June 1966, pp. 68-75.

49. On the Solidaridad Catalana see Pabón, op. cit., Vol. I, pp. 255-80. For the 1907 election, see Miguel M. Cuadrado, Elecciones y Partidos Políticos de España (1868-1931), Madrid, Taurus, 1969, pp. 727-49, mainly 745. Of 511,694 voters in Catalonia 60 percent voted and 41 percent (211,791) of the votes went to parties in the Solidaridad Coalition; 19 percent went to other parties. Within that heterogeneous anti-system coalition the Lliga obtained 54,910 votes, 26 percent, and the Nationalist Republicans (Esquerra) 23,065. The Carlist still obtained 27,387 votes, 13 percent, and the Federal Republicans 34,416, 16 percent; Unión Republicana obtained 32,567 or 15 percent.

Due to the electoral system under the Republic (1931-1936) it is almost impossible to determine the strength of the different Catalan parties in the whole principality, since in some provinces they ran the candidates on coalition tickets with either left or right non-Catalan parties. For the elections returns in 1933 and 1936, the electoral propaganda, the making of coalition slates, and so on in 1936, see Javier Tusell Gómez, Las Elecciones del Frente Popular en España, Madrid, Edicusa, 1971, 2 vols., and José A. González Casanova, Elecciones en Barcelona (1931-1936), Madrid, Tecnos, 1969 and Isidre Molas, "Les eleccions parcials a Corts Constituents d'Octubre del 1931 a la ciutat de Barcelona", in Recerques. Història, Economia, Cultura, I (La formacio de la Catalunya moderna), Esplugues de Llobregat, Ariel, 1970, pp. 201-237.

50. Pabón op. cit., Vol. II, part 2, p. 491.

51. José Ortega y Gasset, España Invertebrada, Madrid, Revista de Occidente, 1948, First published 1920, pp. 45-48 and passim. English translation by Mildred Adams, Invertebrate Spain, New York, Norton, 1937, pp. 36-45.

52. Francisco Cambó, Por la Concordia, Madrid, Compañía Ibero-Americana de Publicaciones, 1927.

53. Albert Balcells, El Problema Agrari a Catalunya: 1890-1936. La Qüestió Rabassaire, Barcelona, Nova Terra, 1968.

54. Pabón, op. cit., Vol. II, part 2, p. 403.

55. Antonio Ramos Oliveira, Politics, Economics, and Men of Modern Spain: 1808-1946, London, Victor Gollanz, 1946, Ch. X, pp. 374-405. See also his La Unidad Nacional y los Nacionalismos Españoles, Mexico, Grijalbo, 1970.

56. Pabón, op. cit., Vol. II, Part 2, p. 356. There is no monograph on the Catalan policy of the Republic, particularly the enactment of the Estatuto in the frame work of the 1931 Constitution and its implementation, nor of the relationship between Azaña and Companys. The reading of Manuel Azaña on the question in his Obras Completas, Mexico, Editorial Oasis, 1967, edited with an introductory analysis by Juan Marichal, is essential, Vol. II, pp. 41-43; and the speeches on the Estatuto, pp. 249-309; Vol. III, pp. 12-13, 16, 19-23. The dilemmas internal to Catalanism that made consociational solutions difficult are well analysed in his "Mi rebelión en Barcelona," see pp. 44-52, and throughout his extensive memoirs and notebooks.

On Companys, see Angel Ossorio y Gallardo, Vida y Sacrificio de Companys, Buenos Aires, Losada, 1943, by his defense lawyer after the 1934 events.

57. Pabón, op. cit., Vol. II, Part 2, pp. 335-36.

58. Stanley G. Payne, The Spanish Revolution, op. cit., Ch. 3, pp. 37-61. The problem posed by teaching in the regional languages for the working class, native and immigrant, was well formulated by Antonio Fabra Rivas, an intimate collaborator of the Socialist Minister of Labor, Largo Caballero, in an article in Crisol, November 5, 1931, when he wrote:

> With respect to teaching, not only of Castilian, but also in Castilian, the Republic cannot make the slightest concession, unless it fails in one of its most sacred duties, specially in relation to the workers. The upper and middle classes of the Basque provinces, of Catalonia and Galicia will always learn—out of self-interest—Castilian, but on account of their interests they would try very probably that the working classes should know only the vernacular. In that case the workers of those three regions would find themselves, so to say, confined in their own country or at least with great difficulties to move to other regions, or to go to any of the Hispanic-American countries and, above all, to establish connections and exercise collectively their solidarity with their comrades of the rest of Spain.

Quoted by Gonzalo Redondo, Las Empresas Políticas de Ortega y Gasset, Madrid, Rialp, 1970, Vol. 2, p. 374.

59. Arend Lijphart, "Consociational Democracy," World Politics, Vol. XXI, January 1969, pp. 207-25; "Typologies of Democratic Systems," Comparative Political Studies, Vol. I, April 1968, pp. 3-44; see pp. 28-29. Also see his book The Politics of Accommodation. Pluralism and Democracy in the Netherlands, Berkeley, California, 1968. See also Hans Daalder, "On Building Consociational Nations: the Cases of the Netherlands and Switzerland," Internation Social Science Journal, Vol. XXIII, No. 3, 1971, pp. 351-70.

60. Cambó, op. cit., pp. 103-09.

61. See José Múgica, Carlistas, Moderados y Progresistas. Claudio Antón de Luzuriaga, San Sebastián, Biblioteca Vascongada de Amigos del Pais, 1950, pp. 170-76, provides evidence how the municipality of San Sebastian stood against the Carlists and prefered the new liberal individualistic freedom to the fueros. Rodrigo Rodríguez Garraza, Navarra de Reino a Provincia (1828-1841), Pamplona, University of Navarre, 1968, pp. 153-60, 233-39.

62. Maximiano García Venero, Historia del Nacionalismo Vasco, Madrid, Editora Nacional, 1968, rev. Ed., pp. 210-11.

63. Ibid., pp. 211-13.

64. That provision would become an issue in 1934 when the central government faced with an overproduction of wine asked for a lowering of the tax, provoking an illegal meeting of representatives of the three provinces.

65. On integrismo see N. Schumacher, S. J., "Integrism," The Catholic Historical Review, Vol. XLVIII, October 1962, pp. 343-64. For the Basque nationalist critique of Fuerism, Carlism, and Integrism, see Ami Vasco, by P. Evangelista de Ibero, in F. Sarrailh de Ihartzu, op. cit. pp. 563-77.

66. On Sabino Arana, see Pedro de Basaldúa, El Libertador Vasco, with a foreword by José A. de Aguirre (the prime minister of the autonomous Basque country during the Civil War), Buenos Aires, Editorial Vasca Ekin, 1953.

67. Pedro González Blasco, "Modern Nationalism in Old Nations as a Consequence of Earlier State-Building: The Case of the Basque-Spain", chapter 24 in Wendell Bell and Walter E. Freeman (eds.), Ethnicity and Nation-Building: Comparative, International and Historical Perspectives, Beverly Hills, California, Sage Publications, 1973. See also William A. Douglass and Milton da Silva, "Basque Nationalism" in Oriol Pi-Sunyer, op. cit., pp. 147-87.

The best scholarly ethnologico-historical study of the Basque country is Julio Caro Baroja, Los Vascos, Madrid, Minotauro, 1958. This work corrects without passion the misleading interpretations of the historical past, particularly in the Middle Ages, advanced for political purposes, and sketches the historical phases in the development of the region, pp. 514-517.

See Luis Michelena, Historia de la Literatura Vasca, Madrid, Minotauro, 1960, for a balanced view of the folk and educated literary tradition, the relatively late appearance of the second, its limited importance, and the religious character of many publications in Basque.

68. Antoni M. Badia i Margarit, La Llengua dels Barcelonins. Resultats d'una Enquesta Sociológico-Lingüística, Barcelona, Edicions 62, 1967, and FOESSA. Informe Sobre la Situación Social de España 1970, op. cit., Chap. 18, pp. 1261-268, and Tables 18.42 to 18.93, pp. 1302-347. Spanish censuses have never asked questions about language used or cultural identification.

For a history of language use, from a sociolonguistic perspective in the Catalan regions, see: "Aproximacion a la historia del bilingüismo en Cataluna" in Francesc Vallverdu, Ensayos sobre bilingüismo, Esplugues de Lobregat, Ariel, 1972, pp. 7-97. This work includes a survey of writings on bilingualism in the Catalan speaking area.

69. Amando de Miguel and Juan J. Linz, "Movilidad Geográfica del Empresariado Español," Revista de Estudios Geográficos. Vol. 25 94, 1964, pp. 2-29.

70. On the regional origin of different elites, see Linz and De Miguel, "The Eight Spains," op. cit., pp. 301-06, and Juan J. Linz, "Spanish Cabinets and Parliaments from the Restoration to the Present," in a volume on political elites ed. by M. Dogan, and J. Linz, in progress.

71. A. de Lizarra, Los Vascos y la República Española, Buenos Aires, Editorial Vasca Ekin, 1944, p. 24.

72. For further information on the ETA program and those of other underground movements, like ELNAS, Euskal Langile-Nekazarien Alderdi Sozialista (Socialist Party of Basque Workers and Peasants), as well as of the French Basque Enbata, and those of the prewar organizations, see Fernando Sarrailh de Ihartza, Vasconia, op. cit., George Hills, "ETA and Basque Nationalism", Iberian Studies, vol. I, no. 2, Autumn 1972, pp. 83-90. In the same issue, see: Tudor H. Rawkins, "The Geographical Background of Basque Nationalism", pp. 90-93 for a description of the criss-crossing of political, administrative, historical and linguistic boundaries in the Basque country with a useful map.

The trial of ETA members accused of terrorism in Burgos in December 1970 by a military court had great international resonance and provoked a serious crisis in the life of the country, polarising attitudes and leading to a mobilization of the supporters of the regime under the leadership of a resurgent extreme right. On the trial, its antecedents, statements of ETA spokesmen and the accused, world reaction, the impact on Spanish public opinion, see Kepa Salaberri, El Proceso de Euskadi en Burgos. Sumarísimo 31-69, Paris, Ruedo Ibérico, 1971, and Gisele Halimi, Le Procès de Burgos, Paris, Gallimard, 1971 (with Foreword by Jean-Paul Sartre). From a pro-regime point of view: Federico de Arteaga, *"ETA" y el proceso de Burgos. (La quimera separatista)*, Madrid, E. Aguado, 1971.

73. For a very informative historical monograph on the minor Valencian nationalist parties and the attitudes toward regionalism of other parties, the tensions with the Catalan nationalists of Catalonia, and the differences in outlook on autonomy between the provinces of the kingdom of Valencia, see Alfons Cucó, El Valencianisme Polític 1874-1936, Valencia, Garbi 2, 1971. This work also reproduces party platforms, legislative proposals, and the like.

74. For the place of the Baleares in Spanish culture and society, see Josep Melià, Els Mallorquins, Forward by Joan Fuster, Palma de Mallorca, Daedalus, 1967.

75. On the history of Valencia, see Joan Reglà, Aproximació a la Historia del país Valencià, Valencia, L'Estel, 1968. Joan Fuster. Nosaltres els Valencians, Barcelona, Edicions 62, 1962 (by a Valencian-Catalan nationalist); see ch. IV on the Valencian Renaixença in contrast to that of Catalonia. For the parties, elections, and campaigns under the Republic, see Javier Tusell Gómez, op. cit.

76. Reglà, ibid., p. 143.

77. Vicente Risco, El Problema Político de Galicia, Madrid, Biblioteca de Estudios Gallegos, CIAP, 1930. For a left Galician nationalist, see El Pensamiento Político de Castelao, Antología, ed. by Alberto Mínguez, Paris, Ruedo Ibérico, 1965. On June 28, 1936, less than a month before the Civil War, the Estatuto, initiated with limited enthusiasm in 1932, submitted to the Cortes on February 1, 1936, was submitted for a plebiscite and approved by 73 percent of those voting. See Jose Vilas Nogueira, El proyecto de Estatuto de Autonomía de Galicia bajo la Segunda República, Ph.D in Law, University of Santiago de Compostela, in manuscript.

78. Santiago Fernández and Maximino Arocos, eds. Galicia Hoy, Buenos Aires, Ruedo Ibérico, 1966, p. 135.

79. Oscar Jászi, The Dissolution of the Habsburg Monarchy, Chicago, Phoenix Book, University of Chicago Press, 1961, first published 1929, p. 3.

80. Hedwig Hintze, Staatseinheit und Föderalismus in Alten Frankreich und in der Revolution, Stuttgart, Deutsche Verlagsanstalt, 1928.

81. S. Rokkan in this volume.

82. Oscar Jászi, op. cit.

83. Juan Plaza Prieto, "Conciertos Económicos," in Anon., Notas Sobre Política Económica Española, Madrid, Publicaciones de la Delegacion Nacional de Provincias de FET y de las JONS, 1954 (a collection of articles published in the newspaper Arriba), pp. 395-98.

84. Val R. Lorwin, "Segmented Pluralism: Ideological Cleavages and Political Cohesion in the Smaller European Democracies," Comparative Politics, Vol. 3, No. 2, January 1971, pp. 141-75.

85. See Richard Rose, "The United Kingdom as a Multi-National State," University of Strathclyde, Survey Research Centre Occasional Paper No. 6, 1970. The Spanish liberal intellectual-politician and long-term resident in the U.K., Salvador de Madariaga, refers often to this difference in Memorias de un Federalista, Buenos

Aires, Editorial Sudamericana, 1967, for example pp. 44, 26-28, 168-69.

86. Cambó, op. cit., pp. 116-18, 126-28.

87. Madariaga, op. cit., passim. The anarcho-syndicalists, some left-fascists, and now some partisans of European unification, such as the "Europe des Patries," think in those terms.

88. Pierre Vilar, op. cit., pp. 158-59.

89. On the regional-nationalist question in present and future Spanish politics, see Juan J. Linz, "Opposition in and under an Authoritarian Regime: The Case of Spain" in Robert Dahl ed. Regimes and Oppositions, New Haven, Yale University Press, 1973, pp. 171-259. See pp. 240-252 and the bibliographic references given there. Our analysis there should complete this paper for the period after 1936. See also Sergio Vilar, Protagonistas de la España Democrática. La Oposición a la Dictadura, 1939-1969, Paris, Ediciones Sociales, n.d., with chapters on left, center and right in both the center and the regions, and a section on "form of the state," based on interviews with men of the opposition, from a leftish perspective.

It could be argued that under the conditions of semi-or pseudo freedom under an authoritarian regime it is particularly difficult to organize a nationwide opposition and that therefore some of the opposition sentiment is channeled into cultural linguistic nationalism. It can find an "apolitical" expression in cultural, folkloristic, language use, etc. forms and in a critique of the central government, more difficult to repress, rather than in more organized nation-wide forms. Paradoxically, the Franco regime, despite its "anti-separatism," centralism, and support for the Castilian language, has indirectly reinforced the appeal of particularistic peripheral nationalisms.

90. Robert A. Dahl, Polyarchy, Participation and Opposition, New Haven, Yale 1971, University Press, pp. 120-21.

91. José Calvo Sotelo in a speech in 1934, quoted by Felipe Acedo Colunga, José Calvo Sotelo. (La Verdad de una Muerte), Barcelona, AHR, 1957, p. 227.

92. José María Fontana Tarrats, Abel en Tierra de Caín. El Separatismo y el Problema Agrario Hoy, Barcelona, Ariel, 1968, p. 57.

93. José Ortega y Gasset, Invertebrate Spain, op. cit., La Redención de las Provincias, "El Concepto Deportivo del Estado". See the texts quoted by Carlos M. Rama. La Crisis Española del Siglo XX, Mexico Fondo de Cultura Económica, 1960, p. 97.

Ramón Menéndez Pidal. The Spaniards in their History, New York, Norton, 1950, ch. IV, "Centralization and Regionalism," pp. 75-101, and throughout his work.

Américo Castro as quoted by Sergio Vilar, Cataluña en España. Aproximación desde Cataluña al espíritu y los problemas de las Regiones Españolas (País Vasco, Galicia. Catilla, Andalucía), Barcelona, Ayma, 1968, pp. 18-19.

94. Robert A. Dahl (ed.), Political Opposition in Western Democracies, New Haven, Yale University Press, 1966, Ch. 11, "Patterns of Opposition," p. 358.

95. This requires a rejection of a position well reflected in the following text of the great historian Ramón Menéndez Pidal:

The federalism, cantonalism, and nationalism of modern days have come to destroy the unity of many centuries and have not succeeded in establishing themselves. Far from representing authentic Spain they belong only to an abnormal and transitory moment, a period of weakness that cannot be prolonged without grave danger to the country. They appear as a disease which attacks a nation, when its strength is low, for all disease consists in the struggle for autonomy of some organ which refuses to co-operate with the unified functioning of the body. Localism has always existed side by side with unitarism, but in moments of pathological weakness both one and the other become exacerbated . . . On the other hand, in the unified state there often is a failure to appreciate the problems of the region; there is, in fact, a lack of that strong and just spirit of co-ordination whereby each part of the nation feels itself assisted in a way which it is forced to recognize as equitable. Sometimes what happens is that extravagant concessions are made to the autonomous regions, and they are given protection which injures the other regions. On other occasions there is a severe repression of legitimate aspirations and attempts are made to suppress violently the symptoms of the disease without trying to cure it at its roots by wise and steadfast government.

The nationalisms of the periphery might have been the undesirable result of the Spanish crisis of the last century and a half, but today they are a permanent reality that has to be seen in a positive light, incorporated into the state. Perhaps an emphasis on multilingualism, rather than multinatioalism would be more fruitful for compromise solutions. Trudeau's position in Canada favoring linguistic rights rather than a two-nation federalism, would also be applicable to Spain, where Catalan speakers constitute large minorities outside of Catalonia, and Basque speakers live in Navarre outside of the three provinces seeking autonomy.

96. Salvador de Madariaga, Memorias de un Federalista, Buenos Aires, Editorial Sudamericana, 1967, p. 11.

97. F. Cambó, Por la Concordia, op. cit. pp., 117-18.

98. In addition to the already quoted writings of Lorwin, Lijphart, and Daalder, see Gerhard Lehmbruch, Proporzdemokratie: Politisches System un Politische Kultur in der Schweiz und in Oesterreich, Tübingen, Mohr & Siebeck, 1967; Jurg Steiner, "Conflict Revolution and Democratic Stability in Subculturally Segmented Political Systems," Res Publica, Vol. XI, No. 4, 1969, pp. 775-98; and Gewaltlose Politik und kulturelle Vielfalt: Hypothesen entwickelt am Beispiel der Schweiz, Bern, 1970. Also see Dahl, Polyarchy, op. cit., Ch. 7, "Subcultures, Cleavage Patterns, and Governmental Effectiveness," pp. 105-23, where he poses the tragic dilemma: "Thus the price of polyarchy may be the breakup of the country. And the price of territorial unity may be a hegemonic regime," p. 121.

CHAPTER 3

VARIETIES OF NATION-BUILDING IN THE BALKANS AND AMONG THE SOUTHERN SLAVS

Najdan Pašić

NAJDAN PASIC is Professor of Political Science and Director of the Institute of Social Sciences at the University of Belgrade. He has done extensive research on social structure and politics in Yugoslavia and has also been active in international study groups. He was elected a member of the Executive of the International Political Science Association in 1970.

If Europe was the cradle of nations in the modern sense of the word, the Balkans were the part of Europe where the process of nation-building progressed more slowly and unevenly than elsewhere, and under most complex conditions. It is, therefore, paradoxical that the complicated historical process of nation-building in the Balkans, which embarked on its final phase only with the Second World War, has not been the subject of broader and more comprehensive sociological and political research.

In recent years, the national phenomenon has captured the interest of research workers and is becoming an area for fruitful application of interdisciplinary approaches. This occurrence is understandable in view of the place that nations and national relationships hold in the development of the present-day world. The modern study of these problems, launched by, among other books, Karl Deutsch's *Nationalism and Social Communication,* has been oriented largely in two directions: toward certain cases of nation-building within the fold of multinational states in Europe and in other parts of the world, and toward the problems of nations and nationalism among the so-called new states, those that have taken shape in Africa and Asia with the collapse of the worldwide colonial empires.

It has been noted, and rightly so, that these studies have not been sufficiently linked with the search for common patterns of nation-building and that knowledge of the factors involved in the formation of classic nations in Europe has not yet been applied to the so-called new states.[1] It would appear that the highly divergent situations under which the historical processes unfolded and the long intervals of time separating them discourage efforts to find what is general and common to them. Comparative studies still lack the links that could tie up the historical experience of "classic" nation formation in Europe during the transition from feudalism to capitalism with the formation of the "new nations" characterizing the contemporary epoch. Future research may show that the experience of the Balkan nations is, in a sense, a missing link. In other words, it may turn out that nation-building in the Balkans is a transition between the way nations were formed in Europe at the beginning of the present era and the nation-building now going on in the developing countries. However, in view of the scarcity of previous systematic politico-sociological research in the area and the author's own personal limitations, this chapter on nation-building in the Balkans, particularly among the Southern Slavs, is necessarily modest in its scope.

We propose to select a number of key factors relevant to nation-building and to consider the role these played in developing the Yugoslav nations and internationality relationships in the Balkans. Obviously, this exposition does not represent conclusive scientific evidence, but it may offer an introduction to discussion and study of these problems.

The creation of states and the building of nations in the Balkans, as elsewhere, were not parallel or identical processes. However, the establishment of continuous state organizations and authority, especially during the period when primitive tribal organization was in decline and barbarism was giving way to civilization, played an exceptionally important role in shaping national consciousness and in the integration of ethnically divergent elements.[2]

The Yugoslav tribes settled the Balkan Peninsula in the fifth, sixth, and seventh centuries A.D. and formed their independent states in a period lasting from the eighth to the thirteenth century.[3] Within the Byzantine Empire, we see the parallel or successive appearance of a number of centres around which states were constituted. Numerous small states emerged, declined, and emerged again. Alternately, they gained power over broader areas where conditions of tribal organization still prevailed and where the people had not yet developed national consciousness or differentiated national features. Even after the formation of independent states comprising the Southern Slav settlers, the shadow of the Byzantine Empire hovered over the entire region until the Empire's final collapse. Until that collapse, it did not renounce its claim to supreme authority over the Balkans, and even then retained some influence in political, ideological, and cultural life.

The numerous nuclei, the multitude of rival centres of growing statehood and the attendant national consciousness, the continual pretentions to conquest of tribally organized states by the older and economically more developed ones—these were factors setting a specific stamp in the Middle Ages on the formation of relations among the Balkan nations, particularly among the Southern Slavs. These factors made the Balkans, in the distant and in the recent past, an area notorious for unceasing tribal and national friction and political instability. The English language even took the word "Balkan" to form the verb "balkanize," which, according to the *Oxford Dictionary*, means "to divide a region up into small, antagonistic states."

The nuclei of the separate states created by the association of ethnically related tribes, and the parallel disintegration of their tribal economic and social structure, provided the framework for the formation of the mediaeval Southern Slav peoples who, in the nineteenth and twentieth centuries, were to emerge as modern nations. Each nation in the Balkans today has developed a separate national individuality in its own specific way. Substantially this individuality has produced the special national pretensions of each of these peoples as well as their mutual relationships and is an important and lasting determinant in their political history.

After settling in the Balkans, the Slav tribes in the eastern Alps and the Macedonian Slavs in the Valley of the Vardar River and around the lakes of Prespan and Chrid encountered the harshest conditions and showed the least success in forming independent states. The proximity of powerful states—the Western Roman Empire and the early feudal German states—to the Slovenes, and the Byzantine Empire near the Macedonians, made it very difficult for these tribes to create independent states and to emerge as separate national entities. In the eighth century and the first half of the ninth, the tribal alliances and the independent Carinthia of the Slovenes, as well as Samuil's Empire in Macedonia in the early eleventh century, were not in a position to maintain themselves for long. However, the Croats, Serbs, and Bulgarians had their internationally recognized feudal states in the Middle Ages.

The state of Croatia, which lasted from the ninth to the end of the eleventh century, created a significant tradition of separate statehood among the Croatian people. At various periods, that state included not only the larger part of Dalmatia but also all of Bosnia and other parts of the Balkan Peninsula. In 1102, when Croatia lost its independence, it entered, as a legal entity, into a state community with Hungary, a status recognized by treaty.

Early in the ninth century, after assimilation with the Hun and Avar tribes that subjugated the Slavs in the eastern Balkan Peninsula, the Bulgarians set up a powerful state capable of defeating Byzantium and spreading out over a large part of the Balkan Peninsula. Under Emperor Simeun, Bulgaria reached out to encompass not only Macedonia, and Serbian lands but sections of Bosnia as well.

A strong and independent Serbian state was formed towards the end of the twelfth and the beginning of the thirteenth centuries under the Nemanjić Dynasty. The culmination of its expansion and development was reflected in the Empire of Dušan, a state that covered the larger part of the Balkan Peninsula and was officially named the Empire of Serbs, Bulgars, and Greeks. The independent state development of the Southern Slav peoples was interrupted by the Turkish invasions of the fourteenth century, and by the definitive consolidation of Hungarian and Austrian power in the Western regions of the Balkans, and of Venice along the Adriatic Coast.

The mediaeval history of the Balkan states significantly influenced the development of the national question in these areas and the formation of the national consciousness and aspirations of various Balkan nations. Areas of belated national awakening and ethnical mixtures became the scenes of struggle for influence by state and national centres that had been formed earlier. Until the late nineteenth and early twentieth centuries, the Turkish occupation acted to preserve regions in which a clear national orientation was nonexistent. The smallish Balkan states emancipated from Turkish domination—Serbia, Bulgaria, and Greece—began their struggle for the "Balkan apple of discord," Macedonia; and rivalry developed between Serbia and Croatia over Bosnia.

Like the big powers, the Balkan states were drawn into the bitter struggle for the Turkish inheritance. Under the circumstances, any alteration in the borders, or the inclusion of various territories freed from Turkish rule into one of the Balkan states could and often did have a decisive influence on the national orientation of the population in those areas. Thus, for instance, the expansion of the Serbian state in the late nineteenth century to areas along the Southern Morava River was instrumental in determining the national character of those regions that were ethnically and linguistically in transition between Serbia and

Bulgaria.[4] The educational system and organized national propaganda were important tools of national conquest intensively used by the already formed Balkan states of Serbia, Bulgaria, and Greece.

The national struggle of the Serbs, Bulgarians, and Greeks over Macedonia was particularly bitter.[5] However, international cohesion among the Macedonian people and their national awakening had already progressed so that they ultimately triumphed over the hegemonistic aspirations of the other three Balkan states.[6] Their goal was achieved only in the national liberation struggle during the Second World War,[7] whereas in the thirty-year period between emancipation from the Turks and the creation of the new Federal Republic of Yougoslavia, the Macedonian people had to endure yet another era of negation of their existence under the former Yugoslavia in which Macedonia was considered to be "southern Serbia."

The formation of a separate Montenegrin nation is characteristic of the decisive influence that separate statehood can have on the establishment of a nation. Montenegrin tribes were part of the Serbian nation and the Serbian mediaeval state. Serbian national tradition and the national myth, bound up with the medieval kingdom and empire and its tragic defeat in the Battle of Kosovo, were retained in their purest form in Montenegro. After the collapse of the Serbian state, and during the rule of the Turks in the Balkans, the Montenegrin people met a separate historic fate. Throughout centuries their isolation from the other section of the Serbian nation, their ceaseless struggle against the Turks and the Venetian hegemony, and especially the formation of a separate, independent Montenegrin state and dynasty by the end of the eighteenth and into the nineteenth century also led to the formation of a separate Montenegrin nation.[8] Although of Serbian descent and Serbian ethnic affiliation, the Montenegrins developed a separate national consciousness and found their place, as an independent nation, within the federated Yugoslav community of nations in which Montenegro is one of the six constituent and equal republics.

There is among the Southern Slav peoples a high degree of ethnic and linguistic similarity. This factor has played an important but also a contradictory role in the historical process of nation-building in the Balkans. This similarity, the virtually identical historical destinies and common interests in the struggle to preserve national independence and the right to unfettered development against the constant threat of external aggression gave impetus to the strivings of the Southern Slav peoples to come together. But it likewise provided food for hegemonistic aspirations on the part of certain tribal and national groups and later of particular nations toward each other.

In the nineteenth and twentieth centuries, during the era of national awakening and struggle for national independence, the Yugoslav nations demonstrated a desire for closer ties and for unification in a common state. However, from the outset, opinions have differed as to how that unification should be implemented and what should be the nature and function of the common state. What was known as the "Yugoslav idea" appeared in various forms among all the Southern Slav peoples, but in the interpretations of the ideologues and politicians of various classes and social groups, it acquired different and even contradictory meanings. We find the parallel existence of and conflict between the tendency toward unification on the grounds of equality, voluntary union, and recognition of specific national individuality, and the tendency toward imposition in the name of unity, nationalist, hegemonistic, unitarian, and great-state concepts of a unified national and state community. The creation of a common state gave various Yugoslav nations their historical chance to achieve and preserve their national independence and liberty, but in that common state they also ran the risk of losing their own national individuality to larger and more developed nations.

In the 1830s the Illyrian Movement came into being as a reflection of the desire of the Yugoslav nations for unification. Having emerged from the resistance to "Hungarianization" and the imposition of the Hungarian language on the Croats, this romantic literary, cultural, and political movement strove, under the common name of the Illyrians, to unify all Yugoslav peoples, first culturally and then politically. One of its principal weaknesses lay in the fact that it practically negated the individuality of the various Yugoslav nations. Consequently, it was accepted by only a relatively small section of intellectuals in Croatia and had few followers among other Yugoslav peoples.[9]

In Slovenia, the Illyrian Movement could not enjoy broad support because it implied renunciation of the use of the Slovenian national language and the adoption of the Serbo-Croatian literary language. For Slovenes, therefore, a common national struggle on the basis of the Illyrian Movement meant renunciation of their national individuality.[10]

In Serbia, too, which won national independence through the popular revolts in the early nineteenth century and which sought to achieve its broader national aspirations, the idea of the Illyrian Movement could not become very attractive or popular.[11] By the mid-nineteenth century the young Serbian bourgeoisie had become carried away by the idea of creating a great Serbia, a kind of Piedmont providing a rallying point for the unification of all the Southern Slavs.[12] The national liberation of the Southern Slav lands was thought of as restoration of the Empire of Dušan and the annexation of the Yugoslav countries to Serbia.

Different ideas about the unification of the Southern Slavs and Balkan nations were developed by the socialists in Serbia, and by the founder of the socialist movement and Socialist Party, Svetozar Markovic. He demanded that a difference be made between the liberation and unification of the Balkan nations, and the desire to increase the number of subjects of the Serbian dynasty of Obrenović. Against the idea of a great Serbia he pitted the idea of a Balkan federation of equal peoples.[13]

When the Hungarian Empire was destroyed and when a common state of Southern Slav nations was finally formed,[14] the genuine similarity and solidarity existing among them was exploited by the Serbian bourgeoisie to impose a unitarian form of state order on them, based on the theory of a single people bearing three names: Serbs, Croats, and Slovenes, the three tribes of a single nation. Speculating on this ethnic and linguistic relationship, the rulers of prewar Yugoslavia forced upon others the conception of integral "Yugoslavhood," negating the existence of separate nations within the framework of Yugoslavia and leading to their national deindividualization and unification. While the Serbs, Croats, and Slovenes were treated as tribes, as sections of the same nation, the national existence of the Montenegrins and Macedonians was denied altogether.[15]

Naturally, when the common state was formed and during the period when it was being constituted there were political forces that supported the idea of creating a federated or confederated community of Yugoslav nations. However, owing to the overall ratio of political forces and above all to the fact that the Serbian bourgeoisie had control over the army and the organized state machinery, this federalist orientation suffered defeat and was rejected.

It is interesting to note, however, that neither the workers' movement nor the newly formed Communist Party of Yugoslavia had clear conceptions of the national question and the organization of the common state.

At its early congresses in 1919 and 1920, the Communist Party practically adopted the idea of Yugoslavia as the common state of a nation with three names. Later, when the Great Serbian hegemony provoked widespread unrest and national dissatisfaction in the country, the Communist Party, under the influence of the Third International, adopted in 1928 another extremist conception to the effect that Yugoslavia should be broken up into separate and independent national states. Only in the thirties did the Communist Party arrive at a clear position on the subject of the national problem in Yugoslavia and seek to reject the unitarian state order while advocating the formation of Yugoslavia as a federated community of equal peoples.[16] This idea was realized in the National

Liberation War and Revolution. It was expressed for the first time, and most significantly, in the second session of the Anti-Fascist Council of the National Liberation of Yugoslavia in November 1943, when a resolution was passed to constitute Yugoslavia as a federated state community of Serbs, Croat, Slovenes, Montenegrins, and Macedonians.[17]

The National Liberation War and Revolution demonstrated that the desire of the people for equality and freedom and for winning independence through a common struggle under a single political leadership had generated a tremendous revolutionary force. Had this situation not been the case, it would have been unthinkable to mobilize on a broad basis the progressive forces of all the Yugoslav nations and to engage them in the National Liberation War under the leadership of the Communist Party, the only party with a clear and developed conception of how the national question in Yugoslavia had to be solved.[18]

Thus in the most decisive hours in the life of the Yugoslav peoples from the standpoint of their destiny, unitarianism and separatism suffered historical defeat. It was demonstrated that the ethnic similarities and relatedness of the Yugoslav peoples could be an important component in creating a joint state, but only if that common state were not a framework for enforced unification. Rather it had to be a common instrument for the defense of liberty, independence, and equality of each of the constituent peoples.

As is everywhere the case, ideological and cultural factors figured significantly in the formation of individual nations in the Balkans and among the Yugoslav nations. This fact was even more true here because the Yugoslav peoples lost their national independence early and for centuries were subject to foreign domination and attempts to denationalize them. Under those conditions, oral folk literature and folk dancing and singing were highly instrumental in transmitting the national consciousness from one generation to another, as a way of preserving and developing national traditions, myths, and customs. Of particular interest is the role of heroic folk poetry among the Serbs.[19] Serbian folk poetry, nurtured for centuries among the people by the guslars—the folk singers with their one-string instruments—preserved in advanced artistic form the Serbian national myth that was a constructive element in Serbian nationalism.

Among all the Southern Slav peoples, national awakening and national renaissance were linked with the struggle for a national literary language and the creation of a literature in the vernacular. National awakening among the Slovenes was produced by the reform headed by the prominent figure, Primoz Trubar, an ardent fighter for the Slovene tongue and

Slovene schools. The major Slovene writers, from the poet Franc Prešern to Ivan Cankar, were also leading national ideologues.

Among the Croats, vernacular literature by Avgust Senoa and other prominent writers of the eighteenth and nineteenth centuries, and particularly mediaeval literature developed in Dalmatia, also had their "national mission." Of the Montenegrins, the greatest national poet, Negos, was simultaneously the most influential standard-bearer of Serbian and Montenegrin national consciousness.

Throughout the entire historical period, from the first activity by the Byzantine missionaries among the newly settled Slav tribes to the most recent times, the Church has played an important role in the complex process of national integration and division and in the development of national relationships among the Southern Slavs and in the Balkans generally.[20]

Initially, the work of the Christian Churches, the Byzantine and the Roman, bore the hallmark of foreign ideological influence. Finding it impossible to hold back the wave of Slav settlers flooding its territories, the divided Roman Empire endeavoured to bring them under its ideological and political influence through dissemination of the Christian religion. This desire was the original motive for training and sending missionaries who, apart from their general ideological influence, always played an important political role as vehicles for the political arrangements concluded between Byzantium and the Christian Church of the West with the newly arrived Slav settlers. The Church soon became a bridge between the advanced societies of Greco-Roman civilization and the primitive tribal communities of the settlers. The Christian Church, both East and West, had a ramified, firm, and stable organizational structure, and a hierarchy suited to the relationships existing among the already developed feudal society. The very establishment of a church organization among the Slav tribes had a devasting effect on the backward clan and tribal relationship. It lent impulse to social differentiation and stimulated elements of feudal relations, thereby paving the way for the creation of broader national groups and firm state organization.

During a somewhat later phase, the strong church organization, the moral and political authority of the church, and its enormous ideological influence were to become the principal pillar and support of the newly formed feudal states struggling for stabilization and international recognition. Church autonomy (that is, independent national churches) was, therefore, a major concession that debilitated Byzantium had to make to its powerful neighbours in the north, the Bulgarian and Serbian states. There is no doubt that the granting of autonomy to the Church in the early thirteenth century played an exceptionally important role in strengthening the Serbian mediaeval state, contributing to its swift military, political, and cultural development in the course of a century and a half. Among the Slovenes and Croats, the struggle for national affirmation and independent statehood was continually linked with, and dependent upon, relations with the Catholic Church and its powerful international organization. In this respect, the coronation in the eleventh century of the Croatian King Zvonimir, who received his crown from the hands of the Papal Nuncio, was highly significant from the standpoint of consolidation and international recognition of independent Croatian statehood.

Of course, the Church was not simply a factor of unification and national integration but also one that directly influenced national divisions, national conflicts, and friction. It should not be forgotten that the Balkans were an area of major church and religious confrontations. It is a fact that the boundary line between the Orthodox and the Catholic Churches and between Islam and Christianity ran for centuries through the Balkan Peninsula. The political and ideological repercussions of this phenomenon were far-reaching and manifold and counted significantly in the development of national relations among the Southern Slavs and in the Balkans. The Catholic Church consolidated its position among the Slovenes and Croats, as did the Orthodox Church among the Serbs, Bulgarians, Montenegrins, and Macedonians. Affiliation with different churches also meant different alphabets and different ideological and cultural influences that extended down through the centuries, leaving a profound imprint on the culture, the mentality, and the national consciousness of various nations and smaller groupings, especially those of mixed religious affiliation.

In areas where Serbs, Croats, and Moslems mingled and where, though belonging to different confessions, they were bound together by a common tongue and other anthropological and ethnic similarities, religion frequently was and remained the fundamental feature of national identity—hence, the significance attached to such questions as whether or not one crossed oneself and how.

In certain historical situations, religion was also the principal basis for constituting separate ethnic groupings and even separate national consciousness, as in the case of the Moslems in the central section of modern Yugoslavia—in Bosnia and Sandzak. The Moslems are Slavs and, in a large sense, the descendants of mediaeval Bosnian feudal landowners who, during the Turkish onslaughts, converted to Islam in order to retain their property and social position. The language of the Moslems is the same as that spoken by Bosnians, Serbs, and Croats. However, during Turkish rule, belonging to the Moslem religion meant holding a privileged social position. As a result, the Bosnian Moslems thought of Turkish authority as their own. They were linked to a much greater extent than other sections of the population with the ruling classes in the Turkish Empire and remained for centuries under the strong impact of Turkish and Arabic oriental culture. All of these factors tended to separate the Moslems into a special ethnic community. For a long time the question of whether or not the Moslems could be considered a separate nation aroused considerable controversy. Today the opinion prevails that the Moslems cannot be denied a special national individuality.[21]

Another question deserving special study is the role of the Church in preserving national consciousness during long centuries of foreign rule. This role was particularly significant among the Southern Slav peoples who were under Turkish domination. The politically disenfranchised Christian population of the Ottoman Empire found in the Church its sole representative and protector. The rights granted by the Ottoman Empire to the Christian Church on its territory included a certain degree of jurisdiction over its own followers, and the right to found schools and to develop certain forms of educational activity. Thus, under certain historical conditions the national church organization replaced the lost state organization. For this reason, it appeared important to preserve the independence of the national Church. At one time, the Serbian and Bulgarian Orthodox Churches lost their independence to the Byzantine-Greek Church and Greek clergy. Consequently, the restoration of the Patriarchate of Pec and therby the independence of the Serbian Church in the sixteenth century was of prime national significance.

Later, in the nineteenth century, when the Bulgarian-Greek-Serbian struggle flared up over Macedonia, the Church was an important instrument of national hegemonistic policy. This struggle was above all a conflict between the Greek and the restored Bulgarian national churches (1870). Serbia, which had rid itself of Turkish rule by a series of insurrections in the early nineteenth century naturally had its own national church, but the church was not allowed to function legally in the European part of Turkey. The strategists of Serbian nationalist policy (Stojan Novaković, for one) thought this situation highly inconvenient. They considered it a sign of the wisdom of Bulgarian policy-makers that Bulgaria, after winning independence in 1878, did not transfer the seat of its national church from Constantinople to Bulgaria but rather permitted its church to function side by side with the Greek Church in the European part of Turkey, thereby bringing considerable pro-Bulgarian influence to bear in Macedonia.

In Croatia and Slovenia, the influence of the Catholic Church predominated, that is, the activity of the Church was sometimes positive, sometimes negative, but always a significant factor in the formation and maintenance of national consciousness, although as the upholder and standard-bearer of legitimacy, it represented a strong basis for foreign rule over the Slav lands in Austria-Hungary. At the same time, the Catholic Church, in its desire to entrench itself more firmly among the people, demonstrated considerable sensitivity to certain popular demands, particularly regarding writing. language, and customs. An important feature in the struggle to preserve the national character of the Croatian and Slovenian peoples was the struggle for the right to worship in the vernacular languages rather than in Latin. This struggle enjoyed the support of a large section of the Catholic clergy, especially the lower clergy. From Bishop Grgur Ninski, who led the struggle for worship in the vernacular and for the use of the Galgolithic alphabet in the tenth century to Bishop Strossmayer of the mid-nineteenth century, who was a great protagonist of the Yugoslav idea and the founder of the Yugoslav Academy of Arts and Sciences in Zagreb, the national struggle proved to be, under certain conditions, closely linked with the Church and church organization.

When the church was the fundamental ideological force and the most important spiritual force in society, religion divided people into relatively narrow, exclusive, endogenous groups existing side by side for centuries in the same settlements and regions. In the nineteenth century, when the process of more intensive formation of national consciousness began, national identification as a rule followed the lead of religious affiliation. Rivalry between the great church organizations—Orthodox and Catholic—created obstacles to formation of a comon state of Yugoslav peoples and hampered consolidation of the joint state once it was firmly established by the end of the First World War. At times, rival pretensions to a privileged status and to a position as a state religion gave rise to internal tensions in the newly created state and offered a wide margin for political speculation. Thus did religion and the influence of church organizations render heterogeneous the otherwise considerable homogeneous social milieu and favor intolerance and conflict. In pre-Second World War Yugoslavia, then a country of national oppression and refusal to recognize the existence of a variety of nations, the influence of the Church exacerbated national conflicts. In this sense, the Churches represented a destructive force in the Yugoslav state, abetting the occupiers' policy of setting the Yugoslav people against each other. During the war, the church organizations, considered as a whole, made common cause with the ultra-nationalistic, quisling movements: the Chetniks in Serbia, the Ustashi in Croatia, and the White Guards in Slovenia.[22] Consequently, in the new Yugoslav state that emerged from the national liberation struggle and revolution, and that raised the slogan of brotherhood and unity among the Yugoslav peoples, one of the conditions for political consolidation was introducing religious tolerance and strict separation of Church from state.[23] After the war in which the attempt to incite fratricidal struggle among the peoples of Yugoslavia suffered defeat, special sanctions were needed against the incitement of national, religious, and racial intolerance.

Throughout several centuries, all the nations of Yugoslavia and all Slav peoples in the Balkans were deprived of political independence and made to live under foreign rule in politically subordinate and dependent territories, thereby slowing down the process of nation-building in the Balkan area. By different means and with varying intensity, the states that gained power over the Balkan lands made efforts to stifle national consciousness and break the national resistance of the Yugoslav peoples. For centuries a deliberate policy was to maintain and deepen national divisions, dissensions, and quarrels. Nowhere in Europe was the imperialistic principle of "divide and rule" implemented so systematically and successfuly as in the Balkans.[24] On the other hand, the attempts at "denationalization" provoked organized resistance that went on more or less without ceasing, for it sprang from powerful social and class sources. Virtually the entire ruling class and the government were alien, both in language and origin. Social and national suppression were handmaidens, giving rise to dissatisfaction and revolt against economic and social exploitation, which regularly acquired the features of national revolt and struggle against foreign rule, aimed at the alien class of exploiters.

The major peasant revolts and uprisings in Croatia and Slovenia and the peasant wars in the sixteenth and seventeenth centuries and later, were clearly national in character; these were the rebellions of the downtrodden peasant masses against alien masters, against the Austrian and Hungarian nobles and landlords. The unceasing guerrilla warfare of the Haiduks and Uskoks in Serbia, Bosnia, Croatia, and Macedonia was similar in motivation and clearly national in character.[25] Throughout the entire Balkan area, social rebellion merged and intermingled with resistance to national oppression and to attempts at denationalization explaining both the vigorous force of these resistance movements and the harsh methods used to quell them.

On the other hand, it must be kept in mind that for centuries the Balkans were a region where the big powers, above all Austria-Hungary and Russia, met and clashed over the so-called Turkish legacy. All the big powers engaged in this strife sustained and incited dissension among the Balkan nations and later among the small Balkan states by playing on nationalistic ambitions and desire for expansion, thereby transforming the Balkans into pawns. Striving first to achieve national liberation and later to attain their hegemonistic aspirations, the Balkan nations sought patrons among the big powers. By this very fact, however, they became the tools of those powers. For centuries, especially in the nineteenth and even in the twentieth century, when competition among the imperial nations intensified and the ratio of forces changed considerably, and also when it became apparent that the collapse of Turkish rule over the Balkans was only a matter of time, the fate of the Balkan peoples and their states was decided outside the Balkans by bargaining among the big powers who sat in judgment when controversies broke out among those states. From the Holy Alliance and the Congress of Berlin to the Yalta Conference, where spheres of influence in the Balkans were calculated in percentages, the Balkan peoples had their destinies carved out by others. The parceling out of political and national structures in the Balkans was in a substantial part the product of such external forces.

In this respect, the historical circumstances surrounding nation-building in the Balkans bear a close resemblance to those in which nations and independent national states have taken shape in other parts of the economically underdeveloped world, on continents where socio-economic development came late.

In each of the Balkan countries, the big powers set up their own political groups through which they interfered directly in the policies of these states, pushing them into endless mutual conflicts and wars. It was for this reason that the idea of consolidating national relations in the Balkans through various forms of association and confederation won followers among the most progressive social forces and sections of the population.[26] However, the sources of conflict, including constant interference from the outside, were too powerful for these tendencies to prevail. The big European powers had available to them an abundance of means for exploiting the bickering among the Balkan nations. As a result, the successful common struggle by the Balkan nations against outside enemies most frequently ended in mutual conflict, as was the case with the Balkan wars of 1912 and 1913.[27]

The Second World War represents an important historical turning point in this sense. From the resistance to the policy of exploiting national friction and national intolerance pursued by the fascist occupiers, in which most of the political forces of the ruling class followed suit, emerged the solidarity of the Yugoslav peoples.[28] The policy based on this solidarity proved to hold a great attraction for the people and finally triumphed over the policy of division and the quarrels of the Slav nations in the Balkans.[29]

The economic underdevelopment and the backwardness of the Balkan countries compared with other parts of Europe provide the background for the process of nation-building. All the Balkan countries, those which had been under Turkish occupation, those which had belonged to Austria-Hungary, and those once dominated by Venice, represented a backward periphery and agrarian appendix to the great feudal-military and mercantile empires of Turkey, Austria-Hungary, and Venice. The regime of alien political domination frustrated normal economic development of the Balkan countries and the formation of progressive national economies over a broader economic area. The countries that had lived under Turkish occupation were retarded by the widespread devastations of constant warfare and the primitive, backward forms of an economy organized along military and feudal lines. Political insecurity, underdeveloped lines of communication and economic relations based largely on brute force and plunder banished all thought of economic prosperity and the development of processing activities and trade encompassing broad masses of the domestic population. The result was the restoration and conservation of regional autarky and an economic structure and way of life based on tribal and family cooperative organization and barter. Large areas lived isolated from each other in primitive self-sufficiency.

The poorly differentiated social and class structure and the primitive tribal forms of life were suited to agricultural production, barter economy, and seminomadic livestock raising. Over large and sparesely settled areas the population was forced to shy away from roads and lines of communication in order to keep out of the way of hostile, alien authorities and frequent military incursions.[30] Members of the ruling class belonging to the local population were few and far between or nonexistent. By and large, the inhabitants were a simple, illiterate mass of peasants. The feudal lords, mercantile bourgeoisie, and government officials were regularly, or even exclusively aliens. This situation retarded the development of a market economy and the social and class differentiation based on it. In Serbia, Bulgaria, and Macedonia, the towns were, ethnically speaking, not part of the nations on the territory in which they existed. Most of the urban population consisted of Turks, Greeks, Jews, and Cincars—that is, elements foreign to the peasant mass.[31] Thus for instance, the towns captured by the rebellious Serbian peasants during the first uprising (1804-13) were actually foreign in the composition of their populations. In Serbia, during the first uprising, there was one literate person per 1,000 inhabitants. One of the first two Serbian princes was himself illiterate. The uprising was, therefore, led by a small group of well-to-do peasants, prominent villagers, and merchants.

Consequently, until Turkish rule was overthrown it was impossible to form urban centres that would at the same time be centres for rallying the nation and integrating it. The situation in the lands under Austro-Hungarian rule was only slightly different. In those areas, Austria introduced an up-to-date administration, built roads and laid railway lines, and set up post offices and other forms of communication. But all of these improvements were designed above all to exploit those regions and to transform them into agrarian and raw materials bases for the industrial and commercial capitals concentrated in Vienna and Budapest. A testimony to this fact was the entire policy of constructing lines of communication, precluding the maintenance of direct ties between towns and districts belonging to the same national region while connecting these up with the economic and political centres of the Habsburg Monarchy in Austria and Hungary.

And so it happened that within the national territories of the more or less compact Slav peoples, enclosed economic regions were spontaneously and artificially formed, isolated from each other by political boundaries and communication barriers. Even when modern methods of economic activity and the first industries began penetrating into these marginal sections of Austria-Hungary, the distribution of economic wealth was extremely uneven, to the detriment of the Slav population. The land and all other sources of economic power and wealth were largely in the hands of foreigners. In areas under Austro-Hungarian domination, the domestic bourgeoisie was small in number and to a great extent economically and politically dependent. In Zagreb, which since the Middle Ages had been a powerful urban centre, both economically and culturally, theatrical performances were given in German until near the end of the nineteenth century.

In the struggle for national rights and national liberation, the bourgeoisie provided an undecided and faltering leadership, always living in fear of radical, determined social demands by its own masses and therefore ever ready to compromise with the bourgeoisie and state authorities of the foreign ruling power. All the Balkan lands under foreign domination were within an economic periphery, which was parceled into relatively small segments, with lastingly negative consequences for the economic development of the Balkan countries. This circumstance also presented an obstacle to the indispensable processes of economic integration within the broader political entities set up later within the Yugoslavian state.

Nonetheless, the urban centres were important points of national integration, while the national cultural autonomy granted in Austria-Hungary offered certain possibilities for developing organized national action at the cultural and educational levels.

With the cessation of foreign political domination and with national liberation, the towns in the Balkans, practically without exception, experienced a period of rapid transformation,[32] expressed in the economy, in politics, and in culture, indicating the degree of national maturity already achieved. The previously retarded process of national maturation and nation-building in the Balkans followed an exceptionally turbulent and revolutionary course in the last few decades of the last century and the first half of the present one.[33]

But the negative heritage of history, the parceling out of the region's economy and its links with outside centres of economic and political power, generated serious and lasting problems for the Yugoslav state and for relations among the Balkan nations generally. For centuries some of these nations or sections of them lived under conditions of primitive autarchy, in isolation from each other, developing at various paces and under divergent external influences. The process of national liberation, which did not proceed in an even or synchronized fashion, found itself dealing with various areas formerly under the rule of alien empires with greatly differing capacities for independent economic existence in the context of Europe with its advanced capitalist economy and its established powerful national states. The larger part of the Balkan Peninsula, which had been under Turkish occupation for some time, shared the fate of the Turkish Empire itself: decadence, retrogression, and backwardness in relation to Western Europe. And these sections, which had been peripheral and provincial even for Turkey, remained at the level of a barter economy, never attaining even an advanced feudalism.

In the areas which had been under the domination of the Austro-Hungarian Empire there had been an infusion of capital, especially in Slovenia and in Zagreb, but nowhere had any large-scale industrial centres on a contemporary model come into being. The accent had been on small- and medium-scale industries, based on the supply of domestic raw materials but economically dependent on the large concentrations of capital outside the national territory. These concentrations were branches of Viennese and Budapest industrial and financial concerns. In agriculture, semifeudal, semicapitalist land holdings in the hands of foreign owners dominated the scene. The general level of economic development of those sections of the Balkans that had been under Austria-Hungary—as indicated by the numerous working class and industrial proletariat, the developed infrastructure and communications, and the level of national income—was incomparably higher than that of the areas and regions that had languished for centuries under Turkish rule. Hence, integration into the socio-economic entities of the newly formed states was a complex, long, and contradictory process that has not been completed to this very day.

In a highly complicated national structure, economic questions always have an explicitly national-political aspect and weight. There can be no genuine national equality without equal conditions for the economic development of each nation and each minority nationality. Therefore it is of the utmost importance in a multinational state like Yugoslavia to assure that the conflicting interests of the developed and underdeveloped parts of the country do not become internationality conflicts and that relationships of economic inequality are not created. Each nation must enjoy not only the political but also the economic advantages of living in a joint state with a common economy. Economic policy must, therefore, pursue two goals. On the one hand, it must assure the most rapid and comprehensive economic integration possible on the basis of the free play of commodity-money relationships, the freest possible flow of the capital accumulation of society, and the development of self-managed enterprises and free-commodity producers. On the other hand, economic policy and the economic system itself must include measures and instruments for securing relatively rapid advancement for the economically underdeveloped parts of the country.

The more society rids itself of coercive administrative centralism as economic and political life is democratized, the more necessary it becomes to develop new integrational and cohesive forces linking immediate with long-term interests and assembling the various parts of the country into a single integrated economic whole ensuring a position of equality and equal prospects of development for all. The focus of national problems is consequently transferred from the political and cultural to the economic sphere.

The radical socio-political change that occurred in the course of the Second World War and particularly the events of the national liberation struggle and the Socialist Revolution, gave internationality relations in Yugoslavia and in the Balkans a new dimension and new perspectives. The participation of all the nations of Yugoslavia in the National Liberation War confirmed their historical orientation toward a federated state community guaranteeing their national integrity and equality. In contrast to the prewar Yugoslavian state, the new Yugoslavia, in its constitutional, legal, and state development along federal lines, has laid special emphasis on the principle of full national equality. In this respect, all possible measures were taken to guarantee this equality in practice in economic, political, and cultural life. Various social and political practices have been introduced to substantiate the principles adopted for the development of an equal community of peoples. A central parliament has been created in which the most prominent role—no law can be passed without its approval—belongs to the Chamber of Nationalities, a group composed of an equal number of representatives from each republic. The principle of negotiation and consensus, rather than voting, was accepted as the basis for solving problems concerning the entire country. The strict adherence to what are known as national "keys" in the composition of all federal organs; the restriction of the functions and competence of the federal government to those matters that have explicitly been entrusted to it in the common interest of all the republics, as formulated in the Constitution; and the abolition of a state language, the granting of legal and real equality of all languages, and the possibility of using them in public and private communication have also been adopted.

However, as experience has shown, neither legal and political measures and normative solutions nor the appropriate political practice can entirely resolve the problem of internationality relations once and for all. Removing centralistic administrative shackles in economic, political, and ideological affairs, through the development of self-management as a global system of social organization, creates possibilities for the fuller expression and affirmation of special national interests and internationality relations. The states are therby invested with a new dimension and substance that transcends by far the point from which they started when the principal goal was to guarantee the formal and legal equality of nations and republics and to preclude the possibility of national discrimination.

A society that endeavours to base its existence less and less on state coercion and more and more on the freely expressed interests of the associated workers (that is, on the enterprises and associations organized along the lines of self-management) encounters new problems in the sphere of internationality relations. Among these problems are the relationship between the integral economic region and the various national economies as narrower, politically constituted entities within that region; between the economically advanced and less advanced, the big and the small, the historically "older" and the historically "younger" nations; and between those that had in the past been deprived of the right to use their language and had no independent state organization, and those that had achieved independent statehood earlier but on that basis had also developed pretensions to national hegemony and domination.

For a society that is becoming increasingly democratic, thereby creating the possibility for freer expression and pursuit of different interests, solving the national question means promoting and coordinating all these relationships on the basis of free will and full equality. Consequently, internationality problems cannot be solved completely, but their solutions can be approached democratically.

In view of these considerations, the Yugoslav experience can serve as a basis for the empirical testing of certain historical hypotheses and conceptions in accordance with which the mass of the population (workers, peasants), is becoming active in economic and social processes, strengthening national consciousness and the sentiment of belonging to a specific nationality. Consequently, national relations become more highly differentiated, complex, and substantial. This thesis had already been developed by the Austrian socialist theoretician, Otto Bauer, in his well-known work *Socialism and the National Question.* Although differing in scope and presented in a different context, Karl Deutsch's book, *Nationalism and Social Communication,* advances the interesting thesis that social mobilization and the modernization of economic and political life, as well as the strengthening of the role of the state as an instrument of collective needs, adds new dimensions and substance to nationalism and the problem of international relations.

What is happening in various parts of the world today seems to confirm this hypothesis to a growing degree. Apparently, social progress does not negate national differences, but rather affirms and permits the self-assertion of separate national individualities.

NOTES

1. Stein Rokkan, "Models and Methods in the Comparative Study of Nation-Building," Acta Sociologica, Vol. 12, No. 2, 1969.

2. A typical case was the feudal Serbian state under the Nemanjić Dynasty, during which period the Serbian people represented a relatively stable social community—a "nation being created"; also, there was the state of Croatia during the Trpimirović Dynasty (ninth-eleventh century A.D.).

3. For the genesis and development of feudalism in the countries of Yugoslavia, source material is scarce and research problems only partially solved. For literature about the Croats, see F. Rački, T. Smičiklas, F. Sišić, M. Kostrenčić, V. Klaić, L. Hauptman, O. Mandić, M. Barada, V. Novak, and others; about the Bosnians, see C. Truhelka, V. Cubrilović, B. Djurdjev, N. Filipović, and others; about the Slovens, see B. Grafenauer, L. Hauptman, and M. Kos; about the Serbs, see S. Bovaković, K. Jiriček, S. Corović, T. Taranovski, N. Radojčić, D. Janković, and others.

4. Prominent Balkan historians have submitted differing data on the national affiliation of well-known participants in liberation movements at the beginning of the nineteenth century, owing to ethnical intermingling and nebulous national orienta-

tion. For purposes of illustration, we might take the assertions of various historians that Petar Ičko was a Serb, a Macedonian, a Bulgar, and a Greek respectively: V. Corović, History of Yugoslavia, Belgrade, 1933, pp. 417-18 (original in Serbo-Croatian); History of Bulgaria, Vol. I, Sofia, BAN, 1961, p. 327, (original in Bulgarian); M. Laskaris, Le Rôle des Grecs dans l'Insurrection Serbe sous Karageorges, Les Balkans, 1933. Or, for instance, the Serbian hero, Haiduk Veljko, is considered Bulgarian, and Marko Botzaris is variously described as a Greek, Bulgar, Albanian, and Macedonian.

5. Ljuben Lape, A short Survey of Macedonian History from the Second Half of the 17th Century to 1914, Skopje, 1953 (monograph) (original in Macedonian); History of the Macedonian People, Vol. II, Belgrade, 1970, pp. 117-23, (original in Serbo-Croatian).

6. The standard bearers of these aspirations, known as the Macedonists (the Miladinov brothers, teachers from Struga; Bishop Partenije Zografski from Galičnik; Kuzman Sapkarov, publisher of eight textbooks in the Macedonian language; and others), called for the introduction of the Macedonian language into schools and literature.

See K. Misirkov, On Macedonian Questions, Skopje, 1946 (original in Macedonian); Aleksandar Hristov, "The Socio-political Foundations of the Emergence and Development of the Idea of Macedonian Statehood (1893-1912)," Legal and Social Science Archives, Vol. 2, Belgrade, 1968 (original in Serbo-Croatian), and "The Organization of Revolutionary Government during the Ilinden Uprising (1903)," Legal and Social Science Archives, Vols. 1 and 2, Belgrade (original in Serbo-Croatian); Dragan Taškovski, The Emergence of the Macedonian Nations, Skopje, 1967 (original in Macedonian; and D. Miljovska, Class Forces of the National Liberation Movement of the Macedonian People in the Second Half of the 19th Century, Skopje, 1961 (original in Serbo-Croatian).

7. During its session held on 2 August 1944 the Anti-fascist Council of the People's Liberation of Macedonia (ASNOM) constituted its legislative and executive organs. After the establishment of the Provisional Government of Democratic Federal Yugoslavia, the first government of the Republic of Macedonia was also formed. See A. Hristov, The First Session of ASNOM, Skopje, 1968 (original in Macedonian).

8. "At the beginning of the twentieth century, the concept of Serbhood in Montenegro had no concrete historical substance, but was rather an ideological remnant of the past in the consciousness of a patriarchal environment." (From D. Vujović, The Unification of Montenegro and Serbia, Titograd, 1962 (original in Serbo-Croatian).)

For the liberation movements, the process of the decline of tribal society in Montenegro towards the end of the eighteenth century, and the emergence of statehood, see also G. Stanojević, Montenegro on the Eve of the Creation of a State, Belgrade, 1962 (original in Serbo-Croatian); B. Pavičević, The Creation of the Montenegrin State, Belgrade, 1955 (original in Serbo-Croatian); P. Popović, Montenegro during the Period of Petar I and Petar II, Belgrade, 1951 (original in Serbo-Croatian); Dušan Vuksan, Petar I Petrović Nejegos and his Times, Cetinje, 1951 (original in Serbo-Croatian).

9. R. Warnier, "Illyrisme et nationalisme croate," Le Monde Slave, Vol. XII, 1935; F. Sišić, "On the One Hundredth Anniversary of the Illyrian Movement," Arnual JAZU, No. 49, 1937 (original in Serbo-Croatian); J. Sidak, "The Yugoslav Idea in the Illyrian Movement," Yugoslav Historical Magazine, No. 3, 1963, Belgrade

(original in Serbo-Croatian) and "Contribution to the Development of the Yugoslav Idea up to 1914," Our Themes, Zagreb, 1965, pp. 1290-1317 (original in Serbo-Croatian); Miroslav Krleža, "Introductory Remarks at the Scientific Consultation in Zagreb—13th Anniversary of the Croatian National Renaissance, March 29-31, 1966," Kolo, Zagreb, 1966 (original in Serbo-Croatian); D. Surmin, Croatian Renaissance, Vols. I-II, Zagreb, 1903-04 (original in Serbo-Croatian); F. Sišić, Bishop Strosmajer and Yugoslav Thought, Belgrade, 1922 (original in Serbo-Croatian); T. Smičiklas, "The Defence and Development of the Croatian National Idea 1790-1835," Works of the Yugoslav Academy, Vol. LXXX, Zagreb, 1885 (original in Serbo-Croatian); M. Gross, "On Some Aspects of the Development of the National Idea during the National Renaissance in Dalmatia," Historical Review, Vol. I, Zagreb, 1963, pp. 11-18 (original in Serbo-Croatian); G. Novak, "On the One Hundredth Anniversary of the National Renaissance in Dalmatia, "Works of the Institute of the Yˑ goslav Academy of Sciences and Arts, Vol. VIII, Zadar, 1961 (original in Serbo-Croatian).

10. F. Petre, The Experiment of Illyrism among the Slovenes (1835-1849), Ljubljana, 1939 (original in Slovenian); E. Kardelj, The Development of the Slovian National Question, Belgrade, 1957, pp. 251-63 (original in Serbo-Croatian). In a letter to the Illyrian, Stanko Vraz, the eminent Slovian poet, France Prešern, replied in the negative to an invitation to join the Illyrians ("Ich bin von der Unausfürbarkeit diser Idee überzeugt").

11. The resistance of the Serbs to Illyrism was strongest in 1840, so that in 1841, Stjepan Moyses, who sent instructive reports on the situation in Croatia to Vienna, was able to observe:

> Der Illyrismus nämlich kann um desto weniger eines Trachtens sich mit Serbien zu vereinigen beschuldigt werden, je klarer es aus der Literatur der Serben erhellt wird, dass sie der illyrischen Benennung feind sind. Dadurch bleibt also natürlich und gesetzmässig der Illyrismus auf die Kroaten und Slavonier beschränkt.

See J. Sidak, "The Croatian National Renaissance, Ideas and Problems," Kolo, Zagreb, 1966 (original in Serbo-Croatin). Of the Serbian writers, from Vuk Karadžić, Branko Radičević, to Sima Milutinović Sarajlija, Jovan Sterija Popović, and Mušicki, not a single prominent author adopted the ideas of Illyrism.

12. D. Pavlović, "Serbia and the Serbian Movement in Southern Hungary—1848 and 1849," Belgrade, 1904 (original in Serbo-Croatian); G. Jakšić and V. J. Vučković, "Serbia's Foreign Policy During the Rule of Prince Mihailo," Programme of Yugoslav Policy Proposed by Garašanin to Strosmajer (March 1867), Belgrade, 1963 (original in Serbo-Croatian); V. J. Vučković, "Contribution to the Study of the Emergence of the Project" (1844) and the "Basic Thought" (1847), Yugoslav Review for International Law, Vol. VIII, No. 1, Belgrade, 1961 (original in Serbo-Croatian); D. Stranjaković, Serbia's Political Propaganda in the Yugoslav Provinces 1844-58, Belgrade, 1936 (original in Serbo-Croatian), Serbia, the Piedmont of the South Slavs 1842-53, Belgrade, 1932 (original in Serbo-Croatian) and "The Yugoslav National and State Programme of the Principality of Serbia from 1844," Herald of the Historical Society, Vol. VI, Novi Sad, 1931 (original in Serbo-Croatian).

13. The Serbian socialists saw the process of national liberation as unfolding in a revolution of emancipation, in a coherent programme of social and national freedom, and in a Balkan federation.

Svetozar Marković, Serbia in the East, Belgrade, 1892 (original in Serbo-Croatian);

Dimitrije Tucović, Serbia and Albania, Belgrade, 1914 (original in Serbo-Croatian) and "The first Balkan Social-Democratic Conference," "The Balkan Conference," "On a Federation of Free Balkan Peoples," Selected Writings, Vol. 1, Belgrade, 1949 (original in Serbo-Croatian); Vlado Strugar, Social Democracy and the National Question of the Yugoslav Peoples, Belgrade, 1956 (original in Serbo-Croatian); J. Marjanović, The Emergence and Development of the Workers' Movement in the Yugoslav Countries up until the First World War, Belgrade, 1958 (original in Serbo-Croatian); and S. Marković, "Socialism or the Social Question," Radenik, No. 22, Belgrade, 1874. (It would be more useful for the development and progress of federal organization for each one of these three main sections (Serbia, Bosnia, and Herzegovina and Montenegro) of the Serbian people in Turkey to have its own internal, independent order in which it would develop autonomously. The more progressive part—Serbia—would not impose its institutions on the more backward parts, as would have to be the case in a single state.)

14. F. Sišić, Documents on the Emergence of the Kingdom of Serbs, Croats and Slovenes 1914-1919, Zagreb, 1920 (original in Serbo-Croatian); Fran Barac, Les Croates et les Slovénes ont été les Amis de l'Entente pendant la Guerre, Paris, 1919; D. Janković and B. Krizman, Material on the Creation of the Yugoslav State, Belgrade, 1964 (original in Serbo-Croatian); Milada Paulova, "The Yugoslav Committee," The History of the Yugoslav Emigrants during the World War 1914-1918, Zagreb, 1924 (original in Serbo-Croatian) and Dejiny Maffie—Odboj Ceshu i Jihoslovanu za Svetove Valky 1914-1918, Prague, 1937; Dragoslav Janković, The Yugoslav Question and the Corfu Declaration, 1917, Belgrade, 1967 (original in Serbo-Croatian); S. Budislavljević, The Creation of the State of Serbs, Croats and Slovenes, Zagreb, 1958 (original in Serbo-Croatian); Vlado Strugar, "Social-Democracy in the Creation of Yugoslavia," Labour, Belgrade, 1965, p. 379 (original in Serbo-Croatian); V. Bogdanov, The Historical Role of Social Classes in Solution of the South Slav National Question, Sarajevo, 1956 (original in Serbo-Croatian); A. Arnautović, De la Serbie à Yougoslavie, Paris, 1919.

15. In contrast to many Serbian scientists of those times, the prominent Serbian geographer, Jovan Cvijić, did not consider the Macedonians as Southern Serbs, but rather emphasized their individuality, calling them "Macedonian Slavs," "a floating Slav mass," and so on (Jovan Cvijić, La Péninsule Balkanique, Paris, 1918); also see his Bases for the Geography and Geology of Macedonia and Old Serbia, Vol. III, Belgrade, 1906, 1911 (original in Serbo-Croatian) and his General Geography and Anthropogeography, Belgrade, 1907 (original in Serbo-Croatian).

16. At the fifth Country-wide Conference of the Communist Party of Yugoslavia in 1940, in Dubrava (near Zagreb), stress was laid on it being the task of Communists to fight for the national equality of all the Yugoslav peoples and against chauvinistic and separatist movements and the agents of foreign fascism.

17. Vojislav Simović, The Anti-fascist Council of the Peoples Liberation of Yugoslavia (A legal-political study), Belgrade, Kultura, 1958 (original in Serbo-Croatian).

18. Josip Broz Tito, The Struggle for the Liberation of Yugoslavia 1941-45, Belgrade, 1959 (original in Serbo-Croatian).

19. V. Cubrilović, The Development of Political Thinking in Serbia in the 19th Century, Belgrade, 1958 (original in Serbo-Croatian).

20. L. Hadrović, Le Peuple Serbe et son Eglise sous la Domination Durque, Paris, 1947; Cubrilović, op. cit.

21. Avdo Humo, "The Moslems in Yugoslavia," Komunist, Belgrade, Vols. 11, 18, and 25, July 1968.

22. On the activities of the Roman Catholic clergy, see Viktor Novak, Magnum Crimen, Zagreb, 1948 (original in Serbo-Croatian); and Branko Petranović, "The Activities of the Roman Catholic Clergy against the Settlement of Conditions in Yugoslavia (March 1945, September 1946)," in Institute of Social Sciences, Zbornik, Vol. V, Belgrade, 1963.

23. The proclamation of the Central Committee of the Communist Party of Yugoslavia, relating to the initiation of the uprising, states: "The peoples of Yugoslavia must unite irrespective of political and religious conviction and, through their united struggle, expel the despised occupiers from their country" (original in Serbo-Croatian). See also E. Kardelj, The Problems of our Socialist Development, Vol. II, Belgrade, pp. 299-300.

24. The young men of Bosnia suffered as a result of "Bosnian hatreds"—the fanatical national and religious hatred existing in Bosnia at the turn of the century.

25. V. Cubrilović, The Bosnian Uprising of 1875-78, Belgrade, 1930 (original in Serbo-Croatian) and Revolts and Uprisings in Bosnia and Herzegovina in the 19th Century, ed. by Military-Historical Institute of the Yugoslav Army, Belgrade, 1962 (original in Serbo-Croatian); M. Ekmečić, "The External Factor in the Process of the Maturing of Balkan Revolutions 1849-1878," The Yugoslav Historical Magazine (Belgrade), Vol. 3, No. 12, 1964 (original in Serbo-Croatian); Dimitrije Djordjević, Révolutions Nationales des Peuples Balkaniques, 1804-1914, Belgrade, Institut d'Histoire, 1965; La Question d'Orient, ed. by Driault, Paris, 1921; V. Kallay, Geschichte des Serbischen Aufstandes, 1807-1810, Vienna, 1910; R. W. Seton-Watson, The Southern Slav Question and the Habsburg Monarchy, London, 1911.

26. L. Stavrianos, Balkan Federation, North Hampton, Mass., 1955, p. 46. The federalist idea in the Yugoslav movement was linked up with a series of projects on the confederation or federation of Balkan and Danubian peoples, which took shape in the period between 1849 and 1862 among the Hungarian, Polish, Rumanian, and Italian emigrants.

27. Lenin, who touched on only the problems of national relations in the Balkans in some of his articles, gave an exceptionally acute and accurate assessment of the role played in national conflicts in this area by the European bourgeoisie, which exploited the class and political relations in the small Balkan states:

> What is the historical reason for the vital problems of the Balkans being solved by war, governed by bourgeois and dynastic interests? The principal reason is the weakness of the proletariat in the Balkans, and also reactionary influences and pressures by the powerful European bourgeoisie. It fears genuine liberty in the Balkans and in its own house; it strives for only easy profit at the expense of others; it incites chauvinism and national hatred to make it easier for it to pursue the policy of plunder, to obstruct the free development of the suppressed Balkan classes.

From V. I. Lenin, "The Balkan War and Bourgeois Chauvinism," Pravda, No. 74, 29 March 1913 (original in Russian).

28. Jovan Marjanović, "The Bourgeois Forces on the Eve of the Armed Struggle against the Occupiers," The Uprising and National Liberation Movement in Serbia. 1941, Belgrade, 1963 (original in Serbo-Croatian).

29. "Federation and Relations Among the Peoples of Yugoslavia. Consolidation of the Spirit of Socialistic Internationalism," The Programme of the League of

Communists of Yugoslavia, Chapter VIII, Belgrade, 1957 (original in Serbo-Croatian).

30. In the sixteenth century, the country was sparsely settled and poorly developed. Serbia was poorly cultivated.

31. In the seventeenth century, towns in Serbia had a distinctly Eastern atmosphere and a predominantly Moslem population. According to Evlija Celebija, Belgrade in 1660 had 38 Moslem districts, 3 Gypsy, 3 Greek, 3 Serbian and 1 each Armenian and Jewish. See The History of the Peoples of Yugoslavia, Vol. II, Zagreb, 1958 (original in Serbo-Croatian).

Jewish merchants of Spanish descent are mentioned as living in Belgrade as early as the sixteenth century. During the Austrian occupation of Serbia (1718-39, the Spanish Jews were joined by German Jews from Pozsony (Bratislava), Mannheim, and Prague. There were about 2,000 Jews in Serbia in the 1830s, when Prince Miloš ruled the country. See N. Vučo, The Decline of the Guilds in Serbia, Vol. I, Belgrade, 1954 (original in Serbo-Croatian). See also B. Kunibert, The Serbian Uprising and the First Period of Rule by Prince Miloš Obrenović, Belgrade, 1901 (original in Serbo-Croatian).

"Several decades ago," wrote M. D. Miličević in the 1870s, "the principal town in Serbia, Belgrade, was part Turkish, part Greek, part cosmopolitan and probably least of all Serbian. . . . The houses, stores, shops, clothing, ways of life and customs were Eastern." From M. D. Miličević, The Principality of Serbia, Belgrade, 1876, p. 23 (original in Serbo-Croatian).

32. F. Zvitter, Les Problémes Nationaux dans la Monarchie des Habsbourgs, Belgrade, 1960; J. Sidak, "The Croatian Question in the Habsburg Monarchy," Historical Review, Zagreb, Vol. IX, 1963 (original in Serbo-Croatian).

33. D. Djordjević, Revolutions Nationales des Peuples Balkaniques 1804-1919 (including the first Serbian uprising, the Greek Revolution of 1821, the uprisings in Herzegovina, the liberation struggle against Turkey in Montenegro, the April uprising in Bulgaria, struggles in Macedonia, and the Ilinden uprising of 1903); L. Ranke, Die Serbische Revolution, Darmstadt, 1897; S. Novakovitsch, Die Wieder-gebuhrt des Serbischen Staates 1804-1820, Sarajevo, 1912; R. Guzina, The principality and the Emergence of the Serbian Bourgeois State, Belgrade, 1955 (original in Serbo-Croatian); V. Cubrilović, The First Serbian Uprising and the Bosnian Serbs, Belgrade, 1939 (original in Serbo-Croatian); S. Novaković, The Uprising against the Dahis 1804, Belgrade, 1954 (original in Serbo-Croatian); D. Pantelić, The Belgrade Pashalic Before the First Serbian Uprising 1704-1804, Belgrade, 1949 (original in Serbo-Croatian); D. Novaković, The Turkish Empire before the First Serbian Uprising 1780-1804, Belgrade, 1906 (original in Serbo-Croatian). Thus, for instance, under the Habsburg Monarchy, Hungarian and German landholdings in Vojvodina accounted for 93.5 percent of the land, while per capita income in 1911-13 in Austria and Hungary was 695 crowns and only half that (350 crowns), in the Yugoslav areas.

Political power was also in the hands of the upper sections of the German and Hungarian population. In 1910, Hungarians and Croatians held 405 of a total of 413 seats in the Hungarian Parliament. The total of 35.6 percent of Germans in Austria (1910) accounted for 95 percent of the officer corps and 81 percent of state administration employees. Dimitrije Djordjević, "Collapse of the Habsburg Monarchy in 1918," Yugoslav Historical Magazine, Belgrade, No. 1-2, 1968 (original in Serbo-Croatian).

II.

THE AMERICAS

CHAPTER 4

EMPIRE, LANGUAGE, AND NATION:
THE CANADIAN CASE

Kenneth D. McRae

KENNETH D. McRAE is Professor of Political Science at Carleton University in Ottawa. He served as a research supervisor for the Canadian Royal Commission on Bilingualism and Biculturalism and has done comparative studies of linguistic and cultural diversity with special reference to Switzerland, Belgium, Finland, and Canada.

In the case of Canada the concepts of nation-building and state formation must be applied to a single, modern polity covering a vast territory, and in such a context, we cannot take full advantage of the comparative method that is possible where several polities have emerged under roughly similar conditions, as in Latin America or Africa. Yet, certain wider comparative perspectives suggest themselves and merit closer study. First and foremost, there is the example of the United States, sharing the same continent and similar political and social traditions, but differing sharply from Canada in its early and decisive acquisition of political independence. Second, there are examples of other federal polities, possessing similarly weak centralizing tendencies and correspondingly strong or geographically distant peripheral communities. Finally, there are other plurilingual countries, characterized by a degree of linguistic and cultural diversity between two or more communities such that the nation-building process finds limits in counter-movements favoring the linguistic community over the polity. However, in a paper focusing on Canada, these wider comparative perspectives can only be touched on rather briefly.

[144]

PRELIMINARY CONSIDERATIONS

Several broad background factors in the Canadian situation deserve to be noted at the start. In the first place, Canada (and North America generally) have been "developed" societies, in an economic sense at least, since the beginnings of European expansionism. One can even argue that to a certain degree, economic development *precedes* European settlement. By this I mean that Canada has been integrated into the European and Western market economy since the sixteenth century onwards, and that the production for export of primary staples—the Atlantic fishery, the fur trade, timber, grain, minerals, and pulp and paper—has gone hand in hand with the development of a domestic economy. This has meant that even the most marginal areas of settlement in colonial times were never completely outside the orbit of the world economy, though transportation difficulties could make these links rather tenuous.

A second factor in Canadian development has been a rather difficult environment. Geography has imposed deterrents on state-building, the first and most obvious being physical distance. Unlike the case of Australia, where the major problem was the distance of the whole continent from its trading partners, Canada's problem has been the internal distance that separates a small, widely scattered population. Distance, even when physically overcome, remains a continuing economic cost. It is no exaggeration to say that state-building in Canada was scarcely conceivable before the age of the railroad. Unlike Australia, Canada has no easy water routes to link east and west, and the prior development of American transport routes worked against nation-building rather than in its favor. Another environmental aspect is climatic severity: for a country of settlement the level of economic rewards had to be sufficient to offset the attractions of other countries of immigration possessing less rigorous climates.

Third, the deep-seated consequences of the immigration process need to be considered. Modern Canada is a polity formed by extensive immigration from Europe under the colonial regimes of France and Britain; in the formative stages, the indigenous peoples played only a marginal role. In general, it may be suggested that a society of immigrants tends to dissolve or weaken the regional particularisms characteristic of the country of origin and to pave the way for further social and economic mobilization. Geographical mobility is easier for a man who has already moved once. The need for cultural adaptation to a new environment probably facilitates further cultural adaptation to developments in technology. In short the mobilization of both American and Canadian society in the industrial age was in all likelihood prefigured and made easier by the adaptive processes experienced as a result of their migratory foundations.

There is a fourth background factor of crucial importance. Unlike the United States and many other countries whose legal autonomy was established decisively at a given point in time, Canada, along with the other countries of the old Commonwealth, achieved a sense of political independence only gradually over a period of approximately a century. Further, the process was rendered more complex for Canada than for the others by the preponderance of the United States in North America and the continentalist tendencies that have derived from the American presence. Indeed, one can maintain that the segregative or differentiative aspects of state-building in Canada are at least as important as the aggregative or combinatory ones, and possibly of greater interest in a comparative context.

There are some parallels here with the formation of European nations in the sixteenth century. We should not forget that nation-building in Renaissance Europe was a twofold process, not only of overcoming local and regional particularism but also of reducing traditional medieval loyalties to empire and papacy. There are parallels between King Henry VIII's statute of 1533 declaring England an "empire" not subject to any higher jurisdiction, and Mr. Mackenzie King's fight for full dominion autonomy culminating in the Statute of Westminster of 1931. On the other hand, these former settlement colonies seem basically different from the former colonies of the developing world, in most of which the feeling of wider imperial allegiance was far less developed.

Of course, the more usual problems in state-building of aggregating local and group interests have existed in Canada as in other countries, and indeed certain of these problems have intensified in recent years. We can thus discern certain analytically separate processes in the Canadian experience of state formation, and hence, it seems useful to review these different processes under four distinct categories, as follows:

(A) The gradual emergence of a Canadian identity in relation to imperial and Commonwealth unity.

(B) The long-run tension between Canadian autonomy and North American continentalist tendencies.

(C) The accommodation of regional and provincial diversity in a federal polity.

(D) The accommodation of religious, linguistic, and cultural diversity in a pluralist society.

This list is not exhaustive. Certain further aspects, such as the integration of class or economic interests, could still be explored, but in the Canadian setting the four categories listed above appear to be paramount. Though there are subtle interrelationships to be traced among these four broad themes, each of the four seems to play a separate and identifiable part in the nation-building process, no matter whether that process be conceived primarily as a question of allegiance, of economic integration, of communication networks, of administrative capacity, or of consciousness of group identity.

BRITISH IMPERIUM AND CANADIAN IDENTITY

It is worth noting that a sense of separate Canadian identity emerged well before the end of the French regime. Even in the early eighteenth century one can find references to a growing divergence of perspectives and attitudes in New France between the French and the *Canadiens.* However the British conquest cut short the development of Canada as a French colony in 1759, and by Article IV of the Treaty of Paris those with French interests and connections were permitted to leave.

The foundations of a polity based on cultural and linguistic duality were only created as a consequence of the American Revolution. In this sense modern Canada is the product of two separations, the first between Great Britain and her American colonies in the eighteenth century, the second a slower, more gradual separation of Britain and her British North American colonies in the nineteenth and twentieth centuries.

The nature of the first of these splits is crucial to an understanding of Canadian society. Much of the historical and ideological tradition of English-speaking Canada has stressed the loyalist, antirepublican, and conservative characteristics of the American refugees whose arrival at the close of the Revolutionary War constituted the first major wave of English-speaking settlers in the remaining British North American colonies. The political circumstances of their arrival in New Brunswick, Nova Scotia, and Quebec afforded a strong base in each colony for legitimating continued colonial rule and counteracting American influences. All this, however, tended to obscure the extent to which loyalist refugees and Americans shared a common social heritage and common values, a topic which has been probed and debated in recent years (Hartz, 1964, ch. 7; Horowitz, 1966; Bell, 1970).

There is, of course, practically no sense of a common British North American identity after the American Revolution. Life was rudimentary, pioneering, and largely self-sufficient, and the colonies were remote from one another. For several decades all of these small societies could be classified as peripheral, with London and the Colonial Office being the obvious centre.

Yet even from an early period elective legislative assemblies were available as an instrument for development and change. These were established in Nova Scotia in 1758, in Prince Edward Island in 1773, in New Brunswick in 1784, in Upper and Lower Canada in 1791. By the late 1820s these representative assemblies had begun to call for ministries responsible to them rather than to the governor and the Colonial Office, and after various vicissitudes, including armed rebellion in the Canadas in 1837 and 1838, the principle of ministerial responsibility was conceded in the Province of Canada and in Nova Scotia in 1848 (Martin, 1929). Once achieved in British North America, the new principle was sought by and conceded to other settlement colonies throughout the empire. As envisaged by Britain, responsible government was to apply to the domestic affairs only of each colony, excluding all matters of imperial interest, but once the principle of local autonomy had been conceded the line of demarcation between local and imperial interests proved impossible to stabilize.

In the protracted struggle for ministerial responsibility in the Canadas, one of the most strongly contested issues was the control of appointments of public servants. Ministerial control meant the displacement of imperially appointed career officials by local supporters of the ministry of the day. While administratively less efficient in the short run, the wider distribution of the rewards of office probably contributed to a faster mobilization of the population at a time when few other means were available for this purpose. At the same time, it reduced the network of imperial administration and heightened political participation within each colony.

But the process of disentanglement from the imperial administrative structure was a slow one, and various vestiges of the imperial network remained long after the conceding of responsible government. The colonial governors and governors-general remained as agents of the British government and guardians of imperial interests until well into the twentieth century, and British military garrisons and naval bases existed in Canada until 1906. The last formal components of the imperial administrative network, those concerned with defence and diplomacy, were phased out only gradually as the dominions developed their own structures in the 1920s and 1930s.

From a strict legal standpoint, the process of imperial disengagement for Canada is even today incomplete, in that the written Constitution has not been "repatriated" and must, therefore, still be amended formally through the agency of the United Kingdom Parliament. This, however, is a constitutional anomaly, arising from the fact that unsettled provincial-federal differences have overshadowed the question of formal legal disengagement from the empire. The effective dates for the completion of Canada's legal, administrative, and structural "statehood" in relation to the British Empire and Commonwealth should be considered the Imperial Conference of 1926 and the Statute of Westminster of 1931.

Thus Canada realized only slowly, through gradual but deliberate development over approximately a century, the characteristics of formal legal independence that the United States had achieved decisively and immediately by the Treaty of Paris in 1783. Hence in their sudden acquisition of legal statehood the United States and most developing countries today stand in sharp contrast with the countries of the older British Commonwealth, all of which underwent a very gradual evolution from colonial status towards the same goal. The pressures to complete the legal details of sovereignty were stronger in South Africa than in Canada, weaker in Australia and New Zealand, and closer study of the domestic histories of the four countries suggests that the ethnic diversity of South Africa and Canada was one significant factor in accounting for the difference of tempo.

To trace the evolution of concepts and attitudes concerning colonial, national, and imperial relationships is a complicated task. We must be content with sketching the broad outlines in rather impressionistic terms. The first large wave of English-speaking settlers, the American Loyalists, had been closely identified with the cause of imperial unity and had suffered for it. These circumstances gave the colonies a strong identification with the mother country. These feelings were further promoted by official policy and strengthened by the successful defense of Canada against American invasions in 1812-1814. The decades following the Napoleonic Wars saw massive immigration from Britain to British North America, particularly to Upper Canada. Though most British immigrants sought to improve their social and economic status by migration, the literature of the period suggests that they did not see migration as involving a change of allegiance. They remained simply British subjects who lived in the colonies.

By the 1850s the colonial society had developed very considerably. Local self-government had been achieved, population had multiplied, canals and railways had eased the major difficulties of transport, and economic development had been extensive. The best farming lands in the eastern colonies had been largely occupied. It is in this decade that one finds the first clear legislative assertion of colonial economic interests (a colonial tariff against British manufacturers) and also a growing interest in the undeveloped lands of the western prairies. The 1860s and 1870s saw a period of active "nation-building" (which will be discussed more fully below), but this did not preclude sharing in the renewed interest in imperialism and the Imperial Federation Movement in the 1880s and 1890s (Berger, 1970). The significant point is that many Canadians felt no real conflict between an allegiance to the "new nationality" supposedly created at confederation and their membership, as British subjects, in the empire. This period of dual allegiance lasted for several decades, probably down to the First World War for the majority of English-speaking Canadians. It was an attitude especially prevalent among the British-born section of the population, which accounted for 11 percent of the total population in 1931, or just half of those born inside Canada (Coats and Maclean, 1943, p. 2).

More recently these ambiguities of allegiance have tended to diminish among English-speaking Canadians. For the generation born and educated in Canada after 1920 it is doubtful if they have ever existed; for these age groups the primary identification is clearly with Canada. And yet the earlier heritage of divided loyalties may perhaps be discerned in another form. Canada's easy acceptance of extensive commitments in NATO and the United Nations after 1945 might be explained in part as a continuation of this English-Canadian tradition of allegiance extending beyond the territorial polity.

The slow evolution of a sense of "nationhood" among English-speaking Canadians may also be traced in their sensitivities about the symbols of national identity, particularly in their quest for a Canadian flag and a national anthem. The Canadian red ensign, which had long been used but without parliamentary sanction, carried a Union Jack on its quarter and was not popular among French-speaking Canadians. An attempt to find an acceptable, less obviously British-oriented design led to a long, bitter, paralysing parliamentary debate in 1964 that parallelled the similar controversy over the South African flag forty years previously. The new design was eventually adopted, but one result was an immediate upsurge in the display of provincial flags, including an Ontario design which bears a curiously close resemblance to the superseded red ensign. On the question of an anthem, policy has been more cautious. For many years the British anthem (God Save the Queen) and a native one (O Canada) enjoyed joint recognition, but it would appear now that opinion is inching slowly towards recognition of O Canada as the sole anthem without precipitating a confrontation similar to the flag debate.

In general every public debate over symbols—including coats-of-arms, postage stamps, the designation "royal," and similar matters—will show that the older tradition of a dual allegiance to Canada and to Britain and/or the Commonwealth is far from dead in some regions and among some age groups, though it is clearly much diminished. But the survival of these attitudes has direct links with domestic issues, with the unwillingness of some English Canadians to make the more liberal accommodations with French Canada that have become urgently necessary since 1960. For if Canada remains a "British" country in the traditional sense, how can it also be a bilingual one? This issue will be examined below.

CANADIAN IDENTITY AND NORTH AMERICAN CONTINENTALISM

One of the factors that gave the idea of imperial federation a good deal of strength in Canada was the apparent unfeasibility of its alternative: independence. To many, independence seemed an impossible goal if Canada were to be the unprotected neighbour of a major power with ten times her population, a power that had more than once invaded her territory. For these people the empire and later the Commonwealth seemed a strong counterweight to otherwise irresistible American pressures, and most opinion in Canada, to all appearances, has always had resistance to "Americanization" as one of its central tenets. Yet surface appearances can be deceptive, and any analysis in depth would find that the full picture of American-Canadian relations is extraordinarily complex.

It does not seem possible, within the confines of this essay, to do full justice to this complicated question. Yet it is clearly of importance to nation-building theory, for here is a case where two centuries of contiguous territory, common language and culture (for English-speaking Canadians at least), intermigration, trade, travel, and communication have *not* produced formal political integration. Perhaps the most useful contribution for the present is to attempt to indicate the range of issues that would need to be examined in a full-scale study of these inter-relationships.

There are, in the first place, certain military, political, and diplomatic themes. These include not only the wars, invasions, political tensions, boundary disputes, and diplomacy between the two polities, but also the development of formal mechanisms for conflict resolution, such as the International Joint Commission. They include the role of dissentient groups in each society and the reception of support found by these groups across the border, from American support of the Canadian rebellion of 1837-1838 down through the Confederate raid on St. Alban's in 1864, the Fenian raid in Canada in 1866, to the reception of draft evaders and deserters from the American forces in recent years. They also include the respective roles of Canada and the United States in wider diplomatic ventures, in world politics, and in international organizations. Nor is this usually a bilateral relationship. In many aspects, as Brebner has insisted in a broad-ranging study (1945), the interplay has been more frequently triangular with Great Britain as a third participant.

In the second place, there are eocnomic relationships to be considered. Although the United States and Canada have behaved in economic and commercial policy as separate polities for much of their history, they have also experienced a decade of partial free trade under the Reciprocity Treaty of 1854, the termination of which by the United States served as a powerful stimulus to Canadian confederation. Free trade or full reciprocity with the United States was a central plank in the platform of the Liberal Party at the federal elections of 1891 and 1911, though it was defeated on both occasions. After the Ottawa Conference of 1932 Canada entered into tariff preferences with other Commonwealth countries, but the Canadian-American automobile agreement of 1965 and a number of other special economic arrangements have pointed to further integration of the two economies in recent years. The long-term trend of Canada's foreign trade has been towards increasing dependence on the United States as the role of the United Kingdom and the Commonwealth has diminished, as may be seen from Table 1. This dependence has left Canada extremely vulnerable to changes in American trade and monetary policies, as exemplified by President Nixon's economic measures of August 1971. On the other hand, Canada is now the lowest of all the Commonwealth countries in its percentage of trade carried on within the Commonwealth. In 1969 less than 12 percent of Canadian exports and 10 percent of imports were with other Commonwealth countries, as compared to an average of 23 percent for the Commonwealth as a whole (*The Commonwealth in Brief*, 1970, p. 43).

In recent years attention has focused more directly on the degree of American ownership of Canadian industry and natural resources. For decades Canada admitted foreign capital freely and through this means became an industrialized society. However the decline of Britain as a financial power during World War II has meant that the great bulk of investment has become American in origin, and many of the industries that grew up under protective Canadian tariffs are simply branch plants of large American firms. Until quite recently Canadian economic policy paid

TABLE 1
CANADA'S FOREIGN TRADE (excluding gold) BY MAJOR
TRADING AREAS, 1886-1969 (in percentages)

Year	Imports From				Exports To			
	Total	Common- wealth	United States	Other Countries	Total	Common- wealth	United States	Other Countries
1886	100	43.1	44.6	12.2	100	51.4	44.1	4.5
1891	100	39.8	46.7	13.6	100	53.2	42.6	4.3
1896	100	33.4	50.8	15.8	100	60.9	34.4	4.7
1901	100	26.2	60.3	13.4	100	56.8	38.3	4.9
1906	100	29.5	59.7	10.8	100	58.8	35.5	5.7
1911	100	28.6	60.9	10.5	100	54.3	38.0	7.7
1916	100	20.7	73.0	6.3	100	65.1	27.1	7.8
1921	100	21.4	69.0	9.5	100	33.9	45.6	20.5
1926	100	21.3	66.3	12.4	100	44.0	36.3	19.7
1931	100	24.2	62.7	13.1	100	37.4	40.9	21.7
1936	100	29.8	58.1	12.1	100	51.1	35.6	13.3
1941	100	24.8	69.3	5.8	100	54.2	37.0	8.8
1946	100	17.7	72.9	9.4	100	39.1	38.4	22.5
1951	100	17.8	68.9	13.3	100	22.3	58.7	19.0
1956	100	12.4	72.9	14.7	100	22.0	58.8	19.1
1961	100	15.8	67.0	17.2	100	21.5	54.0	24.5
1966	100	10.7	72.3	16.9	100	16.5	59.9	23.6
1969	100	9.6	72.6	17.8	100	11.7	70.7	17.6

SOURCES: 1886-1956: calculated from M. C. Urquhart, ed., **Historical Statistics of Canada** (Toronto, 1965), pp. 181-182. 1961-1969: **Canada Year Book,** 1970-71, pp. 1081-082.

little attention to these developments, and despite growing public concern no general policy has yet taken shape. Different sectors of the economy produce sharply divergent attitudes on the question, and economic interpenetration is by no means one-sided, though it is disproportionate due to the disparity in population and sources of capital. However, some limited policy measures have evolved in recent years, usually in response to specific situations, notably in the fields of banking, communications media, and uranium mining, and more general policies are under consideration.

A full study of economic relations between Canada and the United States would have to weigh not only broad patterns of international trade and cross-ownership of industry and financial assets but also the many minor and sometimes subtle ways in which the economies and technologies are interlocked. As examples of this one could mention standard railway gauges and couplings; the uniformity or near uniformity of standards, weights, and measures; the North American telephone network (with standardized direct long distance dialing); the near equivalence of currency units and the interchangeability of coins; freedom from exchange control; and many others.

Beside the political, military, and economic approaches should be placed certain demographic and social themes. In terms of population movement, the interplay across the frontier has been studied and documented by Hansen (1940), Truesdell (1943), and Coats and Maclean (1943). In summary, the international boundary has proved a minimal barrier to migration in either direction for the last two centuries. After the Revolution, American Loyalists poured into Canada, and for three decades they were followed into Upper Canada by thousands more Americans seeking land. Later on Canadians poured into the American midwest as westward expansion continued, and later still the frontier moved from the American midwest to the Canadian prairies. Later emigration and immigration reflected differential prosperity at different periods. Nor was the migration confined to the English-speaking population; French Canadians moved to New England in far greater numbers than they did to other parts of Canada. The overall picture, as reflected by the country of birth of the population, may be seen in Table 2, which shows that the peak of Canadian emigration occurred during the 1890s, when there was

TABLE 2
CANADIAN-BORN RESIDENTS IN THE UNITED STATES AND AMERICAN-BORN RESIDENTS IN CANADA, 1851-1961

Year	Total Population of Canada (millions)	Canadian-Born Residents in United States[a]		American-Born Residents in Canada	
		(000s)	As % of Total Pop. of Canada	(000s)	As % of Total Pop. of Canada
1851	2.4	148	6.1	63	2.6
1861	3.2	250	7.7	70	2.2
1871	3.7	493	13.4	65	1.7
1881	4.3	717	16.6	78	1.8
1891	4.8	980	20.3	81	1.7
1901	5.4	1,180	22.0	128	2.4
1911	7.2	1,205	16.7	304	4.2
1921	8.8	1,125	12.8	374	4.3
1931	10.4	1,286	12.4	345	3.3
1941	11.5	1,065	9.3	312	2.7
1951	14.0	994	7.1	282	2.0
1961	18.2	942	5.2	284	1.6

SOURCES: 1851-1931: Coats and Maclean, 1943, p. 24. 1941-1961: Canada Year Book, 1970-71, p. 238; Statistical Abstract of the United States, 1962, p. 34, and 1969, p. 31.
a. Figures in this column are based on the U.S. census, one year earlier than the corresponding Canadian census.

roughly one expatriate Canadian in the United States for every five residents of Canada. It may be noted further that French-speakers represented 31 percent of the total Canadian-born population in the United States in 1890, 34 percent in 1900, 32 percent in 1910, 28 percent in 1920, and 29 percent in 1930, so that in this period the French-speaking Canadians showed roughly the same propensity to migrate as the English-speaking (Truesdell, 1943, pp. 45-47). More recently, however, the proportion has fallen to 26 percent in 1940 and 24 percent in 1950, which is below the proportion of French Canadians in Canada.

It can be argued that the patterns of transborder migration, short-term travel for business or pleasure, and communication—to say nothing of less tangible factors such as common cultural and political heritage—afford a considerable base for the development of common values and attitudes. This subject is too large for full exploration here, but we may note the findings of one study as to perceived similarities. In a survey of a national sample of French-speaking and English-speaking young people from 13 to 20 in 1965, both groups inclined firmly to the view that Canadians and Americans are "alike in most ways" rather than "different in most ways," the English-speaking by 79 percent to 18, the French-speaking by 56 percent to 37 (Johnstone, 1969, p. 23). Further, all respondents were asked whether French Canadians and English Canadians respectively had more in common with each other or with Americans. Both groups saw French-speaking Canadians as having more in common with English-speaking Canadians than with Americans, but both groups also tended to see English-speaking Canadians as having more in common with Americans than with French-speaking Canadians. English-speaking respondents perceived this common tie between English Canadians and Americans by a considerable majority—68 percent to 20 percent; French-speaking respondents perceived it only marginally—41 percent to 39 percent (Johnstone, 1969, p. 33).

In a further question which allows some comparison of continentalist, Commonwealth, and foreign orientations, these teen-aged respondents were asked to name the country that is Canada's "best friend." As table 3 indicates, the results for both major language groups suggest clearly the overwhelming strength of continentalism in comparison with all other possible foreign alignments.

Another national survey, which dealt with adult opinion but used the same households as the Johnstone study, had direct questions on political and economic union with the United States. On economic union, 51 percent were in favor and 29 percent were opposed, the percentage in favor being higher among those identifying as French-Canadians (59

TABLE 3
YOUNG PEOPLE'S PERCEPTION OF CANADA'S "BEST FRIEND" BY LANGUAGE SPOKEN AT HOME (in percentages)

Country	English	French
United States	65	72
Great Britain	29	6
France	1	8
All others	1	1
No reply	4	13
Total	100	100

SOURCE: Johnstone, 1969, p. 14.

percent) than among those identifying as English-Canadians (47 percent). On political union—"joining together as one country"—the majority in each group were clearly opposed, 69 to 19 percent among English Canadians, 54 to 25 percent among French Canadians, and 64 to 21 percent for the entire sample. Yet what is notable is that in 1965 one Canadian in five favored political union with the United States and one in two favored economic union. Curiously enough, an overwhelming majority (95 percent of English Canadians and 92 percent of French Canadians) also agreed with the proposition that "more effort should be made so that all citizens of Canada feel they are one people" (Social Research Group, 1965, pp. M 6, M 79). Some respondents therefore appeared to feel no inconsistency between a desire for stronger nation-building measures, presumably of an internal nature, and further North American economic or even political integration. Just as Canadians of an earlier generation could feel a simultaneous and nonconflicting allegiance to Canada and to the empire, it would appear that many of their descendants can favor both a stronger Canadian polity and more contintentalism.

But the range of attitudes is wide, and public discussion on Canada's relations with the American colossus is never-ending. Nor can these attitudes be linked automatically with political affiliations. There is today a strong anti-Americanism of the Canadian left, and there are older traditions of anti-Americanism in Canadian conservatism, but equally there have been periods of accommodation and alliance on both the left and the right. There is also anti-Americanism which can be classified as simply tactical manoeuvring in interest-group conflict, such as opposition to specific American unions or industries.

How can one explain this absence of clear-cut attitudinal patterns? The point seems to be that for English Canadians at least some differentiation from American value patterns is absolutely central to the definition of Canadian identity, and this process is made difficult by the strong similarities in the cultural and institutional inheritance of the two countries. The typical English Canadian has both nationalist and continentalist elements in his life style. In most circumstances he can reconcile without difficulty an allegiance to national symbols with a pragmatic acceptance of continentalist economic benefits, but the slightest change in the complex array of forces touching his own life can activate either nationalist or continentalist responses and involve him as a partisan in the continuing debate on Canada's relationship with the United States.

STATE-BUILDING, REGIONALISM AND FEDERALISM

If nation-building and state formation in Canada have involved the rejection of certain wider alternatives, they have also demanded the integration of local, regional, religious, linguistic, and cultural interests within the Canadian territory. This is perhaps the more conventional aspect of nation-building, and certain aspects of it may be passed over rather lightly here. These include the building of a federal state out of some widely scattered components, a process that has been duplicated elsewhere often enough. I shall reserve for more detailed comment in a separate section the questions of religious, linguistic, and ethnic diversity, on which there is a variety of data available through the work of the recent federal Royal Commission on Bilingualism and Biculturalism.

Although the term "British North America" was in common use before 1867, and although there had been a "governor in chief" (usually resident in Lower Canada) for the colonies as a group, the situation in fact was one of minimal contact among the colonies. Just as Acadians and French-Canadians had remained far apart during the French regime, so did the maritime and inland colonies of the second British Empire have little to do with one another. Even more isolated were the small Red River colony and the settlements on the West Coast. The maritime colonies had some degree of intercommunication among themselves, and perhaps as much with the New England states, but only Upper and Lower Canada, divided by religion and language but linked by a common dependence on the St. Lawrence River system, had a relatively high level of intercommunication. These statements are impressionistic only, however, since no systematic study of levels of communication or economic transactions appears to have been attempted.

The confederation of these scattered colonies was promoted by a combination of internal and external factors. For the Canadas, it was important as an escape from the legislative union of 1840, which had produced ministerial instability and chronic political deadlock. For the Atlantic provinces it was an alternative to a smaller and less ambitious scheme of maritime union and a possible solution for structural economic problems. But more important than all this was the fact that during the early 1860s the United States was mobilized in civil war, and there was universal apprehension that the victorious Northern armies might be turned against Canada at the conclusion of hostilities. Further, the imperial authorities, subject to the pressures of the Little England movement, were prepared to push for federation in the belief that a single, larger dependency would be less costly to the home government. But confederation was not a movement based on mass support. The proposals were never specifically submitted to the electorate in any of the original colonies. New Brunswick defeated the government that negotioted on its behalf, and Nova Scotia at the first federal election chose 18 out of 19 members pledged to repeal. If the colonies concerned had been independent at the time, it is doubtful whether confederation would have been effected.

Nevertheless, confederation was achieved, chiefly through negotiotions among the colonial political elites. Mindful of the breakdown of American federalism, the colonial delegates who worked out its terms believed that they were creating a strong central government, but one which left scope for ethnic and regional diversity. Certainly the list of enumerated federal powers in the Constitution of 1867 includes a number that are obviously relevant to state-building, including among others defence; banking and currency; navigation; the postal service; railways, canals, and telegraphs extending beyond a single province; regulation of trade and commerce; and unrestricted powers of taxation. Moreover, to all appearances the federal government received all residual powers not explicitly allocated to the provinces. The provinces for their part received a more restricted and localized range of powers, which nevertheless included jurisdiction over property and civil rights (to safeguard the respective domains of common and civil law), over welfare and charitable agencies, and over municipal and local government. The fathers of confederation, with misplaced confidence, felt that they had established in 1867 a clear line of demarcation that avoided the pitfalls which had led to crisis and breakdown in the United States; as events were to demonstrate, their system was open to considerable change and conflict over the following century as the role of government was expanded and transformed.

The years that followed 1867 can be viewed as a period of positive state-building in a number of specific ways, and indeed these tendencies can be seen as the extension of an expansionist mentality that is discernible in the province of Canada as early as the 1850s. One of the first priorities was to round out the new state in a territorial and political sense. The vast Hudson's Bay Company lands of the west and north were acquired by Canada in 1869; new provinces were admitted (Manitoba in 1870, British Columbia in 1871, Prince Edward Island in 1873) or created from federally administered territorial lands (Alberta and Saskatchewan in 1905). Once again the process was a slow one. The definition of boundaries was not completed, insofar as Alaska and the Arctic islands were concerned, until the twentieth century (Nicholson, 1954), and Newfoundland, whose entry into confederation was provided for in the Constitution of 1867, did not enter until 1949.

By far the most important aspect of state-building after 1867 was the construction of railways, and particularly the Canadian Pacific. Without it, the political changes would have had little significance. An undertaking on this scale was a major challenge to Canada, and the issue dominated federal politics for more than a decade until the first transcontinental line was completed in 1885 (Berton, 1970-1971). The 1870s also marked the beginnings of a "National Policy" that gave tariff protection to domestic industry.

These political and economic measures were accompanied by some related intellectual developments. The 1870s saw the rise of the Canada First movement, the first significant expression of English-Canadian nationalism. From this time on there is a more or less continuous expression of opinion focusing on Canadian rather than provincial or local loyalties. However, we must note two things. First, this early nationalism found nothing incompatible with the wider rights and obligations of imperial citizenship, and some leaders of Canada First are later found in the Imperial Federation movement. Second, these same leaders invariably saw Canada as an Anglo-Saxon nation, a second Britain. Their vision was defective in that the movement underrated the influence of a full third of the Canadian population, the French Canadians.

But state-building measures did not remain unopposed. There was a ready organization for resisting them and for maintaining regional interests in the provincial governments, and the first comprehensive reaction culminated in the Interprovincial Conference of 1887, to which five out of seven provinces came to protest and resist federal politics of centralization. The pattern of resistance is not simple, however, for it was the strong central provinces of Ontario and Quebec, not the periphery, which were foremost in the revolt.

One can reasonably maintain that the post-confederation period saw the emergence and consolidation of a territorial centre for Canada, founded on the central provinces of Ontario and Quebec and more specifically on the two rival commercial-industrial centres of Montreal and Toronto. Certainly there have been strong feelings from the beginning in the Atlantic provinces and in the West that confederation has chiefly benefited the two populous central provinces. It is therefore tempting to interpret Canadian development in terms of a relationship between centre and periphery, between metropolis and frontier. However, the full picture is complex and needs some major qualifications to make all the pieces fit into place. While the West developed separate political parties of protest (the Progressive Party, the Social Credit, and the Cooperative Commonwealth Federation, or C.C.F.), maritime grievances have always been expressed through traditional federal parties. One finds at certain stages the anomaly that policies allegedly favoring the centre were carried on by federal administrations whose political strength was dependent upon the periphery. Besides, the centre-periphery concept, which applies most obviously to a federal state in a geographical sense, could also be looked at in an ethnic or linguistic sense, and here the lines of division diverge sharply. Basically, the geographic and economic centre is not ethnically or culturally homogeneous, and never has been. This raises questions which will be considered more fully in the next section.

In the second half century after confederation the role of the provincial governments increased more rapidly than the federal role. In part this was due to the increasing interest of the state in the welfare field, and in part to judicial interpretation of the division of powers of 1867, which upheld an enlarged provincial jurisdiction and tended to relegate the residual federal power to an emergency power applicable only in time of war or similar crisis. In recent years the emphasis on provincial activities has increased even more rapidly. The vast increases of expenditures on education, health, and welfare in the 1960s have raised the level of provincial expenditures from a level of roughly half of federal expenditures in 1960 to one apparently slightly *exceeding* federal expenditures in 1970.

It is clear that the provinces today play a role of a significance apparently never envisaged in 1867. Moreover, two surveys sponsored by the Royal Commission on Bilingualism suggest that this enhanced provincial role accords closely with the expectations and preferences of the public. In the national survey of adults, respondents were asked which level of government (federal or provincial) "takes best care of the interests of people like you." Of the total sample a plurality named provincial government, by 31 percent to 19, the remainder being neutral, undecided, and so on. Closer analysis by ethnic group and region shows that this provincial preference is found among those identifying as French Canadians in every region, and among English Canadians in every region except Quebec (Social Research Group, 1965, pp. M-78, 291). In the corresponding youth survey, respondents were asked which level of government (federal, provincial, or local) "does the *most* for people." Here too the provincial level outranked the federal, only marginally among English speakers, but by almost two to one among French speakers, who ranked the federal government in third place behind local government (Johnstone, 1969, p. 18). Johnstone (1969, p. 22) also found that provincial orientations increased sharply by age groups from 13 to 20, suggesting that in Canada "the adolescent years . . . could be characterized as the period of emergent sectionalism."

In the adult survey respondents were also asked a question as to their relative level of interest in federal or provincial politics, and here the regional patterns differ. English Canadians in Central Canada (Ontario and Quebec) expressed greater interest in federal politics, while the periphery (the West and the Maritimes) was more interested in provincial politics. French Canadians expressed greater interest in provincial issues in all regions except Ontario (Social Research Group, 1965, p. 290). Similarly, in the youth survey, when respondents were asked which level of government would be best to work for, more French speakers preferred provincial government, while more English speakers chose the federal level; but here no regional breakdowns were reported (Johnstone, 1969, p. 18).

Any interpretation of these survey data should probably be done cautiously, since many underlying factors may be involved. However, it may be suggested tentatively that in terms of trust and protection of interests, more Canadians tended to think in sectional than in pan-Canadian terms, the sole exception being English Canadians in Quebec. However when viewing government as an instrument for social action there was a split: English Canadians at the periphery and practically all French Canadians (Ontario excepted) still prefer the provinces, while English Canadians in the centre and French Canadians in Ontario favor the federal level by quite substantial margins.

THE ACCOMMODATION OF RELIGIOUS, CULTURAL, AND LINGUISTIC DIVERSITY

The commercial-industrial centre of modern Canada, located along the St. Lawrence River system, first exerienced European settlement as a colony of France. During a century and a half of development a distinctive French-Canadian society was implanted which has firmly resisted cultural assimilation. At the last census of the French regime in 1754, the population of the colony numbered 55,000. The colony was ceded by France to Britain in 1763, but its first significant English-speaking settlement occurred only in the 1780s after the War of American Independence. From this time on the rapidly increasing population of British North America was characterized by a deep social cleavage, which had religious, linguistic, and cultural dimensions, and which stemmed from the circumstances of colonization. In the terminology of Louis Hartz, French and English Canada are two distinct fragments generated under different historical circumstances in the process of European expansion and characterized by different ideological underpinnings (Hartz, 1964). The fourth and final aspect of this essay is to consider some of the dimensions of this cleavage and how it has been accommodated to the extent necessary for state formation.

The most immediate problem of accommodation after France's cession of Canada to Britain was religious. In Britain, Catholic emancipation was not to be conceded until 1829; what would be the status of Roman Catholics in the new colony? The question was an important one because after the disappearance of French civil administration the Church had become the major rallying point for the French-Canadian elite. In the end the British colonial system adjusted to the new situation, allowing the free exercise of the Catholic faith, consecration of bishops, collection of customary Church dues, modified oaths of allegiance, and in general latitude to the Church to fill the broad social role that it acquired after the displacement of the French secular authorities. This policy led the ecclesiastical hierarchy to support the British civil regime, especially after the French Revolution cut off ties with Old France.

A second problem lay in the legal systems. Again adjustments were made so that the Custom of Paris could continue as the basis for the law of property and civil rights. An adjustment of a different order occurred in 1791, when the English-speaking American Loyalist settlements west of Montreal were made a separate colony, Upper Canada, which immediately adopted a common-law legal system and freehold land tenure. By these early measures foundations were laid for the separate development of French and English Canada, a development which juxtaposed throughout the nineteenth century a society that was predominantly seigneurial, Catholic, and French-speaking against one that was predominantly Protestant, English-speaking, and contractual. But the separation was imperfect; for each line of cleavage there was at least one substantial minority, and these minorities grew in numbers and proportions as time went on. Territorially, there was a significant Protestant, English-speaking minority in Lower Canada, and they were the dynamic, entrepreneurial element in the nineteenth century. Religiously, there were English-speaking Catholics in both Upper and Lower Canada, particularly after the Irish migration of the 1840s. Linguistically, the Catholic population was split between English-speaking and French-speaking components. As Canada developed, these lines of cleavage were to be found in varying degrees in every province.

Though Canada was still a British dependency, the system began to develop a certain dynamic of its own. What happened after the reunification of Upper and Lower Canada in 1840 is instructive. Following the rebellions of 1837-1838, the British government accepted Lord Durham's recommendation to reunite the two colonies in the belief that the French Canadians would therby be assimilated by the more dynamic English-speaking population. But imposed legislative union quickly gave way to de facto federalism. The intent of the imperial authorities was frustrated by a new series of accommodative techniques, including bi-ethnic political parties, double ministerial portfolios and split administrative departments, separate legislation for the two portions of the United Province, parity in budgetary allocations, and so on.

Thus even before confederation the accommodation of diversity through territorial autonomy was well enough established to override formal institutional provisions for unity. With the formalization of federalism in 1867 these tendencies became much stronger, to the extent that cross-cutting religious or linguistic cleavages were usually subordinated to provincial autonomy. One must distinguish here, however, between Quebec and the other provinces, because in Quebec the English-speaking Protestant minority, prosperous, well-educated, articulate, and backed by its majority position in Canada as a whole, was never in the weak position of the other religious or ethnic minorities, and it could usually uphold its own interests.

The exact nature of the confederation settlement of 1867 has been much debated in Canada. Insofar as it represented imperial legislation, it was simply a decision of the British government for one of of its numerous dependencies. Insofar as these decisions represented elements of consensus reached at two preceding intercolonial conferences at Charlottetown and Quebec, it represented an agreement or compact. But a compact of what? The delegates came as members of colonial legislatures, and most of the discussion concerned the interests of their respective provinces, particularly fiscal and economic questions. The element of compact is first and foremost a compact of provinces, and only indirectly a compact among religious or ethnic interests. As a result the powers, fiscal rights, and institutions of the provinces are set out in some detail, while other guarantees are rather rudimentary. The only special cross-cutting religious protection was a federal power of intervention to protect denominational schools—a power which three decades later was to prove ineffectual before the forces of provincial autonomy. The only cross-cutting language protection in the 1867 Act was at the level of the federal Parliament and federal Courts, and also—to protect the English-speaking Protestant minority—in the province of Quebec.

Basically, then, the most significant accommodation of linguistic and religious diversity at confederation was through provincial autonomy, especially in educational and cultural matters. Within that framework, most provinces left Protestants and Catholics a considerable freedom to finance and run their own school systems as they saw fit, but linguistic and ethnic diversity received less attention (except in Quebec where it largely coincided with religious cleavage). Such a settlement was suitable for a society that was still largely rural and technologically uncomplicated, but later it came under strain when the same cleavages had to be reconciled under conditions of industrialization and urbanization involving closer contact of heterogeneous populations. In particular the linguistic and cultural cleavage between French Canadians and English Canadians, each group stabilized in its own fragment and committed to its own core values, was to prove an increasing source of tension as society became more complex and urbanized.

The transition to industrial society placed greater stress upon core values in French Canada than in English Canada. The agrarian and ultramontanist ideal, which was strongly defended until the 1940s, proved increasingly unable to provide a standard of living in keeping with rising economic expectations. In one sense the industrialization of French Canada antedated the industrialization of Quebec itself; it began with the outflow of French-Canadian workers to the New England towns in the second half of the nineteenth century. After 1890 more rapid industrialization appeared in Quebec itself, and the proportion of the active population employed in agriculture in Quebec dropped from 46 percent in 1891 to 31 percent in 1911 (Hughes, 1943, p. 23). More recently the agricultural segment has continued to decline, falling to 13 percent of the work force in 1951 and to 7 percent in 1961, by which year the percentage was the same as in Ontario and below that of Canada as a whole (10 percent).

But entry into the industrial system did not solve all problems; the

French Canadians found themselves at a considerable disadvantage which is reflected in lower incomes and a lower-status occupational structure. Rising levels of discontent led to the appointment in 1963 of a federal Royal Commission on Bilingualism and Biculturalism with a wide mandate to study language policy and interethnic relations both generally and in certain designated domains including the federal public service, the mass media, and education. This commission undertook an extensive programme of data collection and research concerning many aspects of interethnic relations, with the result that it is now possible to analyse the ethnic and linguistic dimensions of Canadian society to a degree that is possible for few other countries.

In particular the commission's research programme conducted special analyses of 1961 census data classified by ethnic origin and language. In economic terms it was found that French-Canadian males had an income index of 88 percent of the Canadian average while those of British origin reached 110 percent of the Canadian average. Similar disparities were found in levels of education; 53 percent of French Canadians, compared to 31 percent of those of British origin, had only elementary education, while the proportion with some university training was 12 percent for the British and 6 percent for the French. Occupational structures reflected these differences, the British being somewhat more concentrated than the French in the professional and managerial categories. More detailed analysis in selected cities found that interethnic income differentials were in part due to differences in the age structure, industry structure, and levels of unemployment of the groups concerned. Another approach by regression analysis suggested that in Montreal the ethnicity factor accounted for higher than average incomes among those of English-Scottish, Irish, and Northern European origins, and for lower than average incomes among those of French, Italian, Eastern European, and other origins (R.C.B.B., 1969, Book III, Chs. 1-5; Raynauld, Marion, and Béland, 1966).

The religious variable and the value systems attaching to it have not been examined with the same degree of attention. Nevertheless in the Montreal area Roman Catholics of British origin occupy a midway position between British non-Catholics and French in the upper and lower occupational groups (R.C.B.B., 1969, Book III, p. 44). By comparison of census tracts in major cities another study found suggestive correlations between income levels and Protestant-Catholic religious affiliation even in cities where ethnic diversity was relatively low (Porter, 1965, pp. 98-103). We may summarize a considerable range of data now available by suggesting that most major ethnic groups and most major religious denominations participate extensively in the modern, industrialized, urbanized economic structure of Canada, but that ethnic, linguistic, and religious differences coincide to some significant degree with differences in occupational status and rewards.

In general the political integration of French and English Canada preceded economic integration. French Canadians received the franchise in Lower Canada in 1791, and ever since have elected their own legislative representation, including federal representation after confederation. In the twentieth century the level of voter turnout has not been significantly different in Quebec from the levels in Ontario or in Canada as a whole; for the twenty federal elections from 1896 to 1965 the average turnout was 72.4 percent for Quebec, 72.0 percent for Ontario, and 72.6 percent for Canada as a whole (Courtney, 1967, pp. 200-01). Since 1867 the formation of federal ministries has been subject to certain clearly understood conventions guaranteeing minority religious and linguistic representation (Gibson, 1970; Van Loon, 1966). While this has led in some instances to token representation in unimportant portfolios, the trend since 1963 has been towards a more balanced distribution of the more important ministries between French-speaking and English-speaking members.

How have religious and linguistic diversity been accommodated in political associations? Canada has shown no tendency to develop distinctive ethnic political parties, as in Finland or South Africa, nor does religious diversity find formal expression in the party structure, as in Belgium, Switzerland, and other countries. In part this may be due to the electoral system, based on single-member constituencies. Nor has French-Canadian nationalism found any significant expression as an independent force in federal politics. Instead the majority of French Canadians have looked to the province of Quebec—where they are themselves a strong majority—to articulate and protect their interests, and the level of frustration or disillusionment with federal politics has tended to coincide with the intensity of nationalism in the provincial arena. At higher levels of discontent, the more disaffected think in terms of a more decentralized or even radically restructured federal system or of an independent Quebec. Such solutions ignore the nineteen percent of French-speaking Canadians who live outside Quebec, but they are in keeping with the historic tendency to accommodate the major lines of cleavage in Canada primarily through federalism and provincial autonomy.

The level of opinion favoring separatism is of course important, and it serves as a prime indicator of the strength of the integration challenge. The national survey carried out for the Royal Commission on Bilingualism in

1965 found that 7 percent of those identifying as French Canadians favored separation. This may be compared with the 6 percent of those identifying as English Canadians who favored it, or with the 21 percent of the entire sample who favored political union of Canada with the United States (Social Research Group, 1965, pp. M-79, M-80). Since 1965 the proportion has undoubtedly grown, and the merging of several smaller separatist groups into the Parti Québecois has helped to polarize the issue. At the April 1970 Quebec provincial election this party obtained 23 percent of the popular vote. On the other hand the Liberal Party, campaigning on a federalist platform and with emphasis on economic, nonnationalist issues, showed unexpected strength in winning a decisive victory over its three major rivals. A public opinion survey taken just before the election indicated higher than average support for the Parti Québecois among those under twenty-four years old, in Montreal area French-speaking constituencies, and among union members. Occupationally, it showed relative strength among professionals, white-collar workers, unskilled labor, and students, and relative weakness among managers, sales personnel, farmers, housewives, and retired people, with other occupations closer to the general average (*Ottawa Citizen,* April 24, 1970). This suggests that unlike the older French-Canadian nationalist movements, which were almost exclusively of middle-class interest, the Parti Québecois as a party of social reform had significant support among some sections of organized labor.

Traditionally, linguistic and cultural diversity in Canada have been accommodated not through the federal government but primarily through the provinces. In practice, because of the relative strength of the interests concerned, this has meant a Quebec which was institutionally bilingual both in law and practice and nine other provinces in which all linguistic minorities were submerged in the vast English-speaking expanse of North America. The appointment of the Royal Commission on Bilingualism and Biculturalism in 1963 terminated a century of almost total linguistic *laissez faire* on the part of the federal government. The work of this commission is now at an end, and in its wake there has been federal legislation which expresses for the first time a federal interest in Canada's ethnic and linguistic diversity.

The mandate of the commission called for it to recommend measures based on the concept of "equal partnership" of the two founding groups, but taking into account also "the contribution made by the other ethnic groups to the cultural enrichment of Canada." Up to the present (1971), six books of the *Final Report* and two series of research studies have been issued, with other studies still to appear. The first volume recommended that French and English be accorded full formal equality as official languages and proposed that a system of bilingual districts be established wherever substantial official language minorities existed, in which all federal services would be available in both languages. The provinces would not be bound by this system, but the commission saw possibilities of coordinating provincial and municipal practices with federal policy by intergovernmental negotiation. The principles of linguistic equality and of bilingual services in districts having an official language minority of 10 percent or more, which are analogous to the language legislation adopted by Finland in 1922, are now embodied in Canada in the Official Languages Act of 1969.

In education, the commission urged all provinces to accept the obligation of providing minority-language schooling wherever numbers warrant it, and while it recognized that education is strictly a provincial responsibility, it proposed a series of federal subsidies to meet the additional costs to the provinces of providing minority-language instruction, teacher training, and so on. For the federal public service and the armed forces, the commission made a series of recommendations to promote a more balanced representation of linguistic groups, to increase the linguistic capacity of the personnel, and to establish units in which French would be the normal language of work. Similarly for the private sector of the economy the commission proposed major changes in the language of business and industry in Quebec, as well as further studies in Ontario and New Brunswick to widen the opportunities for the use of French in bilingual districts. Further books of the *Report* have dealt with the position of those of other than British or French origins, with linguistic policy for the federal capital, and with the role of voluntary associations in interethnic relations, but the commission was dissolved without publishing its last four projected books on the mass media, arts and letters, federal institutions, and general conclusions (R.C.B.B., 1967, Book I, p. xviii).

If the recommendations of the commission and their legislative implementation to date are considered in perspective, it can be said that the primary accommodation of linguistic and cultural diversity through extensive provincial autonomy remains unchanged, but an additional dimension has been added through the expression of a federal interest which will supplement provincial action. This new federal role is bound to be of greatest significance in aiding the linguistic minorities in each province, and particularly the French-speaking minorities, which have hitherto been relatively weak politically and economically. In Quebec the problem is different. There the question is how the linguistic and cultural aspirations of the French-speaking majority can be reconciled with a modern industrial society in a North American environment. Though the federal government can help to some extent, the crucial arena of action here is unquestionably provincial, and a Quebec provincial commission on language policy, established in 1968, has yet to publish its report. Nevertheless the new federal role in linguistic and cultural matters, while clearly more limited than the wide range of provincial activities in the linguistic and cultural area, has important implications for nation-building. By establishing linguistic equality at the federal level and offering special assistance to the linguistic minorities in each province, the federal government can utilize cross-cutting linguistic cleavages to stop the cultural chasm between Quebec and the other provinces from widening further.

This section would be incomplete without a mention of two other components of Canadian society, the "other ethnic groups," that is, the population of other than British or French origin, and the indigenous peoples, Indians and Eskimos. The other ethnic groups, which constitute 25 percent of Canada's population, are sometimes referred to as a "Third Force" in relation to those of French or British origin, but this is in some ways misleading in that this component is made up of many distinct ethnic groups which show varying rates of mother-tongue transfer to the official languages. To some degree the concept of "other ethnic groups" arises from the Canadian census itself, which has always stressed ultimate ethnic origin over mother tongue or home language in its major tables, but the census in turn perhaps reflects an emphasis on cultural maintenance in the Canadian value structure. Overall, the population of other than French or English *mother tongue* fell from 15.7 to 13.4 percent between 1931 and 1961 while the figures for non-British, non-French *ethnic origins* rose from 19.9 to 25.8 percent in the same period.

A more detailed relationship between ethnic origin and mother tongue for the larger ethnic groups in Canada is shown in Table 4. For each ethnic group represented in column 1, one may compare the percentage of persons having the corresponding language as mother tongue (column 2) and the percentage born abroad (column 4). It will be noted that while in some groups the proportion retaining the mother tongue is very close to the proportion born abroad, for others it is considerably higher. Among Ukrainian Canadians more than half of those born in Canada retain Ukrainian as mother tongue. In column 3 are listed the *total* number of

TABLE 4

ETHNIC ORIGIN, MOTHER TONGUE, AND KNOWLEDGE OF
OFFICIAL LANGUAGES, PRINCIPAL ETHNIC GROUPS,
CANADA, 1961

Ethnic Group and Language	Ethnic Origin[a] (000s) Col. 1	% of Col. 1 Having Corresponding Mother Tongue Col. 2	Total Having Corresponding Mother Tongue as % of Col. 1 Col. 3	% of Col. 1 Born Abroad Col. 4	Official Language: % of Col. 1 Knowing Neither English nor French Col. 5
British (English)	7,996.7	98.6	133.3	14.4	0.1
French	5,540.3	89.6	92.5	1.6	0.2
German	1,049.6	39.4	53.7	27.4	1.3
Ukrainian	473.3	64.4	76.4	23.3	2.5
Italian	450.4	73.6	75.4	58.9	17.4
Dutch	429.7	37.6	39.6	36.2	1.6
Scandinavian[b]	386.5	28.8	30.2	27.1	0.2
Polish	323.5	45.5	50.0	39.9	2.5
Native Indian and Eskimo	220.1	71.4	75.6	—	19.2

SOURCE: Calculated from Census of Canada, 1961.
a. The census definition is based on the "ethnic or cultural group" to which the person himself or his male ancestor belonged on coming to North America.
b. Includes Norwegian, Danish, Swedish, Icelandic.

persons having the respective languages as mother tongues, again listed as a percentage of column 1, and these figures are higher than those in column 2 because they reflect origins listed under other categories (e.g. Austrian, Belgian, Swiss), mother tongues derived from the maternal side, and linguistic transfers to that language.

Column 5 of Table 4 concerns the knowledge of official languages: the census asks all persons whether they can speak English, French, both, or neither. In the Canadian context this question is one of the best indicators of integration. Of the total population only 1.3 percent knew neither official language in 1961, and the only large immigrant group to be substantially above that level were the Italians, who had been entering Canada in large numbers in the 1950s.

One may conclude that while some groups (including some of the smaller ones not listed here) have firm aspirations to retain their ethnic identity, culture, and language, the vast majority of members of every group have integrated to the extent of learning at least one official language. The two processes are not incompatible. The official Canadian symbol of integration is a variegated mosaic rather than a melting pot. This may be in part a conscious recognition of a society that makes fewer demands on its members than does the typical nation-state. In any case it seems likely that in any country of two major cultures it is easier for another ethnic group to find its own middle way short of full assimilation.

One problem of some significance is that the great majority of those of other origins have identified—linguistically at least—with the English-speaking community. Official-language data from the census of 1961 shows that 86 percent of those born outside Canada could speak English compared to 8 percent for both English and French and only 2 percent for French. The predominance of English among immigrants can be demonstrated even in Montreal, with its predominantly French-speaking majority. Some see this as a failure of federal immigration policy; some explain it as a form of economic opportunism that will change as language usage changes in Quebec industry. However, one study for the Royal Commission on Bilingualism showed that even French-speaking immigrants encounter obstacles to integrating in French-Canadian society, especially if they are non-Catholics (Kattan, 1965). One can conclude that the high level of immigration of other groups into Canada has not constituted a significant integration challenge in itself, but that the disproportionate identification of these immigrants with the English-speaking community has tended to intensify existing tensions in French-English relations, particularly at a time when the French-Canadian birth rate is no longer high enough to offset immigrant acculturation into the English-speaking sector.

The Indians and Eskimos of Canada are in quite a different position from all other groups. Historically most Indians retained their hunting economy and drew back into undeveloped areas as the agricultural frontier advanced, and the Eskimos lacked contact with the modern economy until very recent times. Today both groups have sharply lower levels of participation in the developed sectors of the economy. As Table 4 shows, 19 percent of the combined Indian-Eskimo total knew neither English nor French in 1961, the highest proportion of any major ethnic group. Although the total numbers involved are relatively small—just over 1 percent of the total population in 1961—there is an integration issue here that has yet to be solved. A federal policy paper issued in June 1969 proposed the ending of reserve rights and speedier integration of Indians into wider Canadian society (*Statement,* 1969), but it has been almost unanimously rejected by Indian groups. Any generally acceptable integrative solution appears to be many years away, but because of the numbers involved, this question—complex as it may be in terms of human rights—has been one of the marginal issues of state formation in Canada.

CONCLUSION

How should one summarize Canadian experience in state formation and nation-building in a general and comparative perspective? One must note at the start the relative scarcity of Canadian studies specifically addressed to this question, which is perhaps significant in itself. Though there is much historical material on various aspects of Canadian development, most of it is not oriented in a theoretical direction. Since the empirical ground work to date is rather sketchy, any explicit formulations or revisions of theory therefore seem rather premature, and it is perhaps better simply to call attention to those aspects of Canadian experience which merit further attention from the standpoint of theory formation. The more important of these might be summarized as follows:

1. Canadian society is the product of European expansionism, and the precolonial history of Europe—particularly France and the British Isles—is in some senses the history of Canada as well. Unlike Latin America, interaction with the indigenous peoples has been of slight significance until very recent times.

2. Canada has faced no decisive challenge or break with tradition such as the American revolution and hence nation-building has been slow, gradual, and often indecisive to the point that the completion of certain stages (e.g. withdrawal of imperial military forces, completion of legal autonomy) can be dated only in approximate terms. There has been no crisis of identity, but certain continuing ambiguities. Unlike Latin America, most Canadians acknowledge and accept their colonial past, and they find no significant psychological barriers to building upon it. Much the same may be said, *mutatis mutandis*, for the other settlement-states of the British Commonwealth. Australia and New Zealand, however, faced no conflict between state and geography, nor any significant linguistic cleavage, but had more trouble in outgrowing the imperial tie.

3. Social mobilization has always been relatively high compared even with European societies. This may be related to the prior mobilization involved in immigration and settlement, and also to continuing economic links between Europe and its North American periphery.

4. Economic development begins early and is continuous. The market economy precedes settlement and remains characteristic of all the frontiers of settlement, whether in mining, forestry, fisheries, or agriculture. Exports and imports account for a proportion of national product far above the average.

5. Political development came early; some aspects were part of the original settler heritage. Major institutions such as legislative assemblies, a

wide franchise, political parties, and ministerial responsibility all precede political unification (confederation). Most provinces developed a strong base for aggregating regional interests before confederation, and this base was never surrendered despite later centralizing pressures.

6. The concepts of centre and periphery are rather ambiguous in the Canadian setting. The Ontario-Quebec industrial complex is to some degree a territorial centre, but it faces strong counterforces both above (continentalism) and below (regionalism) the level of the Canadian polity. Further, the "centre" is divided geographically (Montreal, Toronto, Ottawa), functionally (administrative, economic-financial, cultural), and also in terms of language and religion. Excessive centralism has frequently evoked strong regional reactions, and some federal ministries have had their power base disproportionally in the electorate of the periphery. In wider perspective, however, this shapelessness of the centre is no doubt to be expected in most federal states, in some plurilingual states, and in some religiously heterogeneous states. Canada reveals all these lines of cleavage, and hence the centre is weak.

7. Political unification and administrative consolidation in 1867 were followed by economic measures for nation-building, most notably trans-continental railways, removal of interprovincial trade barriers, uniform tariffs, and protection of domestic secondary industry. These measures in turn were a response to the loss of American markets and decreased continentalism after 1866. Nevertheless economic centre-building has also faced strong counter forces, including high levels of international trade (particularly with the United States) and North-South travel patterns. Canada's principal capital market was London, until the latter was displaced by New York.

8. Given the levels of religious and linguistic cleavage in Canada, the potential for conflict has always been high and has become higher with urbanization, mobility, and industrialism. The model of consociational democracy is appropriate here, and indeed some elements of consociation-alism may be indentified in federal political institutions and processes. Perhaps the most obvious manifestation of this was the elitist nature of the confederation settlement and various later regional, religious, and linguistic adjustments. However, in practice the consociational model has been less than fully realized, the problem being that religious or linguistic compromises attempted at the federal level cannot always be implemented at the mass level, and this in turn undermines confidence in the federal elites. On current linguistic issues (as on past religious ones) English Canadians have been too deeply imbued with a belief in majority rule and French Canadians have turned away from their federal leadership in favor

of a stronger majoritarian position in Quebec. It is worth noting, however, that when consociational approaches fail at the federal level, there is a safety value in a revitalized provincial autonomy and federal restraint.

9. A partial explanation for the depth of religious and cultural cleavage in Canada may be found in certain cross-national comparisons of the structure of cleavages. Tentatively, we may estimate that religious, linguistic, and regional cleavages in Canada overlap and reinforce each other more than in Switzerland. Religious cleavage seems to coincide with linguistic cleavage more than in Belgium (where religious cleavage is between levels of commitment to Catholicism). Ideological (conservative-liberal-socialist) cleavage seems less important absolutely in Canada than in Belgium or Switzerland, where it is both strong and cross-cutting. Hence in Canada the mutually reinforcing religious-linguistic cleavage is offset by no other cleavage of comparable strength. The cumulation of major cleavages may be seen partly as a consequence of Canada's historical evolution as two Hartzian "fragments" of Europe, each established and developed through its crucial early stages independently of the other.

10. By almost any criterion, the process of nation-building understood in terms of developing allegiance to the federal polity has always been at relatively low levels in Canada, and has always faced strong counter-tendencies both inside and beyond the Canadian state. In the face of strong competing claims that have become deeply engrained in the political culture, the Canadian political system makes perhaps fewer demands of allegiance from its citizens than any other Western society. The result has been an advanced level of "stateness" combined with a relatively low level of "nationness." One may well raise questions about vulnerability, capacity to respond to crises, and prospects of long-run survival; nevertheless, the Canadian political system has so far demonstrated considerable stability, perhaps more than if the nation-building pressures had been stronger. But whether this stability owes more to an absence of serious challenge or crisis, or rather to some intricate equilibrium or balancing of the various cross-pressures opposed to nation-building, requires a more extensive analysis of both Canadian and comparative data, and possibly in addition a more advanced theoretical understanding of the complex relationship between state-building and nation-building.

REFERENCES

Bell, D. V. J., "The Loyalist Tradition in Canada," Journal of Canadian Studies, Vol. 5, May 1970, pp. 22-33.

Berger, C., The Sense of Power: Studies in the Ideas of Canadian Imperialism, 1867-1914, Toronto, University of Toronto Press, 1970.

Berton, P., The Great Railway. Vol. I. 1871-1881: The National Dream; Vol. II. 1881-1885: The Last Spike; Toronto and Montreal, McClelland & Stewart, 1970; 1971.

Brebner, J. B., North Atlantic Triangle: The Interplay of Canada, the United States and Great Britain, New Haven, Yale University Press; Toronto, Ryerson Press; London, Oxford University Press; 1945.

Coats, R. H. and M. C. Maclean, The American-Born in Canada: A Statistical Interpretation, Toronto, Ryerson Press; New Haven, Yale University Press; 1943.

Commonwealth in Brief, The, London, Central Office of Information, 1970.

Courtney, J. C., ed., Voting in Canada, Scarborough, Prentice-Hall of Canada, 1967.

Gibson, F. W., ed., Cabinet Formation and Bicultural Relations, Studies of the Royal Commission on Bilingualism and Biculturalism 6, Ottawa, Queen's Printer, 1970.

Hansen, M. L., The Mingling of the Canadian and American Peoples, New Haven, Yale University Press; Toronto, Ryerson Press; London, Oxford University Press; 1940.

Hartz, L. et al., The Founding of New Societies, New York, Harcourt, Brace & World, 1964.

Horowitz, G., "Conservatism, Liberalism and Socialism in Canada: An Interpretation," Canadian Journal of Economics and Political Science, Vol. 32, 1966, pp. 143-71.

Hughes, E. C., French Canada in Transition, Chicago, University of Chicago Press, 1943.

Johnstone, J. C., Young People's Images of Canadian Society, Studies of the Royal Commission on Bilingualism and Biculturalism 2, Ottawa, Queen's Printer, 1969.

Kattan, N., "L'Immigrant de Langue Francaise et Son Integration a la Vie Canadienne," study prepared for the Royal Commission on Bilingualism and Biculturalism, Montreal, 1965. (mimeo)

Martin, C. B., Empire and Commonwealth, Oxford, Clarendon Press, 1929.

Nicholson, N. L., The Boundaries of Canada, Its Provinces and Territories, Ottawa, Queen's Printer, 1954.

Porter, J., The Vertical Mosaic, Toronto, University of Toronto Press, 1965.

Raynauld, A., G. Marion, and R. Beland, "La Repartition des Revenus selon les Groupes Ethniques au Canada," study prepared for the Royal Commission on Bilingualism and Biculturalism, Ottawa, 1966. (mimeo, 4 vols.)

Royal Commission on Bilingualism and Biculturalism, Preliminary Report, Book I, The Official Languages, Ottawa, Queen's Printer, 1967.

———, Preliminary Report, Book II, Education, Ottawa, Queen's Printer, 1968.

———, Preliminary Report, Book III, The Work World, 2 vols., Ottawa, Queen's Printer, 1969.

———, Preliminary Report, Book IV, The Cultural Contribution of the Other Ethnic Groups, Ottawa, Queen's Printer, 1970.

———, Preliminary Report, Book V, The Federal Capital, Ottawa, Queen's Printer, 1970.

———, Preliminary Report, Book VI, Voluntary Associations, Ottawa, Queen's Printer, 1970.

Schwartz, M. A., Public Opinion and Canadian Identity, Berkeley and Los Angeles, University of California Press, 1967.

Social Research Group, "A Study of Interethnic Relations in Canada," study prepared for the Royal Commission on Bilingualism and Biculturalism, Montreal, 1965. (mimeo, 6 vols.)

Statement of the Government of Canada on Indian Policy, Ottawa, 1969.

Truesdell, L. E., The Canadian-Born in the United States, New Haven, Yale University Press; Toronto, Ryerson Press; London, Oxford University Press; 1943.

Van Loon, R. J., "The Structure and Membership of the Canadian Cabinet," study prepared for the Royal Commission on Bilingualism and Biculturalism, Ottawa, 1966. (mimeo)

CHAPTER 5

NEW STATES IN THE CARIBBEAN:
A GROUNDED THEORETICAL ACCOUNT

Wendell Bell

WENDELL BELL is Professor of Sociology at Yale University, serving as chairman from 1965 to 1969, and is Director of the Comparative Sociology Training Program. His research has been in the fields of urban sociology, social change, and political sociology. He has authored or edited *Social Area Analysis, Public Leadership, Decisions of Nationhood, Jamaican Leaders, The Democratic Revolution in the West Indies, The Sociology of the Future,* and *Ethnicity and Nation-Building.*

The purpose of this chapter is to summarize a theory of nation-founding and nation-building grounded on a decade of research by myself and my associates in the new states of the Caribbean. My field work in the Caribbean began in the summer of 1956 with an exploratory trip to Jamaica that lasted three months. Data collection began in earnest on a second field trip during the spring and summer of 1958 with the bulk of specific studies being completed during a third period of field work in 1961-1962. Active interest and minor data collections, along with analyses of previous data and writing of research reports, continued through 1966. One of our number, Ivar Oxaal, has sustained his research activities in the area until the present, his most recent writing being a documentary interpretation of the 1970 Black Power revolt in Trinidad.[1]

The period of data collection and writing for our studies occurred during the time that the territories under study were in transition from politically dependent colony to politically independent nation-state, although the outcome of that process for some has been stalled and for others did not turn out as expected. With the formation of the West Indies Federation in 1958 it looked as if the British territories of the Caribbean—or most of them since British Guiana (now Guyana), British Honduras, and the British Virgin Islands were excluded—faced the transition together to compose a single state made up of the islands of Antigua, Barbados, Dominica, Grenada, Jamaica, Montserrat, St. Kitts-Nevis-Anguilla, St. Lucia, St. Vincent, and Trinidad. But such was not to be the case. A referendum in Jamaica in September 1961 resulted in the withdrawal of the largest island in favor of "going it alone." Dr. Eric Williams, prime minister of Trinidad, figured that ten minus one equaled zero, and the Federation collapsed, leaving, in addition to Guyana (which became politically independent on May 25, 1966), the new states of Jamaica (August 6, 1962), Trinidad and Tobago (August 31, 1962), Barbados (November 30, 1966), and the leftover "orphans" of the other islands in a "half-way house" of suspended development, still more or less dependent on Great Britain.

In this chapter, I focus on this period of political and social change in the life of the English-speaking Caribbean. My purpose is not to give a narrative account of events but rather to give a theoretical account using concepts that can be applied to the rise of nation-states at other times and places, concepts that at the same time are valid representations of the particularities of the West Indian case. Different levels of theory will be used. At the most abstract level, some notion of the movement of history, of long-term trends, even of evolutionary processes are relevant and useful, although they may usually remain beyond the horizon of consciousness of many historical participants. Lack of space precludes more than a brief description of general theory here, but there seem to be important connections between this general notion of the direction of long-term change and the less abstract levels of theory that will be used. The latter we have called the "cybernetic-decisional theory of social change," and, within the specific context of nation-forming and nation-building, we have formulated, rather concretely, the "decisions of nationhood." After a summary description of the West Indian setting and, then, a brief discussion of theory, I will discuss the new states of the Caribbean as illustrative of the decisions required of nationhood. Our conceptualizing and theorizing at every level, however, resulted from our efforts to understand the transition to nationhood in the twentieth-century Caribbean and, therefore, are grounded in particular data experiences.

THE WEST INDIAN SETTING[2]

The Caribbean Sea stretches for about one thousand five hundred miles between Cuba on the north and Panama on the south and varies in width from four hundred to seven hundred miles. The islands that bound it on the north and east were—and most still are—dominated by European powers and, more recently, by the United States. Although geographically close (for example, Jamaica is ninety miles from Cuba at the nearest point), they are separated today in part because they are socially and culturally distant. The language barrier is itself a considerable problem to any effort to create unity. Spanish, English, French, Dutch, and a variety of local dialects of Creole languages are scattered throughout the area.

There is also a dizzying variety of political forms. The republic of Haiti was founded in 1804 and after nearly two centuries of independence remains traditionally despotic and economically stagnant. Independent Cuba has fidelista communism intent on transforming what remains of the colonial past into a socialist future. In the presumably independent Dominican Republic, there is corrupt politics on the one hand and the withdrawal from the electoral process of the largest mass party on the other; there is also the oligarchic dominance of church, business, and military as well as the illegitimate influence of the United States that intervened in the civil war of 1965. The tiny American Virgin Islands are partially self-governing colonies of the United States, and so is Puerto Rico, although with a more exalted commonwealth status and a variety of economic benefits largely derived from open migration and free trade with the United States. The islands of the Netherlands Antilles and Surinam constitute a federative state to some extent integrated with the Netherlands and to some extent still separate and dependent. In a seemingly progressive act the full consequences of which are yet to be seen, the French Antilles and French Guiana in 1946 were incorporated as overseas departments into the structure of metropolitan France with their people achieving full political equality of citizenship. And in the 1960s, four parts of the English-speaking Caribbean added to this political diversity by becoming independent nation-states—the first new states in the western hemisphere since Panama in 1903—as part of the same post-World War II breakdown of the colonial empires that saw the creation of so many new states in Asia and Africa.[3]

The history of the Caribbean in an important sense began at the end of the fifteenth and beginning of the sixteenth centuries with "discovery" by Europeans and colonization by immigrants that were to shape future Caribbean societies and cultures. The history of the Caribbean includes sea battles of European navies, European adventurers seeking their fortunes to spend in Europe, torture and pain for mistreated Indians, ships and trade, derringdo of buccaneers, production of sugar and rum, rich plantations and absentee owners, wealth that financed the industrial revolution in Europe, exploitation of indentured servants and Negro slaves, imperial rape of the colonies, and sexual mixing of many races of people.

The Europeans came, the Amerindians were practically exterminated, and by 1502 the first African slaves arrived in the Caribbean, beginning a flow of forced migration and servitude that was to last for more than three centuries. Following emancipation, a new source of labor was found in persons indentured from India. The ironies of history have left us with a number of different types of "Indies" and "Indians" which may be confusing to the uninitiated. In the former British West Indies, all of the present-day inhabitants may be referred to as "West Indians," although the particular island identities are also widely used, e.g. "Jamaicans" or "Trinidadians." The original inhabitants, the Amerindians, have been wiped out, except in Guyana where a considerable number still exist, especially in the interior. The vast majority of today's West Indians, then, are the descendents of African slaves or indentured laborers brought from India, both Hindus and Moslems. The latter, called "*East* Indians" (although they are also *West* Indians) were brought chiefly to Guyana and Trinidad; in Guyana they outnumber the Negroes and in Trinidad they constitute over one-third of the population.

The West Indies constitute a cultural and racial mosaic of various types and mixtures, including, in addition to Africans and East Indians, descendants of English, Irish, Welsh, Scottish, French, Portuguese, German, Chinese, Lebanese, and Syrian immigrants. Trinidad, for example, the most polyglot island of the former British Caribbean is the home of a dialect which has been described as "Spanish in origin, French by tradition, English by adoption, and not without traces of the languages of India, Pakistan, China, Syria, and Palestine" (Moosai-Maharaj, 1957, p. 79). The population and approximate racial composition of the West Indian territories during the 1960s are given in Table 1.

The class structure of the area—in oversimplified terms—consists of a small white or near-white upper class, a mostly brown-skinned middle class, and predominantly dark-brown or black lower class (Smith, 1965). These designations, however, no longer show the same high degree of correlation between color and status as has held in the past. Brown and black men are today found in large numbers as leading professionals, politicians, labor leaders, educators, clergymen, and civil servants. Aside from East Indians, however, they are heavily underrepresented in

TABLE 1

POPULATION AND APPROXIMATE PERCENTAGES OF PERSONS IN DIFFERENT RACIAL GROUPS IN THE BRITISH WEST INDIES BY TERRITORY

Territory	Population (1964 estimates) (in 000s)	Racial Composition in Percentages (based on 1960 census)					
		White	Colored	Black	East Indian	Chinese	Amerindian
Jamaica	1,730	1	15	80	3	1	—
Trinidad and Tobago	947	2	16	44	37	1	—
Guyana	,630	2	11	32	49	1	5
Barbados	242	4	6	90	—	—	—
British Honduras	103	a					
Windward Islands:	336	1	26	70	3	—	—
Dominica	64						
Grenada	93						
St. Lucia	94						
St. Vincent	85						
Leeward Islands:	141	1	5	94	—	—	—
Antigua	60						
Montserrat	13						
St. Kitts-Nevis-Anguilla	59						
Virgin Islands (British)	9	a					
Total British West Indies	4,130	2	14	64	18	1	1

SOURCE: From Moskos (1967, pp. 8-9).
a. Racial composition for British Honduras and the British Virgin Islands is not given.

management of business firms where the lighter-skinned minorities still prevail. Thus, the classic West Indian color-status pattern is to be found most pronounced in the economic sphere, particularly in the commercial community, where family capitalism remains an important mode of organization. This tendency toward ethnically based polarization of political and economic power has not, however, resulted in a chronic pattern of critical conflict between light and darker-skinned elites.

Although many nonwhite politicians identify themselves as "socialists" and lead parties based on organized labor, they have generally adhered to a conception of economic development which stresses the need for partnership and cooperation between government and business, and between the latter and organized labor. A recent major exception is Guyana where the bauxite industry was nationalized.

There has been a definite trend toward increasing equality in many spheres with the transition to independence, as we shall see; but widespread inequalities in employment, income, wealth, property, educational opportunity, and levels of living remain. And, although brown and black persons can be found in the upper levels of the stratification iceberg among the white elite minorities, and although they dominate the political roles, below the surface the masses are largely black. Perhaps as many as a hundred thousand, for example, are submerged in shantytowns in Western Kingston, Jamaica.

The West Indian economy, today as always, is largely dependent on agricultural production for the world market, with all the vulnerability to fluctuation and chronic uncertainty that this entails. The major export crop remains sugar although such tropical specialities as bananas, coconuts, spices, and citrus fruits are also marketed abroad. The major extractive industries are bauxite in Jamaica and Guyana and petroleum in Trinidad. Some small-scale manufacturing is conducted locally—notably in Jamaica and Trinidad—and tourism has become an important source of income for some of the islands—especially Jamaica and Barbados. There has been some success in Jamaica and Trinidad toward economic development and the raising of per capita income but, despite the general modernity of the area compared to some underdeveloped countries, the West Indies are poor and suffer from high rates of under- and unemployment, widespread poverty and growing populations, low per-capita productivity, often poorly utilized land, illiteracy, and inadequate educational facilities. The revolution of rising expectations is so much an accomplished fact in the West Indies that, between 1955 and 1960, Jamaica alone sent over a hundred thousand migrants to the United Kingdom—an exodus curtailed by the 1962 Commonwealth Immigration Act (Davison, 1962).

The modern political history of the British West Indies began in the late 1930s when outbreaks of poverty-induced strikes and riots spread throughout most of the area. The economic discontent of the West Indian people was given voice by new labor leaders and nationalist politicians and led to a series of constitutional advances which got underway in the mid-1940s. The old Crown Colony system gave way to modified ministerial forms of government, and by the early 1950s all of the colonies had achieved universal adult suffrage and were being primed for self-government. These measures were aimed ultimately at bringing all of the British territories in the area into a federation, which would be the vehicle intended to take them collectively on to dominion status. This, at any rate, was the expressed wish of both British colonial authorities and leading West Indian politicians at the Montego Bay conference of 1947. As we have seen, the federal plan was fated for failure.

THEORETICAL ORIENTATION

The Equality Revolution

My thesis is that the nationalist revolution of our time—of which the new states of the Caribbean are part—is a manifestation of a long-term trend toward equality; that there is another more basic revolution, an equality revolution which in some important sense, is a cause of twentieth-century nationalist movements that have resulted in over sixty new states since World War II. Political independence has been primarily a means to achieve equality of citizenship with people of other nations of the world; to replace the vulgar degradation of "subject" and the subtle defamation of "native"; and to achieve distributional reforms, social justice, and more equal rights for people within the new states as well. The nationalist movements generally were led, joined, and fought for by people who believed in progress, in rationality and the use of reason in the conduct of human affairs, and in human control of the future. They believed that people can learn, can be taught, can improve. And they believed in liberty and fraternity, but most of all in equality. People who opposed the movements had contrary beliefs and values.

Since such beliefs and values form part of the thinking of the philosophes of the eighteenth-century Enlightenment, this thesis clearly needs elaboration. The nationalist revolution of our time is not only *an* equality revolution, it is also a direct continuation of *the* democratic revolution of eighteenth-century Western Europe and North America. The historian R. R. Palmer (1959, 1964) among others, documents the view that "what happened in the world of Western Civilization in the forty years from 1760 to 1800" should be seen

> as a single movement, revolutionary in character, for which the word "democratic" is appropriate and enlightening; a movement which, however different in different countries, was everywhere aimed against closed elites, self-selecting power groups, hereditary castes, and forms of special advantage or discrimination that no longer served any useful purpose (Palmer, 1964, p. 572).

Palmer uses the term "democratic" to refer to this movement because it was the last decade of the eighteenth century "that brought the word out of the study and into actual politics" (Palmer, 1959, p. 20). He points out that then the words "liberal," "radical," and "progressive" did not exist, and that when "moderates or conservatives wished to indicate the dangerous drift of the times, or when the more advanced spirits spoke of themselves, they might very well use the words 'democrat' or 'democracy' " (Palmer, 1959, pp. 13-14).

The word "revolution" he uses because the movement posed a conflict between incompatible images of the future, between opposing views of what the community ought to be and what it was, because it included serious political protest, and because it involved a series of rapid changes that resulted in the reconstitution of government and society. Violence and destruction need not necessarily accompany a movement or situation for it to be called a "revolution," although, of course, brute force, civil war, and a reign of terror sometimes dominate the scene.

Palmer restricts his discussion to what is now called the Atlantic community, Europe and America (mostly Anglo-America) of the last forty years of the eighteenth century. At the end of his final volume, however, he suggests a wider application to all revolutions since 1800 in Europe, Latin America, Asia, and Africa. In the laboratories of the new states, one may find the evidence to verify this view. How much of the political, economic, and social change going on throughout the world in the last half of the twentieth century can be understood as a continuation of the democratic revolution—especially as an extension of the drive toward equality—to which Europe and America of the latter part of the eighteenth century gave birth as a realizable human aspiration?

I choose to call the revolution an "equality" revolution rather than a "democratic" revolution for several resons. First, equality was a key value in the movement from the very beginning. Palmer, for example, refers to the ubiquity of the concept of equality in a variety of different situations:

> It could mean an equality between colonials and residents of a mother country, as in America; between nobles and commoners, as in France; patricians and burghers, as at Geneva; ruling townsmen and subject country people, as at Zurich and elsewhere; between Catholic and Protestant, Anglican and Dissenter, Christian and Jew, religionist and unbeliever, or between Greek and Turk. . . . It might refer to the equal right of guildsmen and outsiders to enter upon a particular kind of trade or manufacture. For some few it included greater equality between men and women. Equality for ex-slaves and between races was not overlooked. For popular democrats, like the Paris sans-culottes, it meant the hope for a more adequate livelihood, more schooling and education, the right to stroll on the boulevards with the upper classes, and for more recognition and more respect; and it passed on to the extreme claim for an exact equality of material circumstances, which was rarely in fact made during the Revolutionary era, but was feared as an ultimate consequence of it by conservatives, and expressed in Babeuf's blunt formula, "stomachs are equal" (Palmer, 1964, p. 573).

Second, if "democratic" is interpreted in the sense of parliamentary politics and public liberties, then clearly some new nationalist regimes, while maintaining their efforts to create more equality in other spheres, have become undemocratic. Thus, "equality" seems more accurate than "democratic" to describe the revolution that is taking place.

And third, a related reason is the split between various ideologists of different camps of the Left, especially the broad one between the Marxist and the non-Marxist, which in many of the new states has tended to take the form of a difference between those committed to Western democratic forms and those favoring authoritarian and coercive "people's democracies." Yet both remain—to the extent to which they are Left groups—committed to important aspects of the ideal of equality, and both design governmental action that is justified in its name and oriented toward its achievement.

The meaning of equality, of course, has been elaborated in the last two hundred years. The concept itself has been broadened as has both the range of institutional settings to which it applied and the scope of its application to different sections of the population. In the first instance, the meaning was largely restricted operationally to the civil and political community, referring to such things as equality before the law or equal rights to vote; then it was gradually expanded to include nearly all spheres of human organization: the economic, the social, and the cultural. Thus, among other things, the right to work; to adequate food, clothing, and housing; to free choice of a marriage partner; to rest and leisure; to equal access to educational opportunity, and to take part in the cultural life of the nation were added to the original conception.

In the second instance, the groups to which the current concept of equality applies have been enlarged. At first, there were restrictions on who was considered a full-fledged citizen, restrictions of property, religion, race, or social class. In the United States, for example, despite Thomas Jefferson's declaration "that all men are created equal," it was understood that Negro slaves, American Indians, women, children, and men without sufficient property were not to be included. Today, however, it is increasingly agreed that the doctrines of equality should apply to all people regardless of class, race, color, creed, sex, age, intelligence, attitudes, knowledge, length of hair, shortness of skirt, or state of cleanliness. These two facts permit us to define a trend over the last two hundred years: there have been rising minimums of civil, political, economic, social, and cultural rights—especially as they have defined the status of the lower social classes and subordinate ethnic and racial groups—that have been equally applied to larger and larger percentages of the world's population.

The rise of the new states was an important recent stage in this trend. As the empires crumbled and the proconsuls packed their bags, the political hegemony of privileged, foreign elites ruling over a mass of people who were denied full inclusion into the society of their own countries was broken. In their place, came the new states where society was generally redefined to include all—or nearly all—the people who were to constitute the new national citizenries.

Such a redefinition of society places the equality revolution squarely within the trend toward the increase in the scale of society. Despite discontinuous interruptions, temporary reactions and setbacks, it seems clear that there has been a global trend toward increases in the range of social relations, in the scope of social interaction and interdependency. The breakdown of empires, though a reduction of political scale from one point of view, nonetheless ushered in an age of increased scale by bringing many of the people of earth into a national political community for the first time as equal citizens, thereby breaking down the barriers both of communal groups and imperial caste. Both domestic and international dialogues became wider in scale and more intense than before, as the new national communities formed.

It is not presumed that the trend toward equality and increasing scale occur automatically as cosmic principles or mystical determinants. Rather, it is assumed that, as is obviously the case, there is considerable conflict and repeated struggles. But at least since the eighteenth-century Enlightenment, there has been spreading from the Europe and North America of two hundred years ago an interrelated set of values with equality at the core that has now reached global dimensions. These values, among others, one assumes further, have evolutionary implications that derive from the survival, health, and dignity of humankind and from the fact that the advantages of group living at the highest levels of cooperative organization far outweigh the advantages of solitary living or of levels of organization of lesser scope.

Yet it is only the choices and decisions of human beings, and most directly the action that results from them, that create social trends and shape the future. Thus, if there is an equality revolution and if it is to continue, one must further assume that human consciousness—or some humans' consciousness—has become aware of the advantages of larger scale and has learned to value those things that contribute toward human welfare and dignity. The values and images of the future they hold and the actions they base on them function as a kind of feedback control system directing the course of change. The evolution of human organization is the result of the intervention of humankind, just as nationalist leaders intervened to found and create the new states.[4]

Images of the Future

Elsewhere, James A. Mau and I (Bell and Mau, 1971) have formulated a cybernetic-decisional theory of social change. Our immediate purpose was to state a general theory that would be isomorphic with our research results from the West Indies. The theory involves the reciprocal effects of social structures on behavior and, in turn, behavior on social structures, and is designed to explain the creation, restructuring, and destructuring of social organizations, institutions, and social systems. It is based upon individuals' beliefs about the past, beliefs about the present, and beliefs about causes and effects, since such beliefs importantly orient individuals' actions. It importantly includes values, the decision-making process, and individual and collective action as determinants of the shape of social systems. Most centrally, it focuses on images of the future. Such images are expectations about the state of things to come at some future time, a range of differentially probable possibilities for the future that people act to bring about, to prevent, to adapt to, or, in some cases, simply to accept fatalistically. Images of the future may vary in a variety of ways, such as the amount of information on which they are based or how they are evaluated (as desirable or undesirable). But they can be usefully viewed as a steering mechanism that guides particular individuals, groups, and entire societies along certain courses of development and toward certain presumed end-states rather than others.

Wherever time is split in the awareness of human beings, images of a future state of affairs can be created that differ from the past and the present. Then, the routines of interdependency can be broken, blind repetition ended. Goal-seeking, problem-solving, utopia-constructing humans can transcend the limits of structural determinism (and B. F. Skinner's box) into the world of plans, goal setting, value creating, institution building, and nation founding. The fan of alternative futures can become known and the most desirable future selected by self-actualizing and semiautonomous humans.

The cybernetic-decisional theory of social change can be invoked to understand a wide range of behavior and structural change and can be applied to a variety of units of analysis, such as an individual deciding on an occupational career, a family buying a new house, a university changing its admission policies, or a city planning its zoning regulations. It was devoloped, however, out of an analysis of the decisions of nationhood in the West Indies, and our reasoning can be most easily explained in that context.

DECISIONS OF NATIONHOOD

Should We Become Politically Independent?

Among the first questions that must be raised by any people destined by their own actions to create a new state is whether or not to strive for the formation of a politically independent state. The terms of framing the question and the possible answers are, of course, shaped by the definition of the nature of the state. What it means to be a state is in part arbitrary, yet it is also an understandable product of a particular set of historical circumstances and events. The appeal of nationhood for the former colonies is, perhaps, a final obeisance to the imperial masters, since it is an image of the future derived most directly from European roots. Nonetheless, as we shall see, for the most part it was an act of liberation.

In the West Indies, as in other places, there was considerable disagreement over the question of independence. For example, Moskos (1967) interviewed one hundred twelve top leaders in Jamaica, Trinidad, Guyana, Barbados, Grenada, and Dominica during the end of 1961 and the beginning of 1962 and found only 39 percent whom he could classify as true nationalists. These were persons who favored political independence, who wanted it at once, and who had actually engaged in some action to help bring it about, such as helping to organize nationalist parties, giving speeches, or writing articles and pamphlets. Conversely, nearly as many West Indian leaders, 36 percent, were colonialists, people who completely opposed independence and wanted to maintain the colonial system indefinitely. At the time of the interviews, the colonialists had pretty much given up trying to change the course of events since the British government was supporting the transition and since most of the territories were well on the road to self-government. Yet on the eve of independence, over a third of West Indian elites opposed the political changes then taking place and rejected the image of a future independent West Indies.

The remaining 25 percent Moskos classified as acquiescing nationalists. These were reluctant leaders (11 percent) who said that they favored independence but didn't want it so soon; dutiful leaders (5 percent) who privately opposed independence but felt, with an air of noblesse oblige or enlightened self-interest, that they should publicly favor it because it was the will of the people and that their skills were needed to help make it work now that it was coming; and opportunistic leaders (9 percent) who privately opposed independence but engaged in proindependence activity. The latter were either long-time political leaders who had to match the activities of the militant nationalists to stay in office, or businessmen who gave financial support to nationalist parties to protect their interests in the future.

Leaders having different attitudes toward political independence, of course, were differentiated by a number of social correlates: compared to colonialists, the true nationalists were more likely to be younger; to have a provincial middle-class, West Indian variant of European life-styles; to be divided between only grammar school or university educations; to be dark-brown or black in skin color, including some East Indians particularly in Guyana; to be relatively not wealthy; and to be leaders of mass-based organizations such as trade unions and political parties.

Conversely, compared to true nationalists, colonialists were more likely to be older, well-off economically, planters and merchants, white and near white in skin color, Anglo-European in life-style, and secondary-school educated rather than having more or less education. Acquiescing nationalists generally held intermediate positions. Although there were exceptions, support of the colonial system was most likely to come form the traditionally dominant groups while support for the nationalist movements was most likely to come from leaders whose characteristics were more like those of the general population, leaders who led mass-based organizations, or who were intellectuals.

A full understanding of the rise of the new nationalist movements must take into account more variables and more historical events than we have been able to do in our studies. The objectives of the British government, for instance, that led to relaxation of the British hold on the reins of empire and in many cases to a cooperative transition to self-government for some former colonies, may not be fully understood until archives are opened. Nor can we take into account in any exact way the effect of World War II on colonial peoples, yet it must have changed the world views of many of them and altered their conceptions of the possibilities for the future. What we have tried to explain is who led nationalist movements and why they did so, who opposed them and why, and the context of social values and images of the future that helped shape the important decisions of nationhood during the transition to independence.

The cause of nationalist attitudes is in part a configuration, the coming together of several things. Most important is the structure of inequality on the one hand and the ideology of equality on the other. A past of oppression; invidious distinctions; and systematic status differences, institutionalized by the colonial situation, clashes in the present with an image of a better, more egalitarian future. The economic exploitation of the masses was perhaps the most glaring aspect of inequality in the West Indies, but the brown middle and educated classes were also subject to a variety of discriminatory practices, from job ceilings and income differentials to exclusion from social clubs, in relation to the white ruling groups.

The image of a better future was largely defined by the values of the eighteenth-century Enlightenment as they had evolved to be applicable to modern times, especially the rights of man: liberty, equality, and fraternity. Young West Indian intellectuals educated abroad became the carriers of ideas that negated the colonial stratification system. For those who didn't travel the ideas were imported, for example by Left book clubs and earlier by European missionaries. And some of the white imperial rulers brought them too, since such ideas were, after all, part of their own professed values in another context. The leaders of nationalist movements, giving rise to the inchoate economic discontent of the masses and their own experiences of the injustices of inequality, set as their primary goal the restructuting of society along more democratic, egalitarian, and socially inclusive lines. The historical circumstances of colonial status determined the means: past and present inequalities were viewed as resulting from colonialism and the apparatus of government was viewed as the instrument for transforming their societies. Thus, colonialism had to go; they had to take the reins of government into their own hands. Then, they intended to increase the scope of government. With the control of their own government of expanding size they would achieve the power to make the changes necessary to create a future egalitarian society.

Considerable evidence from our various studies supports this view. To give just one example, Table 2 shows attitudes toward independence by an Index of Enlightenment. The latter is composed of attitudes toward equality of opportunity, attitudes toward democracy (defined as favorable

TABLE 2

NATIONALIST TYPES BY AN INDEX OF ENLIGHTENMENT
(in percentages)

	West Indian Leaders Who Were:				
Index of Enlightenment[a]	Colonialists	Acquiescing Nationalists	True Nationalists	Total	Number of Cases
High 3 (enlightened)	0	0	100	100	(29)
2	0	22	78	100	(18)
1	25	71	4	100	(24)
Low 0 (unenlightened)	83	17	0	100	(41)

SOURCE: From Moskos (1967, p. 57).
a. Based on attitudes toward equality, political democracy, and reducing social barriers within the local society.

attitudes toward a parliamentary system and the maintenance of public liberties), and attitudes toward social inclusivism (defined as favorable attitudes toward reducing social barriers within the local society rather than for increasing social contact abroad). Egalitarians, democrats, and inclusivists were considered "enlightened" in the sense that these three notions are part of Enlightenment thought. Responses were scored 0 or 1 on each of the three measures, thus a score of 3 is most enlightened and shows that those respondents favored equality, democracy, and inclusivism (or fraternity), and a score of 0 is most unenlightened and shows that those respondents rejected each of the three values.

From Table 2, note that the correlation between enlightenment as defined by the rights of man and attitudes toward independence is very high. One hundred percent of the most enlightened leaders were true nationalists, and 78 percent of the next most enlightened leaders were true nationalists. Contrariwise, 83 percent of the most unenlightened leaders were colonialists, and none of them were true nationalists.

Since some reviewers of our work have accused us of being overly optimistic, I should point out a disheartening fact: the number of unenlightened leaders (scores 0 and 1) outnumbered the number of enlightened leaders (scores 2 and 3), by 65 to 47 in Moskos' sample. Such a finding or related findings are repeated over and over again in our data. For example, in my questionnaire study of 238 Jamaican leaders in 1958, half of the respondents were clearly undemocratic in their cynical attitudes concerning political democracy. Furthermore, although enlightened attitudes motivated the drive to independence on the part of some local elites, one must point out that "the equalitarian and democratic promise of West Indian nationalism may not be fulfilled" (Bell, 1964, p. 173). There are two reasons. First, the considerable number of inegalitarians, authoritarians, and exclusivists may succeed in sabotaging the efforts to achieve an egalitarian future. Second, one wonders if the true nationalists themselves can remain true to their goals and whether they have the competence, will, and courage to carry out the rather radical changes that are necessary to make the future an egalitarian one. It is, perhaps, too early to tell, but subsequent events, such as the February Revolution in Trinidad, show that some West Indians have decided that some of the promises made by the now-aging nationalist leaders have not been fulfilled.

There is much that could and should be said to elaborate the above propositions about the intersect of the structure of inequality and the ideology of equality, goals and images of the future, and the means of political independence to achieve the power to transform society, but space precludes a further discussion here. The reader is referred to the references at the end of this chapter, especially to the independent test of the theory by Murch (1967, 1971) in the contrary case of the French Antilles. There he found enlightened leaders and considerable support for more local autonomy, but the ground had been cut out from under dissatisfaction with the amount of equality by a more socially open system, by better educational opportunities than had been available to West Indians under the British, and especially by incorporation of French Antilleans into the larger political community of France as equal citizens. Such satisfaction, of course, may change to dissatisfaction and mass protest unless additional changes are made to create additional equality in other spheres of life.

It remains to point out, however, that feasibility is also an important variable. That is, political independence must be viewed by relevant actors as a real possibility for the future. If it is not, then a movement aimed at the creation of a nation-state cannot develop. Rather, under such a circumstance, perceived inequalities and the ideology of equality combine to generate either a desire for subgroup autonomy and local self-determination of some kind within an existing state or equality within the larger state by demands for full citizenship rights. Such, for example, is typically the case with subordinate racial and ethnic groups that are not territorially bounded in a way that makes creating a new state practical. Such "quasi-nationalist" movements, however, such as those of the Canadian Indians (Boldt, 1972) and American blacks, may have all the other defining characteristics and their correlates that are typical of the nationalist movements that have created the new states.

How Much National Sovereignty Should the New State Have?

Perhaps by definition the new states have opted for full political sovereignty, although this may be in some cases more apparent than real. Yet we should explicitly take note of the variety of half-way houses that exist where varying amounts of internal self-government can be combined with varying amounts of dependence especially in the spheres of foreign affairs and military protection. Puerto Rico represents such a mid-position as do the smaller English-speaking islands of the Leewards and Windwards.

Within the new states of the Caribbean over the last few years a new version of this question has been raised. It constitutes an attack on the economic domination of the new states by North Atlantic investment patterns and a desire for economic self-determination which constitutional independence has not brought (McDonald, 1971). Both the 1970 Black Power Revolt in Trinidad and the nationalization of bauxite in Guyana can be seen as efforts to end economic colonialism and as such they are continuations of the same images of a more egalitarian future that fueled the earlier transition to nationhood.

What Should the Geographical Boundaries of the New State Be?

One of the defining characteristics of nation-states is that they distinctively occupy mutually exclusive geographical territories. The location of some of the existing borders of the new states defies logical explanations if one looks to the facts of history and geography; religion; language; tribe, race, caste, and class; and patterns of consumption, communication, and custom. On the one hand cultural groups have been split into different states and on the other the new state boundaries often contain a goulash of social and cultural diversity. In general, the fairly arbitrary geographical divisions convenient for the European administration of the former colonies seem to have been largely carried over by the fathers of the new states. There were exceptions, of course, such as the division of the Indian empire into the two states of India and Pakistan (and now three with Bangladesh). And in the West Indies the outcome of this decision of nationhood was both problematic and subject to considerable deliberation and conscious decision-making.

As we have seen, in 1958 ten island-territories of the West Indies were headed for nationhood as a single state. Yet even then, a few months after its formation, some cabinet ministers in Jamaica told me privately that they did not favor federation but preferred to see Jamaica become an independent nation in its own right. These leaders were members of the People's National Party and were giving public support to federation out of deference to the views of the then-Chief Minister, Norman W. Manley. Furthermore, my 1958 survey showed that Jamaican leaders generally were far from enthusiastic about federation. For example, note the answers to the following question: "Does Jamaica have more to gain or lose as a result of being part of Federation?"

Jamaica has more to gain	41%
Federation makes no difference	4
Jamaica has more to lose	51
Gain in some ways, lose in others	4
Total	100%
Number of Cases	(232)
No answers	(6)

The major factor underlying the antifederation feeling was the belief that Jamaica had more to lose economically by being part of the federation than she did by being independent. The cost of the federal government itself (Jamaica was to provide 43 percent of the general revenue) and particularly the economic liabilities of the smaller, less developed islands with which Jamaica would be saddled in federation were cited as reasons. Other reasons for opposing federation were the geographical isolation of Jamaica from the other islands and the belief that the self-government and independence of Jamaica would not be fully complete under a federal government. When the opposition party made federation a partisan issue. Manley, perhaps unwisely, called for a referendum. The results were no surprise.

For some West Indians, there remains a deep regret over the collapse of federation and they retain a dream of a future West Indian nation. Even as I write, informal discussions are taking place between Guyana and Grenada, though next week, a Jamaican leader will surely be quoted in the Guyana *Graphic* as doubting that Jamaica would join. Yet regional cooperation does exist and is growing. The University of the West Indies survives. There is the Caribbean Mental Health Association and the recently formed Caribbean Free Trade Association. And despite all the diversity in the West Indies, there is a West Indian identity.

To complete the record, one must add that there have been some suggestions for drawing what amount to national boundaries *within* some of the individual territories, suggestions that most West Indians considered to be on the lunatic fringe. The relatively isolated Maroons of Jamaica, descendants of escaped slaves, constitute an enclave with proud but threadbare national sentiments; some extreme East Indian nationalists in both Guyana and Trinidad have occasionally spoken in favor of ethnic partition. Partition and communal representation were actually suggested by some Hindu leaders in Trinidad on the eve of independence, but these suggestions provoked far more hilarity and derision than serious discussion among the majority of the Negro and Muslim populations.

Should the State and the Nation Be Coterminous?

This decision of nationhood hinges on the distinction between the state as a political entity and the nation as a cultural entity. Should the political boundaries of the state also define a single, homogeneous cultural unit? This is a question most of the new states have had to face with the realization that their peoples were beset by a number of crisscrossing cleavages and considerable cultural diversity. Von der Mehden (1964 p. 2) summarizes the situation as follows:

In South-Southeast Asia, the former colonial area with the longest history of political independence, not a single country has escaped the problem of dissident groups. Pakistan has her frontier peoples [and now the Bengali civil war]; Ceylon, the Tamil-Sinhalese conflict; Burma, her hill peoples; Thailand, her Chinese and southern Malays; Laos, the non-Mekong Lao; Cambodia, the Vietnamese; Vietnam, the Cambodians and other ethnic and religious groups; Malaysia, a delicate balance among Malays, Chinese, and Indians; while India, the Philippines, and Indonesia must cope with a multitude of different ethnic, language, and religious groups. In many Middle Eastern countries, tensions have arisen over alienated groups such as the Kurds, the Armenians, and various Muslim sects. In Africa, many of the new states are torn by tribal rivalries.

There are, of course, spatial modes of making a nation and a state coterminous. Thus, this question can be linked to the previous one: juggle the geographical boundaries, shift peoples *en masse* from one locale to another, or do both. In the West Indies, the only scheme for shifting populations within the region that has ever been advanced has been the sometime suggestion that Trinidad and Guyana should exchange their Negro and East Indian populations, so that Guyana would become an all-East Indian country and Trinidad an all-Negro country. Negro, East Indian, and other ethnic minorities from time to time have advocated removing themselves from the West Indies altogether on the grounds that the nation with which they identify exists elsewhere in the world. The Negro Ras Tafari Brethren of Jamaica view Emperor Hailie Selassie of Ethiopia as God and Africa as the homeland to which they desire repatriation; East Indians in both Trinidad and Guyana have tended to view themselves as exiles from Mother India, but among the few who have visited India many have found that they are far better off, and more at home, in the West Indies than they had realized, and have therefore returned. The majority Trinidadian sentiment on the question of repatriation was probably best expressed in a calypso of Mighty Dougla (a Negro-East Indian mixed-blood) who speculated whimsically on which parts of his body might be repatriated back to Africa, which to India.

Generally, the new national elites in the West Indies are trying to change social and cultural boundaries. They have said, "Yes, we want the state and the nation to be coterminous," and they have set about trying to make nations out of their states, as presently geographically defined, in a socially inclusive manner. They are trying to include all local persons as equal citizens in their new states and to build a sense of national identity and unity. The promotion of such unity can be seen, for example, in the national motto of Jamaica, "Out of Many, One People."

What Should the Form of Government Be?

Carl Becker claimed for the American Revolution that the question of home rule was also a question of who should rule at home. This was also the case in the West Indies. There is no doubt but that the British Government during the tutelary period promoted a democratic form of government, that is a parliamentary system based on universal adult suffrage and public liberties. Yet political democracy was also an important part of the future that most nationalist leaders in the West Indies were trying to create.

For example, we constructed a typology of political types from Moskos' data from leaders' beliefs about the competence of the typical West Indian voter and their attitudes toward the democratic form of government being best suited or not for the West Indies. The results (Bell, 1967, p. 71) were as follows:

Political Types (n = 111)	*% of Total*
Democrats (voters competent, democracy best)	22
Authoritarian idealists (voters competent, democracy unsuitable)	6
Cynical parliamentarians (voters incompetent, democracy best)	28
Authoritarians (voters incompetent, democracy unsuitable)	44
Total	100

One must conclude from this distribution alone that the foundations of democracy as reflected in the beliefs and attitudes of West Indian leaders are somewhat shaky, there being twice as many authoritarians as there were democrats.

Yet the point at issue is how preferences toward different forms of government related to the nationalist movements and to the waxing and waning of different elites. Seventy-nine percent of the democrats were true nationalists compared to only 8 percent of the authoritarians, and none of the democrats were colonialists compared to 76 percent of the authoritarians. Thus, waxing elites were more likely to be democrats that were waning elites, since the nationalists were coming to power. In the biographies of the West Indian leaders, one finds considerable evidence of the time priority of democratic over nationalist attitudes and behaviors; nationalist leaders were democrats before they were nationalists. This, of course, is consistent with our earlier conclusion that political independence was viewed and sought as a means of achieving the rights of man.

Yet, looked at another way, it is clear that democratic values were not held by all nationalists: only 44 percent of the true nationalists were democrats. As we shall see, it was the value of equality even more than democratic values that spurred the drive toward independence.

How Much of a Role Should Government Play in Society, Especially in Economy Affairs?

True nationalists wanted independence in order to obtain legitimate control over governmental power. The exercise of such power was to serve their goals of transforming society. Additionally, they wished to increase the scope of government so that the instrument of change would become increasingly effective and powerful. For example, the West Indian leaders interviewed by Moskos were classified into five categories according to their views on the proper role of the government in the economy of their territories: *reactionaries,* those who thought the state's role should be about what it was before the rise of the nationalist movements and should not extend beyond providing basic services such as a postal system, roads, police and fire protection; *conservatives,* those who wished to maintain the present situation, with the state in addition to providing basic services also being responsible for welfare schemes for the ill, aged, and unemployed, for public works, and for a general educational system, but with the reservations that taxation should be less discriminatory against the entrepreneurial class and that government should be less protective of labor union interests; *populists,* those who lacked long-range economic policies, and who were pragmatically concerned with immediate bread and butter issues, although accepting a belief in a market economy geared to the demands of labor unions or mass-based political organizations; *liberals,* those who wanted greater intervention of the government in the economy, but who did not foresee radical changes beyond the achievement of modern welfare capitalism; and *radicals,* those who advocated fundamental changes in the present system so that the state would become the major factor in determining local economic life, with the extreme radicals seeking the abolishment of all private property.

The high correlation between these economic ideologies and nationalist attitudes can be seen from Table 3. "Left" economic ideologies went with true nationalism and "Right" economic ideologies went with support for the colonial system: all of the radicals were true nationalists, and none of the reactionaries or conservatives were. Moreover, the acquiescing nationalists tended to be concentrated in the intermediate economic ideologies.

What Kind of Social Structure Should the New State Have?

At least since Durkheim, sociologists have tended to take social structure as given and have focused their attention on how structure shapes human behavior. This is perfectly legitimate and has resulted in an impressive growth of knowledge. Yet it has been one-sided in encouraging a rather static view of the social world and in ignoring how individuals acting individually and collectively are constantly in motion creating, changing, and dismantling social structures. Although society may shape individuals, individuals also shape society.

The problematic aspects of the nature of society are dramatically protrayed during the transition to nationhood when the possibilities for alternative futures different from the past or present are forced upon the consciousness of new national decision-makers. What kind of a society should they strive to construct? What are the choices that can be made?

In the West Indies, the terms of this decision concerned the nature of the stratification system, both with respect to class and color. In fact, our major claim is that the inequalities of the stratificaiton system combined with an image of a more egalitarian future to spark the nationalist movements as soon as political independence appeared to be feasible. Although all of our studies show significant proportions of inegalitarians among West Indians—students and current leaders alike—nationalists had egalitarian attitudes and colonialists were inegalitarians. This correlation has already been discussed as part of the relationship between Enlighten-

TABLE 3
NATIONALIST TYPES OF ECONOMIC IDEOLOGIES
(in percentages)

Economic Ideologies	West Indian Leaders Who Were:				
	Colonialists	Acquiescing Nationalists	True Nationalists	Total	Number of Cases
Reactionaries	86	14	0	100	(22)
Conservatives	58	42	0	100	(33)
Populists	18	36	46	100	(11)
Liberals	0	28	72	100	(25)
Radicals	0	0	100	100	(21)

SOURCE: From Moskos (1967, p. 46).

ment values and nationalist types, but it is of some note in its own right since it is one of the highest of any in all of our studies. One hundred percent of the egalitarians in Moskos' study were true nationalists while none of the inegalitarians were. The latter were split between acquiescing nationalists (41 percent) and colonialists (59 percent).

Leaders were queried further to find out if these two attitudes could be temporally differentiated in their past experiences. Attitudes toward equality were prior to desires for political independence. For example, most leaders could remember when they first began to think of the possibility of nationhood. Often, some particular date, event, or period in their lives was involved when independence occurred to the respondents as a solution to rather long-standing perceptions of inequality and commitments to equality. For example, one true nationalist said:

> It's hard to say when I first started to think this way [favorably toward political independence], but it certainly was based on the injustices of the West Indies. It seemed natural when political independence became an issue that I would be for it. I remember when I was still in school listening to a sermon given by a white minister. He based it on one of Paul's epistles where something like the following was said, "there shall be neither Greek or Barbarian, Jew or Gentile, slave or free and all shall be of one Spirit." I was particularly moved by that sermon. Several days later my father sent me to deliver something to the minister at his house. As I approached the front door, he waved to me through the window to go around the house to the back door. I think my concern with social injustice might have been given a big push then. The hypocrisy of the whole system became apparent when I was able to continue my studies in England. It was there I realized that political independence was the only means to bring about a society with no discrimination and equal opportunity for all (Moskos, 1967, p. 68).

It would take another paper of equal length to this one to assess the question of the success of the West Indian nationalist leaders in achieving more egalitarian societies since they have come to power. There are obvious areas where minimums of civil, political, economic, social, and cultural rights have been raised, thus contributing toward greater equality. Also, there are policies in education, welfare, and agriculture aimed at the same end. The big question, I think, is an economic one, and involves both the question of foreign capital and the more effective mobilization of local labor sources. The present changes in Guyana directed toward the control of their own resources and self-help cooperatives based on volunteer labor may offer a glimpse into the future.

What Kind of People Should the New State Have?

The first generalization to be made about decisions involving the national character of the West Indian people is the obvious observation that a people resident in the same confined insular region for many generations has already acquired some sort of collective character. If one asks a Jamaican, Barbadian, or Trinidadian what his people are or ought to be like, one will usually receive a definite answer. Such questions are meaningful both at the level of the common man and at the highest official levels. Further, as might be expected in an area swept by a momentum toward change and progress, there are often sharp discrepancies perceived between what the national character *is* and what it *ought to be.* It is the mark of a new state—as of all nations undergoing rapid social change—that there is a rather high degree of ferment and controversy on this question. In the midst of this ferment stand those who will make the major decisions affecting its initial direction (Bell and Oxaal, 1964).

West Indian nationalists are likely to see the defects in West Indian character as stemming from the twin heritages of slavery and indentured labor on the one hand and colonialism as an authoritarian political and social system on the other. They are in part the consequences of social pluralism and ignorance and are combated by education designed to foster identical national ideals among young citizens, the values and precepts of the Enlightenment, and *enlightenment* in the simple sense of inculcating the skills by which a rational-scientific orientation toward the world might be forwarded. New national heroes are honored who embody the national ideals, in which colonial versions of local character are often reversed.

Another presumed crucial flaw in the West Indian character is the belief that West Indians, partially as a result of the antiwork attitudes engendered by slavery, are incorrigibly lazy and inefficient. This critique of the national character has long been a subject for exasperated commentary by West Indians and colonial officials alike, so much so that one member of our research team, Andrew P. Phillips (1963), directed his worker study of the Antiguan sugar factory to it. His findings show that when a worker believed that his individual life goals could be achieved by working hard, then he would be a good worker. Contrariwise, if he could see no such thing, then he tended to adopt a dilatory attitude toward work. The regrettable conclusion is that for many of the poor workers, their beliefs about the lack of effectiveness of good work habits in realizing their hopes for a better life may be accurate—at least under the present structure of the situation. Clearly, here is an opportunity for leadership to change the structure of the situation.

What Should the New State's
Cultural Traditions Be?

As Marriott (1963, p. 27) says, "No state, not even an infant one, is willing to appear before the world as a bare political frame. Each would be clothed in a cultural garb symbolic of its aims and ideal being." The conscious manipulation of cultural traditions may involve the problem of selecting from a rich and varied cultural background of inherited civilizations those elements to be stressed, as in the case of India which has an *embarras de richesse;* or it may entail creating the wherewithal to fill a historical void, as in the case of some of the new states of sub-Saharan Africa; or it can involve overturning European versions of the colonial past, as it has in most of the new states.

Voltaire said that "History is only a pack of tricks we play on the dead." But watching the rewriting of history in the new states, one must conclude that it is more. It is a form of cultural management in which past, present, and future interpenetrate each other, in which the struggle to control the future shapes the way the past is viewed. It is, perhaps, not so much the dead but the unborn on whom we play the tricks. New national histories reflect the meaning of independence and reveal the beliefs and values that lie at the foundation of the other decisions of nationhood. They become part of the more or less integrated set of images of the future that are congealed in national flags, dress, anthems, pledges, songs, mottos, and other national symbols.

Trinidad and Tobago—with a renowned historian, Dr. Eric Williams, as prime minister—gives a convincing demonstration of the importance of the intellectual and moral decisions involved in writing cultural history and of its importance in relation to national decisions. On the very first day of national independence, Williams issued his *History of the People of Trinidad and Tobago* (1962) which was explicitly committed to providing a unifying theory for a society marked by major racial and cultural divisions. Although cognizant of these divisive tendencies, Williams—like some other West Indian nationalists—stressed the idea that tendencies toward social and cultural pluralism need not weaken the nation, that there is strength not only in unity but in diversity, and that these factors are not irreconcilable. Most of the major ethnic groups in Trinidad, he asserted, are bound together by a common history of exploitation and subordination under colonialism, and all should therefore unite to build the new nation. Thus, he perceived the existence of cultural differences as requiring a "closing of ranks" rather than separate national allegiances. This argument is supported by the Enlightenment values of which he was a leading West Indian exponent: the presence of ascriptive ethnic social barriers need not and should not be a bar to equality of opportunity; the maintenance of a multiplicity of subcultural units can be reconciled with the goals of nationhood as long as all groups share a basic loyalty to the nation and to the democratic and egalitarian, if not the inclusivist, values that guided the nationalist movement (Bell and Oxaal, 1964).

What Should the New Nation's External Affairs Be?

Any organization has the problem of managing its external affairs, and for the new states this has meant taking part in international relations, establishing networks of communication with other nations. Under colonialism, these were matters for the imperial power—the European metropole—to decide. With nationhood, the question of the most desirable and beneficial international relations from the point of view of local benefits and welfare could be raised by the new national leaders. Although existing flows of trade, of language and culture, and of tradition had to be taken into account, some choice seemed possible.

Important features of the international scene at the time of West Indian independence were the facts that it was global in scale and prominently divided into Western or communist blocs, with the possibility of alignment with the so-called neutralist nations. Moskos (1967) asked the West Indian leaders that he interviewed, "When [Jamaica, or other appropriate territory] becomes fully independent, with which group should (Jamaica) align itself, the Western nations, the communist countries, or the neutralist countries?" The responses were:

Western nations	77%
Neutralist countries	19
Communist countries	4
Total	100%
Number of cases	(112)

There is some evidence to suggest that between 1958 and 1962 there was a slight shift of opinion away from the West, although neither the data nor the sample of leaders are strictly comparable. In my 1958 study 83 percent of the Jamaican leaders thought the United States had been morally right more often than the Soviet Union as an actor on the world scene. In the 1962 data reported above, 70 percent of the Jamaican leaders preferred alignment with the West.

But which leaders were most likely to support the West? Table 4 shows attitudes toward global alignments by the Index of Enlightenment. Note that enlightened leaders were much less likely to favor alignment with the West than the unenlightened leaders. In fact, 100 percent of the most unenlightened West Indian leaders preferred a Western alignment compared to only 50 percent of the most enlightened leaders. That is, the West Indian leaders most committed to the Western ideals and values of liberty, equality, and fraternity were least likely to favor alignment with the Western nations.

Many of the enlightened leaders no longer regarded the countries of the West as egalitarian forces on the international scene. To some extent they share Juan Bosch's (1965) view of the United States during the occupation of the Dominican Republic, "This was a deomcratic revolution smashed by the leading democracy of the world, the United States." Or as Cheddi Jagan, communist and former premier of Guyana, told Ivar Oxaal and me in Georgetown, Guyana, "I held office but was never in power." He was referring to several things including, I assume, the fact that the United States Central Intelligence Agency poured over a million dollars (U.S.) into Guyana through an international labor organization to support a strike against Jagan's democratically elected government (Meisler, 1964). Jagan's ability to rule was seriously impaired. The British government forced a system of proportionate representation that resulted in Jagan's losing the elections held in December 1964.

Of course, the nationalists among the West Indian elites were committed to the ideas of self-determination for their territories and of freedom from the political domination of the United Kingdom. For many of them such commitments carried over into their foreign-policy attitudes and led them to prefer the more "independent" posture of neutralism rather than following along after the United States, the United Kingdom, or the other nations of the West, or for that matter after the nations of the communist world either. To them, neutralism involved the least dilution of

TABLE 4
ATTITUDES TOWARD GLOBAL ALIGNMENTS BY THE INDEX OF ENLIGHTENMENT (in percentages)

	The New State Should Align Itself With:				
Index of Enlightenment	Western Nations	Neutralist Countries	Communist Countries	Total	Number of Cases
3 (enlightened)	50	43	7	100	(30)
2	41	47	12	100	(17)
1	96	0	4	100	(24)
0 (unenlightened)	100	0	0	100	(41)

SOURCE: From Moskos and Bell (1964 p. 37).

their countries' newly achieved or soon hoped-for national sovereignty. At the same time, as we have seen, nationalists' hopes and ambitions were in fact inspired by Western ideals, by the commitment to the rights of man—especially by the desire for equality.

At the other extreme, the colonialists among the West Indian leaders were authoritarians, inegalitarians, and social exclusivists. The same configuration of factors which produced their anti-independence attitudes also produced their 100 percent preference for Western alignment. Their fear of what the nationalists would do in the years after independence and their hope for policies which would not undermine their generally well-established socioeconomic positions in the society were linked to their desire for Western alignment, their opposition to nationalist movements, and their preferences for the conservative or reactionary versions of the Western models of polity, economy, and society. They opposed progressive change; they represented the status quo; and they found the basic values of Western Civilization, as expressed in the three rights-of-man variables, abominations. Ironically, such "abominations," according to their views, characterized the communist countries to a much greater extent than the Western nations.

CONCLUSION

Today, as I write, Jamaica and Trinidad have been politically independent for more than nine years, Barbados and Guyana for about five, and my early field work in the West Indies in 1956 and 1958, even the longer period of 1961-1962, seems to have been a long time ago. Actually, it has been but a short time by any reasonable scale of historical perspective, too soon for the evenbalanced, leisurely informed opinion of the historian to come into play and, of course, too soon for the judgment of future events that are still to come.

For these new states of the Caribbean, constitutional independence has been achieved. Reacting to the social injustices of the colonial stratification systems—especially the many oppressive inequalities—and giving voice to the economic discontent of the masses, nationalist leaders and their supporters viewed political independence, as our studies have shown, as a means to get the power to achieve their ends: righting the wrongs of colonialism, raising minimums of human rights, creating equal opportunities and inclusivist societies, and generally advancing democratic participation of the people.

It is, perhaps, time for someone to make a full-scale assessment of progress toward these goals. Although I feel confident in speculating that any fair evaluation would conclude that considerable progress has been made—from universal suffrage and opening social clubs to increased national pride and dignity—there is one growing sore point about which not enough has been accomplished if the nationalist leaders are to be held to their own professed values and stated promises. Much of the West Indies is still foreign-owned. Despite the brown and black faces in the parliaments, for the most part white imperialism—and increasingly U.S. imperialism—is still dominant. At the aftermath of the February Revolution in Trinidad, C.L.R. James (1970) said,

> What we have here is the traditional example of recognition of what is wrong but refusal to face the issue of power, power against the foreign powers that dominate the Caribbean, and against the black regimes which protect the domination exercised for centuries by foreign powers. That protection is now in danger."

The image of a future egalitarian West Indies appears to be very much alive, but the means have changed. The goal of constitutional independence has been replaced by the goal of economic nationalism. This has been to some extent confused by the arrival of the Black Power movement into the West Indies in the last few years in that the continuing high correlation between race and class permits a rhetoric of race war to mask the real issue. At Carnival in Trinidad in February 1970, three of the participating bands dedicated their entries to socio-political protest, one carrying a banner on which the message was "Black blood; black sweat; black tears—white profits" (Oxaal, 1971 p. 22). But one is tempted to agree with Cheddi Jagan. In the West Indies "Black Power" demands may be, in the nature of the case, demands for socialism. They are, at least, demands for local ownership, an end to foreign exploitation, and more distributional reforms.

As Ivar Oxaal (1971 p. 38) says of Dr. Williams and the P.N.M. in Trinidad, West Indian nationalist leaders during the transition to political independence "made a considerable contribution to raising the level of mass awareness and the cumulative effect over the years of continually expanded educaitonal opportunities was undeniable." It is from this new level of mass awareness that the confrontation with economic imperialism has begun and from which some West Indian leaders—many new and emergent—continue the struggle for equality.

NOTES

1. See I. Oxaal, Race and Revolutionary Consciousness. . . . The 1970 Black Power revolt is also known as the "February Revolution," since the first major protest march was on February 26th.

2. For this description of the West Indies, I've drawn from Bell, The Democratic Revolution in the West Indies. . . also see Maingot, "Social Life of the Caribbean."

3. For a review, see Lewis, "The Politics of the Caribbean."

4. Compare with Fallers' discussion of the politics of equality: "Equality, Modernity, and Democracy in the New States." In addition to the equality revolution, there was also involved in the rise of the nationalist movements a corresponding rise in West Indian romanticism. It was, however, more of an effect or a concomitant process than it was a cause. Yet its importance should not be denied. It was, like the equality revolution, also a desire for an increase in the scale of society, an increase to be brought about by closer interaction with the ancestral background of West Indians, an increase in historical scale. It was part of the search for cultural identity. Thus, among true nationalists, there was a desire for more West Indian history to be taught in the schools, especially with an emphasis on the African origins and slavery (and for many in Trinidad and Guyana—on the Indian origins and indentured labor); there was also a desire for a uniquely West Indian future cultural development rather than a basically Anglo-European one; and there was a flowering of West Indian *belles lettres* that occurred after the initial political awakening. See Moskos. The Sociology of Political Independence . . . , p. 67.

REFERENCES

Alger, J. M., "The Sociology of the American Revolution," Ph.D. dissertation, New Haven, Yale University, 1972.

———, "Impact of Ethnicity and Religion on Social Development in Revolutionary America," in W. Bell and W. Freeman (eds.); Ethnicity and Nation-Building, Beverly Hills, Calif., Sage Publications, 1973.

Bell, W., ed., The Democratic Revolution in the West Indies: Studies in Nationalism, Leadership and the Belief in Progress, Cambridge, Schenkman, 1967.

———, "Social Change and Elites in an Emergent Nation," in H. R. Barringer, G. I. Blanksten, and R. W. Mack (eds.); Social Change in Developing Areas: A Reinterpretation of Evolutionary Theory, Cambridge, Schenkman, 1965, pp. 155-202.

———, Jamaican Leaders: Political Attitudes in a New Nation, Berkeley, University of California Press, 1964.

———, "Equality and Attitudes of Elites in Jamaica," Social and Economic Studies, Vol. 11, December 1962, pp. 409-32.

———, "Images of the United States and the Soviet Union Held by Jamaican Elite Groups," World Politics, Vol. 12, January 1960, pp. 225-48.

———, "Attitudes of Jamaican Elites toward the West Indies Federation," Annals of the New York Academy of Sciences, Vol. 83, January 1960, pp. 862-79.

—— and J. A. Mau, eds., The Sociology of the Future: Theory, Cases, and Annotated Bibliography, New York, Russell Sage Foundation, 1971.

Bell, W. and I. Oxaal, "The Nation-State as a Unit in the Comparative Study of Social Change," in W. E. Moore and R. M. Cook (eds.), Readings in Social Change, Englewood Cliffs, N.J., Prentice-Hall, 1967, pp. 169-81.

———, Decisions of Nationhood: Political and Social Development in the British Caribbean, Denver, Social Science Foundation, University of Denver, 1964.

Boldt, M., "Nationalist Attitudes among Canadian Indian Leaders: A Study in Ambivalence," Ph.D. dissertation, New Haven, Yale University, 1972.

Bosch, J., in New York Times, May 8, 1965.

Davison, R. B., West Indian Migrants, London, Institute of Race Relations, Oxford University Press, 1962.

Duke, J. T., "Equalitarianism among Emergent Elites in a New Nation," Ph.D. dissertation, Los Angeles, University of California, 1963.

Fallers, L., "Equality, Modernity, and Democracy in the New States," in C. Geertz (ed.), Old Societies and New States, New York, Free Press, 1963, pp. 158-219.

James, C. L. R., "The Caribbean Confrontation Begins," Race Today, September 1970.

Landis, J. B., "Race and Politics in Guyana," Ph.D. dissertation, New Haven, Yale University, 1971.

Lewis, G. K., "The Politics of the Caribbean," in T. Szulc (ed.), The United States and the Caribbean, Englewood Cliffs, N.J., Prentice-Hall, 1971, pp. 5-35.

McDonald, F., "The Commonwealth Caribbean," in T. Szulc (ed.), The United States and the Caribbean, Englewood Cliffs, N.J., Prentice-Hall, 1971, pp. 126-56.

Maingot, A. P., "Social Life of the Caribbean," in T. Szulc (ed.), The United States and the Caribbean, Englewood Cliffs, N.J., Prentice-Hall, 1971, pp. 36-68.

Marriott, M., "Cultural Policy in the New States," in C. Geertz (ed.), Old Societies and New States, New York, Free Press, 1963, pp. 27-56.

Mau, J. A., Social Change and Images of the Future, Cambridge, Schenkman, 1968.

———, "The Threatening Masses: Myth or Reality?" in F. M. Andic and T. G. Mathews (eds.), The Caribbean in Transition: Papers on Social, Political, and Economic Development; Rio Piedras, Puerto Rico, Institute of Caribbean Studies, University of Puerto Rico, 1965, pp. 258-70.

———, "Social Change and Belief in Progress: A Study of Images of the Future in Jamaica," Ph.D. dissertation, Los Angeles, University of California, 1963.

———, R. J. Hill, and W. Bell, "Scale Analyses of Status Perception and Status Attitude in Jamaica and the United States," Pacific Sociological Review, Spring 1961, pp. 33-40.

Meisler, S., "Dubious Role of A.F.L.-C.I.O. Meddling in Latin America," Nation, No. 198, February 10, 1964, pp. 131-38.

Moosai-Maharaj, S., "Problems of Race and Language in the British Caribbean, " in P. A. Lockwood, (ed.), Canada and the West Indies Federation, Sakville, N.B., Canada, Mt. Allison University Publication No. 2, 1957.

Moskos, C. C., Jr., The Sociology of Political Independence: A Study of Nationalist Attitudes among West Indian Leaders, Cambridge, Schenkman, 1967.

———, "British Guiana: Can Jagan Hold On?" New Republic, March 21, 1964, pp. 10-11.

———, "The Sociology of Political Independence: A Study of Influence, Social Structure and Ideology in the British West Indies," Ph.D. dissertation, Los Angeles, University of California, 1963.

Moskos, C. C., Jr., and W. Bell, "Cultural Unity and Diversity in New States," Teachers College Record, No. 66, May 1965, pp. 679-94.

———, "Some Implications of Equality for Political, Economic, and Social Development," International Review of Community Development, Nos. 13-14, 1965, pp. 219-46.

———, "Emergent Caribbean Nations Face the Outside World," Social Problems, Vol. 12, Summer 1964, pp. 24-41.

———, "West Indian Nationalism," New Society, No. 69, January 23, 1964, pp. 16-18.

———, "Igualdad, Democracia y Guerra Fria en la Zona Britanica del Caribe," Revista de Estudios Politicos, No. 137, 1964, pp. 125-55.

———, "Attitudes towards Democracy among Leaders in Four Emergent Nations," British Journal of Sociology, Vol. 15, December 1964, pp. 317-37.

Murch, A. W., "Black Frenchmen: A Comparative Study of Equality and Nationalism in the Caribbean," Cambridge, Schenkman, 1971.

———, "Political Integration as an Alternative to Independence in the French Antilles," American Sociological Review, Vol. 33, August 1968, pp. 544-62.

———, "Political Integration as an Alternative to Independence in the French Antilles," Ph.D. dissertation, New Haven, Yale University, 1967.

Oxaal, I., Race and Revolutionary Consciousness: A Documentary Interpretation of the 1970 Black Power Revolt in Trinidad," Cambridge, Schenkman, 1971.

———, "The Quest for Utopia: A Case Study from El Dorado," in W. Bell and J. A. Mau (eds.), The Sociology of the Future, New York, Russell Sage Foundation, 1971, pp. 294-323.

———, Black Intellectuals Come to Power: The Rise of Creole Nationalism in Trinidad and Tobago, Cambridge, Schenkman, 1968.

———, "Neo-Nationalism in the West Indies," New Society, No. 176, February 10, 1966, pp. 24-25.

———, ed., Trinidad and Tobago Index: An Informal Review of Social History and Research, 1965-1967.

———, "West Indian Intellectuals Come to Power: A Study of the Colonial Heritage and Nationalist Action in Trinidad and Tobago," Ph.D. dissertation, Los Angeles, University of California, 1964.

Palmer, R. R., "The Struggle," The Age of the Democratic Revolution: A Political History of Europe and America, 1760-1800, Princeton, Princeton University Press, 1964.

———, "The Challenge," The Age of the Democratic Revolution: A Political History of Europe and America, 1760-1800, Princeton, Princeton University Press, 1959.

Phillips, A. P., "The Development of a Modern Labor Force in Antigua," Ph.D. dissertation, Los Angeles, University of California, 1963.

Smith, M. G., The Plural Society in the British West Indies, Berkeley, University of California Press, 1965.

Williams, E., History of the People of Trinidad and Tobago; Port of Spain, Trinidad, P.N.M. Publishing, 1962.

Von der Mehden, F. R., Religion and Naitonalism in Southeast Asia: Burma, Indonesia, and the Philippines, Madison, University of Wisconsin Press, 1964.

CHAPTER 6

REGIONAL CONTRASTS WITHIN A
CONTINENTAL-SCALE STATE: BRAZIL

Simon Schwartzman

SIMON SCHWARTZMAN is Director of Research at the Brazilian School of Public Administration of the Getulio Vargas Foundation in Rio de Janeiro. He has been engaged in cross-national research on problems of social and political change, and he is the author of the forthcoming book, *Regional Cleavages and Political Patrimonialism in Brazil.*

If one wants to go deeper into the study of a given political system, one should move from the analysis of the overall political system into the study of regional differences and subsystems; and the larger the population and geographical area covered by the national system, the more important this analysis becomes: the closer and deeper we look into something we are trying to understand, the better. The idea in this chapter however, goes much further than that. The proposition is that the analysis of regional subsystems, when properly performed, implies a profound theoretical shift of perspectives in such a way that the kind of knowledge acquired is not simply "better" than before, but qualitatively more adequate. The gain is not a simple matter of added knowledge, but of a new way of understanding.

This notion of a new theoretical approach stemming from an analysis of regional differentiations, with reference to the role of the state of São

Author's Note: This chapter is a revised version of a paper presented in the Social Sciences Research Council Seminar on Social Indicators of National Development,

Paulo in the Brazilian national system has already been indicated by Warren Dean.[1] The idea was that it is impossible to consider São Paulo either as a "deviant" case in the national picture, or as a representative one of a "more advanced" stage of development in the country. Two facts suffice to illustrate this point. One is the weakness of the national political parties in the state of São Paulo during the 1945-1964 period, reflecting the relative marginality of the country's economic center regarding the national party system.[2] The other is the relative equilibrium between the processes of urbanization and industrialization, which the state underwent during this century. This condition differs markedly from urbanization without industrialization in other metropolitan areas of the country. To consider São Paulo a deviant case would explain away the historical role of the most important area of the country in terms of its economy and population; this action is obviously not acceptable. And there are no reasons to imagine that the present metropolitan areas of the country such as Rio, Belo Horizonte, Recife, and others, will eventually replicate the Paulista pattern of intensive industrialization leading to a process of urban concentration.

Nor is São Paulo the only deviant case. The state of Rio Grande do Sul, bordering Argentina, Uruguay, and Paraguay, has historically played a political role in the national system quite out of proportion to its size and economic weight.[3] Rio Grande do Sul is not a region of traditional politics based on local bonds and loyalties in a stagnant economy, held to be by many as the core of traditional Brazilian politics; it has never been a dominant economic pole, and was never the administrative center of the country. On the contrary, it is a frontier state, thousands of miles away from the country's capital, but this geographical marginality seemed to have placed the state in the very center of national politics from the beginning of the twentieth century on. The special role of Rio de Janeiro as the seat of the national government is probably easier to understand;

Rio de Janeiro, May, 1972, and is part of a broader study of the Brazilian political system in historical perspective. Earlier published papers include "Representação e Cooptação Política no Brasil," *Dados,* Vol. 7, 1971, and *Desarollo Economico,* Vol. 41, 1971; "Veinte Años de Democracia Representativa en Brasil," *Revista Latino-americana de Ciência Política,* 1971; and "Desenvolvimento e Abertura Política," *Dados,* Vol. 6, 1970. The emphasis has always been in the theoretical perspective, rather than in factual data. Excellent studies have recently come out on Brazilian regional history, and they provide the indispensable empirical reference for my interpretations. I am grateful to Antonio Octavio Cintra, Glaucio A. D. Soares, Gustavo Bayer, and Peter McDonough for suggestions, comments, and criticism, with the usual "no blame" clause.

the same applies to the state of Minas Gerais, which is closer to evincing what traditional politics is supposed to be, in historical terms.

We have, in short, at least four main regional actors in the political system which behave in quite different ways and have important but sometimes unexpected impact on the national system: the economic center (São Paulo), the urban and administrative center (Rio de Janeiro), the traditional countryside (Minas Gerais), and the frontier state (Rio Grande do Sul). To describe the theoretical framework of their interaction is the objective of this chapter.[4]

STATE AND SOCIETY

Stein Rokkan has presented us with a highly sophisticated and complex framework for the study of nation-building and the development of political and party cleavages in Western Europe.[5] It would probably be unwise to apply his whole analytical framework directly to the study of the Brazilian political system; but it will be essential to bear it in mind as we try to unfold the variables that characterize Brazil's regional differences and national integration process in a more inductive and, as it were, "natural" way.

The point of departure is the classic distinction between state and society. It is well known today that there are substantial differences in the meanings of the word "state" in the Anglo-Saxon and other intellectual traditions; these differences reflect real historical differences, and explain the relative "statelessness" of Anglo-Saxon political theory. J. P. Nettl has argued in favor of using the "variable degree of stateness" as a central variable in cross-national studies;[6] Reinhardt Bendix, in an earlier paper, made a similar suggestion.[7]

The essential idea is that the state is not only a concept referring to the integration and sovereignty of a given population in a given territory—in which case the notion of different levels or degrees of stateness would be meaningless—but is also a specific institution within a country which not only performs the functions of boundary maintenance and sovereignty, but can also be smaller or bigger, stronger or weaker, independent or controlled by other social groups and institutions. In other words, there is here a shift from a functional to a more structural perspective, that is, the state is considered an institution endowed with a changing structure of its own.

Both Bendix and Nettl place these different conceptions of the state in historical and theoretical perspectives. Bendix emphasizes the existence of two main approaches in political theory since Machiavelli. The first and older of these approaches is Machiavelli's own: he thought of political facts and events as functions of the abilities and virtues of the political leader, the prince. Generally speaking, this tradition leads to a perception of the state as a unit that organizes the wills and aspirations of the society as a whole, defining and working towards its goals. The ruler is not responsive to the ruled, whereas the social structure seems to offer no resistance to the prince: the only limitations to his will are his own fancy and wit. This conception, of course, is an extreme that has the absolutist state as its implicit empirical reference.

The other theoretical tradition stems from Rousseau: the power of the state is delegated by the population and the state must act in accordance with an explicit and well-limited social contract. The idea of a social contract has an ideological and normative meaning, since it appeared in the struggle against Absolutism; but it also has sociological value in that it is an empirical statement on how politics is performed when social groups are strong and the government is weak. The contractualist notion of the state was equivalent to a Copernican revolution in political thought, leading to a shift in perspective which in turn quite often led to the very annihilation of the state as an autonomous variable worthy of the political analyst's attention. As a matter of fact, in this extreme view, the state is nothing but the locus through which the dominant groups or classes exercise their will: it has no political texture of its own.

As seen through the criticism that Marx addresses to his *Philosophy of Law,*[8] it is Hegel who opens the way for the analysis of the relationships between the state and civil society as separate and often contradictory structures. Hegel distinguishes between civil society, which is the state of necessity, and the state, which represents the general will, the unity of political life. More specifically, civil society is for Hegel the "phenomenon" of the state, while the state is the "idea" of society. The idea is incorporated in the sovereign and the constitution, and the mediation between the idea and society is performed by several intervening institutions, such as public opinion, the representation of civilian groups in the state, the bureaucracy, and so on.[9]

One of the main points of Marx's criticism is the stress he places on the private character of bureaucracy. For Hegel, bureaucracy is the soul of the state, and the private activities of civil servants perform a universal function. In Marx's opinion, however, the bureaucrat ends up making this universal function his private business. For Hegel, bureaucracy has as its first assumption the autonomy and organization of civil society in private corporations. The choice of civil servants and public authorities is conceived as a mixed choice, initiated in the private sector and approved by the sovereign. The fact is, says Marx, that this kind of penetration by civil society into the state leads to nothing but the creation of another kind of private corporation, the bureaucracy:

> The corporations are the materialism of the bureaucracy, and the bureaucracy is the spiritualism of the corporations; but the corporation is the bureaucracy of civil society, and the bureaucracy is the corporation of the state.

And later on:

> The bureaucracy keeps in its power the being of the State, the spiritual being of society: it is its *private property*. The general spirit of the bureaucracy is its *mystery;* this mystery is kept inside the bureaucracy by its hierarchy, and kept from the outside because the bureaucracy has the characteristics of a private corporation. To make the spirit of the State known to everybody is thus perceived by the bureaucracy as a treason to its mystery. The principle of the bureaucratic science is thus the *authority,* and the *idolatry* of authority its *sentiment.* Kept within the bureaucracy, this *spiritualism* becomes a *sordid materialism,* the materialism of passive obeisance, of faith in authority, of the *mechanism* of fixed formal activities, of fixed principles, ideas and traditions. For the bureaucrat taken as an individual, the goals of the State become his private goal, which is *the hunting for higher positions, the push in the way up.*

This notion of a bureaucracy with private interests includes, of course, the conception of the state as the political arm of a given social class, but it is more general than that. Nettl discusses this notion in some length, and shows how

> Marx partially lost interest in the problem of the state when he moved intellectually as well as physically from Europe to England and when, in writing *Das Kapital,* he concentrated on the much more "English" analysis of economic forces and consequent class relations rather than on the problems of ideological consciousness and revolution in a state-dominated Europe.[11]

Bendix shows how Machiavelli himself recognized the existence of two types of government, one carried on by "the Prince and his servants" and the other by "the Prince and by Barons."[12] While, in the first type, the prince is the only source of power, in the latter there are rights of political influence that are obtained through heritage and do not depend on the prince's favor. This second type of political power characterizes a state of equilibrium between the central power and what would later be called "civil society"; each has some autonomy of decisions and initiative, and tries to limit and direct the behavior of the other. The fact that the barons are just a tiny group of aristocrats is less important, theoretically, than the notion that their sources of power do not come from the prince.

Once this duality of power sources is established, it expands and differentiates in several directions. What is important is the idea that this is not a simple matter of functional differentiation, in which the state performs the political functions of vertical authority and domination, while the barons retain the horizontal functions of solidarity interest aggregation, and articulation. What happens, in fact, is that aggregation and articulation of private interests are carried on within the structures of authority, while systems of authority develop in the "private" sector of society and reach towards the control of the state. The actual balance between these two tendencies varies, and has to be determined empirically. The more significant theoretical point here is that the characteristics of a given state's structure cannot be fully deduced from the characteristics of its civil society (or, in contemporary terms, its class structure), just as society cannot be fully understood from the formal characteristics of its governmental organization.

PATRIMONIALISM AND THE GROWTH OF THE STATE

In the contractual model, the government does not have power of its own; it acts by delegation and with resources provided by civil society. In fact, as demonstrated in Marx's criticism of Helgel's *Theory of Law,* the organization that performs this delegation develops private resources and private interests. This development occurs when the state acts by delegation of the whole society, as well as when it behaves more or less clearly as "the instrument" of a given class. One of the reasons for this occurrence is, of course, the sheer growth and differentiation of the government. From the theoretical role of a simple gendarme and mediator, the stateless state of the nineteenth century referred to by Nettl develops into a giant that makes the simple interest group approach to political analysis little more than an historical relic. E. E. Schattschneider stressed this point very strongly:

> While we were looking the other way, the government of the United States became a global operation a decade or two ago. The budget is about two hundred fifty times as large as it was seventy years ago . . . . In a purely formal sense we can say that the government of the United States is the same one that was established in 1789—in about the same way in which Henry Ford's bicycle repair shop is the same as the Ford Motor Company today.[13]

What is more remarkable about the American system is not so much this development in itself, as the fact that it did not lead to a more thorough annihilation of independent power sources. American liberalism, according to one of its critics, Theodore J. Lowi, means just the opposite, since it leads to the privatization of the public sector.

Referring to the agricultural sector, for instance, Lowi sees it as an extreme case of "private expropriation of public authority." "This is the feudal pattern," he continues; "fusion of all statuses and functions and governing through rigid but personalized fealties. In modern dress, that was the corporativistic way."[14] The difference between this neocorporativism of the liberal state and the corporative state as such is that, in the latter, the state behaves explicitly and legitimately on behalf of a group that has control of the state apparatus as the basis, rather than as the instrument, of its social, economic, and political power.

The idea of economic power based on the state, and not the opposite (that is, political power based on economic resources), is difficult to accept in stateless political theories, and this difficulty helps to explain the odyssey of the "Asian mode of production" in Marxian literature.[15] As it appears in the relatively recently rediscovered *Grundrisse,*[16] this concept applies to some precapitalist forms of economic organization, which are characterized by the partial or total nonexistence of private property, or at least by the existence of a predominant public sector in the economy:

> Etant le veritable proprietaire et la veritable condition de la proprieté collective, l'unité peut elle-même sembler *distincte* et au-dessus de la multitude des communáutes particulières: l'individu est allors, en fait, sans proprieté.[17]

Marx distinguishes two subtypes of these precapitalist forms, one which is generally based on the large-scale organization of rural economies, usually through nationally integrated systems of water irrigation works, and others based instead on urban centers, where:

> La guerre est donc la grand tâche collective, le grand travail commun, exigés soit pour s'emparer des conditions matérielles d'existence, soit pour défendre et pérpetuer l'occupation.[18]

There is no need to go further into the expanding debate that still revolves around the concept of "Asiatism." It is enough to keep in mind that this type of economic and political organization does not fit the evolutionary model that goes from slavery to serfdom to wage labor and capitalism, a model in which the interest group politics concept belongs, and a model that is more or less implicit in the stateless theories of social development.[19] It is a fact that the Western States that attained high levels of development during this century have more or less followed that pattern, and there is a high correlation between a decentralized and feudallike system in the past and high economic development in this century. "Hydraulic societies," bureaucratic and centralized empires of the past, were way above medieval Europe, according to almost any standards of development, but they did not seem to be able to adapt themselves to modern industrial society, while countries with a feudal past (the only one in Asia that comes close to it being Japan) were much more able to adopt modern and efficient forms of economic organization. Thus—contrary to what is sometimes held—feudalism does not seem to have been a factor of underdevelopment, but on the contrary, it was its absence, and the dominance of a bureaucratized and overgrown state, which seemed to have been one of its determinants. Having arrived late to a world developed through capitalist initiative, these countries have only their own inflated states to bring them to the world of industrial development.[20]

CLEAVAGES IN PATRIMONIAL STATES

The concept of "patrimonialism" aquires its full characterization in Max Weber, who refers to a type of traditional domination where the government "is an extension of the ruler's household." It is essential to recall that this concept is used as an alternative to another major type of traditional domination, feudalism.[21] There are a few characteristics of patrimonialism which lead more or less directly to the political cleavages that are bound to appear in states with this type of domination.

First, patrimonial states tend to be urban-based and to develop urban civilizations. These urban centers can be either the capital of an empire, or a city-state with trade and military interests abroad. These centers tend to have a sizable floating population, and an aristocracy that has to be fitted somehow into the governmental bureaucracy. The first political problem of patrimonial states is keeping the urban masses content, and keeping the government jobs open to the urban aristocracy.

Second, there is the classic tension between the ruler and its officers:

> All patrimonial states of the past have involved a pattern of decentralization that has been determined by the struggle for power between the ruler and his retainers and officers.[22]

As the patrimonial realm grows, so grows the need to delegate power and authority, and at the same time the feasibility of central control is reduced. Moreover, retainers of patrimonial delegation tend to receive their posts as political prebends, and to use them as their private property. When the patrimonial state is based on military conquest and occupation, this pattern leads to the development of private, or praetorian military bodies, which have more loyalty to their own captains than to the ruler. When the patrimonial state is based on agriculture, regional atomization occurs and semiautonomous satraps emerge.

The third type involves a pattern of continuous belligerency between the patrimonial state and other states at its borders. It is reasonable to suppose, in fact, that military occupation and direct exploitation are simply extreme cases of patrimonial military expansion. The history of the old empires, including the Roman Empire, shows a clear pattern of expansion that includes, first, military occupation, looting, and enslavement of part of the local population and afterwards, the establishment of some kind of federation between conqueror and conquered, very often maintaining the local ruling class in its positions. The rationale for this arrangement is obvious, since the maintenance of the local economic and political structure assures a continous flow of revenue towards the patrimonial state, through levies and taxes of all kinds, which cannot be kept flowing in predatory conquests. The maintenance of this kind of local autonomy means that some power remains outside the state, and that tensions and conflicts are bound to arise.

A not altogether different situation occurs when some forms of autonomous activity emerge within the patrimonial dominion, with or without the ruler's consent and intention. One pattern here is the emergence of some industry or agriculture for the foreign market, which is heavily taxed by the state. The state stimulates this activity, but at the same time functions as a parasite that limits and eventually kills autonomous activity. This situation is different from the patrimonial state in the hydraulic type of society, where the government plays an active role in the organization and administration of the economy. Here, all the initiative comes from the private sphere, and the role of the state is almost purely fiscal. In absolutist Europe, this process was evidenced in the emergence of strong trade and industrial centers, which paralleled the progressive decay of feudal power. Eventually, it led to the emergence of bourgeois aspirations and values that brought about the destruction of the patrimonial state. Actually, in his analysis of Weber's theories on the emergence of legal rationality, Bendix shows that

> in western Europe patrimonial power eventually promoted the formal rationality of law and administration, and this conflicts with the tendency of patrimonial rulers to promote substantive justice and personal favoritism."

This process is explained by Weber, as are other things, as a consequence of the central government's need to restrain the power pretensions of vassals and officeholders. This restraint was accomplished through the establishment of a "centrally-controlled officialdom," and "in the struggle against the entrenched position of the states, patrimonial rulers were frequently supported by the rising bourgeoisie."[23]

It is fairly clear from the foregoing discussion that patrimonialism of the Western European kind, as it existed in the absolutist regimes, was very different from other versions. The main difference lies in the fact that Western European patrimonialism was strengthened together with the emergence of the bourgeoisie; at the end of the process, the system of legal domination, inherited by the absolutist regimes, was mostly contractual and most suited to modern capitalism. It would certainly be possible to trace the differences between state and stateless societies, suggested by Nettl, back to the varying balances between bourgeois and patrimonial powers in the struggle against the remains of the feudal, corporatist society. It is remarkable how Weber himself does not seem to have elaborated on the structural conditions that could explain the differences in legal rationality and authority between the Anglo-Saxon and the continental European countries. These differences are minimal, nevertheless, when compared with the states that changed from an original patrimonial system to a modern centralized state without the mediation of a bourgeois revolution. These states are certainly able to modernize and rationalize their bureaucracies, but their power bases and political systems must necessarily be quite different from those of the Western democracies. And these make up, of course, the bulk of today's non-Western countries.

A FOURFOLD REGIONALIZATION

The previous discussion presents a theoretical framework for the interpretation of the four types of Brazilian regions suggested at the beginning. The gap between the theoretical discussion and the Brazilian case can now be covered by showing how Brazilian regions belong to a more general type, a species related to the historical presence of a patrimonial state.

That Portugal did not fit the classic European type of feudal organization seems fairly established among historians:

> [Portuguese] nobility, according to Antonio de Souza, never plunged its roots in the countryside, nor had it ever had a civilizing, directive and protective role for the local population; it was rather a parasite living off the population and the central power.[24]

Power was concentrated in the House of Avis, and this fact helps to explain the remarkable entrepreneurial push that fifteenth- and sixteenth-century Portugal showed. The centralized, bureaucratic, and patrimonial structure of government was transplanted in Brazil, first with the establishment of the General Government in 1548, and much later with the migration of the whole Portuguese court to Rio in 1808.[25] Made independent in 1822 by a member of the Portuguese royalty, the line of continuity was never completely broken, and this fact is important for an understanding of the stable institutionalization of the Brazilian government during the colonial period, and later, in the second half of the nineteenth century. It is worth noting that prior to the establishment of the General Government in 1548, a system of feudallike captaincies was promoted, without success. These captaincies were to be transmitted from father to son, and the Portuguese Crown had to buy one of them back when the General Government was to be created.[26] The system of captaincies did not work out, the historicans say, but two of them enjoyed some success. One was Pernambuco, where the sugar culture flourished as the colony's main product during the sixteenth and seventeenth centuries. The other was São Vicente, later known as the Province and State of São Paulo.

This brief overview sketches three of our main region types. One of these is the government capital, which at first was Salvador, and later Rio de Janeiro. This is the country's most modern area: it has more direct contact with European life, and it's culture and consumption are more conspicuous. This also tended to be an area of marginal population and underemployment. According to the 1890 Census of Rio de Janeiro, for instance, about 50 percent of its employees were in "domestic services" or had "undeclared professions." Race was obviously a related factor since slavery had been abolished only two years earlier. But the differences are not that great: 76 percent of the blacks and 53 percent of the mulatoes were in this group, but also 43 percent of the whites, which represented 62.5 percent of the whole "employed" population.[27] This mass of marginal population was certainly a nuisance for the elite that had to reckon with them occasionally when they became restless.[28] Usually, however, Rio presented a picture of popular politics and mass participation which had little to do with how things were really decided. In this sense it did not differ much from the other administrative capitals of nonindustrial societies. Its economic resources were derived from trade and governmental employment, and its political life was characterized by some degree of tension between the urban bureaucrats and tradesmen on the one hand, and a dependent regional gentry on the other, with occasional mobilization of the populace. Election turnout never went above five percent of the total population before 1930; this fact gives us the overall pattern of political participation.

Nineteenth and early twentieth-century Rio de Janeiro can be broadly described as a preindustrial city. This concept was used by Gideon Sjoberg to characterize the urban structures that developed, according to him, in feudal societies where industrial development had not yet begun. In a footnote, Sjoberg tries to reduce the difference between European and non-European preindustrial towns:

> Henri Pirenne, in Medieval Cities, and others have noted that European Cities grew up in opposition to and were separate from the greater society. But this thesis has been overstated for Medieval Europe. Most industrial cities are integral parts of broader social structures.[29]

The main difficulty with the preindustrial city notion is, of course, the theory of unilinear development which it implies, and which takes the feudal system as the sole predecessor of modern societies. This point is made in a rebuttal to Sjoberg's book by Oliver C. Cox,[30] who states that even in medieval Europe the cities developed outside the feudal structure; Cox considers that Sjoberg's preindustrial city notion is little more than a residual concept.

Cox's criticism of Sjoberg's argument is convincing, but has little to offer as an alternative. The best theoretical clue, not surprisingly, is to be found in Max Weber, with his difference between occidental vs. oriental city.[31] For him,

> the residence of the ruler or of any administrative body being the focal point for the whole country or region is the most important feature in the structure and functioning of oriental cities.

In contrast, occidental cities are endowed with "corporate autonomy and autocephaly.[32] The theoretical consequences of these differences are manifold, and have to do with differences in social stratification, the role of the army, the existence of autonomous economic activities, education, and so on. These differences are not, of course, a matter of geography, but have to do with the differences between the patrimonial and the feudal variants of traditional domination. City politics in Rio de Janeiro was most certainly "local," in the sense that its bearing on national events was minimal; but the same cannot be said of the politics of its elite, which was eminently national.

The second region is the so-called "traditional" reverse of the bureaucratic and urban capital. Brazilian traditional regions have little in common with what appears as traditionalism in the standard literature on underdevelopment and modernization. This literature usually takes as traditional those peasant or otherwise nonindustrial societies that suffer the impact of modernization and industrialization.[33] These traditional societies are supposedly in a primitive stage of social and economic development, and the corresponding sociological literature deals with the cultural, emotional, and social obstacles to modern values, life-styles, and patterns of behavior.[34]

In Brazil, as in some other countries, traditional areas are not those that have not modernized, but, on the contrary, tend to be areas that have had a period of progress in the past, and then suffered a process of economic decay. The old sugar culture area of the Northeast and the former mining areas of Minas Gerais are probably the best example of Brazilian traditionalism: both have a past of wealth and national economic preeminence. One of the most obscure, but more interesting questions about Brazilian economic and political history is what happens with these areas when they lose their export capabilities and recede into the shadow of history.[35] In the case of Minas Gerais, the exhaustion of the mining activities by the second half of the eighteenth century left the province with the largest population in the country, mostly centered in urban settlements, and with no major economic activity of high profitability.[36] The other thing that remained was, most probably, the bureaucratic structure of the Portuguese administration, and this administration was certainly the means through which the political vocation of the Minas Gerias elite was born.

V. O. Key's *Southern Politics* is probably the best description of a political system that survives a process of political decay—in this case, the period after the South's defeat in the Civil War. (The eleven states studied by Key are also those of the Southern Confederacy.) He shows that these studies have at least one common trait with the Brazilian states of the Old Republic, namely the one-party system. Key's analysis of the behavior of Southern senators suggests a very consistent pattern: they unite whenever the state's autonomy is at stake, whenever the racial status quo is threatened, and whenever the national Democratic government needs their support. The arrangement is fairly clear: the Southern Democrats support the government in exchange for control in their own states. In spite of these well defined patterns, Southern politics is usually "issueless," since even the racial question tends not to be raised. One-party systems, oligarchic control of the state political machinery, little popular participation, large rural properties in a decaying economy—all these similarities with traditional Minas Gerais are not purely coincidental. The main difference, of course, is that while the Confederate states had been defeated by the industrialized North, in Brazil the political hegemony of the industrial center was never the case.[37]

The smallest unit in traditional politics of this kind is the local community in the countryside, where the local chieftain (in Brazil, the coronel) exerts his power. A sizeable portion of Brazilian political literature has been devoted to examining the patterns of political traditionalism at the grass roots.[38] The most successful theoretical attempts are those that interpret local and regional political preeminence as a function of the brokerage roles played by the political leaders among local, state, and national governments.[39] It is important to note that this interpretation does not imply that the control of the land, family ties, loyalties, and personal allegiances did not have a role to play. All of these traditional elements were certainly present in different degrees, but they worked in a context of economic decay and predominance of bureaucratic government at the state and national level.

The third region, represented by São Paulo, shows most important differences. Since the very beginning of the country's history, the former captaincy of São Vicente developed independently of central administration. São Vicente was the first settlement that moved from the coast to the hinterland, in open contradiction of the general settlement policy of the Portuguese Crown.[40] The history of the expansion of São Vicente includes Indian hunting expeditions that penetrated further and further south, resulting in a military clash with the Spanish Jesuit Missions; expeditions in search of gold and gems, until the clash over the mining areas with other immigrants from Rio and the north during the Emboabas War;[41] and a conspicuous absence of the Province of São Paulo from the first front of national events until the explosion of the coffee plantation in the nineteenth century.

This chapter is not the place for a history of the spectacular development of São Paulo from the late nineteenth century onwards, nor for the area's political role in the national picture. It is enough to recall that, after the 1940 census, it was the largest Brazilian state in terms of population, and it had for a long time been the main source of taxes for the central government and the center of the country's industrialization. Politically, São Paulo has been less important than its size and economic weight would suggest; and, in 1932, it was the last Brazilian state to rise in arms against the central government.[42]

This pattern of relationships between administrative and economic centers is not a Brazilian peculiarity; it is a more general phenomenon shared by those countries that experienced some development in the setting up of a strong patrimoniallike state.

Juan Linz finds in Spain the same paradox that we find in Brazil:

> Paradoxically, in the recent history of Spain, the most developed regions have felt alienated from the nation-state. Having "economic power" and well-being, they felt, rightly or wrongly, deprived of "political power."[43]

TABLE 1
SPAIN: BARCELONA AND MADRID

	"Bourgeois" Spain (Barcelona)	Madrid
Population 1960	24.20%	7.67%
Per Capita Income (national average = 100)	164	131
Recruitment of Cabinet Members of Franco Regime[a]	.85	6.25
Judges (1958)[a]	.58	3.24
University Professors[a]	.95	2.87

SOURCE: Juan Linz, "The Eight Spains," in R. L. Merritt and S. Rokkan, **Comparing Nations,** New Haven, Conn., Yale University Press, 1966.
a. Ratio of the proportion born in each "Spain" and the proportion of the population living there in 1910 (taken as a date close to the birth year of the elites).

The differences between Madrid and Barcelona, as expressed in Table 1, are strikingly similar to those we could find between Rio and São Paulo (see Table 2).

Italy seems to be another case in point, with differences among the industrial northern area, the urban and administrative center, and the rural south, as can be seen in Table 3.

A. F. Organski is aware of the regional discontinuities in Italy, and links the emergence of Fascism with them:

> Some regions modernize faster and further than others because of advantages in resources, available skills, communications with the outside world, or other

TABLE 2
BRAZIL: REGIONAL DIFFERENCES IN FOUR STATES
(in percentages)

	Population (1970)		Income			
	Urban	Total	From Industry	From Agriculture	From Public Sector	Total Income
São Paulo	27.3	19.0	56.8	19.5	23.5	35.3
Minas Gerais	11.7	12.3	7.5	12.2	8.3	10.0
Rio de Janeiro (Guanabara)	8.2	4.6	9.7	0.6	25.2	11.4
Rio Grande do Sul	6.8	7.1	5.9	12.6	8.9	8.5
Sum of Four States	54.0	43.0	79.9	44.9	65.9	65.2
Brazil	100	100	100	100	100	100

SOURCE: Fundacão IBGE, Instituto Brasileiro de Estatística, **Anuário Estatístico de Brasil, 1971.**

TABLE 3

ITALY: RESIDENT FAMILIES BY BRANCH OF ECONOMIC ACTIVITY OF THE HEAD OF THE FAMILY AND REGIONS (in percentages)

| Regions | Population | Number of Families with Head of Family Working in: | | |
		Industry	Agriculture	Other Activities
Settentrionale	44.8	56.5	35.5	47.1
Centrale	18.5	17.5	16.0	22.4
Meridionale	24.5	18.0	31.8	20.2
Insulare	12.2	8.0	16.7	10.3
Total	100	100	100	100

SOURCE: Calculated from Instituto Centrale de Statistica, **Compendio Statistico Italiano**, Rome, 1971, pp. 21 and 28-29.

reasons. Some nations modernize politically and remain backward economically. Other nations are highly urban before they are economically developed or politically modern . . . In the degree of symmetry and the degree of continuity in the changes of these three sets of variables (social, economic and political modernization) lies a very large portion—certainly a major portion—of the explanation for the appearance of fascist systems, the duration of their tenure, the variation in fascist political attitudes and behavior, and the manner and timing of the termination of the system.[44]

The assumption of unequal, but nevertheless unilinear development is probably the main weakness of this notion. Indeed, if "no nation develops in such a fashion that all regions and all aspects of national life keep in step with all the rest," it remains to be explained why only a few of these nations fall in the fascist pattern of political organization. The fact is that the differences are not just a matter of varying regional and functional rates of growth, but mostly a question of regional structural differentiation that the imbalances of development reflect.

The fourth region is Rio Grande do Sul, the southernmost state in the country. Its history starts with the establishment of the Portuguese colony of Sacramento at the border of the Rio de la Plata; an attack by the Spanish governor of Buenos Aires followed almost immediately. During most of the eighteenth century the region was the main point of friction between the Portuguese and the Spanish empires in America. After Brazil's independence, the military nature of the province remained because of the conflicts between Brazil and Argentina concerning the control of what is today Uruguay, as well as because of the separatist revolutionary movements in Rio Grande, which always involved dealings with Argentine and Uruguayan rulers and *caudillos*.[45]

Stein Rokkan has captured an important aspect of European nation-building which to some extent parallels the process that Rio Grande underwent. He shows essentially two types of city-states developing in Europe:

> The Swiss and Dutch confederations were essentially defensive in character: there was no strong conquest centre ... but a network of strategically placed cities willing to pool their resources in defense of their trading privileges.[46]

To these typical, occidental cities, he opposes another type, developed "at the edges" of the Old Roman Empire. "Paradoxically," he says, "the history of Europe is one of centre formation at the periphery." More specifically:

> These power centers at the southeastern and northeastern corners of the territories of the Roman Church built up crusading frontier empires against the rival world region of the South. This helps to explain the very close symbiosis of Church and State in these empires: the military might of the State was a decisive instrument in the struggle for the expansion of Western Christendom ... The Iberian empires brought the same fervour of orthodoxy across the ocean to the New World: the conquest of Latin America produced an even stronger fusion of religious, political and economic institutions.[47]

As in a system of Chinese boxes, Rio Grande seemed to have played in Brazil the same role that Portugal and Spain did in Christian Europe: as a frontier military outpost, it developed its own orthodoxy, Positivism—a peculiar combination of military tradition and cattle-raising culture—and a strong state oligarchy that gathered strength for the fights against the Spanish and porteño enemy for autonomy regarding the Brazilian Empire. The region was (and still is) the basis for the most important wing of the Brazilian army, and furnished a sizeable part of its cadres. It played a very active role in national politics since the creation of the *Partido Republicano Riograndense* in 1822, during the military overthrow of the Empire in 1889, and thereafter. It came to national power in 1930 with Vargas, governor of Rio Grande in behalf of the state boss, Borges de Medeiros; with Vargas, the *gauchos* literally hitched their horses in the national capital.[49] Vargas came to power again in 1950, Goulart in 1961, Costa e Silva and Medici after 1964: all these gaucho presidents testify to Rio Grande's remarkable vocation for national power, either through its civilian or its military sons.

This outline is too short to account for other important aspects of Rio Grande's role in Brazilian history. It would be important to take into account the state's internal cleavages, and its special economic role as a supplier of goods to the national market, as well as the importance that early European migration to the state had on the development of a highly productive agricultural system.[49] But the fact seems to remain that Rio Grande's political role at the national level has much more to do with its military, caudillo, revolutionary, and oligarchic traditions than with the modern and European-like aspects of its economy and society.

CONCLUSION

Granting that the fourfold regionalization suggested here is relevant to the study of Brazilian political history, one might still wonder about its usefulness in the analysis of future outcomes in Brazilian politics.

The Brazilian political picture suffered a drastic change after 1945, with the granting of political suffrage to the entire adult literate population. The system of mass politics that emerged after 1945 was superimposed upon the regional cleavages, creating a rather complex pattern that I analyze elsewhere.[50] To the cleavage between the patrimonial and the capitalist areas of national politics, and the cleavages among center, periphery, and frontier in the patrimonial state, another cleavage, involving issues of popular participation, was added. Basically, two dominant types of political participation emerged: one along the Minas-Rio axis, the other in the industrial areas of the country. The first was what can be called a "cooptation system," which was defined as a system of political participation in which governmental positions are sought not so much as resources for implementing sectoral interests, but rather as a means of social mobility in themselves. The second was closer to the classic concept of interest-group politics. There are rural and urban, as well as capitalist and working-class cleavages in each of these systems, making the number of possible combinations quite high. I believe that the regional context for the emergence of mass politics in Brazil is an essential clue to the understanding of this experience of representative democracy, if one intends to go deeper than what the simple concepts of modernization, mobilization, massification, or radicalization would allow.

Furthermore, the correct understanding of the 1945-1964 system is indispensable if predictions about the political future of the country are to be made. It is clear, for instance, that this discussion shows the naiveté of expecting a new party system to emerge in Brazil in terms of interest group representation. The present restrictions on political activity in the country cannot be taken as a simple consequence of the ideological preferences of the government; rather they should be seen as the development of an historical tradition of governmental centralization and weak autonomous organizations. This view means that, if the restrictions on political participation and mobilization are lifted, any workable political arrangement will have to be based on newly created forms of political organization, more in accordance with the realities of the country, and less as a function of the old-fashioned, interest-group imagery. Once the search for these new forms begins, a correct view of the history of political cleavages in the country will be indispensable.

NOTES

1. For the Role of São Paulo in the Brazilian political and economic systems, especially before 1945, see Warren Dean, The Industrialization of São Paulo, 1880-1945, Austin, University of Texas Press, 1969, and my discussion in "Representação e Cooptação, Politica no Brasil," Dados, Vol. 7, 1971.

2. See Simon Schwartzman, "Veinte Años de Democracia Representativa en Brasil," Revista Latinoamericana de Ciencia Política, Vol. 11, No. 1, April 1971.

3. For the role of Rio Grande do Sul in Brazilian regional politics, see Joseph L. Love, Rio Grande do Sul and Brazilian Regionalism, 1882-1930 Stanford, Stanford University Press, 1971. For a scholarly account of the social and political fabric of Rio Grande do Sul in the nineteenth century, see F. H. Cardoso, Capitalismo e Escravidão no Brasil Meridional, São Paulo, Difusão Europeia do Livro, 1962.

4. It is important to notice that I am leaving Bahia and Pernambuco out of the picture: these states were national political and economic centers in the colonial period, but have suffered a marked process of political "atimie." I am assuming that they fall in the traditional pattern typified by Minas Gerais, but this assumption is certainly a simplification that should only be accepted with caution.

5. See Stein Rokkan, "Dimensions of State Formation and Nation Building, A Possible Paradigm," in Charles Tilly (ed.), The Formation of National States in Western Europe (forthcoming under the sponsorship of the Committee on Comparative Politics, Social Science Research Council); and "Cleavage Structures, Party Systems and Voter Alignments: an Introduction" (with S. M. Lipset) in S. Rokkan and S. M. Lipset, Party Systems and Voter Alignments, New York, Free Press, 1967. Charles Tilly has suggested an extermely interesting framework for the analysis of Western European nation-building which is within the same perspective. Cf. "Reflections on the History of European Statemaking" and "Postscript: Western Statemaking and Theories of political Development," in Tilly, The Formation of National States in Western Europe.

6. See J. P. Nettl, "The State as a Conceptual Variable," World Politics, Vol. XX, No. 4, 1968, pp. 559-92.

The relative "statelessness" of American social science coincides with the relative statelessness of the United States, with the long period during which the egalitarian and pluralistic society predicted with sensitive fingertips by Tocqueville was becoming institutionalized over a vast continent. One has only to read Lipset or Mitchell to see that an American socio-political self-examination simply leaves no room for any valid notion of state..

7. Reinhard Bendix, "Social Stratification and the Political Community," in R. Bendix and S. M. Lipset (eds.), Class, Status and Power, New York, Free Press, 1966.

8. Cf. G. W. Hegel, Principes de la Philosophie du Droit, trans. by Andre Kaan, Paris, Gallimard, 1940, especially after p. 255.

9. I am following here the discussion of Jean Hippolyte, Etudes sur Marx et Hegel, Paris, Marcel Rivière, 1965, which refers to the classic work of G. Luckacz on the young Hegel.

10. This extract is a free translation of the French version of the "Critique de la Philosophie d'Etat de Hegel," in K. Marx, Oeuvres Philosophiques, Vol. 4, Paris, Molitor, p. 103.

11. See Nettl, op. cit., p. 572. The main reference here is Eugene Kamenka, The Ethical Foundation of Marxism New York, 1962.

12. N. Machiavelli, The Prince, New York, Modern Library, 1940, p. 15, quoted by R. Bendix, Max Weber—An Intellectual Portrait, New York, Doubleday, 1960, p. 360.

13. E. E. Schatschneider, The Semi-Sovereign People, New York, Holt, 1966, pp. 116-17.

14. Theodore J. Lowi, The End of Liberalism, New York, Norton, 1969, p. 102.

15. For a lengthy discussion of the concept and its history and fate in the Marxist literature, cf. Karl A. Wittfogel, Oriental Despotism, New Haven, Conn., Yale University Press, 1957, ch. 9.

16. This work was first published in Russia in 1939. It was translated into French by Roger Dangeville, as Fondements de la critique de l'Economie Politique, Paris, Anthropos, 1967. The reference is from Vol. 1, p. 437.

17. Ibid., p. 439.

18. Ibid.

19. This model is explicit in Engels' The Origin of Family, Private Property and the State. See the discussion in Wittfogel, op. cit., pp. 382 ff.

20. Behind this thesis is, among other things, the debate created by Barrington Moore's Social Origins of Democracy and Dictatorship, Boston, Beacon Press, 1966. Previous relevant works that lead to the same notion include Alexander Gerschenkron, Economic Backwardness in Historical Perspective, Cambridge, Mass., Harvard University Press, 1962, and R. Bendix, Work and Authority in Industry, New York, John Wiley, 1956, which deals with the role of the state in the class relations of industrial society. For a broader reference, see Simon Schwartzman, "Desenvolvimento e Abertura Política," Dados, Vol. 6, 1969, 36-41.

21. R. Bendix, Max Weber—An Intellectual Portrait, New York, Doubleday, 1960, p. 360.

22. Ibid., p. 348.

23. Ibid., pp. 405-06.

24. Sergio Buarque de Holanda, ed, História Geral da Civilização Brasileria, Vol. I, São Paulo, Difusão Européia do Livro, 1960, p. 18 (my translation).

25. The main source for the analysis of Portuguese patrimonialism in Brazil is Raymundo Faoro, Os Donos do Poder—Formação do Patronato Político Brasileiro, Porto Alegre, Editora Globo, 1958. For an overview of Spanish patrimonialism, see Magali Sarfatti, Spanish Bureaucratic Patrimonialism in America, Berkeley, Institute of International Studies, University of California, 1966.

26. See Burns, A History of Brazil, New York, Columbia University Press, 1970, p. 24:

Those inalienable land grants transmitted by inheritance to the oldest son brought to the New World some of the residues of feudalism long on the wane in the Iberian peninsula.

27. Data recalculated from Herbert S. Klein, "The Colored Freedmen in Brazilian Society," Journal of Social History, Vol. 3, No. 1, 1969, p. 50. The original source is the Diretoria Geral de Estatística, Recenseamento Geral ... de 1890, Distrito Federal, Rio de Janeiro, 1895, p. 416-21.

28. Rio has traditionally been the place for popular mobilization on political issues. One of the most well-known examples is the abolitionist campaign in the late nineteenth century; another was the rebellion of the Rio population in 1904 against compulsory smallpox vaccination. Edgar Carone gives a good example both of public proximity and public impotence in political issues in a quotation from an eyewitness of the 1889 coup that established the Republic:

> For the time being, the Government is purely military, and will remain this way. Theirs was the event, only theirs, because the cooperation of the civilian element was almost inexistant. The people followed all that stupified, surprised, without knowing what it meant. Many believed that it was a military parade. It was something worth seeing, the enthusiasm came later.

This extract is from a letter of Aristides Lobo, a newsman, quoted in Edgar Carone, A Primeira República, São Paulo Difusão Europeia do Livro, 1969, p. 288. (The translation is mine.)

29. Gideon Sjoberg, The Preindustrial City, New York, Free Press, 1960.

30. Oliver C. Cox, "The Preindustrial City Reconsidered," The Sociological Quarterly, Vol. V, 1964, p. 133-44.

31. Max Weber, The City, trans. and ed. by Don Martindale and G. Neuwith, New York, Free Press, 1958.

32. Vatro Murvaer, "Some Tentative Modifications of Weber's Typology: Ocidental vs. Oriental City," Social Forces, Vol. 44, March 1966, pp. 381-89.

33. Classic references here are E. Banfield, The Moral Basis of a Backward Society, New York, Free Press, 1958, and Daniel Lerner, The Passing of Traditional Society, New York, Free Press, 1958. Implicit in Banfield's work is the assumption that, as people become less backward, their frame of reference expands from "amoral-familism" to "public regardiness." (The presence of public-regardiness in the North American upper strata was tested, quite unsuccessfully, in J. Q. Wilson and E. C. Banfield, "Public Regardiness as a Value Premise in Voting Behavior," American Political Science Review, Vol. 58, No. 4, December 1964, pp. 876-87.) Lerner's relevance in the sociology of development also should not be minimized. According to Bendix, "the great merit of Lerner's study consists in its candid use of Western modernization as a model of global applicability" (R. Bendix, "Tradition and Modernity Reconsidered," in Embattled Reason, New York, Oxford University Press, 1970, p. 250).

34. For instance, see Lucien Pye, Politics, Personality and Nation Building, New Haven, Conn., Yale University Press, 1962.

35. This process of economic decay and the mechanisms of adjustment are the subject of Antonio Barros de Castro, "A Herança Regional do Desenvolvimento Brasileiro," Ensaios sobre a Economia Brasileira, Vol. II, Rio de Janeiro, Forense, 1971. For an analysis of the economic mechanisms behind the growing inequalities between the Northeast and the Southwest of Brazil, see Nathaniel H. Leff, "Desenvolvimento Econômico e Desigualdade Regional: Origens do Caso Brasileiro," Revista Brasileira de Economia, Vol. 26, No. 1, January-March 1972.

36. In the 1872 census, 20.54 percent of the Brazilian population was concentrated in Minas Gerais, as against 13.89 percent in Bahia and 8.43 percent in

São Paulo. São Paulo takes the lead only in the 1940 census, with 17.4 percent of the population compared to 16.4 percent in Minas.

37. V. O. Key, Southern Politics, New York, Knopf, 1949, especially ch. 16, "Solidarity in the Senate."

38. For a review of this literature, see José Murilo de Carvalho, "Estudos de Poder Local no Brasil," Revista Brasileira de Estudos Políticos (Belo Horizonte), No. 25-26, June 1968, pp. 231-48. Glaucio Soares, in a forthcoming book on the 1945-64 period, has shown in a typology of Brazilian grass-roots politics that the traditional coronel type of local politics is just one kind of local power, more typical of Minas Gerais than of São Paulo. Cf. Glaucio A. D. Soares, A Democracia que Passou mimeographed, Brasília, 1971.

39. The best theoretical interpretation of local politics in traditional Brazil is certainly Antonio Octavio Cintra, "A Integração do Processo Político no Brasil: Algumas Hipóteses Inspiradas na Literatura," Revista de Administração Pública, (Rio de Janeiro, Fundação Getúlio Vargas), Vol. 5, No. 2, 1971.

40.

> But São Paulo's case, where the colonos and their descendants—white or mestiço—preferred the interior to the coast is, in any case, an exception. In the rest of Brazil, for a long time, the rule was to follow the classic settlement patterns of Portuguese colonizing activities which had been dictated by mercantils convenience and by the African and Asian experiences."

See Sergio Buarque de Holanda, História Geral da Civilização Brasileira, Vol. 1, pp. 129-30.

41. For a description of the Emboabas War against the Paulista explorers in Minas Cerais around 1700, see Holanda, Ibid., pp. 297-369.

42. Actually, after 1932, Minas Gerais rebelled twice against the central government, once, through a "Manifesto dos Mineiros," against the Vargas dictatorship, and later with the government of Magalhães Pinto against João Goulart in 1964. In both cases, the central government was soon to be overthrown by the army. The São Paulo Governor, Adhemar de Barros, also threatened to set his state against Goulart in 1964; but this attempt was less consonant with the national civil-military movement, and his own political survival was not maintained The differences in pattern are significant.

43. Juan Linz, "The Eight Spains," in L. Merritt and S. Rokkan, Comparing Nations, New Haven, Conn., Yale University Press, 1966, p. 278 ff. See the tables comparing Brazil and Spain. Juan Linz gives some "soft" data that cannot easily be reproduced for Brazil. Alfred Stepan, nevertheless, makes an explicit parallel between Madrid-Barcelona and Rio-São Paulo when referring to the recruitment of cadets for Brazilian Military School. He shows that, in the 1964-66 period, São Paulo had 18.3 percent of the Brazilian population, but only 8.26 percent of the Army cadets, giving a ratio of about 5 to 10. The ratio for Rio de Janeiro was 90 to 10, and for Rio Grande do Sul, 19 to 10. The ratio for Rio Grande in an earlier period is much higher. Alfred Stepan, The Military in Politics, Princeton, Princeton University Press, 1971, p. 38.

44. A. F. Organski, "Fascism and Modernization," in S. D. Wolf (ed.), The Nature of Fascism, New York, Vintage Books, 1969, pp. 19-41.

45. The best study on Rio Grande do Sul's political history in the twentieth century is certainly Joseph L. Love's Rio Grande do Sul and Brazilian Regionalism, Stanford, Stanford University Press, 1971. The Brazilian bibliography on the early

period is quite extensive. For a detailed account of the conflicts with the Spanish colonies since the establishment of the colonia de Sacramento, see Alcides Lima, História Popular do Rio Grande do Sul, Porto Alegre, O Globo, 1935.

46. Stein Rokkan, "Dimensions of State Formation and Nation Building," op. cit.

47. Ibid.

48. For the relationships between the Rio Grande caudillos and the army, see Sylvio Romero, O Castilhismo no Rio Grande do Sul, Porto, 1912. J. Love gives a detailed account of the role of Rio Grande in the "military question," that eventually led to the fall of the empire. He also reproduces a photo of the guachos hitching their horses to the obelisk on Rio's Avenida Rio Branco on November 1, 1930.

49. For the economic role of Rio Grande as a supplier of the internal market, see the section headed "Extremo Sul-O precoce desenvolvimento Voltado para Dentro," in The Chapter entitled "A Herança Regional do Desenvolvimento Brasileiro," in Antonio Barros de Castro, Ensaios sobre a Economia Brasileira, Vol. II, Rio de Janeiro, Forense, 1971.

50. Cf. S. Schwartzman, "Veinte Años de Democracia Representativa en Brasil, op. cit.

CHAPTER 7

DIVERSITIES AMONG DEPENDENT NATIONS:
AN OVERVIEW OF LATIN AMERICAN DEVELOPMENTS

José A. Silva Michelena

JOSE A. SILVA MICHELENA is Professor of Political Science at the School of Sociology and Anthropology at the Central University of Venezuela in Caracas. He has worked closely with Frank Bonilla at the M.I.T. Center for International Studies; out of this collaboration was published the series *The Politics of Change in Venezuela.* He is co-editor of Volume I, *A Strategy for Research on Social Policy,* and author of Volume III, *The Illusion of Democracy in Dependent Nations.*

THE CURRENT STATE OF RESEARCH

There is no doubt that a new trend in political science has developed over the past fifteen years. This new trend may be characterized, in general, by the use of diverse relevant social sciences to explain a given theme, by greater and more systematic comparative efforts, and by a renewed interest in social dynamics. According to Almond and Powell[1] this new trend has been beneficial to political science because it has helped to defeat the old parochial, configurative, formalistic approach and stimulated the emergence of a new, more comprehensive, realistic, and precise approach, tending to seek out a new theoretical order.

AUTHOR'S NOTE: The focus of this paper on Latin America as a whole is limited by the examples chosen to illustrate specific points. Whenever possible we looked for cases located in the northern part of Latin America (Mexico and the Caribbean) inasmuch as other papers presented to the meeting on State formation and

One of the themes where this theoretical order has reached an advanced stage of crystallization is the so-called modernization or political development field. In the last five years more and more political scientists have reached a virtual consensus about a general definition of modernization and about the main processes underlying political development.[2] Much widely accepted literature refers to one or several of the following main processes: identity, rationalization of authority, structural differentiation, political participation, and center formation.[3]

A critical analysis of these theories reveals that, on the whole, we have not yet found an explanatory theory. Two main limitations may be pointed out here. In the first place there is no clear definition of the interrelations between those key processes. The question why in some cases we had a particular sequence and in others a quite different one has not been tackled. Often we have no explicit formulation of the effects of one type of crisis on others, and there is no clear-cut definition allowing us to recognize when we are faced by one or another type of crisis. To avoid this problem, some scholars assume that these crises represent permanent processes and that they develop at different speeds. Even so, the differential pace of chance of the different processes remains to be explained. The alternative of "measuring" them by a set of indicators, assuming that this can be done for long periods of time, offers only a superficial solution to the problem. Indicators, as the name clearly reveals, are merely the most obvious manifestations of some structural, underlying phenomenon. If we lack the appropriate knowledge of such a structure, the indicator is left drifting like a meaningless buoy. To summarize this criticism, identity, rationalization of authority, structural differentiation, political participation and center formation are useful categories which help the political scientist to describe the process of nation-building, because they themselves are the manifestations of other processes that, within specific historic frames, are altering the structure of society.

Perhaps the most serious flaw that the theoretical perspective just examined introduces into the analysis of political scientists seeking to explain the process of nation-building in the underdeveloped world is that it insensibly leads them to consider underdeveloped nations as wholes, to be explained without references to the global context in which they exist. It is common to find studies of underdeveloped national political "systems" without serious references to the international relations of such

nation-building (Cérisy-la-Salle, France, 7-11 August 1970) dealt with examples from the rest of the continent. This paper rests heavily on parts of two chapters of a larger work of mine entitled *The Illusion of Democracy In Dependent Nations,* Vol. 3 of Frank Bonilla and J. A. Silva Michelena (eds.), *The Politics Of Change In Venezuela,* Cambridge, MIT Press, 1968.

systems. Since, as will be shown later, such international relations (which we may call dependency) constitute the most important variable for understanding the system, the explanations given are very limited.

Such limitations do not happen casually or because the scholars making those studies are not well trained. They arise from the limitations of the more general theory to which, consciously or not, they subscribe. What is this more general theory?

We are not, of course, referring to a general or even partial model, which explicitly maps the interrelations among the important political processes described earlier. Such a model does not yet exist. We are referring to the more general formulation known today as the theory of modernization. This theory attempts to explain the process of the transition of society from a traditional to a modern pole. This trend of thought has a long tradition in the social sciences and among its more coherent exponents was Ferdinand Tönnies; we will not here trace the history of the traditional-modern continuum theory. The most recent and comprehensive versions of this model have been formulated by Rostow, and Milikan et al., in the series of studies in political development sponsored by the Committee on Comparative Politics of the Social Science Research Council, and by Almond and Powell.[4] One of the basic features of this model is that it assumes a unilinear mode of evolution of societies. If one knows the initial and ending points, one can "explain" any society, at any given time, as a transitional society, more or less advanced, depending on the particular combination of traits that one finds in it. Since a purely traditional or a purely modern society can never be found in reality, because they are ideal types, the most advanced Western societies are inevitably transformed into the models which set the pattern of development for the rest of the world.

Some scholars, also following a long tradition in the social sciences, have identified definite stages of development. The variety of approaches depends more on which particular aspect of society is emphasized than on anything else. Thus, one may find explanations which underline the role of motivational factors such as achievement, or social processes such as communication, or the importance of normative orientations (pattern-variables), or economic processes. All of these approaches share the same basic theoretical assumption of unilinearity. A consequence of adopting this basis assumption is to believe that if the necessary reforms are done internally, any society can evolve toward higher levels of development.

For each underdeveloped area of the world, there exist more or less explicit formulations which take this perspective. In the case of Latin America, there are several studies that in one way or another have taken this perspective.[5] We shall here proceed to summarize briefly the most serious and up-to-date formulations.

According to these formulations, underdevelopment is simply a stage in the relatively long road to development. At the end of this road lies the affluent society, in which the most urgent needs of all are fulfilled, a society that today's conservatives would oppose as a serious danger to traditional social values—a welfare state. Clearly then the task before those espousing developmentalism would be devising and developing political support for a series of steps, which would result in a country's active movement in the desired direction. What policies would that involve?

The endemic illness of Latin America, it has been said, arises from the fact that from its earliest colonial days, it grew outward, because its economy was based on primary exports. This not only prevented modernization, it ensured that the centers of economic decision-making would be located outside the countries. It was assumed that the building of a national industry would increase the growth of the economy, provide jobs for the growing marginal populations being driven from the rural areas by the crass inhumanity of the agrarian structure, and finally, transfer decision-making power to groups within the national boundaries.

A national bourgeoisie would emerge, which would then be the active agent of industrialization. This national bourgeoisie, in developing the material base of the country, would in the process become the ruling elite and fulfill its historical role: it would ally itself with most modern sectors of the middle classes and of the proletariat.

Merged in multiclass parties, this group would take the reins of political power from the traditional ruling classes. It was assumed that once this heterogeneous developmentalist group had achieved real political power, the democratization of the country would be accelerated: redistribution of income would be accomplished by means of programmes such as land reform, radical expansion of education, and increased political participation. This would lead to the reaffirmation of a sense of autonomy which, along with the structural changes mentioned above, would crystallize in the formation of a true national state. On this basis, the struggle for better international trade terms would be facilitated. It would be possible to denounce unfavourable commercial treaties with other countries and to supplant with domestic capital the international loans and foreign investments which had been the initial compromises necessary to acquire the funds to initiate the programme of internal growth and development.

AN HISTORICAL APPROACH:
THE PROCESS TOWARD UNDERDEVELOPMENT

Even to the uninformed it is obvious that what has happened in Latin America in the past two decades sharply contradicts the expectations of the theory just outlined above. Instead of reaching a take-off stage, Latin America seems to be in an even more profound crisis than before. That crisis is dramatically expressed in several forms: a sharp reconcentration of power by repressive military elites, increase of the marginal population in cities, denationalization of the economy, enormous concentration of growth in terms of employment and income[6] and progressive reduction of the growth rate of per capita income in Latin America as a whole.[7] In other words, why did the anticipated take-off toward development never come about? What was wrong with the modernization or developmentalist theory? The answer to these questions may be found, if one reconsiders the entire historical process that brought about the underdevelopment of Latin America.

Colonial Stage

The area which today is called Latin American was discovered when the economically most powerful European nations were expanding throughout the world in search of new trade routes, new markets, and primary resources. At that time, Spain and Portugal had some industry and carried on minor trade with other European countries, some of which were under the dominion of Spain. The prolonged internal crusade, which led to the reconquest of Spain from the Moors and the expansion of the dominion of the Spanish Empire, imposed upon the metropolis the need for precious metals to finance the enormous expenditures made necessary by the new conditions of the country. The inflow of gold and silver that soon started from the West Indies, provoked an inflationary process in Spain which, along with the competition from the growing industrial mercantilism taking place in Holland, France, and Great Britain, contributed to the deterioration of the incipient Spanish industries.

England, for example, permitted sizeable emgiration to its colonies not only to ensure supplies of raw materials but also to enlarge export markets. These markets could be maintained and broadened only if colonists to the new world were permitted reasonable latitude in the development of the lands they had occupied. Their purchasing power, obviously, depended upon their own economic growth. However, unequal development of the American colonies cannot by explained by ethnic origin alone; if that were the only factor, then one would expect the south of North America, India, and other British colonies to reach a level of development similar to that of New England, The fact that New England, in contrast to the south of North America, Mexico, New Grenada, Peru, and other Spanish-American colonies, was able to reach a higher level of development may also be imputed to the fact that there was practically no organized labour force in the former area and therefore the exploitation of the available land was done by immigrants, who not only worked in relatively free conditions but also were permitted to have comparatively high salaries.[8]

The economies of the Luso-Spanish colonies were organized according to a different and extremely rigid pattern. The colonies were viewed by the mother countries as sources of wealth in the form of gold, silver and later, raw materials, not in the form of potential markets. On the other hand, especially in the areas rich in silver and gold mines (Mexico and Peru), there was, to begin with, a sizeable and organized labour force which was enslaved or reduced to serfdom. Therefore, growth could only take place by means of exporting the products which were assigned to the colonial economies in the international division of labour. Production for export thus became the principal generator of surpluses. The greater part of these surpluses was shipped to the metropolis and what remained in the colony, if not conspicuously consumed, was reinvested in activities that yielded the biggest profits. Therefore, a mono-productive and mono-exporting economic structure developed.[9]

Colonial policies of the mother country were tailored to ensure that the colonies would develop no national sense of their own. Forms of guaranteeing dependency were various: Spain established intermediary centres (e.g. Mexico, New Grenada, Lima, and later on Rio de la Plata) between the colonies and the metropolis. This guaranteed Spain both a monopoly of trade and an effective political control over the colonies.

The Spaniards, in this drive to keep their colonies both separate from and dependent on predetermined power centres, granted exclusive trading rights to Spaniards sent out from Spain. This policy was also aimed at maintaining the largest possible margin of profit for Spain. The second major technique for averting any possibility of the development of independent political structures in the colonies was the policy of appointing Spaniards only to important political positions. For a long period, these arrangements effectively excluded any possibility that the *criollos* would be able to develop local voluntary associations and control their own destinies. Despite their Spanish descent and what would seem to have been their logical right to benefit from their economic activities and to control their political destiny, they were limited to agrarian activities—albeit on large plantations—and to minor political offices in the city.

Although such general traits are common to all of Latin America, it is obvious that even in colonial times important differences developed among the colonies. These differences emerged from the timing in which the main thrust of colonization was carried forward. But the timing depended on the type of natural and labour resources available. The colonies which developed first were those where abundant gold and silver mines were found and where a sizeable labour force was available. These colonies became the political centres of the overseas territories. Later on, Spaniards dedicated themselves to expanding their control of the colonies by means of developing the exploitation of exotic tropical products. The economy of plantations was thus developed. Mexico, Peru, Bolivia, and to a lesser degree, Colombia, represented the first type of areas while the second category covered the rest of Spanish America.

There is a trend of thought which maintains that the mode of production developed by Spanish policies in Latin America was a feudal one. This is a mistake since it constitutes an attempt to force the Latin American reality into a concept developed to describe a European situation. To begin with, at the time of the discovery of America, Spain was at a stage which could rather be described as mercantile and financial capitalism, although it is true that the old feudal structures were not totally liquidated and Spanish feudalism was fundamentally different from the classical French feudalism. Moreover, the Spaniards' "own colonization experience in the south of Spain opened the possibility of conceiving a new type of settlement" for Spanish America.[10]

The transitional situation of Spain, the innovative thrust together with the differentiated resources and the cultural and social structures found in Latin America resulted in the formation of a new and heterogeneous mode of production in which different relations of production coexisted. But what was common to all of them was the overexploitation of the labour force.

The heterogeneous Latin American mode of production was more oriented toward the satisfaction of the needs of the metropolis than to inducing internal development of the colony, and it resulted in the formation of a specific class structure and a nucleated distribution of the population centres.

Apart from the place which each group occupied in the productive structure just described, the ethnic criteria also operated to shape the hierarchical structure of classes. Thus, Spaniards, who were at the top of the pyramid, reserved for themselves the import-export activities and higher political positions, and the white criollos, directly descendant from Spaniards, took over mining, agriculture, and cattle raising. Marginal whites (blancos de orilla) who came from the periphery of the Spanish Empire, and those whose purity of blood was dubious, usually devoted themselves to minor internal commerce and crafts. Then followed the pardos, the racially mixed population, who worked in the haciendas as "free" workers in a variety of forms. Some of the pardos were able to manage small shops, while others, although a minority, were enslaved. Then followed the Indians who were subject to the system of mita (obligatory labour) and who worked as labourers in agriculture or were enslaved. Finally, there was a large group of black slaves. The social rigidity of this structure varied according to the place of the colony in the politico-administrative scheme imposed by Spain, which in turn was designed according to the wealth of the territory. In the richest territories (Mexico, New Grenada, Peru) main centres of powers (Viceroyships) were created, with a socially rigid society.

Since the entire system was rather outwardly oriented, a true internal centre never developed, but rather a system of internally isolated regions having more contact with the metropolis than with other colonies. This system delayed the formation of a sense of identity in the population of the colony. However, towards the beginning of the nineteenth century, the colonial system was already being weakened by several factors. Internally, the growing conflicts between the Spanish merchants and criollo land-owners, each of whom was attempting to obtain a larger share of the excedents produced, together with the growing aspirations of the pardos and the frequent revolts of Indians and slaves were gradually bringing about the disintegration of the colonial system. This climate of tension made the dominant classes of criollos sensitive to the revolutionary ideas which had earlier emerged from the American movement for independence and from the French Revolution. Externally, the Spanish control of the colonies was gradually being loosened by British and Dutch piracy and contraband. But the coup de grace was given by the loss of the Spanish control of Spain due to its occupation by Napoleon's troops.

In view of the latent, and in some places quite overt, conflicts between the criollos and the Spaniards, the criollos took advantage of the opportunity to launch the war of emancipation. This war, of course, developed according to the peculiarities of the different colonies; a common factor was that, although for the criollos the enemy was clearly the Spanish, for the rest of the population (pardos, Indians, and slaves) this was not quite as obvious. Their interest lay chiefly in liberating themselves from the unjust system of exploitation to which they were subjected. This heterogeneity of conflicting interests affected the future course of events.

With political independence for Latin America came the possibility of transforming the former colonies into automonous centres, since the development of an indigenous capitalism was finally possible. But this alternative was never adopted, because the criollos clung to the economic and social patterns of the past and facilited a new form of dependency on the growing British Empire.

The Formation of Nationality

By the end of the eighteenth century British industrial products, especially textiles, had already conquered a large portion of the Spanish American markets and by 1815, had already saturated these markets. The criollos, both during the war of independence and afterwards, concentrated on keeping the economy linked with the world capitalist market through the exploitation and export of primary products, which constituted the main source of the badly needed economic growth. But the impact of British commerce differed according to the nature of the raw materials extracted and the size of the local markets. This impact was more extensive in those places which were climatically suitable for producing the materials most needed by British industries or consumers and which, in turn, had the largest markets for British products: the Atlantic countries and those in the south cone of Latin America.

In mining regions like Mexico and Peru, or regions with a very small potential market, like Central America, the Antilles, and Venezuela, an almost completely outwardly oriented economy was fostered. These economies remained enclaves throughout the nineteenth century.[12]

In the mining countries, foreign investments in services, energy, and transportation helped create some internal markets and even stimulated the emergence of local industries, creating the necessary conditions to foster a process of national integration. In the enclave economies, on the contrary, their kind of dependency on the world market not only prevented the significant inward-oriented impact of foreign commerce but also prevented the early formation of a national market.

It has become part of common wisdom that Western political institutions were not created by chance. They were structured to meet the needs to administer, guide, and facilitate the development of the new capitalist relations of production and distribution being established throughout Europe. The development of European industry created not only a new mode of work, "free work", but also a new form of organizing production: a hierarchical system. This system was ultimately imposed on society through state bureaucracy. Along with the consolidation of markets, national boundaries were defined and competition, established for capturing the world market, fostered national economic and political development.[13]

In Latin America the process of state formation has followed different lines. Since the basic economic mechanism is derived from the relationship between exports and imports, the society as a whole is outwardly oriented. The state and the bureaucracy are not seen as necessary instruments to improve the national position in the world competitve market; on the contrary, it is the world market, by means of the dominant powers, which imposes the conditions of existence on a given country. No internal class is able, therefore, to see the nation as a project or economic development as a reason of state.

Moreover, the nucleated urban structure, created during colonial times and based on a hinterland of plantations (*haciendas*), led to the formation of competing regional caudillos who, in the course of the nineteenth century, fought incessantly to gain control of the central power. In general, the nations which, during colonial times and in the first years of independent life, were able to reach the highest level of development, were those which first reached the stage of national integration of markets and the concentration of power by means of centralizing caudillo. At this stage, three dominant classes developed: the latifundistas (big landowners), the importers and their administrators, and the latifundista generals. Although they held considerable local control, they were still under a dependent structure, subordinate to decisions which they did not control. The backwardness of the productive forces made the organization of the masses almost impossible. Instead, the masses were used alternatively as soldiers or as semifree workers. The lowest classes, then, were subjected to a double domination, internal and external, and did not profit at all from their own work.

During the nineteenth century, in almost every nation of Latin America, the process of gradual secularization of society, or rather, the gradual loosening of church power upon society, represented one of the most generalized conflicts, which usually appears superimposed on the problem of concentration of power. Mexico is perhaps one of the cases where all these conflicts or crises appear most acutely.[14]

The history of most Latin American countries during the nineteenth century as a whole is a history of the frustration of national formation: the legacy of the colonial period and the new relations of dependency on the British led to the destruction of crafts and local industries and prevented the emergence of a national class which would have been capable of articulating objectives of economic autonomy.

Neocolonial Stage

With the advent of the twentieth century the United State rapidly emerged as the dominant world economic power. Latin American markets were rapidly taken over by United States enterprises. North Americans also invested directly in enterprises related to primary production: sugar mills in Cuba, Santo Domingo, and Puerto Rico, banana plantations in Central America, oil industry in Venezuela, copper mines in Chile; and so forth. A process of technological transference began to take place from United States corporations to growing Latin American industries. The economic collapse of the 1930s had significant repercussions on most of the Latin American economies, with the exception of Venezuela. This crisis fostered the idea that Latin America should develop its own industry, carrying out the process known as industrialization by means of import substitution.

The process of industrialization proceeded more swiftly in nations such as Argentina and Chile which, economically speaking, were already more advanced and had already solved the problem of concentration of power. In these nations industrialization followed three definite stages. At first, industry grew quickly due to the fact that a market for consumer goods already existed, the technology employed was rather simple and capital requirements were small. A new class of local industrial entrepreneurs began to emerge and participational and integrational aspirations were encouraged in the masses through the stimulation of consumption. Populist governments such as those of Getulio Vargas in Brazil, and Perón in Argentina politically canalized these aspirations. But the inadequacy of such development was soon apparent, through the limitations of the "national" bourgeoisie, when it came to tackling the second or third stages of import substitution, industrialization (substitution of intermediate and capital goods), as well as through the further concentration of economic activities.

In contrast to the first stage, the technological requirements for producing intermediate or capital goods were high and required large capital investments. Since local entrepreneurs had neither, industry gradually began to be denationalized under the increasing advances of American and other foreign multinational corporations. The kind of technology used in this connection also brought about several deforming structural consequences. First, the goods produced with this advanced technology were intended for a diversified, sophisticated market. The market was therefore limited to the upper income strata representing from 10 to 30 percent of the population. Since the patterns of consumption of this limited, sophisticated market required a diversified production, factories usually operated at levels where it was impossible to attain economies of scale. Prices were therefore necessarily high, since industries usually operated at half capacity. In other words, badly needed capital resources were not fully used or, to put it more crudely, were wasted. But industry intended for this kind of market is very dynamic, due to incessant imported innovations. Entrepreneurs are forced to improve their factories before they reach full capacity and the phenomenon of waste becomes permanent. Finally, since the technology used is labour saving, a structural problem of unemployment emerges. All of these factors—restricted market, high prices, wasted capacity and labour saving—mean that an increasingly large sector of the population is becoming a potentially explosive urban mass.

Because of the importance of the issue, we shall consider in detail some of the questions involving the role of technology in furthering dependence. Let us assume for the moment, that the bourgeoisie were culturally and politically able, autonomously, to confront and undertake the second phase of import substitution, industrialization. What would be the likelihood of their success? Up to now there has been little or no capacity within Latin America to generate the technology required to establish such industrial complexes. Inevitably then, under the present form of political organization, the country would have to adopt methods of production and forms of organization and control dictated by those who own the technology, and it would continue to be subordinate to foreign interests.

Although a number of theorists recognize the risk of adopting technology produced in advanced countries, they feel that such use also has great advantages. The Brazilian economist, Celso Furtado, recently pointed out the fallacy in this assumption. Latin American entrepreneurs (assuming that they have accumulated the capital and have the cultural disposition to do so) may choose from a wide spectrum of ready-made technology, which makes it unnecessary for them to invest in creating it. But how real is this advantage in the light of the needs of society? The technology of advanced countries is developed primarily around the goals of saving both labour and raw materials—perhaps the only abundant resources in underdeveloped countries. The adoption of technology only tends, therefore, to worsen unemployment structurally, among the classes in which it is the greatest problem, and to diminish the overall impact of new investments on the national economy. Furthermore, the adoption of a foreign technology is almost inevitably linked to dependence on the foreign groups which produce it, leading, in the end, to the denationalization of the economy.

The adoption of alien technology has further consequences for underdeveloped societies. Armando Córdova, for example, points out that alien technology imposes alien patterns of consumption which, in turn, brake the development of national productive forces. Marx had already pointed that out:

> Production not only provides materials to fulfill needs it also provides needs for materials. . . . The need for an object which consumers experience has been created by perception of such an object. . . . Thus production not only produces an object for a subject, but also produces a subject for an object,[16]

Interdependently and dynamically then, both processes reinforce the dependency of the peripheral country on a technologically and economically dominant one.

In addition, within the dependent country, the local bases of production of science and technology and, in general, of the culture which emerges from developments in the productive process are judged according to foreign patterns and standards. This situation not only reinforces the use of alien technology, it gradually eliminates the possibility of developing an autonomous mechanism for producing the technological innovations allowing the development of an indigenous production structure. Moreover, since increments in productivity and, therefore, in workers' income, are linked to technological advances made in other countries, the workers tend to perceive dependency as necessary to their personal betterment. This idea is generally reinforced by the alien culture that is diffused through the mass media. In this way the effects of alien, and alienating, technology are propagated through the productive process, to social classes, culture, and society.[17]

Dependency is thus revealed as a particular form of relationship between advanced dominant economic centres and peripheral dependent economies.

This general process has taken place in different ways in different countries. It is more advanced in countries like Argentina, Brazil, Chile, and Mexico, which in the last century were able to take advantage of an early process of national economic and political integration. In other countries, such as Venezuela, Colombia, and Peru, the process is midway. In others it is still at its beginnings.

The foregoing analysis of this relationship was made from the standpoint of dependent countries. It also, of course, has to be viewed within the framework of relations among the dominant world powers.

These relations have changed during the years since the Second World War. Furtado has admirably described the dissolution of the alliance between the United States and the Soviet Union after the war and the emergence of the rivalry between the great powers which has dominated the structure of world politics for many years.[18]

More recently, the so-called "bi-polar" structure of world politics has changed into a more complex multipolar situation with the growth of Chinese power, the growing autonomy of Europe, and the rise of new independent states in Africa and Asia. In the multipolar world, the United States and the Soviet Union have shown tendencies to accept, on the one hand, a kind of pragmatic coexistence and avoid direct confrontation and, on the other, to seek to ensure their position over their special spheres of influence, the Soviets in Eastern Europe and the Americans in Latin America and the Caribbean.

Within this changing situation, the policies of the United States exerted great pressure on the internal developments of Latin American countries. Indeed, any analysis of these developments has to take these external pressures into account. A complex analysis of this relation is beyond the scope of this chapter, but should be noted as one begins to consider future research needs.

PRIORITIES FOR FUTURE RESEARCH

The historical analysis advanced in previous sections points to some general hypotheses, which need further research in order to be refined and tested. The first of these hypotheses refers to the formation of underdevelopment in Latin America as part of the process of world economic expansion. However, within this unity, diversities stem both from differences in structural situations, motivations, and policies of the dominant countries and from the peculiarities emerging from the specific economic, social, and political conditions of dependent societies.

The general question which needs to be explained is the old problem of unequal development of different regions of the world. A comparative historic study of the formation of underdevelopment in Asia, Africa, and Latin America is needed in order to elaborate, if possible, a long-range theory of unequal development of human societies. We saw that the theory of modernization is inadequate both as an explanatory theory and as a guide for policymaking oriented toward the suppression of under-development.[10]

Focusing on contemporary world politics, it is obvious that the destiny of any underdeveloped society depends, to a great extent, upon what happens in world politics and on the economic and political tendencies of the dominant countries. The study of the implications for underdeveloped societies of both internal and world politics of the dominant countries is another area of research priority. These studies, in order to be useful, in the sense of delineating, from the perspective of underdeveloped societies, the framework within which the national formation and development processes take place, have to concentrate in detail on the study of regional policies of dominant countries. (For instance, in the case of Latin America, it does not suffice to study the United States policy toward Latin America. This policy needs to be studied in relation to the United States policy toward other underdeveloped regions of the world. Then, the linkage between these two sets of policies and the United States relations with the Soviet Union and other world superpowers needs to be established.)

A final area of research priority is the detailed study of national societies. If it is true that what happens among the dominant world powers to a great extent determines the course of events in the rest of the world's nations, it is also true that the outcome in each particular case depends, to an even greater extent, upon the particular conditions of internal situations. To make it more explicit, dependency is not an external factor but a phenomenon with manifestations in the internal structures of each underdeveloped nation. This is so, because these internal structures have been constituted throughout centuries of dependency. The structures of these societies are generally adapted to such situations, as can be seen, for instance, in Latin America through the system of cities which emerged with the primary function of serving as colonial ports. For that reason urban centres remained isolated from each other for a long time. As the system developed, its different centres became interconnected under the main impulse of international commerce. However, urban systems have grown so much in complexity that it becomes an academic exercise to distinguish between "primary" and "secondary" functions. But detailed studies of the historical process as well as of the operation of the system in a more complex situation, such as the present one, are lacking. The same can be said, to an even greater extent, of the function of the system in any particular sector of the economy, such as agriculture, and of the main political processes and structures. Therefore, the study of the internal manifestations of dependency in any given underdeveloped country clearly becomes a study of the political capacity of that country to solve the basic problems involved in taking an autonomous path toward development.

NOTES

1. G. Almond and G. B. Powell, Comparative Politics: A Developmental Approach, Boston, Little Brown, 1966, p. 1-15.

2. See Susanne J. Bodenheimer, "The Ideology of Developmentalism: American Political Science's Paradigm-surrogate for Latin American Studies," Berkeley Journal of Sociology, Vol. XV, 1970, pp. 95-137.

3. For the sake of brevity we will not summarize this theory here; however, the reader may find an excellent summary in the article by S. N. Eisenstadt included in this issue. See, for example, S. P. Huntington, "Political Development and Political Decay," World Politics, Vol. XVII, No. 3, April 1965, and "Political Modernization: America vs. Europe," World Politics, Vol. XVIII, No. 3, April 1966; Almond and Powell, op. cit., especially Ch. XI; R. E. Ward and D. A. Rustow, "Introduction," Political Modernization in Japan and Turkey, Princeton, Princeton University Press, 1964; and Pye, op. cit., pp. 46-48. A good summary of the various approaches is to be found in Stein Rokkan, "Models and Methods in the Comparative Study of Nation-Building," Acta Sociologica, Vol. 12, No. 2, 1969.

4. W. W. Rostow, States of Economic Growth: A Non-Communist Manifesto, Cambridge, Cambridge University Press, 1960; D. Blackmer and Milikan, (eds.) The Emerging Nations, (Boston, Little, Brown, 1961; G. A. Almond and James S. Coleman (eds.) The Politics of the Developing Areas, Princeton, Princeton University Press, 1960; L. W. Pye (ed.) Communications and Political Development, Princeton, Princeton University Press, 1963 J. LaPalombara (ed.) Bureaucracy and Political Development, Princeton, Princeton University Press, r. d. (in the Introduction to this volume LaPalombara criticizes the West-centered character of political development theory); R. E. Ward and D. A. Rustow (eds.) Political Modernization in Japan and Turkey, Princeton, Princeton University Press, 1964; L. W. Pye and S. Verba (eds.) Political Culture and Political Development, Princeton, Princeton University Press, 1965; J. LaPalombara and M. Weiner (eds.) Political Parties and Political Development, Princeton, Princeton University Press, 1969; Almond and Powell, op. cit.

5. R. N. Adams, Social Change in Latin America Today: Its Implications for United States Policy, New York, Vintage, 1960; A. Boecke, Economics and Economic Policy of Dual Societies, New York, 1953; F. Bourricaud, Poder y Sociedad en el Perú Contemporaneo, Buenos Aires, 1967; G. Germani, Politica y Sociedad en una Epoca en Transicion, Buenos Aires, 1965; Jacques Lambert, Os Dois Brasis, Rio de Janeiro, 1958; S. M. Lipset and Aldo Solari, Elites en América Latina, Buenos Aires, 1968. Some of the contributions of the Economic Commission for Latin America (ECLA) can also be included here.

6. See Pedro Vuskovic, Observaciones para el Debate Lationamericano. Concentracion y Marginalización en el Desarrollo Latinoamericano, Santiago, 1969 (mimeo).

7. See CEPAL, "Estudio Económico de America Latina" (E/CN-12/696), E/CN-12/967, and E/CN-12/825/Rev. I).

8. André Gunder Frank, "Hacia una Teoria Histórica del Sub-desarrollo Capitalista en Asia, Africa y América Latina," Conferencia dictada, en la V Reunión de Facultades y Escuelas de Economia de América Latina, Maracaibo, Venezuela, November 1969 (mimeo).

9. Ray Mauro Marini, Subdesarrollo y Revolución, México, Siglo XXI, S.A., 1969, p. 7.

10. Orlando Fals Borda, La Subversión en Colombia: El Cambio Social en la Historia (1st ed.) Bogota, Tercer Mundo, 1967, p. 63.

11. Tulio Halperin Donghi, Historia Contemporanea de America Latin, Madrid, Alianze Editorial, 1969, pp. 147-55.

12. Fernando Henrique Cardoso and Enso Faletto, Dependencia y Desarrollo en America Latina, México, Siglo XXI, 1969, ch. III.

13. H. Marcuse, "Sobre Max Weber," ECO: Revista de la Cultura de Occidente, June 1968, pp. 202-35.

14. A good description of this period is found in Alonso Aguilar Monteverde, Dialética de la Economía Mexicana, Mexico, 1968, Ed. Nuestro Tiempo, ch. 5 and 7.

15. Celso Furtado, Subdesenvolvimento e Estagnaçao na America Latina, Rio Janeiro, Civizaçao Brasileira, 1968, ch. 2.

16. Cited by Héctor Silva Michelena, Necolonialismo y Universidad (unpublished manuscript). p. 14.

17. Ibid., pp. 15-47

18. Furtado, op. cit., pp. 21-40

19. Alternative formulations have begun to appear recently: Darcy Ribeiro, The Civilizatory Process, Wash., D.C., 1969, Smithsonian Institute, Frank, op. cit.

III

ASIA

CHAPTER 8

NATION-BUILDING AT THE EDGE OF AN OLD EMPIRE: JAPAN AND KOREA.

Joji Watanuki

JOJI WATANUKI is Professor of Sociology at the Institute of International Relations, Sophia University, in Tokyo. He has carried out extensive research on social structure and politics in Japan and has contributed chapters on Japanese developments in such collections as the Lipset-Rokkan volume on *Party Systems and Voter Alignments.*

Compared to the rest of the world, China, Korea, and Japan all developed distinctive politico-cultural systems remarkably early.

In the case of China, such distinctiveness can be traced back to the Chou (1122-255 B.C.) and the Ch'in (255-206 B.C.) dynasties. Chinese characters, Confucianism and other Chinese philosophies that influenced not only the Chinese people but also the Koreans and the Japanese until the nineteenth, or even the twentieth century; the idea of the "Middle Kingdom," which contained the assumption of the cultural unity and supremacy of China over "external barbarians"—all these were the products of the period of the Chou dynasty. In terms of political integration, the first emperor of the Ch'in dynasty, Shih Huang Ti, took such important steps as the creation of a centralized administrative organization; the unification of weights and measures; and the construction of roads leading to the capital, canals connecting north and south, and the famous Great Wall that constituted part of the "boundary" of its empire. As for administrative organization, it was nearly a thousand years

later, under the T'ang dynasty (A.D. 618-907), that the next decisive
development occurred: the founding emperor of the T'ang, T'ai Tsung, set
up the famous civil-service examination system, the rudimentary form of
which can be traced as far back as the Han (206 B.C.-A.D. 220), making it
the sole channel to all official positions; he also effected an elaborate
reorganization of the central and local administrative establishments. (As
will be noted later, the T'ang's political institutions served as a model both
in Korea and Japan.) The basic cultural unit and home of the Chinese
(Han) people was the Middle Kingdom, which has continuously expanded
through their migrations and conquests. Since the Middle Kingdom has
been basically a cultural definition rather than an ethnic or geographical
one, its physical boundary has remained vague. However, because of this
cultural definition, political conquests by non-Han rulers—the most
durable ones were those by the Mongol in the period of the Yuan dynasty
(A.D. 1206-1368) and by the Manchu in that of the Ch'ing dynasty
(1644-1911)—have not affected Chinese cultural, and consequently
political continuity and unity, into which the minority non-Han rulers
have been absorbed.

In the case of Korea, the date of political unification can be traced back
to A.D. 670 when the Silla kingdom came to encompass the whole region
of Korea. This political unification has been maintained and developed
through the succeeding Koryo (918-1392) and Yi (1392-1910) dynasties,
in spite of occasional invasions from the north (by the Chinese of the Sui
and T'ang dynasties in the seventh century, the Khitan in the late tenth and
early eleventh, the Mongolia of the Yuan Empire in the thirteenth and
fourteenth centuries) and from the south (the Japanese under Hideyoshi in
the late sixteenth century). Thus in 957 under the Koryo dynasty, a
civil-service examination system was instituted, and later under the Yi
dynasty it was elaborated and perfected. The Yi dynasty seems to have
achieved a high degree of centralized bureaucratic rule. In terms of cultural
unity, Korea, like Japan, has enjoyed almost complete ethnic and linguistic
homogeneity from the beginning of her history. The spoken language has
been one with no dialects except that of Choju Do, an island to the south
of the Korean peninsula. A system of writing the Korean language using
Chinese ideography was used from the fourth to the fifteenth centuries,
until the Korean alphabet, *hangul* was devised. Thereafter, although many
Chinese characters continued to be used, writing based on *hangul* spread
gradually.

In Japan's case, historians agree that initial political unification was
achieved around the fifth century,[1] being reinforced in the seventh
century when Prince Shotoku launched the Taika reform (A.D. 645), and

the Taiho code was promulgated (A.D. 700). The ensuing period—generally known as the Nara (710-793) and Heian (794-1192) eras, taking their names from those of the capital in each era (Heian is the ancient name for Kyoto)—is sometimes referred to as that of the *ritsu-ryo* system or the ritsu-ryo state, meaning a uniform and centralized state under the emperor *(tenno)* by law *(ritsu)* and code *(ryo)*. Before that period, the tenno was the head of the most powerful clan, and his power and authority were restricted by the existence and autonomy of other clans. The Taika reform and Taiho code aimed at and achieved, to a certain degree, the restriction of the power of other clans by abolishing all the great private holdings of land, and by setting up a uniform and centralized administrative apparatus. The T'ang system in China was considered as exemplary in these reforms. Ethnically speaking, in spite of the existence of various clans, Japan already seems to have enjoyed a high degree of ethnic homogeneity over most of its territory, the sole exception being the Northern part of Honshu where clashes with an alien tribe called the *Ezo* were recorded in the eighth and ninth centuries (whether the *Ezo* were the forbears of the present Ainu living in Hokkaido has not yet been determined). At that time, Hokkaido was an unknown land to the Japanese. As in Korea, one language was spoken from the beginning of the known period. In developing its written language, Japan took over the Chinese ideography, rapidly making the necessary modifications, and in the early Heian era, Japanese syllable letters were developed. During the Heian era much literature was written using these Japanese letters—literature that is still read, the most famous example being the *Genji-monogatari (The Tales of Genji)* written in the early eleventh century.

In Japan, political unification and centralization did not go as far as in China and Korea. Under the Taika reform, local administrative units such as provinces (*kuni*) and counties (*gun*) were established, the heads of which were appointed by the central government. However, it was quite symbolic of the lesser degree of political unification in Japan that, as Burks mentions,

> the Japanese term for the province, *kuni,* uses the same ideograph as the Chinese character *kuo,* which to the Chinese means realm, kingdom or country. The scattered topography of Japan and the tradition of clan independence made it easy for the Japanese to think of their newly reformed Empire as a composite of many small realms.

No civil-service examination system after the Chinese model was attempted. Finally, the Heian era ended in a struggle between two warrior clans and the establishment by the victorious clan of a kind of military government in Kamakura (1193). From 1193 to the end of the Edo era

(Tokugawa era), a dual government was maintained: the emperor, the court, and the nobles were in Kyoto going through the ceremonial motions of ruling, while the actual ruler was the generalissimo (*shogun*). The first holder of this title, appointed by the emperor, was the leader of the most powerful warrior group; but the title became hereditary, remaining in the same family until a rival group managed to usurp control. The Tokugawa Shogunate, maintaining its capital in Edo (Tokyo), lasted for 265 years with fifteen successive inheritors of the *shogun* position. Even the Shogunate, however, did not achieve complete centralization. Under the Tokugawa Shogunate, which was the most stable and centralized compared to those preceding it, there were 260-70 feudal lords (*daimyo*) with their own territory over which they exercised a fairly autonomous rule in spite of certain regulations imposed by the Tokugawa Shogunate.

The impact of the West in the nineteenth century and the necessity for modernization made it impossible for the traditional system to survive in any of the countries of East Asia. The Ch'ing dynasty in China, the Yi dynasty in Korea, and the Tokugawa Shogunate in Japan all collapsed. After the collapse, however, these three followed quite different routes to modernization. The most tragic case was Korea, which had taken various measures to cope with the external pressures and to bring about modernization. In 1882 it adopted what is still the national flag of the Republic of Korea, the *Taegukki,* and various attempts at reform were made: the Taewongun reform of 1867, the Kaewadang reform of 1884, the Tonghak rebellion of 1894, and the Independence Club movement of 1896-98. Nevertheless, Korea became a pawn in the international struggles of the Western states and China and Japan. It was finally annexed by Japan in 1910, ceasing to exist as an independent political unit for the next thirty-five years. In China, the final and belated fall of the Ch'ing dynasty in 1911 was followed by political chaos; provincial warlords (*tuchuns*) played prominent roles, especially in the north, for over a decade, until the Kuomintang brought about political unification in 1927 under the "sun-in-the-blue-sky" flag. In contrast to China and Korea, the downfall of the Tokugawa Shogunate in Japan was followed by the expeditious formation of the Meiji State and rapid progress in modernization.

Looking at the different routes followed by these three East Asian countries in the modern world, one is impressed with the fact that a long, historical existence of cultural and political unity per se was not a sufficient condition for building and developing a nation or state capable of surviving and developing in the modern world. From these examples, one is led to raising the following questions: what were the factors that made it possible to build a viable nation in Meiji Japan, and what were the factors that hindered the same development in China and Korea? As for the first question, a number of analyses and arguments have been presented by both Japanese and non-Japanese scholars.[3] Several studies have tried to compare the case of Japan with that of other countries— Britain and France,[4] Germany,[5] and Turkey.[6] However, there has been no study comparing the three countries in East Asia in terms of political modernization or modern nation-building. There are some studies referring to China and Japan,[7] but no comparative studies including Korea,[8] so far as the author knows, although there is an increasing number of studies on Korean political development.

As for the second question, the answer can be sought in two approaches. One is to look into internal factors in China and Korea which hindered or at least delayed the development of a viable nation in the modern period. The studies by Levy and Henderson can be regarded as such efforts. Another is to see external factors as the main cause of failure. Thus, Japan's rapid formation of the Meiji State and subsequent "development" directly affected China and Korea. On the one hand, some regarded Japan as a model of development for China and Korea, but on the other hand, Japan's annexation of Korea, possession of Taiwan, and invasion of Manchuria undeniably showed that Japan was the direct enemy of the independence and political unity of China and Korea. Studies of East Asian political history between 1868 and 1945 are full of descriptions and analyses of Japan's impact on China and Korea, that is, the negative impact of the development of one political unit in the region on the political development of other units, or to put it in another way, the consequences of unbalanced political development within the region.

Viewed in this way, one can doubt whether Japan between 1868 and 1945 is an example of political development in the positive sense. As a matter of fact, not only Barrington Moore[9] but others also—especially Japanese scholars[10]—regard the political development of Japan from 1868 to 1945 and especially from 1930 to 1945 as the development of Asian fascism or ultranationalism or capitalistic imperialism or something else negative. Others attempt, as S. N. Eisenstadt did,[11] to introduce such concepts as breakdown or decay of modernization in order to explain Japan's external action and internal structure especially from 1930 to 1945.

Necessary Conditions for State-Building

So far I have focused on the given historical, cultural, and political situation of each of the three countries. The important question to be asked is: What were the conditions necessary for building a viable nation or state that could coexist with the other nations in the modern world? Put in these terms, the historical existence of cultural and political unity is not sufficient; in fact, it can be counter-productive.

Take the example of China. The idea of the Middle Kingdom, which had been the symbol of the cultural and political unity of China, functioned in the nineteenth century to enhance the unrealistic and suicidal response to the Western powers. Chinese political leaders, mesmerized by the concept of the Middle Kingdom, found little to learn from the West, rejecting technological progress; they even treated the diplomatic delegation from the victorious British as a tributary mission, making realistic diplomacy impossible. In China's case, as has often been pointed out,[12] in spite of long political centralization and cultural unity, the family and kinship had provided the focus of loyalty for the vast population living in villages; loyalty to the family and kinship transcended all other social obligations. Perhaps we should say "because of long cultural unity and centralization" instead of "in spite of . . . " Confucian philosophy, which constituted part of the cultural unity of traditional China, endorsed such a family-centered standard of morality. Political centralization seems to have been facilitated by a social and moral vacuum beyond the family and kinship level; the rulers did not attempt to mobilize mass support, being content with the chance of ruling with relatively small forces as a result of the vacuum.

With regard to Korea, in order to analyse the causes of her failure to build a viable nation or state in the nineteenth century, we must not ignore the external factors—especially the threats from Japan and the final annexation by Japan in 1910. However, if we engage in a kind of speculative experiment and assume for the moment that the external threats were small or nonexistent, we can ask whether Korea could have built and developed a viable nation-state anyway, taking advantage of her ethnic, linguistic, and political unity.

One is tempted to give an affirmative answer to this question, considering such characteristics of the Korean society and people as the spread of education, their diligence, and so on, in addition to their ethnic, linguistic, and political unity. However, Gregory Henderson in his book, *Korea: The Politics of Vortex,* develops a rather paradoxical logic: "because of" ethnic, linguistic, and political unity, a political dynamic he calls "the politics of vortex" was generated and resulted in factionalism, indecision, and lack of political leadership. Let us follow Henderson's logic a little further.

I argue here that the unity and homogeneity of Korea acted to produce a *mass* society, much, perhaps, as they acted for the population of the core area of her neighbor, China. By mass society, I mean a society lacking in the formation of strong institutions or voluntary associations between village and throne; a society that knows little of castle town, feudal lord and court, semi-independent merchant societies, city-states, guilds, or classes cohesive enough to be centers of independent stance and action in the polity.

. . . Compactness of the territory, absence of ethnic, religious, political, linguistic, or other basic sources of cleavage within Korea, and a universalistic value system have created a society in which groupings are artificial.

. . . Grouping is hence an opportunistic matter concerned only with access to power for its members, and, because other differences are not present, each group tends to be distinguished from the others only by the personalities of its members and by their relationship to power at the time. Hence groupings are factional; for the issues and interests that forge true parties from factions are absent from the homogeneous, power-bent society . . . The result is a pattern of extreme centripetal dynamics . . . The physics of Korean political dynamics appears to resemble a strong vortex tending to sweep all active elements of the society upward toward central power . . . intermediary groupings find it difficult to achieve aggregation. Vertiginous updraft tends to suck all components from each other before they cohere on lower levels and tends to propel them in atomized form toward the power apex.[13]

As Henderson himself admits, this is a very bold, ambitious and provocative theory in comparing China, Korea, and Japan. Also it has tremendous significance for the theory of nation-building and political development. As Henderson hints, we have to raise the question: "Is it possible that the unity, centrality, and homogeneity now sought by emerging nations may set in motion, as they did for Korea, a vortex similarly destructive to political amalgamation and pluralism?[14] Or as Samuel P. Huntington put it in the foreword to Henderson's book, we might be able to propose a more general proposition saying that "what is good for national integration is not necessarily good for national development.[15] Let us examine Henderson's "Korea—mass society— politics of vortex" theory, taking into consideration China and Japan for comparison. As for China, in the above quotation Henderson seems to regard it too as a "mass society" in his sense, and we might infer, therefore, that to use Henderson's expression, China would be regarded as having been caught in the politics of vortex, resulting in factionalism, indecision, incompetent political leadership, and inability to build a viable nation. Certainly that was proved by the history of the late Ch'ing dynasty in the nineteenth and early twentieth century. However, I hesitate very much about using the mass society concept in this context, for it is also used in contemporary sociology, where it denotes the existence of atomized individuals, subject to easy manipulation by the state or ruling minority. In other words, the basic assumption is complete penetration by the state or the ruling elite into the mass as atomized individuals, and a high degree of modern manipulation through state-sponsored organizations and media made possible by modern techniques of communication. To apply the same concept to a traditional, centralized society inevitably causes confusion. Take the example of the Chinese and Korean societies of the nineteenth century, where apparently the unit was not an individual, but the family or kin group. Penetration by the central government or by a ruling elite was not complete in the modern sense, because the techniques of manipulation were not available. To apply the concept of mass society to this sort of situation seems untenable. In terms of social relationships, people in those societies were not scattered, isolated individuals, but were tightly drawn into small social units of family, kin group, and village. Thus there was a peculiar combination of traditional segmentation and centralization. In this sense, we might use the concept of traditional mass society.

Viewed in terms of this theory of a traditional mass society, and contrasting Japan with Korea, what were the characteristics of Japanese society in the premodern period, and what were their consequences? In scattered and occasional references to Japan, Henderson in his book points to the existence of more regional differentiation and specialization than in Korea, to the existence of a more pronounced hierarchy, and to the greater prevalence of upward loyalty. Certainly these were characteristics of Japan's Tokugawa society, because it was a feudal society where the feudal lords had their own territory, demanded that their vassals pay homage to them, and attempted to get more revenue by encouraging or manipulating commerce and industry within their territories. On the other hand, because it was a centralized feudalism, the political unity of Japan as a whole was maintained, and trade and commerce developed on a nationwide scale. In addition, the emperor served as the magnet for feelings of unity, and served as a renewed source of the legitimacy of political power when the Tokugawa Shogunate fell.

In Japan's case, both of those elements (feudal regionalism and centralization) happened to be so arranged that they facilitated nation-building after the Meiji Restoration of 1868. However, it was not so much the mere existence of these elements as the conscious manipulation of them that was more important for the Meiji nation-building. We must therefore pay more attention to that manipulation, which on the one hand contributed to rapid nation-building, but on the other led to aggressive activities that so seriously impeded nation-building in Korea and China.

As is often pointed out,[1] the manipulative measures taken in Meiji Japan were peculiar; they succeeded in transforming the traditional attachment to family, kin group, and village to loyalty to the nation by means of the doctrine and myth of a "family state" led by the emperor. Utilizing loyalty to feudal lords, and the spiritual authority of the imperial family, these measures caused traditional and somewhat primitive attachments to primary groups and the immediate environment to be linked to loyalty to the Emperor and the state. This proved to be a highly successful short cut to the building of a viable nation ("a prosperous nation and a strong military" as the Meiji leaders said), but at the same time revealed its own contradictions and strains. Internally, since the political power of the Meiji State was legitimized by the spiritual authority of the emperor and implemented by the bureaucratic apparatus, power tended to invade the private and spiritual world of the citizens and to forestall any participation or control by the people. As a matter of fact, in the "family state" ideas and practices associated with civil liberties and popular participation were not fully recognized, and finally in the "Imperial State" of Japan in the 1940s they were declared to be without value.[18] Only after the defeat in the Second World War, and in the presence of the Allied Occupation Forces, could Japan rebuild her state in a form fully compatible with civil liberties and popular participation.

Japan's external behavior between 1868 and 1945 can be explained in various ways and certainly reflects multiple causes. However, given the present purpose of identifying the consequences of the Meiji way of nation-building, we have to pay special attention to the nature of Meiji nationalism, and its grotesque outgrowth, the ultra-nationalism of the Imperial State during the Second World War; for nationalism as an ideology, an integrative political symbol, and a popular sentiment was and is one of the important factors in nation-building. As Maruyama points out, the first thing to be noticed is the lack of a sense of membership in an international community in the East Asia of the nineteenth century.[19] In spite of long, historical contacts among China, Korea, and Japan (and partly because of the seclusion policy of Yi Korea and Tokugawa Japan, both of which closed their doors to foreigners for over two hundred years) there was no sense of international community even among these three. Moreover, the traditional Chinese concept of the Middle Kingdom, applied to international relations, was based on the idea of superior and inferior relationships between nations, especially in cultural terms. Faced with threats from the Western powers, all three East Asian countries—China, Korea, and Japan—reacted in a similar way to the initial impact. The rulers in all three, believing in the superiority of their own nation, showed a strong sense of repugnance for the West. "Repel the barbarians" was commonly used as a slogan in all three. Once defeated by the overwhelming military strength of the Western powers, the rulers of the three countries soon recognized the need to learn and absorb from the West. In this respect too, all three reacted in similar ways. Distinguishing between the material and the spiritual, the technical and the cultural, and believing in the cultural superiority of their own nations, the rulers tried to take from the West only the material, the technological, and the military. The point is that this sort of situation led the ruling group in Japan, and also, to a considerable degree, the people, to see the world as an arena, a power struggle, where there were conquerors and conquered, superiors and inferiors. According to this view, and due to the lack of a sense of community among the three East Asian countries, the Japanese, after their success in nation-building and industrialization following the Meiji Restoration, began to think that Korea and China were inferior, and were there to be conquered. Supported by this sort of logic and popular sentiment, the Meiji State annexed Korea. It also intervened in China in the second decade of the twentieth century after the downfall of the Ch'ing dynasty, among other things making demands on China in 1915 in the form of twenty-one points. After 1930, this sort of Japanese view of international relations was combined with the idea of the family state and the Imperial Way and developed into that notorious idea of a "Great East Asia Co-Prosperity Sphere." According to this idea, Japan was supposed to be the leader or the father of Asian nations. Inside this sphere, a hierarchical relationship among the states was assumed, and outside this sphere, the rule of the conqueror and the conquered, the strong and the weak was supposed to work.

Implications of the East Asian Cases

What are the implications for the theory of nation-building? The East Asian cases suggest the following points. First, what the three countries experienced in common was the impact of Western powers in the latter part of the nineteenth century. I have not discussed the nature of the Western powers at that time, but it is quite apparent that they did not behave in a way favourable either to the maintenance of the traditional political unity of these countries or to their rebuilding in modern form. In dealing with the problems of nation-building, we have to take into consideration this sort of world situation.

Second, the East Asian cases give us an example of unbalanced development among neighbouring units within a region. This unbalanced development had an unfortunate and unfavourable consequence in that the most successful unit terminated the independent existence of one neighbour and impeded development in another through intervention. Attention must be given to this sort of political dynamics within a region and between neighbouring units, and its causes and consequences assessed.

Third, Japan's seemingly successful attempt at nation-building after the Meiji Restoration—if we take into consideration the internal and external consequences of that mode of nation-building—suggests that there is a grave danger in making too great a use of the traditional social structure and ancient myths (such as Japan's emperor myth) in modern nation-building, and that nationalism or national consciousness should be combined with some elements of internationalism or belief in the existence of an international community. Given the world situation of the late nineteenth century, Japan was perhaps justified in adopting the goal of a prosperous nation and a strong military. But, if so, it only meant that a later rebuilding and reorientation was imperative if Japan was to accept equality as a basis of her relations with her East Asian neighbours and if she was to permit civil liberties and popular participation in government at home. Actually in Japan's case, some move toward such rebuilding appeared during the 1920s. Externally, the Foreign Minister Kijuro Shidehara, who served successively in five cabinets from 1924 to 1931, took the policy of nonintervention toward China. Internally, universal manhood suffrage was introduced in 1925 and the Party Cabinet based on the majority in the Diet emerged in 1924. However, as is well known, these moves touched off counter-moves from the political forces and values built into the Meiji State. The result was the emergence of the Imperial State, which was a grotesquely developed form of the Meiji State. The rebuilding and reorientation finally took place only after complete defeat in the Second World War.

Fourth, the (traditional) mass society theory presented by Henderson breaks down into the following elements:

(1) As is often pointed out, the political rule of the traditional Chinese (and Korean) dynasties was a combination of centralization at the top and decentralized agrarian village communities at the bottom. This rule differed from the rule of feudalism in both Western Europe and Japan, where there was considerable decentralization; it also differed from the political rule of the centralized ancient empires, such as the Roman Empire or the Egyptian Empire, which were characterized by the direct use of slave labour on large estates of the *latifundium* type. This fact has been repeatedly pointed out by Karl Marx and others.[20] In this respect, Henderson's theory is another attempt to focus on, and assess the consequences of, the vacuum or gap between political centralization and self-sufficient village life.

(2) However, if we focus on village life and trace its effects on political culture even in today's Japan, we find several features similar to those that Henderson attributed to the historical existence of (traditional) mass society.

My point is that these features, such as lack of association, prevalence of factionalism, and so on, can be found in Japan, too,[21] which has not been the (traditional) mass society in Henderson's sense. Therefore, the historical origin of these features should be sought in the behaviour patterns nourished in villages with their small-scale farming methods, close social relationships, and communal character. Stated more generally, the question is how democracy, which emphasizes individual rights, can develop in Asian societies having a communal political culture based on small-scale farming and agrarian village life.

(3) As for ethnic, linguistic and cultural homogeneity, certainly in Japan's case too, this was one of the factors that contributed to the rapid building of a centralized state after the *Meiji* Restoration. As a matter of fact, after the Second World War when the rebuilding of the nation was attempted with emphasis on local autonomy, a strong tendency toward uniform and centralized administration persisted and later revived. From the viewpoint of encouraging local autonomy and grass-roots democracy, this sort of homogeneity can have some disadvantages. We can also argue that the existence of a certain degree of heterogeneity can contribute toward checking excessive centralization if properly handled.[22]

Fifth, looking at contemporary East Asia as a whole, we become aware of particular problems. One is the existence of historical societies divided into more than one state. Korea is a typical example, and China shares the same problem. However, in the case of China there exist some ethnic minorities and geographical and social boundaries are still somewhat vague, especially on her western frontier. In addition, the large number of Chinese living in various countries in Southeast Asia poses very important problems with regard to nation-building and political development. The different facets of the problem of foreign China deserve special attention and research in both a theoretical and a practical sense.[23] Apart from China's special features, the existence of divided states reminds us again to take the world situation into consideration in dealing with the problem of nation-building.

The second problem in East Asia is the weakness of the sense of an international community, shared by the political units of the region, which might keep them compatible and contribute to their common development. Various factors have produced this situation. Historically, it traces back to the premodern era, and has been accentuated by Japan's external behaviour since the Meiji period, especially towards Korea. In addition, tensions arising from the creation of divided states in the area after the Second World War are another factor. However, in this respect, other regions in the world are plagued with a similar problem. Its solution requires both prudent action by each nation concerned and research by social scientists.

PROBLEMS FOR FURTHER RESEARCH

Generally speaking, whenever we try to undertake a comparative study of this sort, we are bothered by the limited amount of knowledge and data available. In particular, there is, as Rokkan points out, a tendency towards "large nation bias," and very little knowledge about small units is available in the international scholarly world.[24] As a matter of fact, in the case of East Asia, a fairly large amount of knowledge is available about China and Japan, but not enough for sophisticated comparative studies. Quite inadequate knowledge about Mongolia and Korea is available to scholars who are not specialists in these areas but who want to make comparative studies encompassing these countries. To improve and advance the field of comparative studies, we need to accumulate and codify the social histories of particularly the smaller units in the world.

Another question concerns the advantages and disadvantages of proceeding by regions in accumulating our comparative knowledge. The advantages are the following: (a) this method provides the opportunity to take into consideration the small units that otherwise are often ignored; (b) it compels researchers to give their attention to the various interactions among the units in the region and the resulting consequences; and (c) the units in the same region often have some similarities in terms of their internal social and cultural structures. Therefore, intra-regional comparison can provide useful clues for inter-regional or worldwide comparison.

However, on the other hand, the definition of region cannot avoid some vagueness and arbitrariness. Take the example of East Asia. Naturally East Asia has not been and is not an isolated region. Historically, through succeeding Chinese empires, it has had contact and interaction with other regions, and more recently Japan's action in the Second World War has had important effects on the nation-building of various units in Southeast Asia.[25] Moreover, in terms of the problem of the formation of an international community, relationships among the units of East and South Asia become very important.

Comparative study should not be hindered by "region-parochialism." It should proceed to broader typologies and generalization, as a sequel to the identification of regional problems and the accumulation of regional data.

NOTES

1. Mitsusada Inoue, Nihon Kokka no Kigen [The Origin of the Japanese State], Tokyo, Iwanami Shoten, 1960.

2. Paul M. A. Linebarger, Djang Chu and Ardath W. Burks, Far Eastern Government and Politics: China and Japan, Princeton, Van Nostrand, 1967, p. 285.

3. The study of the Meiji Restoration and the modern nation-building following it has attracted many Japanese historians and social scientsits. There has been a vast amount of literature on this topic published in Japanese. See Rekishigaku Kenkyukai (Research Association of Historical Science), Meiji Ishin Kenkyushi Koza [A Series on the History of Researches on the Meiji Restoration] Vol. 6, Tokyo, Heibon Sha 1958; new supplementary vol., 1969. An example of the study on this topic by non-Japanese scholars is Robert E. Ward, ed., Political Development in Modern Japan, Princeton, Princeton University Press, 1968.

4. Takeo Kuwabara ed., Burujowa Kakumei no Hikaku Kenhyu [A Comparative Study in Bourgeois Revolutions], Tokyo, Chikuma Shobo, 1964; Kenji Kawano, Furansu Kakumei to Meiji Ishin [The French Revolution and the Meiji Restoration], Tokyo, Nippon Hoso Shuppan Kyokai, 1961; Shunpei Ueyama, Meiji Ishin no Bunseki Shiten [A Framework for the Analysis of the Meiji Restoration], Tokyo, Kodansha, 1968.

5. Reinhard Bendix, Nation-Building and Citizenship, New York, Wiley, 1964.

6. Robert E. Ward and Dankwart A. Rustow, eds., Political Modernization in Japan and Turkey, Princeton, Princeton University Press, 1964.

7. The classical example by a Japanese scholar is Goro Hani, Toyo niokeru Shihonshugi no Keisei [Formation of Capitalism in Asia], Kyoto, San'ichi Shobo, 1948, which was originally published as articles in a journal in 1932. This is a comparative study of Japan, China, and India focusing on politico-economic modernization. More recent examples in English are Robert T. Holt and John E. Turner, The Political Basis of Economic Development, Princeton, Van Nostrand, 1966; Marion J. Levy, Jr., "Contrasting Factors in the Modernization of China and Japan," in Simon Kuznets, Wilbert E. Moore, and Joseph J. Spengler (eds.), Economic Growth: Brazil, India, Japan, Durham, Duke University Press, 1955. Holt and Turner examine four cases, those of England, France, China, and Japan, focusing on the take-off stage of economic growth.

8. Three recent publications are especially relevant to the present topic of nation-building and political modernization: Chong-sik Lee, The Politics of Korean Nationalism, Berkeley and Los Angeles, University of California Press, 1963; Hahn-been Lee, Korea: Time, Change, and Administration, Honolulu, East-West Center Press, 1968; Gregory Henderson, Korea: The Politics of Vortex, Cambridge, Mass., Harvard University Press, 1968.

9. Barrington Moore, Jr., Social Origins of Dictatorship and Democracy, Boston, Mass., Beacon Press, 1966. Moore's perspective on the problem differs from the one found in most discussions of political modernization or nation-building. As the title of the book indicates, the question Moore raises is: what are the factors that lead to different routes and to different political forms in the modern world? He points to three routes: the first is a combination of capitalism and parliamentary democracy achieved after a series of revolutions; the second is a combination of capitalism and a succession of reactionary political structures culminating in fascism; and the third is communism. Moore puts Japan in the second category, analysing it under the title "Asian Fascism." He puts China in the third category.

10. A large number of books and articles are written in Japanese in this sort of tone. In 1955, a book that severely criticized Japanese history in the Showa period

(1926–) was published and attained a wide circulation: Shigeki Toyama, Seiichi Imai, and Akira Fujiwara, Showa Shi [A History of Showa Period], Tokyo, Iwanami Shoten.

11. S. N. Eisenstadt, Modernization: Protest and Change, Englewood Cliffs, N.J., Prentice-Hall, 1966.

12. Levy, op. cit.; C. K. Yang, Chinese Communist Society: The Family and the Village, Cambridge, Mass., MIT Press, 1959. As Dr. Yang writes (pp. 173-74):

all modern Chinese reformers have tried to shift the center of loyalty from the family to the state. K'ang Yu-Wei in his Ta T'ung Shu (The Great Commonwealth) pointed out the incomparibility between family loyalty and national interest. Sun Yat-sen in his San-min Chu-i (Three People's Principles) exhorted his countrymen to broaden familism to nationalism by widening the centre of loyalty from the family to the nation. The defeats China had suffered from foreign powers made the adoption of nationalism and patriotism a matter of urgent necessity. The Japanese invasion and the ensuing eight years of devastating war (1937-1945) extended the influence of nationalism from the intelligentsia to other classes of the population. The state as a morally higher center of loyalty had been an established factor in the modern trend of social, economic, and political events prior to the rise of the Communist regime, but in no previous period has the interest of the state and its been sharply defined and loyalty to it more drastically demanded than under the Communist rule.

13. Henderson, op. cit., pp. 4-5.

14. Ibid., p. 3.

15. Ibid., p. viii.

16. William Kornhauser, The Politics of Mass Society, Glencoe, Ill., Free Press, 1959.

17. For example, Masao Maruyama, Thought and Behavior in Japanese Politics, New York, Oxford University Press, expanded ed., 1969.

18.

What we normally refer to as "private life" is, in the final analysis, the way of the subject. As such, it has a public significance, in that each so-called private action is carried out by the subject as part of his humble efforts to assist the Throne. . . . Thus we must never forget that even in our personal lives we are joined to the Emperor and must be moved by the desire to serve our country.

Ministry of Education, The Ways of the Subject, 1941, quoted in Maruyama, ibid., p. 7.

19. Before the modern nation-state was born, Europe had already established one form of universalism. The foundations had been laid by the Roman Empire, which bequeathed its ideas to the doctrine of a European corporate body—the Corpus Christianum—symbolized by the Roman Catholic (Universal) Church and the Holy Roman Empire. The development of modern nation-states beginning in the Renaissance and Reformation periods was no more than a pluralistic disruption that had originally been one. National consciousness in Europe therefore bore from its inception the imprint of a consciousness of international society. It was a self-evident premise that disputes among sovereign states were conflicts among independent members of this international society. . . . How does this compare with the so-called Asian world? . . . it is . . . clear that the nations of the East have never constituted a corporate body or international society in the European sense, although various forms of diplomatic intercourse have existed among them. Maruyama, ibid., pp. 138-39.

20. Karl Marx, Einleitung zur Despotism, New Haven, Conn., Yale University Press, 1957.

21. Cf. Takeshi Ishida, "The Development of Interest Groups and the pattern of Political Modernization in Japan," in Robert E. Ward (ed.), Political Development in Modern Japan, Princeton, Princeton University Press, 1968.

22. The arguments on "consociational democracy" have some bearing on this point; cf. Arend Lijphart, "Consociational Democracy," World Politics, Vol. 21, 1968-69, pp. 207-25, and Hans Daalder chapter in this volume.

23. Eberhard and Collings both argue, taking the example of historical Chinese society, that the concept of social system or political system is difficult to apply to societies with vague boundaries. Collins proceeds to advance a "historical sociology" approach that analyses society or politics in terms of interest groups and layers, without assuming the interrelationship of all the elements of society or any boundaries. Wolfram Eberhard, "Problems of Historical Sociology," Randall Collings, "A Comparative Approach to Political Sociology," in Reinhard Bendix (ed.), State and Society: A Reader in Comparative Political Sociology, Boston, Mass., Little, Brown, 1968.

24. Stein Rokkan, "Models and Methods in the Comparative Study of Nation-Building," Acta Sociologica, Vol. 12, No. 2, 1969, pp. 54-55.

25. Cf. Gunnar Myrdal, Asian Drama, Vol. I, New York, Pantheon, 1968, part 2.

DIAGNOSING PROCESSES OF NATION-BUILDING: AN OVERALL PERSPECTIVE AND AN ANALYSIS OF DEVELOPMENT ON THE INDIAN SUBCONTINENT

R. Mukherjee

R. MUKHERJEE is Research Professor of Sociology in the Indian Statistical Institute, Calcutta, and President of the Indian Sociological Society. He has carried out extensive research on kinship, social structure, and change in the subcontinent of India and elsewhere, and has been active in the development of archival facilities for the social sciences in India. Among his major publications are *The Rise and Fall of the East India Company, The Problem of Uganda, The Dynamics of a Rural Society, The Sociologist and Social Change in India Today, Data Inventory on Social Sciences: India,* and *Concepts and Methods for the Secondary Analysis of Variations in Family Structures.*

However we may examine the phenomena of nation-building and state formation, the following postulates will be found appropriate:

(1) The existence of a "state" or a "nation" is a *matter of interpretation* of (a) the integration of a group of people at a particular level of their ideology and action, and (b) the corresponding distinction of this set of people from analogous sets of people.

(2) Nation-Building is a *matter of diagnosis* in a situation of diverse possibilities. A set of people identified on operational grounds at a particular point of time and space may or may not exhibit, over the relevant time span, the constellation of ideological and action characteristics necessary for interpreting the set as having reached the status of a "nation." Also the set may continue to maintain its distinctive identity or merge with an analogous set in the process of "nation-building." In the

latter case, the analogous sets of people may not be confined to the space originally defined on operational grounds.

(3) State formation, in the same context, is a *matter of speculation* with reference to one or more sets of people. A state, at a given point of time and space, may contain one or more nations, or one segment of a nation, while the process of nation-building may lead to (a) new state formations out of the existing state, (b) alterations in the articulation of the existing state, or (c) the formation of a new state out of more than one existing concurrently.

STATE AND NATION CONCEPTS

The first postulate refers to an historically accomplished phenomenon, viz. a state, comprising one or more nations (or nation-units), is in existence at a given point of time and space. Variations, therefore, may occur in (a) the political attributes regarded as representing a state in operation, and (b) the attributes of ideology and action, as well as in the level at which these attributes are to be integrated, to denote that a set of people has attained the status of nationhood. These variations appear to be redundant in our present discussion since the states are present *ipso facto,* and it is taken for granted that the people of a state have attained the status of nationhood. Also, contextually, we are not concerned with questions such as whether the German Democratic Republic should be recognized as a sovereign state by the United Nations or whether the U.S.A. should recognize the Peoples Republic of China. However, even at the diachronic level of identification of states and nations (or nation-units) in the Third World, an overview of the situation prompts us to ask two questions: (1) Can we presume that the states invariably represent mutually distinguished nations (or sets of nation-units)? and (2) What will be the criterion to denote that a state is composed of a set of subnational units, or comprises only one subnational unit, or is a multinational entity?

To illustrate the first question: Do the North and South Korean Republics represent two different nations? If they do, what is the crucial attribute of their differentiation, or is there a set of such attributes? It will be recalled that in the 1930s and 1940s the Koreans were regarded as a nation striving for a sovereign state of their own. They have now formed two states considered to be different in ideology and practice. Has this difference in ideology, or in any particular practice (e.g. in the economic organization of the respective societies), or in both, led to different nation formations of the North and South Koreans? If the answer to this question is "no," what is the viability of the two states for one nation? If, on the other hand, the answer to that question is "yes," what is the attribute (or the set of attributes) to denote differential nation formations? Also, have the two state formations preceded the corresponding nation formations? Or, is it the other way round?

These questions may be repeated for North and South Vietnam, and we may examine, consequently, whether the same set of attributes has played the causal role in their context. We may also ascertain the particularistic or the universalistic role of these attributes in other societies, for example with reference to any distinction drawn between the respective sets of nation-units in Malaysia and Singapore, the national identities of the Chinese in mainland China and in Taiwan (or Formosa).

Logically, such a course of study will bring us to the second question posed earlier, which may be illustrated as follows: Do the republics of India, Pakistan, Uganda, and so on represent undifferentiated nations, respectively? If not, are they composed of subnational units or nation-alities? Alternatively, do they represent multination states, or are they the components of larger configurations which would denote respective nations?

We know, for example, that while in the British period of its history, the subcontinent of India was regarded as one nation, the two-nation theory is considered to have become established with the partition of the subcontinent in 1947 into the Indian Union and Pakistan. The theory seems to be validated by the Indians and the Pakistanis in their recent conflict. However, under this theoretical construct, do the Bengalis in the eastern wing of Pakistan represent a subnational unit, a nationality or a nation(?), as against the Pathans, the Punjabis, and so on, in the western wing of Pakistan? Correspondingly, how should we characterize the Bengalis in the state of West Bengal as against the Bengalis in East Bengal (the eastern wing of Pakistan), on the one hand, and the Assamese, the Oriyas, the Biharis, and all such other "peoples" in India, on the other?

Unless we bring up these questions, we cannot appreciate the movements which flared up in East Bengal soon after the partition of India and which have continued since then in one form or another, viz. for the recognition of Bengali as a state language, for the change of name of the eastern wing of Pakistan to *Bangla Desh* (literally, the land of Bengal). Also, without taking note of the above questions, we cannot explain the support these movements receive from the people of West Bengal in spite of their gruesome experience of the Hindu-Moslem riots at the time of the partition and thereafter, the spontaneous welcome given to the litterateurs and others who visit West Bengal from East Pakistan, the genuine praise showered by the West Bengal intelligentsia upon the growth of Bengali literature in East Bengal, and so on. Furthermore, the two questions are extremely relevant to the understanding of the incipient but growing movement for a United Bengal, which gathers support from both the state of West Bengal in the republic of India and the eastern wing of Pakistan.

Potentially, West Bengal and the eastern wing of Pakistan present problems similar to those of Korea and Vietnam, although the situation is not at all drastic and the solution to the problem may be akin to that for West and East Germany. A similarity to this situation may be found in Africa if we examine the suggestion that the contemporary African states do not represent nations or sets of nation-units, respectively, but the analogous segments of "a great African nation which embraces the continent as a whole or at least everything south of the Sahara" (Emerson, 1963, p. 102). These possibilities refer to the last of the four alternatives posed earlier, characterizing one or more of the currently identified nation-states in the Third World.

Other possibilities of intrastate differences are apparent from an overview of the Third World. We find, for example, more and more evidence of tension among the constituent groups of many nation-states. The tension may occasionally take a violent form: in India, between the Maharastrians and the "south Indians," between the Assamese and the Bengalis; in Pakistan, between the East and the West Pakistanis; in Malaysia, between the Malays and the Chinese; and so on in Nigeria, Kenya, and others. Specific economic concession may be demanded to resolve such tensions, for example, in India, the demand for the establishment of the fourth steel plant in Andhra, although this territory has neither iron nor coal. The demand may also be explicitly of a political character, such as for Pakhtoonistan in Pakistan, for the hill states in Assam, or West Bengal in India.

The people producing such tensions are identified as tribal, racial, or ethnic groups, or merely as "people" with different nomenclatures. This manner of identification, however, does not indicate the role of the social groups in terms of a nation or an existing state. The generalized term "people" precludes any national identification. The outmoded "racial" classification may be accepted to denote ethnic difference in the present context, but the question remains: What will be the criterion to distinguish a subnational unit, a nationality, or a nation from an ethnic or a tribal unit?

This question attains added significance when we concern ourselves with the situation in Africa. The common image of this continent is of a multitude of tribal organizations until the emergence of sovereign states in recent times. But this image nullifies the analytical relevance of the "tribe" concept in social development, and overlooks the inherent dynamism of any society. However slow its rate of social change, even the most isolated society cannot remain, at any period of its history, in a state of *static equilibrium.* Did the African societies remain in the static state of tribal organization until they were helped by the "civilized powers" to become "nations" in the contemporary world? Much of the evidence we possess on the social development of the African people, before the continent was shared among the colonial powers, does not warrant this assumption (see, for example, Frobenius, 1923; Westermann, 1952; Panikkar, 1963).

Also, with reference to the Uganda Africans, for example, we learn that before the advent of the colonial powers on the scene, the Baganda, Banyoro, Banyankole, Batoro, and others were sharply distinguished among themselves in many more ways than can be attributed to intertribal or ethnic difference. Referring to these people, Lowie (1950, p. 341) wrote:

> Here we even find a curious analogy to European feudalism: the chief of the ruling pastoralists, now king of a sizeable population, claims in principle all the subjects' livestock as a medieval monarch claimed all their land.

Oberg (1949, p. 122) wrote with reference to the Banyankole and the neighboring people:

> Although it is said that the Bahima were once united and held sway over a great empire called Kitara, in historic times this territory was split up into kingdoms stretching from Bunyoro through Toro and Ankole to Ruanda in Belgian territory.

A large number of intrasocietal economic and political differentiations were also noticeable within the respective kingdoms, markedly in that of Buganda (Mukherjee, 1956, pp. 46-105). In the last named state, while external trade was rapidly developing, "the kings and the chiefs were turning into traders, and new ideas about social and spiritual life were also gaining ground in the society" (Mukherjee, 1956, p. 98).

Obviously, to consider all the people of Uganda to have remained at the tribal stage of social development in the pre-British and the British period of their history would be unrealistic, just as it is with regard to the great majority of African people. Emerson (1963, p. 97-98) wrote that "the extended family, the clan, and the tribe are the communities in which Africans have lived their lives and which continue to play a very large role today." He also stated, however, that "the tribal system has already undergone serious change in a few decades of European colonial rule"; and, further, he parenthesized the appellation "tribe" by "nationality."

Evidently the classificatory point cannot be bypassed in this way. It also cannot be glossed over by merely stating that the "Europeans of a later era (when nation had become associated with the modern nation-state) called correspondingly African groups 'tribes'" (Rustow, 1968, p. 8). It would be equally wrong to consider the classificatory problem we have raised to be of no relevance to the present discussion. For the germ of nation-building lies dormant in these distinctions which, for a while, may not assert themselves.

Thus the peoples of Uganda developed a common loyalty against the British rule, and their internal conflict remained submerged in the process (Mukherjee, 1956, pp. 215-66). This conflict, however, has not necessarily disappeared altogether. In India, on the other hand, the internal conflict ran concurrently with common loyalty against the British rule, and the former left a lasting imprint on state formations in the subcontinent. But with regard to this part of the world also, the previous citations suggest that the internal conflicts have not been fully resolved. Similar investigations may be appropriate to many other places in the Third World: the recent conflict in British Nigeria, British Malay with the formation and consolidation of Malaysia and Singapore.

It follows that for the Third World, at any rate, the first of the three postulates we have stated at the beginning of this chapter does not refer to a simple matter of identification of things as they are. This is because, barring a few exceptions (e.g., Thailand and Afghanistan), a common feature of virtually all societies in the Third World is that their specific ways of economic, social, and political development were cut short at one stage of their history by the imposition of a foreign rule. Also their emergence as sovereign states after the Second World War was, in many instances, decisively influenced by external forces. As a result, even from the diachronic aspect, the states and nations already emerged are still in flux. The diachronic aspect of state and nation in the Third World is, therefore, intricately linked with the synchronic aspect of nation-building and state formation in the societies under discussion.

Hence, instead of treating the first postulate as irrelevant to our discussion, it should be synchronized with the second and the third postulate stated at the beginning. It follows therefrom that the problem of state formation and nation-building in the Third World should not be examined from the present as the base line but in accordance with the processes at work from their historical antecedents. How should we, then, enquire into these processes, and what should we consider to be their historical antecedents?

DEVELOPMENT SCHEMA

It is tempting to presuppose a unilinear course of sequential development up to the stage of nationhood: for example, the schema of "tribe-caste-nation" for India; the schema of "tribe-confederation of tribes-nation" for various African nation-states; the schema of dispersed ethnic groups and their amalgamation into a nation for, say, Indonesia; the schema of eventual fusion of different sets of immigrants (with or without the autochthones) into a nation for, say, Guyana and Cuba; and so on. Such a *deductive and positivistic* approach may be appropriate for an explanatory proposition when (1) nation-building has already taken place, (2) sufficient data are available to specify the terminal points of change and to trace unambiguously the course of alterations from the base to the apex, and (3) a particular schema is seen to give the *best fit* to this course of sequential alterations. As a diagnostic proposition, however, the method is fallacious for reasons pointed out under the second postulate stated at the beginning of this paper. Also, even while dealing with an accomplished phenomenon of nation-building, the three conditions noted above are not invariably met in the Third World as a whole or in one of its nation-states.

Nearly a century ago, Alfred Lyall (1882, p. 135) spoke of "the gradual Brahmanising of the aboriginal, non-Aryan, or castless tribes" of India, and a few years later Risley (1891, Vol. I, pp. xv-xxx, lxxxiii-lxxxv) described how the tribes were transformed into Hindu castes in eastern India. However, the evolution of the Hindu caste structure does not represent a simple case of transformation of tribes into castes. It refers to a period in India's history when the bulk of the Indian people had already passed beyond the tribal stage of social development and were settled in village communities (for some details, see Mukherjee, 1957, pp. 61-80; 1958, pp. 143-74). This point has been equally stressed by Marx (1949, pp. 350-52) and Weber (1958, pp. 111, 130-31). Even for the Hindu community, therefore, the schematic alteration from tribe to caste presents an oversimplified picture, while its relevance to the other religious communities in India is negligible or virtually nil. On the other hand, the formation of ethnic groups (like the Telegu, Gujarati, Bengali) has cut across the religion-caste boundaries and may be of distinctive significance to any study of nation-building in India. Hence, as an accomplished phenomenon, the schema of tribe-caste-nation may be suitable for an appreciation of local political dynamics, as Bailey (1960) has attempted to demonstrate, but for the whole of India it cannot presume general validity for either the past or the present.

The fallacy of applying the schema of tribe-confederation of tribes-nation to all parts of Africa is clear if we give a precise meaning to the word "tribe" in the course of the social development of any people. As we have pointed out, any attempt to identify nations or to ascertain a course of nation-building will be inadequate without that precision. The schema, therefore, may be useful to the examination of nation-building in some particularly secluded areas where the people may still be living as different sets of "tribals." But how many such areas are there in the Third World, or in the world at large?

Unlike previously, precision in defining and identifying a tribe is generally avoided these days (see Mukherjee, 1956, pp. 48-54). A wider connotation is given to the term although it may be acknowledged that the term "tribe" refers to "that social and political unit which is above the kin group and is still small enough to claim common descent although it is large enough to permit intermarriage" (Deutsch, 1963, p. 4). More precisely, tribe is identified, contemporarily, if as a set of people with tribal nomenclature they still "have direct command over resources, and their access to the products of the economy are not derived mediately through a dependent status on others," and "they are a relatively large proportion of the total population in the area" (Bailey, 1960, p. 265). Under these or similarly specific conditions, very few sets of people will be identified as tribes in present times. Also, even if the scope for the identification of tribes is loosely enlarged, not many people will fall under the above schema.

For example, the people in the northeast frontier region of India are commonly denoted as tribals. These people have come together, and for the last two decades have developed a vigorous separatist movement. In terms of nation-building, can that movement be put under the schema of tribe-confederation of tribes-nation? Can we employ the same schema to explain the Jharkand movement in Bihar? Even if the answer to the two questions is "yes," which a careful study of the level of integration of ideology and action of these people may or may not indicate, the schema will be of local importance only. The "hill people" of Darjeeling and the sub-Himalayan belt in West Bengal, who are virtually neighbors to the aforementioned people in the northeast frontier region of India, have also become distinctly vocal in favor of regional autonomy; but they cannot be fitted into this schema by any stretch of imagination. As an exploratory survey conducted by the Sociological Research Unit of the Indian Statistical Institute in 1969 showed, the movement of these people is led by those identified as Nepalis, who constitute the bulk of the hill people and who are certainly not tribals even under a loose interpretation of the term. The Lepchas (who are being absorbed into the Nepali community by intermarriage) and a sprinkling of other people, like the Bhutanese, have joined the movement as allies (Munshi and Das Gupta, 1970). It is questionable, however, whether they (as well as the people in the northeast frontier region of India and those involved in the Jharkand movement in Bihar) can also be considered tribals according to the precise meaning of this term in the process of social development.

Thus, it appears that even with reference to the commonly regarded "tribal pockets" in the Third World, the schema of tribe-confederation of tribes-nation cannot attain general validity for either the past or the present.

The schema of amalgamation of ethnic groups into a nation may be appropriate to specific situations, but it loses its usefulness as a tool of analysis unless the *what, how,* and *why* of the process of amalgamation are substantiated precisely and unambiguously. For example, what about the spill over of particular ethnic groups beyond the border of Indonesia while all those falling within the territory of the Dutch East Indies evolved into the nation of Indonesians? How should the schema be applied to India and Pakistan in view of the splitting of some important ethnic groups (like the Punjabi, Sindhi, Bengali) at the time of partitioning the subcontinent? Why should the nation of Nepalis be considered in terms of amalgamation of the Newars and other ethnic groups? The importance of this schema also becomes merely nominal in the general perspective of identification of nations and the course of nation-building in the Third World.

The schema of eventual fusion of different sets of immigrants (with or without the autochthones) is applicable only to some particular areas in the Third World where the social structure has been built that way. But, there again, the schema may not be invariably applicable. It may be appropriate to national development in Guyana or Cuba, but it appears to fail where the Chinese and Indian immigrants in many nation-states of South Asia are concerned. Also it has certainly failed in many nation-states in Africa, such as in Uganda and Kenya with reference to the Indian immigrants, in Rhodesia with reference to the African autochthones, in South Africa with reference to the Indian immigrants and the African autochthones. Both in the possible areas of its application and in its order of applicability, the usefulness of this schema is almost as limited as those labelled tribe-caste-nation and tribe-confederation of tribes-nation.

As a corollary to the schema of amalgamation of ethnic groups into a nation, we may consider the possibility of transformation of respective ethnic groups into nations. This may happen in some instances, but will also be of nominal importance to the identification of nations and the examination of any course of nation-building, as will be obvious from our previous discussion of the Koreans and the Bengalis. Thus, we are not in a position to pick and choose *deductively* any schema to depict the historical antecedents of a nation and the course of development into nationhood.

In fact, we cannot depend on any variant of the deductive and positivistic approach to ascertain nation-building in the Third World because the possibilities for any given set of people are too many and the courses of development of these possibilities, respectively and jointly, are uncharted. Therefore, we have to adopt an *inductive and inferential* approach based upon the logic of probability, to ascertain the level of integration of the people, in their ideology and action, at which they may be considered to form a nation or to be on the way toward it.

Viewed in this manner,

> What appears as a process of nation-building from the point of view of governments here appears as a matter of nation-choosing by the individual. As Weilenmann [1963, pp. 33-55] sees it, it is an act of personal choice, or rather a sequence of choices, made in terms of the needs inherent in an individual's personality as well as in his external situation. Both personality and situation may be changed to some extent and made and remade by the consequences of each choice (Deutsch, 1963, p. 10).

How then, should we proceed to ascertain any course of nation-building and to infer, probabilistically, any possible state formation?

ATTRIBUTES OF NATIONHOOD

The frequently adopted manner of identification of nations is by means of a number of discrete attributes which, when striking a balance, is regarded to form the compound known as nation. These attributes have been categorized as "objective" and "subjective" and are enumerated by Marxists, non-Marxists, and anti-Marxists as territorial identification, common history, community of culture and language(s), common economic organization, and so on under the objective category, and a distinct psychological identity, the willingness to assert that identity vis-à-vis analogous identities, and so on under the subjective category. Admittedly, this is an ideal-typical construct since one or another of the objective attributes have been found to be missing from, or rendered futile to, the identification of nations in the past or present, for example, the Jewish or the Pakistani nation before Israel or Pakistan was founded, or the British and the American nations of the same language in contradistinction to the

Swiss nation of three languages. The mutually distinct Indian and Pakistani nations, although they had a common history for centuries, had developed a community of culture and languages and were living under the same economic organization all through their period of existence in the subcontinent (for details, see Mukherjee, 1957; 1958, pp. 140-212, 300-50; and other writings).

Also the same objective attribute may operate differently in separate situations. For example, all those who from the most ancient times migrated into the subcontinent of India—the pre-Aryans and the Aryans, the Sakas, Hunas, Yavanas, Pathans, Mughals—made this territory, identified as Bharat or Hindusthan, their homeland. But this age-old attribute of territorial affinity did not forbid separate nation-building of the Indians and the Pakistanis, and the eventual partitioning of the subcontinent. Contrariwise, the territorial identification of the Africans in Uganda is less than a century-old phenomenon after the formation of the Uganda Protectorate by the British, yet this attribute has a positive role to play in the nation-building of the Uganda Africans.

We may consider another attribute, viz. religion, which played the role of alienation in British India but that of consolidation in the Dutch East Indies in the context of nation-building and state formation in these respective areas. Religion was certainly a factor in separating the bulk of the Hindus from the bulk of the Muslims in the Indian subcontinent, although (1) the Mughal state power from the time of Akbar to Shah Jahan adopted various social and religious measures to ensure coexistence of the two communities of Hindus and Muslims in the subcontinent; (2) the Bhakti movement, which spread all over pre-British India, generated social and religious force to unite the two communities; (3) the social and political movements against the British rule repeatedly attempted to foster amity between the Hindus and the Muslims; and (4) in the historical process of developing a community of culture and languages in India, the caste system—the basis of Hindu social organization—permeated the Muslim community and still persists in Pakistan through the operation of many Muslim functional castes (Mukherjee, 1957; 1958; Bessaignet, 1960). In Indonesia, on the other hand, where there has been an infrastructure of Hindu culture since ancient times and where the Muslims select their names from the Hindu epics of the Ramayana and Mahabharata, Islam became the "fermenting agent for the revolutionary process which has taken place in the twentieth century" (Wertheim, 1956, p. 196).

Similar examples can be cited for other countries and people in the Third World to confirm that the objective attributes to define a nation or to appraise a course of nation-building will have to be regarded as variables both in their occurrence and implication. The subjective attributes, on the other hand, appear to function as a constant in the same context. Unless a human group is "bound together by common solidarity—a group whose members place loyalty to the group as a whole over any conflicting loyalties" (Rustow, 1968, p. 7)—there cannot be any nation-building.

We are not concerned, however, with any form of ascriptive loyalty arising out of an individual's affiliation to a family, kingroup, clan, caste, tribe, or religion. Neither are we concerned with those forms of achieved loyalty based on an individual's affiliation to a social class (as defined by Max Weber) or to a class identified in terms of his role in the social relations of production for the society (as defined by Karl Marx). The loyalty considered here cuts across or supersedes these kinds of loyalty and motivates a mass of people characterized by diverse socio-economic traits. Its power derives from the will of the human group thus constituted to aspire for or sustain self-government without interference from analogous groups but within the confines of international understanding stipulated by the United Nations charter and, if applicable, according to the constitution which a set of such groups may lay down for their mutual benefit.

This characterization of loyalty is implicit in the identification of nation-states. Likewise, we should examine the diachronic aspect of nation and state in the Third World simultaneously with the synchronic aspects of nation-building and state formation within or beyond them, because the assumption that this loyalty is *singularly* operative in each nation-state in the Third World may not be warranted. Concerning nation-building and state formation, therefore, this form of loyalty will have no analytical relevance so long as there is no "feeling of alienation" within the given set of people from the state power in operation. Its analytical relevance begins with the onset of that feeling of alienation within one or more segments of the given population attaining group-cohesion as described above and as specified by the previously mentioned objective attributes of nation formation. The analytical relevance of this form of loyalty ends with its resolution within or beyond the currently operating state power. In the former case, either the feeling of alienation disappears (by suppression or of its own volition) or new nations (or nationalities) appear on the social scene. In the case of the latter, the course of nation-building attains its climax in new state formations.

It follows that in order to diagnose any course of nation-building and state formation in the Third World, our attention should be focused on cases of "alienation" from the currently operating state power. This research orientation, however, may appear to keep the field of variation deliberately concealed with regard to the forces operating to build nations and form states. It may also seem that the cover might be lifted were our attention not focused on alienation but on the consolidation of the existing state power. In that way, nation-building would be examined as a constructive, not as a disruptive process, with new state formations as a possible corollary to that process.

Possibly because of the above assumptions, the consolidation model is popular with the majority of social and political scientists, as suggested by the statement, "The central fact of nation-building is the orderly exercise of a nation-wide, public authority" (Bendix, 1964, p. 18). This point of view is also implicit, and sometimes explicit, in the studies undertaken by several reputable researchers on the political perspective of the nation-states in the Third World (e.g., Shils, 1961, 1962; Kahin, 1959, Almond and Coleman, 1960). However, if we examine how this research orientation can be put into practice, we may find that it will not serve our needs efficiently or adequately in case (1) we wish to study the phenomena of nation-building and state formation as a diagnostic proposition in the contemporary perspective, and (2) we want to examine the relevant processes objectively, that is, without any ideological bias.

If the objective of a study is to explain how nation-building and state formation have *already* taken place in a territory and with reference to a set of people, it can be designed to focus one's attention on how the public authority has been exercised on a nationwide scale. The study refers to a *post facto* situation in which any previous course of alienation has been succeeded by a phase of consolidation in the social, economic, and political structure of the given society and the people. There is, thus, no unintended ommission of the alienation phase from a study conducted objectively. Also the perspective of such a study will be the backward projection of a segment of reality of which the end-results of nation-building and state formation are known. Therefore there will be no possibility for interpreting nation-building differently according to the ideological bias of the researchers. At a certain point of time, the goals have been attained.

For purposes of explaining a historically accomplished situation, the study of nation-building and state formation can focus on the orderly exercise of the public authority found to be operating *ultimately* on a nationwide scale. This focus may be regarded particularly appropriate to the task since, within the time span under consideration, there may have been a series of alienations from the corresponding public authorities, and so attention (it may be claimed) should be directed towards the results of all such alienations and consolidations. The validity of this focus of attention is substantiated by the explanatory (and not diagnostic) studies made on (1) the emergence of nations and states in Europe and North America in the historic past, and (2) the phase of nation-building in the Third World in the colonial or semicolonial phase of its history, leading to the formation of the presently operating nation-states (e.g. Wertheim, 1956; Desai, 1948; Padmore, 1958). These studies may be enriched by additional facts, but at any stage of our knowledge, they will be efficient and adequate. In the contemporary perspective also, this research orientation would have been adequate if the phenomena of nation-building and state formation could be examined against one, and only one, *predetermined* goal of social and political development, because under this proviso, nation-building would be equal to only one particular configuration of national integration, and, with "an orderly exercise of a nation-wide, public authority," to meeting that goal. So a study like that of Bendix on public authority in contemporary India becomes an efficient one on nation-building under the stipulation made by Bendix himself that *"Modernization* (sometimes called *social and political development*) refers to all these *social* and *political* changes that accompanied industrialization in many countries of Western civilization" (Bendix, 1964, p. 5).

Such a stipulation, however, may not be universally accepted because it is value-charged, as the concepts of modernization and "development" will have to be (for a relevant discussion, see Mukherjee, 1970a, pp. 29-41). The value-load may be different from person to person, and this may attribute different meanings to nation-building (national integration, in the present context). Concerning India, this is partly exemplified by the studies of Bendix (1964) and Shils (1961) in terms of the abovementioned value-load as against studies on the theme of national integration from the point of view of a Gandhian (Bose, 1967), a follower of Nehru (Thirtha, 1964), and an Indian Marxist intellectual (Mukerji, 1964). Obviously, other meanings to national integration (nation-building) in India could be provided by studies conducted on the basis of, say, the Russian and the Chinese interpretation of the Marxist point of view.

Thus, since the end-results of nation-building and state formation are unknown in the contemporary perspective, the ideological bias of the researchers to formulate them will turn the appraisal of the two phenomena into a subjectively variable task. At the same time, if we persist in the investigation of nation-building in terms of the "orderly exercise of a nation-wide, public authority," we cannot eliminate or omit that bias from our study. Bendix and Bose, for instance, are seen to be particularly conscious of this point in their studies on India, and it has been strongly underlined in a critical appraisal of "tribal integration" to the Indian society at large (Chattopadhyay and De, 1969, pp. 1985-994). This focus of attention, therefore, will not be conducive to an *objective* appraisal of the phenomena in the contemporary perspective.

Also, it will not serve our purpose adequately. In the contemporary perspective we cannot assume that along with the instances of alienation from the corresponding state power, the subsequent cases of consolidation invariably will be accounted for in the course of investigation. While the very fact of alienation from the currently operating state power draws our attention to the study of nation-building and state formation, the course of alienation has not yet come to any conclusion. Therefore, if we focus our attention on a course of consolidation instead of on the corresponding course(s) of alienation, our scope may be too circumscribed and lead to neglect of vital areas of investigation. The consolidation model may keep the field of variation concealed, while the concealment will be lifted by the alienation model.

For example, national integration as a research theme has been current in India for some years, as it has been with many social and political scientists interested in the study of political developments in the Third World (e.g. Shils, Kahin, Almond and Coleman). In regard to India, most of the studies under this head concentrate on the question of kinship-caste-religious-regional loyalty, the role of the social and political elites, the voting behavior of the people in the general elections, and so on. These issues have their due importance in specific social and political contexts. In the context of "national integration," however, they are upheld without stating why they deserve the topmost priority. And we find concurrently that several potential or *post facto* cases of "alienation," which strike one as salient in the question of nation-building and possible (or achieved) state formation, hardly receive any attention. There is practically no serious study of the conflict situations in the northeast frontier region, in Goa before and after it became a part of the Indian republic, and so on. The Naxalite movement, which is said to be inspired by the Chinese way of life, is steadily gaining ground in India; but we have no objective study of this movement yet. Even the analysis of the Kashmir situation is left to the politicians, administrators, and journalists.

Similar situations can be enumerated for many other nation-states in the Third World, such as those concerning recent conflicts in East and West Pakistan, and in Nigeria. We may also note that the drastic changes in recent years in Ghana and Indonesia may have been anticipated by some politicians and journalists, but they were hardly indicated in any serious study of political developments in these countries. We may make the same comment concerning the formation of the United Arab Republic, or, more contemporarily, concerning recently raging world issues like the conflict in Vietnam.

It is true that not many studies have been made on the political situation in the nation-states of the Third World. It is equally true, however, that there has been a spate of such studies in recent years which have dealt, directly or indirectly, with the question of nation-building and state formation. In most of these studies, however, the focus is on *what* the public authority is and *how* it is exercised. Except in a few instances, the forces antagonistic to the public authority are located at the fringe of the illuminated area of discussion or beyond its range. Seldom is the focus on *why* that public authority is denounced, through which societal media the force of "alienation" is operative, and whether that force is gathering momentum or disintegrating. Since the dynamics of political development are out of focus, our knowledge of nation-building and state formation in the Third World remains segmental and sometimes distorted. This limitation on our appraisal of the two phenomena in the current perspective is partly illustrated by Silverstein's account of Burma vis-a-vis that of Leach, or Coleman's account of Africa vis-a-vis that of Servoise; Leach and Servoise did not remain constrained by the use of the "consolidation" model and made *prima facie* use of some cases of alienation in Burma and Africa (Silverstein, 1959, pp. 75-152; Leach, 1963, pp. 121-53; Coleman, 1960, pp. 247-368; Servoise, 1963, pp. 181-294).

Thus the need for shifting our focus of attention from the consolidation of the currently operating state power to alienation from that state power is indicated for the diagnosis of nation-building and state formation in the Third World. This shift will also provide effective meanings for the notions of "center-periphery relations," "state-ness and nation-ness," "polycephality versus monocephality," in the dynamic sense of the forces involved in the emergence of these two phenomena (Learner, 1966, pp. 259-63; Merritt, 1966, pp. 321-36; Rokkan, 1969, pp. 88-91). We may note, further, that if we focus our attention on the courses of alienation from the currently operating state power, we shall automatically take note of the corresponding courses of consolidation of that state power; but the reverse arrangement is not equally automatic. "Deviations" cannot be identified without appreciating the contextual "norm," but to focus on the latter need not enjoin taking the former into account. As Bendix (1964, p. 19) also stated: "Order in a political community can be understood in terms of its opposite—anarchy."

Alienation, however, may not necessarily end in anarchy. Since alienation and consolidation are complementary aspects of the same phenomenon at every stage of its dynamic presence, the former will culminate in anarchy only when the latter is reduced to zero. Otherwise the relative strength of the two aspects, at any point of time and place, will register a particular level of nation-building and any one of all possibilities of state formation. The cases of alienation may be resolved and consolidation may be effected within the operating state power, as has recently happened in Nigeria. Alternatively, they may lead to the consolidation of the alienated segment of the society by evolving its own state power, as happened in the case of Pakistan. Or the alienated segment may merge within another state boundary, as is happening in the fringe areas of many nation-states in Asia and Oceania. The cases of alienation also will make it possible for the alienated segments from different state powers to form an analogous set and become so forceful as to impart a new meaning to nation-building and state formation, as has happened in the United Arab Republic.

The plasticity of the concepts of nation-building and state formation, which we have discussed in the first section of this paper, will thus be maintained unambiguously by our focus on the deviations from the norm, and not the other way round, for reasons already pointed out. Also, by accounting for all possibilities in nation-building and state formation, this focus will be value-free and conform to the inductive-inferential approach to the study of the two phenomena. Contrariwise, the focus on consolidation cannot but be value-loaded and conform to the deductive-positivistic approach, which we have described in the second section of this paper as inefficient for a diagnostic appraisal of the two phenomena in the contemporary perspective. The fact of alienation, therefore, attains cardinal importance for our course of research. How, then, should we prepare a research design for our observation, analysis, interpretation, and inference in that context?

THE RESEARCH DESIGN

Obviously, alienation can be observed only in situations of conflict of one or more particularly characterized groups of citizens in a state against the state power. Any form of alienation, however, will have its own course of development. The antagonism it expresses or implies—through voting behavior, desire or demand for autonomy or independence, or any other channel—may be overtly noticed or may not have come out in the open yet. Also all conflict situations may not refer to the kind of alienation stated above. Therefore, we may either take into account only those conflict situations which, for our purpose, are overtly noticed, or prepare a research design in such a manner that the course of development of all those conflict situations which should fall within the gamut of our analysis (whether or not we are presently aware of all of them) are brought within the field of observation. Since the first will give us a distorted or, at any rate, a truncated appraisal of any course of nation-building and state formation, we should choose the second alternative.

The field of observation we are to identify, accordingly, should be characterized as a theoretical space bounded by its three dimensions of variation in the *place,* the *time,* and the *object,* viz. the society under reference, the point of time at which the investigation begins, and the conflict situations enumerated in that society and at that point of time. After having thus identified the field from operational considerations, we will allow each of the dimensions to vary in the light of our need to appraise the phenomena of nation-building and state formation respectively, so that any course of examination of the two phenomena will not suffer from constraints in the demarcation of the field (in its extent and depth) or in the characteristics of its content, while the arrangements will suit the operational needs of research conducted at any point of time and in any society.

The limits of the society and the population will be treated as variables because the course of nation-building and state formation may spill over a nation-state, as we have already discussed. The time dimension will obviously be a variable since we cannot appreciate any course of nation-building and state formation precisely and objectively without appraisal of the roots and the development of the process from its germination at, say, t_i to the point of time t_n = the terminal point at which the investigation is focused. The object dimension of conflict situations should also be treated as a variable since all these situations in a society, and at a point of time, may not be relevant to the study of the two phenomena (as stated above) or demand priorities for investigation.

We need not discuss further the dimensions of variation in place and time because as we refer to the demarcation of the field of observation, we will take care of them when an empirical investigation is conducted. As to the object dimension of variation, we should conceive of the field of observation as comprising an *infinite but enumerable* number of conflict situations. To be sure, the field for any empirical investigation can contain only a finite number of conflict situations since it will be bounded in operational considerations by its spatial coordinates and the time point t_n. However, the concept of infinite but enumerable objects of observation, analysis, and inference will be suitable to the formulation of appropriate *null hypotheses* and the corresponding *alternate hypotheses,* without imposing any restriction upon the given field of variation. This requires some explanation, as given below.

Conflict situations are *sui gereris* to the analysis (and not a mere description) of the societal *processes,* whether or not these situations are overtly noticeable or submerged in the processes. Otherwise, subjects for analytical research on structural and/or functional changes in a society would not materialize. Therefore, alienation as the *null point* in an inductive-inferential course of investigation tends to equate the study of nation-building and state formation with the study of social change in a society, so that even if social change is studied precisely and unambiguously, which is not always the case (see, for a relevant discussion, Mukherjee, 1968a, pp. 31-55), the study of nation-building and state formation attains only peripheral importance in that context. All forms of social change (and thus all conflict situations referring to a society at a particular point in time) need not be *causally,* or even *concomitally,* related to the phenomena under reference. They may be of *contingent* relevance only; that is, their role in nation-building and state formation is virtually nil or cannot be ascertained yet.

This point has been noted with respect to nation-building in Latin America (Scott, 1963, pp. 73-83); it can also be illustrated from our stock of a priori knowledge. For example, the peasants' and workers' struggle for economic bargain in a society may be of contingent, concomitant, or causal importance to the study of nation-building and state formation at different points of time. Up until the 1950s, the movement of the tea plantation workers in the Darjeeling district of West Bengal may have been of only contingent importance since it registered a mere potential relevance to the process under discussion. In the 1960s it may have attained importance concomitant to the process, with the growth of the demand of the "hill people" for a regional autonomy. In the 1970s, it may maintain that importance, or revert back to its contingent role in the process, or attain a causal importance in the context of the separatist movement in the northeast frontier region of India. The growth of the sharecroppers' movement in undivided Bengal, and later in West Bengal under the banner of *tebhaga* struggle, can also be examined in the same manner in a time-perspective, leading to the currently developing Naxalite movement.

Also, diachronically, the conflict situations noticed at a particular point in time may be of contingent, concomitant, or causal relevance, respectively, to the appraisal of any course of nation-builidng and state formation. For example, in the contemporary perspective of Pakistan, the demand of the East Bengal intelligentsia for better representation in civil service (as compared with the West Pakistanis employed as civil servants) may be of contingent importance to the development of the separatist movement in the eastern wing of Pakistan. The demand of the East Bengal people to declare Bengali as a state language may be of concomitant importance to the same effect, and the demand for renaming the eastern wing of Pakistan as *Bangla Desh* may be of causal importance in the same context. Obviously, similar categorization of conflict situations, in their synchronic or diachronic aspects, is possible with reference to any nation-state or an operationally identified territory such as Vietnam.

However, to which of the three categories a conflict situation belongs is a matter for investigation. The categorization of some causal, concomitant, or contingent importance to nation-builidng and state formation may appear to be obvious, as illustrated above, but the assumption may be wrong. For the present, therefore, the three categories of conflict situations constitute a mental construct for the formulation of suitable hypotheses for empirical verification. Hence the field of variation in conflict situations will have to be appropriately characterized, according to this mental construct, for the appraisal of any course of nation-building and state formation.

For this purpose, we should, first, conceive of the field as comprising an infinite but enumerable number of conflict situations, and then formulate the appropriate null hypothesis that all conflict situations are of only contingent importance to our study. With the field thus characterized and the null hypothesis formulated, all possible alternate hypotheses can be formulated to unravel the properties of the field with respect to nation-building and state formation without imposing any restriction on our systematic accumulation of knowledge on account of these two phenomena. And since the alternate hypotheses will refer to the concomitant or causal relevance of the conflict situations to nation-building and state formation, the inferences drawn probabilistically from the test of all these hypotheses will provide us with a precise and objective appraisal of the two phenomena in any nation-building or operationally identified territory.

The inference may be exclusively on the contingent role of the conflict situations in nation-building and state formation. In that case, any new state formation is out of the picture and nation-building also loses its analytical relevance, at least for the time being. The inference may also be on the concomitant role of some or all the conflict situations in nation-building and state formation. In that case, the nature and extent of the relevant conflict situations, which have already been observed, analyzed, and interpreted will indicate whether the currently operating public authority can still consolidate its power on a nationwide scale. Some of the inferences, however, may be on the causal role of certain conflict situations in nation-building and state formation. In that case, the magnitude and momentum of these conflict situations, as ascertained from their observation, analysis, and interpretation will indicate whether they can be resolved within the confines of the existing socio-economic-political structure, or whether a different course of nation-building and state formation is in the offing. The appraisal of nation-building and state formation thus requires primarily the formulation of precise and comprehensive alternate hypotheses.

Obviously, the previously described subjective attributes of nationhood are axiomatic to the formulation of alternate hypotheses. They characterize the "feeling of alienation" without which there cannot be any new course of nation-building or state formation, although this feeling may be in the incubative phase regarding the concomitant role and overtly expressed regarding the causal role of the conflict situations. Our attention, therefore, is directed towards the previously described objective attributes since they lead to the crystallization of the subjective attributes to register alienation.

In certain circumstances, it may appear that the subjective attributes are antecedents of the objective attributes. For example, it is usually believed that the Pakistani nation owes its origin to the inherent feeling of alienation of the Muslims from the Hindus in India. Evidence has been cited to support this notion from the time the Muslims came to the subcontinent; counter-evidence, however, is profusely available (see Mukherjee, 1958, pp. 163, 172-212, 315-35). Moreover, from the time the idea of Pakistan began to permeate the activities of the Muslim League, the role of the objective attributes in rousing, nurturing, and sustaining the feeling of alienation became noticeable. In Bengal, where the movement for Pakistan was particularly strong and possibly played a decisive role in partitioning the subcontinent after the communal massacres in 1946-1947, the overwhelming majority of the landlords, well-to-do farmers, owners of big business, and top-ranking white collar workers and professionals were Hindus, and the bulk of the Muslims were sharecroppers, poor peasants, or sundry workers. The Muslims were not only economically deprived but were socially discriminated against by their overlords. The ground for the germination and a rich harvest of the feeling of alienation was thus well prepared.

To be sure, once the feeling of alienation has developed into a social force through establishment of a psychological identity and expression of group loyalty, its objective antecedents may turn out to be of little relevance. We cannot, however, conceive of the development of that feeling in a vacuum, and we are also not in a position to assume it to be an innate quality of human beings. Psychological identities cannot be achieved in a rarefied atmosphere; group loyalties evolve out of objective circumstances. On the other hand, if we conceive of the subjective attributes as innate to the study of nation-building (not as derived from the objective attributes in that context), then they lose all analytical relevance to social research by becoming either a random phenomenon in the society or a genetic constituent of the people concerned. We should consider, therefore, that (1) mutually antagonistic groups are logically formed (and are not ordained by suprasocietal agencies or produced accidentally) out of the total number of individuals in the given society or the operationally identified territory, and (2) the force behind this course of group cohesion, on the one hand, and the corresponding group divergence, on the other, is supplied by the objective attributes of nation-building and state formation.

Thus, a conflict situation, which represents one (or more than one) manner of expression of the feeling of alienation, will provide one (or more than one) set of reference groups for the formulation of the alternate hypotheses; the content of these hypotheses will vary according to the objective attributes taken into account to assume, hypothetically, the emergence of these reference groups. For example, the previously mentioned conflict situation in the Himalayan region of West Bengal can be examined under several reference groups according to the possible manifestation of conflict within and between the hill people and the plains people: the former category can be split into its components of different groups of Nepalis (the Newars, Chettris, Rai, Limbu), Lepchas, Bhutanese, and others; the components of the latter category can be enumerated as Bengali, Marwari, Bihari. Afterwards, according to each pair of reference groups, alternate hypotheses may be formulated in terms of a set of objective attributes, e.g. the role of the respective reference groups in the economic organization of the area, their cultural relations, political alliance or opposition, territorial affinity or distinction, religious unity or animosity.

Obviously, the constitution of the reference groups will vary according to the nature of the conflict situation brought under examination. For example, if we examine the conflict situation created by the previously mentioned Naxalbari movement, we may find on the basis of our a priori knowledge that the reference groups are suitably denoted by the economic and political affiliation of the people concerned, while the ethnic affiliation of the relevant people is appropriate to the constitution of reference groups for the initial examination of the conflict situation in the Himalayan region of West Bengal. Correspondingly, the reference groups concerned with the separatist movement in the eastern wing of Pakistan or with the creation of Pakhtoonistan in West Pakistan may be constituted by the ethnic-economic-political affiliation of the people in the society or the territory under reference. However, concerning the conflict between the whites and nonwhites in the Union of South Africa, white and black in Rhodesia, and the Africans and Indians in Kenya or Uganda, the constitution of the reference-groups will have virtually nothing to do with the ethnic or political affiliation of the people involved.

It follows that the objective attributes employed to formulate alternate hypotheses will vary according to our a priori knowledge of their contextual relevance to different conflict situations and allied theoretical considerations. However, given a set of alternate hypotheses formulated in the above manner, the test of the hypotheses will lead to valid inferences on (1) those group-distinctions chosen to formulate the hypotheses, which indicate their causal or concomitant role in any ongoing process of nation-building and state formation, and (2) those objective attributes chosen to formulate the hypotheses, which denote intergroup distinction and thus register, by their relative power of discrimination, the constitution of group cohesion, on the one hand, and group antagonism, on the other.

The inference will be precise and comprehensive as any course of research undertaken in successive phases yields information on (1) which reference groups are *relevant, necessary,* and *sufficient* to depict the causal or the concomitant role of the conflict situation with respect to nation-building and state formation; (2) which objective attributes are, correspondingly, *relevant, necessary,* and *sufficient* to discriminate the reference groups formed in the given context; and (3) what is the nature and degree of interaction among the objective attributes to rouse and foster different expressions of the feeling of alienation. However, the constitution of the reference groups for one phase of the investigation may not be flexible enough to be recast differently if that is required for the succeeding phases of investigation. Also the manner of assessment of the nature and degree of interaction among those objective attributes enumerated for the preceding phase of investigation may not permit including other relevant and necessary attributes in the succeeding phase of investigation, although the consideration of additional attributes *along with* those already considered may be found desirable.

Next, we should examine how the proposed research design can be applied so that (1) the formulation of all possible alternate hypotheses (concerning the reference groups formed to denote their structure and the objective attributes selected to denote their content) does not put any constraint on the systematic accumulation of our knowledge from the given field of variation, and (2) the relative power of discrimination of all possible objective attributes to denote nation-building and state formation can be ascertained precisely, unambiguously, and objectively. Otherwise, any study on the two phenomena will not be efficient or comprehensive, although we may (a) examine them in light of their *historical antecedents* for reasons stated in the first section of this paper; (b) follow the inductive-inferential approach to avoid fallacies in their appraisal in the *contemporary* perspective, as discussed in the second section; (c) adopt the alienation model for an unambiguous course of *diagnostic* investigation, as explained in the third section; and (d) as described in this section of the chapter, conceive of the field of variation as comprising infinite but enumerable conflict situations and formulate the null hypothesis of their contingent importance in order that no *restriction* is imposed upon the investigation of the properties of the field for our purpose.

For two reasons it is not always appreciated that we should consider the issues involved in (a) the formulation of the alternate hypotheses for a free flow of information on nation-building and state formation, and (b) the manner of assessment of the relative power of discrimination of the objective attributes in the same context. One reason is that empirical research is sometimes equated to a "hit and run" undertaking and, therefore, alternate hypotheses are formed spontaneously and tested by whatever methods are available, without systematization of the issues involved. The other reason is based on the assumption that the reference groups and objective attributes required to formulate the alternate hypotheses emerge *pari pasu* with the formulation of the conflict situations to be examined. The two reasons are not mutually exclusive. However, the first may lead to incomplete research; the second to a distorted appraisal of the course of nation-building and state formation under examination. We shall, therefore, examine the second reason in some detail, while dealing more generally with the first.

There is no reason to doubt that the reference groups and the objective attributes to be taken into account for the formulations of alternate hypotheses are indicated prima facie by the characteristics of a conflict situation. However, any uncritical emphasis on preconceived notions of them, without due scrutiny and empirical verification, may seriously jeopardize the efficiency of a course of research. For example, the separatist movement in the Himalayan region of West Bengal spontaneously suggests the alternate hypothesis that since the hill people have a distinctly different territorial affiliation and community of culture and languages from the plains people, they feel alienated from the latter group and wish to develop their own public authority. This hypothesis is also strongly endorsed by the largest political party of the hill people. However, as previously illustrated, an initial but objective examination of the conflict situation indicates that such an omnibus constitution of the reference groups in unsatisfactory, and the above enumeration of the objective attributes to formulate the alternate hypotheses is neither exhaustive nor effective.

Fallacies of this nature are found to occur even when dealing with the question of nation-building and state formation on a macro-scale. Our a priori knowledge is expected to be ample and extensive in that context; yet we tend to overemphasize one or another of the objective attributes and thus fail to ascertain the root cause of the conflict situations under discussion. For example, if we overemphasize the attribute of religion in nation-building of the Pakistani people (as is not infrequently done in Pakistan today), we shall be unable to ascertain the root cause of the conflict situations in the eastern and western wings of Pakistan. It is also not uncommon to explain African-Indian conflict in East Africa in terms of the different ethos of the Africans and the Indians. But if we overemphasize the ethos of the Uganda Africans vis-à-vis the Indians in Uganda, and do not pay sufficient attention to their respective roles in the economic organization of the country in British and post-British times, we shall not only fail to appreciate the root cause of the African-Indian conflict but also that of the incipient (and sometimes explicit) conflict situations among the respective peoples of Uganda (see, for instance, Mukherjee, 1956, pp. 215-74).

Similarly, if we overemphasize the Indian ethos in terms of the territorial, social, cultural, and ideological unity of the people of India, we may merely harp on the prescription of emotional integration for nation-building in the Indian republic. Some topmost Indian intellectuals stress this characteristic of Indian unity one-sidedly and suggest the aforementioned policy for national integration (see Mukerji, 1964, pp. 8-9). There is evidence, however, to substantiate the facts that (a) regional and ethnic distinctions have been registered from ancient times in spite of the concurrent territorial integration of Bharat and the emergence of Indian ethos through an all-India spread of the caste system and the values propagated by the epics, *puranas* (see Mukherjee, 1965, pp. 193-94); (b) mutually distinct linguistic-cultural areas emerged in the subcontinent by the seventeenth century, which also catered to separate markets for commodity production (see Mukherjee, 1958, pp. 187-212); and (c) conflicts between different linguistic-cultural areas have been a chronic ailment in the British and post-British period of India's history, and this called for specific resolutions to be passed by the Indian National Congress before and after independence.

Several such examples can be cited to illustrate the obvious fact that for all cases of conflict we should consider the reference groups and objective attributes to vary not only in their relevance but also in their usefulness to the appraisal of nation-building and state formation. During a course of empirical investigation, the attributes not found relevant will be left out of consideration, as will be those reference groups found irrelevant when examined according to the relevant attributes. Also, while the relevant attributes enumerated at one phase of investigation may not exhaust the total of such attributes, all of them may not be found necessary for the study in hand because of their comparatively low power of discrimination. Their role may be negligible in the given context or it may already be indicated by their high correlation with other attributes found necessary for the particular study. On the other hand, a few attributes may be found which are relevant, necessary and sufficient to denote a course of nation-building and state formation. Following such an appraisal of the objective attributes as is necessary or sufficient for the present purpose, appropriate reference groups will be constituted.

In order to accommodate all these possibilities, we should conceive of an infinite but enumerable field of variation of the objective attributes from which they are selected, successively, on a priori grounds and retained or rejected according to the inferences drawn, after investigations, as to their relevance and relative usefullness to the particular course of nation-building and state formation. Correspondingly, we should conceive of an infinite but enumerable field of variation of the reference groups constituted with the objective attributes selected and retained after properly conducted empirical investigations. It is only by a systematic interlocking of the three infinite but enumerable fields of variation in conflict situations, reference groups, and objective attributes that we may satisfactorily apply the proposed research design to appraise any course of nation-building and state formation precisely, unambiguously, and comprehensively.

This piece of engineering should start from the bottom, as it were, by looking into all possible compositions of the objective attributes. Obviously, each one of them is composed of a number of elements which, in the ultimate stage of categorization, are indivisible. For example, the attribute of ethnic affiliation of the people in the Himalayan region of

West Bengal refers to the Nepalis as a composite element which may be further divided into its components of Newar, Chettri, Rai, Limbu, and so on. A further division of the components may be possible and necessary for investigation; alternatively, a composite element may be adequate. Therefore, the reference groups will be recast or reconstituted for successive phases of an investigation provided the possibilities for the objective attributes are (1) freely enumerated, (2) characterized by their respective elements up to the stage where these elements become indivisible, and (3) analyzed to denote their relevance, necessity, or sufficiency in the course of an appraisal of nation-building and state formation.

The categorization of the individuals to produce the reference groups will successively incorporate the elements characterizing those attributes which have been ascertained to be necessary or sufficiently important to the course of analysis and which have been further rated prioritywise according to their relative power of discrimination in the given context. For example, the ethnic distinction of the people in the Himalayan region of West Bengal appeared from a preliminary examination of the conflict situation to constitute the reference groups, say, $(g_1, g_2, \ldots, g_n)$. The first-phase investigation of the issue, however, points out that further distinction of the ethnically distinguished reference groups is necessary according to their role in the economic organization of the area. For both ethnic affiliation and role in economic organization are ascertained to be relevant and necessary attributes for the appraisal of nation-building in this operationally identified territory. The reference groups, therefore, may now be constituted as say:

$$g_{11}, g_{12}, \ldots, g_{1n},$$
$$g_{21}, g_{22}, \ldots, g_{2n},$$
$$\ldots \quad \ldots \quad \ldots \quad \ldots$$
$$g_{k1}, g_{k2}, \ldots, g_{kn}.$$

Some of the reference groups thus identified may be identical; others may not occur at all. For example, the Nepalis of the previously illustrated case may refer to distinct orbits of economic organization along with their separation into the aforesaid components of Newar and so on, while the Marwaris *en bloc* may refer to only one role in the economic organization of the area. However, the reference groups thus distinguished can incorporate further groupings as other attributes are taken into account for their constitution, so that the theoretical configuration of all possible reference groups may be schematically presented as:

$$g_{1..11}, \quad g_{1..12}, \quad \cdots, \quad g_{1..1r},$$

$$g_{1..21}, \quad g_{1..22}, \quad \cdots, \quad g_{1..2r},$$

$$\cdots \qquad \cdots \qquad \cdots, \qquad \cdots$$

$$g_{1..n1}, \quad g_{1..n2}, \quad \cdots, \quad g_{1..nr},$$

$$g_{2..11}, \quad g_{2..12}, \quad \cdots, \quad g_{2..1r},$$

$$\cdots \qquad \cdots \qquad \cdots \qquad \cdots$$

$$g_{2..n1}, \quad g_{2..n2}, \quad \cdots, \quad g_{2..nr},$$

$$\cdots \qquad \cdots \qquad \cdots \qquad \cdots$$

$$g_{k..11}, \quad g_{k..12}, \quad \cdots, \quad g_{k..1r},$$

$$\cdots \qquad \cdots \qquad \cdots \qquad \cdots$$

$$g_{k..n1}, \quad g_{k..n2}, \quad \cdots, \quad g_{k..nr}.$$

It follows from the above that if we wish to formulate all possible alternate hypotheses without imposing any constraint on the application of the proposed research design, we should consider the objective attributes to form an infinite but enumerable series of mutually distinct but analogous elements. The elements will go into the formation of all possible reference groups. Therefore, we should also consider that the reference groups thus constituted form an infinite but enumerable series of mutually distinct but analogous entities, as schematically presented, so that the successive consolidation and differentiation of all possible reference groups into a few pooled ones (which will ultimately depict the effective group-cohesion and group-antagonism for nation-building and state formation by their complementary aspect) will follow from (1) the enumeration of all possible relevant, necessary, and sufficient objective attributes for the study in hand, and (2) the assessment of their relative powers of group consolidation and group discrimination in terms of the expressed or implied feeling of alienation from the currently operating public authority.

Next, therefore, we should examine what will be the appropriate method for the proposed course of research, what kind of analytical tools and data we require, and which of them are available to us.

RESEARCH METHODOLOGY AND TOOLS

The frame of reference we have developed shows that the application of the research design requires increasingly precise and comprehensive *group distance*—the groups being constituted as described above—in a *social space* characterized by conflict situations. We need for this purpose a set of indicators to denote the feeling of alienation in particular reference to the conflict situation(s) under examination. The indicators will refer to the opinion, attitude, action, and behavior pattern of all the people concerned and, thus, of the constituents of the reference groups. Initially formed qualitatively or quantitatively, as they occur in their primary form, the indicators can be made more and more quantifiable provided the implication and the intrinsic characteristics of the qualitative indicators are not lost during their abstraction into quantities.

Hasty quantification may affect a study adversely, as has been illustrated with respect to radio listening as denoting communication of social or political values in the developing societies (see Mukherjee, 1968a, pp. 32-33, 44-45; 1970a, pp. 3-4, concerning the quantified indicators in Russet et al., 1964, pp. 118-25). Also it may not be appropriate to quantify all the indicators, as Friedrich (1966, pp. 57-72) has aptly pointed out regarding political data. However, fully quantified or not, the indicators can be employed as discriminant functions to elicit the properties of the social space.

If the indicators are fully quantified, a discriminant function analysis may be attempted by the use of, say, Mahalanobis's D^2 statistic. Such an analysis will not only bring out the group constellations in the social space but also place the reference groups evolved out of the process within a precise measure of their intergroup distances. This measure will take note of only the exclusive effect of each objective attribute to produce, complementarily, group cohesion and group divergence. Also, the introduction of new objective attributes during the course of analysis will register their *net* discriminating effect and thus indicate their relevance, necessity, or sufficiency to the task. The relative power of discrimination of the attributes, therefore, will be registered precisely and comprehensively and lead in the course of successive trials to the detection of the most effective group consolidation and group antagonism in reference to the conflict situation(s) under examination.

D^2 statistic has been successfuly employed in the above manner not only for anthropometric analysis (which was Mahalanobis's first interest) but also for economic and psychometric analyses as well as to ascertain social class distance, intercaste divergence, and the like. (For some details, see Mukherjee, 1951, pp. 47-56; 1955; 1968b, pp. 508-26; and Mukherjee and Bandyopadhyay, 1963, pp. 259-82). For the appraisal of nation-building and state formation also, the D^2 statistic can be effectively employed to conform to the proposed research design in case the indicators are fully quantified in their primary form or can be duly quantified subsequently.

Even if the indicators are not quantifiable, group constellations can be ascertained in terms of proportional representation of the indicators by the people concerned who are, concurrently, categorized by a panel of objective attributes into a set of reference groups. Suitable analytical tools can be devised to show how, in this manner also, the operationally evolved reference groups form group cohesion and group distinction complementarily and how the course of consolidation and divergence can be made more and more precise and comprehensive (for instance, see Mukherjee, 1965, pp. 76-94, 100-101), so that the qualitative indicators will be employed (although not as efficiently as is possible for the quantified indicators) as discriminant functions to elicit the properties of the given social space.

Obviously, in the case of partly quantitative and partly qualitative indicators, appropriate analytical tools may be found from those available, or new ones will have to be devised to meet the specific requirements. However, the point to note regarding all tools of analysis is that, like Mahalanobis's D^2 statistic, they should elicit the *net* discriminating effect of each and every objective attribute brought to account, and thus constitute the reference groups effectively, without subjective judgement. Thus, any course of research on nation-building and state formation will always be amenable to a systematic accumulation of our knowledge in that context.

The information we require to pursue this course of research will refer to the following specification of the units of observation, analysis, and interpretation with respect to any conflict situation. At any phase of our investigation, the *unit of observation* is each person in the society, or the operationally identified territory, who is mature enough to develop and react to a feeling of alienation from the currently exercised public authority. He or she will be characterized by the applicable elements of the objective attributes taken into account to formulate the alternate hypotheses. Correspondingly, therefore, the *unit of analysis* is each reference group characterized by the elements of the objective attributes taken into account, and the *unit of interpretation* in the light of the inference drawn from the test of each alternate hypothesis, is the configuration of the given reference groups into mutually distinct but analogous clusters of group cohesion and group divergence. The use of indicators in this context is like mortar in a masonry work. We need, therefore, information to (a) devise the indicators, (b) enumerate a set of objective attributes which appear to be relevant to the study, and (c) constitute the reference groups out of the total population (the units of observation) by a cross-classification of the elements of the attributes.

Needless to say, all three kinds of information will have to be collected during empirical investigation as it proceeds from its exploratory to an optimally deterministic phase. To begin with, however, we must depend on our stock of a priori knowledge which we will gain, both in extent and depth, from the experience of the preceding phases of investigation. Therefore, inasmuch as our a priori knowledge will be more and more consolidated as the investigation proceeds, so it is necessary to consolidate whatever a priori knowledge is available at the beginning of the course of research. This point is mentioned because we are sometimes tempted to adopt the so-called "open minded" approach and thus fail to benefit fully from the labor of our forerunners.

At the beginning of a course of research, our stock of a priori knowledge refers to two sources: (1) the background information available on the society and the people under reference, and (2) the theoretical overview we obtain from research conducted in this and the other two parts of the world. The point to consider, therefore, is how effectively we may make use of them.

The sources of background information are generally considered to be the census, sample surveys, and data-collecting agencies, so that data inventory is now accepted as a useful appendage to any empirical research undertaking. Another no less important source, however, will be relevant books, papers, reports, documents, manuscripts, and the like. The coverage of this source, both in extent and depth, varies for different nation-states in the Third World. It is however, appreciable for any one of them, while for India, at any rate, the usefulness of such material for empirical research has been substantial (for instance, see Mukherjee, 1969; 1970b). There is no reason why similar benefit cannot be derived from them in appraising nation-building and state formation in the Third World. Therefore, along with data inventory, bibliographical research should constitute another useful adjunct to any program of empirical research on the two phenomena.

Along with the consolidation of our background information in the above manner, the theoretical overview obtained from research conducted in the other two parts of the world will constitute our a priori knowledge comprehensively. The notions of center-periphery relations mentioned earlier, as well as the concepts and models suggested for empirical verification (for instance, see Rokkan, 1969b, pp. 53-73) will be of immense value to research on nation-building and state formation in the Third World, for they will help us to systematize our background information at each stage of investigation and look for the nuances of the two phenomena in a sea of details.

The theoretical overview will also provide us with arguments to formulate the alternate hypotheses. However, it cannot be employed deductively to prove or disprove a thesis or to explain nation-building and state formation according to one's inclination or value judgement, just as background information on the indicators, objective attributes, and reference groups cannot substitute for first-hand empirical investigation. It is necessary to underline this point, even for those researchers who wish to examine the two phenomena objectively and impartially, because the current theories on nation-building and state formation have emerged mainly out of studies of the European and North American situations. Their imitative and acontextual application in the Third World will either confuse the appreciation of political dynamics or produce disastrous results, as has been noted with regard to corresponding social and economic theories (for instance, see Alatas, 1969; Mukherjee, 1969, 1970a; Myrdal, 1969; Odaka, 1964). The fallacy of any such uncritical attempt was also pointed out in the symposium organized in Sweden by UNESCO in August-September 1968 (Rokkan, 1969a, pp. 87-97). The appraisal of nation-building and state formation in the Third World, therefore, will have to be based on empirical research with ancillary help from all available sources, as indicated above. Also, if the problems posed in this chapter are found to be of decisive importance, and the method proposed to solve them is acceptable, then the course of research will be a rigorous and sustained undertaking. There is, however, no shortcut to success.

REFERENCES

Alatas, Syed Hussein, "The Captive Mind in Development Planning," presented at the eleventh world conference of the Society for International Development, New Delhi, November 14-17, 1969.

Almond, Gabriel A. and James S. Coleman, eds., The Politics of the Developing Areas, Princeton, Princeton University Press, 1960.

Bailey, F. G., Tribe, Caste, and Nation, Manchester, Manchester University Press, 1960.

Bendix, R., Nation-Building and Citizenship, New York, John Wiley, 1964.

Bessaignet, Pierre, ed., Social Research in East Pakistan, Dacca, Asiatic Society of Pakistan, 1960.

Bose, Nirmal Kumar, Problems of National Integration, Simla, Indian Institute of Advanced Study, 1967.

Chattopadhyay, Gouranga and Barun De, "Problems of Tribal-Integration to Urban Industrial Society: A Theoretical Approach," Economic and Political Weekly, Vol. IV, No. 52, pp. 1935-94. (Bombay)

Coleman, James S., "The Politics of Sub-Saharan Africa," in G. A. Almond and J. S. Coleman (eds.), The Politics of the Developing Areas, Princeton, Princeton University Press, 1960.

Desai, A. R., Social Background of Indian Nationalism, Bombay, Oxford University Press, 1948.

Deutch, Karl W., "Some Problems in the Study of Nation-Building," in K. W. Deutsch and W. J. Foltz (eds.), Nation-Building, New York, Atherton, 1963.

Emerson, Rupert, "Nation-Building in Africa," in K. W. Deutsch and W. J. Foltz (eds.), Nation-Building, New York, Atherton, 1963.

Friedrich, Carl J., "Some General Theoretical Reflections on the Problems of Political Data," in R. L. Merritt and S. Rokkan (eds.), Comparing Nations, New Haven, Yale University Press, 1966.

Frobenius, Leo, Das Unbekannte Afrika, Munich, C. H. Becksche, 1923.

Kahin, George McTurnan, ed., Governments and Politics of Southeast Asia, New York, Cornell University Press, 1959.

Leach, Edmund, "The Political Future of Burma," in B. de Jouvenel (ed.), Futuribles, Geneva, Droz, 1963.

Lerner, Daniel, "Some Comments on Center-Periphery Relations," in R. L. Merritt and S. Rokkan (eds.), Comparing Nations, New Haven, Yale University Press, 1966.

Lowie, Robert H., Social Organization, London, Routledge & Kegan Paul, 1950.

Lyall, Alfred, Asiatic Studies, London, John Murray, 1882.

Marx, Karl, Capital, Vol. I, London, George Allen & Unwin, 1949.

Merritt, Richard L., "West Berlin—Center or Periphery?" in R. L. Merritt and S. Rokkan (eds.), Comparing Nations, New Haven, Yale University Press, 1966.

Mukerji, Nirod, Standing at the Cross-Roads, Bombay, Allied Publishers, 1964.

Mukherjee, Ramkrishna, Development of Sociology in "Developing Societies:" Some Observations, Calcutta, Indian Statistical Institute, 1970. (mimeo)

———, Data Inventory on Social Science—India, Calcutta, Indian Statistical Institute and Statistical Publishing Society, 1970.

———, "Empirical Social Research on Contemporary India," Social Science Information, Vol. 8, No. 6, 1969. (Paris)

———, "Some Observations on the Diachronic and Synchronic Aspects of Social Change," Social Science Information, Vol. 7, No. 1, 1968, pp. 31-55. (Paris)

———, "Socio-Economic Factors in Children's Body Development," in L. P. Vidyarthi (ed.), Applied Anthropology in India, Allahabad, Kitab Mahal, 1968.

———, The Sociologist and Social Change in India Today, New Delhi, Prentice-Hall of India, 1965.

———, The Rise and Fall of the East India Company, Berlin, Verlag der Wissenchaften, 1958.

———, The Dynamics of a Rural Society, Berlin, Akademie-Verlag, 1957.

———, The Problem of Uganda, Berlin, Akademie-Verlag, 1956.

———, A Study on Differences in Physical Development by Socio-Economic Strata," Sankhya, Vol. 11, No. 1, 1951, pp. 47-56. (Calcutta)

―――, and Suraj Bandyopadhyay, "Social Research and Mahalanobis's D^2," in C. R. Rao (ed.), Contribution to Statistics, Calcutta, Statistical Publishing Society and Oxford, Pergamon Press, 1963.

Mukherjee, Ramkrishna, C. R. Rao, and J. C. Trevor, "The Physical Characteristics of the Ancient Inhabitants of Jebel Moya, Sudan; Cambridge, Cambridge University Press, 1955.

Munshi, Surendra and Atis Das Gupta, "Groups and Group Conflict in Darjeeling Town: An Exploratory Study, Calcutta, Indian Statistical Institute, 1970. (Sociological Research United Working Paper, mimeo)

Myrdal, Gunnar, "Cleansing the Approach from Biases in the Study of Underdeveloped Countries," Social Science Information, Vol. 8, No. 8, 1969, pp. 9-26. (Paris)

Oberg, K., "The Kingdom of Ankole in Uganda," in M. Fortes and E. E. Evans-Pritchard (eds.), African Political Systems, London, Oxford University Press, 1950.

―――, Terena and the Caduvco of Southern Mato Grosso, Brazil, Greenwood, 1949.

Odaka, K., "Traditionalism and Democracy in Japanese Industry," Transactions of the Fifth World Congress of Sociology (Louvain, Belgium), International Sociological Association, Vol. III, pp. 39-49.

Padmore, George, The Gold Coast Revolution, London, Dennis Dobson, 1958.

Panikkar, K. Madhu, The Serpent and the Crescent, Bombay, Asia Publishing House, 1963.

Risley, H. H., The Tribes and Castes of Bengal, Calcutta, Bengal Secretariat Press, 1891.

Rokkan, Stein, "Centre Formation, Nation-Building and Cultural Diversity: Report on a Symposium Organized by UNESCO," Social Science Information, Vol, 8, No. 1, 1969, pp. 85-99.

―――, "Models and Methods in the Comparative Study of Nation-Building," Acta Sociologica, Vol. 12, No. 2, 1969, pp. 53-73.

Russett, Bruce M., Hayward R. Alker, Jr., Karl W. Deutsch, and Harold D. Lasswell, World Handbook of Political and Social Indicators, New Haven, Yale University Press, 1964.

Rustow, Dankwart A., "Nation," in D. L. Sills (ed.), International Encyclopaedia of the Social Sciences, New York, Glencoe, 1968, pp. 7-14.

Scott, Robert L., "Nation-Building in Latin America," in K. W. Deutsch and W. J. Foltz (eds.), Nation-Building, New York, Atherton, 1963.

Servoise, Rene, "Whiter Black Africa?" in B. de Jouvenel (ed.), Futuribles, Geneva, Droz, 1963.

Shils, Edward, Political Development in the New States, Netherlands, Gravenhage, Mouton, 1962.

―――, The Intellectual Between Tradition and Modernity: the Indian Situation, The Hague, Mouton, 1961.

Silverstein, Josef, "Burma," in G. M. Kahin (ed.), Governments and Politics of Southeast Asia, New York, Cornell University Press, 1959.

Thirtha, N. V., National Integration, Jullundur-Delhi, University Publishers, 1964.

Weber, Max, The Religion of India, Glencoe, Free Press, 1958.

Weilenmann, Hermann, "The Interlocking of Nation and Personality Structure," in K. W. Deutsch and W. J. Foltz (eds.), Nation-Building, New York, Atherton, 1963.

Wertheim, W. F., Indonesian Society in Transition, The Hague and Bandung, W. van Hoeve, 1956.
Westermann, D., Geschichte Afrikas, Köln, Greven-Verlag, 1952.

CHAPTER 10

NATION-BUILDING AND NATIONAL IDENTITY
IN SOUTHEAST ASIA

Chan Heng-Chee and Hans-Dieter Evers

CHAN HENG-CHEE is Lecturer in Political Science at the University of Singapore. She is engaged in research on Singapore's political system and is the author of *Singapore, the Politics of Survival.*

HANS-DIETER EVERS was educated in Germany, has taught at Yale University, and is currently Professor of Sociology at the University of Singapore. He has done extensive research on class formation and social development in Southeast Asia and is the author of *Monks, Priests and Peasants* and *Kulturwandel in Ceylon.* He edited *Modernization in Southeast Asia* and *Loosely Structured Social Systems–Thailand in Comparative Perspective.*

The ideas of the nation-state and of national identity are intimately connected with European political history of the nineteenth century, and have been exported to the colonial territories of the Western powers as part of the process of cultural expansion and westernization. It is, therefore, quite understandable that concern for nation-building through the development of a national identity and eventually an identity crisis are phenomena found only, or at least predominantly, amongst the westernized elites of Asian countries who at the same time constitute most of the ruling elites. The insistence of Western political scientists on emphasizing the importance of these questions is probably largely fostered by their own social background as well as by their method of interviewing members of westernized elites, if only to overcome linguistic difficulties and for the sake of convenience. We do not want to argue that these concepts are useless; after all, we are about to embark on this very subject, but we wish to make a few cautionary remarks. Many Asian political leaders, and specifically all members of traditional elites, are perfectly clear about their identities. They do not experience any identity crisis and in many cases would look with some exasperation upon the keen social scientist presenting questions out of his carefully constructed questionnaire to test his theory of national identity crisis. There is, therefore, no need to search for identity as identity is clearly established (and usually, minorities that might challenge the established identity are suppressed).

NATIONAL IDENTITY IN SOUTHEAST ASIA

National identity, we maintain, is only a problem of westernized elites that are alienated from their own cultural tradition. Traditional elites tend to be sure of their own identity and of the identity of the state they try to maintain or to build. There is, therefore, *no* major problem of national identity in those states that have an unbroken tradition of statehood, that have maintained their symbols of identity and are governed by elites that combine a low degree of westernization with a high degree of identification with their own cultural tradition. Ethnic homogeneity of the respective society is, of course, a further major factor that decreases the importance of identity problems.

The Southeast Asian countries that approximates this type are Thailand and to a somewhat lesser extent, Cambodia and Laos. The coalescence of being ethnic Thai, Theravada Buddhist, and governed by an unbroken lineage of Thai kings have made the question of a national identity largely irrelevant to Thai elites.

There is a very strong and clear identity of being Thai which is maintained both in popular culture, in religious activities, and in school curricula. No search for national identity is necessary in the Thai population except among the ethnic minorities of Muslim Malays in the South, hill tribes in the North, and Chinese in Bangkok. In the case of the latter, assimilation to Thai culture has proceeded very fast and a Thai identity or at least a "double identity" has been established. It was consequently very difficult to illicit any comments on national identity from Thai leaders during interviews on this problem.[1] Thailand's escape from European colonialism was, however, often ascribed to the quality of Thai national symbols, especially that of the king and a national karma in Buddhist terms.

But theorists of national identity and nation-building have tended to look at these concepts with a very different premise. Major emphasis is placed on the need to create a national identity because it is seen to be inextricably bound up with social and cultural pluralism which in turn is thought to be associated with political instability.[2] Nation-building through identity formation would entail a process through which an individual of a political system is taught to subsume his cultural, social, and ethnic identity under a broader and more general national identity.

Hence, replacing primordial sentiments with national ones is viewed as a means of fostering stability and order. In this chapter, we will attempt to understand the policies of the new nations from this perspective. We wish to address ourselves to the following questions: Which political elites make use of a deliberate policy of national identity formation for the purpose of nation-building? If they make use of such policy, what sort of national identity will they try to create?

The search for national identity and the attempt to use it as an instrument of nation-building was generally pronounced in those countries where colonial domination left behind a westernized elite faced with the problem of building nation-states. These elites tried to perpetuate in most cases the political system of a somewhat "decolonized colonialism": Legally independent states deriving their identity from the model of their previous colonial masters. This identity always remained an identity of a minor westernized elite and never penetrated the masses of the population. Sooner or later the westernized political elite had to establish an identity that was *different* from that of the colonial mother country. There appears to have been two major alternatives for elites trying to shed a colonial or neo-colonial identification.

(1) *Regressive identity*. All Southeast Asian countries (with the possible exception of the Philippines) can look back upon a long and proud cultural and political tradition. The revival of this tradition, the attempt to link the present with a precolonial state, is therefore a distinct possibility. The focus of the search for identity becomes the "golden" past.

(2) *Progressive identity*. The past is seen as detrimental to progress; lack of development is ascribed to remnants of the feudal or colonial past; and a new society, a new state, and a new national identity is sought. Socialism and communism are seen as the major options, and a new identity as a socialist state is desired.

These two basic variants of establishing a national identity can, of course, be found in the same country championed by different elites contending for political leadership. (The case of Indonesia is particularly relevant here.) They can also lend themselves to quite different political systems and can find expression in various political forms. In recent years, a third variant has emerged. The case of Singapore is especially intriguing in this respect. During the period when Singapore was part of Malaysia, the question of a separate identity did not come up. Some faint attempts were made, however, to implement the "identity policies" of the central government in Kuala Lumpur, e.g. by making use of Malay as a national language. When the separation between Malaysia and Singapore was forced, the Singapore People's Action Party leadership found itself in an acute dilemma: A nation-state was created and a national identity was deemed essential to integrate a multiracial society. What sort of identity should the leaders have implemented and fostered?

The two basic Southeast Asian variants mentioned before were not viable: Singapore, founded as a trading post by the British in 1819, has only a short and total colonial past that could hardly have been used for creating a national identity; with 76 percent of its population being ethnic immigrant Chinese, a "regressive identity" would mean the creation of a third China, a solution totally unacceptable to Singapore's neighbours Malaysia and Indonesia and to both the westernized Chinese and the other ethnic groups in Singapore. The path of a "progressive identity" was originally instigated by the ruling party, the People's Action Party (PAP) leadership but could not ideologically be maintained for two major reasons: British forces still stationed in great numbers on the island would have thwarted any pro-Communist take over, and the economic survival of Singapore depended on the attraction of foreign capital and the maintenance of Singapore's entrepot trade. The slightest sign of a leftist or Communist ideology in government policies would have destroyed, in the view of the PAP leaders, both Singapore's trade monopoly and its chances for rapid industrialisation.

What, then, was the solution to Singapore's identity dilemma? A national identity had to be created, nation-building through national identity was deemed essential, but two major ideological options were closed. The solution lay in an attempt to create a nonideological identity, or if this seems to be a contradiction in terms, an identity through an "ideology of pragmatism." Discussion of basic questions of political philosophy and ideology, even political discussion in general, was severely curbed until it flowed at a low ebb out of public purview. Some of the main tenants and symbols of this nonideology of pragmatism and development were the "HBD flats" (high-rise and low-cost buildings), the Jurong industrial estate, and the "keep Singapore clean and pollution free" campaign.

The decisive question is, of course, whether a nonideological national identity is viable over a long period of time and what political forms will be attached to it in the long run. We, therefore, propose to take a closer look at the case of Singapore which appears to bring out in a very clear manner one of the major problems of nation-building through national identity formation in Southeast Asia.

SINGAPORE–COLONY TO NATION-STATE

A necessary preface to any discussion on Singapore must be an introduction to its unique geopolitical features. The island republic lies at the tip of the Malayan Peninsula and is the smallest state in Southeast Asia although it is not the smallest in the world. Encircling Singapore within a radius of 1,100 miles, are the major Indonesian islands of Java, Sumatra, Kalimantan, Cambodia, South Vietnam, southern parts of Thailand, just under half of Laos, and part of Burma, and only three-quarters of a mile of causeway separates the island from West Malaysia.

Historically, the island has always looked toward peninsula Malaya (or West Malaysia, today). In the nineteenth century during British colonial rule, Singapore was governed as part of Malaya, although after the Malayan Union proposals in 1945 she was progressively treated as a unit separate politically from the mainland. The establishment of the Federation of Malaya and the subsequent development of the two territories confirmed the dissociating trends.

The population of Singapore is of a complicated ethnic mix. The Chinese form 76 percent of the total population of 2.2 million; the Malays, 15 percent, the Indians and Pakistanis, 7 percent.[3] This simple division into the three major ethnic groups, however, obscures the heterogeneity of the population. For instance, the Chinese may be subdivided into five different dialect group communities: Hokkiens, Teochew, Cantonese, Hakka, and Hainanese. The first three are each more numerous than the Malay population. The Indians and Pakistanis include people of differing religions, customs, and languages; and even the Malay community, the most homogeneous of the communities, includes people of different immigrant stock such as Javanese, Buginese, and Boyanese.

The ethnic cleavages are further emphasised by the socio-economic cleavages. The Malays are not only a minority group in the numerical sense, they are also a socio-economic minority. *The Singapore Sample Household Survey, 1966* gives a vivid picture of the social stratification of the entire population. The Chinese form the bulk of the upper and middle class as indicated by their occupational rankings. The Indians and Pakistanis enjoy social and economic influence exceeding the size of their population. But the bulk of the Malays, about 71 percent of the economically active, are engaged in occupations connected with service, transport, communication, production, process work, crafts, and labour while the Indian and Chinese percentages are 58 percent and 54 percent for the same category of activities. The problems of integrating the three major racial divisions into one political community and creating a nation out of this diversity are probably familiar to most students of integration in new states, but there is an added aspect to the problem of pluralism in Singapore.

The population complexity of Singapore does not simply end in the presence of different racial groups. Another way of looking at the population is to divide it according to the education medium. Thus, one can discern the English-educated group, the Chinese-educated, the Malay-educated (which is strictly speaking, Tamil-educated). With language of instruction as the differentiating factor, many points of differences may be observed between the Chinese-educated Chinese and the English-educated Chinese, and along the same lines, the Malay-educated Malay and the English-educated Malay, the Tamil-educated Indian and the English-educated Indian.[4] A breakdown of the school enrollment according to medium of education is roughly as follows:

	1959	%	1967	%	1970	%
English-educated	153,486	50.9	304,651	58.9	317,335	64.3
Chinese-educated	140,231	43.6	175,278	33.8	162,111	31.8
Malay-educated	15,804	5.0	36,142	7.0	28,340	5.6
Tamil-educated	1,456	0.5	18,114	0.3	1,472	0.3

The trend is toward an increase in the enrollment in the English stream of education.

One fact that has not escaped notice is the existence of a greater degree of similarity and agreement in terms of values and attitudes among the English-educated groups whatever their racial origin than, say, between an English-educated and the mother-tongue educated member of the same community. These cross-cutting cleavages merely add another dimension to the existing racial, cultural, and linguistic problems of the infant nation. There is also the converse argument that the cross-cutting alignment of the English-educated, in fact, alleviates the situation of separate racial compartmentalization. It is becoming increasingly clear in Singapore that among the Chinese, the interests, values, and attitudes of the Chinese-educated Chinese and the English-educated Chinese are not congruent. The political elite in Singapore, at present an English-educated one, is making attempts to reduce some of these differences. The national education system is expected to reduce the gap between the groups.

Meanwhile, a "great cultural divide" exists between these two groups of people of the same ethnic stock. A solidarity pattern based on the Chinese medium of education is potentially extremely powerful. If the Indians and Pakistanis are suspected of loyalty to their homeland and are encouraged to break their own home ties, the Chinese are suspected of being powerfully drawn to China. It is generally believed that the Chinese-educated Chinese are highly susceptible to China's influence. It is their common usage of the Chinese language, the enthusiastic manifestation of the Chinese culture by this particular group that has embarrassed political leaders of Singapore in the past and led less discerning neighbouring powers to see the island as a "third China." It has been the policy of the Singapore leadership to discourage the Eastward political orientations of the Chinese.

An Independent State

In the early calculations of the People's Action Party (PAP) government, the definition of a national identity for the island was in terms of a larger federation of Malaya and Singapore, and in the early sixties, one of the main efforts of the Singapore government was made in working toward union with Malaya. The Federation of Malaysia was formed in 1963, but nearly two years and several political crisis later, the partnership between Singapore and Malaysia ended, and Singapore became an independent republic in 1965.

The problem faced by the Singapore leadership thereafter was how to consolidate a new identity—a Singapore identity—never deeply rooted in the island and never accepted as eminently rational by the PAP leaders themselves.[5] Initially, the Singapore leaders still hoped for reunification at a future date, but it appears that when the expected economic and political co-operation with Malaysia did not materialize, the Singapore leaders decided to define a separate and distinct identity for the republic and dropped all references to reunification altogether.

In projecting a new identity, the leaders obviously asked themselves what sort of Singapore they wanted and the type of individual the Singaporean should become. In selecting the values that are to be adopted as the national values, three factors were primary considerations: (1) the geographical context of Singapore, (2) the ethnic composition of the island and (3) the PAP analysis and understanding of how small nations survive, which is based on their close study of Israel, Finland and

Switzerland. Most of all, these had to be values that, in the final outcome of a crisis situation, whatever the community, the individual would still identify his future and fortune with.

The Singapore Identity

In the Singapore situation, the option of selecting a regressive identity, to emphasize past glories and traditional culture, was not really available. The population is made up of largely immigrant stock and the early immigrants were themselves not the culture-bearers since they were all traders or coolies. Thus the profound appreciation and grasp of the Chinese, Indian or Indonesian cultures and consequently the drive to propagate these traditions were never evident. Pride in Singapore's history is not a conscious phenomenon with this immigrant island. Besides its history has been relatively short and uneventful. In fact, the leadership has pointed out that in the case of Singapore, ruminating on the past would merely emphasise the differences among the races, and Singaporeans are exhorted to look toward the future and their destiny together.

In selecting the values that would express the Singapore identity, the choice fell on what would appear to be nonideological, pragmatic values.

Multiracialism

For a predominantly Chinese island state to survive in Southeast Asia, it was essential for Singapore not to be labeled a third China. Further, to inculcate a sense of commitment to the state in the various racial groups and to exist in racial harmony, multiracialism and multilingualism were to be emphasised as the fundamental beliefs of the state. By multiracialism, the Singapore leaders meant the practice of cultural tolerance toward the various communities; acceptance of differences in religious practices, customs and traditions of the different communities without discrimination; and according each community equality before the law and equal opportunity for advancement. Although never explicitly stated, the PAP leaders were obviously thinking of the retention of traditional values that did not clash with the new values that were to be embodied in the new state. The nature of these old values has never been really elaborated. The prime minister has, however, emphasised the importance of the family unit.

The PAP leaders further advocated that the concomitant value of multiracialism is meritocracy, that merit and performance rather than ethnic identification should be the criteria for authority and upward social mobility. In fact, the PAP interpretation of equal treatment has been so stringent that spokesmen for special treatment for the generally recognised backward and underprivileged Malay community have been outrightly turned down, if these special concessions entailed lowering standards of performance. Government critics point out that this assumes that every community can compete at the same level, which is simply untrue of the Malay community. Thus, if the policy remains unchanged, the Malays as a group will be left behind. The government, however, is not prepared to relent on this principle.

Multilingualism

The PAP leaders must have realised how vulnerable Singapore would be in Southeast Asia if she accorded the Chinese language a predominant status. It has always been the party's policy to advocate multilingualism. Immediately after separation, the prime minister emphasised categorically that the island would continue to maintain this principle. The Singapore government was forced to take a strong stand because the influential Chinese Chamber of Commerce, probably reading this period as a turning point in Singapore's destiny, sought to have written into the new Singapore Constitution the continued use of the Chinese language. This action was, in fact, the first open attempt by the more Chinese culture-oriented sector to shape the image of the new Singapore. The official policy was to establish the multilingual society in which English, Malay, Chinese, and Tamil were to be the official languages.

Within the schools greater emphasis was placed on bilingualism. The thinking behind this policy was that the monolingual person in Singapore would not have the facility to communicate with any group other than his language community, and bilingualism would increase the opportunity of contact between communities. The new generation, products of the PAP educational system, would therefore be equipped with an added skill. In practice, it meant that in non-English language schools, mathematics, science, and technology would be taught in English, and in the English schools the humanities would be taught in one of the other languages.

With time and deeper thinking on the issue, the PAP leaders began to formulate more definite views on bilingualism. In November 1970, Mr. Lee delivered the Dillingham lecture at the University of Hawaii's East-West Center.[6] This speech represented for the first time the single most explicit summary of the Singapore leader's thoughts on language. Mr. Lee underlined the need for developing countries to acquire access to new knowledge, the sciences and technology. This inevitably meant that developing nations must acquire the languages of the developed countries: English, Russian, German, or French. The easiest course would be to continue using the language of the former metropolitan power. His entire argument is succinctly expressed thus.

> The deliberate stifling of a language which gives access to superior technology can be damaging beyond repair. Sometimes this is done not to elevate the status of the indigenous language, as much as to take away a supposed advantage a minority in the society is deemed to have because that minority has already formed a greater competence in the foreign language. This can be most damaging. It is tantamount to blinding the next generation to the knowledge of the advanced countries.

In Singapore, English is emphasised as the language of development, and it is now increasingly clear with regard to the policy of bilingualism that when PAP leaders speak of bilingualism, they do not mean *any* two of the four official languages. They are not simply advocating the study of Malay and Chinese or Chinese and Tamil or Malay and English. There is no ambiguity whatever that bilingualism means English and the mother tongue. Thus, it is the intention that in future Singaporeans of whatever racial origin should retain their cultural identity through education in their own language and culture and yet gain a common ground through the English language, the base on which all can compete equally.

The values that have been described and discussed deal with the cultural aspects of Singapore's identity. The self-image and image the island wants to project is that of a multiracial and multicultural society, albeit a society which is basically an English language state with Chinese, Tamil, and Malay preserved.

The economic-cultural aspects of the national identity evolve from and revolve around the same goals and themes. Ultimately, the leaders hope to see Singapore established as a highly successful industrial state with a high level of technology and skill, a state which is able to sustain economic growth, maintain social progress and bring about the elimination of poverty. To achieve these goals, the PAP has proposed a strategy of development. Briefly paraphrased, it could be stated thusly:

(1) Strong leadership and organisation equal achievement of goals, but a continuing political stability must exist in the region.

(2) The leadership should inculcate in the population the right values and attitudes that are supportive of or may even quicken the pace of modernisation and development. Some of these values and attitudes include a sense of future orientation, achievement orientation, efficiency, social discipline, self-discipline, willing acceptance of change as part of life, and inclination to hard work.

(3) When initial success is achieved the pace of development must not slacken; to maintain growth, creeping complacency must be fought.

(4) It is extremely important to create an atmosphere of confidence, as success breeds success. Thus the spirit of dynamism and political stability must be preserved.

(5) With time, this development will be institutionalised.

The Singapore leaders are highly conscious of the fact that during the course of development in which there is heavy borrowing of Western experience and technology, the problem for the developing nation is simply how to retain a part of the traditional identity—its uniqueness—so that it is not just a poor imitation of the West "with all the fads and fetishes, the disorders and abberations of contemporary Western societies." If she could, Singapore would want to import the technology, but not the culture. To prevent the "infection" of Singapore by the "promiscuous" and "permissive" ideas of Western society, the Singapore government has taken action periodically whenever "counterculture" tendencies manifest themselves. The official campaign against long hair and the current drive against drug pushers and drug takers is an attack launched against hippism which is seen to be a phenomenon undermining the process of development.

In keeping with the nonideological pragmatic identity, effectiveness and efficiency have been the major qualities pursued, and the celebrated Singapore symbols are the Housing and Development Board flats which is the massive, successful, low-cost housing achievement of the PAP government, and the industrial establishments at Jurong, Redhill, Kallang, and others on the island. Another identity symbol is the Singapore Armed Forces because of its important role in the defence of the island.

The Singapore government has deliberately set out to fashion an identity for Singapore, based partly on some of the constraints of its geographical and political considerations. It appeared impossible to elevate the cultural identity of one particular racial group to national status and to create, as Geertz has suggested, a national identity by an extension of primordial loyalty to a more inclusive group identity in ever widening circles which would eventually embrace the entire population.

Each segment of Singapore's population is too distinct and exhibits too strong a cultural tradition to warrant any hope that these traditions would merge into a single cultural and national identity. The pragmatic solution was to create a double identity—a somewhat subdued cultural identity based on English.

This approach has not remained unchallenged precisely because the remaining cultural identity can still be activated for political purposes.

Challenges

If the Malays find it difficult to accept the values and attitudes of the new Singapore identity or to keep up with the pace of development, they are unable to offer any strong resistance. The militant *Utusan Melayu* ceased to circulate in Singapore in 1969. The Malay community seems to lack political leadership, and the most coherent is that offered by the PAP Malay leadership. Dissatisfaction with present national policies is therefore confined to perennial expressions of grievances at conferences and seminars that discuss the problems of the community. The difficulty with any lengthy exposition of the underprivileged position of the Malays is that it is liable to be discouraged or curtailed on the grounds that it suggests dangerous communalistic analysis.

The aspirations of the Malay community have been trimmed with time, and one indicator of the process is the recent proposal by the Malay Teachers' Union. In September 1970, the union submitted a proposal, through the Malay Educational Council, to the Singapore government. According to the proposal, English should be the medium of instruction in the republic's education system, but Malay—being the national language— should be a compulsory subject.[7] In other words, the Malay teachers were prepared to see the abolition of Malay schools altogether. This position was undoubtedly taken because of the awareness that the enrollment in Malay schools is falling by significant numbers yearly; in the future, Malay parents, discerning that English is the language of economic opportunity, may cease sending their children to a Malay school altogether. It would seem that the Malay community may see that it has no choice but to adjust to the system since it is unable to exert any meaningful influence upon it. The Malay community is only too aware of its own numerical disadvantage; it knows that the Singapore government is prepared to use its coercive powers to deal with any major disruption and to maintain law and order in the society.

Further criticism of the Singapore government's policies came from two directions. These were, however, not political parties or politically organised groups. Though 14 parties exist in Singapore, only four may be considered real entities; the rest are either shadow or phantom political parties. Yet in 1971, none of the four—the United National Front, the Workers' Party, the Barisan Sosialis, and the Pekemas (the former Singapore UMNO)—offered any real opposition or serious sound criticisms of the PAP.

The Chinese-educated Chinese seemed uneasy and unhappy over some of the developments within the island. It is necessary to go back in history to understand the position and problems of the Chinese-educated Chinese. Since World War II, Chinese language and education have emerged as major socio-political issues in Malaya and Singapore. To the Chinese, language and consequently education is the expression of their identity and culture. Thus, overseas Chinese have set up Chinese schools, whenever they were in large enough numbers, to transmit their heritage to their siblings.[8] The Chinese Peoples Republic's establishment and its achievements had the effect of increasing political awareness of the Chinese in general and increasing cultural pride. Chinese education organised independently for some time, until the colonial government realised that it would have to do something toward the creation of a national system of education. The attempts to "domesticate" the Chinese education system led to student unrest in the Chinese Middle Schools in and after 1954. The leading body responsible for the political militancy of the Chinese students was the Singapore Chinese Middle Schools Students' Union. In an attempt to solve the problem, a committee representative of all political parties was appointed in 1955 to look into the situation in the Chinese schools in Singapore; they were to make recommendations for the improvement and strengthening of Chinese education in the interest of the Chinese and in the interest of orderly progress toward self-government and independence. The committee recommended equal treatment for all schools—English or "vernacular"—and that common textbooks be produced for all media of instruction. This report remains the basis of the education system today. It cannot be said that Chinese education is in any way being eliminated in Singapore. In the schools, it is the policy to achieve bilingualism in the primary schools and trilingualism in the secondary schools. At the moment, the standards for teaching the second language are low, and students graduate with only low proficiency in the language. Therefore, it is common to find that Chinese school graduates do not as yet have a fluent command of English.

Today in postcolonial Singapore, the English language still remains the language of greatest economic value and job opportunities, particularly since jobs with better prospects are available mainly to those who are well versed in English. The trend is toward a gradual decline in enrollment in the Chinese schools as parents become more calculating and realistic. The implication is the Chinese schools are unable to compete with their English counterparts in open competition.

Many grievances were accumulated by the Chinese-educated Chinese, although they had no serious spokesman until the *Nanyang Siang Pau*, toward the last quarter of 1970, highlighted its dissatisfaction by publishing letters and opinions from the readers, editorialising and featuring articles on the issue areas.[9] The Singapore government responded swiftly. On 2 May 1971, four senior executives of the Chinese daily were detained on orders of the government for having launched "a deliberate campaign to stir up Chinese racial emotions." Thus, the Singapore government delivered the first of the three stikes against the press in Singapore.

The blow against the *Eastern Sun,* an English language daily in Singapore, was of a different kind, but also led to the closing of the newspaper. Following the *Nanyang* arrests, the *Eastern Sun* was charged with being a Hong Kong Communist newspaper. The managing director was accused of receiving the initial loan to start the paper from Communist sources. The plan, it was alleged, was that the paper, at some future date, after becoming established and acceptable, would be used to subvert Singapore. The public charges were never denied by the managing director, and the seven editorial staff members promptly resigned. The paper ceased publication. It is not the intention of the chapter to try to discuss the press crisis in detail. The episode has been mentioned only as it concerns the identity creation of a new state, but it is suggested here that, in fact, this was the central issure of the entire press crisis.

The *Singapore Herald* was the next newspaper to receive political attention. This newspaper, established in 1969, was distinguished by its slightly more critical editorials and independent thinking and writing on government policy. It also published an extremely outspoken readers' letter page, particularly on bureaucratic inefficiencies and maladministration. The PAP leaders insinuated that again foreign capital was financing the paper with an intention of undermining the political stability of the republic. The *Singapore Herald* was accused of "taking on" the Singapore government by eroding the will and attitudes of the people with regard to certain fundamental national matters, such as national service; agitation over labour laws; the Internal Security Act; and advocating "with-it" isms and permissiveness in sex, drugs, and dress styles. Thus while the *Nanyang Siang Pau* was clearly seen in opposition to the officially sponsored cultural linguistic identity by advocating a regressive Chinese identity, the *Eastern Sun* was potentially an advocate for the radical communist identity. The *Singapore Herald* was viewed as opposing the pragmatic development identity favoured by the PAP leadership.

SOUTHEAST ASIA—OVERVIEW AND CONCLUSIONS

Singapore, the case we discussed at some length, is certainly not representative of the whole region, though the Singapore experiment in nation-building is closely watched and might produce a "demonstration effect" for other Southeast Asian nations. The implications of this experiment are, nevertheless, intriguing.

The option to create a national identity in relation to the past was not open, but neither was an expressive rejection of the past nor a revolutionary image of the future a viable alternative. Singapore leaders, faced with the problem of integrating a highly pluralistic society, chose another option, namely, the deliberate construction of a pragmatic identity with development and economic success as the symbols of identification. The most striking feature of this endeavor is that a highly particularistic value system (Singaporean national identity) is to be established by using highly universalistic values that are not connected with any particular cultural tradition. This attempt of the Singapore PAP leadership is suspected by members of individual ethnic communities as being in fact nothing but the expression of values prevalent among the English educated elite, and by those with socialist leanings as being an ideology of a capitalist economic system with authoritarian political features.

Despite these critical views, the preliminary success of Singapore's attempt at nation-building are impressive. Bilingualism is on the rise, and the symbols of Singapore's pragmatic identity are widely accepted.[10]

In Indonesia, also a highly pluralistic society, a similiar type of pragmatic identity is now promoted, though the option of a regressive identity with the past still remains open and finds its expression in cultural revivalist movements, especially in the religious sphere. The period of Sukarno, during which a strongly regressive identity was fostered, has left its mark on political thought. During this time, ideas and organizational principles that were thought to have been prevalent in precolonial days or alledgedly still prevalent in traditional (Javanese) village society, were used to build a state ideology and new political institutions. The principles of neighbourly help *(gotong rojong)* and of unanimous decision after deliberation *(musjawara dan mufakat)* were declared typically Indonesian and contrasted to western capitalist individualism and democratic voting systems. The political style of Sukarno has also been described as "kraton politics" after the name of the traditional Javanese court *(kraton)*. The ideology of the Communist Party that was utterly crushed in the 1965 GESTAPU putsch, was of course combined with a progressive identity, which, however, appears to have merged in the minds of Javanese peasants with millenarian ideas about the reestablishment of a just society, ideas which were traditional or regressive as they linked a golden past with a golden future. Also Sukarno was seen by large sections of the population as the "just ruler" *(ratu adil)* who would bring about the new and just society. Though the empirical reality of Indonesian politics was and still is extremely complex, the *intention* of political elites to use national identity as a means of nation-building are very clear: Sukarno's national identity was regressive, Aidit's Indonesian Communist Party was progressive, and President Suharto's exhibits—as far as it exists at all—pragmatic tendencies. A complete return to a regressive identity, though likely if one takes the utterly Javanese character of General Suharto's personality and social background into account, is made difficult because such a regressive identity has been discredited by the economic mismanagement of the Sukarno period. Adopting a progressive identity is similarly made impossible by the PKI's (Indonesian Communist Party) involvement in the 1965 coup attempt. Indonesian identity formation is thus in a dilemma not entirely different from the above analysed Singaporean one—in contrast to the situation in Malaysia and Thailand but at least vaguely similar to the Burmese political scene.

Malaysia's policy of identity formation is still largely regressive. Many traditional Malay values are revered, the Malay language is fostered as the national language, and the glory of Malacca and Malay folk heroes is frequently evoked and publicized. After the racial riots of 13 May 1969 which were in fact rooted in the differing concepts of the national identity, Parliament legislated on the question of national identity. Essentially, the opposition non-Malay parties, more specifically the Chinese supported parties—the Democratic Action Party (DAP) and some elements of the Gerakan Rakyat Malaysia (GRM)—were pressing for a revision of the concept of the nation. The DAP in particular sought to establish a multiracial society that adopted and implemented "the principle of racial equality at all levels of national life and all fields of national endeavour—political, social, economic, cultural and educational."[11] In keeping with this principle, it asked for the establishment of English, Chinese, and Tamil as official languages, thus denying Malay national and sole official language status. It also asked for the establishment of the other languages as media for instruction and examinations in schools. The response to the challenge culminated eventually in bloody riots which led to emergency military rule for twenty months.

The return to parliamentary democracy in the country also saw the legal enforcement of an identity that the political leadership wanted to see established. The *Rukunegara,* an ideological statement embodying the fundamental assumptions upon which the state rests, asserts that Islam is the official religion of Malaysia, that Malaysia is a constitutional monarchy, and that loyalty to the *Yang di-Pertuan Agong* (the King) and the other sultans is expected of every citizen; it further asserts that Malay is the national and official language of Malaysia and that it recognizes the special position of the Malays and the legitimate interests of the other ethnic communities. The *Rukunegara* was translated into law when the Constitution was amended in February 1971 to embody its goals and place them beyond debate.

In our discussion of nation-building through identity formation in the Southeast Asian countries of Thailand, Malaysia, Indonesia, and Singapore, we have concentrated primarily on the last because we see Singapore both as a new type of national identity and as a new type of political system that is taking shape. It now remains to show, at least in outline, what impact an ideology of pragmatism might have on the political system, i.e. on nation-building as such.

The pragmatism to which the national identity refers is one of purposive rational action, one of means-end calculation, one of technology and science. Citizens are admonished to identify with the economic success of the state which demonstrates that the correct policies have been applied. As these policies are not based on an explicitly stated ideology nor even on purely political considerations, but on rational and scientific principles, any criticism of these policies can be branded as irrational. The prestige of science and technology is thus used to buttress not only the day to day policies but also the social and political system resulting from such policies, because leaders will ask if such a system is not derived from the very principles of scientific and rational action. The supremacy of this pragmatic identity or technocratic consciousness can thus be used to legitimize tight political control and eventually an authoritarian political system. In Indonesia, attempts at tight political control through the military government are somewhat mediated by the inefficiency of the bureaucracy, by traditional organizations and regional sentiments. In Singapore the still fairly strong tradition of British parliamentary democracy and the compliance of a generally upwardly mobile population have cushioned extreme authoritarian tendencies and policies. The fact remains, however, that an ideology of pragmatism is eminently suited to legitimise a political system of domination and suppression, both within a nation and within an international system. As this technocratic rationality and pragmatism

> extends to the correct choice among strategies, the appropriate application of technologies, and the efficient establishment of systems (with presupposed aims in given situations), it removes the total social framework of interests in which strategies are chosen, technologies applied, and systems established, from the scope of reflection and rational reconstruction.[12]

Moreover, this rationality extends only to relations of possible technical control and, therefore, requires a type of action that implies domination, whether of nature or of society. The peculiar fusion of technology and domination, of rationality and oppression, to which analysts of modern capitalist society have referred might thus find its early realization in developing nations following a policy of nation-building through an ideology of pragmatism. The formation of a national identity of pragmatism is consequently nothing but a means of legitimizing the power of a ruling elite and of an existing economic system.

NOTES

1. Interviews in 1963 during a UNESCO sponsored study on the self-image of elites in Southwest Asia. See Hans-Dieter Evers, *Higher Thai Civil Servants, Social Mobility and Attitudes towards their own Cultural Tradition.* Freiburg: Arnold Bergstraesser Institute, 1964 and Hans-Dieter Evers and T. M. Silcock, "Elites and Selection," in T. M. Silcock, ed., *Thailand, Economic and Social Studies in Development.* Canberra: Australian National University Press and Durham, N.C.: Duke University Press, 1969.

2. See Haug's study on pluralism and political stability in 115 countries: Marie Haug, "Social and Cultural Pluralism as a concept in social systems analysis," *American Journal of Sociology* 73 (1967): 294-304.

3. *Census of Population 1970. Singapore Interim Release.*

4. A Chinese who attends a Chinese-medium school learns the Mandarin language which is, in fact, not his mother tongue. Singapore Chinese are normally brought up with a Chinese dialect.

5. Problems faced by Singapore's political leadership during this time are discussed in Chan Heng Chee, *Singapore, the Politics of Survival 1965-1967.* Singapore: Oxford University Press, 1971.

6. This lecture contained many of the PM's insights on the modernization process of the developing countries. It revealed tough, clear thinking on very sensitive but fundamental issues that affect development. Mr. Lee showed he was devoid of any traditional cultural identity crisis about language.

7. The PAP Government rejected the proposed national system for obvious political reasons. In the Prime Minister's words: "In effect, it means closing down the Chinese schools and teaching Chinese as a third language, next to first English and second Malay. If any government is mad enough to accept this proposal, it can only provoke the Chinese-educated to hostility" (quoted in *The Mirror,* Vol. 7, No. 22, May 31, 1971, p. 8).

8. See Current Affairs Bulletin, Vol. 47, no. 3: "Malaysia: Contending Elites" by Wang Gungwu, for an insight into the motivations of the Chinese-educated and the development of the Chinese educational system.

9. The Nanyang Siang Pau (South Seas Commercial News) is one of the two major Chinese dailies on the island. It has a circulation of 134,000, 45,000 in Singapore, the rest in West Malaysia, Indonesia, and Thailand.

10. Results of a recent national sample survey show "high levels of national identity among Singapore's electorate." This so far unpublished study was carried out in 1970-1971 by Chiew Seen Kong, a graduate student in Sociology and Dr. John A. McDougall, lecturer in Sociology, University of Singapore.

11. The Setapak Declaration, manifesto of the Democratic Action Party, Malaysia, p. 4.

12. Jürgen Habermas, Towards a Rational Society. London: Heinemann, 1971, p. 82. Habermas refers to Marcuse's critical analysis of Max Weber's concept of "purposive rational action."

IV.

THE OLD AND THE NEW AFRICA

CHAPTER 11

NATION-BUILDING IN THE MAGHREB

Abdelkader Zghal

ABDELKADER ZGHAL is Director of the Sociological Division of the Center for Economic Research at the University of Tunis. He has carried out extensive anthropological research on nomads and peasantry in the Maghreb and is currently engaged in studies of processes of modernization and mobilization in this area.

It often happens, in political sociology, that such notions as nation-building, socialism, bourgeoisie, lose their original meaning and become transformed in the hands of ideologists into weapons—whether offensive or defensive—instead of being used, in the first place, as instruments of scientific analysis. That is why, in this chapter on nation-building in the Maghreb, we shall set aside all disputes, academic or otherwise, regarding the idea of the nation as a form of integration, within a specific social context, of a variety of individual groups (ethnic, socio-professional, religious) in order to confine ourselves to the study of nation-building considered as a process whereby the social and cultural distance separating regions and social groups within a given context known as a nation can be reduced.

This chapter has been prepared with the object, on the one hand, of explaining the characteristics of nation-building in the Maghreb and, on the other hand, of furnishing material for comparative studies on nation-building in regions with different socio-cultural characteristics. Such comparative studies are, in fact, a prerequisite for establishing the necessary foundations upon which to develop a general theory relating to nation-building in the various regions of the world.

STATE OF RESEARCH ON NATION-BUILDING
IN THE MAGHREB

An introductory remark seems necessary: French publications on the subject of nation-building are practically nonexistent. It is mainly English-speaking political theorists who have taken an interest in the problem.[1] So it is not surprising that, so far, no systematic study exists on nation-building in the former French colonial territories, especially the Maghreb. We should mention, however, Balandier's efforts to encourage French-speaking sociologists to include this subject in their field of interest. Thus the theme for the sixth Symposium of the Association Internationale des Sociologues de Langue Francaise, Royaumont, 28-30 October 1965, was Sociological Problems of Nation Building in the New States,[2] and in the working group organized by Balandier during the sixth World Sociological Congress, Evian, 1966, certain papers presented dealt more or less directly with the subject of nation-building. However, it was especially the ideological problems of nationalism which formed the main subject of discussion at both those meetings.

It is true that nationalism, considered as an ideology explicitly formulated by elites, represents a highly important dimension in the process of nation-building among the former colonies. However, even in order to understand the factors which go to make up the ideologies of nationalist elites, it is useful to know the precise role in the nation-building process played by other, less articulate social groups. If we restrict ourselves to what the elites have to say in our efforts to understand the ideology of certain human societies, such as the Arab world, we shall be failing to take into account the considerable role played by the ethos of the peasantry in the conditioning, structural development, and expression of the explicit ideologies formulated by elites.[3]

Our aim, in the present phase of research on nation-building in the various regions of the world, is to try to discover, as it were, the structural (i.e. socio-historical) foundations of nation-building within a relatively uniform regional context (the three former French colonies of the Maghreb: Morocco, Algeria, and Tunisia). I think the necessary material exists for this type of approach. For that, we must consult authors who, without using the essentially modern notion of nation-building, tried nevertheless to elucidate problems of Maghrebian society which are very closely related to our subject.

THE MAGHREB AND THE MEDITERRANEAN WORLD

In order to understand Maghrebian society and its particular history, we must consider the Maghreb against its natural background, which is the Mediterranean and the Mediterranean world. It is, of course, true that the Maghreb forms within the Mediterranean world a clearly marked geographical unit with its own special characteristics that distinguish it from other parts of that world. Physically, it constitutes as clearly defined a geographical unit as an island, bounded as it is by the Atlantic Ocean to the west, the Mediterranean to the north and east, and the Sahara to the south. The Arab geographers found a good definition when they named it Djaziret-El-Maghreb—the Isle of the Setting Sun. However, it is an island which since the Middle Ages has maintained uninterrupted relations with Africa south of the Sahara, the Middle East, and the countries of Mediterranean Europe.

So we must begin by taking up again a question which has often been raised since the colonial conquest: how is it that Maghrebian society, which in the Middle Ages was not backward by comparison with the feudal societies of Europe, should nevertheless not have succeeded, either in the period of the Renaissance in Western Europe or in modern times, in radically transforming its structures dating from mediaeval times and in laying the foundations of one or several nations in the classical sense of that term?

The works of the fourteenth-century Maghrebian sociologist, Ibn Khaldūn, have provided the basic source material for all those—and they have been many—who have attempted to answer that question. Ibn Khaldūn's central idea was that the stagnation of the Maghreb in his time was essentially due to the structural instability of the Maghrebian state and to the cyclical and noncumulative character of the changes that it underwent. The dynasties wielding power in the Maghreb in mediaeval times were all of tribal origin. After attaining power and establishing themselves in the capital (often a new one of their own choice), the dynasty-founding tribes, which had previously led a marginal existence, progressively lost the esprit de corps that was the source of their strength and allowed themselves to be overthrown by other tribes.[4]

It is on the basis of this interpretation of the traditional Maghrebian state that twentieth-century European authors have tried to understand the fundamental reasons which have caused the nation-building process in states on the southern shores of the Mediterranean, and especially the Maghreb, to lag behind that in states north of the Mediterranean. Broadly speaking, two widely accepted interpretations of this phenomenon exist:

(a) that of the classical orientalists, uniting at the time when the colonial system was at its zenith, and (b) that of the anticolonialist Marxist, uniting towards the end of the colonial era.

THE ORIENTALISTS

E. F. Gautier is probably the most representative author among the orientalists prior to the Second World War.[5] According to him, a nation is the result of cooperation between peasantry and townsfolk, as European experience bears out. However, in Gautier's view, such cooperation was only possible in the Maghreb if, among the peasantry, one or more groups of settled peasants had managed to subdue the nomadic tribes which were a permanent threat to city life. Thus, it is the bitter struggle between the Sanhadja Kabyles (settled peasants) and Zeneta nomads (nomadic peasants) which, according to Gautier, "provides the clue to the obscure vicissitudes of Maghrebian history." He goes on to assert that "it is not simply a question of warring individuals, tribes or dynasties, but of two irreconcilable conceptions of society and of life. The Kabyles (settled peasants) are an agglomeration of small, quasi-urban democracies. The nomad is a disciplined communist with the outlook of an aristocrat."

So the "effort of national concentration," to use an expression of Gautier's, depends on the state of equilibrium between these two opposing forces. From the time of the Arab conquest up to the beginning of the tenth century, neither of these two forces was able to maintain itself consistently in power without being overthrown by the other. At the beginning of the tenth century, however, the founding of the Fatimid Empire by the settled peasants of the Ketama tribe (in Kabylia) gave the Maghreb the opportunity "for the first and only time—to shape its own destiny, to extract or fail to extract from within itself the ingredients of a nation." This dynasty successfully resisted the attacks of the nomad peasants who had embraced the Kharidjite heresy. But this attempt at nation-building on the European model (through cooperation between settled peasants and city-dwellers) failed as a result of the invasion of the Hilali nomads from upper Egypt in the middle of the eleventh century, followed by the renaissance of the Zeneta, or nomadic Berbers. After the collapse of the Sanhadja dynasty (settled peasants), the "evolutionary curve" in the Maghreb "takes a rapid and definite downward plunge. The end of the Middle Ages was a period of complete and hopeless disintegration."

To sum up, Gautier's theory is as follows: the marked disparity in the twin processes of nation-building to the north and south of the Mediterranean occurred from the eleventh century onwards because the Arab nomads had put down the first attempt on the part of settled Berber peasant communities to set up an autochthonous national State based upon an alliance between peasantry and townfolk.

THE MARXISTS

Thus Gautier argues as though the Maghreb had always been an island completely cut off from the outside world, but kept in a state of constant ferment by two mutually antagonistic social forces (settled and nomadic peasants), and as if it were the arrival of nomadic Arab tribes in the middle of the eleventh century which finally destroyed the area's internal equilibrium at the expense of the settled peasants and at the same time put an end to any chances that Maghrebian society may have had of evolving progressively towards a nation of the modern type, based upon the alliance of settled peasants and townsfolk.

Marxist writers, however, reject this line of argument and relate the Maghreb to its true geopolitical context—the Mediterranean world. Within this clearly defined area, the volume and flow of foreign trade and the location of the principal trade routes exercised a considerable influence on the development of the internal social structures of the countries north and south of the Mediterranean. Owing to its geographical situation, the Maghreb in the Middle Ages served as an essential link between Mediterranean Europe and Black Africa and controlled the gold traffic between the Sudan and the two most "developed" regions of the time—the Middle East and Mediterranean Europe. It thus derived immense profits from its role as an intermediary between regional units which had reached different stages of technological development, and the least advanced of which (Africa south of the Sahara) possessed natural resources that were greatly in demand—gold, spices, ivory, and slaves—and was prepared to take in exchange such products as salt from the Maghreb, cloth from Europe, linen and cotton goods from Egypt and, to an increasing extent, iron goods, especially weapons.[6]

In these circumstances, the evolution of Maghrebian society towards modern nationhood was to a very large extent conditioned by the balance of political forces within the Mediterranean zone. That is why in the eleventh century "the rise of the Italian republics—Pisa, Genoa, Amalfi, Venice, and so on, and the expansion of Norman power in Sicily" intensified the internal difficulties of the Maghreb.[7] But it seems that it was in the fourteenth century that "the Maghreb relinquished by degrees its control over the gold routes and, in fact, ceased to be the necessary intermediary between the Sudan and Egypt."[8] In 1316, the overthrow of the Christian kingdom of Nubia by the Mameluke dynasty of Cairo provided the opportunity for "the great trading centres of the Orient . . . to enter into direct contact with the gold-producing kingdoms of the Sudan, without being obliged any longer to deal through the Maghrebians."

However, supposing that the "crises" occurred in the fourteenth century and not in the eleventh century, a question still remains unanswered: How is it that Maghrebian society proved to be incapable of utilizing the profits derived from trading in gold and other commodities, for economic activities which could have served as a material basis for the nation-building process, as happened in the case of the countries north of the Mediterranean, whose level of technological development in the Middle Ages was not notably superior to that of the Maghreb?

It cannot be said that this question has engaged the attention of many Marxist writers. Generally speaking, and until quite recently, Marxist—and even some non-Marxist—historians tended to assimilate mediaeval social structures in the Maghreb with those of European feudalism.[9] But feudalism considered as a "social type," to use Marc Bloch's expression,[10] is something unknown to Maghrebian society. No doubt there existed despotic local chieftains and peasants whose social status bore certain resemblances to that of serfs. But these elements, by themselves do not form a feudal social system, or, to use a Marxist expreseion, a feudal mode of production. At least two component elements of feudalism *qua* social system, without which feudalism loses its essential characteristics are lacking in Maghrebian society of the Middle Ages, or rather possess a social content structurally opposed to that of feudalism. These two elements are:

(1) Lineal solidarity, as a system of protection for the individual, was very weak in feudal society but highly effective in the Mahgreb. As Marc Bloch has pointed out, "it was as a kind of substitute for or complement of lineal solidarity, *which had become insufficiently effective,*" (my italics) that relations of personal dependence made their appearance upon the scene of history. . . . For the individual threatened by countless dangers in an age of violence, *the ties of kinship, even during the early stages of feudalism, did not seem to offer sufficient protection* (my italics). No doubt such ties were of too vague and imprecise a nature, too deeply eroded from the inside by the dual system of descent through both the male and the female line.[11] That is why men were compelled to search for or submit to other ties.

(2) Military traditions and practices of the time afforded the peasant the opportunity of becoming a soldier out of his own resources. According to

> Bloch: "In places where a freeman, whoever he might be, remained a warrior who could be called upon for military service at any time, and whose arms and equipment were indistinguishable in all essential respects from those worn by professional fighting men, it was easy for the peasant to escape from the clutches of the feudal lord." That is precisely what happened in the Maghreb, where any peasant could turn himself into a soldier, in contrast to feudal Europe, where mediaeval soldiering became more or less a professional monopoly of the vassal-knight owing to "the preponderance which the horseman, with his massive offensive and defensive equipment, acquired on the field of battle at the expense of the foot-soldier. In addition, a long apprenticeship was required in order to learn how to handle one's charger in battle and carry out complicated fencing manoeuvres in heavy armour." Hence there was "the demand for professional warriors who had been brought up in a group tradition and were primarily horsemen."[12]

Thus we can understand why the European peasant, insufficiently protected by kinship ties and lacking the material resources enabling him to arm himself like a professional warrior, was in a situation such that his personal safety and means of existence depended primarily on the protection of an overlord sufficiently powerful to defend him and at the same time exploit him. In the Maghreb, on the other hand, the peasant was protected by his kinship ties and the very strong feeling of solidarity they inspired. Furthermore, all adult males could, without changing their social status, turn themselves into warriors. In the Maghreb, horses and guns never became the privileged possessions of a warrior class. To compare Maghrebian society to feudalism is to empty the notion of feudalism of all social content. At first sight, such an attitude seems incomprehensible on the part of writers claiming to be Marxists. But the origin of this serious confusion becomes less mysterious when it is discovered that the same mistaken interpretation has been applied by Marxist historians in the case of other regions where feudalism in the classic sense of the term never existed either, such as India, Vietnam, or black Africa.[13] It was, in fact, essentially for political reasons that from 1931 onwards, as the result of a major discussion organized in Leningrad on the "Asian mode of production" and the official rejection of this notion, that orthodox Marxists began to postulate a feudal stage as the necessary antecedent of the capitalist stage in the history of every society.

After Stalin's death, however, and especially after the XXth Congress of the Communist Party of the Soviet Union, a new school of Marxist thought emerged, according to which the capitalist stage had generally been preceded in non-European regions by a mode of production which, while precapitalist, had not been feudal. The notion of an "Asian form of production" was resuscitated[14] and some authors went so far as to describe the Maghrebian social system during the Middle Ages as comparable to an "imperfect [sic] form" of the Asian mode of production.[15] This is as serious a confusion to fall into as that of those writers who have made a mechanical use of the notion of feudalism. If the notion of an Asian mode of production is not widened so as to include all precapitalist social systems which did not pass through the stage of feudalism as such—in other words, if one adheres to Marx who regarded capitalism, feudalism, and the Asian mode of production as social systems each with its own individual characteristics—one must necessarily reject the application of this concept to a social system such as that of the Maghreb.

The essential feature of the notion of an Asian mode of production consists in the role played by the central power in the organization and control of production, often on the basis of an irrigated system of agriculture which is only possible through extensive engineering works far beyond the capacity of local communities. Under these conditions, it is the state and its bureaucracy (as in Egypt under Pharaonic rule) which effectively manage the economy and make their presence felt in every local community. Under this social system, the situation of the peasants is one of "generalized slavery," to use Marx's expression. But in the Maghreb, right up to the time of its colonization, the various States never possessed the resources that would have enabled them to manage the economy at the level of the local communities; on the contrary, they were continually obliged to accept the refusal to pay taxes by a considerable number of tribes as a fait accompli. If the Asian mode of production is characterized, inter alia, by the stability of the central power and the breadth of its authority, the Maghrebian social system is on the whole characterized by the instability of the central power and the limited scope of its authority throughout the Middle Ages and up to the very eve of the colonial conquest.

And so, neither feudalism nor the Asian mode of production is the answer.[16] But what in that case was the nature of this Maghrebian system, which remained radically unchanged up to the eve of colonization and thus proved itself incapable of adapting to the structural and cultural changes of its environment, and in particular of the countries on the northern shores of the Mediterranean?

THE CONTRIBUTION OF FRENCH ETHNOLOGISTS AND ENGLISH-SPEAKING ANTHROPOLOGISTS

Just as Marxist writers are fond of producing outlines of the general evolution of society in which they endeavour to identify different stages and modes of production, so the ethnologists seek on the contrary to eliminate the time factor by concentrating on the areas of research least subject to change, in the hope of discovering, through a study of the social institutions and cultural behaviour patterns most resistant to the erosion of time, the basic structures of the traditional social system of the Maghreb. If we accept, as a working assumption, that nation-building may be interpreted as reducing the social and cultural gap between the different regions and social groups in an entity defined as a nation, we are bound to pay special attention to the work of the ethnologists. By studying the zones least affected by modernization, the ethnologists can, in fact, reconstruct for us some of the components of the traditional social system and help us to appreciate the importance, and the geographical and social distribution of the segments of society whose relatively marginal condition indicates how much needs to be done in order to increase the pace of the nation-building process.

A COMMON CULTURAL BASIS

One of the most significant features of the traditional Maghreb is the almost permanent existence of the Bled Siba side by side with the Bled Makhzen. These two expressions denote two types of relationship between the local Maghrebian communities and the precolonial central power. The communities in the Bled Makhzen are those willing—or rather unable to refuse—to pay taxes to the central authorities: the Makhzen.[17] The areas which are marginal, or to which the central power can have access only with difficulty, constitute the Bled Siba (the zone of dissidence). In general there is no clearly defined frontier between the two. Powerful dynasties succeed, by means of violence or cunning, inconsiderably reducing the zone of dissidence, but in moments of crisis the Bled Makhzen is confined to the towns and the immediately neighbouring plains. The irreducible strongholds of the zone of dissidence are the mountain regions, such as the Atlas and the Rif in Morocco, Kabylia and the Aurès in Algeria, and the predesert regions inhabited by nomadic tribes whose mobility is a first-class guarantee against the action of the central power.

This division of the precolonial Maghreb into three zones—towns, government-controlled plains, and marginal areas—is a fundamental fact to be kept in mind if we are to understand the local and regional peculiarities of nation-building in the Maghreb.

Thus the Bled Siba (zone of dissidence) is ideal ground for ethnological research. There is no urban life. Communications with the outside world are practically nonexistent. Age-old institutions are maintained almost intact right up to—and even for some years after—the colonial conquest. Moreover, the inhabitants of these regions are usually people who have retained their Berber language and who have not as a rule been in permanent contact with Arab or Arabized population groups—hence the considerable value of ethnological writing on the Berber world and the rarity of ethnological studies on the Arab or Arabized population.

But this ethnological research has brought to light an important fact for the understanding of nation-building in the Maghreb. Beyond the particularisms which distinguish Berber from Arab, and the differences between the life of a nomad and that of a settled peasant, we ultimately encounter the same structural forms at the level of family and political organization in the various peasant communities of the Maghreb. In the extended family the preponderance of the group of agnates is indisputable. In lineal descent, marriage with a parallel cousin (the daughter of the paternal uncle) is preferred even if not automatically practised. It is in patrilineage that we meet with the basic political unit of all the peasant communities of the Maghreb—a unity which at the same time offers the structural model for the larger political groups. As a rule, important political decisions are taken unanimously at an assembly of the adullt males.

Such are the basic groupings, but it is possible, by conscious or unconscious manipulation of the genealogical model, to break up these units still further or merge them into larger groups, as circumstances dictate. The names of this structural model, and the forms it assumes in daily life, change from region to region, according to the groups and the circumstances; but what is important is the existence of a common cultural background. That explains why, even in the zone of dissidence (the Bled Siba), the Sultan's spiritual authority is not questioned in theory, even though the peasants there may refuse in practice to pay their taxes because, as a result of the marginal position of their region in relation to the central authority, they are in a position to refuse.[18] The importance accorded to the unanimity of the decisions taken at the assemblies of the basic political group (patrilineage), serves as an example and standard of reference for all other political groups. The result of this is the absence of any legal standing for minority political opinions, and a lack of norms for deciding quickly who should succeed the head of a community instead of waiting to obtain the unanimous consent of the representatives of that community. The word "community" is used here to mean all types of political groups regardless of their size, for we know that, beyond the patrilineal unit, all other political groups have very uncertain limits and an existence that is conditioned by circumstances. There is no word in Arabic for a stable political unit with fixed boundaries lying between the basic political group and the Umma (the Moslem community). It follows that the sentiment of belonging to a nation or national state, in the modern sense, is constantly being challenged by two kinds of identification: (a) identification with kindred and (b) identification with the Moslem community as a whole (the Umma).

Nevertheless, intermediate political groups between these two poles (kindred and Umma) have played a considerable political role in the Maghreb. According to the earliest research of French ethnologists in Kabylia (Algeria)[19] and in the Atlas (Morocco),[20] it is these intermediate political groups and the way in which they are organized that are responsible for maintaining order in the zones of dissidence (Bled Siba), where no specialized institutions exist for this purpose in the local communities. R. Montagne, in particular, has made a systematic analysis of data regarding local political life in the zones of dissidence, such as the Moroccan Atlas, and explained the maintenance of order in that region by the fact that the political alliances between the various local groups are not formed at random but follow a certain structural pattern, in which all the basic groups of a given region fall into two leagues or two political parties (the *leff* or the *çof*) in a way resembling the layout of the black and white squares on a chessboard. The anarchy of the zones of dissidence is consequently an anarchy regulated by the balance of political alliances. Each group is entirely surrounded by hostile groups of practically equal strength. Careful research in the High Atlas has not, however, confirmed Montagne's thesis. In the region of the Seksawa "there is no sign of a balanced dualism setting Taqbilts of the same group against one another, like pieces on a chessboard."[21]

A dual organization certainly exists in certain regions, but it is not the only pattern of segmentation. Political groups are very often divided into a larger number of sub-groups—three or even five in the case of several large tribes. In reality, as Gellner has pointed out, French research on the political life of the Berbers was badly hampered by the lack of an explicit formulation of the notion of "segmentary society."[22] It is, in fact, the English-speaking anthropologists who have developed and systematized this old concept of Durkheim.[23] Research on segmentary societies is relatively recent.[24] But it is not my intention to describe here all the sociological implications of this form of social organization. Suffice it to say that the concept of segmentation provides a more general answer than R. Montagne's thesis of moieties (the *leffs*) to the problem of the maintenance of order in the zones of dissidence. This interpretation is valid only in the case of the conflict between the groups forming the basic units of the two opposing leagues, but conflict may break out at all levels and mobilize groups of all sizes. For present purposes we shall take only some principles of segmentary organization. One of these principles is that "loyalty to, and membership of, a group depend on the conflict in question and the size of the groups involved."[25] This is illustrated by the Arab proverb: "I against my brother, my brothers and I against my cousins, my cousins, my brothers and I against the whole world." According to circumstances, the groups, at no matter what level, either remain, as groups, in a situation of institutionalized hostility, or else they form a temporary alliance in order to fight an equivalent group. In a segmentary society, "equivalent groups issuing from the same stock oppose one another, but are associated and united within the group next above, which in turn is in opposition with its equivalent."[26] But the basic idea to bear in mind about segmentation as far as our subject is concerned, is that "there cannot ... be any absolute authority vested in a single Shaikh of a tribe when the fundamental principle of tribal structure is opposition between its segments. ... Authority is distributed at every point of the tribal structure and political leadership is limited to situations in which a tribe or a segment of it acts corporately."[27]

To what extent does this ideal model of a segmentary society resemble the real political life of the Bled Siba (zones of dissidence) before colonization? To a very large extent, says Gellner, and there can be no doubt that he is right. But it must be added that it was also in one of these areas of dissidence, or regulated anarchy, that the lords of the Atlas emerged: individuals whose despotic behaviour was probably one of the causes which prompted certain observers of the Maghreb to apply to that society such notions as feudalism and the Asian mode of production.

If we are to understand this, it should be mentioned that, up to the nineteenth century, the segmentary organization of the zones of dissidence proved efficient enough to render the attempts of the despotic chiefs to consolidate their authority precarious and unstable. These ambitious leaders were often eliminated following a change of alliance aimed exclusively at preventing any one political group from acquiring a monopoly of authority and power and obtaining permanent mastery over all the other groups. But in the nineteenth century, certain families succeeded in imposing their authority on a large sector of the population. It should be noted, however, that this form of despotism is rather that of a group over other groups, and that within the despot's own group the despot is forced, if he is to maintain the cohesion of this group, to behave "democratically." "In his native Khoms, the Idaw Talilt, the Great Abdelmalek Mtuggi is only an amghar, the first of his peers. At the level of the Mtugga, he is a patriarchal centralizer. At the level of the whole body of dependent tribes, an authoritarian and crafty exploiter. . . . At the level of the Moroccan South, he even ventures upon international intrigue. But the political weight he brings to it depends ultimately on the fidelity of his own jemaâ."[28]

In the precolonial Maghreb, even the Lords of the Atlas were thus consequently subject to the control of their own jemaâ (assembly of all adult males of the patrilineal group).

THE NEW DRIVE TO BUILD A NATION AFTER THE SUBJECTION OF THE BLED SIBA

At the time of the conquest of Algiers (1830), the entire Maghreb, except for Morocco, was under the control of the Ottoman Empire. It was by withdrawing into itself and to a certain extent revivifying its traditional instututions that Morocco succeeded in preserving its independence up to the opening years of the twentieth century. The Ottoman conquest of Algeria and Tunisia in the middle of the fifteenth century did not lead to any radical change in the traditional structures of these two countries. Of the Maghreb as a whole it may be said that the Middle Ages continued up to the nineteenth century, but that the social organization of the three countries displayed certain differences. On the eve of colonization by the French, Tunisia, as at the time of the Roman occupation, was the most highly urbanized region of the Maghreb, the one in which the traditional zones of dissidence (Bled Siba) were the smallest. Communications and exchanges between the townsfolk and the sedentary peasants were more highly developed in Tunisia than in the rest of the Maghreb. The old city families and the tribal leaders enjoyed a far more considerable share of power in Tunisia than in Algeria, where the Turks behaved as foreigners in a conquered land (though as Moslem foreigners who had something in common with the native population and were trying to defend that part of the Umma world—Moslem community—against interference from the Catholic powers).

On the eve of the French colonization, the ingredients of a nation in the modern sense existed, but there was no single, consistent current of national feeling. That the idea of nationhood meant different things to different people can be seen from a significant event that occurred in the 1860s.

In the most highly urbanized country of the Maghreb, Tunisia, where the nation-building process was most advanced, two slogans in use during a general uprising of the country against the Bey of the time (1864) enable us to understand the mood of the various categories of the population. The head of the insurrectionist movement, a peasant from a traditionally dissident region (the High Plateaux) was, at one moment, designated by the peasants in revolt as the Bey of the Arabs (that is, the Bedouins), in opposition to the lawful Bey, the Bey of the Turks and the Mamelukes (slaves brought up in Turkish families). It was certainly not by chance that the insurgents spontaneously hit upon the expression "Bey of the Arabs" rather than the more nationalistic "Bey of the Tunisians." On the other hand, one of the slogans of the insurgent population of Sfax (the second town of Tunisia) is also significant. To express their hostility to the central authority, the inhabitants of Sfax cried: "Down with the Bey! Long live the Ottoman Sultan!" These two slogans show the inconsistency of the idea of nationhood in the middle of the nineteenth century in the most highly urbanized region of the Maghreb. What, then, can be said about the situation in Algeria and Morocco prior to colonization, when we consider that very large areas traditionally lay outside the control of the central power?

It is undeniably colonization which, by breaking up the traditional structures, involuntarily—and against its interests—set the stage for a new drive towards nationhood. One of its first actions in Algeria was to define the frontiers of the Central Maghreb and confer upon the area thus demarcated an Arabic name—that of the city of Algiers; but the decisive act in all three countries was to subject the traditional zones of dissidence (Bled Siba) to the powerful politico-military administration of the French colonial authority. This does not mean that these zones were brought up to date economically; however, by imposing security even on the marginal zones and developing communications between all the regions, colonization eliminated the traditional brakes on advancing national awareness. Nevertheless, when the time came for the three Maghrebian states to attain independence, the progress achieved in nation-building was not identical in all three, any more that it had been on the eve of colonization.

This is explained by a combination of two series of factors: (a) the internal situation in each country at the time of colonization and (b) the style and duration of colonial rule up to the time of independence.

It is in Algeria, the first French colony in the Maghreb and the least urbanized at the time of the conquest (1830), that the impact of colonization on nation-building was particularly complex and contradictory. Algeria was officially a French département, and the French colony there felt almost as if it were at home. Hence, while it did far more to build up the conditions of a modern state than in Morocco or Tunisia, it also did far more than in either of those countries to slow down the emergence of a modern nation. That explains the difference between the role played by the city elites of Algeria and those of Morocco and Tunisia in the movements for national liberation and in the process of nation-building. In Morocco and Tunisia, which were protectorates and not colonies, the city elites (upper-middle and lower-middle classes) were regarded by the colonial power as partners in a dialogue—interlocuteurs valables—even if they occasionally suffered short periods of persecution. Their Algerian counterparts had to choose between an existence on the fringe of legality, with all its physical dangers, or assimilation, with all its humiliations. This explains the poor standing of the city elites in Algeria, the absence there, on the eve of independence, of a national party as solidly built as the Istiqulal in Morocco and the Neo-Destour in Tunisia, and lastly, the violence with which the Algerian Revolution broke out.

In Tunisia, where urban life is more developed and more stable than elsewhere in the Maghreb, independence was to a certain extent the culmination of a process in the course of which the movement for national liberation had gradually attained maturity. The movement was successively led by the Mameluke (assimilationist) and nationalist middle-class (traditionalist) elites and finally, after 1934, by lower-middle-class intellectuals (modernists).[29] In Algeria, these three currents existed on the eve of the outbreak of armed conflict. In Morocco, the brief duration of the colonization and its official ideology—respect for indigenous traditions—prevented the emergence of a lower-middle class intellectual elite as numerous as that in Tunisia. On the eve of Moroccan independence, the leadership of the national liberation movement lay in the hands of the traditionalist urban middle class.

In the countryside, colonization did not take the same form in all three countries. The colonists sought to occupy as much land as possible everywhere, but it was in Algeria that the peasants were most effectively uprooted; which explains to a certain extent the mass participation of the peasantry in the Algerian Revolution.[30] In Tunisia, colonization continued a trend that had begun long before the colonial conquest. In Morocco, it not only made no systematic attempt to overturn the traditional structures of the peasantry, but even used the peasants in the regions of traditional dissidence (the Atlas) to counteract the movement in the nationalist cities.

But in all three countries of the Maghreb, it was the union of forces between the peasants and the urban elites that made the movement for national liberation irreversible.

INDEPENDENCE AND THE REACTIVATION OF
THE SEGMENTARY STRUCTURES

At the time of their accession to independence, as on the eve of colonization, the three countries were not in the same situation as far as nation-building was concerned. As in the nineteenth century, there continued to be a common cultural stock based essentially on the Moslem religion and the almost total preponderance of the Malekite rites. Furthermore, these three countries had gone through essentially the same type of colonization.[31]

However, the differences between the three countries are significant. Tunisia has practically no Berber minority. In Algeria and Morocco, the Berber populations generally inhabit the mountain regions (the former zones of dissidence). The difference between Arabs and Berbers is not an ethnic one, because most of the people known as Arabs in the Maghreb are Arabized Berbers. Colonization speeded up the Arabization of the Berber population with the expansion of means of communications. It is estimated today that one-fifth of the population speaks the Berber dialect (which has no alphabet). There is no Berber problem in the Maghreb as there is a Kurdish problem in Iraq, but there is a possibility of the Berber population's being manipulated by certain urban elites.

The independence of the three countries offered, in fact, an occasion for reactivation of the segmentary structures, with a reappearance of the old "Siba" in the traditional zones of dissidence (the mountains and predesert regions). In Tunisia, however, the phenomenon (with Ben Youssef's movement) failed to assume as definite a regionalist dimension as in the case of the risings in Kabylia or the Aurès in Algeria,[32] or the Atlas or the Rif in Morocco.[33] However, while the form of these revolts strangely resembles that of the old traditional Siba, the content is different. In the past, peasant rebellions in the zones of dissidence were directed against the direct intervention of the central authority. Since independence, peasant insurrections in the same region have been mainly aimed at attracting the attention of the central authority to under-administration and to the scarcity of investments and of new jobs created by the state in its capacity as principal employer.

This reactivation of the segmentary structures is tempered in Tunisia by the existence of a very old established political party with deep roots in the country. In Algeria, the absence of a political party such as the Tunisian Neo-Destour, explains both the internecine fighting with no ideological basis that took place between the various clans at the time of independence, and the seizure of power by the army which was the only organization possessing a relatively stable structure.

In Morocco, the traditional-style legitimacy of the Alaoui Dynasty and the reactivation of the segmentary structures at the level of the political elites seem to be blocking the functioning of the institutions and preparing the way for an explosive situation in the medium-term or distant future.[34]

Such instances of the reactivation of segmentary structures with a contemporary political content can be explained by the existence in Maghrebian society of a structural imbalance between the mass of the population, which has been torn from its traditional way of life, and the modern sector, which is unable to offer it any possibility of coming to terms with its new situation. In such circumstances, the social stratification arising from modern economic activity loses its coherence, and even at times its sense. Nobody knows who represents whom, or who are the real allies or real enemies of men in public life, who were friends ten years ago, have been enemies for the last five, but continue to meet socially on the occasion of the traditional feast days.

The reactivation of the segmentary structures after independence is not limited exclusively to the political life of each country. Relations between the Maghrebian states continue to be dominated to a large extent by the segmentary approach. Will the Greater Maghreb—to employ an expression quite common in all three countries—be, in the near future, a nation in the modern sense of the word, a confederation of national states, or merely three states?

At present, one has the impression that the specific nationalism of each of the three national States is what is most deep-rooted in the collective mind. This may, however, be an erroneous impression, induced by the explicit ideology of the elites of the three countries. What can be said is that, between the reactivation of regionalist sentiment (at the local level) and pan—Arabism, there still exist a number of intermediate choices, and that in the Maghreb everything, or almost everything, is still possible.

NOTES

1. The reader will find an excellent account of research work on this subject in an article by S. Rokkan, "Models and Methods in the Comparative Study of Nation-Building," Acta Sociologica, Vol. 12, No. 2, 1969.

2. The chief papers presented at this symposium were published in the Revue de l'Institut de Sociologie, No. 2/3, 1967.

3. As an example of this tendency, see A. Laroui's L'Idéologie Arabe Contemporaine. Essai Critique, Paris, Maspero, 1967. See also the criticism by .G. Labica of Laroui's thesis, published in the Revue Algérienne des Sciences Juridiques, Politiques et Economiques, No. 4, December 1967.

4. I have tried to explain Ibn Khaldūn's notion of the Maghrebian state in somewhat greater detail. See "La Participation de la Paysannerie Maghrébine à la Construction Nationale," Revue Tunisienne des Sciences Sociales, No. 22, July 1970.

5. E. F. Gautier, Le Passé de l'Afrique du Nord, Paris, Payot, 1952.

6. Cf. F. Braudel, La Méditerranée et le Monde Méditerranéen à l'Epoque de Philippe II, Paris, Armand Colin, 1966; M. Lombard, "L'or Musulman du VII au XI siècle," Annales (Economies, Sociétés, Civilisations), No. 2, April-June 1947.

7. J. Poncet, "Le Mythe de la Catastrophe Hilalienne," Annales (Economies, Sociétés, Civilisations), No. 5, September-October 1967.

8. Cf. Y. Lacoste, Ibn Khaldoun: Naissance de l'Histoire du Passé au Tiers-Monde, Paris, Maspero, 1966.

9. Cf. A. Ayache, Le Maroc, bilan d'une colonisation, Paris, Editions Sociales, 1956; Y. Lacoste, A. Nouschi, and A. Prenant, L'Algérie–Passé et Présent, Paris, Editions Sociales, 1960; M. Lacheraf, L'Algérie–Nation et Société, Paris, Maspero, 1965; P. Sebag, La Tunisie–Essai de Monographie, Paris, Editions Sociales, 1951.

10. Marc Bloch, La Société Féodale, Paris, Editions Albin Michel, 1968.

11. As opposed to the Arab system of kinship, in which the preferred form of marriage is to the patri-lateral parallel cousin; cf. J. Cuisenier, "Le Mariage Arabe," L'Homme (Revue Française d'Anthropologie), May-August 1962.

12. Bloch, op. cit.

13. Cf. P. A. Dange, India from Primitive Communism to Slavery, Bombay, People's Publishing House, 1949; J. Chesneaux, Contribution à l'Histoire de la Nation Vietnamienne, Paris, Editions Sociales, 1955; J. Suret-Canale, Afrique Noire, Paris, Editions Sociales, 1961.

14. R. Gallissot, "Essai de Définition du Mode de Production de l'Algérie Pré-Coloniale," La Pensée, No. 142, December 1968.

15. Cf. with regard to this notion and its utilization with respect to non-European regions the publication by the Centre d'Etudes et de Recherches Marxistes, Sur le Mode de Production Asiatique, Paris, Editions Sociales, 1969.

16. Note that in K. Wittfogel's book, Oriental Despotism. Comparative Study of Total Power, New Haven, Yale University Press, London, Oxford University Press, 1957, some maps show the Maghreb as forming part of the regions governed by the Asian mode of production. Yet agriculture by irrigation in the Maghreb, as in mediaeval Spain, requires no extensive engineering works or permanent state control.

17. The word makhzen originally meant "warehouse" and has produced the French word magasin. In the Maghreb it came to mean "the central power," the state. The word shows how the central power was seen by the Maghreb in general, and the zones of dissidence in particular: as a military force responsible for making them pay their taxes. The other functions of the central power (foreign relations, the defence of Islam) were not generally challenged by the Bled Siba.

18. M. Lahbabi's interpretation of this situation seem to me somewhat overidealistic; cf. his book, Le Gouvernement Marocain à l'Aube du XX siècle, Rabat, 1968 (Editions Techniques Nord-africaines). See also the reservations on this point expressed by M. Ben Barka in his preface to Lahbabi's book.

19. A. Hanoteau and A. Letourneaux, La Kabylie et les Coutumes Kabyles, Paris, 1872-1873, 3 vols. (Editions Challanel).

20. R. Montagne, Les Berbères et le Makhzen dans le Sud du Maroc, Paris, Alcan, 1930.

21. J. Berque, Structures sociales du Haut Atlas, Paris, Presses Universitaires de France, 1955.

22. E. Gellner, Saints of the Atlas, London, Weidenfeld & Nicolson, 1969.

23. E. Durkheim, De la Division du Travail Social. Etude sur l'Organisation des Sociétés Supérieures, Paris, Alcan, 1893.

24. In addition to the above study by Gellner on Morocco, mention may be made of the following publications: E. E. Evans-Pritchard, Les Nueur, Paris, Editions Gallimard, 1968 and The Sanusi of Cyrenaica, London, Oxford University Press, 1949; I. G. Cunison, Baggara Arabs: Power and Lineage in a Sudanese Nomad Tribe, London, Oxford University Press, 1966; J. Middleton and D. Tait, Tribes Without Rulers. Studies in African Segmentary Systems, London, Routledge & Kegan Paul, 1958; S. M. Salim, Marsh Dwellers of the Euphrates Delta, London, Athlone Press, 1962. See also the following articles on the Maghreb by J. Favret: "La Segmentarité au Maghreb," L'Homme (Revue française d'Anthropologie), Vol. VI, No. 2, April-June 1966; "Relations de Dépendence et Manipulation de la Violence en Kabylie," L'Homme (Revue Française d'Anthropologie), Vol. VIII, No. 4, October-December 1968.

25. Gellner, op. cit.

26. G. Balandier, Anthropologie politique, Paris, Presses Universitaires de France, 1967 (collection SUP).

27. E. E. Evans-Pritchard, The Sanusi of Cyrenaica, op. cit.

28. J. Berque, Structures sociales du Haut Atlas, op. cit.

29. C. H. Moore, Politics in North Africa, Boston, Little, Brown, 1970; A. Zghal, "Construction Nationale et Nouvelles Classes Sociales en Tunisie," Revue de l'Institut de Sociologie, Brussels, University of Brussels (167-2/3).

30. P. Bourdieu (in collaboration with A. Sayad), Le Déracinement. La Crise de l'Agriculture Traditionnelle en Algérie, Paris, Editions de Minuit, 1964.

31. That is why the case of Libya, which can be regarded as belonging either to the Maghreb or the Middle East, has not been considered.

32. J. Favret, "Le Traditionalisme par Excès de Modernisme," Archives Européennes de Sociologie, VIII, 1967.

33. E. Gellner, "Patterns of Rural Rebellion in Morocco: Tribes as Minorities," European Journal of Sociology, Vol. 3, No. 2, 1962.

34. J. Waterbury, The Commander of the Faithful, The Moroccan Political Elite. A Study of Segmented Politics, London, Weidenfeld & Nicolson, 1970.

CHAPTER 12

UNIQUENESS IN THE CULTURAL CONDITIONS FOR POLITICAL DEVELOPMENT IN BLACK AFRICA

Jack Goody

JACK GOODY is Professor of Social Anthropology at Cambridge University and has been, until recently, Director of the African Studies Centre. He has carried out extensive field research in Northern Ghana and has made major theoretical contributions to the comparative study of kinship and inheritance, political succession, and the functions of script in the development of social structures. He has recently edited two forthcoming works: *Changing Social Structure in Ghana* and *Essays in Kinship*.

The concepts we use to discuss development, whether political, economic, or cultural, tend to fall into dichotomies. There are developed countries and developing ones, modern and modernising, contemporary and traditional, industrial and preindustrial. In part, this is simply a result of the binary character of the elementary opposition between what is A and not A, a simplistic way of categorising a situation for the purposes of intellectual shorthand. However, it is a mode of discourse into which one is much more likely to fall when more precise modes of "measurement," more sensitive judgements, are absent.

AUTHOR'S NOTE: Much of this chapter is drawn from earlier publications of mine, specifically the following: "Consensus and Dissent in Ghana," *Political Science Quarterly* 83 (1968): 337-52. "The Myth of a State," *Journal of Modern African Studies* 6 (1968): 461-73. "Inheritance, Property and Marriage in Africa and Eurasia,"

Whatever its origins, the idea that there is a single category of "developing nations," the inhabitants of a Third World (the lapse into a tertiary division concealing the basic dualism behind the assumption), is dangerous not only for the purposes of intellectual discussion but also for social policy. It assumes that one can establish a single model for changing a polity or economy from a developing to a developed state, whether we are dealing with Cambodia or the Cameroons.

Put in this bald fashion, the proposition is patently suspect (though this does not stop reputable social scientists from making the assumption of a common point of departure). But what precisely arouses this suspicion? It would be easy to adopt a holistic standpoint and assert that all cultures are unique or to search for specific cultural features, such as the Muslim taboo on pork, to account for the failure of pigfarms in the Middle East. Here I want to adopt neither of these approaches, but to try to elucidate some of the general aspects of the African situation which make it different from other continents, but specifically from Europe and Asia.

Let me begin by pointing out that the history of colonial development in Africa was different from almost all other continents except parts of Asia. The history of European expansion differed fundamentally depending upon the economic structure of the earlier population. Where hunting societies existed, as in Australia, North and South America, and South Africa, the population was small in relation to the land, both initially and after conquest, and European penetration took the form of colonies of settlement. Where agricultural populations existed, the history of colonial rule was very different. Most land was already farmed, and therefore not so easily acquired for European expansion. Without the wholesale slaughter or expulsion of sitting tenants(who fell into a different conceptual category from scattered hunters or shifting nomads), the conquerors had less land to exploit, and the colonists were inevitably a small proportion of the total population. In the former kind of colonies, Europeans have stayed; in the latter kind, they have mostly withdrawn. Moreover, in Africa they withdrew after a very short occupation. While coastal settlements had been established for up to four hundred years, the new colonial territories were products of the last decade of the nineteenth century. Hardly more than a jubilee separated conquest from independence.

Sociology 3 (1969): 56-76. "Succession in Contemporary Africa," *European Journal of Sociology* 10 (1969): 118-32. "Marriage Policy and Incorporation in Northern Ghana," in R. Cohen and J. Middleton, eds. *From Tribe to Nation in Africa,* San Francisco: Chandler, 1970. *Technology, Tradition and the State in Africa,* Oxford University Press, 1971.

Clearly the differing history of colonisation has meant a different history of development. In colonies of settlement, the influx of individuals from societies that were already advanced in a technological, administrative, and educational sense meant that they were presented with a ready-made prescription for development. In other societies, such as India and some in Africa, the colonialists withdrew leaving the indigenes to build upon their own resources.

The point I want to make here is that those traditional resources which were available before and to some extent after the period of European colonisation were very different in Africa south of the Sahara is in some ways very deceptive regarding technological development. From one standpoint, precolonial Africa could be said to be in the Iron Age. It had techniques of smelting iron and other metals, and it could fashion these metals into slashing and throwing weapons, and into hoes with which to farm the land. And it also used metals for artistic purposes as with the fine gold work of the Ashanti or the superb bronze sculptures of the Ife. What never reached Africa, however, was that cluster of human inventions that appeared in the Middle East about the fourth millenium B.C. and which was associated with the rise of what archaelogists call "civilisation," referring not to any built-in mode of behaviour but rather to some aspects of life that accompanied the birth of cities.

WRITING AND THE TECHNOLOGY
OF THE INTELLECT

An important cluster of inventions included writing, the wheel, and intensive farming. It is difficult to separate the effects of these inventions one from another. The development of intensive farming, whether by the animal-drawn plough or by irrigation, meant the possibility of specialisation in jobs that were not directly involved in the production of food. While there were considerable difficulties marking the kind of writing which first developed, nevertheless this system of communication was of fundamental importance in the recording of human thought, in the development of technology, science, and other forms of knowledge about the universe. The wheel permitted greater mobility as well as greater craft productivity, and the use of the principle of rotary motion affected many other activities, such as the irrigation of fields and the manufacture of pots. The neolithic advances in agriculture and animal husbandry had spread throughout Africa. Later on, the techniques of iron working also had a profound influence throughout the continent. But these important inventions connected with the Bronze Age and "rise of civilization" hardly touched Black Africa south of Ethiopia. It is true that in some areas, beginning effectively about the year 1000 A.D., writing did spread below the Sahara with the advance of Islam. Indeed it brought a superior form of writing to that which emerged in the Bronze Age of Mesopotamia, for Arabic made use of the alphabetic principle, at least as far as the consonantal structure was concerned. But what spread was a religious literacy in which the primary aim was to teach individuals not so much how to read and write as how to read the Koran. While a few Africans continued with further studies and made some contributions to scholarship, such efforts were rare and lay outside the field of "science," however broadly defined. Even where it existed, literacy was everywhere restricted, both in the numbers of those able to read and write and in the content of the literature available. Outside the Muslim sphere, a few embryonic systems of writing have been reported, but where these are at all developed the inspiration appears to have been of recent origin.

The absence of literacy had a number of implications. Except for certain states on the East African coast and in the savannah region of West Africa, states which had been influenced by Islam, administration had to be carried out without the aid of writing. This meant the absence of a great deal of the apparatus of a modern administration: record-keeping, filing system, sending letters, decision-making by memoranda. Not only was the adminstration affected, but also the organisation of law, since the rules in operation were those that could be transmitted by oral communication and held in memory store. The absence of writing for law and government had certain advantages: it gave greater flexibility and meant that laws which were out of tune with contemporary thinking simply slipped out of the repertoire of judges, but the limitations were equally clear. Consequently the advent of colonial government in the shape of the district officer and his network of communications made a much more radical change in Africa than it did in those areas of the world which already possessed writing. This remained true even of the Muslim areas, where it had often been the magical and religious, rather than the more pragmatic, aspects of writing which were predominant.

While the absence of literacy was a considerable disadvantage in the process of political and economic development, it was one that was relatively easy to overcome. For example, in northern Ghana, fifty years passed between the coming of the colonial troops and the graduation of the first university student; despite the perjorative comments of many contemporary nationalists, the colonial regimes achieved a considerable amount of educational development in a comparatively short time. Here social change was easy to effect, even though the kind of instruction that was introduced, and is still being taught, leaves much to be desired, since it presents major problems of adaptation to local conditions. Indeed, one might say that the rapid spread of the modern educational system was actually assisted by the absence of preexisting schools of a religious kind; it has been in the Islamic areas that educational development in the Western sense has been slowest. "Pagans" converted to Christianity more easily, constituting a spur to social change, not only because of the values Christianity inculcated but because its missionaries were anxious for all to read the Book and were consequently in the vanguard of those establishing schools and literacy programmes.

THE PLOUGH AND THE MEANS OF PRODUCTION

There were other areas of social life where change was more difficult to effect because of the low level of earlier technologies. I refer here primarily to the argricultural systems. In certain places agriculture changed drastically, primarily because of the introduction of new crops which were of value in the European markets, e.g. cocoa in West Africa. But overall, Africa south of the Sahara presents much greater problems for agricultural development than, for example, the countries of Asia. Farming was and still is primarily carried out with hoe and machette. The plough never penetrated south of the Sahara. Animals were not used for any kind of traction, whether for the plough or for wheeled vehicles. The principles involved in raising water for irrigation in the Middle East, namely, rotary motion and the lever, were scarcely utilised. All this meant that agriculture was extensive rather than intensive. So it remains today. Shifting cultivation prevails in large parts of the continent. With it goes a simple type of farming, low productivity, and greater land use per individual(on the whole) than is the case with more intensive systems. The density of population is low by the standards of other agricultural regions, and so too is productivity.

We may contrast the African situation with that in Europe and Asia where most farming was done by the plough. With a plough a single man can cultivate a large area of land, up to one hundred acres. With a hoe he can hardly keep more than five under cultivation. While the full capabilities of the plough are in practice rarely realised (many plough farms are even smaller than African plots), its potentialities for increasing productivity are clearly much greater than those of the hoe. Hence differences in land holding mean much more to individuals under a system of plough farming than they do to those using the hoe. In the latter case, the limitations of the technology ensure a degree of equality; neither the acreage of holdings nor their product is likely to vary very widely. On the Eurasian continent the population of rural areas was heavily stratified, largely in accordance with the amount of land owned. In rural Africa this was rarely the case; the acquisition of rights of usufruct presented few problems. There has never been a landless rural proletariat in the continent of Africa, though one is now emerging. However, even today most individuals can leave their employment in the city, can exercise their claim to rights in land in their natal villages and can become subsistence farmers. They are thus in the position of the Scottish crofters, whom Lord Leverhulme regarded as an impediment to his attempt to modernise the Hebrides; the development of industry needs a disciplined labour force and control is greater if there is no independent access to the means of production.

It is fundamentally misleading to compare the position of Africa, either in the towns or in the country, to that of Europe, Asia, or North America in their preindustrial phases. Elsewhere in the world the transformation of agriculture involves the mechanisation of plough cultivation. In Africa it means the more radical transformation of a hoe agriculture. In this situation, there are again some advantages. Land reform has not been an issue because there has been little or no landlordism. Moreover, much can be achieved simply by introducing the plough, whose import cost is low, but such halfway measures are not to the taste of many modernising politicians. They prefer to go straight to the tractor, and here the problems become significantly more complicated than they would be in Europe or Asia. The introduction of mechanised farming is not just a question of importing a specified number of machines from an industrial nation. There is the whole question of the plant and technology that is required to support their operation in rural areas. Absent from Africa was the array of rural crafts which arose around the Bronze Age technology. For example, carpenter's tools, other than the knife, were few and far between. While iron working was a central aspect of the economy throughout the continent, the absence of rotary motion and the lack of any control of nonhuman sources of energy meant a low-level of technical development.

THE GUN AND THE MEANS OF DESTRUCTION

The consequences of the introduction of guns were profound for the political history of the continent, especially in the military field. The point can best be seen in juxtaposing the reactions of Africa and Asia to European conquest.

When the Portuguese spearheaded European expansion into other continents, they succeeded largely because of their use of gun-bearing sailing ships. Through these they could dominate their African opponents who were armed only with sword, spear, and bow. By the end of the fifteenth century, when the expansion of Europe began, their guns could also dominate Asia as well. These technological innovations soon spread from Europe, just as simpler forms of gunpowder and "cannon" had earlier diffused to Europe from China and the Middle East, but the way in which they did so is of great interest. The African, it seems, never learned to make fire-arms as good as those of the Europeans, unlike the sixteenth and seventeenth-century Japanese and Sinhalese, who soon achieved virtual parity with the Portuguese in this respect. Already in the mid-sixteenth century the Japanese were producing matchlocks, and they were soon followed by the Koreans; Ceylon had become a centre of production by the end of the sixteenth century, when muskets and cannon were made at many different points in the Indian subcontinent. By the seventeenth century the inhabitants of the Malabar coast were exporting muskets to Arabia. The reason for the lack of African success in taking up the manufacture of this powerful new weapon is a simple one. Africans did not possess the requisite level of craft skill in iron-working. As a result, they were at an enormous disadvantage when the scramble for their continent began, since they had to fight against the very people who were supplying them with arms.

One does not have to adopt a position of "technological determinism" to realise that these limitations have had profound implications for political development. Clearly the process of modernisation has been more difficult, not only because of the simplicity of the earlier technology, but also because those concerned with development have failed to realise just what these differences have entailed. Modernising politicians have attempted to jump straight from the hoe to the tractor, often with disastrous results; others have failed to see the advantages of simple measures by which productivity could be significantly increased. The absence of an intermediate technology has its advantages as well as its disadvantages, but only if the nature of the gap is realised in advance.

The particular situation in Africa displayed some other features which could be turned to advantage and which again derived from the nature of the productive system and its relationship to political organisation. Shifting cultivation by means of the hoe meant that each man could utilise only a limited amount of land. Population was relatively sparse, and while the land was plentiful, it was also less productive than in Eurasia, partly because of the technological limitations, and partly because tropical soils are often of poor quality. Moreover, since processes of soil regeneration (either by manure or by special cropping) were limited in nature, the fertility of land soon fell off. Under these conditions, the answer usually lay in moving one's farm (though not necessarily one's residence) to a new site; it led to the practice of shifting cultivation.

The social consequences were twofold. Politically, chiefship tended to be over people rather than over land; a leader had to try to attract people as well as restrain them. The conditions for the forms of domination that obtained in the European Middle Ages hardly existed, except for slavery itself. In slavery, labour is controlled by political force; in serfdom, economic controls, such as land tenure, are of equal importance. It is significant that only in Ethiopia, which had the plough, was there any landlordism in Africa.

If you have landlords, you can also have tenants and serfs; unfree tenancies mean little unless land is highly valued and the peasantry has nowhere else to go. Under conditions of shifting cultivation, it means little. Slavery was important throughout most of Africa; war captives were given household or agricultural work to perform for their captors or their purchasers. But ties of subordinations arose not out of shortage of land but as the result of purchase or conquest, thus giving rise to slavery rather than to serfdom.

The limited surplus in the productive system meant that whatever political differences existed between chief and commoner, the economic differences were small. There was little tendency for gentry subcultures to emerge, except in a few areas; within any state, men tended to speak the same language, practise the same customs, eat the same food, and marry the same women. The latter was important. In Europe and Asia, property distinctions often entered directly into marriage arrangements through the mechanism of the dowry (or else by a prospective inheritance); by this means a woman from a rich family could marry a man of similar standing; the match was the criteria of a good marriage. In Africa the dowry was absent and marriage payments tended to be standardised; economically it mattered little where one's daughter married, since the immediate return in bridewealth would be virtually the same. Whereas marriage in Europe and Asia tended to be enclosed (endogamous), marriage in Africa was outward looking (exogamous). Most ruling dynasties had to take their wives from outside, that is, from commoners, from neighbours, and often from slaves. In a polygynous household, women from different social estates would share the same compound, the same supplies, the same kitchen. So too would their children. Under these conditions, cultural differences tended to merge rather than emerge; the development of a gentry subculture was strangled at birth, especially in view of the attention people gave to their maternal as well as their paternal kin.

Such a widespread system of marriage clearly led to a strong identification between the different groups in the political system. The ruling dynasties, which were in any case "mass" dynasties through which high office sometimes passed in circulating succession, were linked by many cross-cutting ties to the other elements of the population. It is critical to note that in all the post independence upheaval that has taken place in that continent, little violence has been directed towards superior strata, apart from the colonial rulers themselves. The peasants have revolted in two countries, Ruanda and Zanzibar, exactly those places where the marriage system stressed the isolation of the political elite. In other areas, the emphasis on out-marriage has tended to produce great horizontal homogeneity, though this in turn has perhaps increased the vertical differentiation of the "tribe." Thus the greater fluidity of status is counterbalanced by greater rigidity of tribe; the results of the one are as apparent as those of the other.

The immediate reason lies in the marriage system, but beyond that lies the basic differences in the nature of agricultural production; in Eurasia a much greater isolation of the ruling strata was possible, giving rise to the socio-political problems that marked the feudal regime. Under Eurasian conditions there is a tendency toward closer rather than distant marriages, toward in-marriage and endogamy rather than out-marriage and exogamy. In Africa, on the other hand, the ownership of land was not the main key to economic achievement, which in the agricultural field varied within fairly confined limits. As a result, social life was relatively homogeneous, and marriage policy was less firmly directed toward the matching of like with like.

E. B. Tylor pointed to the fact that exogamy created ties between groups and increased interaction, whereas endogamy was a policy of isolation. When differences in land holding are a major factor in the social hierarchy and when property is conveyed through marriage and inheritance, a premium is placed upon in-marriage rather than out-marriage, upon endogamy rather than exogamy. This is particularly the case where, to preserve the standing of daughters as well as of sons, property is distributed "bilaterally" (that is, to both sexes) by the process of "diverging devolution" (that is, by dowry as well as inheritance). This policy of isolation in terms of property leads to variations of behaviour within the culture, variations that tend to crystallise out in gentry subcultures or in differences between richer peasants, poorer peasants and those with no land at all, rural proletariat.

In Africa this kind of differentiated situation is only now emerging with the introduction of larger-scale commercial farming, the enclosure and sale of lands, the emergence of educational stratification. In the case of all these forms of differentiation, whether at the rural, industrial, or educational levels, men and women make strenuous efforts to hand them on to their children. Differences of subculture are not only emerging but are being perpetuated, by farmers, university lecturers, politicians of all persuasions. Africa still has a long way to go in this respect. Most people have a foot in the country as well as in the town, among the poor as well as among the rich. But patterns of interaction and marriage arrangements are unmistakeably changing among the elite, in a manner that will affect the mode of political communication and the relationships between strata. The pervasive egalitarianism of Africa, characterised by some as "African socialism," is vanishing before the tide of socio-political development.

This development is changing old structures more radically than elsewhere. When the relative political and economic position of a Eurasian aristocracy in the society changes, because of conquest, democracy, industrialisation, or the rise of new skills, then it still has its land and other possessions on which to fall back—providing that the change stops short of complete dispossession. This property gives it a lever on the new dispensation and helps it preserve a privileged position, even if this has been modified by events. Many European writers have tended to see African chiefships in just such a "feudal" mode and ask the same sort of question about the relationship between traditional and modern elites as would be appropriate for the post-Reformation period in Europe; they are anxious to perceive and describe the situation in terms of class conflict. But, except in special cases, African chiefs were sustained by temporary political rather than by enduring economic power, and so could put up little resistance either under colonial rule or after independence. In such a situation, the system of elites, and of stratification generally, is likely to be much more fluid than in Eurasia, and the educational ladder will receive more emphasis as the road to success. The new elite are consolidating their position by the same educational process, and by marrying amongst themselves. The earlier egalitarianism and subsequent fluidity are crystallising into a new hierarchy attempting, like all others, to hold on to the positions it has acquired. However, it *is* a new hierarchy and has none of the legitimacy of age. While office-holders are everywhere collecting the perquisites of office, they are not seen as having any entitlement to these benefits, other than what is gained by the rapid attainment of power. Consequently, their behaviour is openly criticised or silently envied, and their government is correspondingly insecure. While government and elite may achieve a temporary charisma, neither has the aura of tradition. Nor indeed do they have much to fall back on, and hence are reluctant to give up office, even when their support has dwindled.

AFRICA SOUTH AND NORTH OF THE SAHARA

What differences did all this make for nation building in Black Africa as compared with Muslim areas, or rather between Africa north and south of the Sahara? Zghal rightly shows that precolonial North Africa corresponded to the models neither of feudal society nor of Oriental despotism. In particular he calls attention to differences in its kinship systems, in its military organisation, and in its productive system (which did not involve large-scale irrigation works). In addition, there was the open frontier with segmentary nomads to the south.

The presence of these segmentary societies is one of the main similarities between the North and South. As in the Maghreb, the political systems of sub-Saharan Africa consisted of zones of control (states) and of dissidence (segmentary or acephalous societies), corresponding to the Bled Mahkzen and the Bled Siba of North Africa. In trying to deal with the ever-present question of why the countries of North Africa did not develop like Western Europe, writers have turned to the work of the great fourteenth-century historian, Ibn Kahldun. As Zghal notes, his basic theme relates the stagnation of his time to the structural instability of the traditional state and to the cyclical and noncumulative character of the changes taking place. He saw this as resulting from the interplay between the vigorous peoples of the desert and the declining dynasties of the towns. The segmentary peoples are used to resistance to central governments. In the Tibesti region of Chad, their persistence in time has been ascribed to the way they melt before invaders, only to regroup elsewhere. They are the natural guerrillas, having had to adopt these tactics against many conquerors. In Northern Ghana the Tallensi (Frafra) and the LoDagaa (Lobi) provided the British and the French with stiffer resistance over the longer term than did the centralised states. And this resistance to central government has continued to mark the Ibo and the LoDagaa, though at the same time they have seized more eagerly than most upon the benefits to be wrung from "development." Again in the Portuguese colony of Guinea, it is the segmentary peoples that provide the core of the resistance to colonial rule;[1] and it is people with the same kind of political structure who have resisted northern rule in the Sudan and southern rule in Chad. But it seems doubtful whether the existence of such peoples has been a great obstacle to the process of nation-building, and the difficulties they made for the North African states was surely due to their nomadic life and desert habitat as much as to their political structure.

More significant than the similarities with the north are the differences. The absence of writing was of course mitigated immediately south of the Sahara and on the eastern seaboard by contact with Islam, a contact which was certainly not entirely passive. It was associated with the basic differences in the productive system that we have already noted. The system of hoe production strictly limited the amount of land any individual could cultivate, and hence any surplus that could be drawn off for activities not concerned with primary production. Except in certain trading cities of West Africa, this low level of production resulted in a relatively homogeneous style of life, with a system of open connubium. By and large, Africans marry widely; exogamy is more characteristic than endogamy; even where Islam has been adopted, paralled cousin marriage is rare; indeed, many societies forbid close marriage of all description. Consequently, ties of kinship extend across the boundaries of different groups even though these may be separated in terms of access to political office; chiefs are likely to have their mother's brothers in commoner clans. Equally, Muslims often marry outside their own ranks and save a pagan soul by doing so. Again such "distant" marriages between unlikes proliferate the cross-cutting ties. It makes for strong vertical solidarity within communities and between men of differing religious approaches; it makes both for political acquiescence and religious apostasy. But the horizontal solidarity resulting from open connubium is obtained at the expense of ties between local groups. The politically dominant groups tended to marry down rather than out, thus emphasising the internal solidarity of people (tribe) against people. Of course, such independence was modified by trade and conquest, especially by conquest, but the European invasion had no such unifying effect. It provided a ruling group which did not marry locally (nor more did the priests and traders, European, Lebanese, Indian, Greek). Then the dominant group that had initially established the boundaries of the territory withdrew, leaving the original inhabitants in charge. While they had acquired some unity by the adoption of an endoglossic national language of external origin and by common participation in an administrative system, they were still involved in their own more particularistic concerns at the domestic and local levels. So much so that census material often tells one little about local circumstance, since it is often the summation of difference. Equally, much African law is local law and can be applied only locally.[2]

It might be argued that these horizontal divisions between peoples within a nation, tribe, or ethnic group create the conditions for the territorial instability of the state. There is some truth in this statement. The attempt of Katanga to break away from the Congo was not just a matter of external interference and economic interest. Much less was the War of Ibo Secession simply a matter of oil and neocolonialism. In both cases, ethnicity was critical in events leading up to the attempted break-away. Subsidiary nationalisms, based on primordial ties, are a constant feature of the African scene; rightly or wrongly, each dismissal from a cabinet, each military coup, tends to get interpreted in these terms; even where ethnic identification has played little part, the actors often feel such forces are the real key to the interpretation of events.

AFRICAN NATION-BUILDING IN WORLD PERSPECTIVE

In his introduction to this volume Rokkan has pointed to the contrast between the socio-economic conditions facing the state-builders in Europe and those facing the postcolonial states of the mid-twentieth century. They face "a cumulation of challenges in a very different world environment." Indeed so contrary are these conditions that one wonders not simply how these nations were created (indeed the process of internal protest and external reform was fairly straightforward), but how they continue to exist at all.

On the variables he considers Africa always comes low. The old religions are localised; the new tend to be divisive with the exception of Islam. Linguistic unity tended to develop within the boundaries of precolonial states, but the polyglot kingdom was not uncommon. In any case the linguistic unity of the old states is usually irrelevant to the new colonial boundaries. On the economic side, hoe agriculture scarcely provided the conditions for the appearance of large, independent estates. Some degree of urbanisation there was, especially in trading areas, along the coasts and the sub-Saharan fringe. Elsewhere large agro-towns were to be found among the Yoruba. But the level of manufacture was usually limited to craft production, and the independence of professional groups was restricted. The inhabitants were town-dwellers but hardly a bourgeoisie, not at any rate in the sense of developing semi-independent organs of government and administration. Indeed this dependence on chiefs made for a relatively easy take-over both at the colonial conquest and at the coming of independence. It paved the way for the establishment of the administrative or civil-service state, displaying a low level of mass participation, and becoming an easy prey to the military take-over.

The basic problem of nation-building in present-day Africa is not the absence of precolonial states which could provide a basis for further development. A state like Ashanti had a larger population than some of the newly emergent nations in the continent. Others have formed the core of modern nations, as the Mossi empire has done for Upper Volta and the kingdom of Dahomey for the nation of that name, while the inter-lacustrine states of the Ganda (Uganda), Ruanda (Rwanda), and Rundi (Burundi) have constituted the basis of other new members of the international community. But in most cases the units of colonial administration (for in every case this is what the present nations of Africa are, in a territorial sense) were not limited to the boundaries of such kingdoms, but extended further afield into the territory of acephalous neighbours. Virtually none are monoglot; indeed, the selection of a local language as a national tongue might well lead to the destruction of the political unit as it exists. National languages are largely those of the colonial invaders.

But the colonial powers did more than extend the boundaries of previous political units. They also weakened the existing elites, whether in the political, economic, or religious spheres. Colonial overrule, with its district officers penetrating even into the most remote areas, reduced the position of the chiefs by instituting an alternative system of government and by removing the economic supports to their power; their rights to taxes and tribute were abolished, their ability to control trade and acquire booty was ended. Chiefs continued largely as agents of the central government, as leaders in ceremony and rite. Even the power of the larger merchants was weakened. Many of these, like Thomas Brew of Cape Coast, became wealthy in commerce with Europe; others were involved in the trade across the Sahara or the Indian Ocean. With the arrival of foreign trading concerns, none of these groups could develop as they might; Europe had not only the manufacturers and the capital, but the double entry bookkeeping as well.

The high degree of dependence on the European trade is seen in the sites of many of the national capitals which reflect the colonial past and the commercial present. The long line of West African capitals are all coastal towns: Dakar, Bathurst, Bissau, Conakry, Freetown, Monrovia, Abidjan, Accra, Lomé, Contonou, Lagos. The capitals of hinterland nations are usually sited more centrally and in West Africa these countries are correspondingly poorer. Even at its height the trans-Saharan trade did not compare with the vigorous trading by nations of what Rokkan calls the "seaward empire-nations of Western Europe," especially under Protestantism. Liberated by their rejection of Catholicism, they were able to trade freely with the West African littoral, acquiring gold for Europe and slaves for their compatriots in America. They were free, too, to break the ban on supplying arms and technicians to the enemies of Christendom. Queen Elizabeth of England helped the armies of Morocco to traverse the Sahara and conquer Timbuctoo; the guns of Europe helped build up some of the most important states of the Guinea Coast: Dahomey, Akwamu, Denkyira, and Ashanti. There, muzzle loaders, still known as "Dane guns," were exchanged for Guinea gold and black ivory.

What does nation-building mean in the African context? Essentially it is the consolidation of colonial boundaries. The position taken by the Organisation of African Unity of accepting existing frontiers is not simply a question of politicians hanging on to what they have got. It is also a matter of having no apparent alternative, except splitting up into small tribal, linguistic, or ethnic groups as the basis of one's national units. And in Africa there are some 5,000 of these.[3]

The alternative to fragmentation into small, culturally homogeneous units is either making the best of what exists or aggregating the present nations into wider sovereign groups. The latter solution is pressed upon Africa by economists who find the present national markets too small even for many simple manufacturing processes, as well as by political scientists who envy the greater leverage and greater responsibility exercised by larger units. Radical politicians like Nkrumah have called for African unity and for regional pacts. But in reality there has been virtually no delegation of national powers; most of the earlier interterritorial arrangements such as the East African Community have collapsed; new ones such as the Senegal-Mali Union or the Ghana-Guinea pact never got off the ground. And despite warm professions of friendship and elaborate symbolic ceremonies that destroyed frontiers, long-established "aliens" have been expelled and open boundaries have been closed. New laws of nationality are among the most restrictive in the world.

All this is at a time when nations in Europe and elsewhere have grouped themselves into wider units, delegating sovereignty either through the legacy of conquest (or liberation) or because of political and economic necessity. Conquest is no longer a very probable method of building larger political units, though China used it successfully to reestablish herself in Tibet; fragmentation is the more usual outcome of violence, since internal war is not subject to the same controls as external war, but the political and economic advantages of wider groupings are more apparent in Africa than in Europe. So too is the argument from tradition. Since the present nations are arbitrarily defined, their inclusion in larger polities might be thought to present no great obstacle.

Such a supposition is rational but naive. It is not only politicians who feel that the greater the number of units, the more numerous the beneficiaries. The identification with existing nations is not confined to the elite with their calculations of jobs and rewards. Every new literate increases the vested interest in preserving the newly acquired national language as well as the educational and other institutions introduced by the colonial power. Even nonliterates now recognise the reality of the boundary by referring to their fellow tribesmen across the border as "French" or "English." Above all the new unit is recognised in the councils of the world, by the O.A.U. and the United Nations, who deal with any politically independent unit on the same general terms.

In these circumstances, the concept of nation-building has a very different meaning from the process of group definition that occurred in the rest of the world in the period of European expansion. Contemporary political units emerged initially through outside conquest and have tried to acquire the semblance of unity by the adoption of the paraphernalia of nationhood: an anthem, an airline, and often the name of a great kingdom to boot. The paradox of the situation is that despite all contrary signs, nations have been able to establish and continue to operate even under these adverse conditions. The stability of regimes has been low; the politics of mass participation is always difficult to work where primordial ties are strong, but the stability of boundaries and administration has been high. They have neither broken down nor joined up, despite the primordial pressures toward contraction and the international pressures towards amalgamation.

NOTES

1. "Having no central power which left them leaderless when overthrown, the segmentaries sometimes fought harder and longer than the centralised states." Basil Davidson, The Africans, London, Longmans, 1969, p. 262.

2. See for example N. A. Ollennu, The Law of Testate and Intestate Succession in Ghana, London, Sweet and Maxwell, 1966.

3. G. P. Murdock lists some 6,000 tribal names in the Index to his book, Africa: Its Peoples and their Culture History, New York, McGraw-Hill, 1959.

CHAPTER 13

POLITICAL BOUNDARIES AND
POLITICAL COMPETITION IN
TROPICAL AFRICA

William J. Foltz

WILLIAM J. FOLTZ is Associate Professor of Political Science at Yale University. He has carried out extensive research on political development in West Africa and has also studied the structuring of conflicts and the possibilities of reconciliation in East Africa and in Ulster. His publications include *From French West Africa to the Mali Federation,* and he has edited, with Karl W. Deutsch, a volume of essays on *Nation-Building.*

Of the many issues that must be faced both in the study and practice of nation-building, none is so intractable as the delimitation of the nation itself. Despite the evident architectural connotations of the term, or the various organic systems approaches that have often been subsumed under it, both of which should logically lead one to think in terms of variable external dimensions, most discussion has been concerned with the internal elaboration of structure leading to increasing interrelation of segments and their eventual integration into an architectonic of a functionally coherent whole. Public statements of today's real world nation-builders, political leaders, and writers of development plans for example, have for obvious reasons taken the external dimensions of their field of action as given, and those lesser mortals who have not been relegated to such disagreeable categories as "subversives," "neo-colonialists," or "visionaries," have accepted their verdict. Seemingly, however, we may talk of the growing interdependence of all men, or however much the earlier history of mankind or the contemporary rise of the multinational corporation may contradict its assumptions, the normative triumph of the nation-state as the basic, correct, and permanent unit of human organization seems incontrovertible. The Charter as well as the name of the United Nations embodies this triumph.

Conventional wisdom has it that the external boundaries of all of Africa's states are artificial, the product of arbitrary—if not willfully malicious—European decisions made in ignorance of local realities and preferences. Whether these boundaries are any more arbitrary than any others is a difficult question which no scholar has yet answered; indeed, posed in such a form, the question is probably unanswerable. Perhaps because of this seeming artificiality, Africa's national leaders have taken great pains to assure the solidity and permanence of the boundaries their states assumed at independence. The Organisation of African Unity quite explicitly protects the boundaries and the territorial integrity of its member states and has consistently opposed attempts, such as those made by the Somalis and the Biafrans, to alter existing boundaries.[1] However difficult the human and intellectual issues posed by Somali and Biafran claims, the OAU's position reflects both logical consistency and the political realism to be expected of a successful group of national political leaders.

Such logic and realism should not lead to assuming, however, either that the triumph of Africa's present state boundaries was inevitable, or that alterations may not be in the offing. All political boundaries are the product of some political process, and Africa's present boundaries are, of course, no exception. The relevant boundary-establishing political processes in Africa have changed over time from those involving principally competition between European powers with Africans providing limiting conditions, to those involving competition between Africans with the occasional involvement, active or passive, of European or other outside groups. Only occasionally has conflict over boundaries taken a purely African versus outsider form. In recent years the political process within Africa has been dominated by conflict of different social groups for formal positions of political power. This conflict, centering as it has around the struggle for independence and the organization of new states, has taken place in a relatively fluid political environment in which the determination of final institutional structures has been both a means and an end of political conflict—an end because that is what achieving formal independence means, and a means because the sort of structure adopted inevitably influences the relative weight accorded the different bundles of political resources that different groups and individuals bring to political life.

This chapter argues that much recent political conflict in Africa can usefully be understood as conflict over political boundaries, and that the boundaries presently attained can usefully be looked at as the indeterminate result of an ongoing political process involving conflict between a variety of groups possessing different political resources. As such, these boundaries themselves are subject to alteration, and the form their alteration takes will influence the further development of political conflict. After a brief discussion of what I mean by "political boundary," the chapter will demonstrate with historical example the problematic nature of Africa's boundaries. It will then relate the various conceptions of and changes in boundaries to certain features of political life in Africa, and finally try to assess factors likely to sustain or weaken the present political boundaries within which people are trying to build nations.

POLITICAL BOUNDARIES

Establishing political boundaries may be seen to involve three basic aspects, of which two are obvious: establishing relative continuity of political order within a political unit, and establishing relative discontinuity between that unit and the rest of the world. These seem at first glance to be two sides of the same coin in that, logically, change in one side produces an equal and opposite reaction on the other. When one moves beyond logical formulae to political action, however, one finds it necessary to separate the two sides of the coin. Different formal political structures commonly deal with internal as opposed to external questions, and in a world where state sovereignty receives considerable deference (at least if it is out of the path of big power competition) a decrease in internal cohesion may not immediately produce an increase in involvement with the world outside the state's borders, and vice versa. Since state sovereignty receives considerable automatic support from the international system, relatively little attention has to be directed toward maintaining political discontinuity with the outside world once an initial geographical border is recognized, whereas issues concerning the establishment and maintenance of internal continuity—particularly those involving the extension or restriction of political participation and the centralization or decentralization of political decisions—continue so long as political life exists.

The third aspect of political boundaries is no less important for being less obvious; this aspect is the establishment of rules for the control of boundary crossing or boundary permeability. Such permeability is an essential issue in both the above aspects of boundary determination. Domestically, it involves determining the circumstances under which certain irrelevant or nonpolitical resources may legitimately be transformed into relevant political resources; to put it another way, it involves determination of what parts of the border between the national political system and its economic, social, or cultural systems and in some cases its subordinate political system are going to be held firmly, and which parts opened selectively to particular outside groups and resources. Externally, it involves the determination of legitimate political alliances across state borders; it determines what external resources or influences may legitimately be brought into the domestic political system.[2] This third aspect involves one of the grey areas of most political life, and is most subject to manipulation, both by a regime and its opponents, since it involves changing the political environment and the distribution of resources, often in ways that are not immediately apparent to the public eye.

To summarize, determining a nation's political boundary involves answering three questions: The internal question, how is the national political process to be set off from other aspects of life, including conceivably other political processes? The external question, who and what resources are not in the political system and neither subject to its decisions nor legitimately entitled to participate in it? The permeability question, how, and under what circumstances, may the previous rules legitimately be amended, bent, or broken?

INDEPENDENCE BOUNDARIES:
THE NATIONALIST ORDER

In the great majority of cases, the internal and external boundaries established at independence, or shortly thereafter as the result of the same political processes that led to independence, hewed closely to what can be called the "nationalist order." This ideal set of rules may be summarized as follows:

(1) The external boundary of the sovereign political unit shall be that of the largest existing colonial political unit within which a distinct administrative service has been developed, at least one African political party has organized itself, and some political rewards have been allocated.

(2) Internally, there should be no strong regional or local political boundaries. Political power should be centralized, and political and administrative officers should be able to function in any part of the national territory. There should, however, be strong boundaries between the political and other systems within the national territory.

(3) The external boundary should be crossed only through formal government to government contract, through such well established international arrangements as alliances, foreign aid, and the like. Domestically, the boundary between the political and other systems should be readily crossable in one direction only, from the political to the economic or social. While it would under some circumstances be appropriate for a person to achieve high social or economic status or to control social or economic activities as the result of his political position, one should not be able to achieve political distinction solely because of one's wealth or social status.

It is perhaps important to point out here that there is nothing astonishing, or disastrously wrong, or brilliantly correct about such a set of ideal rules. Rather it is their commonality to very different African contexts that strikes one, and that suggests that the processes of decolonization, the development of nationalism, and the consolidation of national power were similar enough throughout tropical Africa to generate similar ideal boundary rules. Let us look at those commonalities.

From the perspective of the colonial powers, the boundary rules implied by the nationalist order could be seen in most points serving their purposes, or at least not significantly contravening them. Although some measure of generosity should not be excluded as a motive for colonial withdrawal strategies, to prevail such generosity had to be rooted in some metropolitan interests, or at least not disrupt bureaucratic routine. "Colonial powers" is a broad category, and in addition to examining Britain, France, and Belgium separately, a full analysis of their purposes would have to consider the sometimes contradictory pressures of colonial service, metropolitan politicians, trading companies, the military, white settlers, the foreign office, and many others, the exact mixture varying for each colony. However, the intra-European political process, both in Africa and in the metropolitan countries, which paved the way for independence achieved agreement on the following interrelated goals. First, negotiate your way out peacefully and in an orderly manner with some "responsible spokesman." Second, leave behind something that will hold together. Among other things, this implies that there ought to be some minimal resource base and, more importantly perhaps, that the spokesman really speak for someone. Third, preserve some of the political and administrative structures you had set up. Reasons for this could vary from simple pride or bureaucratic inertia to feelings that such structures could more easily be manipulated from the outside after independence, and—doubtless most important—the perhaps incorrect but sincere feelings that such laboriously elaborated structures would somehow be "best." The fourth goal is closely related: preserve points of political access both to structures and significant individuals. Fifth, protect significant metropolitan economic or settler interest, if either existed, and in some cases neither did. Finally, maintain a general friendliness between the metropolitan country, with something of a "special relationship" overtone, if the cost would not be too high. The French have been particularly willing to pay to maintain such a relationship.

One of the most striking things about all the nationalist elites who provided the responsible spokesmen and who took over the reins of government at independence, is the great similarity of their backgrounds. In his study of nationalist politicians in French Africa, Seurin noted, "les mémes couches sociales détiennent les résponsabilités dans tous les partis de facon générale, et . . . la 'classe politique' africaine tend à se recruter dans les mêmes catégories."[3] Data from British and Belgian Africa confirm the wider generality of this conclusion. Elsewhere, I have described this group as a nationalist middle class.[4]

In stricter terms of class analysis, this group is a nonproprietary, petty bourgeoisie dependent on its white collar skills and training for its status. The group includes the lower-level civil servants, the primary school teachers, journalists, veterinarians, male nurses, civil servants, clerks in private businesses, and labor union officials who constituted the new elite that emerged in Africa after the Second World War. In the more economically advanced countries, literate petty traders and market middlemen might also be included. They are usually men with some secondary education, but only the rare leader has gone beyond that level. Most of them combined both rural and urban experience; born in rural areas, they came to the city for education or employment and then were usually posted about to several different rural areas in the early course of their careers. Although their standard of living was higher than that of any simple peasant, their life patterns were not so far removed that they were unapproachable. In the course of their daily jobs they came into contact with—and rendered services for—a wide variety of the African population. As the colonial governments came to emphasize rural development and to extend social services to the population in the early postwar years, they did so through the intermediary of the nationalist middle class. The crucial and frustrating nature of their intermediary position between the foreign ruling elite and the local masses led them both into political activity and into a strong sense of their identity as a group.

The nationalist middle class did not account for all the elite positions in the Africa of the middle years of the century. To achieve its dominant position it had to win out against primarily rural traditional leaders with an appeal based on ethnic particularism (and often an early record of close collaboration with the colonial authorities), and sometimes against an older African bourgeoisie, centered in the capital city, and occupying the liberal professions and often strategic economic points connecting the European trading companies with the retail network in the interior. The winners had to eliminate their opponents (or incorporate some of the more cooperative ones as junior partners) through a combination of electoral and agitational activities with the linked goals of convincing the colonial powers that independence should come quickly and that they were the obvious spokesmen with whom to negotiate the transition. The transmutation of leaders like Nkrumah, Kaunda, Kenyatta, M'ba, and Houphouët-Boigny from prisoners or hunted criminals into reputable nationalist spokesmen dramatically signalized this group's acceptance by the colonial powers.

The nationalist middle class's success in the years leading up to independence reflected the political strengths their strategic social position gave them. These strengths may be summarized as follows. Above all, they were political men; they had political experience, a consciousness of themselves as a legitimate political group, and they were politically hungry. They needed political office if they were to rise above their lower middle class station in life. The alternative to office was a marginal and insecure existence. To attain office they had been forced to build political organizations more or less from the ground up, to unite important segments of urban and rural populations of many different ethnic backgrounds, and to remain close enough to a variety of people to understand their grievances and exploit them to political ends. The rules of electoral competition established in the terminal phases of the colonial era had made the capture of a majority in the colonial territorial legislature the key to power. Thus they had been obliged to fight electoral battles over the whole territory and, where they could not defeat a local or ethnic hero, try to incorporate him or someone like him into their party.

Audrey Richards may overstate the case somewhat when she says "African politicians . . . knew they would not be granted independence unless they solved their ethnic differences," but certainly a decent start on the problem, which at least produced agreement among some politicians of the principal ethnic groups, had to be demonstrated.[5] The politicians' modern skills and freedom as a group from strong identification with a particular ethnic or regional base, allowed them to amalgamate people of similar background from most areas of the country. Although the political organization might lack depth and be forced to make a variety of tactical compromises with other elites in many odd corners of the territory, it was capable of mobilizing support for short term tasks, such as elections and demonstrations, and of distributing rewards of office widely enough to build increasing support. In addition, most such parties succeeded in developing a single leader capable of exercising widespread appeal, a process generally helped out by the colonial power's preference for dealing with a single strong individual and for building up, consciously or not, his individual status and political resources.

These very strengths implied certain weaknesses. The nationalist middle class politicians were unable to call on traditional symbols of support, unlike many of their opponents. If they did, they were all too likely to be outbid on such grounds by real traditional authorities who could manipulate such particularistic symbols more effectively than could the nationalists. Second, the nationalists had no solid base in the economic sphere. These men were clerks, not entrepreneurs, and they neither controlled nor understood the intricacies of either the international trading circuits (which might account for up to eighty percent of a territory's monetized trade) or the principal domestic production or trading activities. Such activities were in the hands principally of Europeans, though, particularly in the more developed countries, an African old bourgeoisie might play a considerable role at least in the domestic trading circuits. Such Africans, like the traditional leaders, constituted natural opponents for the nationalist middle class, and the latter's domestic victory was generally at the expense of parties supported by traditional and bourgeois groups. A third weakness of the nationalists, though not one that was politically important before independence, was their lack of technical and administrative training. These men were politicians, not administrators, and while some politicians can become good administrators, most need a reliable technocratic backup if they are to succeed. Finally, at the time of independence, the nationalist middle class as a whole had few connections beyond the borders of their own territory. A few leaders during student days had established personal friendships (and a few animosities) with foreign Africans of similar background, some of whom subsequently became prominent in nationalist movements in their own territories. In the case of the French territories, contacts were much more extensive and explicitly political, as nationalist parties from the different West and Equatorial African countries united in coalitions both at the level of the French Assemblies and at the level of the two federal parliaments in Dakar and Brazzaville. Even here, however, contacts were limited to a few individuals, and strong interterritorial political party structures never developed, much rhetoric to the contrary notwithstanding. Extra-African contacts were almost exclusively with the metropolitan country.

Part of the object of independence negotiations for both sides was to

WILLIAM J. FOLTZ [365]

bolster the strengths and allay the weaknesses of the inheriting elite. With surprisingly few exceptions, once the colonial authorities decided, however reluctantly, that they had found their spokesman, they tried to assure that these men would inherit structures that would permit them to control their territory, often to the accompaniment of outraged opposition cries that the colonial authorities had sold them down the river and betrayed ancient guarantees. Where the colonial authorities did not go far enough, there was little to stop the new regime from altering or reinterpreting the constitution to fit its strengths and weaknesses once it was in power.

The boundary rules of the nationalist order reflect the nationalist middle class's strengths and weaknesses. Internally, centralization and the removal of regional levels of power undercut the territorially limited political advantages of traditional leaders and some of the urban political machines dominated by the old bourgeoisie. It maximized the advantages of an elite without strong ethnic ties which could be posted anywhere within the national territory. By strongly opposing the conversion of traditional social status or of economic resources into political resources, the nationalists again limited the ability of their African opponents to mount a challenge to which the nationalists could respond only at a distinct disadvantage. By enforcing a tight external border they sought to assure that they would control resources brought in from the outside, whether those resources be economic or technical assistance, or political support.

These decisions were formalized most commonly in more or less explicit ideologies advancing the legitimacy of the single—party state and of some variant of African socialism. These ideologies should not be seen in classic "left-right" terms; the distinction between those states hewing to some explicitly socialist policy and those favoring a more capitalist mode of development rather concerns alternate means of achieving similar ends of political control. This control aim is self-evident in the case of African socialist regimes, where the socialism has the political effect of bringing economic decisions under the control of a political elite and preventing the growth of an independent African economic elite which could mobilize its economic resources for independent political purposes. Similar goals are achieved, however, in countries practicing a capitalist "open door" policy, such as Ivory Coast and Liberia. Both of these single-party regimes have maintained strict political control over the economic sector by preferring to leave major entrepreneurial activities to foreign capitalists, operating through explicit agreements with the national government and dependent on that government's forebearance. At the same time they have confined the economic activities of their own nationals to public sector roles or to private sector activities which are either heavily dependent on government licensing and patronage, or, as in the case of those worthies appointed to the directing boards of foreign capitalist enterprises, directly resultant from the political credit one enjoys with the regime. The result in these cases has been "capitalism without entrepreneurs" and "growth without development," prices the regimes have been willing to pay in exchange for continued political control.[6]

If one compares a single-party socialist regime like Guinea with its two neighbors just mentioned, one finds that the government has moved vigorously, and at high economic and human cost, to expropriate the indigenous African traders and bring their sophisticated trading networks under nationalist middle class direction through the creation of state trading companies.[7] At the same time Guinea has signed agreements allowing foreign companies to exploit its principal economic resources, the bauxite deposits. The form is different in each of these cases, but the reality of domestic political control is essentially the same.

Such boundary rules were not established without internal opposition. Where substantial economic elites existed within the African country, they had to be defeated in electoral competition before independence, and then expropriated or bought off by the nationalists. This was, however, perhaps the easiest of the decisions to impose, since the government had the resources to incorporate those economic elites who could prove their loyalty, and then to make them continuously dependent on government patronage for the continuance of their activities.

The imposition of centralization occasioned perhaps the most intense battles in the periods just before and after independence. The conflict in Ghana between Nkrumah's Convention People's Party and its opponents, the United Gold Coast Convention and the National Liberation Movement, centered around the issue of decentralization, and behind it the power that should be given to purely local elites in both rural and urban areas, the opposition parties' leaderships being coalitions of such elites, both traditional and bourgeois.[8] Although the Ghana case is the best documented one in West Africa, no West African state, except possibly Liberia, escaped this same conflict in one form or another.

Although traditional elites as such were not at issue, Kenya produced an East African variant of the same conflict in the dispute between the nationalist middle class politicians of the dominant KANU party, which was based on an alliance of the largest and best educated groups, against the opposition nationalist politicians of KADU, a party based on a defensive alliance of the smaller and peripheral groups. This conflict, which broke into the open during the final transition to independence, reflected the disunity of the nationalist movement caused basically by a colonial policy for too long oriented toward settler interests, and directly by the prohibition of formal African political activity during the "Mau Mau" emergency. KANU accepted a governmental structure giving strong powers at the regional level "as the price of independence, and the KANU Government abolished it as soon as they were politically able."[9] Proceeding as other nationalists did before independence, Kenyatta pressured opposing regional leaders into the governing party, with due attention to their local patronage interests so long as they did not undermine the centralizing policies of the government itself. The legacy of a "frustrated territorial nationalism" was not so easily overcome, however, and the government leaders found themselves increasingly obliged to transfer political power from the party to the civil service. This "was the centralizing agency that the new Executive needed. Not surprisingly they used it."[10]

A direct ethnic challenge to the centralization rule came in Uganda, where the largest ethnic group, the Buganda, was also the most educated and supplied with strong traditional political institutions under the leadership of Kabaka Edward Mutesa. It was a cardinal element of British policy after World War II to keep Buganda within Uganda; the implementation of this policy led to the temporary exiling of the Kabaka in 1953 by the British governor. The overriding task of the nationalist leaders of the central government came to be the removal of the Kabaka and the destruction of Buganda internal autonomy, something accomplished in 1966 only by armed force and considerable bloodshed.[11] The situation of the Barotse in neighboring Zambia is analogous in many points, though the Barotse possessed nowhere near the concentration of modern skills and institutional strength to carry out such fierce resistance to the nationalists' centralizing desires.[12]

Other countries, mainland Tanzania is a good example, have been fortunate in not having large and strong ethnic particularisms to contend with, though even here among the three most economically and educationally advantaged ethnic groups "some tendencies toward autonomy from central control have emerged," and have provoked strong central government responses.[13]

The essential point here is not that there is anything unusual or anachronistic about such local political opposition, but that the widespread success with which it has been overridden—often at high cost—is quite unusual. Although centralization of decision-making has its logic in Africa, so too does decentralization, as W. Arthur Lewis has quite neatly demonstrated.[14] That so many African nationalist regimes have not been interested in seeking the economic benefits that Lewis and others claim can result from wise decentralization of decision-making suggests again that the issue is perceived at heart as political, not economic.

FEDERATION

The issue of federation provided the greatest challenge to the centralization rule, a challenge reinforced by the ambiguities inherent in the rule stressing the desirability of bureaucratic continuity. Since some colonial bureaucracies operated at several different levels of geographic inclusiveness, the boundary choice was not always obvious. In general, when the bureaucratic legacy was ambiguous, the decisive factor was the level of African political organization. Except where the African politicians themselves were divided on the question, the attitude of the colonial power was not the decisive factor.

The complexity was greatest in the case of the French West and French Equatorial African territories.[15] In these areas, colonial administration and, to some extent, political organization had taken place on both the territorial and federal levels. From about 1950 on, African politicians, all of them dependent on territorially based political organizations, used the issue of federation as a major weapon in their contest for political advantage at the territorial level. Since political office and influence at the supraterritorial level depended on political success at the territorial level, no politician could afford to take chances with his territorial political base. Those political organizations which brought together politicians from the different territories in the two federal assemblies and in the preindependence assemblies in Paris never developed beyond the stage of being temporary alliances of territorially based political parties. By deciding in 1956 to devolve executive authority to African governments at the territorial rather than the federal level, the French supported the desires of the strongest African politician from the richest territory, Félix Houphouët-Boigny of the Ivory Coast, and there can be no doubt that French and Ivoirian influence told heavily in the decision of some of the smaller and politically ill-organized territories to stay out of federal arrangements. Still, De Gaulle's formal acceptance of the federal union of Senegal and the French Soudan showed that French preferences were not decisive when strong African politicians chose independence in larger units. The failure of the Mali Federation of Senegal and Soudan was caused not by French pressure, but by the conclusion of the Senegalese leaders that the federal arrangements did not protect their personal territorial base against Senegalese oppositionists able to call in Soudanese as political allies.

Similar political considerations led the Union of Central African Republics to be stillborn, despite initial agreement of the Chad, Central African Republic, and Congo (Brazzaville) national assemblies to cede foreign policy and defense powers to a central confederal organ. A broader Central African States Customs Union (UDEAC), which included Gabon and Cameroun as well, fared better, but was in turn disrupted by Congo (Kinshasa) pressure which in 1969 led the Central African Republic and Chad to join with Kinshasa in a Central African States Union, which itself subsequently fell apart.[16]

In British East and Central Africa the shifting attitudes of African nationalists toward federal arrangements reflected tactically their overriding priorities of attaining independence from colonial and white settler domination and safeguarding their control over their own political bases. In this their calculations mirrored those made earlier by the settlers whose attitudes toward federal arrangements were no less dominated by considerations of avoiding foreign interference and assuring their own local political power.[17]

A sporadic political issue since World War I, the Central African Federation grouping Northern Rhodesia, Southern Rhodesia, and Nyasaland (later to become Zambia, Rhodesia, and Malawi) was established in 1953 as "a bargain between two sides, Britain and the colonists."[18] The Federation was opposed resolutely by the Africans of Nyasaland, a territory with negligible settler interests and the clearest prospect of someday enjoying African political control. However, "many Northern Rhodesian Africans resented [Nyasaland nationalist Hastings] Banda's attempt to take Nyasaland out of the Federation, since it would weaken the overall balance of black against white." The Southern Rhodesian Congress, representing Africans in the territory with the strongest settler population, "was even anxious to maintain Federation."[19] Once Nyasaland was clearly on the road to independence, and Kenneth Kaunda had consolidated a clear nationalist supremacy in Northern Rhodesia, the Federation's fate was sealed, leaving Southern Rhodesian Africans under an increasingly harsh settler dictatorship and Britain with painful responsibilities it had vainly sought to slough off through its earlier support of federation.

By contrast, in East Africa, white settler influence was no longer the dominant issue by the time of independence. Despite considerable popular enthusiasm for the idea of federal unity in 1963, and an unequivocally worded commitment on the part of the political leaders of Uganda, Kenya, and Tanganyika to achieve "a political federation of East Africa" which received public support from the British secretary of state for colonies, the federal idea foundered within the year on the realities of territorial politics.[20] Kenyatta, Nyerere, and Obote all came to see the federation as a threat to the consolidation of the centralized regime he felt he needed at home. In Uganda, Obote was put in a position where it would have been hard to resist Buganda claims to join as a unit separate from the rest of Uganda. In Kenya, federation was roundly welcomed by the opposition KADU politicians as a way of assuring subterritorial regional powers against the greater threat of a KANU dominated territorial government. This welcome quickly chilled the dominant party's enthusiasm for the project.[21] In Tanganyika, TANU's apparently strong political position and Nyerere's confidence were shaken by the January 1964 army mutiny which had to be put down by British troops, and the government was only too glad to conserve its political energies for the task of reorganizing its own house. This task included establishing a weak confederal relationship with revolutionary Zanzibar, which effectively insulated each side's domestic and, to some degree, foreign politics from its partners. It was not until 1967 that agreement among the governments of Nairobi, Lusaka, and Dar-es-Salaam was attained, and then for a purely economic union, the institutional core of which was the continuation of the colonial administration's common services. The text of the Treaty for East African Co-operation makes no mention of any hope for political union, and indeed avoids reference to politics in any form.[22]

The two most difficult and complex challenges to the nationalist order came in Nigeria and in the Congo (Leopoldville), now the Republic of Zaire. Space does not permit even the sketchiest review of these countries' political peripeties, but within the framework elaborated above we can show that conditions prevented the establishment of centralized nationalist political states, despite behavior on the part of politicians that was consistent with that of their colleagues in other African states. Almost sufficient unto themselves as explanatory conditions are the sheer size and human diversity of the two countries, each of which contained ethnic groups larger than the total population of many neighboring states. Furthermore, for different reasons and in quite different ways, both colonial regimes failed to provide administrative and political conditions allowing a territorywide nationalist movement to flourish and build broad support during the postwar years.

As is well known, Nigeria had been the prize example of Britain's indirect rule policy which reinforced—and in some cases created—ethnic political authorities, the most powerful and extensive of which were the Hausa-Fulani emirates who came to control the government of the Northern Region.[23] When, in the early 1950s, the British formally began the decolonization process, it was established "as an axiom of British policy that Nigeria must be kept united, even if this meant concessions to the North.[24] The concessions took the form of entrenchment of regional powers in a federal governing structure, with the practical political result that control over one of the three regions became the price of maintaining influence at the center.[25] Since each of the regions could be dominated by a single ethnic group, ethnicity was intimately linked to political party development. Instead of promoting a concentration of power and political resources at the center, which would encourage the formation of trans-ethnic links at the elite level, the British approach of unity-through-regional-concessions produced a bargaining standoff relationship whose stability would be threatened by any increase of power at the federal center. The Northern politicians' use of federal powers to control the Eastern Region after 1962 was perceived as a direct threat by Eastern Region interests, which saw themselves condemned to a permanent minority position, and produced the beginnings of a defensive reaction akin to that of the Senegalese leaders under the Mali Federation. In the Nigerian case, however, direct action was taken by military officers, not civilian politicians, with quite different long-term consequences.

Throughout most of its history, the Belgian Congo had been subjected to a "centralizing and uniform system of administration," though until 1933 Katanga had enjoyed something of a semiautonomous status.[26] However, "the central institutions devised by the Belgians were . . . for all intents and purposes, a monopoly of the European administration."[27] The Belgians neither permitted African participation in the administration of a paternalist administrative state, nor followed policies which would encourage the development of loyalties either to the Congo as a political or sentimental unit, or to intermediate political structures which themselves were so committed for clear self-interest reasons. Among the political parties, whose open activity was not allowed until 1958, only the Lumumbist branch of the Mouvement National Congolais, attempted seriously to build a national constituency, but both time and the necessary degree of administrative forebearance were lacking. The administrative and military collapse at independence confirmed Belgian inclinations to rescue the essential—Katanga—but secession only exacerbated the chaos and made the Congo the seat of many-sided foreign interventions reflecting cold-war exploitation of Congolese political fragmentation. As Benoit Verhaegen has argued, however, it is quite possible that a centralized nationalist order might have emerged out of postindependence conflict had United Nations and other's interventions not transformed the political situation so drastically.[28]

Despite their many contextual differences, the African political processes in Nigeria and the Congo were both characterized by political groups' search for a solid political base which they could safely control. Within their boundaries, decision-making calculations were similar to those of nationalist middle class politicians in other African countries. Depending on the circumstances in which they found themselves, different political leaders sought political power and security at the regional or territorial level. Thus in Nigeria, Nnamdi Azikiwe and most Ibo leaders moved from strong support for centralized unity to regional secession, while Obafemi Awolowo, a Yoruba, abandoned championship of regionalism in favor of reinforcing central powers. In the Congo, Moise Tshombé, from being the leader of the Katanga secession, attempted to become the apostle of a new Congolese unity. Each of these successive positions may be seen as a political response to a changing balance of structural constraints and opportunities under situations of high uncertainty. Without a relevant colonial tradition of political domination from the center, ethnic and economic interests more easily penetrated the political sector. Unable to mobilize the power of the state, the politicians found the one-way boundary crossing rule difficult to maintain. Once order broke down and the existence of the state was seriously called into question, different political groups were able to call in different outside allies in their attempts to restructure the domestic political balance—at least locally—in their favor. In the end, military-led regimes forced a centralizing solution on both countries, essentially doing what the politicians had been unable to do.

PAN-AFRICANISM

If federalism provided the most difficult conditions for bringing the nationalist order into being, the greatest intellectual challenge has come from the body of ideas summed up in the term "pan-Africanism." Like the other positions we have discussed, pan-Africanism has a strong political and economic logic to it, and in certain quarters at least, even a stronger emotional appeal. Like the other positions, however, it is subject to basic political constraints which no amount of intellectual generosity has overcome. Historically, pan-Africanism has been a movement of people out of power who have sought through a new and larger territorial unit to find the allies and organizational advantage that others have found on the regional or territorial levels. In the decade following World War II pan-Africanism was espoused by many politicians, who later became staunch territorial centralizers, because the apparent strength that would come from unity seemed a good way to force political concessions from the colonial powers, and for the laggard territories to ride the independence coattails of the more advanced. Since the late 1950s, pan-Africanism has been most strongly espoused by exile movements in search of allies from governments opposed to their own nations and by disaffected students and other opposition elements, particularly those abroad. In the case of students and other intellectuals, pan-Africanism has appeared as a powerful slogan to be used against nationalist regimes at home which could be portrayed as selling out a larger African patrimony in exchange for a small-scale, territorial fiefdom.[29]

The great exception to the above generalization was Kwame Nkrumah who stood, until his overthrow in 1966, as the symbol and rallying point for those Africans willing to fight for continentwide political integration. Paradoxically, however, Nkrumah's pan-Africanist initiatives had the effect of diminishing African interterritorial political integration, and among the opposition groups he supported were those working to break up existing large-scale states. Not only did he succeed in alienating the leaders of all the West African states surrounding his own, including those of Guinea and Mali with which Ghana was linked in a paper Union of African States, but he denounced the 1964 East African attempt at political union and supported separatist movements in Nigeria and the Congo on the principle that only after their "neo-colonialist" governments were overthrown could true pan-Africanism be advanced.[30] At home his government refused citizenship to Africans—including those born in Ghana—who did not come from indigenous Ghanaian ethnic groups and deported many leaders of "foreign" African ethnic communities on allegations they were interfering in Ghanaian politics.[31] One need not doubt the sincerity of Nkrumah's commitment to political pan-Africanism to recognize that his policies had divisive, indeed negative effects for his cause.

Nkrumah was unquestionably playing a complex political game in which his Ghanaian base was to be the solid political springboard to launch him to a position of leadership of the whole African continent. At the same time, his actions on the pan-African, and worldwide stage were expected to reinforce his prestige and leadership at home. Their effect, as we know, was the contrary, to divert him from the careful cultivation of his domestic political garden and to leave him a "not-unfeared, half-welcome guest" in Sékou Touré's rigorously nationalist Guinea. Since his fall, no established African political leader has sought to espouse Nkrumah's pan-African approach.

The African leaders' alternative to Nkrumahist pan-Africanism has been the Organization of African Unity whose Charter explicitly disavows any derogation of state sovereignty or existing borders. With a weak secretariat, the OAU's effective operating agency is the plenary meeting of chiefs of state or their personal delegates. In the most difficult cases to come before it, the OAU has refused to accept border alterations either in the sense of splitting up a large unit (by recognizing the Biafran claims) or of reuniting a divided ethnic group (by recognizing the Somali claims against Ethiopia and Kenya).[32] As Nkrumah warned, the OAU has become the most effective international spokesman for the African nationalist boundary order, as much through its reinforcement of the central political position of the chief of state as through the protection of external border lines.

THE FUTURE?

This chapter has argued that the dominant boundary decisions in Tropical Africa have been the product of a particular political process characterized by the rise to power of a nationalist elite in the context of political negotiations for independence with a colonial power. If this is at least partially right, we may expect that major changes in the political process and particularly in the governing requirements of elites dominating politics might bring an alteration in the nationalist boundary rule. Even where dramatic changes have taken place it would be unlikely that boundary rules would rapidly be altered; lag, inertia, and accommodation are too conspicuously parts of boundary-related behavior. To ignore the possibilities of change would, however, seem equally unwise. As the titles and subtitles of too many books remind us, Africa is in "transition." But in transition towards what?

The years since independence have seen the emergence of two powerful new elite groups, and there are signs that two others may be developing in a few countries. The first of these groups is a university educated new intelligentsia with a strong technocratic orientation. The expansion of higher education, and the politicians' need for competent administrators to fill the bureaucratic positions established by the nationalists' centrally directed economic activities have given this group a powerful corporate identity and access to major positions of power in the state apparatus. The second group is, of course, the military. Also technocratic in its orientation, its rise to power has most often helped to advance the careers and group interests of the civilian technocrats at the expense of the nationalists. The third group, most likely to be a force in potentially rich states like Ghana, Ivory Coast, Kenya, Zambia, Nigeria, and Zaire, would be a capitalist entrepreneurial class powerful and secure enough to operate independently of constant central government control. I do not think such a class has anywhere yet emerged to a politically significant extent, but the possibility cannot be discounted. Finally, one must consider the possibility that revolutionary groups may seize power, both in states still under white control and in existing African ruled countries.

So far, the military and civilian technocrats have formed a powerful alliance in several African states. They have emphasized a development-oriented centralization of power which has, in effect, tried to carry out and perfect the work of the nationlists. Mobutu's Zaire is perhaps the best illustration of this, but the same tendencies have been apparent in such different military regimes as those of Upper Volta, the Central African Republic, Nigeria, and Mali.[33] All have reinforced the nationalist approach to nation-building through first building the state apparatus, and some of the new military leaders have attempted to assume the national hero position of the nationalist political leader. Mobutu's emphasis on donning the Lumumba mantle is the most obvious example.

At the same time military rule contains the possibility that decentralizing forces will win out in the form of regional warlordism. Particularly in the larger states with dispersed armies and poor communications, the temptations of regional warlord rule may be hard for ambitious junior commanders to resist. In its "Congo" phase, Zaire has already had considerable taste of such rule, and Nigeria seems far from assured that the powerful forces of ethnic regionalism will not once again find their expression in military-led secession. Indeed, had the Biafran military been willing to settle for less than independence, some such solution could have been implemented within the framework of the Aburi agreements.[34] It is also quite possible that Ethiopia will revert to an earlier regional warlord heritage, following the death of that unusually successful centralizer and pillar of the OAU, Haile Selassie. The strongest opposition to such regionalism may well arise from the civilian technocrats who value the greater adherence to bureaucratic norms and freedom from warlord whims inherent in a single, centralized regime. The degree of civilian influence in military bureaucratic regimes may thus become an important determinant of centralization's survival.

In the economically more advanced states the growth of a powerful entrepreneurial group could raise political pressures for increased decentralization and reduce the dominance of the political sector and its insulation from penetration by economic elites. There have certainly been important links between African economic and political elites in Nigeria, the Ivory Coast, and, more recently, Kenya, although in each case it has been the political sector which has provided the essential security for success in the economic sector, not the reverse.[35] Overall, the economic elites have accepted the politicians' view of the national state and its boundary rules, because so far they have had little power to alter them.

At the present time African businesses are small-scale operations, the vast majority of them local, or at most regional in scope, and mostly organized either in the capital or in the home area of the owner.[36] The larger operations are primarily para-statal corporations, with or without non-African participation, and are heavily dependent on government participation, protection, and/or personnel. The expansion of these larger operations are unlikely to affect political boundaries except as they erase the distinction between entrepreneur and civil servant and increase the political weight of such a group at the center of government decision-making. The proliferation of successful small-scale and local entrepreneurs, inevitably concentrated in a limited number of relatively wealthy areas, is likely to produce increased pressures for decentralization of decision-making. The success of such pressures will depend on the degree to which such men can come to dominate the political sector and use it to counteract the centralizing tendencies of the civil servants, allied with the para-statal bureaucracy. Since such regionalist attempts will most likely resurrect the specter of ethnicity, they will meet with strong opposition from those who must rule from the center.

The strong external border policy of the nationalists is likely to be retained by any military or civilian technocratic government, since no more than their predecessors will they wish to yield control over the admission of foreign resources to those outside the center. There is no reason to think that contacts with the outside world will decline with such changes in regime; indeed, the military may well increase its agreements with non-African powers for the purchase of arms and training provisions, but these are central government decisions. Local African entrepreneurs may possibly provide a challenge to the strong external boundary policy if they are able to establish links with multinational corporations. While such organizations have so far operated through central government licensing, and generally through centrally controlled African subsidiaries, an increase in the domestic power of African entrepreneurial elites may create pressures for direct contact and exchange of resources between African firm and parent company that would by-pass central government control.[37]

Changes in African regimes are likely to have considerable effect on boundary relations with other African states, particularly on the expansion and combination of existing states. Civilian technocrats will increasingly possess the skills to function effectively in joint organizations operating at the supranational level, and as their numbers and group influence rise, one might expect them to place more and more stress on the expansion of the spheres of activity and of the decision-making powers of secretariats of organizations like the East African Community, OCAM, various OAU organs, and so forth. The acquisition of power by inter-African secretariats will be no easy task, however, since national politicians and some bureaucrats will rightly perceive a threat to their own prerogatives and routines.[38] Part of the attraction of such expansion, however, would be that it would provide yet another level of elite bureaucratic jobs, and one reasonably free from constant intervention by political leaders, be they civilian or military. At the same time, technocrats are likely to be much less enthusiastic about pan-Africanist mergers of existing governments which just consolidate governmental structures and do not superimpose a new layer of jobs. Civil servants anywhere can be notorious foot-draggers when it comes to planning the elimination of their own jobs, and mergers negotiated between equals are not likely to receive their enthusiastic cooperation. Clearly unequal mergers, peacefully negotiated or not, in which one side in effect takes over the other, are more likely to be welcomed by the dominant side's technocrats.

On the basis of the scanty evidence available it is difficult to foresee that the triumph of any of the existing revolutionary movements in Africa would bring about major changes in the political boundary rules of the nationalist order, though they may succeed in splitting off part of an existing unit. Where such movements represent ethnic or regional secessionist forces, as in northern Chad, Eritrea, or Southern Sudan, they are likely to hew with even greater determination to the nationalist order within their secessionist states than do the present rulers of those areas, if only to protect their independence and conciliate the different ethnic groups contained within them. Nor is there much reason to suspect that those trying to promote revolution in existing African-ruled states would change boundary rules, whatever else they might do. Zanzibar and the organization of the Congolese rebel areas in 1964-1965 are the two experiences tropical Africa has had of revolutionary territorial organization. Zanzibar, despite its nominal link with mainland Tanzania, has followed the nationalist order, and the Congolese rebels produced a jerry-rigged replication of Congolese central bureaucratic institutions, just as, in their social characteristics, the rebels most closely resembled those against whom they were fighting.[39]

Nor does there seem to be a basis for expecting different results in the eventuality that any existing revolutionary movements succeed in ousting any of the remaining white-led regimes of Africa. With the signal exception of the PAIGC in Guiné-Bissao (Portuguese Guinea), the existing divisions between the revolutionary nationalist movements and the strength of the regimes against which they are fighting mean that success would be dependent on so many intervening contingencies that guesswork is bootless. The PAIGC, for its part, hews very closely to the dominant African nationalist pattern. Despite active international search for allies and assistence, and the occasional use of pan-Africanist appeals, none of these revolutionary movements has established or seems likely to establish firm trans-national ties. As J. Bowyer Bell concludes from his study of such movements,

> very few [African revolutionary groups] foresee the transformation of the existing African state system by revolution and so most prime loyalties are to the national party or the inchoate nation-state. . . . Every revolutionary organization aspires to eliminate the necessity for most "revolutionary" transnational contacts as rapidly as possible and to begin acting as a normal, if militant, government.[40]

As we have seen, militancy does not of itself alter political boundary rules.

The military must be at the center of speculations about inter-African cooperation or national expansion. On the basis of the way military leaders and organizations have behaved elsewhere, one can hazard the prediction that African military leaders are likely to be very unenthusiastic about the construction of new federations or larger unitary states on the basis of negotiated equality between partners. African armies are hard enough to hold together against the pulls of interservice and interrank rivalries, and the merger of national armies, even in the cause of joint military victory, is a notoriously difficult task requiring more political than military skills. This does not mean that military leaders will oppose all larger-scale enterprises. Supranational technical and economic cooperation which does not involve political merger would not seem to have any particular disadvantages, and might appear to military leaders (as it has to their nationalist predecessors) as a convenient way of politely easing inconvenient or incompetent civilian or military technocrats out of their central government positions and into a safely distant and politically irrelevant international body.

The great question is whether or not the military will use its armed power to produce larger political units through the time-honored means of conquest. Looked at from a broad historical perspective, and with attention to the growing military capabilities of armies like the Nigerian and Zairois, such conquest attempts seem unlikely not to come. At present, it would presumably be unthinkable for an independent African state to invade another one that was in good standing within the OAU. With the exception of Amin's Uganda, African military regimes have so far been at least as peacefully inclined as their predecessors toward their African neighbors. But there are other possibilities. In 1971 General Gowon told the OAU that he thought the African states ought to pledge themselves to liberate one African territory from colonialism within the next three years, and implied that the 200,000 man Nigerian army was ready to play a major role in the task.[41] The motives of such an expedition would be impeccably in line with the expressed policies of the OAU, and any success might be expected to bring OAU blessings, and conceivably such formal transitional arrangements as an OAU-sponsored trusteeship until such time as the inhabitants express their will as to their political future. The most obvious candidate for such attention would be Guiné-Bissao, where nationalist forces have denied Portuguese troops free access to substantial amounts of territory. Were Guiné to receive such attention, the PAIGC could quite probably organize a nationalist government, thank the troops, and send them home. But would that be the case in situations where the indigenous nationalists are badly split or fall into disastrous squabbles while the liberating army is still present? [42]

And might not a militant military regime extend the duty of liberation from colonialist to neighboring neo-colonialist regimes? Nkrumah's militant civilian regime engaged unsuccessfully in several such attempts by training and sending out guerillas. Adventurous military regimes are less likely to rely on irregular troops, which threaten established chains of command, and more likely to commit their own forces. Such a commitment could be initiated either by a Napoleonic chief of state or by a less secure general who felt threatened by restless junior officers, eager for glory and a chance to try their skills.

At this point one can only speculate about the possibility of such outcomes, and everyone is free to build his own scenarios, happy or gloomy as he chooses. It is apparent, however, that possibilities exist for substantial transformations in the nationalist order, particularly as economic and military differentials increase between countries, and between regions within countries. The analysis suggests, in sum, that in the attempt to understand how African nations are built and rebuilt, one might start by asking the old Leninist question, "Who-Whom?" Despite the rigidities introduced by the international system and by domestic institutional inertia, the structure of political boundaries in these new states is ultimately dependent on the groups that control such states, or significant parts of them, and on the specific characteristics and powers of those groups. At the same time one must foresee that within a situation of group political competition several secular processes are likely to be at work which will shift the balance of political advantage over time, and therewith contribute to structural change. The spread of education and the development of economic skills and resources are among the most important internal processes, simply because they will produce more individuals equipped with personal and political resources to challenge incumbents and aware enough of new group interests to be motivated to do so.

Finally, looking at newer elite groups, we have suggested that military and civilian technocrats will have sometimes mutual and sometimes conflicting interests in changing existing political boundary rules, and that leaders of large military organizations in particular may be drawn into making dramatic changes. Over time, the growth of independent African entrepreneurial elites may lead to changes both in the internal distribution of power and in the pattern of involvement of non-African interests in African countries. Finally, the success of the various indigenous revolutionary groups is unlikely to produce changes in Africa's dominant boundary rules, whatever important changes they may make in the lives of the people directly concerned, unless they come to power on the basis of military conquest by another African state's army. This increasingly real possibility could begin a process capable of substantially altering existing political boundaries and transforming the relationships among all African states.

NOTES

1. See Zdenek Cervenka, The Organisation of African Unity and its Charter, London, C. Hurst, 1969.

2. Such use of the external world for domestic political purposes may be particularly prevalent in newer and less-developed nations, but it is certainly not absent from great power practice, as witnessed by the "consultations" between British aspirants for the prime ministership and the American president before a British election; or the ritual fact-finding tours of American political candidates to Ireland, Israel, Italy, and increasingly Africa; or any nation's manipulation of foreign threats or obligations as a means of producing popular unity behind a set of national leaders.

3. Jean-Louis Seurin, "Elites sociales et partis politiques d'AOF," Annales Africaines, Dakar, 1958, p. 137.

4. William J. Foltz, "Political Opposition in Single-Party States of Tropical Africa," in Robert A. Dahl (ed.) Regimes and Oppositions, New Haven, Yale University Press, 1972. The following four paragraphs are based substantially on the arguments developed in this article.

5. Audrey I. Richards, The Multicultural States of East Africa, Montreal, McGill-Queen's University Press, 1969, p. 33.

6. On the Ivory Coast, see Samir Amin, Le Développement du Capitalisme en Côte d'Ivoire, Paris, Ed. de Minuit, 1965. On Liberia, see J. Gus Liebenow, Liberia, the Evolution of Privilege, Ithaca, Cornell University Press, 1969.

7. Elliot J. Berg, "Socialism and Economic Development in Tropical Africa," Quarterly Journal of Economics, Vol. LXXVIII, November 1964, pp. 549-73.

8. This competition is well covered in Dennis Austin, Politics in Ghana, London, Oxford University Press, 1965.

9. Cherry Gertzel, The Politics of Independent Kenya 1963-68, Nairobi, East African Publishing House, 1970, p. 13.

10. Ibid, p. 29. See also Carl G. Rosberg, Jr. and John Nottingham, The Myth of Mau Mau, London, Pall Mall, 1966, pp. 188-233.

11. On preindependence Uganda, see David E. Apter, The Political Kingdom in Uganda, Princeton, Princeton University Press, 1961. On the conflict between the central government and Buganda, see Ali A. Mazrui, "Privilege and Protest as Integrative Factors: The case of Buganda's Status in Uganda," in Robert I. Rotberg and Ali A. Mazrui (eds.) Protest and Power in Black Africa, London, Oxford University Press, 1970, pp. 1072-2087.

12. Gerald L. Caplan, The Elites of Barotseland 1878-1969: A Political History of Zambia's Western Province, Berkeley, University of California Press, 1970, especially pp. 191-222.

13. Raymond F. Hopkins, Political Roles in a New State: Tanzania's First Decade, New Haven, Yale University Press, 1971, pp. 76-77.

14. W. Arthur Lewis, Politics in West Africa, London, Allen and Unwin, 1965.

15. For a detailed presentation of the argument of this paragraph, see William J. Foltz, From French West Africa to the Mali Federation, New Haven, Yale University Press, 1965.

16. See Colin Legum and John Drysdale, Africa Contemporary Record: Annual Survey and Documents (1968-1969), London, African Research, 1969, pp. 426-27, 782, 784; and Guy de Lusignan, French-Speaking Africa since Independence, New York, Praeger, 1969.

17. See Rosberg and Nottingham, op. cit., p. 221, and A. J. Wills, An Introduction to the History of Central Africa, London, Oxford University Press, 1967 (2nd ed.), pp. 248-49, 260 and passim.

18. Margery Perham, Colonial Sequence 1949-1969, London, Methuen, 1970, p. 209.

19. Wills, op. cit., p. 339. See also Robert I. Rotberg, The Rise of Nationalism in Central Africa, Cambridge, Harvard University Press, 1965, pp. 214-52.

20. "A Declaration of Federation by the Governments of East Africa, June 5, 1963," text in Donald Rothchild (ed.) Politics of Integration: An East African Documentary, Nairobi, East African Publishing House, 1968, pp. 76-78. Rothchild's argument in "From Federation to Neo-Federation," (ibid., 1-15) parallels my own. For a different perspective, which emphasizes conflict between ideology and "national interest," conceived more in economic than in political terms, see Joseph S. Nye, Jr., Pan Africanism and East African Integration, Cambridge, Mass., Harvard University Press, 1965, pp. 175-210.

21. See the exchange between Ronald Ngala, leader of the opposition, and Tom Mboya and J. G. Kiano, speaking for government, in House of Representatives

Debates (Kenya), Official Report, First Session, Vol. 1, June 27, 1963, Cols. 403-30. Text reproduced in Rothchild, op. cit., pp. 79-88.

22. "It shall be the aim of the East African Community to strengthen and regulate the industrial, commercial and other relations of the Partner States to the end that there shall be accelerated, harmonious and balanced development and sustained expansion of economic activities the benefits whereof shall be equitably shared" (Article 2, section 1). The Treaty for East African Co-operation, Nairobi, Government Printer, 1967. Major extracts from the Treaty are reprinted in Rothchild, op. cit., pp. 303-36.

23. Essential standard works on Nigeria include James S. Coleman, Nigeria: Background to Nationalism, Berkeley and Los Angeles, University of California, 1958; John P. Mackintosh, Nigerian Government and Politics, Evanston; Northwestern University Press, 1966; S. K. Panter-Brick (ed.) Nigerian Politics and Military Rule: Prelude to the War, London, Athlone Press, 1969; Richard Sklar, Nigerian Political Parties, Princeton, Princeton University Press, 1963; C. Sylvester Whitaker, Jr., The Politics of Tradition, Continuity and Change in Northern Nigeria, Princeton, Princeton University Press, 1969. The Federation's collapse is well analyzed in James O'Connell, "The Fragility of Stability: The Fall of the Nigerian Federal Government, 1966," in Rotberg and Mazrui, op. cit., pp. 1012-34.

24. Mackintosh, op. cit., p. 425.

25. O'Connell, op. cit., p. 1016: "The revision of the consitution in 1954 that turned Nigeria into a properly federal structure was meant by the politicians to protect their bases of support and their possibilities of patronage."

26. Among the basic books on the Congo, see René Le Marchand, Political Awakening in the Belgian Congo, Berkeley and Los Angeles, University of California Press, 1964 and Crawford Young, Politics in the Congo, Princeton, Princeton University Press, 1965. See also the invaluable annual series Dossiers du CRISP published by the Centre de Recherche et d'Information Socio-Politique in Brussels.

27. Le Marchand, op. cit., p. 74.

28. Benoit Verhaegen, Rebellions au Congo, Vol. I, Brussels, CRISP, 1966, pp. 32-33.

29. For an opposing view, see Immanuel Wallerstein, Africa the Politics of Unity, New York, Random House, 1967, who sees pan-Africanism as a consistent force based on what he terms "the party of movement" and opposed by a variety of conservative forces that have bought out or otherwise won over sometime pan-Africanists to a territorial status quo orientation. In my opinion the argument suffers from the central weakness of neglecting the difference in behavior between those who want and those who have political power.

30. See W. Scott Thompson, Ghana's Foreign Policy 1957-1966, Princeton, Princeton University Press, 1969, especially pp. 305-56.

31. Enid Schildkraut, "Strangers and Local Government in Kumasi," Journal of Modern African Studies, Vol. 8, No. 2, 1969, pp. 263-64.

32. The OAU's role is sensitively analyzed in Berhanykun Andemicael, Political Settlement Among African States—Roles of the United Nations and the Organization of African Unity, United Nations Institute for Training and Research, Research Report, 1972, and Yashpal Tandon, "The Organization of African Unity as an Instrument and Forum of Protest," in Rotberg and Mazrui, op. cit., pp. 1153-84.

33. Jean-Claude Willame, "Politics and Power in Congo Kinshasa," Africa Report, Vol. XVI, No. 1, January 1971, pp. 14-17. On military orientations to political

power see William J. Foltz "Psychanalyse des armees sud-sahariennes," in Revue Francaise d'études politiques africaines, Vol. 14, February 1967, and Eric A. Nordlinger, "Soldiers in Mufti: The Impact of Military Rule upon Economic and Social Change in the Non-Western States," American Political Science Review, Vol. LXIV, No. 4, December 1970, pp. 1131-48. The best full-scale study of an African army in politics in Robin Luckham, The Nigerian Military: A Sociological Analysis of Authority and Revolt 1960-67, Cambridge, Cambridge University Press, 1971.

34. Ralph Uwechue, "La Crise nigériane: Réflexions sur l'échec du Biafra et l'avenir politique du Nigéria," Politique Etrangére, No. 5, 1970, p. 527. See also Luckham, op. cit., pp. 298-325. The relevant sections of the Aburi agreements may be found as Appendix 2 in Luckham, op. cit., pp. 347-55.

35. On Nigeria, see the perceptive essay by James O'Connell, "The Political Class and Economic Growth," in Peter Kilby, (ed.) Industrialization in an Open Economy: Nigeria 1945-1968, Cambridge, Cambridge University Press, 1969, pp. 372-83. On the Ivory Coast, see Amin, op. cit. On Kenya, see Peter Marris and Anthony Somerset, African Business: a Study of Entrepreneurship and Development in Kenya, London, Routledge & Kegan Paul, 1971.

36. For example, see Marris and Somerset, op. cit., pp. 105-51, and John R. Harris, "Nigerian Entrepreneurship in Industry," in Peter Kilby (ed.) Entrepreneurship and Economic Development, New York, Free Press, 1971, pp. 331-55, especially p. 334.

37. The dynamic first secretary general of the Afro-Malagasy Union was quickly eliminated by jealous politicians after he displayed an excès de zèle for his task. See Albert Tevoedjre, Pan-africanism in Action: An account of the UAM, Occasional Paper No. 11, Cambridge, Harvard University Center for International Affairs, 1965; A fine case study of conflict between national and international authorities in Africa is James Magee, "ECA and the Paradox of African Cooperation," International Conciliation, No. 580, November 1970, especially pp. 19-40.

38. The literature on multinational corporations is now voluminous. For a good survey of some political consequences, see Raymond Vernon, "The Multinational Enterprise: Power versus Sovereignty," Foreign Affairs, Vol. 49, No. 4, July 1971, pp. 736-51.

39. On Zanzibar, see the conclusions of Michael F. Lofchie, "The Zanzibari Revolution: African Protest in a Racially Plural Society," in Rotberg and Mazrui, op. cit., pp. 966-67. On the Congo rebels, see Verhaegen, op. cit., and Crawford Young, "Rebellion and the Congo," in Rotberg and Mazrui, op. cit., pp. 969-1011.

40. J. Bowyer Bell "Contemporary Revolutionary Organizations," International Organization, Vol. XXX, No. 3, Summer 1971, pp. 509, 517.

41. See the discussion in West Africa, No. 2832, 24 September 1971, pp. 1101-02.

42. For an overview, see Richard Gibson, African Liberation Movements, London, Oxford University Press, 1972. Peter Enahoro provides an informal African perspective on the liberation movements' internal splits in "Africa's Forgotten Wars," Africa: An International Business, Economic and Political Monthly, No. 7, March 1972, pp. 18-20.

CHAPTER 14

STATE-BUILDING AND NATION-BUILDING
IN WEST AFRICA

Sheldon Gellar

SHELDON GELLAR is Assistant Professor of Political Science at Indiana University, where he is also associated with the International Development Research Center and the African Studies Program. He has carried out extensive research on developmental politics in French-speaking West Africa and is currently engaged in a study of post-colonial dependency relationships in Africa, with particular reference to Senegal.

Models and theories of state-building and nation-building derived largely from Western experiences have influenced a significant part of the literature on development and modernization in the Third World.[1] Although many of these models and theories are in flux, they generally share some of the following common assumptions that orient their approach towards the developing countries.[2] First, they tend to regard the nation-state as the highest form of political development and the political unit most favorable for promoting modernization in the contemporary world.[3] Second, they stress the crucial importance of nation-building and thereby place a high value on strengthening national identities and loyalties as opposed to subnational identities, often assuming that the two are incompatible and in constant conflict.[4] Third, they tend to focus on state-building as the primary instrument for building the nation and promoting modernization, and to stress the importance of national integration and unity as prerequisites for modernization. Fourth, in these models, state-building is frequently associated with the development of a strong unitary state and efficient centralized bureaucracy. Finally, these models and theories regard state-building and nation-building from the perspective of the political elites controlling the center.

In this chapter the author shall examine the applicability to West Africa of some of these models and theories of state-building and nation-building derived largely from Western experiences. In the first section it shall be argued that the tribe-to-nation approach, which characterizes much of the social science literature on political development and modernization in sub-Saharan Africa, is unsatisfactory because it exaggerates the significance of nation-building both as a primary goal of African political elites and as a prerequisite for modernization while ignoring other possible modes of political organization.

The tribe-to-nation approach is further weakened by the fact that it is based on false assumptions concerning precolonial African history and political organization, assumptions that neglect the contemporary relevance of precolonial modes of political organization and behavior for state-building and nation-building. Moreover, in focusing on the nation-to-be, the tribe-to-nation approach diverts attention from examining the more immediate problem of state-building and decolonization.

In the second part of the essay, two alternative approaches are discussed which seem more applicable to West Africa than tribe-to-nation analyses. The first approach is built around the concept of the inheritance situation which focuses attention on the extent to which the colonial experience continues to shape and define the problems of state-building and nation-building in the postcolonial era.[5] The second approach is built around the concept of neo-patrimonialism[6] and stresses the need to look for and incorporate traditional modes and patterns of political behavior into contemporary state-building and nation-building models.

The third and last part of this chapter concludes, on the basis of the West African case, that the current models and theories of state-building and nation-building derived from Western experience and based on unilinear evolutionary stage theories of modernization need considerable revision if they are to remain useful tools for analyzing the complex processes of modernization.

FROM TRIBE TO NATION?

The tribe-to-nation approach to state-building and nation-building in Africa is based largely upon tacit acceptance of dichotomous theories of modernization in which the categories of traditional and modern are regarded as generally mutually exclusive.[7] In some instances, a third category, transitional, is injected to describe an intermediate stage.[8] In the African context, traditional tends to become synonymous with tribe, and modern with nation-state. Given these assumptions, political development as a process then refers to the evolution of African societies from tribe to nation.

Although there is general agreement among historians, social scientists, and contemporary political leaders that the tribe represents a less complex and more primitive unit than the nation-state, it is problematic as to whether tribe and nation should be the central units of analysis in studying the broad processes of modernization in Africa. The tribe-to-nation approach to state-building and nation-building is based on several questionable assumptions: (1) that traditional Africa was and still is primarily organized in tribal units;[9] (2) that traditional African modes and patterns of political organization and behavior have no significant role in resolving the problems of state-building and nation-building in contemporary African states;[10] and (3) that the political elites in power really regard nation-building as a top priority.[11] In the discussion that follows, the author will attempt to demonstrate that the preceding assumptions underlying the tribe-to-nation approach are not valid for West Africa in particular, nor for sub-Saharan Africa in general.

Although the theoretical concern of anthropologists with the tribe has been diminishing in recent years, "tribe" nevertheless has persisted as a descriptive label. It is applied to a wide variety of African peoples and groups with distinctive ethnic, linguistic, and cultural identities.[12] "Tribalism" has also emerged as a major ideological[13] concept in contemporary African political language which refers to the following: the resistance of subnational ethnic, linguistic, and cultural groups towards incorporation into the larger national society; a reluctance or refusal to accept the legitimacy, authority, and hegemony of the national government and those controlling it; and a penchant for internecine conflict with rival subnational groups. Since those groups labeled "tribe" and those phenomena labeled "tribalism" are by no means found only in Africa or even in the Third World, but also in the most modern nation-states it behooves us to explain why these two terms are applied almost exclusively to Africa and why such usage makes comparative analysis more difficult.

After the development of clear-cut racial stereotypes of Africans,[14] the popular notion of tribe as applied to Africa emerged in Europe and North America during the nineteenth century. In a century diminated by evolutionary and stage theories of history, it was natural for Europeans who knew little about Africa or African history to look for tribes.[15] It was logical to assume that the peoples of Africa, then regarded as the most primitive in the world, would be organized in tribal units. Racial theories that assumed the white race to be biologically superior to other races reinforced the image of a primitive and tribal Africa. The racist stereotypes and claims of white supremacy were well suited to the needs of apologists for colonialism who justified the conquest and subjugation of the African continent as part of Europe's civilizing mission. Ignoring African history, the tribal image evoked an Africa that had been perpetually in the state of nature and economically and socially stagnant until European rule brought "peace and progress" by ending intertribal warfare and integrating Africans into the world market economy.[16]

After the consolidation of colonial rule, colonial officials and ahistorical anthropologists, particularly in the areas under British rule of East, Central, and Southern Africa, perpetuated the myth of a static tribal Africa.[17] Since they considered traditional Africa to be static and stagnant before European contact, the starting point of their analyses of social change was the original tribe and tribesman.[18] This view led them to observe those groups least touched by modern influences before becoming transformed by the modernization process that resulted from colonialism. With the emergence of towns, anthropologists and sociologists began to study changes in the behavior of Africans living in urban settings, regarding these changes as part of the process of detribalization. The detribalized African was often considered as "spoiled" while those with some Western education were regarded as caricatures of the "civilized" European and likely to be troublemakers. At the same time, the rural illiterate tribal African, untouched by Western influences, remained the prototype of the Noble Savage to many colonial officials and anthropologists. When it became increasingly difficult to find "pure" tribes, sociologists and anthropologists dropped "tribe" as a theoretical concept to guide their research and theory-building, but retained it as a descriptive term to refer to clearly distinct, rural-based African groups bound together by ethnic, linguistic, and kinship ties.[19]

Although post-World War II Western scholars rejected the nineteenth-century racial stereotypes and theories[20] that had initially led to the widespread usage of the term, tribe, in Africa, they continued to employ tribe as a loose descriptive term that retained the original connotations of backwardness.[21] Whereas their predecessors regretted the passage of the Noble Savage, the postwar generation of scholars wished to see the processes of modernization accelerated. Moreover, they were far more sympathetic to the educated, detribalized Africans' demands for self-government and independence than were their predecessors.

During the drive towards independence, tribalism gained impetus as an ideological term used by African nationalists to stigmatize as backward and retrograde those ethnic, religious, and regional groups that did not support their movements. In many instances the same African political leaders who attacked the tribalism of their opponents built and led parties based on strong ethnic or regional ties even when they had potentially broader support.[22] After independence, social scientists and African political leaders alike continued to attack subnational loyalties as detrimental to nation-building and modernization. Tribalism was frequently evoked to explain the difficulties that the new states were facing and the apparent failures of modernization. Political scientists, in particular, spoke in terms of the need for integration, penetration, and mobilization, primarily from the perspective and needs of the ruling elites at the center.[23] Political development, thus, frequently became synonymous with the establishment of a strong central government and efficient bureaucracy.

The tribe-to-nation approach can be challenged on several grounds. One can point to African history and demonstrate that much of the continent was detribalized long before European contact and, hence, that it is inaccurate to equate traditional Africa with tribal Africa. This assertion is most correct in West Africa which experienced a wide variety of chiefdoms, states, and empires throughout its history.[24] These political units had to deal with problems of state-building and empire-building. Moreover, the larger units had to face the problem of incorporating diverse peoples at different levels of social and economic development into their states and empires.[25] A cursory look at West African history is sufficient to demonstrate quite convincingly that the problems of state-building and even nation-building are not new to the area and that African political leaders in the past had succeeded in resolving some of these problems. Although the Mali Empire may have been inherently unstable, it managed to survive for several centuries while the Mossi Empire continued virtually intact for nearly a thousand years.[26] The Hausa-Fulani emirates in Northern Nigeria, founded early in the nineteenth century, provide yet another example of state-building, this time undertaken by Muslim religious reformers.[27] One can multiply the examples—the highly centralized and powerful slave-trading state of Dahomey; the small Wolof states of Baol, Djoloff, and Cayor; the extensive empire of El Hadj Umar Tall ranging from the Senegal River to the Niger Bend; the Yoruba states of Oyo and Benin, and so on. Although the colonial conquest destroyed most of the West African states and empires that the Europeans confronted, African political traditions survived.

During the colonial period, religion, caste, past political traditions, language, and kinship ties tended to be far more important in determining individual identities and loyalties than so-called tribal ties. In some instances as was the case with the Ibos, colonialism contributed to the creation of a tribal identity where none had existed before.[28] This fact was particularly true in British West Africa where Great Britain's policies of indirect rule and sympathies to what was perceived as traditional Africa focused undue attention on tribes and tribalism.

West Africa's past and more recent experiences demonstrate quite clearly that the tribe-to-nation approach is based on false assumptions concerning traditional. African political and social organization. If one equates political development with a highly differentiated mode of political organization such as the centralized state, then many parts of West Africa were far more developed than feudal Europe during the medieval period. The disintegration of powerful West African empires like Ghana, Mali, and Songhai suggests that the path to political development is not necessarily an ever upward unilinear progression.[29] Thus one saw what Huntington might call "political decay" taking place in West Africa long before colonialism came to that region and introduced the colonial state followed by the independent nation-state.[30] African history thus contradicts the evolutionary stage theories of modernization and suggests that a cyclical theory might better fit the African context.[31]

The evolutionary stage theories and models of political development, which give such importance to the creation and enlargement of states as hallmarks of progress, have been increasingly adopted by the historians of Africa. As C. C. Wrigley, a prominent African historian has written in a recent article:

> For just as the political scientists have conditioned us to believe that "nation-building" is the great theme of contemporary African politics, so the historians, during the same period, have been teaching us to see state-formation as the dominant and almost the only significant theme of earlier history.[32]

Wrigley further asserts that behind the historians' concern with state-building and nation-building in the precolonial period lies a model that "instructs him that the whole meaning of progress is the transition from tribe to state, from segmentary to centralized political system."[33] And Wrigley vigorously takes to task the historicism of the tribe-to-nation approach which reifies the mode of political organization as *the* determinant of developmental stages.[34]

One can agree with Wrigley that historicism leads not only to partial misconceptions about the past but also to insecure judgments about the present.[35] Hence, if West Africa was not and *is* not primarily tribal, then the main problem cannot be speeding the passage from tribe to nation. Moreover, in looking for a nation-state patterned on the Western model, we neglect the possibilites of other forms of political organization (e.g., empires) which might facilitate modernization, as well as the current use of traditional African norms to promote contemporary state-building. In much of the literature that stresses the tribe-to-nation approach, traditionalism is viewed largely as dysfunctional to modernization and incompatible with state and nation-building.[36] As the reader shall see later, such traditional behavior may be perfectly compatible with modernization, state-building, and the peaceful incorporation of diverse groups within the framework of the new polity.

While historical evidence demolishes the myth of the tribe for West Africa, which was perpetuated in the tribe-to-nation approach to political development, a second criticism is based on quite different grounds. Here, the tribe-to-nation approach with its stress on nation-building and national integration (often used interchangeably) is chided not because of its historicism, but rather because it draws attention away from class analysis while serving as an ideology in defense of the existing state systems inherited from colonialism and the political elites in power. Although this crriticism may acknowledge the existence of tribal sentiments and solidarities, it denies that these sentiments are the main obstacles to national unity and that the major cleavages in African states are tribe versus nation.[37] Instead, it offers class analysis as an alternative approach. Sklar, for example, using Nigeria as his case in point, argues in this vein:

> Tribalism is widely supposed to be the most formidable barrier to national unity. . . . It is less frequently recognized that tribal movements may be created and instigated to action by the new men of power in furtherance of their own special interests which are, time and again, the constitutive interests of emerging social classes. Tribalism then becomes a mask for class privilege. To borrow a worn metaphor, there is often a nontraditional wolf under the tribal sheepskin.[38]

Hence, tribalism per se is not the primary villain and political force in African politics so often indicated in tribe-to-nation approaches. Class analysis reveals that those in power are not necessarily the guardians of the nation but rather men who seek to perpetuate their power and defend the interests of their social class or elite group.[39] Although this critique, which can be loosely labeled Marxian, corrects some of the biases and sins of omission found in the tribe-to-nation approach, it also tends to ignore the lessons of West African history and to regard traditional African modes of political organization and political behavior as dysfunctional to modernization and state-building.[40] Both the Marxian and the nation-building approaches to political development and modernization are European formulations expressed in ideological concepts. Despite their differences, both approaches tend to regard primordial sentiments and loyalties as less "progressive" than national or class identities. Nationalism is thus opposed to tribalism while socialism is opposed to both feudalism and neo-colonialism. Both represent higher states of political development. And both formulations suffer from the sins of historicism. Finally, both the Marxian[41] and nation-building approaches tend to underestimate the staying power and adaptability of nonnational and nonclass identities, norms, and patterns of behavior.

A third criticism of the tribe-to-nation approach is that ethnocentric and historically bound terms like tribe and tribalism, which are applied almost exclusively to Africa, make it difficult to study groups labeled tribes, and phenomena associated with tribalism, and to compare them with similar groups and phenomena elsewhere in the modern world. For example, the demands of diverse groups (nationalities?), for autonomy and/or political sovereignty, living within the framework of nineteenth-century Central and East European empires had much in common with the demands of certain African groups (tribes?) for more autonomy or for their own state in this century.[42] The Rumanians, Bulgars, Poles, and Czechs who demanded independence were considered nations because they had a common culture, language, and territory;[43] on the other hand, African groups like the Baganda who have similar characteristics (i.e., the very same features that defined a nation in the European context) are called tribes and their movements for autonomy or independence labeled tribalism.

In the tribe-to-nation approach, tribes have no rights to self-determination since they threaten the existing state system and represent an inferior level of political development. On the other hand, nations have the right of self-determination when they do not have their own states. However, in the postcolonial African context, nationalism has been associated with strong attachments to the new state rather than to any single homogeneous group of people that might be called a nation. A striking example of the difficulties and ambiguities that arise in applying tribe and nation concepts in West Africa can be seen in the way in which Nigerians, other Africans, and sympathetic outside observers have interpreted and evaluated the causes of the tragic Nigerian Civil War. The Ibos saw themselves as a nation and as such claimed the right to self-determination. The secession of the Ibos and their establishment of the short-lived Republic of Biafra was thus based on the rights that they claimed as a nation.[44] On the other hand, the Nigerian Federal Government regarded the Ibos as a tribe, their secession as a manifestation of tribalism, and the Federal Government as the guardian of national unity. By denying the Ibos' nationhood, the Nigerian Federal Government thus rejected their right to self-determination and secession. Most African governments supported this position because they too wished to discourage secessionist movements, in their own countries, which they denounced as manifestations of tribalism and threats to national unity. In the Nigerian case, terms like tribe, tribalism, nation, and national unity tended to be used ideologically to support the position of one side or the other. Supporters of the federal government viewed the conflict in terms of tribe versus nation with national unity being the main stake, while supporters of the Ibo viewed the conflict as between a nation and a state. Despite the fact that the state claimed jurisdiction for all the peoples within Nigeria, the Ibos claimed that it was either unwilling or unable to maintain their security and survival as a people within Nigeria. Other observers analyzed the Civil War in quite different terms. Some saw it essentially as a struggle over oil with competing neo-colonialist powers lurking behind the scenes. Others saw it more in internal class terms with Biafra representing a dynamic and progressive people in conflict with Northern feudalism and the worst elements of the corrupt Nigerian political class.

Some of the difficulties that arise in using the tribe-to-nation approach to nation-building stem from the failure to distinguish differences between state and nation, and the possible combinations of relationships between the two. As two astute scholars of nationalism working on this question have written recently:

> "Nation," it is clear, is not the same as "state." The latter refers to an independent and autonomous political structure over a specific territory, with a comprehensive legal system and a sufficient concentration of power to maintain law and order. "State," in other words, is primarily a political-legal concept, whereas "nation" is primarily psycho-cultural. Nation and State may exist independently of one another: a nation may exist without a state, a state may exist without a nation. When the two coincide, when the boundaries of the state are approximately coterminous with those of the nation, the result is a nation-state.[45]

In postcolonial West Africa, the state is clearly not coterminous with any single nation. Unlike most, though not all of Europe, the state in Africa preceded the nation. Hence, in West Africa, one finds state-nations rather than nation-states.[46] But to the extent that the nation-state is regarded as the highest level of political development and the best possible unit for promoting modernization, it becomes imperative to transform the state-nation into the nation-state.[47] This view is the rationale behind the high priority given to nation-building by both African political leaders and modernization theorists adhering to the tribe-to-nation approach. In the nation-building model, it is assumed that the national political leadership ought to be the guardian of national unity and to keep a constant vigil against the more "primitive" subnational forces resisting national integration and impeding the way to more rapid modernization. Furthermore, it is assumed that the state and its leaders *ought* to command the loyalties of the diverse peoples under their jurisdication.[48] Since the state at independence does *not* command all the loyalties of the people, it is necessary to strengthen its authority so that it can better carry out the task of nation-building.[49] Moreover, since nations are not built in a day, a decade, or even a generation, distinctions between state-building (penetration of the populations by the national center) and nation-building (surrender of tribal and other ethnic identities in favor of a national one) may become blurred in the period following political independence.

However, if state-building itself can be an essential part of a nation-building process or even a prerequisite for bringing into being a nation-state, state-building need not be used exclusively for that purpose. It is one thing for the political elites controlling the national center to demand that the center's authority be recognized;[50] it is another thing for them to insist that all the peoples under their legal jurisdiction surrender their other subnational identities. The political elites controlling the center could respect the diverse social and cultural identities of the herterogeneous populations under their legal jurisdiction while still insisting upon obedience to the authority of the state. In this case, they would be engaged in empire building rather than nation-building, although they, too, like the proponents of the nation, would be concerned with strengthening the authority of the center.[51] But the tribe-to-nation approach excludes empire building as an alternative way of looking at the state-building processes now going on in West Africa. Nation-building and empire-building are two responses to the same universal political problem of how to incorporate heterogeneous populations at different levels of political, social, economic, and cultural development into a single political system.[52]

Even if one concedes that nation-building may be a long-range goal of many of the new African states, the focus on the nation and the nation-state projects too far into the future and diverts attention from more critical problems facing the new African states today.[53] From the perspective of the political elites in power, their main problem is how to consolidate and expand their political authority. When they speak of nation-building as many often do, the elites make it clear that strengthening the center, either through the state and/or the party, comes first in their order of priorities since the state and/or party is perceived as *the* principal instrument for creating a national consciousness.[54] As shall be discussed in the next section, the question of the political authority of the new state is closely related to the inheritance situation derived from colonialism. State-building in the new African states cannot be dissociated from the decolonization process. Consequently, one must examine the new African state's relationships with the ex-metropole, the staying power of colonial bureaucratic norms, and the inheritance elites' ability to dissociate themselves from these norms.[55] One must also examine the attitudes of the heterogeneous populations towards the new national center and the men controlling it. For while the modernizing African elites in power may be preoccupied with state building and express some desire for nation-building, these concerns are rarely those of the African masses who are primarily interested in the extent to which their new rulers respect their values, permit them a large measure of autonomy and control over their own lives, and fulfill their distributional obligations according to traditional as well as modern norms.[56]

In this first section, the author has rejected as unsatisfactory the tribe-to-nation approach to political development and modernization in West Africa. As ideal types at different ends of a continuum in a theory of modernization, tribe and nation did not correspond to African realities. For nearly a millenium, the tribe has not been the dominant form of political organization in West Africa. The concept of tribe thus takes us too far back in the distant past to be of use. On the other hand, the contemporary African states are not nations in the European sense and will not be for at least several generations, if ever. Hence the concept of nation as employed in the tribe-to-nation approach takes us too far into the future. Even if one accepted the long-range validity of the assumptions underlying the tribe-to-nation approach, one would still be led to look for intermediate stages when looking at the contemporary world.

ALTERNATIVE APPROACHES TO
TRIBE-TO-NATION ANALYSES

In regarding the new African states as authentic nation-states and the political elites in power as primarily modernizing nationalists, the tribe-to-nation approach generally neglects the significance of traditional and colonial African states. Whereas the focus on the nation and nation-building has diverted attention from difficulties of decolonization, the focus on tribe and tribalism tends to regard strong traditional, subnational loyalties as dysfunctional to modernization and effective nation-building. This section presents two alternative approaches to the study of state-building and nation-building. The first is built around the concept of neo-patrimonialism to examine traditional components in postcolonial West African regimes. These two approaches are complementary rather than contradictory; when combined, rather than when used alone, they present a more accurate and complete picture of the processes of state-building and nation-building in postcolonial West Africa.

COLONIALISM AND THE INHERITANCE SITUATION

Nettl and Robertson have elaborated the concept of the inheritance situation as a point of departure for studying concrete, modernizing societies in the Third World.[57] According to them,

> the concept of an inheritance situation has increasingly helped to provide a crucial *starting point* for analyzing processes which the categories of traditional, developing, and modern by themselves do not seem to offer.[58]

In stressing the importance of socio-political and cultural dissociation, the concept of the inheritance situation suggests that an important aspect of state building and even nation-building during the early phases of decolonization must be dissociation from the colonial past. The new national identity must be dissociated from the colonial identity.

The new inheritance situation is essentially a legal concept, the basic attribute of which is the demise, legal or natural, of an owner and the consequent transfer to heirs of rights in property.[59] Under colonialism, the metropole "owns" the colony. When the ownership of the colony is transferred more or less voluntarily from the metropole to indigenous political elites, the former plays the role of benefactor to the beneficiaries who "inherit" the colony at the legal demise of the benefactor (independence). Translated into political terms, this process corresponds to the decision on the part of the colonial power to grant independence, the actual departure (demise) of the colonial rulers, and finally, the takeover of the colonial state apparatus by the inheritance elites (the beneficiaries). The inheritance situation differs from unilateral seizure (revolution) where property rights are taken by force against the wishes of the owner. Such was not the case in West Africa where, despite occasional outbreaks of violence and repression of nationalist movements, the transition to independence was relatively smooth and peaceful and where the colonial rulers willingly transferred control over their ex-colonies to indigenous political elites.[60]

The inheritance elites who took power in West Africa at the time of independence were generally those associated with the dominant political parties in their territory at independence. According to the rules laid down by France and Great Britain, the two main colonial powers in West Africa, the main route to political power was through electoral competition. With the exception of Guinea, the transfer of power from the metropole to the leaders of the major territorial parties went smoothly.[61] After independence, the inheritance elites continued to maintain close and often cordial relationships with their ex-metropoles even when they (the inheritance elites) developed new relationships with other countries.[62] Moreover, the original inheritance elites and their military and bureaucratic successors rarely made radical changes in the legal and bureaucratic apparatus handed down to them. Where innovations were made, they were often superimposed upon the existing legal and bureaucratic structures handed down from the colonial period, indicating, despite much rhetoric to the contrary, that the new West African states were essentially reformist rather than revolutionary in their dissociation efforts.[63]

This high degree of institutional continuity suggests that most of the new African states and their national centers have more in common with the imperial colonial state that they replaced than the incipient nation-state portrayed in the nation-building models. Before independence, the West African colonies could be best characterized as plural societies ruled by alien European elites.[64] These plural societies consisted of heterogeneous groups at different levels of social, political, and economic development whose common political concern was a desire for greater autonomy from alien rule. They did not constitute a homogeneous nation seeking a state of its own. Hence, the so-called nationalist movements when supported by the people were primarily expressions of anticolonial sentiments and aspirations for autonomy rather than expressions of nationalism.[65] In this situation, nationalist leaders were, in fact, territorial leaders with broad support among diverse groups throughout the colony. For most of the African elites competing for power, the main goal was the capture of the colonial territorial center and its resources rather than the establishment of a nation-state within the given territorial boundaries of the colony. The main reference point of preindependence nationalism which transcended parochial solidarities was Pan-Africanism or, as was the case in the French territories, the preservation of the French West African Federation.[66]

Although manifestations of territorial nationalism appeared in some colonies before independence, it was not until after independence that territorial nationalism was fostered by the beneficiary elites.[67] In the so-called moderate states, territorial nationalism as articulated by the elites in power was expressed in terms of loyalty to the new state and pride in its position and status in Africa and in the wider community of nation-states which it had entered.[68] For the masses, nationalism was more frequently expressed in terms of hostility toward Levantines and nonindigenous Africans in eocnomic competition with the indigenous populations.[69] In the so-called radical states like Guinea, Ghana under Nkrumah, and Mali under Modibo Keita, nationalism was expressed more in terms of hostility toward the ex-colonizer, other Western powers, and the moderate inheritance elites ruling other West African nations, as well as toward nonindigenous groups like the Levantines.[70]

However, neither in the radical nor in the moderate states did the inheritance elites perceive themselves as rulers of a homogeneous population with a common language, history, and territory. Besides their general African culture, the most common feature that these hetero-geneous populations shared was their colonial experience under European rule. And even here, their experiences varied because some traditional elites like the Hausa—Fulani emirs of Northern Nigeria and the Fulani chiefs in Guinea were given preferential treatment by the colonial authorities, while other traditional elites, particularly those who strongly resisted the colonial conquest, saw their power and prestige destroyed.[71] Moreover, some groups like the Ibos and Yorubas in Nigeria, the Baoulé and Agni in the Ivory Coast, and the Wolofs in Senegal enjoyed higher levels of social and economic development which were largely the result of greater colonial investments in their areas.[72]

If under colonialism, all West African colonies were, in fact, plural societies, there is little evidence to support their sudden transformation into nation-states or even state-nations after independence. With independence there were no major changes in the multiethnic structures of the plural society contained within the territorial boundaries of the new states. Despite the occasional expulsion of diverse alien groups that comprised only a tiny percentage of the total population, the ethnic composition of society did not change markedly. Nor did the masses become immersed in a postcolonial national identity when they rallied to the banners of the new state.

While there was great continuity in the composition and boundaries of the plural societies after independence, there was also considerable continuity in the patterns, norms, and dependency relationships of the postcolonial centers and inheritance elites. Such was the case not only because of the relative lack of tampering with colonial institutions and procedures after independence but also because of the inheritance elites' attachments to and dependency upon their benefactors which made dissociation difficult. Cultural attachments were strong because mastery and manipulation of the language and culture of the metropole had been, to a large extent, the foundation of elite status and one of the conditions for being eligible to receive the inheritance.[73] No one without these skills, regardless of his traditional status and prestige, could aspire to a position of national leadership or enter the high echelons of the state bureaucracy.[74] After independence, there was an even higher premium on university degrees as the numbers of African university graduates holding ministerial positions steadily increased. This trend was further accelerated by the rash of military coups in which the new rulers replaced many of the ousted politicians with more highly educated technicians with little or no political experience.[75] Mastery of European languages and cultures also became a highly desired skill because the inheritance elites with these skills were better able to enhance their country's reputation at international conferences and at the bargaining table with other states.[76]

Just as important as the cultural attachments that gave them elite status were the political attachments of the inheritance elites to the ex-metropole. Since independence in most West African states was granted by the metropole rather than seized by the colonies, the political leaders who took power in some measure were in debt to their benefactors for transferring ownership of the ex-colony to them. Political loyalties to the ex-metropole were particularly close in the new Francophone states of West Africa (excluding Guinea and Mali) where the national leaders had for the most part served their political apprenticeships in metropolitan as well as territorial politics and felt personally loyal to General DeGaulle to whom they gave credit for accelerating the process of decolonization and providing generous economic aid even after independence.[77]

Dissociation was also discouraged by the fact that the political authority of the inheritance elites was intimately tied to control of the state structures that it took over. These ex-colonial state structures gave the inheritance elites in power the formal authority and the resources needed to rule. These resources included control over the police, the army, and the legal system as well as the economic resources of the state, which accounted for a significant share of the national product; moreover, the state was the largest single source of employment in the country. There were thus strong vested interests involved in not dismantling the inherited state apparatus. Since control over the colonial territorial center and its resources was the main prize of preindependence politics, there was little desire to diminish this prize. On the contrary, the main goal for the inheritance elites after independence was precisely the consolidation and expansion of state authority. In all but one or two West African states, there was rapid expansion of the state bureaucracy at the expense of political parties that went into sharp decline after independence.[78] The relative influence of the state bureaucracy increased and after a few short years of independence came to resemble the colonial state bureaucracy that it had succeeded and that had placed a high value on efficiency, order, and economic development as opposed to political mobilization.[79] These trends were most evident in moderate Francophone West African states like Senegal, the Ivory Coast, and Upper Volta as well as in Ghana after the fall of Nkrumah in 1966.

The various forms of dependency of the postcolonial national centers on their ex-metropoles or other Western countries were also major factors working against revolutionary changes in institutional structures after independence. Economic dependency was strongest in the Francophone states where many of the ex-colonies continued to rely upon France to subsidize their development efforts and in some cases even their operating budgets.[80] Gambia also looked to its ex-metropole for financial support after independence. Even when the new states sought alternative aid and trade partners, they had to conform to the rules of economic behavior prescribed by the donor nations or agencies. Hence the International Monetary Fund turned down Nkrumah's request for loans to refinance Ghana's external debts while it accepted a similar request by Nkrumah's successors after they agreed to pursue more orthodox fiscal policies and to close down several inefficient state enterprises. The dependency of the state upon revenues generated by the export economy introduced by the ex-colonizer was still another economic factor discouraging any sudden, radical change from prior economic policies.[81] Military dependency of many of the new West African states upon their ex-metropole also favored continuity rather than dissociation. The survival of Mauritania in the wake of Morocco's claims to it during the early 1960s was insured by France while Great Britain supported the federal government's suppression of the Biafran secession to preserve the unity of the federation that it had handed down to the inheritance elites. Continuity was also fostered by the fact that many of the leading army officers involved in military coups were trained in Great Britain or France and instilled with the values and outlooks of their hosts.[82]

The state-building that took place in most of the new West African states was firmly based on the inherited colonial foundation. After independence, the inheritance elites in power attempted to Africanize the colonial state rather than dismantle it, expand its resources and broaden its control over the African populations by bringing the administration closer to them. Although the inheritance elites attempted to foster a new national identity built around the postcolonial state by establishing national anthems, flags, holidays, independence monuments, and other national symbols, major efforts to mobilize the populations through the party were few.[83] On the contrary, the role of the party declined in most West African states after independence with the demise of the party hastened by the end of competitive electoral politics. Hence, despite rhetoric about primacy of the party, voiced by many West African leaders, it was the state that became the single most important political institution, and the national leader the most powerful figure after independence.[84]

The inheritance elites in the so-called moderate West African states stressed goals like economic development and national unity as expressions of dissociation from the colonial past.[85] These goals did not require attacking institutions and social structures closely associated with colonialism. On the contrary, these goals were similar to those of the colonizer but were to be carried out within a national rather than colonial framework. The National Development Plan thus affirmed the new state's national identity and reflected aspirations for rapid economic development. While the colonial regime sought order and stability within the framework of the imperial system, the inheritance elites sought similar goals in the name of national unity and integration. Both the goals of economic development and national integration required the strengthening of the state, since the state was the prime organizer of developmental efforts and the main force for maintaining order and promoting national unity.

However, the implementation of these goals and postcolonial state-building depended to a large extent upon external resources and support. Postcolonial developmental programs required large amounts of foreign aid, technical assistance, and foreign investment which were usually supplied by the ex-colonizer, other Western nations, and international agencies.[86] National integration as fostered by the inheritance elite required improvements in communications and transportation networks and an expanding bureaucracy to penetrate the periphery. To maintain order, the state created a national army and expanded the size of the civilian police forces.[87] These measures again compelled the new states to turn to external assistance. The building of the strength of the state, relative to other forces in society, thus had to be achieved at the expense of decreasing the autonomy of the new state vis-à-vis external forces. In some instances, the new state was little more than a client state of its former metropole, despite its nominal independence and international sovereignty.

In the more radical West African states, the inheritance elites made a greater effort to dissociate from the colonial past. This effort often took the form of attacking neo-colonialism and imperialism as manifested in the foreign domination of the modern sectors of the economy, and affirming economic independence as a primary postcolonial goal.[88] Economic independence required economic disengagement from the ex-metropole and other Western countries and establishment of considerable economic relationships with the Socialist camp. Hence, Guinea, Ghana under Nkrumah during the 1960s, and Mali up to 1968 took steps to sharply reduce their economic dependency on their ex-metropoles and other Western countries and to expand trade and aid ties with the Socialist camp. At the same time, they relied less heavily upon the private sector and more upon the public sector to stimulate economic development.[89] Dissociation was also manifested in foreign policies stressing nonalignment, Pan-Africanism, strong support of anticolonial revolutionary movements on the African continent and criticism of the moderate African states alleged to be in league with neo-colonialism and imperialism.

The inheritance elites in these more radical West African states also took stronger measures to crush the power of those groups and social forces that had been most closely aligned with the ex-colonizer. In Guinea, the most radical of the West African states, self-government and independence were followed by a social revolution that destroyed the power of the Fulani chiefs who with French support had dominated traditional Guinean society during colonial rule.[90] The traditional social structures that had been preserved by the French were dismantled and replaced by a more egalitarian social order in which women, youth, and members of low-caste groups were given a greater voice in the conduct of village, regional, and national affairs. Inheritance elites in power in Ghana and Mali also took measures to check the power of traditional leaders and social forces tied to the colonial system. But in contrast to Guinea, there was no frontal attack on traditional social structures themselves; and, consequently no social revolution took place in Ghana and Mali.

Although the radical states, like the moderate states, also adopted state-building as one of their major tasks, the former gave more importance to the party as an instrument for fostering national integration and unity. To the extent that the party was an indigenous institution whose functioning depended largely upon the organizational skills of its leaders and the energies of its followers, it was less tied to colonial institutions and norms and, therefore, could be used as a more popular agent for promoting a postcolonial national identity than could the state. In the radical states, the inheritance elites in power also gave the party a greater role in defending the security of the regime.[91] Party mobilization was most developed in Guinea where the PDG party apparatus governed the country after the sudden disappearance of the French colonial apparatus in 1958.[92] Moreover, it was party mobilization that helped stave off the 1970 invasion of Guinea by foreign mercenaries and which up to now has saved Sekou Touré and his regime from suffering the fate of his ex-allies who were overthrown in military coups in Ghana (1966) and Mali (1968).

Paradoxically, nation-building as contrasted with state-building has been most evident in the only territory in West Africa still under colonial rule. In Guinea-Bissau, Amilcar Cabral and the *PAIGC* have been waging an increasingly successful armed struggle for independence against Portugal.[93] In the rural areas under their control, the National Liberation Movement has accelerated the dissociation process by dismantling colonial institutions and replacing them with indigenous ones. In its nation-building efforts, the liberation movement has stressed the development of a popular culture based on indigenous cultural values and a national culture based largely upon the history and the achievements of the anticolonial struggle itself.[94] In Guinea-Bissau, where Portugal refuses to play the role of benefactor in handing over the colony to an inheritance elite, nation-building becomes a necessary condition for success since it is the best means of involving the masses in the struggle for independence. During the course of the struggle, nation-building takes place as interethnic barriers break down while diverse groups cooperate and unite in the common cause. In the case of Guinea-Bissau, nation-building entails a greater degree of decolonization than in the other West African states where nation-building is tied to the transfer of loyalties to an indigenous national state patterned largely on the colonial model and led by inheritance elites, rather than tied to a liberation movement led by revolutionary elites in intimate contact with the masses. Hence, this condition may mean that Guinea-Bissau, when it becomes independent, will be the only new West African state in which the nation preceded the state and where nation-building revolved around a people rather than a state.

Anticolonial revolutions such as the one in Guinea-Bissau, seem to be more conducive to nation-building than peaceful transitions to independence.[95] Conversely, the examples of the moderate West African states, with their strong continuity with the colonial past, suggest that most inheritance elites are more likely to be engaged in empire-building rather than nation-building.[96]

The concept of the inheritance situation reveals crucial elements of state-building processes in a postcolonial period, which have generally been overlooked in the tribe-to-nation approach: (1) the strong colonial component in postcolonial states as reflected in the high degree of continuity in institutions and basic goals; (2) the high degree of dependency of postcolonial structures upon external norms and resources; (3) the strong attachment of the inheritance elites to external norms and values; (4) the reemergence of the state as opposed to the party as the dominant political institution; and (5) the promotion of a postcolonial national identity around the state rather than the nation.

Notwithstanding their similarities to the colonial regimes that they replaced, the new West African states should not be regarded simply as successor states. One can identify several important differences between the colonial centers and their postcolonial African successors. For example, structurally, the strength of the postcolonial centers and their relationship with the people are different. Hence, the postcolonial centers are often weaker than their colonial predecessors because they no longer have the economic resources of the metropole behind them or the military power that the colonial ruler could mobilize to put down colonial revolts. Postcolonial centers and African rulers are also more responsive and vulnerable to popular demands and domestic political pressures exerted by indigenous social forces than by the autocratic colonial regimes they replaced.[97] Moreover, the inheritance elites, unlike their European predecessors, in their relationships with the African populations, often conform to traditional African political norms and use precolonial organizational techniques in their postcolonial efforts in state-building.

STATE-BUILDING AND NEO-PATRIMONIALISM

While the concept of the inheritance situation in drawing attention to the continuity of colonial influences in new states provides a useful corrective to the neglect of such influences in the tribe-to-nation approach, the concept of neo-patrimonialism underscores the importance and persistence of traditional norms and behavior in the state-building efforts of the new West African states. As used here, neo-patrimonialism refers to certain common features and patterns found in new states similar to those found in the patrimonial regimes and bureaucratic empires described by Weber and Eisenstadt.

The structural characteristics of the postcolonial African states resemble those of patrimonial regimes in several ways.[98] First, patrimonial regimes had relatively small governmental centers with limited resources.[99] The economic resources of the patrimonial center were derived largely from control over trade and regulation of the economy, and hence, varied according to the size of the economy and the amount of trade passing through the territory.[100] The center's size and strength were limited not only by lack of resources, but also by lack of legitimacy with large segments of the populations under its jurisdication.[101] Efforts at state-building and center-formation by patrimonial rulers were hindered both by lack of economic resources and the resistance of powerful local forces seeking to retain their autonomy vis-à-vis the center.[102] The main instrument utilized by patrimonial centers for penetrating and controlling the periphery was the extension of the central bureaucracy whose officials administered the periphery in the name of the center.[103] Lacking economic resources and legitimacy with large segments of the population, patrimonial centers depended heavily upon force to insure compliance with their rule.[104] This dependency resulted in inherently unstable centers.[105]

Political relationships in patrimonial regimes and in precolonial West Africa also had much in common with patterns of political behavior found in the new West African states. In patrimonial regimes, authority was personalized, and patrimonial rulers conducted themselves in a monarchical style.[106] They had courts and entourages to whom they looked for advice, service, and protection. When loyalty to the ruler was not based on kinship ties or devotion to his person, they were cemented by clientelist relationships in which those involved agreed to serve the ruler in exchange for economic, social, and political benefits.[107] Patron-client relationships generally permeated all levels of society, with the patrimonial ruler being the most prominent patron of all. While recruitment to the state bureaucracy in patrimonial regimes was often through examination, access to the highest offices depended more on the ability of the individual to gain the confidence of the ruler.[108] High military office also depended upon demonstrating personal loyalty to the ruler. Although endowed with great formal power, the patrimonial ruler had difficulty in imposing his authority upon powerful local notables. When he could not impose his authority by force, the patrimonial ruler used marriage alliances, cooptation into his court, clientelism, and displays of generosity and grandeur to cement loyalty to his regime.

Senegal provides an excellent example of the applicability of the neo-patrimonial model in examining the processes of state building in West Africa.[109] Since obtaining independence in 1960, Senegal's state-building and modernization efforts have been channeled largely through neo-patrimonial mechanisms. Like most of the West African states, Senegal has a small, weak center with leaders who are trying to extend its control through expansion of the central bureaucracy. As the successor of the French colonial administration, the postcolonial center has little legitimacy for most Senegalese, who still regard it as an alien institution imported by the colonial ruler. Nevertheless, those controlling the center have won the support of important segments of Senegalese society through the judicious use of clientelist mechanisms, cooptation of opposition elements, and respect for traditional authority structures, particularly those of the Muslim brotherhoods. At the same time, the political stability of the center has been menaced by recurrent social and political crises that have led the regime to rely more heavily upon the use of force for survival.

Since independence, Senegal had been led by Leopold Sédar Senghor, head of the *Union Progressiste Sénégalaise* (UPS), the country's governing party. Senghor did not come to power as a charismatic leader enjoying the unqualified support of a highly mobilized population.[110] Nor did he, being a commoner and a Catholic, come to power as the leader of traditionalist forces in a predominantly Muslim and highly stratified caste-oriented society. Instead Senghor owed his rise to his intellectual brilliance, organizational skills, and ability to convince many of Senegal's most influential traditional elites to encourage their followers to vote for him and his party. For example, Senghor's successful wooing of several of Senegal's most prominent Muslim religious leaders *(marabouts)* was a decisive factor underlying the rise of his party to power and the defeat of Lamine Gueye, his main political rival and the man who had dominated Senegalese politics during the early postwar period.[111]

Since assuming the presidency of Senegal in 1960, Senghor has striven to reinforce the authority of his office and to expand the resources and power of the postcolonial center. He has also sought to overcome his lack of traditional social status by taking measures to increase his own personal authority. Hence, he has conducted himself in the style of a presidential monarch. To increase his prestige and that of his office, Senghor transformed the palace of the ex-governor-general into a presidential palace, established an elaborately costumed guard to receive visiting heads of state and other dignitaries, and presided over all national ceremonies and celebrations.[112]

Like patrimonial rulers in the past, Senghor had his own personal entourage that consisted of traditional as well as modern elements: kinsmen; traditionalists who could advise and represent Senghor in dealing with the powerful traditional forces in the country; military officers; young intellectuals and technicians; and foreign advisors (predominantly French). As his political lieutenants, Senghor often chose men who would not be in a position to challenge his political supremacy. Hence, the political figures in his entourage consisted primarily of men lacking an independent political base of their own or men of low traditional status.

After the establishment of a presidential regime in 1963, power came to be increasingly centralized in the hands of the president and his staff. The centralization of power in the hands of the executive coincided with the decline of party activities and party mobilization. Notwithstanding exhortations from Senghor calling on the UPS to mobilize the people for developmental purposes, a constant theme in Senghor's annual reports to the party since 1960, the state bureaucracy became the main agency for promoting and implementing developmental goals while the party atrophied. Following the pattern of patrimonial rulers of the past, Senghor appointed regional governors who owed their loyalties to the center and attempted to reinforce their authority vis-à-vis local authorities.[113] In areas where traditional authority was weak, Senghor replaced local party leaders with men from the center or those in the area completely loyal to him. Where it was difficult to impose the center's will, Senghor prevented local political forces from uniting against the center by skillfully manipulating clan politics and using state resources to increase the dependency of local factions upon the center.[114]

Despite the trend towards centralization and expansion of bureaucratic authority associated with state-building and modernization, Senghor made frequent concessions to traditional forces in Senegalese society. The leading marabouts, for example, insisted upon representation in the government and access to the president, exemption from government regulations detrimental to their interests, and nonintervention of state authority in their districts. Since much of his political support was derived from them, Senghor hesitated to take measures that would antagonize the marabouts. Moreover, Senghor and the government respected traditional African political norms and social structures. The center thus made no frontal attack on the inequities of the existing caste system. Although laws were passed limiting the brideprice and the amount of money to be spent on diverse ceremonies, these laws were rarely enforced. Nor were the campaigns against corruption sustained over long periods of time.[115] In modern Western societies corruption generally refers to public officials who abuse their authority to obtain extra income from the public. In traditional societies, such practices were considered as part of the benefits of the office and hence carried no onus. Severe punishment of offenders whose crime consisted of using public funds to fulfill traditional obligations and life-styles was politically risky and hence used sparingly.

In economic matters, the Senegalese center also had characteristics found in patrimonial regimes. Its economic resources were derived largely from its control over trade, in this case, the peanut trade, which accounted for seventy-five to eighty-five percent of Senegal's total exports and still remains the principal source of cash income for the majority of Senegalese farmers.[116] One of the first acts in Senegal, as in most of the new African states, was to take control of the regulation and operation of trading activities in the country. Since the center depended upon the revenues generated by the peanut trade, it was in its interest to maintain and expand production. When production declined, the center was obliged to use more coercion in order to collect the revenues needed to support it, although in Senegal's case, the pressure to use more coercion in order to maintain state revenues has been somewhat modified by the ability of the center to obtain large-scale foreign aid. To the extent that the center had an expanding resource base or one that was not derived from taxation of the rural populations, it was in a better position to play the role of the patron-state redistributing its largess to the people.[117] However, the Senegalese center was in a poor position to play this role because of a stagnating economy resulting largely from poor crops and negative changes in the external economic environment. To insure the maintenance of the center, Senghor introduced austerity programs and improved tax collection methods during the mid-1960s, measures that did little to enhance the popularity of his regime.

Still another important feature of patrimonial regimes, found in Senegal, was the government's reliance upon force to insure compliance with its rule. Because of its limited legitimacy as a successor state to the colonial regime and limited economic resources, the Senegalese post-colonial center has increased the amount of force at its disposal in order to insure its survival in the face of recurrent political and social crises. This action has meant a steady increase in the size and importance of the military as an integral part of the Senegalese center.[118]

In its state-building efforts, the Senegalese postcolonial center has used many of the techniques used by precolonial West African states, to enhance its authority with, and to discourage revolt by, the diverse populations under its jurisdiction. While gradually extending its authority through its central bureaucracy, its military and police power, and its economic control of the trading economy, the Senegalese state has also respected traditional norms, avoided open confrontations with powerful, traditional social forces and collectivities, and attempted to win support from various sectors of society through clientelist politics.[119]

Although the concept of neo-patrimonialism is fruitful in directing our attention to the persistence of traditional political norms and relationships, and structural weaknesses of regimes in developing countries, it should not be abused by reifying it. The neo-patrimonial regimes that one finds in West Africa today are not simply replicas of precolonial African political systems, reappearing in the twentieth century. Their structures and functions have also been determined, to a large extent, by the colonial experience, the colonial inheritance situation, and the transformations in the broader society brought about through modernization processes. Hence, neo-patrimonial regimes are generally led by inheritance elites imbued with a culture alien to African traditions; the centers themselves are often heavily dependent upon external resources for their survival and expansion.[120] The social forces and political institutions with which the centers deal are modern—e.g., political parties, industrial workers and university students—as well as traditional;[121] and their goals are generally articulated in terms of modernization within the framework of a world community of nation-states. Given the complexity of state-building processes in postcolonial regimes and the inability of any single concept or approach to provide an accurate global model or theory, it therefore seems wiser to incorporate several approaches into our analyses and to use those concepts that are most suitable to answering the specific questions we have relating to these processes.

For example, the concept of the inheritance situation, unlike that of the neo-patrimonial regime, helps to explain colonial influences on the political behavior of those commanding the postcolonial center, the formal composition of its institutions, the center's external dependencies, and the modern economic sector's dependency upon and domination by foreign elements. Yet, it tells us little about the traditional norms of the inheritance elites themselves, the way in which these norms affect the functioning of the postcolonial center, the manner in which the center relates to the periphery, and finally, how those in the periphery regard the center.[122]

Understanding the processes of state-building in West Africa is better furthered by using both concepts in combination so that one can more clearly see the extent to which the success of the state-building efforts of the inheritance elites is closely related to the ability to obtain external resources needed to carry out the postcolonial center's expansion. Moreover, the fact that those inheritance elites who have made the least effort to dissociate the postcolonial regime from the colonial past have also tended to work closest with traditional elites and to adopt a patrimonial style of rule suggests that neo-patrimonialism and neo-colonialism in a postcolonial context may be closely related. They are compatible because weak neo-patrimonial regimes often look towards powerful external patrons to provide them with arms, economic resources, and status, all of which are transformed into the resources needed by the elites to enhance the authority of the regime and to promote economic and social development. Moreover, the fragility of postcolonial regimes, as reflected in the numerous military coups in West Africa and the recurrent political and social crises in states that have not yet experienced military coups or revolutionary overthrow, also contribute to the establishment of neo-colonial ties. Such ties permit the postcolonial African systems to survive despite breakdowns in the centers resulting from their inability to handle all the demands made upon them by contending social and economic forces in the society. Neo-patrimonial regimes thus often willingly become client states of more powerful, developed states.[123] In West Africa, this fact was especially true of most of the Francophone states that remained clients of France after independence.

While neo-colonial ties may provide a short-run stabilizing influence and enhance modest state-building efforts by the postcolonial center, they contribute little to nation-building or to the rapid social transformation of society because they tend to preserve the political status quo and the existing social structures of plural societies.[124] On the other hand, a weak center seeking to implement radical changes in society and a radical break with the ex-colonizer is highly vulnerable to political instability and collapse because it has no neo-colonial protector to intervene to save the regime through political, military, and economic support. Such radical regimes need mass support, mobilization, and participation to pull them through their crises. When the masses become highly activated, one can no longer speak of a neo-patrimonial regime that by definition excludes such direct popular participation.

CONCLUSIONS

The rejection of the tribe-to-nation approach calls for placing studies of state building, nation-building, and modernization processes in Africa within a broader framework of comparative historical analysis. Progress in this direction can be achieved by dropping the inaccurate and culture-bound concepts of tribe and tribalism which discourage comparisons of phenomena occuring in Africa with similar phenomena found not only eleswhere in the Third World but also in industrial and postindustrial societies as well. As the recent upsurgence of ethnic and racial conflict in such highly industrialized societies as Belgium, Canada, and the United States indicates, the problem labeled tribalism when occurring in Africa is by no means confined to developing societies. What is called tribalism in Africa is part of the universal and timeless problem of how culturally pluralistic societies hold together and function within the framework of a single political system. Moreover, the record in Africa as elsewhere indicates that strong attachments and loyalties to subnational collectivities, and rejection of the authority of the central government need not necessarily be a reflection of backwardness.

Rejection of the tribe-to-nation approach towards state-building and modernization also implies a more careful examination of historical processes and traditional modes of political behavior and organization. Historicism is no substitute for the careful study of history. In the West African case, the tribe-to-nation approach was based on false assumptions about precolonial Africa and its historical development. Instead of studying the unfolding modernization and state-building processes in Europe and generalizing the results to conclude that all societies and states must pass through more or less the same stages indicated by the European experience, it might be wiser to pay greater attention to the history of the developing states themselves. Then one could better see the extent to which traditional modes of political behavior and organization have hindered or helped their current modernization efforts and the extent to which traditional societies can adjust to the exigencies of modernity without giving up some of their core values. Indeed, it might be equally profitable to look at the persistence of traditional modes of political behavior—e.g., clientelism, monarchical political styles, and so on—in the developed states as well. Such an examination might reveal that traditional patterns of political behavior die slowly, if at all.

The concepts of neo-patrimonialism and the inheritance situation have proved to be quite useful for studying the West African case. One could further test the fruitfulness of these concepts by applying them to other settings and time periods. The concept of the inheritance situation when applied to Latin America during the early years of independence, the Balkan and Central European successor states, and the new Asian states might tell us a great deal about the early stages of state-building in newly independent countries and the processes of decolonization. It could also be fruitful to examine the applicability of the concept of neo-patrimonialism in non-African settings in greater detail. Such studies would require a strong historical knowledge of the society being analyzed as well as knowledge of current political organization and behavior. The concept should be applied to developed as well as to developing societies. Comparing the results of such studies might suggest, for example, that not only are traits found in neo-patrimonial regimes functional for modernization but also that certain features generally considered to be archaic carry-overs from traditional political systems may in fact be found in all highly differentiated political systems as permanent features of the political landscape.[125]

Finally, the formulation of relevant models and theories of state-building and nation-building calls for more contributions by Third World scholars whose countries are the objects of our modernization studies. Without greater cooperation between Western and non-Western scholars, it will be very difficult to avoid the ethnocentric biases that have hindered previous efforts at model-building and led to formulations like the tribe-to-nation approach to state-building and nation-building discussed in this chapter.

NOTES

1. See Gabriel A. Almond and G. Bingham Powell, Jr., Comparative Politics: A Developmental Approach, Boston, Little, Brown, 1966; Donald Blackmer and Max Millikan, eds., The Emerging Nations, Boston, Little, Brown, 1961; Karl Deutsch and William J. Foltz, eds., Nation-Building, New York, Atherton Press, 1966; Seymour Martin Lipset, The First New Nation, New York, Basic Books, 1963; A.F.K. Organski, The Stages of Political Development, New York, Knopf, 1965; Lucian W. Pye, Aspects of Political Development, Boston, Little, Brown, 1966; and Claude E. Welch, Jr., ed., Political Modernization: A Reader in Comparative Political Change, Belmont, Calif., Wadsworth, 1967.

2. Since the mid-1960s the International Social Science Council and scholars associated with it have been reexamining and refining state-building and nation-building theories that developed earlier. See, for example, Stein Rokkan, ed., Comparative Research Across Cultures and Nations, The Hague, Mouton, 1968, and more specifically the contributions by Reinhard Bendix, Val R. Lorwin, Richard Rose, and Lee Benson as well as the introduction by the editor. The chapters in the present work, originating from the 1970 UNESCO Cérisy Conference, represent a more recent effort.

3. The nation-state is often regarded as the only modern and viable political unit. Moreover, the very survival of the developing countries becomes contingent upon their acceptance of the norms of a "world culture" and the on-going nation-state system. Pye thus writes, "Once we recognize the demands and attractions of both the nation-state system and the world culture we can begin to appreciate the basic stresses that must underlie the nation-building process in the new states. We can see that there is a minimum level of what were Western but are now world standards which the new states must accept if they are to survive in a world of independent nation-states" (see Pye, op. cit., p. 10).

4. Nation-building concerns problems of group identity and loyalty. According to Almond and Powell, "It refers to the process whereby people transfer their commitment and loyalty from smaller tribes, villages, or petty principalities to the larger central political system." (see Almond and Powell, op. cit., p. 36.)

5. The concept of the inheritance situation and its application to the developing countries is the formulation of J. P. Nettl and Roland Robertson. For a full discussion of this concept, see their International Systems and the Modernization of Societies, London, Faber and Faber, 1968 pp. 63-127. For a somewhat different perspective on the inheritance situation, see Frantz Fanon, The Wretched of the Earth, New York, Grove Press, 1966, and René Dumont, L'Afrique Noire est mal Partie, Paris, Editions du Seuil, 1962.

6. For one of the best treatments of Weber's original concept of patrimonialism, see Ch. XI in Reinhard Bendix, Max Weber: An Intellectual Portrait, Garden City, N.Y., Doubleday, 1962, pp. 329-84. For a full treatment of patrimonial bureaucratic empires of the past, see S. N. Eisenstadt, The Political Systems of Empires, New York, Free Press, 1963. More recently, Eisenstadt has applied the concept of neo-patrimonialism to modern regimes in developing societies having structural characteristics similar to those found in traditional patrimonial regimes. See his "Traditional Patrimonialism and Modern Neo-Patrimonialism," in J. S. Jackson, ed., Sociological Studies: Social Change, Cambridge, Mass., Cambridge University Press, forthcoming. For another example of the adaptation of the concept of neo-patrimonialism to contemporary new states, see Guenther Roth, "Personal Rulership, Patrimonialism, and Empire-Building in the New States," World Politics, Vol. XX, No. 2, January 1968, pp. 194-206. For an application of neo-patrimonialism to West Africa, see Aristide Zolberg, Creating Political Order: The New Party-States of West Africa, Chicago, Rand McNalley, 1966, pp. 134-44.

7. For a brilliant and critical discussion of the dichotomous approaches to modernization, see C. S. Whitaker, Jr., "A Dysrhythmic Process of Political Change," World Politics, Vol. XIX, No. 2, January 1967, pp. 190-217.

8. See, for example, MIT Study Group, "The Transitional Process," in Welch, op. cit., pp. 22-47. Fred Riggs's theory of prismatic society is a much more sophisticated conceptualization of transitional societies and the three stage theories of modernization. For a full treatment of the prismatic model, see his Administration in Developing Countries, Boston, Houghton Mifflin, 1964.

9. In referring to recent efforts to rehabilitate African tradition, Rupert Emerson writes, "To go back further than the brief colonial period is to inescapably come upon the tribes and their relations, hostile or friendly, with one another." See "Nation-Building in Africa," in Deutsch and Foltz, op. cit., p. 113. For a spirited defense of the position that tribe and tribal units are still significant in Africa today, see P. H. Gulliver's "Introduction," in P. H. Gulliver (ed.), Tradition and Transition in East Africa: Studies of the Tribal Element in the Modern Era, Los Angeles, University of California Press, 1969, pp. 5-38.

10. When traditional norms of political and social behavior are discussed, they are generally regarded in a negative light. Hence, loyalty to kin is regarded as nepotism when it means preferential treatment in access to public office or position, while clientelist politics based on traditional relationships and norms of reciprocity between partners of unequal status is generally denounced as "clan" politics.

11. This assertion is fostered largely by the fact that the African leaders in power often affirm that nation-building is a top priority item in their development strategy. Whether they actually practice such a policy is another matter.

12. One of the main difficulties with the concept of tribe is that no standard definition has emerged; moreover, the definitions that have emerged are generally not very rigorous. For one of the best discussions of the concept of tribe, see Morton H. Fried, "On the Concepts of Tribe" and "Tribal Society" in June Helm (ed.), Essays on the Problem of Tribe: Proceedings of the 1967 Annual Meeting of the American Anthropological Society, Seattle, University of Washington Press, 1968, pp. 3-20. Fried not only examines the ambiguity of the concept but also rejects the notion that the tribe constitutes a distinct stage in the evolution of political organization.

13. For the best treatment to date of the use of tribalism as an ideological concept, see Archie Mafeje, "The Ideology of Tribalism," Journal of Modern African Studies, Vol. IX, No. 2, 1971, pp. 253-61.

14. Ronald Cohen and John Middleton, eds., From Tribe to Nation in Africa: Studies in Incorporation Processes, Scranton, Pa., Chandler, 1970, p. 2.

15. The tribe was considered to be the first and most primitive form of society in the evolutionary theories of nineteenth-century writers like Henry Sumner Maine and Lewis H. Morgan. See for example, L. H. Morgan, Ancient Society, New York, Henry Holt, 1878.

16. For a discussion of European myths about Africa, see Michael Crowder, West Africa Under Colonial Rule, London, Hutchinson, 1968, pp. 10-17.

17. It is no accident that the concept of tribe was used more widely by British anthropologists than by the French. The conquest of French West Africa had been achieved primarily through military victory over a number of well-organized African states and aspiring empires. Hence, the French knew that they were not dealing with tribes. On the other hand, in the more sparsely populated regions of East and Central Africa conquered by the British, there were fewer African states and more African societies based primarily on kinship relationships.

18. On this point, see Max Gluckman, "Tribalism in Modern British Central Africa," in Pierre L. Van den Berghe (ed.), Africa: Social Problems of Change and Conflict, San Francisco, Chandler, 1965, pp. 348-49.

19. For example, in their landmark volume that made a major contribution to the comparative study of political systems, the authors used tribe exclusively as a descriptive term to identify the groups being studied. The analysis did not require a rigorous definition of tribe. See M. Fortes and F. E. Evans-Pritchard, African Political Systems, London, Oxford University Press, 1940.

20. The rise and fall of Nazi Germany with its racist ideologies had much to do with discrediting these racial stereotypes. In rejecting Hitler's racial theories, the Western democracies were more or less obliged to give up some of their own racial theories about the colonized populations.

21. The use of the term tribal when applied by Europeans as a general descriptive term for Africa was indignantly rejected by Western-educated African elites because of its connotations of backwardness. On the other hand, these same elites took advantage of these negative connotations in using the term against their opponents.

22. For example, Namdi Azikiwe, who had been one of West Africa's leading nationalists during the 1930s, was accused of being an Ibo tribalist by his political opponents during the 1940s and 1950s when he was the leader of the NCNC, the dominant party of the Eastern Region. In fact, the NCNC was a predominantly Ibo-based party. Yet it had pretensions of being a national or territorial party. "Zikism" became the philosophy of many younger nationalists throughout the federation. Obafemi Awolowo, leader of the Action Party, which was the dominant party in Western Nigeria, also aspired to be both a national leader and a leader of the Yorubas. Under different circumstances both men were accused of being tribalists. See Rupert Emerson, From Empire to Nation, Cambridge, Mass. Harvard University Press, 1960, pp. 354-59.

23. During the early and mid-1960s, national integration was perhaps the single most important theme in the political science literature on Africa. See James S. Coleman and Carl G. Rosberg, Jr., eds., Political Parties and National Integration in Tropical Africa, Berkeley, University of California Press, 1964; Aristide R. Zolberg, "Patterns of National Integration," Journal of Modern African Studies, Vol. X, No. 4, December 1967, pp. 449-67; and I. Wallerstein, "Ethnicity and National

Integration in West Africa," op. cit. For a general discussion of the many usages of the concept of national integration, see Myron Weiner, "Political Integration and Political Development," Annals of the American Academy of Political and Social Science, Vol. 358, March 1965, 52-64.

24. The literature on precolonial West African state systems is too enormous to attempt to cite more than a few major general works on the region. See J. F. Ade Ajayi and Ian Espie, eds., A Thousand Years of West African History, London, Ibadan University Press, 1965; Basil Davidson, A History of West Africa to the Nineteenth Century, Garden City, Doubleday, 1966; Cheikh Anta Diop, L'Afrique Noire Pré-Coloniale, Paris, Présence Africaine, 1960; J. D. Fage, An Introduction to the History of West Africa, Cambridge, Mass., Cambridge University Press, 1962; J. Spencer Trimingham, A History of Islam in West Africa, London, Oxford University Press, 1962; and Thomas Hodgkin, Nigerian Perspectives, London, Oxford University Press, 1960.

25. For an excellent general discussion of how precolonial Africa dealt with this problem and a specific study of the Mossi, see Elliot P. Skinner, "Processes of Political Incorporation in Mossi Society," in Cohen and Middleton, op. cit., pp. 175-200. The article is in large part a rebuttal to Rupert Emerson's "Nation-Building in Africa," in Deutsch and Foltz, op. cit., pp. 95-116. After quoting Emerson extensively, Skinner writes,

> scholars go blithely on talking about the problems of "nation-building" in Africa as if similar processes had not taken place there in the past. Thus, in this paper I shall concern myself with identifying and delineating the processes used by African societies in the past to incorporate identifiably different groups so that these groups were able to live in the same society by submerging their social and cultural differences for a common end, or by accepting control of a superior political organization. Perhaps it might be true, as some scholars, though not necessarily myself, are beginning to argue, that there are few structural differences between the processes of incorporation at work in "traditional," "modern," and "post-independent" Africa. (pp. 176-77).

26. The Mali Empire lasted from the thirteenth through the sixteenth century, reaching its peak under the reign of Mansa Musa (1312-1327). Although Islam became the royal cult, there was no effort on the part of the rulers to convert the rest of the populations. Moreover, while Mali was ruled by a Mandinka dynasty, it managed to incorporate non-Mande peoples into the Empire. Its success in preserving peace and security in the vast region under its sway and its prosperity made Mali one of the outstanding polities of the medieval world. For a description of the Mali state system, see Trimingham, op. cit., pp. 60-83. Elliot Skinner's The Mossi of the Upper Volta, Stanford, Stanford University Press, 1964 remains the standard work of the Mossi Empire. In his article, Skinner cites the use of common myths of origins, facial marks, common languages and customs and, above all, common political institutions as means of maintaining the coherence of the Mossi as a people. They had national holidays such as the Annual Feast of the Dead and New Year's festivals of thanksgiving for new crops. Some foreigners were incorporated through intermarriage while other ethnic groups were deliberately kept outside Mossi society.

27. These emirates were conquest states founded by Fulani religious leaders who conducted a Jihad in Hausaland and subjugated and converted most of the Hausa populations. Because of the British policy of indirect rule, these emirates preserved much of their traditional structures right through Nigerian independence.

And until his assasination in 1966, the Sardauna of Sokoto was not only the spiritual leader of Northern Nigeria's Muslim populations but also the most powerful man in the country. For two major studies of the emirates, see M. G. Smith, Government in Zazzau, London, Oxford University Press, 1960, and C. S. Whitaker, The Politics of Tradition: A Study of Continuity and Change in Northern Nigeria, Princeton, Princeton University Press, 1970.

28. On this subject see Charles W. Anderson, Fred R. von der Mehden, and Crawford Young, Issues of Political Development, Englewood Cliffs, N.J., Prentice-Hall, 1967, pp. 29-39.

29. History seems to indicate that no form of polity is permanently stable. Although the old bureaucratic empires are generally regarded as unstable, many of them lasted for several centuries. It remains to be seen whether the nation-state as a form of political development will be the first to endure indefinitely.

30. See Samuel P. Huntington, "Political Development and Political Decay," World Politics, Vol. XVII, No. 3, 1965, pp. 386-430. By political decay, Huntington refers to the decay of political institutions and the increasing dominance of disruptive social forces.

31. Theorists of political development who place the nation-state as the end product of political evolution might argue that this cyclical pattern involved only higher and lower forms of traditional political systems and hence does not negate the progressive stage theory of political development.

32. "Historicism in Africa: Slavery and State Formation," African Affairs, Vol. LXX, No. 279, April 1971, pp. 117-18. Two main factors are behind the recent emphasis on state-building. The first is the adoption of the basic assumption of the political development theorists that the centralized state is a higher form of development. The second is the attempt to demonstrate that traditional precolonial Africa was not primitive, and by extension, to prove that Africans were and are capable of governing large-scale states.

33. Ibid., p. 120.

34. Ibid., pp. 121-24.

The error of the historicists . . . was to combine the social scientist's taxonomic procedures with the evolutionist's concept of inevitable progress, so that classificatory types, formulated in the first place for their heuristic value, were translated into developmental stages, conceived as having real existence and arranged in a hierarchy which is both chronological and qualitative.

35. Ibid., pp. 121-22.

36. For a contrary view, see Whitaker, Jr., "A Dysrhythmic Process," op. cit., pp. 190-217.

37. For recent formulations of this position, see Mafeje, op. cit., pp. 253-61; B. Magubane, "Pluralism and Conflict Situations in Africa: A New Look," African Social Research, Vol. 7, June 1969, 529-54; and Richard L. Sklar, "Political Science and National Integration—A Radical Approach," Journal of Modern African Studies, Vol. 5, No. 1, 1967, pp. 1-11.

38. Sklar, op. cit., p. 6. See also his "Contradictions in the Nigerian Political System," Journal of Modern African Studies, Vol. 3, No. 2, 1965, pp. 201-13.

39. For other examples of class analysis applied to Africa, see Fanon, op. cit.; Jean Ziégler, Sociologie de la Nouvelle Afrique, Paris, Gallimard, 1964; and Seydou Badian, Les Dirigeants d'Afrique Noire Face à leur Peuple, Paris, François Maspero,

1965. Fanon and Badian, like many Marxists, also assert that the men in power—the commercial and administrative bourgeoisie—serve neo-colonialism as well as their own special interests.

40. Traditional Africa is regarded as backward and feudal by Marxists. Feudal and feudalism thus replace tribal and tribalism as terms to describe precolonial African history and surviving patterns of traditional political and economic behavior and relationships.

41. However, Marxist scholars like Jean Suret-Canale and Majhemout Diop, who have lived and worked in West Africa, are notable exceptions. See for example, Jean Suret-Canale, "Touba in Guinea—Holy Place of Islam," in Christopher Allen and R. W. Johnson (eds.), African Perspectives, Cambridge, Cambridge University Press, 1970, pp. 53-81, and Majhemout Diop, Histoire des Classes Sociales dans L'Afrique de L'ouest, Le Mali, Paris, François Maspero, 1971.

42. For a fascinating discussion comparing European nationalism and African tribalism with particular emphasis on Eastern and Central Europe, see W. J. Argyle, "European Nationalism and African Tribalism," in Gulliver, op. cit., pp. 41-57.

43. During the colonial period, the use of the terms nationalist and nationalism was far less restrictive than after independence. Thomas Hodgkin saw African nationalism in all its forms as a response to colonialism:

> My own inclination is to use the term "nationalist" in a broad sense, to describe any organization or group that explicitly asserts the rights, claims, and aspirations of a given African society (from the level of the language-group to that of "Pan-Africa") in opposition to European authority, whatever its institutional forms and objectives. Nationalism in Colonial Africa, New York, New York University Press, 1956, p. 23.

On the other hand, James S. Coleman rejects so broad a coverage and urges its restriction to organizations that were political in nature and that sought independence and the creation of a modern African nation-state. "Nationalism in Tropical Africa," American Political Science Review, Vol. 48, No. 2, June 1954, pp. 404-26. For still another interpretation of the concept of preindependence African nationalism, see Robert I. Rotberg, "African Nationalism: Concept or Confusion," Journal of Modern African Studies, Vol. IV, No. 1, 1966, pp. 33-46.

With independence, the use of the terms nationalist and nationalism to refer to both trans-national and subnational groupings and aspirations tended to diminish. With the termination of colonial rule, the "legitimacy" of these forms of nationalism decreases, particularly in the case of subnational nationalism. Hence, Baganda nationalism directed against the British is acceptable but not Baganda nationalism directed against the state of Uganda.

44. It is very unlikely that the Ibos would have seceded on "national" grounds alone. On the contrary, the Ibo officers who led the first coup spoke of establishing "a free country devoid of corruption, nepotism, tribalism, and regionalism." Okoi Arikpo, The Development of Modern Nigeria, Baltimore, Penguin Books, 1967, p. 149. However, after the May 1966 massacres and the July coup, the Ibos felt very insecure with many thinking that they were in danger of becoming the victims of genocide.

45. Mostafa Rejai and Cynthia H. Enloe, "Nation-States and State-Nations," International Studies Quarterly, Vol. 13, No. 2, June 1969, p. 143. For another interesting discussion of the distinctions between state-nations and nation-states, see Edmund S. Glenn, "The Two Faces of Nationalism," Comparative Political Studies,

Vol. 3, No. 3, October 1970, pp. 347-66. Both articles make it clear that the developing states are state-nations. Moreover, they both agree that a new nationhood can be established around the new state and that it is not necessary for groups to give up their ethnic identities and loyalties in order to be incorporated into the state-nation.

46. According to Glenn, the short-lived Republic of Biafra would be the only example of an authentic nation-state in West Africa, since it was the only one founded by breaking up state boundaries that did not correspond to ethnic realities. All the other countries are state-nations.

47. This transformation is necessary only if one insists that subnational and particularistic identities are incompatible with a national identity. The state-nation can perform the same modernizing functions just as well, as evidenced by Switzerland, the United States, Great Britain, and the Soviet Union.

48. Since in most instances the state-nation and nation-state may be referring to similar things—i.e., loyalty to the state and the development of a sense of nationality around it—perhaps the most crucial distinction is that the state-nation concept permits the survival and modernization of primordial sentiments while the nation-state concept does not. That is to say, the state-nation provides for cultural pluralism while the nation-state seeks to eliminate it.

49. For a very suggestive critique of the nation-state and nation-building model, see Dov Ronen, "Is National Integration Essential to Modernization? An Enquiry into Regionalism in Dahomey," paper presented to the Midwest Political Science Association Conference, Chicago, April 30-May 2, 1970. Ronen argues that there is no need for people to give up their traditional loyalties to the new national state. Instead, he conceives of the national state as essentially a planning unit coordinating developmental efforts of regional units that still command the loyalties of the populations. In Dahomey, this condition would mean recognizing regionalism and stopping the endless battles by regional leaders to take control of the center. In Dahomey, the losers in politics do not regard the center as the national center but the center of the particular opponent in power and his region. In Ronen's scheme, the center would thus become depoliticized by renouncing many of its political roles and its claims to people's loyalties on the basis of a nonexistent national identity.

50. By center, I refer to a society's central political-administrative institutions and the authority and resources embodied in them. As a term, the center encompasses more than the state since it includes party institutions as well as state structures. In another context, it refers to the political-administrative institutions concentrated in the capital and to the elites controlling them.

51. See Roth, op. cit., pp. 203-04:

> Structurally, much of what is today called nation-building should perhaps be called, more precisely, empire-building, if the political connotations of the term do not make it too difficult to use it in a strictly sociological, value, neutral sense. The problem of empire is the problem of establishing political order in the face of social and cultural heterogeneity.

52. For two important volumes of essays dealing with this subject in Africa, see Cohen and Middleton, op. cit., and Leo Kuper and M. G. Smith, eds., Pluralism in Africa, Berkeley, University of California Press, 1969.

53. As one Francophone African statesman put in in referring to the time required to build a nation, "It is a long term enterprise, requiring centuries of effort

and patience. It took France nearly 2000 years—up to Napoleon's time-to become a nation-state, and she was the first in Europe to do so." Leopold Sedar Senghor, On African Socialism, New York, Praeger, 1964, p. 12.

54. See for example, Sékou Touré, La Révolution Guineénene et Le Progrés Social, Conakry, Imprimerie Nationale, 1962, and Mamadou Dia, African Nations and World Solidarity, New York, Praeger, 1961 for detailed discussions of the role of the state in nation-building by West African leaders.

55. These questions all concern dependency relationships between the ex-colonizer and the ex-colonized after independence, and the distinction between decolonization and neo-colonialism.

56. If the inheritance elites rule in a similar manner to their imperial predecessors and if the populations perceive the new state as the successor of the colonial state, then these conditions would strongly suggest that the African political elites commanding the postcolonial center should be ragarded primarily as empire-builders rather than nation-builders.

57. See Nettl and Robertson, op. cit., pp. 63-64.

58. Ibid., p. 66.

59. Ibid., pp. 66-69.

60. For example, in the Ivory Coast and in Ghana, two colonial territories that suffered most from repression of nationalist movements, the colonial authorities and the leaders of the movements eventually made their peace. Hence, Kwame Nkrumah in Ghana was released from prison to become what was then the Gold Coast's first prime minister while Houphouet-Boigny, after being one of the most outspoken and respected nationalist leaders in French West Africa, became one of France's warmest defenders after he and his party (RDA) broke their formal links with the French Communist Party in the early 1950s.

61. In Guinea, Sékou Touré and the PDG, the leading party in the territory, opted for immediate independence in the September 28, 1958 referendum against the wishes of General DeGaulle. The French retaliated by withdrawing all of their technical assistance personnel and by ending economic aid to Guinea. These measures led to a rupture of relations between Guinea and France which has not yet been healed. Although Guinea did not originally intend to leave the French Community, France's reaction gave her the choice of either humbly confessing her errors or seeking alternative aid and trade partners. Guinea chose the latter.

62. Of all the new West African states, Guinea was the only one to break most of its ties with its ex-metropole. Ghana under Nkrumah, while entering into strong links with the Socialist camp, nevertheless maintained correct, if not cordial, relationships with Great Britain. Mali under Modibo Keita maintained its association with the Common Market, kept its close ties with France, and on many occasions, expressed its admiration for the person and policies of General DeGaulle while developing strong links with the Socialist camp. The rest of the new West African states retained much closer ties with their former metropoles.

63. Reform and revolution are the two main analytical categories through which Nettl and Robertson study the inheritance situation. Even Guinea, which has been the most revolutionary of the new African states in terms of its dissociation with colonial structures and norms, has been accused by opponents on the Left of not having dissociated even more. The main sore point here is Guinea's close ties with and dependency upon the international mining firms that dominate Guinea's export economy, and to a lesser extent, Guinea's aid relationships with the United States.

See B. Ameillon, La Guinée, Bilan d'une Indépendance, Paris, Maspero, 1964. For a more general critique along these lines, see Fanon, op. cit.

64. The concept of colonial societies as plural societies was first developed by J. S. Furnival, a colonial administrator and economist. It has been refined and developed by such scholars as M. G. Smith, Pierre L. van den Berghe and Leo Kuper, particularly in the volume edited by Kuper and Smith, Pluralism in Africa, op. cit. Plural societies are characterized by cultural diversity, social cleavage, and dissension. Politically, the plural society is dominated by a unit that is a cultural minority. M. G. Smith writes: "In their colonial phase, all recently independent African states were plural societies; and despite independence, most of these ex-colonies retain their plural character with marginal alteration." "Institutional and Political Conditions," in Kuper and Smith, op. cit., p. 29.

65. For an early distinction between autonomous and nationalist movements in the European sense, see René Maunier, The Sociology of Colonies, Vol. II, London, Routledge & Kegan Paul, 1949, p. 376.

66. Hence, Nkrumah as a nationalist saw his primary role as an apostle of Pan-Africanism. In French West Africa, Francophone elites called for African unity and resisted the balkanization of the French West African Federation. Following Guinea's courageous no vote in 1958, many non-Guinean elites went to Guinea to serve the cause of African nationalism. Shortly afterwards, Ghana allied herself with Guinea in a formal though nonoperational union.

67. Before independence, the Ivory Coast was the most outspoken in its territorial nationalism. As the richest territory in French West Africa, it resented subsidizing the poorer territories as well as the fact that the federal capital was located in Senegal. Houphouet-Boigny played a major role in dismantling the federation. For a further discussion of the conflict between territorialists and federalists, see Ruth Schachter-Morgenthau, Political Parties in French-Speaking West Africa, Oxford, Clarendon Press, 1964, pp. 301-29.

68. This expression corresponds to the reformist orientations elaborated by Nettl and Robertson. Dissociation is strongest in the preinheritance situation. After independence, many of the benefactor roles are transferred to the inheritance leaders of whom statesmanlike behavior is expected (p. 124).

69. Examples of this hostility are the expulsion of Dahomean traders and civil servants from Niger in 1963, the antistranger riots of 1958-59 in the Ivory Coast, the expulsion of aliens from Ghana following Nkrumah's fall, and anti-Levantine measures taken in Sierra Leone following independence.

70. It was precisely this antagonism towards the ex-colonizer and other Western powers which was the principal factor identifying the radical states that were sharper in their criticism of neo-colonialism and more militant in their anticolonialism concerning white-ruled Black Africa.

71. During the post-World War II period, African chiefs and traditional leaders, particularly those who had collaborated closely with the colonial authorities, were often attacked by the autonomist parties. In many colonies, traditional leaders and chiefs who had been the losers under colonialism sided with parties that opposed not only the colonial administration but also their traditional rivals. This alignment was the case with the Union Soudanaise in French Soudan and the PDG in Guinea where both parties opposed the traditional authorities supported by the French. For further details on these two examples, see Schachter-Morgenthau, op. cit., pp. 219-300.

72. In general, the bulk of colonial investments in West Africa took place in the coastal regions where it was easier and cheaper to evacuate colonial exports to Europe. The inland regions and inland colonies received very little capital investment or social services, and their populations generally had lower literacy rates and living standards.

73. Cultural affinities of the Francophone African elites with France and French culture were generally greater than those of educated Africans from the British territories with Great Britain and English culture. Several factors caused this result: (1) the policy of cultural assimilation whereby France pushed the African students to master French by offering it as the only language of instruction at the primary school level; (2) the relatively greater importance of French education in determining one's elite status in the modern sector; and (3) the admiration of Francophone elites for French culture in general and the ideological positions of the French Left in particular. For further details see J. P. N'Diaye, Enquête sur les Etudiants Noirs en France, Paris: Editions Réalités Africains, 1962, and Victor T. LeVine, Political Leadership in Africa, Stanford: Hoover Institution on War, Peace, and Revolution, 1967.

74. For example, the Grand Khalife of the Mouride Brotherhood, who was considered to be the second most powerful man in Senegal after President Senghor, could not aspire to national or even local office because of his lack of literacy in French. Educational shortcomings also placed considerable constraints on the national role that could be played by the Moro Nabe, the traditional leader of the Mossis in Upper Volta. On the other hand, traditional leaders with advanced Western education like Ahmadu Bello, the Sardauna of Sokoto in Nigeria, emerged as national political figures.

75. Hence, the military regimes in Dahomey, Togo, Upper Volta, Mali, Nigeria, and Ghana filled their cabinets largely with young army officers with advanced education, or university graduates not involved in the allegedly corrupt politics of the past.

76. Some critics frowned upon the extent of the involvement of African inheritance elites in the Westernized international culture as a corrupting influence. See, for example, Albert Meister, L'Afrique, Peut-elle Partir? Paris, Editions du Seuil, 1966, pp. 295-97.

77. As the leader of Free France and the man behind the 1944 Brazzaville Conference which initiated the era of decolonization for France's black African colonies, DeGaulle had an excellent reputation among Francophone Africans. His return to power in 1958 was regarded favorably by most of the postwar generation of African political elites who saw DeGaulle as the man to accelerate the drive towards self-government and independence. His success in negotiating the end of the Algerian War, despite strong opposition from the French military and European colons of Algeria, his staunch defense of postindependence aid to the new Francophone states in the light of a strong antiforeign aid current in French opinion, and his government's courteous treatment of visiting African dignitaries were also important factors behind the loyalty to General DeGaulle of the Francophone elites in power. Since DeGaulle's retirement in 1969, his successor, President Pompidou has continued to apply DeGaulle's African policies and maintain high levels of economic and technical assistance to the Francophone states.

78. Again, Guinea was one of the rare West African countries to maintain constant party mobilization after independence. In Mali, the Union Soudanaise during the mid-1960s became an unreliable instrument for the regime which

instituted a National Revolutionary Council, led by Modibo Keita, to become the vanguard of the Malian Cultural Revolution while the party was relegated to a secondary role. The 1968 military coup ended both the cultural revolution and the Union Soudanaise. In Ghana where the CPP was often equated with Ghana itself, the party's role in the administration of the state was almost nonexistent. For a perceptive analysis of the underlying causes behind the decline of party activity, see Immanuel Wallerstein, "The Decline of the Party in Single-Party African States," in Joseph LaPombara and Myron Weiner, eds., Political Parties and Political Development, Princeton, Princeton University Press, 1966, pp. 201-14.

79. For an interesting discussion of the great stress placed on these values in Senegal, see Ch. VIII in Irving L. Markovitz, Leopold Sedar Senghor and the Politics of Negritude, New York, Atheneum, 1969, pp. 212-39.

80. For the best discussion of the economic dependency relationships that shaped their postcolonial ties with France, see Elliot Berg, "The Economic Basis of Political Choice in French West Africa," American Political Science Review, Vol. 44, June 1960, pp. 391-405.

81. In most African states, the great bulk of state revenue came from indirect taxes levied on foreign trade, particularly on imports. Foreign trade itself was propelled primarily by exports that provided most of the foreign exchange for imports. Since most of the West African states were dependent upon one or two export crops that comprised the great bulk of total exports, it was difficult to suddenly shift from these exports without disrupting the economy and government revenues. Ghana and Senegal, the two most industrialized West African states, could not escape their dependency upon cocoa and peanuts which comprised over three-quarters of their exports.

82. This fact was particularly the case with the younger military officers involved in military coups who received their training at Sandhurst, the Ecole Militaire in Paris, or Saint Cyr. These men were generally imbued with technocratic values while the older military officers in power generally had less formal education and were men who had worked their way up through the ranks of the colonial army.

83. The ability of the party to mobilize the populations has often been exaggerated by both African party leaders and scholars because parties have been discussed in terms of party goals and formal party organization rather than in terms of their actual relationships with the rest of society. For an interesting discussion of this point, see Henry Bienen, Tanzania: Party Transformation and Economic Development, Princeton, Princeton University Press, 1967, pp. 3-9.

84. Strong presidential regimes headed by the national leader became the rule throughout West Africa after independence. This trend was strongest in the new Francophone states that patterned their constitutions after the Gaullist model, and in Ghana where Nkrumah became president. It had already been established in Liberia during the tenure of William Tubman. This trend was less marked in countries like Gambia, Sierra Leone, and Nigeria which had greater party competition and no single recognized national leader.

85. For a detailed discussion of the mobilization aspects of goals like economic development and national integration, see J. P. Nettl, Political Mobilization, pp. 232-260.

86. In poor states like Dahomey, Niger, and Upper Volta, foreign aid was virtually the only source of public capital investments after independence. Andrew Kamarck has pointed out that in most African countries at least half and sometimes

all the investment in the public sector is expected to be financed abroad. He also asserts that this high reliance upon external investment funds in Africa is unique among the developing regions of the world whose external dependency, while important, is not nearly so high. The Economics of African Development, New York, Praeger, 1967, pp. 70-71.

87. Of all the West African states, Gambia was unique in not creating a national army, but this fact might be attributed to Gambia's tiny population of 400,000, its short history as an independent state which dates only from 1965, and its poverty, rather than to any antimilitary position.

88. See, for example, K. Nkrumah's Neo-Colonialism: The Last Stage of Imperialism, New York, International Publishers, 1966.

89. While Guinea broke ties with France and adopted the strongest anti-imperialist and anticolonialist stance in West Africa, it nevertheless had to rely heavily upon its foreign-dominated mining sector for economic resources to keep the Guinean economy and state functioning. On the other hand, Mali, which maintained relations with France and the European Economic Community, sought little foreign investment. This stance by Mali was just as much a result of the lack of investment opportunities in a mineral-poor country as it was of its socialist principles. Ghana, while rapidly extending the state sector, nevertheless, accepted foreign private capital when such acceptance suited the government's purposes.

90. For a discussion of the measures leading to the overthrow of the power of the cheffries, see Guinée, Prelude a l'Independence, Paris, Présence Africaine, 1958 and Jean Suret-Canale, "La Fin de la Cheffrie en Guinée," Journal of African History, Vol. VII, 1966, pp. 459-93. For insights into the important role to be played by youth in Guinea, see Sékou Touré, L'Action Politique du Parti Democratique de Guinee en Faveur de l'Emancipation de la Jeunesse Guinéenne, Conakry, 1962.

91. This role meant the establishment of popular militias to counterbalance the power of the professional army. In Ghana and Mali, the establishment of such popular units antagonized the military and was a contributing factor behind the military coups.

92. For a full discussion of the role played by the PDG in the years immediately following independence, see Bernard Charles, "Un Parti Politique Africain: le Parti Démocratique de Guinée," Revue Française de Science Politique, Vol. XII, No. 2, June 1962, pp. 312-59.

93. For more information on this subject, see Basil Davidson, The Liberation of Guiné, Baltimore, Penguin, 1969; Gérard Chaliand, Armed Struggle in Africa, New York, Monthly Review Press, 1969; and Amilcar Cabral, Revolution in Guinea, New York, Monthly Review Press, 1970.

94. For an examination of the important role of culture in the national liberation struggle, see Amilcar Cabral, "National Liberation and Culture," a lecture delivered at Syracuse University on February 20, 1970 and published as Occasional Paper No. 57 by the Maxwell Graduate School of Citizenship and Public Affairs that same year.

95. For a suggestive discussion of the possible positive effects of armed struggles on political development, see Frank J. Popper, "Internal War as a Stimulant of Political Development," Comparative Political Studies, January 1971, pp. 413-23.

96. It should be pointed out, however, that the political elites in power have made a greater effort to build a national identity than their imperial predecessors.

97. In referring to the trend toward one-party systems and military regimes, commentators have referred to the "erosion of democracy" in African regimes. Yet it is not clear that democracy and democratic practices were features of colonial regimes except for a few years during the terminal phases of colonial rule. Even when free and competitive elections were held, ultimate power lay with the colonial government, which often intervened to get the desired results. Moreover, after independence, the most autocratic and centralizing African regimes have generally been more responsive to popular demands than the colonial regimes that preceded them. For a full statement on the concept of the erosion of democracy, see Ch. XV in Emerson, op. cit., pp. 272-92.

98. In the African context, we are speaking of regimes with some patrimonial features which are trying to become modern states in a world dominated by the larger industrialized countries. This factor is crucial in distinguishing the African states from the patrimonial regimes of the past.

99. The limited resources of the center have much to do with the low level of economic development. In Africa, the centers with the most resources have been in Ghana, Senegal, Nigeria, and the Ivory Coast, which are the more developed countries in the region. The weakest centers in West Africa, conversely, have been in countries like Niger, Upper Volta, and Dahomey where most of the populations are still engaged in nonmonetized subsistence farming. The patrimonial regimes of the past lacked the resources because of the low level of economic development and small size of the societies that they governed. For a useful discussion of the limited authority of the modern political sector—i.e., the center-in West African states, see Zolberg, op. cit., pp. 128-35.

100. This characteristic of patrimonial regimes still applies to most of the new African states that remain essentially trading economies despite some modest efforts in industrialization. In precolonial West Africa, the wealthiest and often the most powerful states and empires were those which controlled trade and engaged in mining activities. For a discussion of economic organization in precolonial Africa, see Diop, L'Afrique Noire Pré-Coloniale, op. cit., pp. 98-120.

101. For example, Weber himself writes in describing China:

The hatred and the distrust of the subjects, which is common to all patrimonialism, in China as everywhere turned above all against the lower levels of the hierarchy, who came into the closest practical contact with the population. The "subjects" apolitical avoidance of all contact with "the state" which was not absolutely necessary was typical for China as for all patrimonial regimes.

H. H. Gerth and C. Wright Mills, From Max Weber: Essays in Sociology, London, Routledge & Kegan Paul, 1964, p. 438. In many parts of West Africa, the peasantry who comprise the bulk of the population also regard the state with suspicion and attempt to avoid contact as much as possible. This avoidance is particularly true of the poorer West African states where there is little economic surplus for the center to tap.

102. For a discussion of the relationships between patrimonial rulers and local notables, see Bendix, op. cit., pp. 355-60.

103. See ibid., pp. 344-48, for a discussion of patrimonial administration.

104. Although most West African states have increased the size of their armies and police, these forces have been used to defend the security of the center rather than to administer or intimidate the people of the countryside into compliance.

105. For an excellent discussion of the vulnerability of the new African states, see Aristide Zolberg, "The Structure of Political Conflict in the New States of Tropical Africa," American Political Science Review, Vol. 62, March 1968, pp. 70-87. For a more general discussion of this problem in the developing states, see S. N. Eisenstadt, "Breakdowns of Modernization," Economic Development and Cultural Change, Vol. XII, No. 4, July 1964, pp. 345-67.

106. For an analysis of monarchical tendencies in contemporary Africa, see Ali A. Mazrui, "The Monarchical Tendency in African Political Culture," in Violence and Thought: Essays on Social Tensions in Africa, London, Longmans, 1969, pp. 206-30. On the personalization and sacralization of power in West Africa, see Badian, op. cit., pp. 30-33. For precolonial West Africa, see Diop, L'Afrique Noire Pré-Coloniale, op. cit., pp. 48-59.

107. The crucial importance of clientelism in cementing political relationships in developing nations has been the subject of a growing body of literature. See, for example, John Duncan Powell, "Peasant Society and Clientelist Politics," American Political Science Review, Vol. 64, No. 2, June 1970, pp. 412-25, and Rene Lemarchand, "Political Clientelism and Ethnicity in Tropical Africa: Competing Solidarities in Nation-Building," American Political Science Review, Vol. 66, No. 1, March 1972, pp. 68-90.

108. This situation was not the case in precolonial West Africa, which was largely preliterate. However, it certainly is the case in postcolonial West Africa where diplomas are rapidly becoming the crucial factor in determining rank in the administration and high social status in the modern sectors of society.

109. For background to Senegalese politics and political structures, see Ruth Schachter-Morgenthau, op. cit., pp. 125-65; William J. Foltz, "Senegal," in James C. Coleman and Carl G. Rosberg, Jr. (eds.), Political Parties and National Integration, Berkeley, University of California Press, 1964, pp. 16-64; Madani Seydou Sy, Recherches sur l'Exercice du Pouvoir en Afrique Noire, Paris, Pedone, 1965; Francois Zuccarelli, Un Parti Politique Africaine: L'Union Progréssiste Sénégalaise, Paris, Librairie Générale de Droit et de Jurisprudence, 1970; and Sheldon Gellar, "The Politics of Development in Senegal," Ph.D. dissertation, Columbia University, 1967.

110. Indeed, few African political leaders were charismatic figures in the Weberian sense. In referring to nontraditionalist patrimonial rulers, Roth writes:

> The second type of patrimonialism is personal rulership on the basis of loyalties that do not require any belief in the ruler's unique personal qualification, but are inextricably linked to material rewards and incentives. This second variant has been submerged in much of the literature through the indiscriminate use of "charismatic."

"Personal Rulership, Patrimonialism, and Empire-Building in the New States," World Politics, Vol. XX, No. 2, January 1968, p. 196. And in the same article, he further states:

> Moreover, the treatment of almost all political leaders in the new states as "charismatic" has been misleading on at least two counts: it has obscured the difference between "charismatic authority" and "charismatic leadership" and it has taken at face value the international propaganda claims of some of the new leaders. Most heads of government in the new states do not have the magic of personal charisma for many groups in the society, nor do they have the kind of impersonal, institutional charisma that Edward Shils has stressed as a basic requirement for organization stability (p. 200).

111. For more details about the prominence of the Muslim brotherhoods in Senegalese politics, see Irving L. Markovitz, "Traditional Social Structure, The Islamic Brotherhoods, and Political Development in Senegal," Journal of Modern African Studies, Vol. VIII, No. 1, 1970, pp. 73-96; and the book length studies by Lucy C. Behrman, Muslim Brotherhoods and Politics in Senegal, Cambridge, Mass., Harvard University Press, 1970; Donald B. Cruise O'Brien, The Mourides of Senegal, Oxford, Clarendon Press, 1971; and Cheikh Tidiane Sy, La Confrérie Sénégalaise des Mourides, Paris, Présonce Africaine, 1969.

112. For a succinct description of the political style of a Senegalese traditional ruler and his efforts to impress his subjects, see Martin Klein, Islam and Imperialism in Senegal: Sine-Salou, Stanford, Stanford University Press, 1968, p. 21.

113. The administrative reforms of 1964 strengthened the powers of the seven regional governors and gave them greater influence in local affairs. At the same time they diminished the role of local party leaders. In Senegal, the governors were named directly by the president. Their loyalties were exclusively to the center. In clashes between the regional governors and local party officials, the national leader generally supported the prerogatives of his officials. One of the principal characteristics of patrimonial regimes was the patrimonial ruler's use of state officials as a weapon against local notables. The expansion of state authority led to conflicts between the state officials seeking to impose the authority of the patrimonial ruler and the local notables who demanded immunity against the interference of patrimonial officials. On this point, see Bendix, op. cit., p. 355.

114. For a discussion of Senegalese clan politics and the way in which the center was able to manipulate local factions, see William J. Foltz, "Social Structure and Political Behavior of Senegalese Elites," Behavior Science Notes, Vol. IV, No. 2, 1969, pp. 145-63; Clement Cottingham, "Political Consolidation in Centre-Local Relations in Senegal," Canadian Journal of African Studies, Vol. IV, No. 1, 1970, pp. 101-20; and Jonathan Barker, "The Paradox of Development: Reflections on a Study of Local-Central Political Relations in Senegal," in Michael F. Lofchie (ed.), The State of the Nations: Constraints on Development in Independent Africa, Berkeley, University of California Press, 1971, pp. 47-63.

115. For a thorough discussion of the concept of political corruption and its different forms and functions in a wide range of societies, see Arnold J. Heidenheimer, ed., Political Corruption: Readings in Comparative Analysis, New York, Holt, Rinehart, and Winston, 1970.

116. In patrimonial regimes the expansion of patrimonial administration was determined largely by the development of the money economy. Bureaucratization itself presupposes the existence of a steady income for the maintenance of the administrative apparatus, which calls for the existence of a stable system of taxation.

117. In African precolonial societies and patrimonial regimes, the ruler was expected to provide for the welfare of his people. "That the patrimonial ruler sees to the welfare of his subjects is the basis on which he legitimates his rule in his own and their eyes. The 'welfare state' is the legend of patrimonialism." Bendix, op. cit., p. 365.

118. Since the mid-1960s, the military has increasingly become one of the main pillars of the regime, being entrusted not only with maintaining security but also with administrative and developmental tasks. For a discussion of Senghor's growing reliance on the army, see Markovitz, Leopold Sedar Senghor, op. cit., pp. 220-22.

119. For one of the best discussions of how the new African states must balance their efforts to extend their authority while not directly confronting traditional forces, see H. S. Aynor, Notes From Africa, New York, Praeger, 1969.

120. These dependency relationships are the main focus of a forthcoming book by Sheldon Gellar, The Politics of Dependency: The Senegal Case, Bloomington, Indiana University Press, IDRC, 1973.

121. The duality of structures in modernizing societies has been stressed by many authors. See, for example, S. N. Eisenstadt, Modernization: Protest and Change, Englewood Cliffs, N.J., Prentice-Hall, 1966, pp. 86-96. For West Africa, see Zolberg, Creating Political Order, op. cit., pp. 130-34. In Senegal, people in the modern sectors have been the ones most critical of the regime; and the principal sources of political opposition have been students, industrial workers, intellectuals, and Senegalese businessmen dissatisfied with their small role in the national economy.

122. On center-periphery relations, see Nettl, Political Mobilization, op. cit., p. 66; Daniel Lerner, "Some Comments on Center-Periphery Relations," in Richard L. Merritt and Stein Rokkan (eds.), Comparing Nations, New Haven, Conn., Yale University Press, 1966, pp. 259-65; and Martin Staniland, "The Rhetoric of Center-Periphery Relations," Journal of Modern African Studies, Vol. 8, No. 4, 1970, pp. 617-36.

123. This behavior suggests that the pattern of evolution in many West African states is not from tribe to nation-state but from colony to client state.

124. Regimes with strong neo-colonial ties tend to concentrate their modernization efforts on economic development and expanding educational programs rather than through a radical restructuring of society.

125. Eisenstadt's long essay, "Traditional Patrimonialism and Modern Neo-Patrimonialism," already cited, represents the most serious attempt to date to incorporate the concept of neo-patrimonialism into the comparative study of developing societies.

CHAPTER 15

"TRIBALISM," REGIONALISM, NATIONALISM, AND SECESSION IN NIGERIA

Ulf Himmelstrand

ULF HIMMELSTRAND is Professor of Sociology at the University of Uppsala. He has carried out a number of surveys of ideological orientations and functions of ideology among leaders and rank-and-file citizens in Sweden. He was for several years Professor at the University of Ibadan, and carried out a major survey of conditions for social and political development in Nigeria just before the onset of the civil war. This was part of a cross-national project including India, Japan, the United States, Yugoslavia, and the Netherlands.

Interpretations of political events in the new multiethnic states of Africa often place great emphasis on ethnic or "tribal" affiliations and tribal conflicts. This emphasis was especially obvious during the Congo crisis and during the recent civil war in Nigeria. The standard explanation for these events in terms of tribalism, understood as an extension of traditional ethnic loyalties into politics, may have been less explicit among social scientists than among news commentators.[1] But if any commentators in the mass media had been serious enough to consult the scientific literature on African societies, they would most probably have encountered a number of books and papers based on the notion of tribe. One

AUTHOR'S NOTE: The research underlying this paper has been financed, at various stages, through grants from the Ford Foundation, the Carnegie Foundation, and the Bank of Sweden Tercentenary Fund; I express my gratitude for their support. I also owe thanks to the Center for Advanced Study in the Behavioral Sciences, Stanford, for the period I spent there writing the larger work from which this paper derives.

tribal society would be compared with another regarding social structure, systems of chiefdom and kinship, the basic personality type fostered by such structural and cultural conditions, and so on.[2]

Historically, this focus on tribe is quite understandable even if one might ask whether or not the more general term "people" could have served equally well.[3] Looking at the matter in terms of current social and political change, however, the use of the term tribal is quite misleading.

References to tribe or to the pervasive tribal character of social relations in the context of contemporary African politics are likely to convey an impression of cultural lag, not to say backwardness. Quite apart from being offensive to many Africans the term tribal narrows our span of attention; it conceals much while appearing to explain a lot. The term is holistic and relates to a complex web of cultural and structural variables, which makes it less useful for purposes of scientific analysis.

Furthermore, it is our contention that any interpretation of tribalism in contemporary African politics as an extension of, or a cultural lag from, past tribal societies obscures the impact of so-called modernization and of political systems imported from the modern world.[4] Traditional African patterns are certainly not insignificant in accounting for contemporary African politics, but their encounter with a new political order introduced by Western colonial powers seems to have created a completely new political amalgam that is as much a result of modernization as of traditional elements in the given society. If this view is correct, tribalist politics can not be adequately interpreted as a remnant of traditional backwardness operating independently to disturb the efficiency of modern government, but only as a result of the interplay between traditional and modern elements in African society. We will have more to say about the nature of this interplay later on. Here it will suffice to say that the assumption of interplay, and the rejection of a simple-minded, culture-lag hypothesis are basic to the main approach of this chapter. Clearly, the view does not eliminate the notion of traditional ethnic affiliation from our analytic perspective, but rather looks at it as one of several factors among which there is a considerable degree of causal interaction.

As we have already indicated, ethnicity as a variable relates to a number of various structural and cultural differences in education, economic systems, ascriptive rank, model personality type, and so on. It would seem rational to focus attention on these variables rather than on ethnicity as such, but reducing ethnicity to such a bundle of variables would leave out an important point. In multiethnic political systems in Africa, ethnic affiliation often has a kind of social reality of its own in the political context, not only phenomenologically in the minds of political actors but also in the statistical correlations (though far from perfect) that often exist between ethnic and political positions.[5] As a result of such correlations, both the actors involved and outside commentators come to interpret politics in tribal terms. What is called tribalism may in fact be defined as politically opportune interpretations in terms of tribal affiliation of contemporary competitive politics and economic life. In our view, however, the social reality of tribalism as a political factor is something to be explained, not something to be introduced as an explanation of certain features of African politics. In this chapter we intend to explore not only some mainsprings of tribalism on the macro-level, but also to discuss preconditions and correlates of regionalism, nationalism, and secessionism in Nigerian political development.

An exploration of the social realities of multiethnic politics in contemporary Nigeria, from the point of view of our so-called interplay assumption, requires some background knowledge of Nigerian society. The following thumbnail sketch is intended mainly for those who are not already familiar with the Nigerian scene, but readers more knowledgeable in this area may also find it useful as an indication of our general approach. Detailed documentation and references will not be provided here, however. Those who wish a more detailed and documented discussion of Nigerian society can easily find other sources that meet their demands.[6]

SOURCES OF STRAIN IN THE NIGERIAN POLITICAL SYSTEM BEFORE THE CIVIL WAR

The following types of sources of structural strain will be discerned:

(1) The geopolitical structure of the Nigerian Federation. In a multiethnic federation like Nigeria it might be more adequate to speak of "geo-ethno-political structure." We will see how this structure was further complicated by the extensive migration of certain ethnic groups into geopolitical units distinct from their home areas.

(2) Cultural intersections occur when members of culturally different ethnic groups are involved in the same activities at cross-purpose or with different perspectives derived from different cultural definitions of the situation.

(3) Economic class differentials. Note that even where economic differentials are obvious to the incidental observer, and by him are diagnosed as signs of a fundamental cleavage in Nigerian society, these economic differences often tend to remain hidden or relegated to the background among the actors involved because of the intense popular preoccupation with geo-ethno-political and cultural conflicts.

When we shift our focus from conflicts on the national level to intracommunity conflict in areas that are culturally and politically fairly homogenous, we do find people spontaneously mentioning economic or class differences in response to open questions about the main opposing groups in the community. We will return to these empirical findings in a later section. Here we only wish to reiterate that geo-ethno-political cleavages have attracted more attention than any other form of conflict in Nigeria during recent years. Only when the nature of this type of conflict is properly understood and its saliency reduced will economic class differences come to be seen by Nigerians as another major form of social cleavage.

It is probably fair to say that the nature of geo-ethno-political conflict in Nigeria is badly understood not only by many outsiders—including some social scientists—but also by many Nigerians themselves. Interviews as well as many informal conversations with Nigerians have convinced us that many of them tend to account for the recent turmoil in Nigeria simply by referring to the tribal character and composition of Nigerian society.

Some Popular Notions That Must be Rejected

For many commentators on the Nigerian crisis of 1965-67 an enumeration of Nigerian tribes and their social and cultural differences was sufficient proof of Nigeria's inability to stay together. No wonder there were perpetual conflicts between the tribes, such people would exclaim. Would not the best solution be to let them each go their own way? Contemporary tensions in Nigeria and the recent civil war, according to this approach, were seen as a continuation of traditional tribal wars, and at the same time as an expression of social and political backwardness. This situation could, therefore, best be resolved by letting the combatant parties break loose from the larger national community where they were so recently placed, withdrawing to their respective homelands, and "growing up" a little before taking upon themselves such a difficult task as joining forces to build a nation. Those foreign Africanists who defended Biafran secession would add that Biafra was less backward; but since the rest of Nigeria was so comparatively underdeveloped, the separation might just as well take place.[7]

This approach not only reflected a condescending Western attitude, not too surprisingly shared at that time by some of the educated Ibo elite, but it was also shallow and inaccurate. If we wish, in a few words, to summarize and characterize the events in Nigeria in the years immediately preceding January 1966, we might just as well find suitable and striking parallels in such highly developed countries as Germany and Italy in the 1930s, or in the so-called urban political machines in the United States during the same period.

A hundred years ago several wars took place between the Hausa-Fulani empire in the north and the Yoruba tribes in the south.[8] These might be considered a protracted series of tribal wars, but the Hausa-Fulani never fought any such tribal war with the Ibos; nor did the Yorubas ever fight any with the Ibos. To view the civil war with Biafra as a continuation of traditional tribal wars is thus a total absurdity. The alignments during the civil war were quite different, as were the reasons behind the fighting.

But why, then, bring tribes or ethnic groups into the picture at all? Once again, because we cannot understand the internal strains in Nigeria that have been both created and exploited by previous political regimes (including the colonial one) unless we take into account the interplay between tradition and modern development in Nigeria. The ethnic groups and their geographical locations constitute the basic traditional element in this interplay. Let us, therfore, proceed to discuss certain important aspects of Nigerian geo-ethno-political structure.

Majority-Minority Relations as a Source of Strain

By counting very carefully, it has been maintained, one can distinguish more than four-hundred ethnic groups in Nigeria. This figure is somewhat misleading, however, since the eight largest ethnic groups account for just over three-fourths of the total population. These eight ethnic groups are the Hausas, Ibos, Yorubas, Fulanis, Kanuris, Ibibios, Tivs, and Edos or Binis. Figure 1 indicates roughly where the bulk of these different groups live. The three largest groups—the Hausas, Ibos, and Yorubas—account for about one-half of the population. The other half consists of what are often called minority groups, a category we will have occasion to discuss later.[9]

While the Hausas, Ibos, and Yorubas were each dominant in one of the three federal regions that the British left behind when Nigeria became independent in 1960, the minority groups were spread throughout the regions and came to be politically dependent on the dominant majority ethnic groups. In other words, within the original federation, half of Nigeria's population, the so-called minorities, came to be dominated in many respects by the other half who controlled most political patronage. This situation was one of the major sources of strain in Nigeria.

When, as the result of a plebiscite in 1964, the minority groups living in the eastern portion of the original Western Region were granted their own

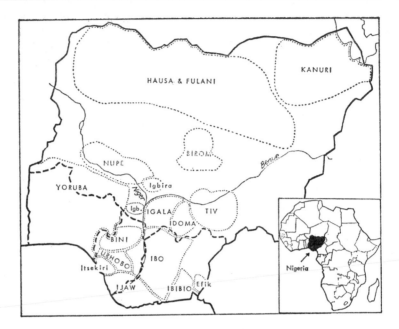

SOURCE: Olav Stokke, Ulf Himmelstrand, and Hans Sjöberg, **Värden, Nigeria och Biafra. Sanningen som kom bort,** Stockholm, Aldus/Bonniers, 1969.

Figure 1: ETHNIC GROUPS IN NIGERIA

region (the Midwestern region), this source of strain was somewhat reduced, but large minority groups were still to be found in the Northern and Eastern Regions, as seen in Figure 1. Once again, we note that it is the interplay among ethnic affiliation, size of ethnic groups, and administrative boundaries that underlies the social strains dealt with in this section. The problem is not ethnicity as such.

Perhaps less important as a source of strain than the minority groups found in all the regions of Nigeria, but still of some interest in that context, were certain overlapping ethnic groups. These were groups that territorially overlapped into regions other than the ones where they were primarily located. In Europe, the irredentism of overlapping linguistic groups in Southern Tyrol is one of the better known cases. In the First Republic of Nigeria there were two clear cases of such overlapping groups: the Yorubas in the southern part of the Northern Region (presently, the Kwara State), and the Ibos in the Midwest. Yorubas are the dominant ethnic group in Western Nigeria, but they also occupied a fairly large area in the southwestern part of the former Northern Region and constituted an overlapping group there. Similarly, the Ibos were dominant in the Eastern Region, but overlapped into the Midwestern Region.

Migration as a Source of Strain

Another source of social and political strain, also relating to the distribution of ethnic groups in Nigeria, was the large number of people from certain groups who had migrated from their own region and settled more or less permanently (or at least taken jobs) in other regions. "Strangers" was the term most commonly used in Nigeria for such aliens from other regions or communities within the federation.

People whose language and culture are different from those of the local population will inevitably constitute something of a problem for societies that are still to some extent dominated by traditional communal values, particularly if such communalism is exploited by politicians competing for power in a "modern," democratic, multiparty system. The stranger problem was thus a third source of strain in Nigeria in addition to the minority and overlapping problems.

In looking more closely at the ways in which these immigrant strangers tended to respond to strains arising from their role as aliens—as we shall do later on—we will find it useful to distinguish between two types of strangers: the minority stranger and the majority stranger.

Strangers who belonged to one of the ethnic minority groups—for instance Efiks from the East or Urhobos from the Midwest who worked and lived in the West or the North—obviously were minority strangers. Majority strangers were persons from one of the "big-three" ethnic groups—Yoruba, Hausa, or Ibo—who lived scattered as immigrants outside their home region.

Strangers should be clearly distinguished from what we have called overlapping groups. In contrast to overlappers, strangers did not live in a distinct, historically inherited territory but instead lived as immigrants scattered in villages and towns in areas outside their home region. Thus Ibos living in Ibadan, the capital of the Western region were majority strangers, as were Ibos and Yorubas living in Northern towns such as Zaria, Kaduna, or Makurdi. In contrast Yorubas in the southwestern part of the Northern Region, as well as Ibos living in the eastern part of the Midwest, were not strangers there but simply an overlapping group in that region.

A Synopsis of Crucial Geo-political
Population Categories

We may now sum up the main population categories that were involved during the last few years proceeding the 1967 Nigerian crisis, both in creating strain and in being subjected to the strain created by the interplay between traditional ethnic and modern political development in Nigeria:

(1) Three majority ethnic groups—Hausa-Fulani, Yorubas, and Ibos, at home both in their traditional territories and in administrative regions ruled by their own elites.

(2) Overlapping ethnic groups—groups that overlapped territorially into administrative regions bordering on the regions in which they were most populous.

(3) Majority strangers—immigrants belonging to majority ethnic groups (Ibo, Yoruba, and Hausa) who lived in other parts of Nigeria than their traditional ethnic domiciles.

(4) Ruling minority ethnic groups—found in the new Midwestern Region that was formed in 1964.

(5) Nonruling minority ethnic groups in their home region—found wherever the elites of a majority ethnic group dominated the population and/or the politics of the region; after the creation of the Midwest Region in 1964 these nonruling minority groups at home were found only in the Northern and Eastern Regions.

(6) Minority strangers—immigrants belonging to minority ethnic groups but living scattered in parts of Nigeria other than their traditional ethnic domicile.

(7) The Lagosians—the ethnically mixed (but Yoruba-dominated) and rather cosmopolitan population of Lagos, the federal capital.

Note that these seven categories are partly nonethnic. To arrive at this classification, traditional ethnic elements have been combined with elements that derive their significance from contemporary, rapidly changing Nigerian society—such as migration, urbanization, new administrative boundaries, regional political power, and the size of ethnic and regional populations as defined by the way in which the Nigerian federal system was constituted before the creation of more states in 1967.

Another way of visually structuring our notions of the above seven population categories is represented in Figure 2.

One way to use this table would be to look for the distribution of relevant dependent variables—pertaining, for instance, to social perception, political allegiance, and political activity—within and between the rows and columns of the table. The extent to which such dependent variables show greater statistical variation along the rows than along the columns in this table would indicate the relative predominance of cultural-ethnic determination over geopolitical determinants of these dependent variables.

Ethnicity Power etc.	Hausa-Fulani	Yoruba	Ibo	Southern Minorities	Northern Minorities
Ruled by Own Elites	1[a] Northern Region	1 Western Region	1 Eastern Region	4 Midwest Region	
Ruled by Other Elites				5 Eastern Region	5 Northern Region
Migrant "Strangers"	3 All regions except the North	3 All regions except the West	3 All regions except the East	6 All regions	6 All regions
Over-Lappers		2 Northern Region	2 Midwest Region		

a. The numbers appearing In this figure refer to the seven population categories mentioned. Category 7 is missing in the figure, it does not quite fit in with the row and column headings.

Figure 2.

With standard statistical procedures we could also detect statistical interaction between cultural-ethnic and political variables in the determination of social perception and political attitudes and activities. To be in a better position to interpret such findings, we will now take a closer look at some of the more important cultural and social characteristics of various ethnic groups in Nigeria.

Cultural Intersections as Sources of Strain

Because of their many centuries of contact with the Arab peoples of the Mediterranean Basin, the history of the Hausa and Fulani peoples is better known than that of any other Nigerian people. Historical sources from the Middle Ages and Arabic documents speak of the lively commerce carried on at that time between Kano and the Mediterranean countries through long caravan routes over the Sahara, work and slaves being the primary exports. The Hausas also have a long tradition of efficient and specialized agriculture and handicrafts. Early in the nineteenth century, the territory of the Hausas was conquered by the Fulanis, who established hierarchically structured sultanates on top of the Hausa feudal system. The sultans had not only military but also economic and religious functions; they collected taxes and spread the Islamic faith.

Certain historians maintain that the Hausa-Fulani empire, which extended over the greater part of Northern Nigeria and attempted to expand southward through wars of conquest in the mid-nineteenth century, was in a period of incipient internal decay when British colonization of Northern Nigeria began. Whatever the case may be, the British colonial administration had the effect of increasing the power of the sultans and emirs by introducing what is generally known as "indirect rule." The sultans and emirs were made a part of the colonial administration, and in this way managed to maintain and even strengthen their positions in most cases. In the same fashion, the stratification of society into distinct classes was preserved: on the top were the sarakuna, or privileged aristocracy, and below the talakawa, or various ranks of ordinary citizens. A certain degree of social climbing or mobility was possible, and the best way to climb was by faithful service to a sarakuna or a highly placed talakawa, showing humble devotion and ability, thereby winning the latter's sympathy and patronage. With the help of such a benefactor, a person could then move on to more and more favoured positions.

In his image of himself and of other ethnic groups in Nigeria today, a highly placed Hausa-Fulani must face a troublesome duality of perspective. Given his historical traditions, his rather highly differentiated and—at least in terms of class—highly refined social structure, his aesthetic culture, his religion, his Arabic literacy, and much else, he feels a sense of pride and self-respect. In the recent past he regarded many of the peoples to the south as savages, but when he now finds himself at cultural intersections with people from Southern Nigeria, he knows that they often regard him as underdeveloped and illiterate, even though he may be able to read part of the Koran in the original Arabic.

The ambiguities inherent in such a dual perspective may be resolved in a number of different ways.[10] One way is to avoid contact with or isolate oneself from the "savage" peoples who by virtue of their presently greater formal education and other characteristics, consider themselves to be of higher status than oneself. If such isolation is impossible or difficult because of the geography of commerce and other necessary contacts, one may ascribe extra significance to one's unique cultural heritage, thereby reasserting one's ethnic identity and compensating for the low rank received from others. Both of these ways of resolving the dual perspective tend to set one apart from other ethnic groups.

On the other hand, it would be at least theoretically possible to solve this identity problem by putting more emphasis on something that one shares with others, irrespective of ethnic or educational status, such as Nigerian citizenship. This kind of solution seems to have been adopted by some Nigerian minorities and migrant strangers.

The Hausa-Fulani leadership and people did not find a Nigerian identity and citizenship either necessary or particularly meaningful, however, except as a convenience to be used, neglected or rejected depending on circumstances. Many factors contributed to this stance, including their distinctive culture, their relative geographical isolation, the cultural shock and rebuff they encountered at their first contacts with the south,[1] and the considerable political power they came to enjoy in the first few years of Nigerian independence as a result of ruling over the most populous region within the federation.

The social structure and life style of the Ibos are in many ways almost the diametrical opposite of those prevailing among the Hausa-Fulanis. While the largest traditional political unit among the Hausas and Fulanis was the great Hausa-Fulani empire with its hierarchical structure, the largest traditional unit among the Ibos was a collection of neighboring villages with a common meeting place that served both as a ritual and political center, as well as a market. Every village had a local council of elders and council of titleholders who enjoyed a certain degree of authority in the village. One of the title holders, called Okpara or Okpala was somewhat more highly placed than the others by reason of being the oldest living descendant from the man who at one time supposedly founded the village.[12] The other titleholders had not inherited their titles, but rather acquired them, through such endeavors as outstanding industriousness in agriculture and the accumulation of wealth, or by distinguishing themselves in games, athletics (such as wrestling), or other spheres of activity.

Just as in many other parts of Africa, there were also institutions based on age; members of a given age group in the village formed an age-grade association and had their special functions within village society. But apart from the limited authority enjoyed by the elders of the village council, authority outside of the family circle had little to do with seniority. An older age grade did not automatically enjoy authority over younger ones, once the latter had been recognized as adults; they simply had different functions. Nor was there any central authority that bound together the clusters of villages, except for a small number of religious oracles whose services were used by villagers throughout Iboland and who, over a period of time, took advantage of their religious power to build up a certain measure of economic and political influence.

The lack of central political authority and of a unified political organization over all of traditional Iboland are characteristic features of what social anthropologists call a segmentary political system. We here disregard the fact unraveled by recent archaelogical findings that central kingdoms existed in ancient Iboland.[13]

In segmentary, uncentralized tribal societies, the settling of internal feuds or disputes poses a problem. Attacks or pressures from outsiders are often helpful in bringing such internal conflicts to a settlement. Among segmentary societies one can, therefore, often discern intricate overlapping sets of concentric systems of definitions of insiders and outsiders. And the more intense the conflict with whomever for the moment is the most outside "outsider" in a particular set—whether Ibos from another clan or some completely different ethnic group—the easier the settling of disputes and feuds on the "inside" of the set. External opposition thus seems to substitute for the lack of central authority in segmentary internal conflict resolution.

Compared to the Hausa-Fulani empire with its finely stratified and ornamented system of social classes, segmental and uncentralized traditional Ibo society may have seemed primitive and undeveloped to the ignorant Western mind. This view is more or less the one British colonial authorities seem to have had of the Ibos in the early colonial years. To them, isolated people, with neither royalty nor an aristocracy or a political hierarchy seemed to be a primitive people.[14]

But in the independent Nigeria after 1960, the Ibos distinguished themselves in science, technology, and administration. Many—and not least the Ibos themselves—were claiming that by the standards of modern civilization, the Ibos had surpassed or at least leveled up to the Yorubas and other groups who had been exposed to Western civilization much earlier than they.

Rather paradoxically the primitive, segmentary structure of traditional Ibo society may have made it easy for an Ibo to adjust to modern society, i.e., to change least while changing the most, as the social anthropologist Simon Ottenberg puts it.[15] Nevertheless, the highly placed Ibo man in modern Nigeria had to face the same kind of dual perspective concerning his self-image that we found in the case of the highly placed Hausa from Northern Nigeria. An Ibo man, with a personality type said to be well equipped for life in a modernizing society, did not always find it easy to introduce himself to highly educated Nigerians belonging to other ethnic groups, and to become accepted as an equal without further ado. The relatively low social evaluation of the Ibo that prevailed in the colonial era seems to have lingered for quite some time—probably to some extent as a result of politically opportune exploitation of this evaluation by competing elites from other ethnic groups.[16]

The place of the Ibo on the social scale in regions other than his own, particularly in Lagos and Western Nigeria, was further affected by his willingness to accept the heaviest and dirtiest of jobs if he could find nothing better. Through hard work he sometimes "expropriated" resources lying idle in areas traditionally inhabited by other ethnic groups. The Ibo's status as a stranger in these parts of Nigeria was naturally brought into focus in this kind of situation. In places where traditional values prevail, or are nurtured for political reasons, a stranger simply does not rank as high on the social scale as does a local person whose qualifications are otherwise on the same level, or, perhaps, even lower. The high degree of self-respect felt by the successful Ibo immigrant as a result of merits acquired through his own efforts, was thus often at variance with the lower regard in which other Nigerians held him. But unlike the relatively isolated Hausa, confronting this dissonant dual perspective, the Ibo man who was constantly in touch with Nigerians belonging to other ethnic groups found it difficult to resolve his dual-perspective dilemma through isolation. Ethnic reassertion or a heavy emphasis on the transcendent status of Nigerian citizenship seem to have been more accessible options among Ibo strangers up to a point. However, isolation was still available as a third option, if the others turned out to be ineffective.[17]

Some social anthropolotists prefer to attribute the difficulties many contemporary Ibos have encountered in fitting in with other Nigerians, to the segmentary type of authority structure in traditional Ibo society, rather than to the psychology of what I have called the dual perspective. Very crudely, their argument is that Ibos do not make friends with other people, nor do they settle disputes easily with anybody unless they have enemies in common with them. In order to maintain solidarity, even among themselves, they must invent or imagine an external opposition where it does not in fact exist.[18]

In accordance with my previous rejection of the cultural-lag interpretation of multiethnic Nigerian politics, I tend to be skeptical of explanations that simply extrapolate notions developed to describe traditional tribal societies to account for contemporary phenomena. I am particularly so when notions of the traditional society are as abstract and simplified as the notion of segmentary social structure, and when contemporary conditions are as complex as they have been in Nigeria. Surely, the notion of dual perspective is simplified as well, but at least it attempts to bridge the gap between the traditional and the contemporary.

Not simply by projecting the past into the present, but by studying the interaction of traditional structures and values with conditions prevailing in contemporary Nigerian society, at both the micro and macro levels, can we understand more fully the paradoxes of Nigerian nationalism and secessionism among the Ibos.

Turning our attention now to the social patterns and life-style of the Yorubas in Western Nigeria we find that they have traditionally shown a mixture of patterns and styles found in Northern and Eastern Nigeria. The hierarchical elements are considerably more evident in most Yoruba communities than among the Ibos. But the small kingdoms and chieftain-doms, with their aristocratic families, that we find in Yorubaland have often been quite independent, or else only loosely united "empires" such as the long-dissolved Oyo empire. In addition, Yorubaland has generally seen a much greater degree of competition on the basis of acquired merits among the many aristocratic candidates for a vacant royal throne than has the Hausa-Fulani empire. Finally, different parts of Yorubaland have rather varying social patterns.[19]

One should also keep in mind that the Yorubas, and the minorities along the Nigerian coast, were the first to be exposed more extensively to the influence of the West, first through the slave trade, and later through the colonial penetration and missionary impact.

The numerous other ethnic groups in Nigeria can generally be placed somewhere on this spectrum from hierarchical to more segmentary societies. Thus the Tiv people of Northern Nigeria are the most segmentary group among all the Nigerian peoples; the Binis in the Midwest have certain hierarchical elements in their social structure, and so forth. At this point we might also mention that the culture of the Midwestern Ibos is in many respects closer to Bini culture than to the cultures of most of the various Ibo peoples to the east of the Niger in the former Eastern Region.

Inherent and Emergent Cultural Differences.

Summarizing the cultural differences indicated by our thumbnail sketch above, we have first the well-known differences between the Hausa-Fulani in the north and the various groups in the south in terms of hierarchical structure, religion, and education. These are inherent cultural character-istics, even though education largely is a result of outside influence.

In addition we have pointed out the larger incidence of migration away from home among some southern groups, particularly the Ibos, and the strain-creating cultural intersections emerging from contacts between such migrants and local populations.

Finally, we have suggested that one must take account of the psychology of the dual perspective in understanding and predicting responses to the structural strain resulting from cultural intersections. When the self-image of a person becomes dissonant as a result of contrasts between (1) a self-evaluation based on standards derived from his own ethnic culture, and (2) the evaluations received from significant others in a migrant setting, he can respond to this dissonance in a number of different ways. He can respond, for instance, with self-imposed isolation or segregation, or with cultural-ethnic reassertion. Both of these responses tend to set him apart from other groups, and to encapsulate him within his in-group. But he may also attempt to resolve the dilemma by redefining his position in terms of some transcendent status, such as Nigerian citizenship, over and above the status inconsistencies resulting from the dual perspective. What line of response is actually choosen would seem to depend on structural and cultural constraints determined largely by the existing power structure and previous historical encounters in situations involving cultural intersections.

In conclusion, we note that tendencies of cultural-ethnic separatism, as well as a transcendent and supraethnic reliance on a nationalist Nigerian identity, emerge from the responses to the strains created by cultural intersections. It is significant that these opposite tendencies are emerging from, but are not, strictly speaking, inherent in the different cultures involved in the intersections. The opposing forces of separatism and nationalism thus cannot be understood or predicted simply on the basis of detailed knowledge of the structural and cultural features of each of the opposing groups. These opposing forces are not just extensions or transpositions of distinct cultures; they are the result of the dynamics of cultural intersections.

The notions of inherent and emergent cultural conflict as well as the psychology of the dual perspective have very definite limitations, however, The cultural intersections and the dual perspectives involved are likely to be found mainly among the more geographically and/or socially mobile part of the population.[20] Overrepresented in this category are middle-class and upper-class people, as well as people who have started careers destined to bring them to such positions. Although some less privileged people are also found in this mobile category, the masses of the people are not covered by any explanation concentrating exclusively on the psychology of dual perspectives and their underlying cultural intersections. Therefore, we should not neglect the political forces arising from the lower socio-economic strata in the Nigerian population, and from the various forms of stratification found in different parts of contemporary Nigeria. In this context, however, we will not attempt a detailed exploration of these matters since they will be dealt with in more depth in other parts of this work.

Strains of Social Stratification

It has been said about African societies that they are classless—that kinship and other kinds of Gemeinschaft-relationships are predominant, while social class has little meaning in the African context.[21] Even in modernizing African societies, where strata become increasingly differentiated, we do not have classes in the strict sense, it is maintained, because people do not think and feel in such terms. Other groupings besides economic ones continue to dominate the African mind. The bonds of family, clan or the village community are still so strong, according to this view, that a successful person often thinks of himself, and others think of him, as a successful native son who symbolically as well as materially gives a measure of grandeur to his village. To the wealthy man himself it may be more attractive (or perhaps opportune) to define himself as a son of his village and his clan rather than to consider himself as belonging to an upper class distinct from the class of his poor relatives and clansmen. Thus, stratification with regard to control over economic resources and political decisions is everywhere crisscrossed by traditional bonds. Modernization has by no means weakened these bonds, and in many cases has strengthened them, since people are now in a better financial position to fulfil many of their traditional obligations to the clan, village, or extended family.

This somewhat romantic picture of classless African societies must be taken with more than one grain of salt. To begin with, Africa has an enormous variety of social structures. Secondly, this talk of classlessness often appears to be a myth encouraged by ruling and possessing strata to smooth over the growing contrast between rich and poor which is there for everybody to see in most contemporary African societies.[22]

Looking at traditional Nigerian societies, it is obvious that the hierarchically structured Hausa-Fulani society has long possessed classlike stratification. A number of Yoruba communities have also traditionally had a similar structure, although much less pronounced. In the segmentary Tiv and Ibo societies, this kind of stratification has been minimal, however.

Regardless of the extent of stratification in traditional societies, contemporary developments have resulted in increasingly pronounced stratification even in societies that traditionally were largely unstratified.

Traditional bonds of community, which in many places have linked together the well-to-do with their poorer relatives, and the peculiar rewards that flow from such cross-cutting bonds, have naturally had a leveling and mitigating effect. This effect has at first obscured the fact of class differences, but not all poor people have benevolent relatives or village compatriots in high positions able to stretch out a helping hand to their poorer relatives. As urbanization and the shift of population from subsistence to cash-crop farming continues, the number of needy or economically insecure persons grows more rapidly than the number of jobs or the number of economically prosperous benefactors available.

Sooner or later ordinary people, first in the cities and later in the countryside, begin to notice that their lot is not really improving, while at the same time the upper class of successful native sons in business and politics is putting on more and more expensive weddings, baptisms, and parties. Even if the splendor surrounding the successful native son may invite admiration from those people from his home village who still derive not only psychological but also more tangible gratification from his success, this splendor is bound to become offensive to all those who find the supply of substantial patronage insufficient.

Here the following hypothetical generalization will be ventured: In a system of social security based on the demand and supply of particularistic patronage along kinship or community lines, when the demand far exceeds the supply, and the prospective suppliers still, at the same time, seem to be gaining in prosperity, the result may be a complete change in definitions of the situation among those demanding patronage. Incapable or unwilling patrons are then no longer defined as successful and admirable native sons, but as corrupt robber barons interested only in their self-enrichment and in material possessions. A quantitative change in demand and supply patronage relationships thus generates a qualitative change in social definitions.

It is notoriously difficult to specify and predict the point at which quantity is transformed into quality in this way. To anyone familiar with the Nigerian scene there is no question, however, that the experience of class-conflict became quite intensive in the years after independence, especially in Southern Nigeria, where class distinctions have traditionally been less pronounced and thus less familar and accustomed than in Northern Nigeria. The successful general strike of government employees in 1963 was the first large-scale expression of this type of conflict. Events in Western Nigeria during the period dominated by the NNDP-regime may also be interpreted partly in terms of class conflict. Clearly this occurrence was not a class conflict in the strict Marxist sense (that is, between a capitalist upper class and an exploited proletariat forced to sell its labor at a low price), but rather a class conflict between a usurping regional political class and the broad masses of the people in the region.[23]

A non-Marxist type of class analysis based on the notion of quantitative and qualitative changes in the demand-supply relationships of particularistic patronage takes us quite far in understanding the strains of social stratification in a country like Nigeria, we believe. Increasingly, however, there is a need to supplement and replace this kind of analysis with an analysis focusing on means of livelihood other than the subsistence and patronage that still account for such a large sector of daily life in Nigeria. We will not here anticipate our later treatment of cash-crop farming, labor in industry and transport, the federal and regional civil service, and the unemployed in all these sectors. But in the present context of analyzing the political forces of tribalism and regional separatism versus Nigerian nationalism, it is important to note that the political demands and supports to be expected in the so-called modern sectors of the Nigerian economy are quite similar in many respects to those resulting from the breakdown of the traditional sector. In other respects there are significant differences.

Among cash-crop farmers specializing in export crops (cocoa, palm oil, groundnuts), we expect to find a demand for an end to corruption, exploitation, and self-enrichment among top functionaries in the regional development corporations. These demands are very similar to those we expect to find among persons disillusioned with the system of patronage, as described earlier. Cash-crop farmers sell their produce to the development corporations that act as middlemen in the chain of distribution; farmers are thus dependent on the efficiency and honesty of development corporation functionaries. It is an historical fact that dishonesty and inefficiency grew rampant in these regional corporations before the military take-over in January 1966.[24]

Simlar reactions and demands could be expected from artisans; craftsmen; and small-scale, self-employed entrepreneurs. Since these occupational categories have a direct access to their own markets without being totally dependent on middlemen, demands arising here for an end to corruption and exploitation would be an indirect result of dishonesty and inefficiency in development corporations and similar agencies. Corruption is quite visible in the urban settings where artisans, craftsmen, and small scale entreprenuers are most likely to be found; and many members of these occupations are also likely to have close relatives in cash-crop farming by whom they are influenced.

Among workers in industry and transportation business who probably constitute less than 2 percent of the Nigerian population, a certain proportion would have no personal reasons for raising the kind of demands just indicated. Instead, we would expect this group to focus their demands more narrowly on higher wages. These demands would be disciplined or inhibited by fears of losing the security enjoyed in a labor market that has very low turnover and is surrounded by insecurity and unemployment in the labor markets outside industry and transport. Furthermore, we can also expect demands for adult education and technical training from these workers. Such demands place these workers in a reformist position within a system they want to use, not to change. This domestication of part of the industrial labor force is a phenomenon that we cannot discuss at greater length in this context. It remains an hypothesis. We are aware that more class conscious and less domesticated workers are likely to be found wherever the turnover is higher and the opportunity structure more open while economic conditions are basically the same. From information more recent than 1966 it seems that a change in this direction has taken place in several parts of Nigeria.[25] To the extent that significant parts of the small industrial labor force in Nigeria still are domesticated, these workers will become involved in the demands and protests of other occupational categories only as a result of exposure to the discontent fermenting among persons in other sectors of the labor force.

What we have said about "domesticated" industrial workers would seem to hold also for employees in the civil service, both at the regional and federal levels. However, there is an additional factor in this sector: the system of accelerated promotions with accompanying frustrations among the unpromoted. It may create the same kind of disillusionment with nepotism and corruption discussed earlier, as well as a demand for an end to nepotism.

An important sector of the Nigerian economy about which very little is known is unemployment. At the very least, however, we must make an important distinction between unemployment as a more comprehensive concept, and de-employment of those who have lost jobs in the modern sector of the economy. Probably the largest category among the unemployed are those who are not de-employed, but who have never had a more enduring job in the modern sector. Those unemployed who are not de-employed probably subsist on the basis of patronage and support from their extended family, and from this kind of predicament we can expect the same kinds of ddisillusionment with patrons described earlier in another context. It is more difficult to predict what we can expect from the de-employed in this respect. Some of those de-employed from private industry might possibly still carry traces of the process of domestication, of which we have already spoken. This situation would imply a readiness to put the blame on oneself for lack of education and training, and a willingness to improve oneself in these regards to find one's way back into employment.

In summing up our rather speculative line of argument, we conclude that one could expect a broad-based disenchantment with the ruling elite of politicians, senior civil servants, and businessmen, and also with the patrons found in this elite category. Nobody who has any first-hand knowledge of the Nigerian scene would be surprised by this conclusion. However, we expect this discontent to be less pronounced among securely employed workers in industry and transportation, and among promoted civil servants in the lower echelons. It should be least pronounced among subsistence farmers, particularly those who earn some extra money from various odd jobs outside farming.

If we tried to express these conclusions in terms of class conflict and class consciousness, we might say that the senses of class and conflict probably are most pronounced among cash-crop farmers growing export crops, and among irregular industrial workers and substistence farmers.

In addition to what we have just said about demands for an end to corruption and exploitation and about class conflict in relation to the Nigerian occupational structure, a few questions should be raised about the supports expected from this occupational base. Will the disenchanted occupational groups support tribalist or regionalist political grouping, or will they look for more broadly oriented national organizations to support? Or will they perhaps withdraw into parochial involvements even more limited than tribalism—such as supporting a kind of communalism that concentrates solely on the welfare of one's own community or clan?

Most disenchanted Nigerians found very little worth supporting among the political parties available preceding the military take-over. Whatever support was forthcoming had to focus on idealized and thus rather false conceptions of the community, on the regional or national-federal governments, or on hopes for the future which were clearly understood as completely unrelated to the realities of the First Republic of Nigeria.

However, some of these ideals seemed at first to come closer to realization after the military take-over. Such was the case, for instance, with the ideal of creating more states within the federation, in order to diminish the power of large, corrupt regional governments, to increase the influence of minority ethnic groups, and to diminish the geographical and social distance between the rulers and large portions of the people.

In the next section we shall discuss such political ideals in terms of the options available to those categories of the Nigerian population we have dealt with thus far in terms of geopolitics, culture, and class. We will focus most of our attention on the geopolitical aspects of the matter, on the argument that clearly crystallized supports for different political options could be identified in this area only in the time period we are considering.

POLITICAL OPTIONS IN THE OLD NIGERIAN FEDERATION: WHO OPTED FOR WHAT?

The following broad political options were available and desirable (but in various degrees) to the different categories of the Nigerian population we have discussed, as they faced the precivil-war Nigerian situation.

(1) Nigerian nationalism: support for supposedly genuine nationalist or national movements and institutions; demands for a national government strong enough to challenge regional governments; demands for help in the form of investments, protection, and the like from such a central national government.

(2) Regionalistic power struggle: a policy of regional security and consolidation of power through varying coalitions between the elites of two regions to reduce or eliminate competition from a third region; the central national government reduced to a manipulated distributor of patronage to the regional ruling elites—that is, to the elites of the more powerful coalition of regions.

(3) Ethnic nationalism within multiethnic regions: support for ethnic cultural associations with political aspirations; demands for redrawing administrative boundaries to better fit ethno-cultural realities; demands for the creation of more states for the benefit of minorities; among majority ethnic groups, ethnic nationalism implies demands for the consolidation of regional power and security for the ruling majority group—note here the probability of transition from option (3) to option (2) among majority ethnic groups.

(4) Ethnic nationalism between regions: interregional irredentism—wanting to join one's own kind on the other side of the regional border.

(5) Secessionism: one region breaking off from the federation to form a nation of its own—which can be seen as an extreme form of option 2.

First, we note that the political elites of all the majority ethnic groups have at one time or another favored, and in the case of the Ibo political elite actually chosen, secession from the Nigerian federation (option 5). It is impossible, historically, to find such an inclination toward secession among any significant section of the minority ethnic group elites. However, the main option of the majority ethnic group elites after Nigerian independence in 1960, and up to about 1965-66, seems to have been the consolidation of regional power and security through a power struggle within the federal structure of the First Republic of Nigeria and with varying coalitions among the regionalist elites (option 2).

The Nigerian nationalism that was pioneered by the country's first political party, NCNC, under Azikiwe's leadership (option 1), probably relied to a great extent on the need among Ibo strangers (who were larger in number than any other stranger group) to establish a political identity valid in all parts of Nigeria. They needed a sense of a nationalism that would be able to overcome, at least temporarily, the dissonance arising from what I have called the dual-perspective self-image of educated Ibo strangers. But other nonnationalist and even secessionist options were also available to these Ibos in a situation of crisis.

In terms of political options we find that majority strangers—Ibo strangers, for instance—and minority strangers were in somewhat different positions. Nigerian nationalism surely would seem to be the option (option 1) best fitting the needs of political identity of both categories of strangers. By supporting and identifying with the development of genuinely Nigerian national institutions, over and above the regionalist loyalties of the area in which they had settled, strangers could hope to protect their rights and find more effective ways of channeling their demands to governmental authorities. But in addition to this option both categories might identify with the sectionalism of the home areas from which they, or their kin, had emigrated. However, the sectionalism, or ethnic nationalism (option 3) of minority strangers was likely to be a sectionalism combined with Nigerian nationalism, while majority strangers had a further option.

If majority ethnic groups, from which majority strangers derive their origin, are led to secede from the federation, taking along in this action the whole region that they dominate politically, then majority strangers in other regions may decide to return home to join the secession (option 5).

The minority ethnic groups could not afford threats of secession much less put them into effect. This situation obviously reflected upon the position of minority strangers. Their position was not complicated by claims and expectations connected with representing a group with significant political power in another region and on a national scale, as was the case with majority strangers. Majority strangers on the other hand, enjoyed the option of invoking the regional power of their home regions and of returning there with secessionist intentions, if necessary.

Of course, a minority stranger could also withdraw to his home area, but it would be highly unrealistic of him or his kin to promote secession, since his homeland was too small, too exposed to more powerful neighbors, and in most cases too lacking in economic viability for independent nationhood. Whatever ethnic nationalism (option 3) may have seemed attractive to the minorities could not find a realistic expression in a modernizing society except through reliance on a larger national unit like Nigeria which could offer support, opportunities, and protection to the minorities, for instance within a federal structure based on the creation of states also for the minority ethnic groups within the nation.

To the extent that minority strangers resolved their problems of political identity by looking at themselves as Nigerian citizens, and not just as members of a particular ethnic group, this Nigerian identity would thus be more reliable than the Nigerian nationalism of majority strangers such as the Ibo immigrants to the West and North. Whereas majority strangers could view withdrawal and secession as a possible way out if and when the inconveniences of being a stranger became too unbearable, this choice was not available to minority strangers.

The significance of distinguishing overlapping groups from strangers becomes obvious as we examine the ways in which such groups could react to pressures from the ruling majority ethnic group in their regions of domicile, as well as to increased administrative differentiation within (or secession from) the federal structure. Their options included demanding the creation of their own states within the federation, and also emphasizing their Nigerian citizenship over and above their regional status as a way of maintaining a meaningful political identity of their own within the region—the latter tendency apparently shared by overlappers, strangers, and minorities. In addition, overlappers had the further option of demanding the right to join their own ethnic group in another federal or seceding region, which is the option of interregional irredentism (option 4).

To give the reader a comprehensive overview of the relationships assumed to exist between population categories and political options, we have summarized our discussion so far in Figure 3.

In this figure we have not attempted to indicate any refined estimates of the extent to which the various population categories favored the different options in the matrix. For the present purpose, this breakdown is not necessary. What is noteworthy in the figure is the fact that some population categories have a larger number of options than others, and that some options are completely out of reach for certain population categories.

By taking account of what we have said earlier about cultural differences and the psychology of the dual perspective, we may, however, qualify some of the crude predictions made in the figure. For instance, we could expect better educated Hausas belonging to population category no. 1, when confronting better educated Nigerians from Southern Nigeria, to

Options: Population Categories:	(a) Nigerian National- ism	(b) Regionalist Power Struggle	(c) Ethnic National- ism	(d) Interregion- al Irredent- ism	(e) Seces- sion
1: Ruling Majority Ethnic Group (North, West and East)	1, 2?	1, 2	1, 2	0	1, 2
2: Ruling Minority Ethnic Group(s) (Midwest)	1, 2	0	1, 2	0	0
3: Nonruling Ethnic Minority in Home Region (North and East)	1, 2	0	1, 2	0	0
4: Overlappers (North and Midwest)	1, 2	0	1, 2	1	0
5: Majority Ethnic Group Strangers (all regions)	1, 2	(1)	(1)	0	1, (2)
6: Minoirty Ethnic Group Strangers (all regions)	1, 2	0	(1)	0	0
7: Lagosians (federal capitol)	1, 2	0	0	1 ⚡	0

Legend: 0 = unavailable option
1 = option available
2 = option actually chosen by significant segments of the given category
() = parentheses indicate that the given option is favored or chosen symbolically by strangers with reference to the "homeland" or expressed in
their place of domicile through homeland oriented cultural associations
and so on
⚡ = the dominant population in Lagos is cosmopolitanized Yoruba; Lagos
is surrounded by Yorubaland

Figure 3.

exhibit more ethnic nationalism (option 3) than would majority ethnic-group elites from other parts of the country. This type of ethnic reassertion could be expected also among literate or better educated Ibo strangers belonging to population category no. 5.

We may now ask whether the predictions made in Figure 3 would be different if we concentrated our attention exclusively on the lower socio-economic strata. From our previous discussion of the impact of social class in this particular context, it should be evident, first, that our predictions in this figure are valid primarily among those persons who are alerted to the problems of regional and federal integration. However, we have also indicated that certain occupational categories in the lower strata—for instance, cash-crop farmers and certain groups of junior civil servants became disenchanted with regional political elites. As a result they probably also became less attracted by the option of regionalist power struggle and more accessible to the appeals of those who supported some idealized brand of Nigerian nationalism. Our main conclusion about the significance of social class is that it is more important in other contexts than the one represented by our set of broad political options like nationalism, regionalism, tribalism, and secessionism.

In conclusion, we would like to draw attention to four different types of Nigerian nationalism, each of which has its own source. Apart from the nationalism of the political elites who were involved in the struggle for independence from colonial rule, nationalism in Nigeria has at least three important sources.

First, some immigrants from one part of the country to another need a valid national identity, and therefore support and identify with the development of national institutions over and above regional or ethnic groupings. This need for identity is the source of Nigerian nationalism that comes closest to the Western interpretation of this phenomenon.

In addition, however, a broader nationalism may also develop as a result of a need for a national center capable of giving support and protection to smaller ethnic groups squeezed between larger and more dominant ones. Note that such nationalism springs from strong loyalties to one's own ethnic group, and from the desire to use the national center as a means of improving the lot of one's own people. While ethnic loyalties and a broader nationalism may seem somewhat contradictory principles among large and dominant ethnic groups, they are supplementary and reciprocally facilitating among smaller ethnic groups.

Finally, nationalism can also result from a need for a rational and honest machinery for social and economic development administered from a strong national center—a quest that emerges in a dialectical fashion from disenchantment with an inefficient, dishonest, and corrupt regional political class. This type of nationalism, like the previously mentioned need for a valid national identity, may seem to be more of an attitude than an organized force; whether this statement is true or not depends on the availability of political parties or other organizations that can absorb the nationalist support rendered by such an attitude, and transform it into political action. No political party in Nigeria before the military take-over, nor any coalition of such parties, seems to have succeeded in bringing about such a transformation. No wonder that when the military took over in January 1966, they were met with such great expectations of national reconstruction, but that subject is a different story, which falls outside the compass of this study.[26]

A NIGERIAN APPLICATION OF ROKKAN'S THEORY OF CLEAVAGE FORMATION AND THE STRUCTURING OF MASS POLITICS

So far, our analysis has attempted to single out some "actors" on the Nigerian political scene, and to understand their political options as seen from the vantage points of their positions in the geo-ethno-political structure of Nigeria. Furthermore, we have attempted to draw attention to the ways in which cultural intersections as well as economic and occupational differentiation form bases for supports and demands directed toward regional and federal establishments and ruling classes. Also on the basis of this analysis, we may distinguish a number of population categories that emerge as actors on the Nigerian scene.

Once we have enumerated the actors, we may ask what is the "play" in which they are acting. What are the themes and the basic cleavages performed as these actors participate in the drama slowly generating the structure of future Nigerian mass politics?

We will here very briefly attempt to apply Stein Rokkan's well-known model of cleavage formation—formulated originally to account for the structuring of European mass politics over the last few centuries—to our analysis of the Nigerian setting.[27]

To simplify our task we will not apply the more elaborate three-dimensional cleavage space more recently developed by Rokkan but stick to his original formulation of two main dimensions of cleavage, namely the territorial axis stretching from the central national establishment to more local and parochial interests, and a cross-local function axis stretching from various types of cultural, that is religions, moral, or ideological

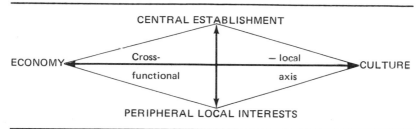

Figure 4.

commitments, to the diverse and specific economic interests that emerge in an increasingly differentiated urban division of labor (see Figure 4).

A closer look at European history from the vantage point of this scheme reveals not only conflicts between the central nation-building, standardizing, and rationalizing machinery of the nation-state, and more peripheral, local interests, but also among central national elites competing for control over the ways in which the system as a whole is to be run. Furthermore, we can discern conflicts among the diverse and specific economic interests identifiable to the left on the cross-local functional axis, as well as conflicts among ideological and religious commitments at the cultural end of the same axis. The scheme also allows the recording of conflicts between the central establishment and various cultural organizations such as the church or ideological movements. In short, this two-dimensional scheme suggests possible conflicts not only along the main dimensions but also within or between any two poles of cleavage. In addition, one can discern positions half way between the poles in different directions.

Rather than illustrating the usefulness of this scheme with reference to Rokkan's own analysis of cleavage formation and the structure of politics emerging in the historical epochs of national revolution and industrial revolution in Europe, we will immediately attempt to place the actors recognized on the Nigerian scene in the various corners and intermediate positions of the diamond-shaped figure suggested by Rokkan. One serious difficulty in trying to place the actors is the fact that Nigeria is a federation. Rokkan has acknowledged a similar difficulty in analyzing, for instance, the political history of Switzerland and the earlier German federation.[28] One way to treat this difficulty is to analyze the separate parts of the country in different diamonds. However, so doing would not serve the purposes of our analysis, since we are concerned primarily with cleavage formation and the structure of politics in Nigeria as a whole. In

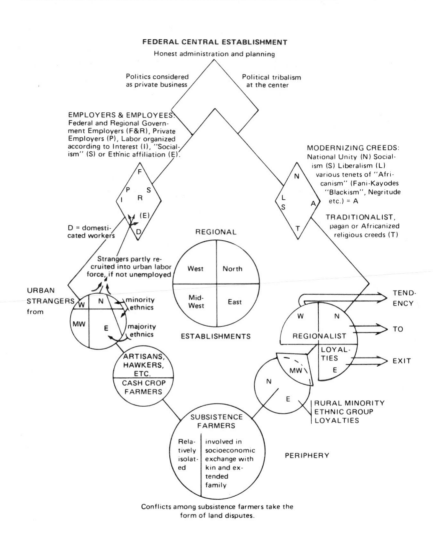

FEDERAL CENTRAL ESTABLISHMENT
Honest administration and planning

Politics considered
as private business

Political tribalism
at the center

EMPLOYERS & EMPLOYEES:
Federal and Regional Government Employers (F&R), Private
Employers (P), Labor organized
according to Interest (I), "Socialism" (S) or Ethnic affiliation (E).

MODERNIZING CREEDS:
National Unity (N) Socialism (S) Liberalism (L)
various tenets of "Afri-
canism" (Fani-Kayodes
"Blackism", Negritude
etc.) = A

F
P S
I R
(E)
D

N
L
S A
T

D = domesticated workers

TRADITIONALIST,
pagan or Africanized
religious creeds (T)

Strangers partly re-
cruited into urban labor
force, if not unemployed

REGIONAL

West | North
Mid-West | East

ESTABLISHMENTS

URBAN
STRANGERS
from

W N
MW E

minority
ethnics

majority
ethnics

W N
MW E
LOYAL-TIES

REGIONALIST

TEND-ENCY

TO

EXIT

ARTISANS,
HAWKERS,
ETC.
CASH CROP
FARMERS

N
E

RURAL MINORITY
ETHNIC GROUP
LOYALTIES

SUBSISTENCE
FARMERS

Rela-
tively
isolat-
ed

involved in
socioeconomic
exchange with
kin and ex-
tended
family

PERIPHERY

Conflicts among subsistence farmers take the
form of land disputes.

Figure 5.

Figure 5, the reader can judge whether we have succeeded in solving at least part of this problem.

From Figure 5, it is obvious that our analysis is complicated not only by the federal structure of Nigeria but also in other ways. As a result of the rather unsettled party political structure in Nigeria before January 1966, and the complete abolishing of political parties after the first military coup, it is impossible in this case to look at the end result of cleavage formation and party crystallization, as Rokkan and others have done for European countries, and trace this back in history. The party political structures were already there, "frozen" fifty years ago in some cases.

As a result of the more unsettled and fluid state of affairs in Nigerian politics, it is impossible to look at the forces operating at the center as strictly representing basic cleavages in Nigerian society. This lack of unambiguous representation at the center makes it necessary to transpose a miniature version of the Rokkan diamond at the top to enable us to discern, say, the fact that top administrators or politicians may represent nothing but their own vested economic and power interests while at the same time claiming to represent, say, the cultural interests of a particular ethnic group.

But there is also another sense in which Rokkan's figure in its original version cannot do justice to the fact of representation in the Nigerian context. Take for instance the existence of ideologies of various kinds toward the right side of the diamond. If we consider culture or ideology as a pole of cross-local, functional cleavage, we cannot effectively take note of the fact that ideologies not only are sides or poles in conflict but also are about conflict. The very content of ideology represents ideas about the nature of conflict, and implies taking sides in conflicts thus interpreted. Quite possibly, we could have an ideology on the right side of the figure which conceives of society as a manifestation of economic class struggle, and which sides with the working class, or which expresses the interests of free enterprise in conflict with state intervention. In terms of content such ideologies are about economy and politics, but not about culture, and should thus be represented in the upper left section of the diagram. But functionally these ideologies are cultural phenomena and should be indicated to the right. Again, by transposing a miniature replica of the diamond on the side of culture we can do justice to the fact that culture may imply a conceptual "representation" of the cleavage structure as a whole, and a commitment to one or the other pole in that representation.

We have tried to do justice to the federal structure at least in some parts of the diagram by taking account of regional establishments, and by indicating the existence of varying ethnic loyalties in the different regions. No claim is made to take detailed account of the federal structure at all levels of the diagram, however.

After having taken a close look at the details of the diagram, the reader may wish to raise questions about the usefulness of this taxonomic exercise for the purposes of our analysis. What do we hope to attain by locating actors on the Nigerian scene in this diagram?

First of all, obviously, this diagram helps to relate our analysis to other chapters in this work. Second, the relative complexity of the social and political structure of Nigeria can be ascertained more readily by means of such a diagram. If the reader attempted to draw lines—dotted, dashed, or continuous—indicating alliances, support, dependence, conflict, and so on, in relationships between actors along the main dimensions of the figure as well as within any pole of cleavage, it is obvious that the picture would soon become extremely blurred. The complexity of such a structure of actor interrelationships would be overwhelming, partly depending on the technique of presentation used. A matrix of actors, each related to all the others in terms of different kinds of relationships, would be more manageable and surveyable. Not even such a matrix, however, would help us to predict what changes to expect in cleavage formation and political change. Such predictions require additional historical and geopolitical information as well as dynamic or dialectical assumptions that "plug" into the matrix, thereby setting it into motion.

In this context, however, we are satisfied to have applied the Rokkan scheme as a taxonomical device that facilitates comparisons between Nigerian and European settings, the latter having been analyzed already along the lines suggested by Rokkan. A few things stand out as crucial for such a comparison.

As a result of the colonial heritage, and the continuous benefits derived by central establishments in the new states from trade and aid with overseas metropolitan economies, it would seem that quite a number of those Nigerians who in the past occupied positions in central as well as regional establishments tended to look at government as part of their own private enterprise, and at government funds as private or family "property." Such property would be used and distributed in ways accepted for property outside government. As we have already indicated, these practices earned both central and regional establishments a well deserved reputation for nepotism and corruption on a large scale well known to most Nigerians. This process has a number of interesting consequences, for instance, in our search for "counter-central" forces as well as forces supporting central and regional establishments.

We can expect to find a very mixed bag of motives both for supporting and resisting the central establishment. Regional governments, loyal mainly to themselves, could still support the center for instrumental reasons, more precisely to obtain their "share of the national cake" in central resource allocations. In addition to this kind of combined dependence and instrumental support, we can distinguish two other sets of actors who for quite different reasons would support the center.

As we have already indicated, several minority ethnic groups as well as the urban stranger category, and also one regional government based mainly on minority ethnic support, namely the Midwestern government, could be expected to support the central establishment not only as a dispenser of patronage but also as a body with distinct state- and nation-building functions. More recently an alignment seems to have developed among these various groups and elements of the army, particularly minority elements making up its rank and file. This support for the state- and nation-building functions of the central establishment is fairly well documented.[29]

Less documented, but intuitively and hypothetically evident, is the support for the center emanating in a dialectical fashion from various dependent strata of the Nigerian population (cash-crop farmers, workers, junior civil servants and the like). Their bitter opposition and disenchantment with regional establishments, and with failing patrons in the regional contexts, made them look for their salvation to a forceful intervention from the center to correct the vices of regional politics. Indirectly the popularity of the new military government immediately after the January 1966 coup would seem to substantiate the existence of such a dialectical reaction in support of the new central establishment.

When some of the population categories mentioned earlier became involved in a general strike in 1964 directed against the federal government as an employer, this action was not an expression of a counter-central tendency. The complaints basic to this conflict were not concerned with the functions of the central establishment as such but only with the failure of the central establishment to effectively meet the demands of its employees.

If those who supported the central establishment for crude opportunistic reasons are eliminated from the picture, we would still have a sizeable coalition of Nigerians supporting the functions of the state- and nation-building central establishment, if not always the actual power holders in this establishment.

However, the common image of Nigeria abroad, and also in many Nigerian circles, has been one of tribal strife tearing the national structure asunder. In Rokkan's scheme, this image could possibly be accounted for as a struggle between various "primordial, peripheral communities" within this multiethnic nation. In previous sections of this chapter, we have argued strongly against the assumptions underlying such an interpretation. We contend that the kind of tribalist struggle for which Nigeria became know, emerged from a calculated regionalist political exploitation, in tribal terms, of discontents arising from competitive strains in the modern economic and political sector of Nigerian society, and translated into stereotyped notions of tribal supremacy, anomaly, and hostility.

In terms of Rokkan's scheme, one interesting feature of this interpretation is the fact that it implies a linkage of opposing poles of cleavage, not in terms of conflict but in terms of causality. The competitive strain mentioned above is supposed to have emerged in that part of society which is represented toward the left and upper parts of the Rokkan diamond: the economic and political sectors. But through the exploitative intervention of regional establishments in the middle of the figure, this strain found an expression in beliefs about the role and nature of ethnicity as represented on the opposite right side of the diamond, namely among the majority ethnic groups—more precisely among those who because of their position, education, and so on were involved in fierce competition involving members of several different ethnic groups. Such competition was enhanced by the attempts made immediately before and after Nigerian independence in 1960, to apply the Western model of liberal, competitive democracy in a situation where cleavages were defined mainly in terms of the crude and unbalanced regional delineations introduced during British colonial rule.

With the cutting up of two powerful and ethnically heterogeneous regions—the Northern and the Eastern Regions—into a larger number of states within the federal structure in May 1967, and after the end of the civil war (which can be viewed as a successful federal response to the attempts by the Ibo elite to retain their regional power base intact), we now have a situation where the structural bases for powerful political tribalism have been destroyed. Within the new Nigerian federation, four regional establishments have been replaced by twelve much weaker state establishments. Whatever tribalism remains is now reduced to a micro-phenomenon in micro-settings, and perhaps to a reasonably wholesome kind of local pride and aspiration. In the broader federal setting where, of course, such aspirations must seek resources and support, old-style tribalism based on the arrogance of power is no longer possible. Solutions must be worked out in coalitions with representatives of other states within the federal structure in order to impress the central establishment.

Once civilian rule is back on the Nigerian scene, perhaps in the midseventies, we will know more about the new coalitions and cleavages that will shape the political future of Nigeria. It is not our task to make predictions about this process. However, implicit in our present analysis is the assumption that the disintegrative forces of political tribalism will turn out to be rather insignificant at that stage while the state- and nation-building functions of the central establishment will be even more widely acknowledged than now. Within this framework, we might see two competing tendencies, namely the tendency to form shifting and pragmatic coalitions to promote economic and social development within the states that make up the federation, and another tendency to form new loyalties along lines of social class and urban-rural distinctions. A coalition between the lower urban classes and the less well-to-do farming population is not unlikely at an earlier stage; but with time this coalition could break up, as it has done elsewhere. A one-party system seems rather unlikely in a nation as complex in its cultural composition, with its multitude of politically creative communities and provinces.

We will conclude this chapter by looking back toward a recent time period of Nigerian history on the basis of substantive empirical data rather than lofty speculation. Our data serve to illuminate only a very limited section of the reality represented in Figure 4, namely the extent or lack of integration of various population categories with four regional establishments and their local agencies.

SOME EMPIRICAL FINDINGS ON LOCAL-REGIONAL STRAIN AND INTEGRATION

Our discussion of the broad political options available among various population categories in Nigeria was based on certain assumptions about what these categories might wish to accomplish and could realistically hope to attain in view of their position in the federal and regional power structure, their size, and their domicile. In Figure 3 we supplemented our conclusions about the options that were theoretically available to the different population categories with some rather crude observations regarding the extent to which these options have been favored or chosen in practice by significant segments of those people. So far, however, we have not linked these theoretical considerations and rather crude observations to our previous discussion about the structural strains to which, presumably, these population categories are exposed. We will try to establish this link in this section.

If we conceive of the alternative lines of political action indicated in the title of this chapter as comprising a push-and-pull process, we can think of the options presented as the pulls operating on the groups and individuals involved, while the strains to which our population categories were exposed provide the driving forces pushing people to act in favor of a particular option, or to shift from one option to another.

In discussing the strains to which various minority ethnic groups, strangers, and overlappers seem to have been exposed, we have particularly emphasized the difficulties these groups have in relating meaningfully and safely to the administrative regions and local communities in which they lived. To operationalize "strain versus integration in region and local community" we have chosen five different indicators from our empirical data which deal with (1) actual local or regional problem-solving contacts, (2) trust in the ability of local and regional government to understand people's needs, (3) absence or presence of tribalists in perceptions of the local community, (4) absence of community divisions perceived in ethnic rather than in political or economic terms, and (5) extent to which help is expected or demanded from local or regional government to solve community problems defined by community members.[30]

These five indicators have been applied to a somewhat more differentiated version of our population categories. With regard to each indicator, a positive sign has been given to any single category exhibiting percentage values higher than the total population percentage for that indicator. In this way we have obtained a matrix very similar to a scalogram, in which our population categories are rank-ordered from those with the largest number of positive signs—that is the highest local-regional integration score—to those that manifest more signs of strain. Note that we have rank-ordered the categories, not the individuals belonging to the categories. This method seems most appropriate for the kind of macro-political analysis which we are here undertaking. In a different context a factor analysis of these and other indicators of strain and integration will be presented where individuals are ordered on the basis of their factor scores.

Our findings concerning the local-regional integration and strain of the urban upper strata are presented in Figure 6:

First, Figure 6 clearly illustrates the point made in the introduction to this chapter, that interactions among administrative, political, demographic, and ethnic factors are as important, or even more so, than ethnic affiliation per se in accounting for important variations in political behavior and perception among the citizenry of Nigeria. Undoubtedly our population categories impose certain constraints on the possibilities of a more detailed analysis of the basic conditions of Nigerian political

Findings in Higher Socio-Economic Strata with Regard to Indicators of Local/ Regional Political Integration (+=more than average)	Non-Ibo Maj Strngr	Ibo Home	Yoruba Home	North Minority	Midwest Minority	Hausa Home	Yoruba Overlap	Ibo Overlap	East Minority	Federal Cap Minor	Ibo Stranger	Minor Stranger
!. Citizen problem-solving contact with local/regional government	+	+	+	+	−	−	−	−	−	−	−	−
2. Regional government said to understand people's needs	+	+	⊖	+	+	+	−	−	⊕	−	−	−
3. Absence of tribalists in perception of community	+	+	+	⊖	+	+	+	⊕	−	−	−	−
4. Absence of community divisions perceived in ethnic terms	+	+	+	+	+	⊖	+	−	−	−	−	⊕
5. Help expected or asked from local/regional government to solve community problems	+	+	+	+	+	+	−	−	−	+	+	−
ORDINAL INTEGRATION SCORE	5	5	4	4	4	3	2	1	1	1	1	1

NOTE: A positive sign indicates that a given population category exhibits percentage values higher than the total percentage for the given indicator. The absolute percentage value could still be quite low. These percentage figures have been used to rank order categories with the same ordinal integration score.

Figure 6.

development. But our empirical results show that these categories still go a long way in accounting for variations in local-regional integration and strain, while a simple listing of different ethnic groups would have accounted for very little of the total variation.

A couple of other things are obvious from Figure 6. First of all, it seems likely that the distribution in the matrix can be attributed to one major dimension of local-regional integration versus strain, even though there are some other dimensions that obviously must be drawn into the picture to account for certain discrepancies in the cumulative scale pattern.

Second, it seems obvious from the figure that, on the whole, majority ethnic groups at home and the ruling minority in the Midwest are best integrated in their local and regional political setting, relatively speaking. The absolute level of integration is not indicated in the figure, however.

Three "deviant" cases stand out at the top of the ranking list:

(1) Non-Ibo majority strangers seem to be the best integrated of all according to our definition of integration. We cannot comment on this finding until we analyze in depth the geographical distribution of these strangers, and the reliabilities of the statistics involved. However, as far as they go, our data suggest that it was not necessarily a disadvantage to be a stranger in 1966, when the survey was carried out, if you belonged to one of the majority ethnic groups, and provided you were not an Ibo.

(2) The Northern minorities, thanks to their higher education probably, were quite well integrated in the North. Possibly they were able to take advantage of the various opportunities resulting from their higher education in competition with less well educated Hausas.

(3) The deviant negative score for "regional government understands people's needs" among the Yorubas in their home region is not unexpected in view of the horrors of the NNDP rule, and the political anarchy that emerged in the West after the Action Group crisis in the early mid-sixties.

Discrepancies in degrees of political integration between any given stranger category and their kinfolk in the home region were smallest for the Yoruba and the Eastern minorities, and largest for the Ibos. But for Eastern minorities these small discrepancies between strangers living in other regions, and their relations at home in the East, were due to the fact that both minority strangers and nonruling minorities at home were very poorly integrated. In contrast, Yorubas were relatively more integrated whether they were at home or strangers.

Ibo strangers were among the least integrated, according to the figure. One can suspect that the vast differences in integration scores between Ibo strangers and their relations back home were somewhat less marked at an earlier period of Nigerian postindependence politics when the NCNC (supported mainly by an Ibo vote) and the NPC of the North were in coalition, so that the Ibos could reap the benefits of being much closer to the sources of federal power, patronage, and protection. Whether these differences ever were as small as the differences, say, among Yoruba strangers and their relations back home, is an open question that we cannot answer in this context, and that would be difficult to answer firmly with any data available today.

We may now ask: If the pattern reflected in Figure 6 is truly

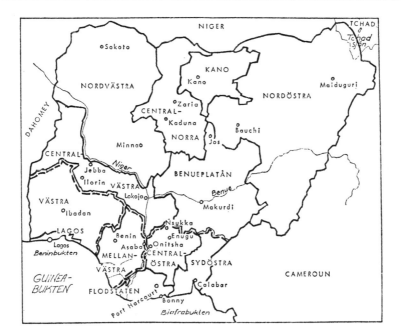

SOURCE: Olav Stokke, Ulf Himmelstrand, and Hans Sjöberg, **Världen, Nigeria och Biafra. Sanningen som kom bort**, Stockholm, Aldus/Bonniers, 1969.

Figure 7.

symptomatic of the lack of political integration on the local and regional levels among important segments of the Nigerian population before the civil war, what are the prospects for an improved local as well as national integration in the new multistate federation that was created on paper in May 1967 and made partly operational rather soon thereafter?

PROSPECTS FOR POLITICAL INTEGRATION IN NIGERIA

Apart from the obvious advantages to nation-building deriving from the fact that no state in the present twelve-state federation can any longer challenge or blackmail the rest of the country in the way that the three large regions could do in the past, the new multistate federation seems to be structured to meet more effectively some of the important problems of the country, and to accommodate the intricate geo-ethno-political texture of Nigeria. There are several bases for this conclusion:

(1) The reduction of political power of majority ethnic groups in the federal context would not seem to change their level of local integration as indicated in Figure 4, since no one of the indicators basic to that figure can be expected to drop lower than occurred during the federal power struggle of the past. One of the majority ethnic groups—namely the Hausa of the North—may in fact derive certain benefits at home from the creation of more states, in spite of the fact that they lost out in the past power struggle for control over the national center. From Figure 5 it is evident that they were less well integrated in their region than the other majority ethnic groups in their home regions. This fact is not surprising in view of the hierarchical structure and the vast territories of the Hausa people, and in view of the cultural differences within the North. The creation of more states among the Hausa can bring about a decentralization of political initiative, and a diminishing distance between government and people. This decentralization, in turn, should make it easier to mobilize genuine problem-solving behavior, and to create a more widespread awareness of the needs and problems of local and state communities without threats to the rest of the country.

(2) Minorities at home in the old regions will now occupy a position more similar to the majority ethnic groups of the past, and to the ruling minorities of the Midwest. Their level of political integration, as here defined, can thus be expected to rise considerably. This increase in integration is one of the most important expected payoffs of the new federation.

(3) The position of strangers in the new multistate federal structure is not as easy to predict as the position of the other population categories just mentioned. By relying on evidence outside the rather restricted frame set by Figure 5 we can say, however, that minority strangers on the whole should find it easier to get along in the new Nigeria than they did in the past, simply because minority peoples play a more dominant role in the new multistate federation than in the previous regionalist federation.[31]

Predictions regarding Ibo strangers are more difficult to make, even though it is well known that more than 50,000 Ibo strangers maintained themselves outside Biafra—in Lagos and in the Western State—throughout the civil war. After the war, numerous reliable sources have reported on the relative ease of Ibo reintegration in various parts of Nigeria outside their home area—not the least in the North. Symptomatically, the only parts of Nigeria where ordinary Ibo strangers confronted serious mistrust and hostility in the immediate postwar period were those minority areas of the former Eastern Region which were made part of Ibo-ruled Biafra.[32]

In terms of our theory of options, the creation of more states within the multistate federal structure of Nigeria implies the complete removal of the options of regionalist struggles for power and "security," and of secession. States within the new federation are more interdependent, and no longer strong and viable enough to choose those options. Instead there is a new option that can more easily be fused with the option of Nigerian nationalism, which we shall call the option of multiple-state coalition-making to win developmental advantages. That these coalitions will no longer consistently follow territorially contiguous clusters of states coinciding with the old regions is already quite obvious, both with regard to the North and the East.[33] It would, therefore, seem rather safe to predict that the reemergence of the old regions and the disintegrative power struggle for regional security and consolidation that characterized the old federation is unlikely in the new Nigeria.

Most important, however, is the fact that the new multistate federal structure promises to reduce the saliency of false issues like tribalism and regionalism, thereby allowing attention to be payed to more basic issues of economic and social development.

NOTES

1. See Olav Stokke, ed., Reporting Africa in African and International Mass Media, Uppsala, Scandinavian Institute of African Studies, 1971, particularly the present author's chapter, pp. 117-33.

2. See for instance Lucy P. Mair, Anthropology and Social Change, Humanities, 1970, p. 100 ff.; "Race, Tribalism and Nationalism in Africa," in W. R. Bascom and M. J. Herskovits (eds.), Continuity and Change in African Cultures, Chicago, University of Chicago, 1959; J. L. Gibbs Jr., ed., Peoples of Africa, New York, Holt, Rinehart and Winston, 1965; Robert A. LeVine, Dreams and Deeds, Chicago, University of Chicago Press, 1966; and Peter C. W. Gutkind, ed., The Passing of Tribal Man in Africa, Leiden, E. J. Brill, 1970.

3. Another suggestion has been made by Chief Awolowo in his Path to Nigerian Freedom, London, Faber and Faber, 1947, p. 48: "It is a mistake to designate them 'tribes.' Each of them is a nation by itself with many tribes and clans."

4. C. S. Whitaker Jr., in his politics of Tradition: Continuity and Change in Northern Nigeria, Princeton, Princeton University Press, 1970, concludes that the social-political processes of modernization are interactional rather than a progressive shedding off of traditional elements. More particularly, he emphasizes that indirect rule, as applied in Northern Nigeria by the British, in actual fact strengthened tradition rather than set Northern Nigeria straight on the road to modernity.

5. K.W.I. Post, in his The Nigerian Federal Election of 1959, Oxford University Press, 1963, p. 13, observed: "Nearly all Ibos supported the NCNC, most Yorubas backed Action Group, all but a small minority of the Hausa and Fulani were associated, if indirectly, with the NPC." But note also the observation by J. P. Mackintosh et al. in Nigerian Government and Politics, London, George Allen Unwin, 1966, p. 296: "When the NCNC established a branch in Enugu one of the first prominent local leaders was Mallam Umaru Altine, a Northern cattle dealer and strong supporter of Dr. Azikiwe. He became President in 1953 and when the NCNC won a majority of the Urban District Council in the following year, he was elected a Chairman."

6. See for instance James S. Coleman, Nigeria: Background to Nationalism, Berkeley, University of California Press, 1958; W. Schwarz, Nigeria, London, Pall Mall Press, 1968; A.H.M. Kirk-Greene, Crisis and Conflict in Nigeria Vols. 1 and 2, New York, Oxford University Press, 1971; and R. Melson and H. Wolpe, eds., Nigeria: Modernisation and the Politics of Communalism, East Lansing, Michigan State University Press, 1971.

7. See for instance the article and the conversation published in Africa Report, Vol. 13, No. 2, 1968.

8. For Nigeria's early history, see Michael Crowder, The Story of Nigeria, London, Faber, 1962 (rev. and expanded ed., 1966).

9. Robert G. Armstrong has even maintained, on the basis of extrapolations from the most reliable census data available, that "the minorities add up to a majority of the country." See his "The Issues at Stake: Nigeria 1967," Ibadan, Ibadan University Press, 1967.

10. Our hypothesis of the dual perspective has also been formulated in terms of so-called rank equilibration theory in Ulf Himmelstrand, "Rank Equilibration, Tribalism and Nationalism in Nigeria," in Melson and Wolpe, op. cit., ch. 9.

11. Much of this information has been amply summarized by Kirk-Greene, op. cit., p. 8 ff.

12. See, for instance, Victor Uchendu, The Igbo of Southeast Nigeria, New York, Holt, Rinehart and Winston, 1965.

13. See, for instance, Thurstan Shaw, Igbo-Ukwu. An Account of Archaelogical Discoveries in Eastern Nigeria, Vols. I and II, London, Faber and Faber, 1970, and R. N. Henderson, The King in Every Man. Evolutionary Trends in Onitsha Ibo Society and Culture, New Haven, Conn,, Yale University Press, 1972, p. 373.

14. See, for instance, I. F. Nicolson, The Administration of Nigeria 1900 to 1960. Men, Methods and Myths, Oxford, Clarendon Press, 1969, p. 85 et passim.

15. See Simon Ottenberg, "Ibo Receptivity to Change," in Bascom and Herskovits, op. cit.

16. The present writer has personally witnessed many educated Yorubas and Hausas report on or express such a low social evaluation of the Ibo. Its saliency seemed to be related to the political climate of the day, which suggests a very delicate cognitive balance in interethnic perception.

17. This argument has been elaborated in more detail in Himmelstrand, op. cit.

18. This kind of argument was heard rather frequently at informal staff discussions in the Faculty of the Social Sciences at the University of Ibadan around 1967. The only place where I have been able to find it in print is in a Preface by Robert G. Armstrong to an incidental publication by Samson O. O. Amali, Ibos and Their Fellow Nigerians.

19. Samuel Johnson, The History of the Yorubas from the Earliest Times to the Beginning of the British Protectorate, edited by Dr. O. Johnson, London, George Routledge, 1921, and N. A. Fadipe, The Sociology of the Yoruba, edited by F. O. Okediji and O. O. Okediji, Ibadan, Ibadan University Press, 1970.

20. For a more detailed discussion of the role of mobility see Himmelstrand, op. cit., p. 267 ff.

21. Until recently references to social class in African societies were rarely found outside the Marxist literature. Aidan Southhall, ed., Social Change in Modern Africa, London, Oxford University Press, 1961, contains a few chapters where the matter is touched upon briefly, and played down. More recent elite studies have put a stronger emphasis on stratification. Peter C. Lloyd, ed., The New Elites of Tropical Africa, London, Oxford University Press, 1966: pp. 49-62 has summarized some arguments about class and elite in tropical Africa.

22. Peter Lloyd (op. cit., p. 59 ff.) has some interesting but noncommittal remarks to make about the "ideology of classlessness," which members of some African elites find it opportune to maintain in the face of the internal exploitation developing in some postcolonial African societies. The works of social anthro-

pologists may have helped to bolster such ideologies. See also Peter C. Lloyd, Africa in Social Change, Harmondsworth, Penguin books, 1967, pp. 313-17, "The non-consciousness of class."

23. This interpretation of events in Western Nigeria is found for instance in Ola Oni, "The Root of the Crisis," Nigerian Socialist, Vol. 1, January 1967, p. 5 ff. A similar interpretation of the background to these events is found in several papers by Richard L. Sklar, for instance, "Contradictions in the Nigerian Political System," Journal of Modern African Studies, Vol. 3, 1965, pp. 201-13, reprinted in Nelson and Wolpe, op. cit., 19, and "Nigerian Politics: The Ordeal of Chief Awolowo 1960-65," in Gwendolen M. Carter ed., Politics in Africa: 7 Cases, New York, Harcourt, Brace & World, 1966, pp. 119-65.

24. For the last few years several tribunals have been investigating irregularities in state corporations and some marketing boards. Their reports are not yet easily available, however.

25. Through personal communications from Gavin Williams, Paul Lubeck, and Adrian Pearce, who have all undertaken research, as yet unpublished, in Nigeria in the early seventies, I have gained the impression that labor unrest and a decreasing labor "domestication" are more obvious today than earlier.

26. A most concise and comprehensive summary of Nigerian reactions to the military take-over in January 1966 is found in Kirk-Greene op. cit., p. 38 ff.

27. Stein Rokkan, Citizens, Elections, Parties. Approaches to the Comparative Study of the Processes of Development, Oslo, Universitetsforlaget, 1970, p. 49 ff. and 96 ff.

28. Stein Rokkan, "The Growth and Structuring of Mass Politics in Western Europe: Reflections of Possible Models of Explanation," Scandinavian Political Studies, Vol. 5, 1970, p. 81, footnote 3.

29. Kirk-Greene, op. cit., p. 61 et passim. See also Armstrong, "The Issues at Stake: Nigeria 1967, op. cit.

30. A more detailed presentation of empirical operations and methodological problems cannot be given here. These will be conveyed in a forthcoming work by the present author and a number of Nigerian coauthors, Options and Constraints of Development: The Case of Nigeria, to be published in 1973.

31. Quite a large number of civilian Commissioners and permanent secretaries in the most important federal ministries come from minority peoples.

32. The irony of this fact—the hostility directed against Ibo Biafrans by former minority Biafrans in Port Harcourt and other parts of the River State immediately after the end of the Nigerian Civil War—did not seem to have much of a sobering effect on the reports of strongly pro-Biafran reporters such as Suzanne Cronjé when in this connection she complained about the failures of the federal government to deliver on its promises of reconcilation with the Ibos. However, she did not mention the relative ease of reconciliation in other parts of allegedly genocidal Nigeria, which had not been under the rule of Biafran leadership.

33. This fact has been particularly obvious in reactions to the so-called Dina Commission's report on derivation and allocation of federal tax revenue. This report, which was made public in 1970, suggested that revenue should be allocated to the various states within the federation not primarily according to the principle of derivation, which earlier had been a cornerstone in federal tax policy, but according to a principle of need. From authoritative circles, I have heard that considerable crisscross between South and North was manifested in responses to these suggestions.

CHAPTER 16

TRADITIONAL CLEAVAGES AND
EFFORTS OF INTEGRATION IN
EAST AFRICA

Ali Mazrui

ALI MAZRUI is now Professor of Political Science at the University of Michigan, after serving for several years as Professor and Head of the Department of Political Science at Makerere University in Uganda. He has written extensively in the field of political theory and political sociology and has made major contributions to the study of African political development. He has been active in the international networks of political scientists and sociologists and is a member of the Executive of the International Political Science Association. Among the books he has published is *Cultural Engineering and Nation-Building in East Africa* (1972).

Nation-building involves in effect five major processes. These are, firstly, some degree of cultural and normative fusion; secondly, the promotion of economic interpenetration between different strata and sectors of society; thirdly, the process of social integration; fourthly, the process of building institutions for effective conflict resolution; and fifthly, the psychological accumulation of shared national experience.

The process of cultural and normative fusion is ultimately the acquisition of shared values, modes of expression, life-style and view of one's place in the universe. Of special importance for this process is cultural interaction among the different subgroups of society. And the

AUTHOR'S NOTE: This paper was written in consultation with Yash Tandon. We are particularly indebted to Victor Uchendu for his comments on an earlier draft.

paramount medium for cultural interaction is, quite simply, language. We shall, therefore, pay special attention in this chapter to the growing restlessness in East Africa over the issue of a national language.

The promotion of economic interpenetration and exchange relationships between subgroups is in part a commitment to the idea of economic interdependence. In other words, the economic dimension of nation-building is the process by which the different subgroups within a country develop a conscious vested interest in the national economy.

The third dimension of nation-building is social integration. Here, we use the term "social integration" to mean that process by which the gaps between the elite and the masses, the town and the countryside, the privileged and the underprivileged, are gradually narrowed.

The fourth dimension in nation-building is a process of acquiring shared national memories, a consciousness of having undergone some important experiences in the past together. When this fifth dimension interacts with the first process of cultural and normative fusion in African conditions, we have the gradual merger of tribal subidentities into a new national identity. Let us now relate these five dimensions of nation-building more specifically to East Africa's experience.

LANGUAGE AND CULTURAL FUSION

Perhaps the most fundamental political problems confronting East African countries are reducible to two crises: the crisis of national integration and the crisis of political authority or political legitimacy. For our purposes the crisis of national integration may be seen as a problem of horizontal relationships. It arises because different clusters of citizens do not as yet accept each other as compatriots. The sense of a shared nationality has yet to be forged.

The crisis of political legitimacy, on the other hand, is a problem of vertical relationships. It arises not because one citizen does not recognize another as a compatriot but because significant numbers of citizens are not convinced that their governments have the right to rule them. Integration is basically a problem of neighbor against neighbor; legitimacy is a problem of the ruled against their rulers.

It can therefore be seen that a process of cultural fusion, leading either to a shared language or to a shared life-style at large, is a contribution towards the integrative process. Swahili in Tanzania is a shared language and in some respects a shared culture. The government's policies on language include a commitment towards developing Swahili to cope with more and more areas of common endeavor. Committees for the compilation of a fuller legal vocabulary in Swahili, the promotion of literary competitions in Swahili, the encouragement of the writing of textbooks in Swahili, and President Nyerere's own work in translating Shakespeare into Swahili, are determined attempts to make the language cope with more of national life and to make national life more systematically interpenetrated by that shared language.

Kenya as an instance of British cultural policy during the colonial period betrays different aftereffects. On attainment of independence, there was a large number of languages recognized both in the educational policies and in the policies of the Department of Information and Broadcasting. But independence itself meant a reduction of this plurality. The languages used on the radio were drastically reduced to English and Swahili, and a few hours of special services were presented. And the debate in the country has gone increasingly in the direction of promoting Swahili. The ruling party, the Kenya African National Union, has already declared itself in favor of the systematic promotion of Swahili as a national language in the country, and President Kenyatta has also come out as a strong champion of Swahili. Only a small minority of Kenyans speak Swahili as their first language, but a large number have increasingly acquired it to use as a medium of communication among mutually incommunicado tribes. The English language is still important in Kenya. It is important as a medium of instruction in the higher education levels, and it is also important as the lingua franca of the elite. But the ultimate basis for Swahili lies in its role as a lingua franca for the masses. And here the promotion of a shared language, with the ultimate ambition of cultural homogenization, becomes once again part of the process of national integration.

Uganda once nearly became another domain of Swahili. In the late 1920's the British colonial authorities were putting forward a strong case for the adoption of Swahili as a medium of education and administration in Uganda. The arguments have since found an echo in some of the current debates in the country about the utility of Swahili. The British administration in Uganda at that time did believe that there was a case for maintaining close cultural ties between the new areas of knowledge that the British were introducing and the traditional background of the people themselves. There was also the view that if Uganda developed an African language other than Swahili for its lingua franca, it would simply be isolating itself. The most sensible thing for Uganda to do, so the British colonial authorities argued in 1927, was to engage in a vigorous pursuit of policies calculated to spread Swahili widely in the life of the nation and to deepen its roots within it.

However, resistance to Swahili came from the Baganda, the largest tribal community of Uganda. The Baganda had a complex system of government with a highly developed cultural heritage. They were also in a strong position to spread their own language and culture to other groups in the country, and thus strengthen their own credentials for leadership in Uganda. The introduction of Swahili would be a threat to the cultural credentials of the Baganda for national leadership, therefore, the Baganda resisted this linguistic intrusion inside their country. The British authorities, after attempting to promote Swahili in the educational system, gave up the endeavor and acquiesced in the Baganda bid to foster their own cultural hegemony in the country.

In 1966 there was a confrontation between the independent Central Government of Uganda and the regional Government of Buganda. The Central Government won, and the king of Buganda fled to England where he lived in exile until his death in November 1969. The political decline of the Baganda has improved the prospects of Swahili in the country. The armed forces had been using Swahili as the language of command since the colonial days, and were by then strongly partial to Swahili as one of the languages of Uganda. In April 1970 the Language Association of Uganda passed a resolution urging the government to take steps to promote Swahili as a potential national language. The resolution was hotly debated in the press, but the very idea of passing such a resolution in support of Swahili would have been almost inconceivable a few years earlier.

In short, all three countries of East Africa are seeking ways to increase cultural intercourse among their different linguistic groups. The quest for a national language, capable of spreading at the grass roots, and identifiable as native to Africa, becomes part of the restless search for greater cultural fusion.

THE ECONOMICS OF NATIONHOOD

The second dimension of nation-building is, as we suggested, the process of economic interpenetration between sectors and groups. The different tribal communities in an African country could conceivably live in a state of bare coexistence. In other words, the boundaries of the country might have put them together on the map, but there could still be little contact between some tribes and others.

A more advanced stage of integration is when the tribes are in. a minimal contact. The process of economic interaction and exchange could increase these contacts and maximize situations for bargaining and compromise.

Tanzania, among the three East African countries, has idealized the concept of self-reliance. Perhaps national self-reliance deserves to be so idealized, provided it does not let itself drift into a form of autarky and isolation. But from the point of view of the integrative process, there is little worse than tribal self-reliance. When each tribe depends solely on itself for its needs, the society is not allowed the opportunity to foster tribal interreliance. Tribal interreliance is achieved when groups from one community find that they have to exchange with groups from another. The market becomes a mechanism for ethnic interpenetration. Goods flow across community boundaries in exchanges of goods or services. The nation moves from a collection of coexisting groups to a collection of interacting groups.

Nevertheless, economic interaction has its dangers to the nation. Karl Marx was right in his assumption that the production and exchange of goods has all the potentiality for generating conflict. Karl Marx was wrong in assuming that this conflict will necessarily be class conflict. In African conditions, ethnic divisions are often deeper and more fundamental than class divisions. And even where economic interaction takes place the tensions created are only partly economic, and quite often secondarily economic.

Exchange and economic interaction as a pathway toward nation-building did have a serious setback in Nigeria's experience. The Ibo as a community were impressive entrepreneurs, and their activities in this sphere did enable them to penetrate other regions and communities as tradesmen. To the extent that the Ibo were so economically mobile—establishing enterprises outside their own regions, establishing business contacts, facilitating movements of goods from one region to another, or movements of money either as capital or as subsidies to relatives—their activities were conducive to a greater degree of interpenetration within Nigeria. They were, in other words, a contribution to national integration.

Yet, tragic massacres in northern Nigeria in May and September 1966 were in part attributable precisely to the entrepreneurial endeavors and the economic mobility of the Ibo. The Ibo had entered the north to fill important sectors of regional life, both public and private. They had provided significant services and helped to enrich and diversify the regional economic system. But partly because of these activities, coupled with their distinctiveness as an ethnic group external to the region, the Ibo generated the kind of tensions that later erupted on such a tragic scale. Of course, the nature of the first coup of January 1966, with special reference to Ibo predominance in its execution, was a major ignitive factor behind the riots and massacres that later took place as the Hausa rose to avenge themselves on the Ibo. Nevertheless, part of the price of economic interaction and exchange as fostered by the Ibo in Nigeria had been the intensification of certain areas of interethnic conflict.

We come now to the third major process indispensable for adequate nation-building: the process of routinizing conflict resolutions. We shall discuss this further later on, but we need to relate it here to economic tensions. We have argued elsewhere that the cumulative experience of conflict resoultion is indispensable to national integration. Conflict itself may have a propensity to force a dissolution of social relationships, but the resolution of conflict is an essential mechanism of integration. The whole experience of jointly looking for a way out of a crisis, of seeing mutual hostility subside to a level of mutual tolerance, of being intensely conscious of each other's position, yet sensing the need to bridge the gulf—these are, as I have argued elsewhere, experiences that over a period of time should help two groups of people move forward into a more highly integrated relationship. It cannot be repeated too often that conflict resolution, even if it is not a sufficient condition for national integration, is certainly a necessary condition.

As for what makes conflict resolution possible, it is sometimes the cumulative power of precedent, of having overcome other crises before. Experience of previous clashes sharpens the capacity to discover areas of mutual compatibility on subsequent occasions of tension. Another factor is awareness of reciprocal dependence. We are back to the function of interaction in promoting ethnic interreliance.

A question that inevitably arises in such a situation is whether or not a market economy with free enterprise is a better mechanism for fostering ethnic interreliance than a centralized economy would be. The situation in East Africa at the moment is that Tanzania and Uganda have opted for a substantial measure of state ownership and state direction of the economy. Tanzania did it in 1967 with the Arusha Declaration and with, initially, the nationalization of banks and other key enterprises, and a greater governmental control of the rest of the economy. Then on May 1, 1970, President Obote of Uganda also announced far-reaching socialistic measures designed in part to give the state a 60 percent share of all the major industries of the country.

Kenya is now the odd one out in this scheme of things. The word "socialism" used to be as recurrently utilized in the rhetoric of Kenya as in that of, say Uganda—perhaps more so at one time. But the word socialism in Kenya is getting rusty. The country under Kenyatta's government is embarked on the path of promoting private enterprise. There is a clear commitment to create an indigenous entrepreneurial culture in the country. Much of the exchange trade on attainment of independence was in the hands of the Indians and the Europeans. Government plans have aggressively initiated measures designed to decrease the share of Indians and Europeans in the nation, and raise the level of participation of indigenous Africans in commercial activity. Institutions have been set up to help African businessmen establish themselves. Legislation has been passed to reserve certain areas for African businessmen, and exclude from those areas the competition of the immigrant communities, especially those who did not take out Kenya citizenship. The immigration regulations both in Kenya and Uganda are designed to indigenize much of the exchange sector of the economy, as well as indigenize other categories of personnel in national life.

The Trade Licensing Acts both in Kenya and Uganda have been designed to increase private initiative by the Africans and protect them from excessive challenge by longer established immigrant business enterprises. In the case of Uganda, however, the Trade Licensing Act of early 1969, which became operational at the beginning of 1970, has in part been overtaken by the socialistic measures announced by President Obote on May Day 1970.

From the point of view of national integration a question still remains whether or not state ownership is a less effective way of promoting ethnic interreliance than a free-market economy would be. On balance, state ownership may reduce the challenge of creating new classes in East Africa, but it may also reduce the degree to which different tribes learn the arts of bargaining with each other and the skills of economic exchange. The market as an institution in East Africa is, on the whole, of briefer historical duration than is found among, say, the Yoruba in West Africa. Premature state control in East Africa, before an adequately vigorous economic culture has been created and before the tradition of rational economic initiative has fully matured, might slow down that aspect of nation-building which relies on maximizing an ethnic interreliance and economic interaction.

It is arguable that state ownership would strengthen governments. If state ownership does have such an effect, it would be contributing towards the consolidation of political legitimacy, even if it does slow down the process of political integration.

Such an assumption, however, might be a little hasty. Does state ownership in situations of fragile central institutions enhance or strain political legitimacy? We are not yet in a position to be sure, but it is at least as arguable that the assumption of major responsibilities by the state might prematurely promote a tendency to hold the state responsible when things go wrong. When the state takes over more and more of the economy it is indeed assuming responsibility for these ventures, but responsibility in this sense implies accountability, and accountability implies the acceptance of blame when things go wrong. As the pace of development in such countries is bound to be slow, and as setbacks are bound to be recurrent, occasions for articulated recrimination or silent grievance are bound to arise from year to year. Setbacks that might otherwise have been blamed on businessmen or blind market forces or immigrant communities are increasingly attributable to failings in state policies. The real danger posed by state socialism in a society with fragile institutions is not the danger of making governments too strong, but the risk of making governments more conspicuously ineffectual. Yet, even the effort itself to make the economy work could, if it includes a significant amount of genuine participation by indigenous workers and peasants, foster the kind of economic interaction necessary for nation-building.

PLURALISM AND SOCIAL INTEGRATION

We have defined social integration as the process by which the gaps between the elite and the masses, the rural and the urban classes, the privileged and the underprivileged, are gradually reduced or leveled out. But here it is worth distinguishing, more explicity, social integration from national integration. For our purposes the term "national integration" has a special sense and a general sense. In its special sense national integration is the merger of subnationalities into a wider national entity. It is the combination of the first dimension of cultural and normative fusion and fifth dimension of cumulative collective experiences on the broad national scale. The merger of tribe with tribe on the slow road to modern nationhood is the meaning of national integration in this narrow specialized sense.

National integration as a broader and more general concept encompasses all five dimensions of nation-building. When a collection of social subgroups are undergoing cultural and normative fusion, economic interpenetration, social integration, institutionalization of their methods of resolving conflicts, and accumulation of countrywide collective experiences, that collection of subgroups is getting nationally integrated in the more general sense.

In this regard too the issue of language policy in East Africa might be illuminating. The critical goals of language policy in relation to social engineering in East Africa are the goals of, firstly, national integration in the special sense and, secondly, social integration. As elsewhere in Africa the creation of a supratribal or supraethnic loyalty to a national homeland is the goal of the integrative process in this national sense.

On the other hand, we have defined social integration partly in relation to social stratification. Yet social integration is not necessarily a process by which the difference in income between the richest man and poorest man in the country is minimized. That absolute difference might remain the same, or even be increased, without implying that there has been no integration. But if the distance between the top and the bottom of the curve of income differences remains the same, the slope of the curve should be gradual and not steep. In a country where there are only very rich people and very poor people and nothing in between, social integration has a long way to go. But if between the pauper and the millionaire there are a lot of people with intermediate rates of income in a gradual gradation, the social integrative process has indeed made progress. We can have a well-integrated traditional society in this social sense of integration, as we can have a well-integrated modern society, but the prerequisites are different in each case. A well-integrated traditional society has to be largely egalitarian, with no major difference in income between the richest and the poorest. A well-integrated modern society need not be egalitarian, but the process of differentiation of structures and specialization of functions must be sufficiently advanced to have created an even or gradual slope of incomes from the top to the bottom.

Can a society move from traditional social integration to modern social integration without passing through the agonies of major gaps of income and life-style between the new elite and the masses, the town and the countryside? Can it move from social equality (the basis of traditional integration) to social differentiation (the basis of modern integration) without passing through a stage of convulsive disparities? These questions present the most agonizing dilemma of contemporary Africa.

Language policy in East Africa is linked to the problems of both national integration in the special sense and social integration, and the place of the English language is critical in both. A case can be made for the proposition that in relation to national integration in Uganda or Kenya the English language is functional, whereas in relation to social integration the English language is dysfunctional. The English language, by providing a means of trans-tribal communication between educated elites drawn from different ethnic groups, does serve the cause of normative interaction and shared acculturation. But the English language, by opening up certain privileges to those who have a command of it, in such countries as Kenya and Uganda, is one causal factor behind a widening gulf between the masses and the elites.

What should be remembered is that both social integration and national integration in the narrow sense are, in essence, processes of depluralizing society. Pluralism itself never completely disappears, but a society ceases to be a plural one when the stage of full national integration is reached. To put it in another way, there is pluralism in every society, but not every society is a plural one; the nature and depth of the pluralism is the determinant factor. After all, it might be true to say that there is some nationhood in every independent African country but not every independent African country is already a nation. Again, the nature and depth of that sense of nationhood are crucial. When Harold Laski rebelled against the notion "man versus the state," what he substituted in its place was a view of society which considers political life in terms of relations between groups, rather than relations between the government and the individual. The theory that Laski was putting forward was a theory of pluralism.

But if a plural society is not simply a soceity with pluralism, what distinguishes plural societies from others? The extreme case of a plural society is a society of total identities, of self-contained cultural systems or exclusive racial groups. Perhaps this kind of plural society as J. C. Mitchell suggests, comes nearest to being "a contradiction in terms." Relationships between the groups are either at the level of bare coexistence or minimal contact. This variety is perhaps the "pure type" of a plural society.[1]

However, as the integrative process gets underway, the total identities are increasingly partialized. By the time coalescence is reached, the society has been substantially depluralized in this special sense. As in England, the society might still have a highly structured class pluralism. Yet England has ceased to be a plural society. England is almost a pure type of an integrated nation. Complete coalescence with the Scots and the Welsh has not been fully achieved, though it is well advanced. The relationship of the English with the Northern Irish is perhaps still basically a compromise relationship, but with substantial areas of coalescence. The preponderant English themselves have achieved cohesion. The process of national integration among the English has virtually come to an end. Yet, for as long as certain forms of pluralism persist, there is still room for further depluralization. England has virtually completed national integration in the narrow sense, but there is considerable room yet for social integration. There is room especially for increased erosion of class distinctions.

While national integration in this narrow sense is finite, social integration is not. The ultimate error of Marxism is perhaps to assume that there is an end to social integration when all classes are abolished. Having made that assumption, Marxism was logical in further assuming that there was an end to the need for the state as well - that the state would "wither history. In some respects, Tanzania is better off than the United Kingdom. When institutions have already acquired primary consensus to back them, they are difficult to change. This situation is all right for as long as the institutions are desirable in themselves and serve the nation well, but many of the British institutions were born in a period of time when men were not engaged in rational and purposeful nation-building. The institutions were not products of reflection, calculation, and rational choice. They were the outcome of the convergence of historical accidents.

The distinctive thing about the last few decades of world history is the greater self-confidence shown by societies in their readiness to experiment with new social institutions. Even among the Tories in the United Kingdom there is now greater preparedness than ever to try things out and to attempt to control factors of production and social change at large.

A country like Tanzania, with wide secondary consensus but as yet uncertain primary consensus, is, in a sense, cast in a situation of real social choice. The secondary agreement behind the leadership and the policies can be used as a basis for experimenting with carefully selected institutions, and for gradually creating primary agreements behind those institutions. The people began in unity behind TANU and Nyerere, but relatively indifferent toward the actual system of government and social organization devised by TANU and Nyerere. TANU and Nyerere had between them, in other words, a wide area of latitude as to the direction in which they wished to take the nation. Because Tanzanians were united on Independence Day behind TANU and Nyerere it made sense for TANU to set up a commission to explore how a one-party unity could be reconciled with democratic values. It was a purposeful engagement in social engineering, but it was social engineering of the most central kind: the decision to erect a structure of government and administration as an act of conscious political choice. Having set up a one-party state de jure, the nation could then set about slowly acquiring primary consensus behind the new system should this be feasible.

But Uganda is in a different situation. It did not emerge into independence either with the sanctity of primary consensus, as in the United Kingdom, or with the blessing of secondary consensus, as in Tanzania. Uganda gradually drifted into a system of greater coercion. There are occasions when coercion is thought of as a functional alternative to consensus. The Congo is less united than Uganda; therefore, the Congo needs more coercion in its system than does Uganda. Tanzania is more united than Uganda; therefore, Tanzania should need less coercion for minimal system maintenance than does Uganda. In this sense coercion and unity or consensus are functional alternatives as bases for governmental action.

away" on attainment of classlessness. Perfect social integration would indeed make the state redundant. Yet, because social integration is an infinite process, the state continues to be necessary for the purpose of giving it direction. Nevertheless, in its formulation of the role of conflict in social change, and in its conception of perfect coalescence, however unrealizable, Marxism still affords useful insights into the nature of the integrative process. As an ideology, Marxism does itself often create conflict; but as a methodology, it helps us to understand it. After all, the integrative process is, in the ultimate analysis, the story of conflict and its role in socializing man.[2] The most fundamental of human institutions have often grown in response to the need to contain conflict of interest, divergence of values, and disputes over rights and duties. It is to this process of conflict resolution in relation to nation-building that we must now turn.

CONFLICT AND INSTITUTION-BUILDING

The routinization of conflict resolution needs not only stable institutions at the center for such purposes, it also needs a diversity of secondary institutions at all the lower levels of national life. The routinization of conflict resolution is, in fact, a process of institution building and the consolidation of procedures. But conflicts and disputes should not all involve the state. Mechanisms for resolving private disputes, or assuring an acceptable outcome of a private bargain, need to grow on all the different levels.

Meanwhile, authority at the center of national life can begin to take root. The problem of political legitimacy, is, in a sense, the old problem of political obligation in social philosophy. It is a problem of why and when one obeys, or ought to obey, the government. Where legitimacy is fully secure, the citizens do not question the government's rights to govern, though they may question the wisdom of this or that governmental action. When it is not secure, challenges to authority may allow little differentiation between dissent, insubordination, rebellion, and outright treason.

The problem facing many African states in the first few years of their independence was in trying to insure that every opposition remained a loyal opposition, that one could challenge decisions of the government but not the government's right to execute such decisions. In the final analysis, consensus was the ultimate problem. As we have argued before, there is a distinction between primary consensus and secondary consensus. Primary consensus is what makes us accept a certain degree of force from the government or even complain about that force without feeling that the government lacks the right to govern at all. Agreement behind institutions is the essence of primary consensus.

Secondary consensus, on the other hand, is consensus on this or that policy, or agreement behind a leader. In this case what is accepted is the substance of a particular policy (for example, a new tax on cigarettes, or greater emphasis on secondary education) or the leadership of a particular individual. The institution that that individual occupies, or through which those policies are arrived at, might remain very fragile, subject to sudden change or collapse, and bereft of the sanctity of widespread and deep acceptance.

In short, then, consensus on policies and behind leaders is secondary consensus, while consensus on methods and procedures and on the sanctity of institutions is primary consensus.

None of the three East African countries has as yet arrived at a situation of secure primary consensus. Tanzania has a highly developed level of secondary consensus behind President Nyerere himself and, for the time being, behind his policies of socialism and self-reliance. Tanzania, in other words, has secondary consensus at the level both of policy and of leadership.

Kenya has substantial secondary consensus at the level of leadership, insofar as there is still acceptance of Mzee Jomo Kenyatta as the guardian of the nation, and there is acceptance of his lieutenants to the extent they they are his lieutenants. But secondary consensus behind policies in Kenya is more fragile, partly because of the greater haziness about concrete national directions in Kenya than is found in Tanzania, and partly because of Kenya's less organized mechanisms of socialization and propaganda in support of policies. In addition, there are factors of tribal nepotism in the course of the implementation of policies which help to aggravate secondary dissension over the very policies themselves.

In regard to this problem of consensus, Uganda's situation is a little worse than Kenya's, let alone Tanzania's. In Uganda there is not quite as much agreement behind either the leadership or the policies as there is in the other two countries; yet Uganda has declared its commitment to a one-party state. It is clear that the reasons for Uganda's choice of the one-party state are radically different from the reasons that led Tanzania to adopt the same system.

In mainland Tanzania the case for a one-party system was based on the observation that the country was solidly united. The Tanganyika African National Union argued that the laws of the country should reflect the realities of the country, and one reality was that Tanganyikans or

mainland Tanzanians had massively voted for single-party dominance. In announcing the intention to form a one-party system *de jure*, President Julius Nyerere defended the decision in 1963 partly on the grounds that without a one-party system, Tanganyika would not enjoy real political contests at election time. TANU was so overwhelmingly supported that opposition candidates stood no chance. Only a one-party system, under whose umbrella candidates belonging to the same party could compete for election, would restore the principle of choice to the Tanganyika electorate—so it was argued.

But Uganda's path toward the one-party system has sprung from entirely different considerations. It seems to have sprung from the conviction that the previous multiparty systems had been basically divisive and prone to violent eruptions. The country needed a one-party system not because, as in the case of Tanzania, the country was solidly united, but because the country was dangerously divided.

When we further compare the two countries, not only with each other but with a more developed and more stable entity, further points of theoretical interest emerge. In mainland Tanzania, people are united in their support for the particular political party and particular political leadership. In Great Britain, on the other hand, people are united in their support for a particular set of institutions and system of rule. Tanzania has more secondary consensus than is normally possible in Britain. No head of government in Britain could hope to have the overwhelming support that Nyerere enjoys in mainland Tanzania, and no sets of policies in the United Kingdom are likely to enjoy as much popular backing as seems to lie behind some of Nyerere's policies on socialism and self-reliance. There is no doubt that in terms of mobilizing support ror a particular personality in politics or a particular set of policies, Tanzania is more mobilizable in peacetime than is the United Kingdom. But clearly, also, the United Kingdom enjoys far greater primary consensus than has as yet been achieved by Tanzania. The system of government under which the United Kingdom is ruled does not pose the question of whether or not it will survive the present head of government. But institutions in Tanzania, devised substantially under Nyerere's inspiration, may conceivably outlive him as a major feature of the country, but that occurrence is by no means certain. For the time being, the institutions derive their authority from the standing of Nyerere rather than Nyerere deriving his authority from the sanctity of the institutions.

In Britain, prime ministers come and go, but the system of government—though always changing in a number of subtle ways—has nevertheless demonstrated stable resilience throughout a substantial period of

Coercion in Uganda is both a response to instability in social values and, to some extent, a cause of further violent plotting and intrigue. On 19 December 1969, there was an attempt on President Obote's life as he was leaving the highly successful annual delegates' conference of his party, the Uganda Peoples' Congress. Who had attempted to kill him? There were three conceivable categories of opponents to the president: ethnic opponents, ideological opponents, and power rivals or those with personal political grievances. The ethnic opponents were conceivably either those who had strong feelings about the president's own tribe, or those who felt that the president had humiliated their own tribe. Theories about Baganda complicity in the attempted assassination were attributing the criminal event to issues of ethnic opposition. In the second category were ideological opponents, perhaps those disturbed by the president's declared intention to turn the country Leftward. The third category included rivals for power, or people with personal grievances against Dr. Obote. This third possibility could amount to a cleavage or tense relationship between powerful political peers at the very commanding heights of the polity.

If the attempted assassination was by an ethnic opponent, then the act itself symbolized the simple fact that the task of national survival was far from complete. In this case the attempted assassination was symptomatic of inadequate national integration, and consequently, it was also symptomatic of inadequate political legitimacy. If, on the other hand, the attempted assassination was by an ideological opponent, it could mean that Ugandans were beginning to feel passionately about political issues other than tribal loyalties and the legitimacy of the regime. Political violence was moving from issues of national survival to issues of ideological preferences. This shift could have great political meaning as a change in the motivation for violence.

We have already discussed the distinction between primary and secondary consensus. There is, in addition, a distinction between primary and secondary violence. To kill because one hates socialism is less fundamental than to kill because one hates the tribe of one's opponent. Tribalistic violence is the violence of identity; ideological violence is the violence of policy. Violence on policy issues is secondary; violence on identity and national survival is primary.

The most primary form of violence is that which concerns the territorial survival of the nation. When one group in a nation is so violently opposed to another that it resents having to share the same frontiers of nationhood, cleavage is at its most fundamental. It affects not only integrative questions, but also brings in the question of whether or not a ruler chosen from one particular tribe has a right to exercise authority over another. National integration and political legitimacy become intertwined in the consequences, although the initial cause of the cleavage is a fracture in the integrative section.

If, on the other hand, the attempt on President Obote's life was a case of ideological violence, resisting the trend towards nationalization and socialistic preferences, then it could conceivably mean that Uganda was moving a little further forward in the process of national integration. Secondary violence, inspired by ideological preference could indicate— though it was still too early to be sure—that the passions of pure tribalism had started on their slow historical road to extinction.

Tribalism in Africa is unlikely to disappear within a single lifetime. But, pessimistic as it may seem, the first signs of its disappearance might have to be sought in the changing types of political violence from primary to secondary. Much of the violence in developed societies is secondary violence, less concerned with national survival than with the issues of policy preferences, but much of the political violence in Africa remains deeply concerned with identity and is therefore primary. The range is from the ghastly experience of the Nigerian Civil War to interethnic resentments between the Batoro and the Bakonjo in one part of Uganda.

Should the difficulties in Uganda have also been concerned with tensions of power rivalry at the top, this circumstance, too, would be secondary violence. It would indicate that President Obote's rivals were sufficiently interested in the central machinery of the nation to wish to control it themselves. A power struggle for control of the center is a confirmation that all rivals are interested in the survival of the system. They simply disagree on who should control it. Violence between political peers for control of the center, or violence by subordinates who have political grievances, are, therefore, normally secondary types, though points of linkage with the crisis of political legitimacy may exist.[3]

TOWARDS A NATIONAL MEMORY

In the long and slow process of national integration, it is not enough that people should interact economically; it is not enough that they should begin to share cultural traits; it is not enough that they should socially evolve a multiplicity of institutions for resolving conflict. There is a fifth dimension required to pull these other four together and focus them towards the center. This fifth dimension might be called the collective cumulation of shared national experience. Economic exchange, though going on all over the country, usually involves relationships between subunits of the nation—a shopkeeper and his customers, a firm with another firm, a parastatal body with its clientele. The spread of the Swahili language, though it does introduce significant cultural interaction in the country, does not ensure that one part of the country knows much about another, or that there is a conscious identification between those who speak Swahili in the northern tip of Tanzania and those who speak it in the southern tip. The routinization of conflict resolution can also be resolution between subunits of the nation, or between the central government and one particular subunit at a given moment in time. None of these experiences really need involve, in any fundamental sense, the population as a whole. They may have repercussions all over the country, but in general the processes of economic interaction, social integration, routinization of conflict resolution, and cultural fusion may be basically processes of integrating subunits into each other but not necessarily of nationalizing them all in a shared moment of particular experience.

In order to give these four other processes a central focus and promote in the population mutual identification as nationals of the same country, some additional area of experience is needed, and this additional centralizing process is what might be called a collective cumulation of shared moments of national experience.

In *Representative Government,* John Stuart Mill defined a nationality in the following terms:

A portion of mankind may be said to constitute a Nationality if they are united among themselves by common sympathies which do not exist between them and any others—which make them co-operate with each other more willingly than with other people, desire to be under the same government, and desire that they should be governed by themselves or a portion of themselves exclusively. This feeling of nationality may have been generated by various causes . . . but the strongest of all is identity of political antecedents; the possession of national history and consequent community of recollections; collective pride and humiliation, pleasure and regret, connected with the same incidents in the past.[4]

Mill is here emphasizing the importance for nationhood of the kind of shared experiences that lead to shared prejudices and shared emotional dispositions. When a group of people begin to feel proud about the same things or humiliated by the same things, pleased or saddened collectively by the incidents, that group of people is acquiring the capacity for collective selfhood. The process of nation-building at the psychological level, therefore, entails the cumulative acquisition of common emotional dispositions and common potential responses to the same stimuli. To be capable of being angry about the same incident is to share an area of fellow-feeling. The shared resentment of colonialism in African countries often constituted the beginnings of national consciousness. And where elections are permitted to take place in independent Africa, the general participation in campaigning and the widespread disputes over policies and personalities are a form of political interaction on a national scale. To that extent, every general election, no matter how painful or even violent, is part of the cumulative acquisition of collective memories by an African people.

Social engineering in the new African states has sometimes taken the form of purposeful collectivization of emotions in a bid to make the populace share a moment of empathy. The collectivization of anger, for example, sometime results in the nationalization of protest. A capacity for what Mill calls "collective pride and humiliation" is a particularly important feature of a sense of shared nationhood. It is precisely because of this feature that anger as an emotion is so central to the growth of nationhood. After all, offended pride gives rise to anger. Collective humiliation is a deeper stage of offended pride. This stage, in turn, generates anger, either overtly or in a subdued silent form. Shared moments of collective anger by a group, by being connected with the cumulative acquisition of a capacity for collective pride and collective humiliation, become part of the process of national integration.

Among political leaders in Africa, Milton Obote of Uganda has been particularly aware of the importance of promoting shared emotional dispositions and potential responses to the same stimuli. Obote, faced with a country deeply divided ethnically, has at times turned precisely to the devices of collectivizing moments of anger and nationalizing protest.

On Saturday, February 13, 1965, some Congolese planes bombed the villages of Goli and Paidha in the West Nile District of Uganda. Obote himself was angry that this should have happened; but, more importantly, he saw the moment as one that afforded the opportunity for collective patriotic anger among Ugandans. Anger against the Congolese for violating Uganda's borders in such a violent way did itself afford some possibilities for patriotic indignation by Ugandans. Yet Obote perceived that being angry with the Congolese was not adequate. The planes that had crossed the border were American-made, sold or given to Tshombe's regime in the Congo by the United States as a conscious high policy. Obote grasped the possibility of collectivizing Ugandan anger and directing it at the United States, in addition to to directing it at Tshombe's regime. The situation did indeed afford possibilities for airing wounded pride. In addition, a diplomatic confrontation between Uganda and the United States had all the air of a David and Goliath meeting. The weak, aroused in proud anger, were confronting the mighty in a posture of defiant protest. Obote said to his countrymen:

away" on attainment of classlessness. Perfect social integration would indeed make the state redundant. Yet, because social integration is an infinite process, the state continues to be necessary for the purpose of giving it direction. Nevertheless, in its formulation of the role of conflict in social change, and in its conception of perfect coalescence, however unrealizable, Marxism still affords useful insights into the nature of the integrative process. As an ideology, Marxism does itself often create conflict; but as a methodology, it helps us to understand it. After all, the integrative process is, in the ultimate analysis, the story of conflict and its role in socializing man.[2] The most fundamental of human institutions have often grown in response to the need to contain conflict of interest, divergence of values, and disputes over rights and duties. It is to this process of conflict resolution in relation to nation-building that we must now turn.

CONFLICT AND INSTITUTION-BUILDING

The routinization of conflict resolution needs not only stable institutions at the center for such purposes, it also needs a diversity of secondary institutions at all the lower levels of national life. The routinization of conflict resolution is, in fact, a process of institution building and the consolidation of procedures. But conflicts and disputes should not all involve the state. Mechanisms for resolving private disputes, or assuring an acceptable outcome of a private bargain, need to grow on all the different levels.

Meanwhile, authority at the center of national life can begin to take root. The problem of political legitimacy, is, in a sense, the old problem of political obligation in social philosophy. It is a problem of why and when one obeys, or ought to obey, the government. Where legitimacy is fully secure, the citizens do not question the government's rights to govern, though they may question the wisdom of this or that governmental action. When it is not secure, challenges to authority may allow little differentiation between dissent, insubordination, rebellion, and outright treason.

The problem facing many African states in the first few years of their independence was in trying to insure that every opposition remained a loyal opposition, that one could challenge decisions of the government but not the government's right to execute such decisions. In the final analysis, consensus was the ultimate problem. As we have argued before, there is a distinction between primary consensus and secondary consensus. Primary consensus is what makes us accept a certain degree of force from the government or even complain about that force without feeling that the government lacks the right to govern at all. Agreement behind institutions is the essence of primary consensus.

Secondary consensus, on the other hand, is consensus on this or that policy, or agreement behind a leader. In this case what is accepted is the substance of a particular policy (for example, a new tax on cigarettes, or greater emphasis on secondary education) or the leadership of a particular individual. The institution that that individual occupies, or through which those policies are arrived at, might remain very fragile, subject to sudden change or collapse, and bereft of the sanctity of widespread and deep acceptance.

In short, then, consensus on policies and behind leaders is secondary consensus, while consensus on methods and procedures and on the sanctity of institutions is primary consensus.

None of the three East African countries has as yet arrived at a situation of secure primary consensus. Tanzania has a highly developed level of secondary consensus behind President Nyerere himself and, for the time being, behind his policies of socialism and self-reliance. Tanzania, in other words, has secondary consensus at the level both of policy and of leadership.

Kenya has substantial secondary consensus at the level of leadership, insofar as there is still acceptance of Mzee Jomo Kenyatta as the guardian of the nation, and there is acceptance of his lieutenants to the extent they they are his lieutenants. But secondary consensus behind policies in Kenya is more fragile, partly because of the greater haziness about concrete national directions in Kenya than is found in Tanzania, and partly because of Kenya's less organized mechanisms of socialization and propaganda in support of policies. In addition, there are factors of tribal nepotism in the course of the implementation of policies which help to aggravate secondary dissension over the very policies themselves.

In regard to this problem of consensus, Uganda's situation is a little worse than Kenya's, let alone Tanzania's. In Uganda there is not quite as much agreement behind either the leadership or the policies as there is in the other two countries; yet Uganda has declared its commitment to a one-party state. It is clear that the reasons for Uganda's choice of the one-party state are radically different from the reasons that led Tanzania to adopt the same system.

In mainland Tanzania the case for a one-party system was based on the observation that the country was solidly united. The Tanganyika African National Union argued that the laws of the country should reflect the realities of the country, and one reality was that Tanganyikans or mainland Tanzanians had massively voted for single-party dominance. In announcing the intention to form a one-party system *de jure*, President Julius Nyerere defended the decision in 1963 partly on the grounds that without a one-party system, Tanganyika would not enjoy real political contests at election time. TANU was so overwhelmingly supported that opposition candidates stood no chance. Only a one-party system, under whose umbrella candidates belonging to the same party could compete for election, would restore the principle of choice to the Tanganyika electorate—so it was argued.

But Uganda's path toward the one-party system has sprung from entirely different considerations. It seems to have sprung from the conviction that the previous multiparty systems had been basically divisive and prone to violent eruptions. The country needed a one-party system not because, as in the case of Tanzania, the country was solidly united, but because the country was dangerously divided.

When we further compare the two countries, not only with each other but with a more developed and more stable entity, further points of theoretical interest emerge. In mainland Tanzania, people are united in their support for the particular political party and particular political leadership. In Great Britain, on the other hand, people are united in their support for a particular set of institutions and system of rule. Tanzania has more secondary consensus than is normally possible in Britain. No head of government in Britain could hope to have the overwhelming support that Nyerere enjoys in mainland Tanzania, and no sets of policies in the United Kingdom are likely to enjoy as much popular backing as seems to lie behind some of Nyerere's policies on socialism and self-reliance. There is no doubt that in terms of mobilizing support for a particular personality in politics or a particular set of policies, Tanzania is more mobilizable in peacetime than is the United Kingdom. But clearly, also, the United Kingdom enjoys far greater primary consensus than has as yet been achieved by Tanzania. The system of government under which the United Kingdom is ruled does not pose the question of whether or not it will survive the present head of government. But institutions in Tanzania, devised substantially under Nyerere's inspiration, may conceivably outlive him as a major feature of the country, but that occurrence is by no means certain. For the time being, the institutions derive their authority from the standing of Nyerere rather than Nyerere deriving his authority from the sanctity of the institutions.

In Britain, prime ministers come and go, but the system of government—though always changing in a number of subtle ways—has nevertheless demonstrated stable resilience throughout a substantial period of history. In some respects, Tanzania is better off than the United Kingdom. When institutions have already acquired primary consensus to back them, they are difficult to change. This situation is all right for as long as the institutions are desirable in themselves and serve the nation well, but many of the British institutions were born in a period of time when men were not engaged in rational and purposeful nation-building. The institutions were not products of reflection, calculation, and rational choice. They were the outcome of the convergence of historical accidents.

The distinctive thing about the last few decades of world history is the greater self-confidence shown by societies in their readiness to experiment with new social institutions. Even among the Tories in the United Kingdom there is now greater preparedness than ever to try things out and to attempt to control factors of production and social change at large.

A country like Tanzania, with wide secondary consensus but as yet uncertain primary consensus, is, in a sense, cast in a situation of real social choice. The secondary agreement behind the leadership and the policies can be used as a basis for experimenting with carefully selected institutions, and for gradually creating primary agreements behind those institutions. The people began in unity behind TANU and Nyerere, but relatively indifferent toward the actual system of government and social organization devised by TANU and Nyerere. TANU and Nyerere had between them, in other words, a wide area of latitude as to the direction in which they wished to take the nation. Because Tanzanians were united on Independence Day behind TANU and Nyerere it made sense for TANU to set up a commission to explore how a one-party unity could be reconciled with democratic values. It was a purposeful engagement in social engineering, but it was social engineering of the most central kind: the decision to erect a structure of government and administration as an act of conscious political choice. Having set up a one-party state de jure, the nation could then set about slowly acquiring primary consensus behind the new system should this be feasible.

But Uganda is in a different situation. It did not emerge into independence either with the sanctity of primary consensus, as in the United Kingdom, or with the blessing of secondary consensus, as in Tanzania. Uganda gradually drifted into a system of greater coercion. There are occasions when coercion is thought of as a functional alternative to consensus. The Congo is less united than Uganda; therefore, the Congo needs more coercion in its system than does Uganda. Tanzania is more united than Uganda; therefore, Tanzania should need less coercion for minimal system maintenance than does Uganda. In this sense coercion and unity or consensus are functional alternatives as bases for governmental action.

Coercion in Uganda is both a response to instability in social values and, to some extent, a cause of further violent plotting and intrigue. On 19 December 1969, there was an attempt on President Obote's life as he was leaving the highly successful annual delegates' conference of his party, the Uganda Peoples' Congress. Who had attempted to kill him? There were three conceivable categories of opponents to the president: ethnic opponents, ideological opponents, and power rivals or those with personal political grievances. The ethnic opponents were conceivably either those who had strong feelings about the president's own tribe, or those who felt that the president had humiliated their own tribe. Theories about Baganda complicity in the attempted assassination were attributing the criminal event to issues of ethnic opposition. In the second category were ideological opponents, perhaps those disturbed by the president's declared intention to turn the country Leftward. The third category included rivals for power, or people with personal grievances against Dr. Obote. This third possibility could amount to a cleavage or tense relationship between powerful political peers at the very commanding heights of the polity.

If the attempted assassination was by an ethnic opponent, then the act itself symbolized the simple fact that the task of national survival was far from complete. In this case the attempted assassination was symptomatic of inadequate national integration, and consequently, it was also symptomatic of inadequate political legitimacy. If, on the other hand, the attempted assassination was by an ideological opponent, it could mean that Ugandans were beginning to feel passionately about political issues other than tribal loyalties and the legitimacy of the regime. Political violence was moving from issues of national survival to issues of ideological preferences. This shift could have great political meaning as a change in the motivation for violence.

We have already discussed the distinction between primary and secondary consensus. There is, in addition, a distinction between primary and secondary violence. To kill because one hates socialism is less fundamental than to kill because one hates the tribe of one's opponent. Tribalistic violence is the violence of identity; ideological violence is the violence of policy. Violence on policy issues is secondary; violence on identity and national survival is primary.

The most primary form of violence is that which concerns the territorial survival of the nation. When one group in a nation is so violently opposed to another that it resents having to share the same frontiers of nationhood, cleavage is at its most fundamental. It affects not only integrative questions, but also brings in the question of whether or not a ruler chosen from one particular tribe has a right to exercise authority over another. National integration and political legitimacy become intertwined in the consequences, although the initial cause of the cleavage is a fracture in the integrative section.

If, on the other hand, the attempt on President Obote's life was a case of ideological violence, resisting the trend towards nationalization and socialistic preferences, then it could conceivably mean that Uganda was moving a little further forward in the process of national integration. Secondary violence, inspired by ideological preference could indicate—though it was still too early to be sure—that the passions of pure tribalism had started on their slow historical road to extinction.

Tribalism in Africa is unlikely to disappear within a single lifetime. But, pessimistic as it may seem, the first signs of its disappearance might have to be sought in the changing types of political violence from primary to secondary. Much of the violence in developed societies is secondary violence, less concerned with national survival than with the issues of policy preferences, but much of the political violence in Africa remains deeply concerned with identity and is therefore primary. The range is from the ghastly experience of the Nigerian Civil War to interethnic resentments between the Batoro and the Bakonjo in one part of Uganda.

Should the difficulties in Uganda have also been concerned with tensions of power rivalry at the top, this circumstance, too, would be secondary violence. It would indicate that President Obote's rivals were sufficiently interested in the central machinery of the nation to wish to control it themselves. A power struggle for control of the center is a confirmation that all rivals are interested in the survival of the system. They simply disagree on who should control it. Violence between political peers for control of the center, or violence by subordinates who have political grievances, are, therefore, normally secondary types, though points of linkage with the crisis of political legitimacy may exist.[3]

TOWARDS A NATIONAL MEMORY

In the long and slow process of national integration, it is not enough that people should interact economically; it is not enough that they should begin to share cultural traits; it is not enough that they should socially evolve a multiplicity of institutions for resolving conflict. There is a fifth dimension required to pull these other four together and focus them towards the center. This fifth dimension might be called the collective cumulation of shared national experience. Economic exchange, though going on all over the country, usually involves relationships between subunits of the nation—a shopkeeper and his customers, a firm with another firm, a parastatal body with its clientele. The spread of the Swahili language, though it does introduce significant cultural interaction in the country, does not ensure that one part of the country knows much about another, or that there is a conscious identification between those who speak Swahili in the northern tip of Tanzania and those who speak it in the southern tip. The routinization of conflict resolution can also be resolution between subunits of the nation, or between the central government and one particular subunit at a given moment in time. None of these experiences really need involve, in any fundamental sense, the population as a whole. They may have repercussions all over the country, but in general the processes of economic interaction, social integration, routinization of conflict resolution, and cultural fusion may be basically processes of integrating subunits into each other but not necessarily of nationalizing them all in a shared moment of particular experience.

In order to give these four other processes a central focus and promote in the population mutual identification as nationals of the same country, some additional area of experience is needed, and this additional centralizing process is what might be called a collective cumulation of shared moments of national experience.

In *Representative Government,* John Stuart Mill defined a nationality in the following terms:

> A portion of mankind may be said to constitute a Nationality if they are united among themselves by common sympathies which do not exist between them and any others—which make them co-operate with each other more willingly than with other people, desire to be under the same government, and desire that they should be governed by themselves or a portion of themselves exclusively. This feeling of nationality may have been generated by various causes . . . but the strongest of all is identity of political antecedents; the possession of national history and consequent community of recollections; collective pride and humiliation, pleasure and regret, connected with the same incidents in the past.[4]

Mill is here emphasizing the importance for nationhood of the kind of shared experiences that lead to shared prejudices and shared emotional dispositions. When a group of people begin to feel proud about the same things or humiliated by the same things, pleased or saddened collectively by the incidents, that group of people is acquiring the capacity for collective selfhood. The process of nation-building at the psychological level, therefore, entails the cumulative acquisition of common emotional dispositions and common potential responses to the same stimuli. To be capable of being angry about the same incident is to share an area of fellow-feeling. The shared resentment of colonialism in African countries often constituted the beginnings of national consciousness. And where elections are permitted to take place in independent Africa, the general participation in campaigning and the widespread disputes over policies and personalities are a form of political interaction on a national scale. To that extent, every general election, no matter how painful or even violent, is part of the cumulative acquisition of collective memories by an African people.

Social engineering in the new African states has sometimes taken the form of purposeful collectivization of emotions in a bid to make the populace share a moment of empathy. The collectivization of anger, for example, sometime results in the nationalization of protest. A capacity for what Mill calls "collective pride and humiliation" is a particularly important feature of a sense of shared nationhood. It is precisely because of this feature that anger as an emotion is so central to the growth of nationhood. After all, offended pride gives rise to anger. Collective humiliation is a deeper stage of offended pride. This stage, in turn, generates anger, either overtly or in a subdued silent form. Shared moments of collective anger by a group, by being connected with the cumulative acquisition of a capacity for collective pride and collective humiliation, become part of the process of national integration.

Among political leaders in Africa, Milton Obote of Uganda has been particularly aware of the importance of promoting shared emotional dispositions and potential responses to the same stimuli. Obote, faced with a country deeply divided ethnically, has at times turned precisely to the devices of collectivizing moments of anger and nationalizing protest.

On Saturday, February 13, 1965, some Congolese planes bombed the villages of Goli and Paidha in the West Nile District of Uganda. Obote himself was angry that this should have happened; but, more importantly, he saw the moment as one that afforded the opportunity for collective patriotic anger among Ugandans. Anger against the Congolese for violating Uganda's borders in such a violent way did itself afford some possibilities for patriotic indignation by Ugandans. Yet Obote perceived that being angry with the Congolese was not adequate. The planes that had crossed the border were American-made, sold or given to Tshombe's regime in the Congo by the United States as a conscious high policy. Obote grasped the possibility of collectivizing Ugandan anger and directing it at the United States, in addition to to directing it at Tshombe's regime. The situation did indeed afford possibilities for airing wounded pride. In addition, a diplomatic confrontation between Uganda and the United States had all the air of a David and Goliath meeting. The weak, aroused in proud anger, were confronting the mighty in a posture of defiant protest. Obote said to his countrymen:

We blame the government of the United States. . . . We have been attacked without provocation on our part. I cannot say whether we are going to retaliate. . . . We must all be prepared to throw sand, and sacks of sands, in the eyes of the mighty.

Even then the question arose as to why Dr. Obote was dramatizing the bombing incident instead of minimizing it. One reason might have been the obvious one: the desire to take a justifiably indignant stand at having had one's frontiers violently violated, but it also seemed likely that Obote perceived the political functions of wounded pride when it is collectivized. An important problem confronting every African government is, after all, how to transform that old race-conscious nationalism of the anticolonial struggle into a new state-conscious patriotism of postindependence days. How could those antiimperialist protests of transformation of yesteryear now be converted into cumulative dispositions of shared national identity?

In the case of the particular incident in Uganda in 1965, there was something very "sovereign" about having to defend one's borders against hostile planes. Perhaps, for that reason, Dr. Obote felt impelled to remind his countrymen of a small point when he spoke on television the night following the bombing of the villages. Obote reminded Ugandans that on October 9, 1962, the country had become independent. There was something rather sovereign about having one's air space protected. To be attacked by enemy planes from across the border could almost be a status symbol in the case of new states. The diplomatic protests that followed inevitably had the ring of newly acquired sovereignty.

If, then, an African leader like Obote was dedicated to creating a state-conscious patriotism in his people, he had to utilize the sovereign symbolism of a variety of different factors—from flags to air space. This fact is what made the destruction of a village in the West Nile District of Uganda something that could be used in the construction of a moment of national cohesion; Ugandans in a moment of joint outrage were Ugandans united.

The government therefore arranged popular participation in national anger. A national demonstration was arranged for Tuesday afternoon, February 16, 1965. There were ministerial appeals to employers to release their workers for the great march to the American Embassy and for the rally to follow. At least metaphorically, Ugandans were up in arms—or so the great march was supposed to demonstrate. And even the wounded soldier in a West Nile village was elevated to a symbolic state hero. As Dr. Obote put it: "Our one officer has already spilled blood for all of us. It will be our duty to redeem that blood.[6]

The Uganda government could have protested directly to the Congolese government or the government of the United States, but such protest would have taken a government-to-government form. Instead, what Obote was out to do was precisely to collectivize anger, and popularize protest as a way of nationalizing it. In the arrangements that were made, there were a number of miscalculations, and not everything went according to plan in that joint endeavor to unite Ugandans in shared indignation, but a demonstration did take place. The American Embassy was momentarily besieged and the American flag was burned. Diplomatic protest at the government to government level was one thing, but Obote was out to give protest some grass roots, and, in so doing, add one more thin layer of experience to that slow cumulative acquisition of a sense of "shared pride and shared humiliation" among Ugandans. The history of Uganda under Obote includes other moments of attempted nationalization of political indignation. The growth of national identity is inseparable from the process by which prejudices become to some extent homogenized in the population, and emotional dispositions become collectivized. Sometimes fear, as a source of protest, is also relevant to this process. The fear of an enemy, the anger arising out of wounded pride, and the ambition to create the foundations of nationhood have often interacted on those occasions of shared responses in new states.[7]

CONCLUSION

These, then, are the five dimensions of nation-building as illustrated by East Africa's experience. The quest for a national language is, in part, a quest for a shared cultural heritage. A collection of individuals or subgroups becomes a people partly when they succeed in forging a common universe of perspectives and a capacity for mutual communication. Cultural and normative fusion does not presuppose an identity of values or uniformity of thought and cultural behavior. It simply presupposes a high degree of mutual influence between groups and individuals in cultural perspectives, tending towards a shared language of cultural discourse.

Economic interpenetration between groups and sectors of society promotes a shared interest in the economic fortunes of the country. In East Africa the issue is also connected with the policies of indigenizing the three economies against a background of expatriate dominance. Put at its most extreme, the approaches have amounted to a choice between black capitalism and African socialism—between state ownership and state control of the economy on the one hand, and the promotion of an indigenous entrepreneurial class on the other. Tanzania is leaning toward a socialistic approach to indigenous economic engagement; Kenya is leaning toward an indigenous private enterprise system; and Uganda seems to be experimenting with both approaches.

Economic interaction is a process that influences other aspects of social change. The issue of class formation looms into relevance. Tanzania seeks to achieve social integration through social equality (as was the case in integrated traditional societies). Kenya, on the other hand, has been pursuing social integration through social differentiation and functional diversification among the African populace. Uganda is again caught between the two approaches. Meanwhile, the policies of progressive depluralization continue, and both language policies and economic policies are central to the whole process.

Class formation, whether encouraged or frustrated, generates areas of conflict. There are other forms of conflict as well in every East African country, ranging from ethnic tensions to ideological disputes. Nation-building must, therefore, include the construction of institutions for the resolution of these multiple levels of conflict. The institutions are entrusted to them. But the experience of institutional experimentation, as well as the constant search for ways of containing conflict at large, are perhaps the most explicitly political of all the dimensions of nation-building. The crisis of political authority and legitimacy is a crisis of institutional fluidity. It is a crisis of incapacity to solve some of the critical disputes of politics. In this respect, nation-building becomes a research for a viable system of tension management.

Finally, we have discussed in this essay the unifying impact of collective experiences on a people. Colonialism itself was for many African countries such an experience, and the struggle against colonialism was another. Having been ruled by the same colonial power for half a century or more was an important factor behind the relative unity and similarity among Uganda, Kenya, and Tanzania, as contrasted with the Congo, which was ruled by a different imperial country. After independence, it has been such phenomena as party politics, electioneering, national service, induced collective indignation, and special central crises, which have focused attention on the country as a whole as a unit of selfhood.

These are the experiences that cumulatively evolve into a shared national memory. And a national memory is the historical dimension of nationhood, giving this particular form of collective identity its roots in time.

NOTES

1. "[I] f [such societies] are 'plural,' can they be societies?" See J. C. Mitchell, Tribalism and the Plural Society, An Inaugural Lecture, London, Oxford University Press, 1960, p. 25.

2. These points are discussed more fully in Ali A. Mazrui, "Pluralism and National Integration," in Leo Kuper and M. C. Smith (eds.), Pluralism in Africa, University of California Press, 1969. Available also as a chapter in Ali A. Mazrui, Violence and Thought, London, Longmans, 1969.

3. These issues are discussed in Ali A. Mazrui, "Leadership in Africa: Obote of Uganda, "International Journal, Summer 1970.

4. John Stuart Mill, Representative Government, 1861, Ch. XVI.

5. Uganda Argus (Kampala), February 15, 1965.

6. Ibid.

7. For a further elaboration of Uganda's experience in this regard, consult Ali A. Mazrui, "Leadership in Africa," op. cit.

APPENDIX
A BRIEF POLITICAL OUTLINE OF EAST AFRICA

I. The United Republic of Tanzania

This republic consists of the mainland, Tanganyika, and the islands of Zanzibar and Pemba. Tanganyika became independent in 1961. It had been a United Nations' trusteeship under the administration of the United Kingdom, having been captured from the Germans at the end of World War I, and having first been a League of Nations' mandate. On attainment of independence, the Tangayika African National Union had overwhelming support in the country under the leadership of Julius K. Nyerere. Julius K. Nyerere became the first prime minister. A year and a half later, he resigned briefly in order to concentrate on the political party and strengthen its institutions. He handed over premiership to a colleague while he completed this task. His resumption of duties was as President of Tanganyika following the proclamation of a republic and the severance of the last link with the British monarch.

In December 1963, a revolution took place in Zanzibar, overthrowing the sultan's regime. The revolution was cheered throughout the three countries of Uganda, Kenya, and Tanganyika; but concern crept in when the violence of the island seemed to spark off an army mutiny in Tanganyika, followed by one in Uganda, and then one in Kenya. The mutinies were suppressed by the intervention of British troops, invited by the three independent governments of East Africa.

In 1965, the first elections since independence took place, mainly in the Tanganyika part of the United Arab Republic. Mainland Tanzania had by that time inaugurated a one-party systeme de jure, following the recommendations of a special commission to inquire into how a one-party system might be made to serve the other ideals of Tanzania. The elections were historical to the extent that they provided a new experiment in single-party democracy. Individual members of the same Tanganyika National African Union stood for elections against each other, and the freedom with which the elections were conducted was illustrated by the fall of an important minister, a Mr. Paul Bomani, several assistant ministers, and some other members of Parliament.

In April 1966, Tanganyika and Zanzibar united to form a new national entity that came to be known as the United Republic of Tanzania.

In February 1967, Nyerere proclaimed the Arusha Declaration of Socialism and self-reliance, which marked an important new phase in the socialistic evolution of Tanzania. Banks and some of the other industries were nationalized, and a greater commitment to internal self-exertion was made by the regime. Although now in some ways the most radical of the three countries, Tanganyika's own road to independence was more moderate than that of the other two. There was not much of a struggle for independence in Tanganyika - certainly not when compared with the Mau Mau insurrection in Kenya, or even the crisis of challenge to authority which littered Uganda's own path towards independence. The mainland of Tanganyika still remains relatively peaceful, with few of the passionate cleavages that one finds in the other two countries. The island of Zanzibar has a less happy experience. This island has been subject to acute mismanagement and poor administration.

II. The Republic of Uganda

Uganda became independent in 1962. The Constitution contains a compromise formula to keep together groups that in some respects seem to have been mutually distrustful. Uganda's history includes the preeminence of the Baganda tribe and Buganda region in national affairs. Indeed the very name of the country is a variation of the dominant tribe. But as independence approached it became clear that Baganda domination could not be maintained any longer in a sovereign country, and popular institutions would have to be introduced. The Baganda became more defensive in their attitude to reform, and even attempted formal secession in 1960 in order to insure their own autonomy. There was a fear that Buganda in a Uganda subject to popular institutions and democratic elections would not only be overshadowed by other communities, but might even be dominated.

It took a good deal of diplomatic maneuvering and negotiation to work out the 1962 Constitution, which gave Buganda a new federal status within the country and seemed to assure her a degree of autonomy within the new political community.

Milton A. Obote's party, the Uganda Peoples' Congress, was the strongest of the three which took their seats in the National Assembly on the attainment of independence; the other two were the Democratic Party and Kabaka Yekka. Kabaka Yekka, meaning "The King Alone," was basically a Baganda political movement, again committed to the dignity and autonomy of Buganda.

None of the three parties could initially form a government on its own. A coalition government was finally negotiated between Obote's Uganda Peoples' Congress and the Baganda party, Kabaka Yekka. It looked like a strange marriage between what was regarded as the most radical of the three parties and what was regarded as the most traditionalist (feudalist).

Partly because of the tendency for some members of Parliament to cross the floor and join the ruling party, the Uganda Peoples' Congress within the legislature got stronger and stronger as more members of the Democratic Party crossed to join the UPC. At the end of 1964 even the parliamentary leader, himself of the Democratic Party, with five others, crossed the floor to join the UPC. Meanwhile, Kabaka Yekka members were also getting restless within their own traditionalist party, and sensing the apparent growing strength of the UPC, some left Kabaka Yekka to join the UPC.

In 1964 the UPC at last felt strong enough to start thinking about ending its alliance with Kabaka Yekka, and did so. A new period of tension was entered between Buganda and the central government. It later appeared that some of the floor crossings, particularly after the breakup of the alliance, were really Trojan horse tactics designed to infiltrate the UPC and change its leadership from the inside.

A moment of crisis was reached in February 1966 when a member of KY, Mr. Daudi Ocheng, advanced a motion in Parliament accusing the prime minister and two of his colleagues of corrupt practices involving the transfer of gold and ivory from the Congo. The prime minister, although conceding to the assignment of a Commission of Inquiry to investigate the allegations made by Daudi Ocheng, nevertheless made certain moves that created a whole new confrontation. Obote suspended the Constitution, arrested five of his colleagues when they were at a Cabinet meeting, relieved the President, Mutesa, of the presidency, and assumed power himself as executive president. Buganda interpreted the suspension of the Constitution as a breach of the national compact that had brought the groups together. Buganda said that with that breach, other parties to the compact had a right to take their own measures. Buganda challenged the central government, and a military confrontation at the palace of the kabaka ended with the fall of the palace. The kabaka fled to England where he remained in exile until his death in November 1970.

Obote inaugurated a new republican Constitution in 1967, abolishing all the kings, but Buganda remained under a state of emergency. In 1968 and 1969 there was a new groping for a socialistic direction to guide the nation. The president announced plans to "move to the Left." A Ministry of National Service was set up, and the president himself issued a blueprint of ideology entitled "The Common Man's Charter" specifying some of the ideals that would animate the regime's policies from then on. At first it appeared that the president, though sounding very radical, was going to be relatively moderate in his leftward moves.

Then in December 1969, an attempt was made on his life. A state of emergency was declared in the country as a whole, all political parties apart from the ruling UPC were banned, and the nation entered its days of uncertainty. By April 1970, Obote seems to have made up his mind that he was going to take a sharper turn to the left than might originally have been planned. It is almost certain that the situation created by the attempt on his life contributed to the greater radicalization of his intentions. In a May Day speech President Obote announced measures to nationalize the export and import trade, and acquire 60 percent of shares in all the major industries of Uganda. Plans to entrust a greater share of the economy to cooperative unions were also announced.

Meanwhile, the idea of setting up a one-party state de jure was in the background, and further details were being awaited as to the form that a one-party Uganda would take.

III. The Republic of Kenya

Kenya emerged independent in December 1963. In the year prior to independence there did seem to be a danger that the country might be divided ethnically between an alliance of the two biggest tribes, the Kikuyu and the Luo, on one side, and some of the smaller tribes on the other. Jomo Kenyatta was released after a long detention, and was the obvious leader for the Kenyan National Union. The opposition party of smaller tribes, the Kenya African Democratic Union, resisted attempts to merge the two parties for the time being.

Not long after independence, however, the Kenya African Democratic Union did decide to join forces with the Kenya African National Union. Kenya became a one-party state de facto, but new cleavages emerged within the single party. The new challenge to the party's leadership came, not from the right, as was the case with the KADU's challenge, but from the left. The leading dissenter in the new group of opposition to KANU's leadership was Oginga Odinga.

In 1966 Odinga at last broke off from the ruling party and formed his own Kenya Peoples' Union (KPU). Kenya had thus once again resumed a two-party system.

As Odinga was a Luo, and as the bulk of the support for his policy came from his province, ethnic factors intruded significantly in Kenya's party politics, but a neat Luo-Kikuyu confrontation was averted partly because of the presence of Tom Mboya, a Luo, within the ruling party. But in July 1969 Mboya was assassinated, and large numbers of Luo concluded that the assassination was part of a Kikuyu attempt to oust all Luo from important positions of power and influence. Tensions between the Luo and the Kikuyu got worse than ever. They culminated in rioting when President Kenyatta visited Kisumu in October 1969, and several people were killed when the security forces opened fire.

The government banned the Kenya Peoples' Union and detained its leaders, including Odinga. The elections scheduled to be a contest between the ruling party and KPU became instead primaries of a one-party election. They took place in Decmeber 1969. The elections were indeed contests between individual members of KANU. Some vigorous debates took place in local constituencies. A large number of members of parliament were ousted as a result of the elections, and new faces appeared in the legislature. Ethnic tensions are still present in Kenya's politics, but there has been an improvement in the atmosphere since the bitter days of October and November 1969.

INDEX OF NATIONS/STATES

N.B.: Roman numerals in brackets preceding each list of page numbers refer to the two volumes of *BUILDING STATES AND NATIONS:* [I] refers to Volume I, [II] refers to Volume II.

INDEX OF AUTHORS